The
Clean Air Act
Handbook SECOND EDITION

Robert J. Martineau, Jr.
and David P. Novello
editors

Cover design by ABA Publishing.

The publications of the Section of Environment, Energy, and Resources have a commitment to quality. Our authors and editors are outstanding professionals and active practitioners in their fields. In addition, prior to publication, the contents of all of our books are rigorously reviewed by the Section's Book Publications Committee and outside experts to ensure the highest quality product and presentation.

The materials contained herein represent the opinions of the authors and editors and should not be construed to be the action of either the American Bar Association or the Section of Environment, Energy, and Resources unless adopted pursuant to the bylaws of the Association.

Nothing contained in this book is to be considered as the rendering of legal advice for specific cases, and readers are responsible for obtaining such advice from their own legal counsel. This book and any forms and agreements herein are intended for educational and informational purposes only.

Printed in the United States of America.

08   5 4 3 2

Library of Congress Cataloging-in-Publication Data

The Clean Air Act handbook / by Robert J. Martineau, Jr., David P. Novello [editors].—2nd ed.
      p. cm.
   Includes bibliographical references and index.
   ISBN 1-59031-289-9
      1. United States. Clean Air Act. 2. Air—Pollution—Law and legislation—United States.
   3. Air quality management—United States. I. Martineau, Robert J. II. Novello, David P., 1957–

   KF3812.C554   2004
   344.7304'6342—dc22

                              2004001471

Discounts are available for books ordered in bulk. Special consideration is given to state bars, CLE programs, and other bar-related organizations. Inquire at Book Publishing, ABA Publishing, American Bar Association, 321 N. Clark, Chicago, Illinois 60610-4714.

www.ababooks.org

SUMMARY OF CONTENTS

CONTENTS

CHAPTER 3
Meeting Ambient Air Standards: Development of the State Implementation Plans 41
Robert A. Wyman, Jr., Dean M. Kato, and Jeffrey S. Alexander

CHAPTER 6
**The New Source Review Program: Prevention of Significant
Deterioration and Nonattainment New Source Review** **131**
Bernard F. Hawkins, Jr., and Mary Ellen Ternes

CHAPTER 7
The Visibility Protection Program
Vickie L. Patton

CHAPTER 8
Hazardous Air Pollutants
Robert J. Martineau, Jr.

CHAPTER 10
**Regulation of Mobile Sources: Motor Vehicles, Nonroad
Engines, and Aircraft** **323**
Michael J. Horowitz

CHAPTER 11
Regulation of Fuels and Fuel Additives **353**
Jonathan S. Martel

CHAPTER 16
Life after Title V Permit Issuance: You've Received Your Permit, Now What Do You Do?

Shannon S. Broome and Charles H. Knauss

CHAPTER 17
Civil Enforcement

Julie R. Domike and Alec C. Zacaroli

CHAPTER 18
Criminal Enforcement **613**
John S. Rudd

CHAPTER 19
Implementation of Clean Air Act Programs by
American Indian Tribes **619**
Jill E. Grant

PREFACE

The Clean Air Act was the first major environmental legislation of the 1970s, and today, several iterations later, it continues to be one of the most complex and comprehensive pieces of environmental legislation ever written. The 1977 and 1990 amendments to the act further expanded the act's breadth and scope into the very fabric of our daily lives. The recent public debate over the Bush administration's changes to the new source review rules, the new source review enforcement initiative, implementation of the new $PM_{2.5}$ and eight-hour ozone standard, measures to deal with interstate transport, the effects on toxic air emissions in our communities, and the massive corresponding public relations effort by environmental groups, industry, and the Environmental Protection Agency alike demonstrate how much clean air has become an issue in all of our lives. Increasingly, the regulations developed to implement the CAA affect our personal behavior patterns and not just large sources of emissions.

This book is a collaborative effort of many. The outstanding contributions of the chapter authors demonstrate their many collective years of experience and the depth of their knowledge of the Clean Air Act's intricacies. Through this book each has selflessly made that knowledge available to others. The authors bring a broad and balanced perspective to the issues and represent a cross section of public and private sector Clean Air Act practitioners. Many individual authors have spent considerable time in both public and private practice; indeed, many were involved in the development of the statutes and regulations about which they have written.

We are particularly pleased to have Mike Barr write the introductory chapter of this Second Edition of the Handbook. Mike is one of the earliest Clean Air Act practitioners, and thirty-three years later, he is as passionate as ever about the issues. He brings a unique and insightful perspective to the pages that follow his chapter. His thoughtful comments about the act's history and its evolution are a most fitting way to introduce the chapters that follow. While we expect most readers to use this book as a reference manual to learn about specific issues, we encourage everyone to read Chapter 1 for context.

As with the first edition, this book is intended to be a reference source for the seasoned Clean Air Act practitioner who needs to brush up on an issue. It is also intended to be a tool for the more general environmental practitioner who needs a quick tutorial on some aspect of the Clean Air Act. This book covers the entire CAA, not just the 1990 amendments. We believe this to be important for two reasons. First, the act before 1990 informs much of the change that occurred in the 1990 amendments, and the importance of those changes must be seen in context. Second, some key areas of the act remain essentially untouched by the 1990 amendments, yet they remain a critical component of daily clean air practice. The controversy over changes to the ozone and particulate matter National Ambient Air Quality Standards and the ongoing efforts to reform the prevention of significant deterioration/new source review regulations are but two examples that come to mind. In this book we have asked the authors to address not only the statutory scheme of the Clean Air Act but also to examine the EPA's implementing regulations and policy guidance.

This leads us to one final observation. This text necessarily must be but a snapshot of the act in time. The EPA issues new regulations on what seems like a weekly basis to implement the myriad statutory requirements; existing regulations are continually amended through notice and comment rule making. Each year the EPA also issues hundreds of policy statements, guidance memoranda, applicability determinations, and other interpretations of the statute and implementing regulations. The courts, through their now numerous judicial decisions, also have shaped and will continue to shape the law. We emphasize this to remind the reader that this reference book should be a starting point, not an end point. The practitioner will want to check for any new rules, EPA pronouncements, or judicial decisions that might be relevant. Appendix 1 is a current list of EPA Web sites containing information on Clean Air Act issues and a list of all regional office Web site addresses.

We hope this book assists you in your practice and increases your understanding of the Clean Air Act. We have certainly benefited from this endeavor.

Robert J. Martineau, Jr.
Nashville, Tennessee

David P. Novello
Washington, D.C.

ACKNOWLEDGMENTS

This book is a collaborative effort by many people without whom it could never have been published. First and foremost, our thanks to the authors for their contributions to this work. Each author's scholarship demonstrates a command of the subject matter that will be of great benefit to the reader. The authors were also uniformly gracious in responding to our editorial suggestions on early drafts of their chapters. Moreover, we appreciate their patience through the time-consuming process of preparing the entire text for publication.

We also want to thank Linda Oldfield for her many hours of assistance, as well as the word processing staff at Waller Lansden. Thanks also to Rick Paszkiet of the ABA publications staff for his assistance, and particularly his patience. We also express our appreciation to Waller Lansden Dortch & Davis, PLLC, for their support (and indulgence) of us throughout the project.

Finally, we express our most sincere gratitude to Marcia Sprague and Pamela Eddy, our respective spouses, for their good humor and support during this endeavor.

Robert J. Martineau, Jr.
Nashville, Tennessee

David P. Novello
Washington, D.C.

ABOUT THE EDITORS

Robert J. Martineau, Jr., is a member of the law firm of Waller Lansden Dortch & Davis, PLLC, in Nashville, Tennessee, and practices environmental law with a particular emphasis on Clean Air Act matters. He has worked with numerous companies in preparation of Title V permit applications, prevention of significant deterioration permits, and other permitting activities. From 1988 through 1994, Mr. Martineau was a senior attorney with the Office of the General Counsel at the U.S. Environmental Protection Agency in Washington, D.C., where he worked on a wide variety of regulations implementing the Clean Air Act as well as a variety of litigation matters related thereto. He received his bachelor of arts degree from St. John's University in Collegeville, Minnesota, in 1980. In 1983, he received his Juris Doctor degree from the University of Cincinnati College of Law. He also served as a law clerk to the late Honorable Harry Phillips, U.S. Court of Appeals for the Sixth Circuit. Since 1990, Mr. Martineau has served as a Vice Chair of the Air Quality Committee of the American Bar Association Section of Environment, Energy, and Resources. He is a frequent speaker on environmental law issues and has written a number of articles on the subject.

David P. Novello is the principal in the Law Offices of David Novello, LLC, in Washington, D.C. He represents corporations and trade associations on environmental issues, with a particular focus on air quality matters. He is also a mediator. From 1987 to 1992 Mr. Novello was a senior lawyer with the U.S. EPA Office of General Counsel, where he worked on a variety of Clean Air Act, hazardous waste, and international environmental issues. He currently serves as Vice Chair of the Air Quality Committee, the Alternative Dispute Resolution Committee, and the Endangered Species Committee of the American Bar Association Section of Environment, Energy, and Resources. Mr. Novello has written many publications on environmental matters and previously served on the editorial board of *Trends*, the section's newsletter. He speaks regularly on environmental topics, and has taught courses on the Clean Air Act at Georgetown University Law Center and the University of Maryland Law School. Mr. Novello is an honors graduate of Dartmouth College and Columbia Law School.

ABOUT THE CONTRIBUTORS

Jeffrey S. Alexander is currently a legal administrator with Universal Pictures in Universal City, California. Previously, he was an associate in the Los Angeles office of Latham & Watkins. He graduated magna cum laude from the University of Illinois College of Law in 2001. He is a 1994 graduate of the University of Michigan.

Richard Ayres is the principal in the Ayres Law Group, in Washington, D.C. Mr. Ayres has shaped the Clean Air Act and its implementation since 1970. He was a leader in the congressional consideration of the Clean Air Amendments of 1977 and 1990, and has participated in most of the major EPA rule makings under the CAA since 1970. He has also litigated a number of air pollution–related cases, taking a lead role in three of the largest enforcement cases in the history of the CAA. He has litigated more than two dozen cases in the U.S. Courts of Appeal and the Supreme Court, including two cases challenging EPA National Ambient Air Quality Standards rules. Mr. Ayres is a graduate of Princeton University and Yale Law School, and holds a master's degree in political science from Yale.

Michael R. Barr is a partner in the law firm of Pillsbury Winthrop LLP in San Francisco. He graduated magna cum laude in the honors chemistry program at the University of Washington, Seattle, and obtained his law degree from Harvard in 1973. He has represented companies, public agencies, and associations on air quality, project development, international matters, and many commercial matters, including Chevron in the leading *Chevron v. NRDC* administrative law case cited in this book, and the Clean Air Act Working Group during the 1990 Clean Air Act Amendments. He has served on many boards, including the board of directors of the California Council for Environmental and Economic Balance, the Golden West Section of Air & Waste Management Association, and the board of trustees of the Golden Gate National Parks Conservancy, and on the governing council of the ABA Section of Environment, Energy, and Resources.

Harold Boo is an associate in the Los Angeles office of Latham & Watkins LLP. Mr. Boo graduated from University of California at Berkeley in 1997 and from UCLA School of Law in 2001.

Shannon S. Broome is a lawyer in private practice in Oakland, California. She is counsel to the Air Permitting Forum, a group of *Fortune* 50 companies dedicated to the smooth implementation of Title V and new source review permitting programs under the Clean Air Act. She has over a decade of experience in legislation and regulatory implementation of environmental laws. While she represents numerous clients before EPA regarding all aspects of implementation of the Clean Air Act, her focus is on assisting plants in the implementation of such requirements, predominantly Title V, new source review requirements, and maximum achievable control technology requirements under Section 112. Ms. Broome graduated from the University of California, Los Angeles, with a B.S. in chemical engineering and obtained her law degree from Boalt Hall School of Law at the University of California, Berkeley, where she is a member of the Order of the Coif. After graduating from law school, Ms. Broome practiced at Swidler & Berlin, Chtd., in Washington, D.C. She then accepted a position as counsel and manager of Clean Air Act programs for the General Electric Company in Fairfield, Connecticut. After five years with GE, she returned to California to resume private practice. Ms. Broome also previously worked as an environmental and construction engineer for Chevron U.S.A. on solid waste and air pollution issues. She has written several articles and given speeches on environmental issues, and is a co-author of *Clean Air Act Operating Permit Program: A Handbook for Counsel, Environmental Managers, and Plant Managers* (ABA, 1993).

Kyle W. Danish is a lawyer in the Washington, D.C., office of Van Ness Feldman, P.C. His practice focuses on environmental and energy law. In the area of global climate change, Mr. Danish has helped to assess and design international and domestic rules for emissions trading and has advised clients on trading transactions in Latin America, Southeast Asia, Africa, and Russia. Mr. Danish is a past co-chair of the American Bar Association's Committee on Climate Change and Sustainable Development. He received his juris doctor cum laude in 1997 from Temple University School of Law. Mr. Danish also received a master in public affairs degree from Princeton University's Woodrow Wilson School of Public and International Affairs, where he was managing editor of the *Journal of Public and International Affairs*. He received a bachelor of arts from Haverford College in 1989.

Julie R. Domike is a partner in the Washington, D.C., firm of Wallace King Marraro & Branson, PLLC. She advises clients on federal and state enforcement actions, EPA rule making under the Clean Air Act, compliance with mobile source requirements, obtaining state and federal permits, defending and challenging environmental permits before the EPA Environmental Appeals Board, the environmental aspects involved in the acquisition or construction of facilities, and the availability of relief under the federal and state audit policies or laws. Ms. Domike is a 1986 graduate of Georgetown University Law Center, and earned her bachelor's degree cum laude from

Mount Holyoke College. She served as attorney-advisor in the Environmental Protection Agency's Air Enforcement Division from 1987 until 1993, when she became the chief of the division's New Source Review, Permits, and Air Toxics Branch. Since October 1996, Ms. Domike has been in private practice in Washington, D.C., first with Piper & Marbury, and with Wallace King Marraro & Branson since October 1999. She is a member of the American Bar Association Section of Environment, Energy, and Resources, and served as Vice Chair of the Air Quality Committee of that section for several years.

Jill E. Grant is a partner with Nordhaus, Haltom, Taylor, Taradash & Bladh, LLP, in the firm's Washington, D.C., office. She works extensively with Indian tribes, assisting tribes in developing environmental programs, codes, and regulations, and in applying to the EPA for "treatment as a state" and primacy approvals. Ms. Grant also represented the National Tribal Environmental Council in its participation in the Grand Canyon Visibility Transport Commission proceedings under the Clean Air Act. Ms. Grant previously worked in the Office of General Counsel at the EPA, where she was on the team that drafted the Clean Air Act Amendments of 1990, and subsequently assisted in developing various programs and implementing regulations under that legislation, including the acid rain program, Indian air rule, and regulation of air emissions from outer continental shelf oil and gas drilling. In addition, Ms. Grant worked on prevention of significant deterioration and radiation protection issues. Ms. Grant earned her J.D. from Harvard Law School and her B.A. from Yale College.

Bernard F. Hawkins, Jr., is a lawyer with Nelson Mullins Riley & Scarborough, L.L.P. Mr. Hawkins practices primarily in the areas of regulatory compliance counseling, administrative hearings and negotiations with federal and state agencies, environmental and toxic tort litigation, and counseling on new or proposed federal and state statutes and regulations with a special emphasis on Clean Air Act issues. In 1986, Mr. Hawkins received a bachelor of science degree in biology from the University of South Carolina, where he was admitted to Phi Beta Kappa and graduated magna cum laude. He attended the University of South Carolina School of Law where he served as Associate Editor-in-Chief of the *South Carolina Law Review* and received his juris doctor cum laude in 1990. Mr. Hawkins was admitted to the South Carolina bar in 1990. He is a member of the American Bar Association Section of Environment, Energy, and Resources, and served as Chair of the Air Quality Committee of that section from 2001 to 2003. Mr. Hawkins appears in *The Best Lawyers in America, 2001–2004.*

Michael J. Horowitz is a lawyer with the Office of General Counsel of the U.S. Environmental Protection Agency. He has worked at the Office of General Counsel (Air and Radiation Division) since 1991. He graduated from Harvard Law School in 1988.

Debra J. Jezouit is a partner in the Washington, D.C., office of Baker Botts LLP. She has extensive experience in Clean Air Act issues, representing clients such as electric generating companies, iron and steel foundries, cement manufacturers, pharmaceutical companies, boat manufacturers, and chemical companies. Ms. Jezouit handles such matters as acid rain compliance, emissions monitoring, air permitting, emissions trading programs, and hazardous air pollutant requirements. She participated extensively in the regulatory development process for the Clean Air Act's Acid Rain Program and led negotiations with the Environmental Protection Agency on the development of various revisions to the acid rain regulations. Ms. Jezouit earned her J.D. from the University of Virginia School of Law and her B.A. from the George Washington University, where she was admitted to Phi Beta Kappa.

Dean M. Kato is managing counsel of Toyota Motor Sales, U.S.A., and was formerly of counsel to Latham & Watkins in Los Angeles. His experience in the air quality area includes mobile and stationary source rule making, permitting, variances, enforcement, and legislative activity. He has handled air quality and other environmental matters before many government agencies, including the Environmental Protection Agency, the California Air Resources Board, and the South Coast Air Quality Management District. Mr. Kato also has experience in alternative fuels and advanced environmental technology regulation, including hybrid-electric and fuel cell vehicle–related matters, as well as strategic advice and counsel related to climate change and environmental corporate communications. Mr. Kato has a B.A. from Columbia University and is a 1991 graduate of the Boalt Hall School of Law of the University of California at Berkeley, where he was an associate editor of the *California Law Review*. He was a Fulbright Scholar at the Faculty of Law of Tokyo University from 1991 to 1992.

Charles H. Knauss is a partner with the law firm of Swidler Berlin Shereff Friedman, LLP, in Washington, D.C. He represents companies and trade associations in complex federal environmental permitting, rule making, litigation, commercial, and legislative matters. Mr. Knauss is a nationally recognized authority on Clean Air Act matters, with almost twenty-five years of experience addressing all aspects of this federal statute, including several years as counsel to the U.S. House of Representatives Committee on Energy and Commerce, where he figured prominently in the development of the comprehensive 1990 Clean Air Act Amendments. Mr. Knauss represents clients in a wide variety of manufacturing and energy sectors, including automotive, aerospace, pharmaceutical, chemical, refinery, power generation, and utilities. Mr. Knauss founded and is counsel to the Air Permitting Forum, a group of *Fortune* 50 companies, to develop practical and effective advice for all aspects of the permit process. He is also the founder of and counsel to the National Sediments Coalition, and maintains a broad practice beyond air quality issues involving sediments remediation, data quality, risk assessment and characterization, and improvements to environmental statutes and regulations generally. Mr. Knauss earned his A.B. degree in biology from Brown University and graduated from the University of Michigan Law School. For the past two years, he has been selected as a leading environmental lawyer by Chambers USA Directory of Leading U.S. Business Lawyers, 2003–2004 and 2002–2003.

Mary Rose Kornreich pursued her interest in scientific legal issues both as an environmental consultant and as an environmental lawyer. After receiving an undergraduate degree from Cornell and a doctorate in toxicology from MIT, she did environmental consulting, first as program manager at the MITRE Corporation and then as division director at Clement Associates. She became director of Bioassay Reports Program at the National Cancer Institute. After earning her law degree from Georgetown University Law Center, she practiced environmental law with Kaye Scholer Fierman Hays & Handler, and later with Jenner and Block. Throughout her career, she frequently spoke and published on scientific legal issues including air quality, chemical regulation, risk assessment, toxic torts, and the use of scientific evidence in the courtroom.

Janda D. R. Kuhnert is an associate in the Los Angeles office of Latham & Watkins. She graduated in 2001 from the University of Texas School of Law. She is a 1997 graduate of the University of California, San Diego, and a member of Phi Beta Kappa.

Troy Sam Lee is an associate in the Los Angeles office of Latham & Watkins LLP. He received his A.B. from Harvard University in 1998 and his J.D. from Columbia University School of Law in 2001.

Jonathan S. Martel is a partner at Arnold & Porter in Washington, D.C., concentrating on Clean Air Act matters, environmental litigation, and counseling. Mr. Martel rejoined Arnold & Porter's Washington, D.C., office in 1994 after serving for three years at Office of General Counsel of the U.S. Environmental Protection Agency. While at the EPA, Mr. Martel was involved primarily in the implementation of the Clean Air Act Amendments of 1990. Mr. Martel is currently an adjunct professor of law at Georgetown University Law Center, where he teaches a course on the Clean Air Act and environmental law. He is also Vice Chair of the Air Quality Committee of the American Bar Association Section of Environment, Energy, and Resources. He is a graduate of Yale Law School and served as a law clerk for Judge Levin H. Campbell on the U.S. Court of Appeals for the First Circuit.

Diane E. McConkey has been an attorney-advisor in the Air and Radiation Law Office of the Office of General Counsel, U.S. Environmental Protection Agency, since 1997. Her work at the EPA has focused on stratospheric ozone, maximum achievable control technology standards for hazardous air pollutants, new source performance standards, and new source review. She previously worked as an environmental lawyer for the Washington, D.C., office of Gardner, Carton & Douglas and served as a law clerk to the Honorable John P. Wiese, U.S. Court of Federal Claims. She graduated in 1993 from the University of Virginia School of Law, where she was an executive editor of the Law Review. She is a 1988 graduate of Amherst College and a member of Phi Beta Kappa.

Vickie L. Patton is a senior attorney at Environmental Defense where she manages the organization's national and regional clean air programs, working out of the group's Boulder, Colorado, office. Environmental Defense is a national nonpartisan, nonprofit environmental advocacy organization representing more than 400,000 members nationwide. Prior to joining Environmental Defense, Ms. Patton worked at the U.S. Environmental Protection Agency's Office of General Counsel in Washington, D.C., where she provided legal counsel on a variety of national air quality initiatives. During her tenure at EPA, Ms. Patton received the Gold Medal for Exceptional Service, the Agency's highest honor award. Ms. Patton is a member of EPA's national Clean Air Act Advisory Committee and the Western Regional Air Partnership's Initiatives Oversight Committee. Ms. Patton has published numerous articles on the Clean Air Act. She earned her J.D. in 1990 from the New York University School of Law.

William F. Pedersen practices environmental law in Washington, D.C. His practice covers all aspects of the Clean Air Act, including counseling and litigation on new source review, Title V permits, maximum achievable control technology standards, state implementation plans, monitoring and reporting issues, fuels regulation, control of ozone depleting substances, and proposals for legislative amendments. During his EPA tenure he served as associate general counsel for Air and Radiation—the government's chief Clean Air Act lawyer. Congress incorporated suggestions from his law review articles into the Clean Air Act in both 1977 and 1990. Mr. Pedersen has been listed in *The Best Lawyers in America* since it began publication.

John S. Rudd is vice president for Regulatory and Legal Affairs at American Biophysics Corporation in North Kingstown, Rhode Island. He is a former member of the Environmental Practice Group at Preti Flaherty, LLC, in Portland, Maine, where his practice focused on compliance counseling, permitting, and litigation in air and hazardous waste law throughout the northeast. Earlier, Mr. Rudd worked in the Office of Enforcement at the U.S. EPA in Washington, D.C., in the areas of Clean Air Act enforcement, rule making, and policy and hazardous waste combustion issues under the Resource Conservation and Recovery Act. Mr. Rudd started his legal career as a law clerk to the Hon. Gregory W. Carman at the U.S. Court of International Trade in

New York City. He is a graduate of Swarthmore College and received his J.D. from the City University of New York at Queens College.

Michael K. Stagg is a member of the law firm of Waller Lansden Dortch & Davis, PLLC, in Nashville, Tennessee. His practice includes many aspects of environmental law but focuses on Clean Air Act and toxic tort matters. Mr. Stagg received his B.S. in natural resources management from Colorado State University, where he received the Honors Senior Award from the College of Forestry and Natural Resources. He is a graduate of the University of Tennessee College of Law, where he served as editor-in-chief of the *Tennessee Law Review* and received the Dean's Citation for Extraordinary Contributions to the College of Law. He has an LL.M. with highest honors in environmental law from the George Washington University Law School, where he received the Randolph C. Shaw Graduate Fellowship and served as advisory editor to *The Environmental Lawyer*. Mr. Stagg is active with the environmental sections of various bar associations and publishes and speaks frequently in the area of environmental law.

Mary Ellen Ternes is of counsel with the law firm of McAfee & Taft in Oklahoma City. She obtained her bachelor's of engineering degree in chemical engineering from Vanderbilt University, Nashville, graduated with high honors from the University of Arkansas at Little Rock School of Law, and participated in the 1994 EPA Office of General Counsel summer honors program. She worked as a chemical engineer for EPA and industry prior to law school, remediating hazardous waste sites and permitting hazardous waste incineration facilities pursuant to the Clean Air Act and the Resource Conservation and Recovery Act. As a lawyer, she has represented companies in air and hazardous waste permitting, development of compliance strategies, and enforcement proceedings, particularly in the context of complex technical applications. She is an active author and lecturer on air topics, particularly Title V and new source review, and is a former chair of the ABA Section of Environment, Energy, and Resources' Air Quality Committee, the technical chair of the Clean Air Act Satellite Seminar, and the 2004 chair of the Annual Conference on Environmental Law.

Peter H. Wyckoff is a lawyer, self-employed since 2000, focusing on air quality law, particularly new source review enforcement. For 2000, Mr. Wyckoff was deputy director and general counsel of the U.S. Commission on International Religious Freedom. From 1989 to 1999, he was a partner in the Washington, D.C., office of Gardner, Carton & Douglas, where he concentrated on international and domestic law relating to stratospheric ozone protection, climate change, the 1990 Clean Air Act Amendments, enforcement matters, and drug regulatory law. From 1978 to 1989, Mr. Wyckoff served as a lawyer and in time as a branch chief in the Air and Radiation Division of EPA's

Office of General Counsel, where he was instrumental in the development of several major regulatory programs, including new source review. Mr. Wyckoff is a 1975 cum laude graduate of Syracuse University College of Law, where he was editor-in-chief of the *Syracuse Law Review*. He is a member of the bars of New York and the District of Columbia.

Robert A. Wyman, Jr., is a partner in the Los Angeles office of Latham & Watkins. As the firm's lead counsel for Clean Air Act matters, he has represented companies and trade associations in a wide variety of rule makings under the statute, including the judicial review of such actions in U.S. Circuit Courts. His litigation practice also includes the civil and criminal defense of environmental claims. Mr. Wyman represented clients during the enactment of the Clean Air Act Amendments of 1990 and the Intermodal Surface Transportation Efficiency Act of 1991. He has testified on several occasions before Congress on the interpretation and implementation of the Clean Air Act. He is a member of the U.S. EPA Clean Air Act Advisory Committee and has chaired subcommittees on market strategies and on the linkages among energy, land use, transportation, and air quality. Mr. Wyman was a principal architect of the Southern California Regional Clean Air Incentives Market. He has also designed a number of other market programs, including the clean air investment fund and the clean air communities programs currently under development by EPA and several states. Mr. Wyman graduated from Princeton University in 1976 and from the University of Virginia Law School in 1980.

Alec C. Zacaroli is a lawyer with the law firm of Wallace King Marraro & Branson, PLLC, in Washington, D.C. His practice covers several areas of environmental law, including regulatory compliance, environmental tort litigation, and environmental enforcement. Mr. Zacaroli specializes in clean air law applicable to both stationary and mobile sources. He also served as a reporter and editor, writing about Clean Air Act issues and environmental litigation, prior to becoming a lawyer. He has written extensively about regulatory and legal developments under the federal Clean Air Act. Mr. Zacaroli is a 1991 graduate of the George Washington University, and received his law degree from the American University Washington College of Law in 1998.

Rick Zbur is a partner in the environmental department in Latham & Watkins's Los Angeles office. Mr. Zbur practices in all areas of environmental law and specializes in air quality compliance, land use, and transportation issues. He has handled numerous matters before federal, state, and regional regulatory agencies, including EPA, the U.S. Food and Drug Administration, the Department of Transportation, the U.S. Army Corps of Engineers, the California Air Resources Board, Cal/EPA, the South Coast Air Quality Management District, and the Southern California Association of Governments, among others. He also has extensive experience advising project developers regarding compliance with the National Environmental Policy Act, the California Environmental Quality Act, and regional air quality and transportation regulations. Mr. Zbur has worked extensively with new source review and emission trading rules and transportation issues under federal and state law. He is heavily involved with multiclient groups in developing new legislation and regulations in the air quality and transportation arenas. He is a 1979 graduate of Yale College and a 1983 graduate of the Harvard Law School, where he was an editor of the *Harvard Journal on Legislation*. In 1996, Mr. Zbur was a major party nominee for United States Congress in California's 38th Congressional District.

CHAPTER 1

Introduction to the Clean Air Act: History, Perspective, and Direction for the Future

MICHAEL R. BARR

Overview

At the dawn of the modern Clean Air Act (CAA)[1] era, the Gipper himself took one of the first momentous steps. On February 21, 1972, California Governor Ronald Reagan submitted the first California state implementation plan (SIP) to the first Environmental Protection Agency (EPA) Administrator, William Ruckelshaus. That primordial California plan emerged in thirteen parts and nearly one hundred chapters combining everything known about air quality in the state that pioneered air pollution control. It promised to implement every control measure then devised. The final draft stood a foot tall.

Governor Reagan hedged his promises in 1972. The State of California expected the national government to share the burden:

> As discussed in the plan, the federal government has to play a key role if the goals of the Clean Air Act are to be achieved. It must assume a major role in developing control measures which are technically sound, and socially and economically acceptable to the citizens of our country.[2]

Citing California's then-established leadership in battling air pollution, Governor Reagan also pledged "California's support and cooperation." Within three years, the EPA disapproved California's first plan, the EPA adopted a Federal Implementation Plan for California including gasoline rationing and land use controls, and Congress amended the CAA to limit the EPA's power and give the states more time to meet the goals of the CAA. A distinctive kind of federalism began to emerge under the CAA.

Thirty years later, states continue to struggle with Clean Air Act mandates, the EPA continues to fill up the Federal Register with Clean Air Act

1

regulations—many of which regulate state planning—and Congress continues to debate clean air. Congress has overhauled the Act twice since 1970, more than doubling the size of the Act in the 1977 CAA Amendments and doubling it again in the 1990 CAA Amendments. The EPA's rulebooks have grown exponentially.

On November 15, 1994, the Executive Officer of the California Air Resources Board (CARB) submitted yet another massive California SIP revision to the EPA—this time in response to the nonattainment provisions of Title I of the CAA as revised by the 1990 Amendments. Echoing Governor Reagan's proviso twenty-two years before, the Executive Officer stated:

> A critical part of the overall control strategy is U.S. EPA's fulfillment of the Act's promise for regulation of national sources pursuant to [Title II of the Clean Air Act]. . . . Volume II of the SIP revision sets forth the specific measures that the 1994 California SIP *assumes the U.S. EPA will adopt and implement on the schedule shown* [emphasis added].[3]

Like Governor Reagan, the CARB executive officer reiterated California's unwavering commitment to clean air. After two decades of experience with federalism under the Clean Air Act, though, the Executive Officer prudently assumed a schedule for his federal partner's performance. This sort of shared responsibility and authority—and mutual finger-pointing, blame, and mistrust—between states and the EPA lies at the heart of the CAA. It also explains much of the rivalry between them and their problems in successfully implementing the Act. From the dawn of the modern CAA era in the early 1970s, Congress has tried to leave the basic authority to achieve clean air with the states while assuring a minimum, federally defined level of clean air quality for all Americans. Congress has always recognized the states'—and since 1990 the Indian tribes'—ability to find the most effective ways of controlling emissions given their unique circumstances. Congress has also insisted that every American must enjoy "clean air," as defined by compliance with the National Ambient Air Quality Standards (NAAQS),[4] standards for hazardous air pollutants, and many other provisions of the CAA.

As many governors and state officials have pointed out over the years, however, Congress also expected the federal government to do its part. The members of Congress who carefully devised the CAA, the Clean Water Act, and other major federal environmental statutes in the early 1970s concluded that they would need a special federal agency to perform the federal government's part in pollution control. Thus, they worked with President Nixon to charter and fund the EPA, its ten regional offices, and its numerous specialized offices to serve every state and address a huge variety of environmental challenges.

Congress chose the EPA from the beginning—rather than the states—to control mobile sources. Congress attempted to minimize adverse effects on interstate commerce. Thus, in Title II of the CAA, Congress established a largely preemptive federal program of motor vehicle control. Congress gave

California special authority to control motor vehicles and fuels because California was already doing so and had worse air quality problems than any other state. Since more than half of the air pollutant inventories of most major metropolitan areas of the country come from mobile sources, the EPA directly and substantially controls the ability of those areas to attain ambient air quality standards.

As a result, from the early 1970s to the present day, the EPA, the states, and local air agencies have had to work together to prepare state implementation plans, emission inventories, air pollution control measures, ambient air monitoring networks, and a host of other elements of the comprehensive air quality management strategy. Actually, the word "host" does not adequately convey the magnitude in sheer number, pages, and words of federal, state, and local air quality rules, regulations, guidance documents, studies, reports, administrative records, and other documents. CAA regulation in this country has developed a deep and almost unimaginably complex history that inevitably challenges the practitioner. Much of the bulk and complexity of this handbook directly reflects the bulk and complexity of air quality law under the Clean Air Act.

Most chapters in this handbook also describe and explain the history of Clean Air Act practice since the 1970 Amendments. Current practitioners might naturally ask: What does the history of the CAA have to do with the current practice of air quality law? Why can't legal practitioners rely exclusively on what has happened since the 1990 Amendments to know everything they need to know about air quality management?

Here are a few reasons why the authors and editors of this Handbook think practitioners should understand basic CAA history and precedents a bit before venturing far into CAA issues:

- CAA history keeps repeating itself, as illustrated by the California quotes, *twenty-two years apart,* provided earlier. Other examples abound: The 1970 federal air toxics program required risk assessment to precede technological controls. The 1990 Amendments flipped the air toxics program, making it a technology-based system with risk assessment now following the installation of the best controls. Now that the residual risk stage of the revised federal air toxics program has been reached, the pre-1990 risk assessment precedents will form the starting point for the analysis—particularly since they are referenced by *Federal Register* citation in the 1990 Amendments themselves! In that instance, Congress expressly *meant* for history to repeat itself.
- The 1990 CAA Amendments were mammoth but incremental. Even the mold-breaking, market-based Title IV acid rain allowance trading system rests on earlier foundations that partly explain the EPA's approach to the Title IV regulations. For example, the EPA pioneered a "usage rights" feature as part of a "banking rule" to facilitate the final phasedown of the levels of lead in unleaded gasoline in the mid-1980s. In turn, the Title IV acid rain allowance system recently served as a model

for the EPA's attempt to require twenty-two states and the District of Columbia to amend their SIPs in a regional ozone reduction SIP call.[5]

- The 1990 Amendments did not repeal the prior CAA provisions, the EPA regulations, or court case holdings. Indeed, the 1990 Amendments included express "savings clauses," saving some things that Congress later decided it should have tossed, such as recent federal implementation plans for three areas in California. Congress, however, is a collector and the CAA's attics and basements remain full of relevant relics from the 1970 and 1977 Amendments.
- Many earlier ideas about air quality management are still good ones. Many current ideas about incentives for reducing traffic congestion, for example, started with the infamous and long-abandoned the EPA transportation control plans from the early 1970s. The EPA's recent new source review (NSR) reforms partly implement a 1982 settlement agreement.
- Congress did not repeal state or local laws or regulations in the 1990 Amendments. Most state or local air quality laws still follow the 1970 and 1977 Amendments. To understand those state and local laws and regulations properly, practitioners often find themselves reviewing EPA regulations and their administrative records from before 1990.
- CAA history is still only about thirty years old. It is still a work in progress. Every CAA practitioner can affect its development.

Practitioners who frequently deal with the CAA will find that they are dealing with many of the country's most pressing problems. CAA provisions and policies affect corn farmers, the Grand Canyon, urban traffic congestion, brownfields redevelopment, regional haze in the Smoky Mountains of Tennessee and North Carolina, recycling to prevent pollution, and, without question, innovation, economic growth and recovery, and international competitiveness. Many Clean Air Act issues are so fundamental to balancing environmental and economic goals that they attract nationwide attention and take decades to resolve. When nine northeastern states sue the EPA over provisions for calculating NSR baseline emissions,[6] it is clear that even seemingly innocuous changes can involve major political, technical, and legal issues.

A Brief History of the CAA

World history provides examples of air pollution problems ever since the roots of civilization. The neighbors probably complained about the smoke as soon as the first tribe invented fire. For CAA practitioners, it is often illuminating and helpful to find earlier examples of current issues.

For example, practitioners often become involved in the search for, and documentation of, the appropriate level of best available control technology (BACT) under the prevention of significant deterioration (PSD) program in Title I of the CAA. For a waste-fired boiler used to produce electricity and thermal energy at a landfill, BACT could include large particulate filters ("bag houses") and controls of gases like nitrogen oxide and sulfur oxide. The waste fuel may consist of the clippings and gardening debris collected by cities, counties, and private waste collectors. In many communities, clippings and garden debris were spiked with fuel oil and fed into large "teepee burners," which routinely blackened the entire area with smoke and soot and had absolutely no emission controls. In recent years, landfills have had powerful incentives to reduce such waste and many communities have welcomed such projects. These beneficial projects may well trigger PSD permitting and/or difficult, time-consuming, and costly BACT reviews.

States, cities, counties, and special districts have experimented with different kinds of air pollution control throughout the industrial revolution.[7] The modern era of air pollution control, though, did not really start until after World War II. For example, not until after 1945 did Los Angeles County seriously address the smudge pots used to heat citrus groves. Regional efforts to address entire air quality basins, such as the nine-county Bay Area Air Pollution Control District in San Francisco Bay, did not start until the 1950s.

The CAA established a major federal regulatory role for the first time with the 1970 CAA Amendments. Before that, the federal government's role was almost entirely devoted to conducting scientific and technical investigations and providing information to the states. In the late 1960s, those functions were performed by the U.S. Health, Education, and Welfare Department and the U.S. Public Health Service.

The federal government took a major step toward national air quality management in 1970 when Congress established the EPA. Congress gathered into the EPA all of the federal resources dealing with air quality management, including the essential public health investigation and control technology work previously done by different, uncoordinated groups within different departments of the federal government. Congress greatly increased the total federal resources devoted to air quality improvement when it created and funded the EPA and, from that time forward, the EPA has coordinated national leadership and provided continuity and institutional memory.

At the same time, the 1970 CAA Amendments charged the EPA with the essential mission of air quality improvement, which has not fundamentally changed to this day. In Title I, Congress directed the EPA to establish "national ambient air quality standards" and to provide guidance to the states on how to develop "state implementation plans" to achieve the NAAQS. States then had a period of time to develop their SIPs, and the EPA was directed to review and either approve or augment the state plans.

The EPA promptly established NAAQS for five air pollutants, relying on previous work done by government and university researchers. The EPA did its work quickly and without the level of support or technical review that the EPA has brought to the process of revising the NAAQS several times since. However, the EPA got the job done on time—an early indication of the tradeoff between congressionally mandated deadlines and the quality of the EPA's technical work.

States then proceeded to develop their "first round" SIPs. States largely got the job done on time, too, and have spent many resources redoing and revising their SIPs ever since.

In those early years of the 1970s, state legislators and state regulators established most of the basic air quality programs. They inserted all of the core program elements into their SIPs: stationary source controls, emissions, inventories, air quality monitoring networks, and procedures like rulemaking and variance procedures.

This first phase of CAA development and implementation probably established the basic air quality management systems and organizations that still exist in the country. Unfortunately, air quality did not improve a great deal in those early years. The EPA found many of the first-round SIPs inadequate and promptly proceeded to augment them, using its authority to adopt federal plans and impose other sanctions under Section 110(c) of the Act. But the EPA concluded that far more drastic measures would be necessary to achieve the NAAQS—especially the NAAQS related to photochemical smog—than any state was willing to propose. As a result, the EPA proposed its own "transportation control plans" to achieve the NAAQS everywhere for everyone at all times.

In places like California, those early EPA plans were truly draconian. For example, the Los Angeles plan, which the EPA proposed in 1973, would have required 100 percent gasoline rationing during the summer months. Even the EPA did not think that anyone would ever implement such a plan.

In response to this halting first round of plans and controls, Congress adjusted the CAA in 1975 and overhauled it in 1977. The 1977 Amendments preserved the NAAQS but provided a much longer and more realistic time frame for states to achieve them. Through the PSD program, the amendments also added protection against air quality degradation for parts of the country already attaining the NAAQS. The 1977 CAA Amendments were clearly incremental and meant to make the original 1970 Amendments work within a time frame that Congress felt was more reasonable. Congress intended to revisit the CAA again in five years and make further "midcourse corrections" in the early 1980s.

The 1980 presidential election, however, resulted in great turmoil at the EPA, and a standoff between Congress and the White House halted any further revision of the CAA. Congress and the President were unable to agree on further CAA amendments, even as the deadlines of the 1977 Amendments approached in the late 1980s and passed. Litigation, chaos, and uncertainty resulted.

Yet states and local air quality regulators, working with the EPA regional offices, did make considerable, quiet progress toward air quality goals throughout the 1980s. Regulators like the San Francisco Bay Area Air Quality Management District implemented policy, enforced control measures, dealt with special cases through limited variances and abatement orders, and actually reduced emissions year-by-year from sources under their control. Similarly, the EPA's federal program for motor vehicle control produced regular, annual reductions in the mobile source inventory. In those areas that made a serious and sustained effort to achieve cleaner air, the air quality began to improve measurably in the early 1980s and markedly improved by the end of that decade.

Air quality management also became institutionalized during the 1980s. People devoted their professional careers to understanding and regulating air quality. Legislators at the federal and state levels began to understand air quality control measures and how to make them work. Legal practitioners gained experience at every level of government and in every part of the country.

Many state and local agencies expanded their programs into new areas—such as the regulation of toxic air contaminants. In many cases, very local concerns about specific facilities forced state and local regulators to respond. Communities became concerned about potential accidents as well as long-term exposure to potential carcinogens. The accident in Bhopal, India, in the early 1980s was the Love Canal of air toxics control.

All of these trends culminated in, and shaped, the 1990 CAA Amendments. The first President Bush started the ball rolling by proposing his own CAA amendments in mid-1989. The Bush Administration bill addressed the three basic components that had to be addressed to appeal to all of the major CAA constituencies: acid rain, air toxics, and nonattainment. Once the President proposed a comprehensive package, Congress did the rest. The 1990 CAA Amendments grew into a legendary legislative "Christmas list" of provisions extending far beyond the President's proposal into areas like these:

- Controls of products that affect stratospheric ozone
- A new federal operating permit program for air pollutant sources, based on the Clean Water Act program
- Special provisions for the Great Lakes
- Controls of "nonroad" mobile sources such as leaf blowers and lawn mowers

In a very important move, Congress greatly expanded the fuel regulatory program, including new requirements for "reformulated gasoline" in the most polluted areas of the country.

At the same time, Congress vastly increased the EPA resources devoted to air quality management. The White House estimated that the CAA would cost the U.S. economy over $21 billion per year, but most observers felt the cost could go far higher. In retrospect, it appears that the observers underestimated the scope and burdens of the CAA.

Directions for the Future

For practitioners faced with problems under the CAA, the 1990 CAA Amendments themselves contain very detailed provisions. The very detail of these provisions can mislead the practitioner into believing that the CAA itself can answer most questions. However, the 1990 Amendments should not be viewed as providing answers as much as direction to the EPA about how to address issues in the future. The CAA delegates most policy-making functions to the EPA. To carry out the 1990 Amendments, the EPA must engage in literally thousands of rulemakings, issue many thousands of guidance documents, and make many more thousands of interpretations.

Even with all of the EPA's activities, most decisions affecting specific industrial facilities are left to state and local permitting agencies. Their decisions in specific rulemakings, permit actions, and enforcement proceedings will determine the performance obligations and financial consequences for most individual facilities.

The EPA has issued a huge number of rules and guidance documents under all of the CAA programs.[8] The EPA has missed some deadlines but has issued more CAA rules in the past ten years than in the previous twenty. The complexity of these rules and their interaction staggers those who must comply.

Several major themes have emerged. The EPA has adopted a variety of processes to issue policy guidance under the 1990 CAA Amendments. The EPA has demonstrated a willingness to sit down with representatives of all affected interests—the stakeholders—to discuss all aspects of its responsibilities under the CAA. As a result, the EPA has received more input, and a greater variety of input, than it ever did before the 1990 Amendments. The EPA professional staff often welcomes stakeholder input. The state and local air quality management agencies that have most of the hands-on experience have had a much larger impact on EPA policy than in the past.

Ironically, just as the EPA seems to be achieving greater consensus than ever in implementing the CAA, the CAA and its programs have received intense scrutiny from Congress. Congress has demanded greater accountability from the EPA, greater responsiveness to state and local concerns, clearer scientific justification, greater justification for costs imposed on regulated entities, and greater explanation for failure to achieve clean air. As Congress increases its demands of the EPA, Congress also proposes to constrain the resources available to the EPA to fulfill its responsibilities under the CAA.

The pressures of increased congressional demands and tight budgets create considerable uncertainty and doubt about whether the EPA will be able to fulfill its duties under the CAA. The EPA is looking more than ever to states, local agencies, industry, universities, and others outside of the EPA to help it develop and shape its policy under the CAA. Unquestionably, this development creates opportunities for practitioners to assist their clients in CAA matters.

While many CAA issues are complex and the outcome uncertain, the stakes remain high. The future of entire industries can depend on whether emission standards are set at levels that can be achieved with current technology or that require technological breakthroughs. The EPA must phase out some products, may ban others, and may regulate pervasive products like consumer goods, autos, and fuels. For company managers to make decisions, they will continue to need skilled practitioners to guide them through the maze.

Practitioners need to understand the variety of tools available to help them do their job. The legislative history of the 1990 CAA Amendments is available from Congress.[9] Each of the EPA's rulemakings rests on elaborate administrative records available through the EPA's Clean Air Docket in Washington and many are now being placed on an electronic docket available to all. The EPA also maintains libraries in each of its ten regional offices. Most of the EPA's rules are developed through workshops, with workshop materials available from the EPA or state agencies.

Less formally, the EPA, state, and local air regulators participate in conferences and sponsor seminars through professional and other organizations. The American Bar Association and its main technical counterpart, the Air and Waste Management Association, sponsor and cosponsor many such events and publish numerous specialized articles, books, and other materials for practitioners.[10]

In recent years, the EPA has significantly upgraded its electronic bulletin board. The EPA's Office of Air Quality Planning and Standards has created a Technology Transfer Network (TTN) of electronic bulletin boards. The network provides information and technology exchange in different areas of air pollution control and is free, except for the telephone charge. It is available to anyone in the world and is accessible from any computer by using a modem and communications software.

The growth of the Internet has included CAA information. The EPA and most states have led the way. The size and variety of CAA documents available on the Internet is staggering. Anyone with Internet access can now electronically participate in rulemakings, monitor workshops, and even apply for a permit.

The EPA, state, and local air quality regulators also have created many new forums for gathering information, discussing policy, and influencing policy makers. Workshops, roundtables, and other forums are now available to almost everyone. Agencies are reaching out to minority groups and others who have not been able to participate in the past.

The EPA has had to focus on implementing the 1990 CAA Amendments in recent years. In its eighth and final progress report in 1999, the EPA dropped its previous statements pledging the necessary support for the states while claiming to have broken the regulatory gridlock of the past. Instead, the EPA lauded the benefits of the EPA's federal efforts—especially the benefits in reducing emissions from the national motor vehicle, fuels, and toxics programs—and claimed credit for assisting the states with programs like "a model NO_x Budget Trading Program" for twenty-two states and the District of Columbia.[11]

The President's selection of a former industrial-state governor as the EPA Administrator in 2001 took state/federal relations under the Clean Air

Act in new directions. In her tenure, Administrator Christine Todd Whitman emphasized partnerships:

> Much of the progress described in the report is a direct result of contributions by our federal, state, local, and tribal partners. Ensuring strong and creative partnerships was a significant focus in FY 2001, and it continues to be a top priority. As a former Governor, I know the importance of providing opportunities for flexibility and innovation to solve local problems in addition to achieving national results.[12]

Former Administrator Whitman's statement repeats many of the themes found throughout the history of the CAA—since Governor Reagan's message to the EPA—and throughout this handbook. The practitioner who masters these CAA themes and the tools available for CAA research will find solutions to most CAA problems.

Notes

1. The federal Clean Air Act is codified at 42 U.S. Code § 7401, *et seq.* There have been three major sets of CAA amendments: Clean Air Act Amendments of 1970, Pub. L. No. 91-604, 84 Stat. 1676; Clean Air Act Amendments of 1977, Pub. L. No. 9-95, 91 Stat. 685; and Clean Air Act Amendments of 1990, Pub. L. No. 10-549, 108 Stat. 2399. The EPA's regulations implementing the CAA are set forth at 40 C.F.R. pts. 50–99.

2. Letter, dated February 21, 1972, from Governor Ronald Reagan to the EPA Administrator William Ruckelshaus.

3. Letter, dated November 15, 1994, from James D. Boyd, Executive Officer, California Air Resources Board, to Felicia Marcus, Regional Administrator, Region IX, U.S. Environmental Protection Agency.

4. The CAA has spawned acronyms and even acronyms of acronyms (e.g., HON stands for "hazardous organic NESHAPs"). NESHAP means National Emission Standards for Hazardous Air Pollutants. See the glossary of acronyms at the end of this handbook. CAA practitioners have developed the habit of pronouncing many of the acronyms as if they were real words rather than spelling them out (e.g., SIP rhymes with *zip* and NAAQS rhymes with *tax*).

5. Finding of Significant Contribution and Rulemaking for Certain States in the Ozone Transport Assessment Group Region for Purposes of Reducing Regional Transport of Ozone, 63 Fed. Reg. 57,356 (Oct. 27, 1998); *see also* Findings of Significant Contribution and Rulemaking on Section 126 Petitions for Purposes of Reducing Interstate Ozone Transport, 65 Fed. Reg. 2674 (Jan. 18, 2000).

6. "Nine States Sue Bush Administration for Gutting Key Component of Clean Air Act," Office of New York State Attorney General Eliot Spitzer, Press Release (December 31, 2002).

7. The literature is rich and includes useful books, articles, and newspaper accounts of very specific environmental conditions in particular states and local areas. Public libraries can often help locate such materials, as can specialized technical and university libraries. Unfortunately, most law libraries do not go back far enough or collect the type of loose-bound reports that may be most helpful to the practitioner in a specific case.

8. The EPA regularly reports on its progress in protecting the environment and implementing the CAA. The latest report is titled "Fiscal Year 2002 Annual Report" and can be found on the EPA's Web site at http://www.epa.gov/ocfo.

9. SEN. COMM. ON ENVIRONMENT AND PUBLIC WORKS, A LEGISLATIVE HISTORY OF THE CLEAN AIR ACT AMENDMENTS OF 1990 TOGETHER WITH A SECTION-BY-SECTION INDEX, S. REP. NO. 103–38, vols. I–VI (November 1993). This compilation includes notable legislation that would have amended the CAA during the 1980s. The history also includes many useful charts and background documents. Though the compilation comprises more than 10,000 pages, the most authoritative explanation of the intent of Congress in enacting the 1990 CAA Amendments is found in the twenty-page "Joint Explanatory Statement of the Committee of Conference" accompanying the final conference report version of the bill. *See* H.R. REP. No. 101-952 (October 26, 1990).

10. For example, the ABA Section of Natural Resources, Energy, and Environmental Law and the Air and Waste Management Association cosponsor the Annual Clean Air Act Videoconference, available at more than eighty down-link sites around the country.

11. Implementation Strategy for the Clean Air Act Amendments of 1990—Update March 1999 (EPA 4-10-K-99-001, March 1999).

12. U.S. Environmental Protection Agency, Fiscal Year 2001 Annual Report.

CHAPTER 2

Setting National Ambient Air Quality Standards

RICHARD E. AYRES
MARY ROSE KORNREICH

The Role of the National Ambient Air Quality Standards

The regulatory scheme established by the Clean Air Act of 1970 (CAA) was based primarily on the concept of nationwide air quality goals and individual state plans to meet those goals. As the statutory scheme has grown more complex, those nationwide goals—the National Ambient Air Quality Standards (NAAQS)—have continued to play an important role. The Environmental Protection Agency (EPA) has promulgated NAAQS for six criteria pollutants: sulfur dioxide (SO_2), particulate matter (PM), nitrogen oxide (NO_x), carbon monoxide (CO), ozone (O_3), and lead (Pb). The NAAQS are codified at 40 C.F.R. Part 50.

For each of these pollutants, the EPA sets standards known as "primary NAAQS" at a level designed to protect the public health with an adequate margin of safety as well as standards known as "secondary NAAQS" at a level designed to protect public welfare. States are primarily responsible for ensuring attainment and maintenance of NAAQS once the EPA has established them.

The NAAQS are not directly enforceable, but they establish ceilings for concentrations of criteria pollutants that are not supposed to be exceeded anywhere in the United States. The NAAQS are implemented through enforceable source-specific emission limitations and other air quality rules established by the states in state implementation plans (SIPs), which are designed to "attain" or "maintain" the NAAQS. (Requirements for these SIPs are discussed in Chapter 3.)

After nearly ten years in which review of the NAAQS was generally considered to be a low priority item at the EPA, in 1996 and 1997 the issue became the most contentious air quality issue since enactment of the 1990 CAA Amendments. In late 1996 the EPA proposed to tighten both the ozone and PM NAAQS. The agency also decided not to revise the SO_2 NAAQS, but proposed a new "intervention level program" to address short-term exposures. Subsequently, the EPA promulgated revised NAAQS for both ozone and PM. Based on studies that were not available when the original ozone and PM NAAQS were established, the new NAAQS place limits on ozone and PM averaged over eight-hour periods.

Promulgation of the new NAAQS was immediately followed by litigation brought by numerous industrial groups in the United States Court of Appeals for the District of Columbia. The D.C. Circuit rejected the EPA's standards, based on the hoary constitutional doctrine of nondelegation. Subsequently, in *Whitman v. American Trucking Ass'ns (ATA II)*, the United States Supreme Court reversed the D.C. Circuit on this point, ruling that the Clean Air Act did not affect an unconstitutional delegation of legislative power to the Environmental Protection Agency, and affirming the fundamental health basis for the NAAQS.[1] Thus it appears that, thirty-one years after the first major federal Clean Air Act was passed, the fundamental health basis for the statute's programs has finally been fully vindicated.

Statutory Requirements for Establishment of Air Quality Standards

Requirements for Listing Pollutants

Section 108 requires the EPA to promulgate a list of air pollutants that are emitted by "numerous or diverse" sources and whose presence in the atmosphere "may reasonably be anticipated to endanger public health or welfare." The CAA does not specify procedural requirements for listing a pollutant under Section 108.

The EPA administrator has a duty to list a substance if he or she determines that (1) the substance is an air pollutant as defined by Section 302(g); (2) the pollutant is emitted by numerous or diverse sources; and (3) the pollutant's presence in the atmosphere "may reasonably be anticipated to endanger public health or welfare."[2] The administrator's duty to list was held to be mandatory in *Natural Resources Defense Council v. Train*,[3] an action to compel the EPA to list lead as a pollutant under Section 108. The U.S. Court of Appeals for the Second Circuit upheld a district court decision requiring that once the administrator determines that a pollutant has an adverse effect on public health or welfare and comes from numerous or diverse sources, a duty to list attaches.

The CAA distinguishes between pollutants from numerous and diverse sources and pollutants that pose dangers only in areas immediately surrounding specific sources of pollutants.[4] Congress intended that NAAQS be established for pollutants that are "generally present in the ambient air in all areas of the nation" and "are generally detectable through monitoring devices and systems."[5] Air pollutants that endanger health and welfare but are confined to a localized area or the emission source and are not generally detectable in the ambient air are regulated either as hazardous air pollutants under Section 112 or pursuant to standards of performance under Section 111 for new stationary sources. Congress's decision in 1990 to list 189 hazardous air pollutants under Section 112(b) probably makes listing of new criteria pollutants under Section 108 less likely.

Requirements for Publishing Air Quality "Criteria"

For each listed pollutant, the EPA is required to publish air quality "criteria" that will "accurately reflect the latest scientific knowledge useful in indicating the kind and extent of all identifiable effects on public health or welfare which may be expected from the presence of such pollutant in the ambient air."[6] The concept of air quality criteria was introduced into the air pollution vocabulary by the Clean Air Act of 1963, which directed the Secretary of Health, Education, and Welfare to "compile and publish criteria reflecting accurately the latest scientific knowledge useful in indicating the kind and extent of such [health and welfare] effects which may be expected from the presence of such air pollution agent."[7] For this reason, substances listed pursuant to Section 108 are referred to as "criteria pollutants." The lengthy document in which the EPA publishes the air quality criteria is referred to as a "Criteria Document." The term "criteria" as used in Section 108 does not have its usual meaning of a standard of judgment; rather, the Criteria Document is a document that provides the scientific basis for promulgation of air quality standards.

The administrator must issue air quality criteria for a substance within twelve months of listing the substance.[8] Criteria Documents are announced in the *Federal Register* when the NAAQS for the pollutant is proposed. Judicial review of a Criteria Document cannot be obtained, except in the context of litigation seeking review of a NAAQS.

Requirements for Establishing NAAQS for Each Criteria Pollutant

Section 109 of the CAA requires the EPA to promulgate regulations prescribing a national primary ambient air quality standard and a secondary ambient air quality standard for each criteria pollutant identified under Section 108. The NAAQS are to be based on the information presented in the Criteria Document. Although the CAA does not define "ambient air," 40 C.F.R. §50.1(e) defines ambient air as "that portion of the atmosphere, external to buildings, to which the general public has access."

The EPA must propose national primary and secondary NAAQS for a criteria pollutant within twelve months of listing the pollutant pursuant to Section 108. The standards are proposed at the same time that the air quality "criteria" are issued.[9]

NAAQS are expressed in terms of concentration of a pollutant in the outdoor ("ambient") air. This may be in the form of mass of pollutant per volume of air or as x parts of pollutant per million (ppm). Concentration levels are to be measured over specific "averaging times." For example, the NAAQS for carbon monoxide (CO) specifies one-hour and eight-hour averaging periods, while the particulate matter (PM) standards are as averaged over twenty-four-hour and annual periods.[10] A NAAQS is not necessarily exceeded upon one reading in excess of the specified concentration. An "exceedance" triggering regulatory attention is expressed in statistical terms. It occurs only when a number of readings (specified in each NAAQS) are registered within a specified period of time. The appendices to 40 C.F.R. Part 50 specify the reference methods for measuring compliance with the different NAAQS.

Primary NAAQS

Section 109(b)(1) defines primary NAAQS as ambient air quality standards that will protect the public health with an "adequate margin of safety." [11] The margin-of-safety requirement expresses a risk avoidance policy. Historically the agency has articulated this policy in terms of setting NAAQS at air pollution levels below those at which adverse health effects have been found or might be expected to occur in sensitive groups.[12] The administrator sets primary NAAQS

> not only to prevent pollution levels that have been demonstrated to be harmful, but also to prevent lower pollutant levels that she finds pose an unacceptable risk of harm, even if that risk is not precisely identified as to nature or degree. In selecting a margin of safety, the EPA has considered such factors as the nature and severity of health effects involved, the size of sensitive population(s) at risk, and the kind and degree of the uncertainties that must be addressed.[13]

This interpretation has support in the legislative history and judicial opinions. The Report of the Senate Committee that crafted this language made clear the broad public health objective of the NAAQS. The term "public health" includes "the health of susceptible individuals as well as healthy adults."[14] The Senate Report stated that the NAAQS are to be established at levels that will protect "sensitive groups" such as "bronchial asthmatics and emphysematics who in the normal course of daily activity are exposed to the ambient environment."[15] The EPA has consistently taken the position that the sole statutory standard for primary NAAQS is protection of the public health.

In *Lead Industries Association v. EPA*,[16] the court rejected the petitioner's claim that the EPA administrator exceeded his statutory authority by promulgating a primary air quality standard that was more stringent than necessary to protect the public health. The court found that Congress "specifically directed the Administrator to allow an adequate margin of safety to protect against effects which have not yet been uncovered by research and effects whose medical significance is a matter of disagreement."[17] In explaining that an administrator must use his or her judgment in the face of uncertainty, the court referred to its previous opinion in *Environmental Defense Fund v. EPA*,[18] which stated:

> If administrative responsibility to protect against the unknown dangers presents a difficult task, indeed, a veritable paradox—calling as it does for knowledge for that which is unknown—then the term "margin of

safety" is Congress' directive that means be found to carry out the task and to reconcile the paradox.[19]

In refuting the petitioner's argument that the administrator had made allowance for a margin of safety by making conservative assumptions at several points in his analysis and should not have added additional safety factors at the end, the court drew a "distinction between scientific judgments based on the available evidence and allowances for margins of safety."[20]

Prior to the *American Trucking Ass'ns* litigation, discussed at length below, the D.C. Circuit held in two instances that the Clean Air Act prohibits the EPA from considering either economic cost or technical feasibility when the agency undertakes a rule making to establish or revise a primary NAAQS.

In *Lead Industries*, the court rejected the industry petitioner's claim that the EPA erred by not considering economic or technical feasibility in setting the primary NAAQS for lead. The court held that "the statute and its legislative history make clear that economic considerations play no part in the promulgation of ambient air quality standards under Section 109."[21] It also explained that Congress deliberately designed Section 109 to force regulated sources to develop pollution control devices that might, at the time the standards are promulgated, appear to be economically or technologically infeasible.[22]

Lead Industries was cited in *American Petroleum Institute v. Costle*, in which the D.C. Circuit held that "[a]ttainability and technological feasibility are not relevant considerations in the promulgation of national ambient air quality standards."[23] The views of these courts were vindicated in *ATA II*.[24]

Secondary NAAQS

Secondary NAAQS are defined by Section 109(b)(2) as ambient air quality standards that will "protect the public welfare from any known or anticipated adverse effects associated with the presence of such air pollutant in the ambient air." Section 302(h)[25] defines public welfare to include effects on soils, water, crops, wildlife, weather, economic values, and personal comfort and well-being.

The sweeping language and legislative history of the secondary NAAQS would suggest that these standards would have important pollution control implications. However, the EPA has administered the secondary NAAQS program in a way that has rendered them largely vestigial. Thus, the EPA set secondary standards at the same level as the primary standards for PM, ozone, nitrogen dioxide, and lead. There is no secondary standard for CO. Only in the case of SO_2 is there a separate secondary standard. Whether this approach would withstand judicial scrutiny has never been tested.

The 1997 NAAQS Revisions and Subsequent Litigation

In 1997, the EPA adopted revised NAAQS for ozone and PM. These standards were immediately challenged by numerous companies and industry associations in the United States Court of Appeals for the District of Columbia

Circuit. This litigation led to the Supreme Court's decision in *ATA II*, which affirmed definitively the EPA position of more than thirty years that health effects are the only permissible basis for primary NAAQS. This position was initially affirmed by the D.C. Circuit in *American Trucking Ass'ns, et al., v. EPA (ATA I)*, wherein the court affirmed the long-standing law of the circuit that the EPA was prohibited from considering economic costs when determining the appropriate level of a NAAQS.[26] But in a two-to-one divided opinion, the circuit court then overturned the NAAQS on the basis of a Depression-era constitutional interpretation that has lain unused since the "Court packing" controversy of President Franklin Roosevelt's second term. The court held that on its face, Section 109(b)(1) of the Clean Air Act unconstitutionally delegated legislative power to the Environmental Protection Agency. Section 109(b)(1)'s direction that the EPA set NAAQS "requisite to protect the public health, with an adequate margin of safety" did not provide sufficiently clear direction to the EPA, according to the court, and therefore delegated the legislative power to the agency.

Despite concluding that the statute was unconstitutional, the court did not strike down Section 109(b)(1). Instead, curiously, the court remanded the NAAQS to the agency, to provide the EPA the opportunity to reinterpret the statute to cure the unconstitutional delegation. In light of its ruling on the constitutionality of the statute, the court declined to review whether the standards chosen were arbitrary, as claimed by the petitioners. It did, however, remand the ozone NAAQS to the EPA to consider the potential benefits of tropospheric ozone in shielding humans from ultraviolet radiation.

The EPA sought review of the Court of Appeals constitutional ruling, while the industry groups cross-petitioned, asking the Supreme Court to reverse the lower court's ruling on the role of economic considerations in establishing NAAQS. The Supreme Court ruled unanimously in the EPA's favor.

In a strongly worded opinion,[27] Justice Scalia affirmed the lower court's holding that the EPA was barred by the Clean Air Act from considering cost:

> The text of § 109(b), interpreted in its statutory and historical context and with appreciation for its importance to the CAA as a whole, unambiguously bars cost considerations from the NAAQS-setting process, and thus ends the matter for us as well as the EPA.[28]

Having disposed of the primary issue, the Court went on consider to two other issues. First, the Court gave the back of the hand to the Court of Appeals' nondelegation holding. Dismissing the idea that an agency can cure an unlawful delegation of legislative power by adopting a limiting construction of the statute, the Court went on to hold that "The scope of discretion § 109(b)(1) allows is in fact well within the outer limits of our nondelegation precedents."[29]

Second, the Court overturned the decision of the Court of Appeals that the implementation of the new ozone NAAQS must be carried out under the rules of "Subpart 2" of Title I of the CAA. Finding that neither Subparts 1 nor 2 entirely governs implementation of a newly adopted NAAQS, the

Court ruled that the EPA could use its discretion in fashioning a means to harmonize the two subparts, but cannot treat either as a nullity. Thus the Court determined that the EPA implementation plan for the ozone NAAQS was unlawful, and remanded to the agency to "develop a reasonable interpretation of the nonattainment implementation provisions insofar as they apply to revised ozone NAAQS."[30]

Subsequent to the Supreme Court's ruling in *ATA II*, most of the parties in that litigation again asked for review of the ozone and particulate matter NAAQS by the D.C. Circuit. Since in the first *ATA* case the D.C. Circuit had held Section 109 of the Clean Air Act unconstitutional, it had not reached the question whether, assuming the statute constitutional, the EPA's NAAQS could pass muster as reasoned decision making.

In these consolidated cases, *American Trucking Ass'ns v. Environmental Protection Agency (ATA III)*, the D.C. Circuit considered and rejected claims that the EPA's decisions on the two NAAQS were arbitrary and capricious, thus ending, as a practical matter, all challenges to the revised NAAQS.[31] In language that could be foreseen in future NAAQS challenges, the court held that the EPA need not identify a "perfectly safe" level of pollution, "rely on specific risk estimates, or . . . specify threshold amounts of scientific information."[32] The agency's "inability to guarantee the accuracy or increase the precision of the $PM_{2.5}$ NAAQS in no way undermines the standards' validity."[33] To rule otherwise, the court concluded, would "thwart[] the Clean Air Act's requirement that the Agency err on the side of caution by setting primary NAAQS that 'allow[] an adequate margin of safety[.]'"[34]

Most recently, the EPA responded to the court of appeals' direction in *ATA I* to review the ozone NAAQS in light of the possibility that tropospheric ozone would provide protection from ultraviolet radiation.[35] In its response, the EPA concluded that the relationship between changes in tropospheric ozone concentrations and changes in relevant patterns of ultraviolet radiation "are too uncertain at this point to warrant any relaxation in the level of public health protection previously determined to be requisite to protect against demonstrated direct adverse respiratory effects of O_3 in the ambient air."[36]

While the issues surrounding the 1997 NAAQS rule making were being settled in the courts, the five-year interval provided in the Act[37] for review of the NAAQS passed. On March 31, 2003, the American Lung Association and others sued the EPA for enforcement of the deadline. In a consent decree announced May 19, 2003, the EPA agreed to issue a proposed rule setting forth the results of its review of the PM NAAQS and propose any revisions by March 31, 2005, and issue a final rule by December 20, 2005. The agency also agreed to issue a proposed rule with regard to the ozone NAAQS by March 31, 2006, and to promulgate a final ozone NAAQS rule by December 20, 2006.[38]

The NAAQS Review Process

Section 109(d)(1) requires review of existing NAAQS at five-year intervals and, if appropriate, revision. Since the EPA has not listed any new criteria pollutants under Section 108 in recent years, the standards review process is where nearly all of the EPA's work on the NAAQS has taken place. The complexity of the review process and other competing concerns have led the EPA to take much longer than five years for its review of NAAQS. As the American Lung litigation mentioned previously suggests, the timing for the reviews has usually been driven by deadline suits brought by environmental organizations. The review process is composed of several phases.

The Scientific Assessment Phase

During the scientific assessment phase, the EPA assesses scientific and technical data and provides opportunities for public and expert review of relevant staff documents. Criteria Documents are revised to incorporate information that has become available since the previous Criteria Document was prepared. As the amount of information on effects of the criteria pollutants has increased, Criteria Documents have become comprehensive, multivolume assessments of medical, scientific, and technical information.

The review process for a Criteria Document begins with an extensive search of the scientific literature on the health and welfare effects of the air pollutant. The EPA publishes a *Federal Register* notice announcing the commencement of the review and inviting submission of relevant scientific and technical papers for consideration in the preparation of the Criteria Document. When new information appears to justify revision of a Criteria Document, teams of experts, both inside and outside of the EPA, prepare a "workshop draft" of a revised document.[39] This draft is reviewed by peer-review workshops, involving experts in the areas covered in each draft chapter. The workshop draft is also made available for public review and comment. Chapter authors revise the workshop draft in response to comments received. The EPA then integrates chapters on health and welfare effects and prepares an executive summary.

Successive drafts of the revised Criteria Document are reviewed by the public and the Clean Air Scientific Advisory Committee (CASAC) of the EPA's Science Advisory Board (SAB), an independent scientific review committee established to advise on NAAQS pursuant to Section 109(d)(2). The CASAC meetings are ordinarily attended by representatives of concerned industries, environmental organizations, and other interested parties. The public is given an opportunity to present written comments to the committee and to make brief oral presentations. These public meetings may last several days. CASAC provides detailed comments on each chapter of the document. EPA staff and contracted chapter authors revise the draft document to incorporate CASAC's advice and recommendations and to address issues raised by the public. Public and CASAC comments on an external review draft may be so extensive that the EPA and CASAC agree that a revised draft should be prepared for review at a future CASAC meeting.

As the process of revising NAAQS evolved, the EPA found it useful to prepare a document that bridges the gap between the scientific review of health and welfare effects contained in the Criteria Document and the judgments required of the administrator in setting the standards. This document, referred to as the Staff Paper, has become an important element in the standards review process. It provides an opportunity for the public to comment on proposed staff recommendations before they are presented to the EPA administrator.

The EPA's Office of Air Quality Planning and Standards (OAQPS) uses the Criteria Document to prepare the Staff Paper. The Staff Paper is an evaluative document that assesses the implications for standard setting of information in the Criteria Document and presents staff recommendations for NAAQS decision making. A draft of the Staff Paper is submitted to staff experts in pertinent EPA offices for internal agency review. The EPA staff members then incorporate comments and recommendations produced through the agency review process and prepare the external review draft.

The draft Staff Paper is made available both to CASAC and to the public for external review. The purpose of this review is to ensure that the staff has correctly interpreted the scientific data presented in the Criteria Document and that the staff's recommendations on the indicators, averaging times, forms, and levels for the primary and secondary NAAQS are supported by the underlying scientific data. CASAC and its consultants meet to review the Staff Paper. The public is given the opportunity to submit written comments to CASAC and to present oral comments at the meeting. The EPA staff revises the draft Staff Paper in accord with CASAC recommendations.

The revised drafts of both the Criteria Document and the Staff Paper are submitted to CASAC and released to the public for review. CASAC and its consultants meet to review these revised drafts. The public is again invited to participate. When CASAC completes its review, it formally submits its advice and recommendations to the administrator in the form of a closure letter. In preparing the final Criteria Document and Staff Paper, the EPA incorporates appropriate revisions recommended by CASAC and addresses any remaining issues raised by the public.

The Regulatory Development Phase

When the EPA considers revising a NAAQS, the EPA staff prepares a number of regulatory decision packages for the administrator to consider. A NAAQS decision package will include the staff's recommendations on the indicators, averaging times, forms, and levels for primary and secondary NAAQS. The decision package will also present appropriate alternatives raised during the review process, along with the basis for each alternative and the rationale for the staff's recommendations. In addition, separate decision packages are prepared on key aspects of SIP requirements and monitoring requirements necessary to implement staff recommendations on the NAAQS.

The administrator considers the revised Criteria Document, the Staff Paper, and the advice of CASAC in deciding whether to propose revising a NAAQS. Once the administrator decides to revise the NAAQS, he or she must reach decisions on the key issues raised in the decision packages. A crucial decision is determining an appropriate level for the primary NAAQS, which must incorporate an "adequate margin of safety" that, in the administrator's judgment, is requisite to protect the public health.

Rule-making procedures for proposing revision of a NAAQS are governed by CAA Section 307(d). (See Chapter 20 for a detailed discussion.) The proposal must set forth or summarize CASAC's advice and justify any significant departures from that advice.

Under guidance from the administrator, the EPA staff prepares a draft *Federal Register* notice of the proposed NAAQS. After issuing the proposal and evaluating comments on it, the EPA must determine whether any revisions are warranted. The EPA then drafts the final decision and supporting technical documents.

The EPA's revision of a NAAQS often involves steps beyond the statutory requirements. Such steps might include preparation of supplements to Criteria Documents and Staff Papers incorporating recent advances in scientific research, additional CASAC meetings, the extension or reopening of comment periods, reproposals, and petitions for reconsideration.

The Implementation Assessment Phase

When the EPA considers revising a NAAQS, it will usually also develop related rule-making packages to implement the contemplated revision. A rule-making package will include guidance for states to use in developing SIPs, reference methods for measuring concentrations of the pollutant in the ambient air, and monitoring and surveillance requirements. Development of the regulatory implementation package proceeds in parallel with proposed revisions of NAAQS so that interested parties can examine the implementation package when they are preparing their comments on the proposed NAAQS.

Executive Order 12866 requires the EPA to prepare regulatory impact analyses. Cost and technological feasibility cannot be considered in setting NAAQS, but costs and benefits can be considered in developing control strategies. The EPA must submit the regulatory impact analyses to the Office of Management and Budget (OMB) for review.

Expediting the NAAQS Review Process

Administrator Carol Browner placed a high priority on accelerating the periodic reviews of air quality criteria and NAAQS. She directed the EPA staff involved in the most recent review of the criteria and NAAQS for ozone to examine ways of accelerating the review process while assuring a scientifically sound and legally defensible decision. This effort involved the Office of Air and Radiation, the Office of Research and Development, the Office of Planning and Evaluation, and the Office of General Counsel. The EPA staff scrutinized each step in the NAAQS review process to evaluate whether the step was necessary for the ozone review and whether the step could be executed in less than the usual time. The American Lung Association was also given an opportunity to offer suggestions for expediting the review process.

The administrator adopted measures recommended by the EPA staff and publicly announced the accelerated ozone review schedule. These measures include the following:

- Developing the Staff Paper and preparing risk assessments concurrently with revising the Criteria Document;
- Adhering to strict schedules for external review of draft Criteria Documents and Staff Papers;
- Involving senior-level EPA management throughout the process to expedite internal agency review;
- Discussing regulatory options with the OMB and other federal agencies earlier in the review process;
- Reducing the volume of information included in the revised Criteria Document by focusing on the most important new studies.[40]

Ozone and Photochemical Oxidants

Rationale for Control of Tropospheric Ozone

Ozone forms in the troposphere as a result of chemical reactions of volatile organic compounds (VOCs), NO_x, and oxygen in the presence of sunlight. The rate of these reactions increases at higher temperatures. Tropospheric (ground level) ozone is chemically identical to stratospheric ozone, which is produced miles above the earth's surface and provides a shield protecting the earth from excess ultraviolet radiation. The EPA controls tropospheric ozone because of the harmful effects it produces as a result of its oxidative properties and its proximity to humans and other living things. Tropospheric ozone is the primary constituent of smog.

Ozone, a highly reactive gas, can produce a wide variety of harmful effects. Ozone adversely affects human health, vegetation, materials, economic values, and personal comfort. Ozone damages lung tissue, reduces lung function, and sensitizes the lungs to other irritants.

Hourly average ambient ozone levels range from 0.03 ppm in remote rural areas to 0.30 ppm and occasionally higher in the most polluted urban areas.[41]

A History of Ozone Regulation

In 1971, the EPA promulgated the first NAAQS for photochemical oxidants (ozone is one of a number of chemicals that are common atmospheric oxidants).[42] These NAAQS were based on a 1970 Criteria Document issued by the Department of Health, Education, and Welfare. Both the primary and secondary NAAQS were set at an hourly average of 0.08 ppm total photochemical oxidants, not to be exceeded more than once a year. In 1977, the EPA announced its first review and update of the NAAQS for photochemical oxidants.[43] Two drafts of the revised Criteria Document were made available for public comment and peer reviewed by the Subcommittee on Scientific Criteria for Photochemical Oxidants of the EPA's SAB. The EPA published the final revised Air Quality Criteria for Ozone and Other Photochemical Oxidants in June 1978. At the same time, the agency proposed revisions to the primary and secondary NAAQS for photochemical oxidants.[44] The proposed standard included changing the chemical designation of the standards from photochemical oxidants to ozone and switching to standards with a statistical form (i.e., expected exceedances) rather than a deterministic form (i.e., not to be exceeded more than x number of times a year). The new proposed primary standard was 0.10 ppm and the proposed secondary standard was 0.08 ppm. The final rule making, announced in February 1979, revised the level of the primary standard from 0.08 ppm to 0.12 ppm, set the secondary and primary standards at identical concentrations, changed the chemical designation for the standards from "photochemical oxidants" to "ozone," and revised the definition of the point at which the standard is attained to "when the expected number of days per calendar year with maximum hourly average concentrations above 0.12 ppm is equal to or less than one as determined by Appendix H."[45]

In 1982, the EPA announced plans to revise the 1978 Criteria Document.[46] CASAC reviewed drafts of the revised Criteria Document at open meetings in 1985 and 1986 and sent the EPA administrator a closure letter on October 22, 1986. In December 1987, while reviewing a draft Staff Paper, CASAC concluded that sufficient new information existed to recommend incorporating relevant new information into a supplement to the 1986 Criteria Document and preparing a new draft Staff Paper.

In October 1991, the American Lung Association and other plaintiffs (environmental organizations and some states) filed suit under Section 304 of the CAA to compel the EPA to complete its review of the criteria and standards for ozone.[47] The complaint noted that the EPA had failed to review the standard every five years as required by the CAA. On February 28, 1992, the U.S. District Court for the Eastern District of New York signed a consent order requiring the EPA to announce its proposed decision on whether to revise the standards for ozone by publishing it in the *Federal Register* by August 1992 and to announce its final decision by March 1, 1993. The order required the EPA to use rule-making procedures in making the proposed and final decisions.

On August 10, 1992, the EPA announced that, in addition to having missed both the 1985 and 1990 deadlines for completion of review cycles under Section 109(d), it would not be able to meet the deadlines under the court order in the *American Lung Association* case.[48] In that announcement the administrator proposed to determine that revisions of the existing primary and secondary ozone standards were not appropriate at that time based on information in the 1986 Criteria Document and its supplement, which contained studies available through early 1989. Studies available after that could not be assessed in the time available under the court order in the *American Lung Association* case.[49]

On March 9, 1993, the EPA published a final decision not to revise the primary and secondary ozone NAAQS.[50] In reaching that decision, the agency considered only data available through 1989, saying that more recent data had not been adequately reviewed and assessed in a Criteria Document. As a result of its reexamination of the NAAQS review process, however, the agency did adopt measures to accelerate the next ozone NAAQS review.

Three years later, on December 13, 1996, after completing an expedited review, the EPA proposed a major change in the form of the ozone standard, together with a more stringent primary standard concentration level. The agency proposed to drop the one-hour averaging time and replace it with an eight-hour averaging time.[51] The EPA also proposed lowering the acceptable concentration from 0.12 ppm to 0.08 ppm and solicited comment on a range of alternative eight-hour concentrations, from 0.07 ppm to 0.9 ppm, as well as alternative forms for the standard. In support of its proposal, the agency cited (1) "a significant body of information available since the last [NAAQS] review" that showed "clear evidence from human clinical studies that O_3 effects of concern are associated with the 6- to 8-hour exposures tested"; (2) numerous epidemiological studies that reported excess hospital admissions and emergency department visits for respiratory causes; and, (3) laboratory animal studies that "suggest that changes in lung biochemistry and structure may, under certain circumstances, become irreversible."[52] The eight-hour, 0.8 ppm level standard was chosen based on evidence that it was necessary to protect the health of children and asthmatics.[53]

As with the proposed new particulate matter NAAQS (discussed in the next section), the EPA proposed a new way to measure attainment of the ozone NAAQS. The agency stated its desire to abandon the current "one-expected exceedance" test, under which an area is considered to be in nonattainment if the expected number of days per year on which the level is exceeded is greater than one, averaged over a three-year period. Instead, the agency proposed a concentration-based statistic. Under this methodology, which the agency said would be more statistically "stable," the standard would be measured as the three-year average of the annual third-highest maximum eight-hour ozone concentration.[54]

The EPA solicited comments on two options for the secondary NAAQS. One would have made the secondary standard consistent with the primary NAAQS. The alternative would have been a 0.06 ppm seasonal standard—based on a twelve-hour period, but measured only during the three-month period of maximum ozone concentrations (i.e., the summer).[55]

On July 18, 1997, the EPA issued a final rule adopting the 0.08 ppm eight-hour level for both primary and secondary ozone NAAQS.[56] Under this rule, an area will be considered in attainment of the ozone NAAQS when the three-year average of the annual fourth-highest daily maximum eight-hour average ozone concentrations is less than or equal to 0.08 ppm.[57]

Explaining its choice, the agency pointed to the support of CASAC, as well as the evidence reviewed by its staff and the comments received during the comment period. The EPA noted that it "took extensive and unprecedented steps to facilitate the public comment process." A national toll-free hotline was installed, as well as a system to facilitate comments by Internet. The EPA received over 14,000 calls and over 4,000 e-mails. The agency also held public hearings and meetings across the country, at which over 400 citizens testified, as well as two national satellite broadcasts. In all, the agency said, it received over 50,000 written and verbal comments on the proposed standard.[58]

The EPA explained its approach to choosing the level and averaging time for the standard as follows:

> The Administrator's task is to select a standard level that will reduce risks sufficiently to protect public health with an adequate margin of safety since a zero-risk standard is neither possible nor required by the Act. As CASAC and the Administrator recognize, the selection of a specific standard level for such pollutants requires public health policy judgments in addition to determinations of a strictly scientific nature.[59]

The agency described its approach to standard setting as integrating evidence of health effects from a number of sources, including the following: clinical studies showing effects of concern associated with six to eight hours of exposure at exposure levels as low as 0.08 ppm; numerous epidemiological studies reporting excess hospital admissions at ozone concentrations below the previous ozone NAAQS; and long-term laboratory animal studies suggesting changes in lung biochemistry and structure that may, under certain circumstances, become irreversible.[60]

The EPA responded at length to commenters who argued that when revising the NAAQS, the agency should take the cost of attainment into account.[61] The agency stated that the EPA has consistently interpreted Section 109 of the Clean Air Act as precluding consideration of cost or technical feasibility in setting NAAQS, based on the language, structure, and legislative history of the statute. It cited the court decisions in *Lead Industries* and *American Petroleum Institute v. Costle*,[62] as well as *Natural Resources Defense Council v. Administrator*[63] and *Natural Resources Defense Council v. EPA*.[64]

Particulate Matter

Rationale for Controlling Particulate Matter

"Particulate matter" is the generic term for a broad class of chemically and physically diverse substances that exist as discrete particles (liquid droplets or solids).[65] Particles may be emitted directly from a variety of stationary and mobile sources or formed in the atmosphere by transformations of gaseous emissions. Those formed in the atmosphere are sometimes referred to as "secondary particulates."

In establishing PM NAAQS, the EPA specifies (1) the particle size fraction that is to be used as an indicator of particulate pollution; (2) the appropriate averaging times and forms of the standards; and (3) the numerical levels of the standards. All of these factors are considered in evaluating the margin of safety assured by PM standards.

A History of Particulate Regulation

In 1971, the EPA promulgated the original primary and secondary NAAQS for PM.[66] The reference method for measuring these standards was the "high volume" sampler,[67] which collects PM up to a nominal size of 25 to 45 micrometers (µm) (referred to as "total suspended particulate," or TSP). The primary standards were 260 µg/m^3, twenty-four-hour average, not to be exceeded more than once per year; and 75 µg/m^3, annual geometric mean. The secondary standard was 150 µg/m^3, twenty-four-hour average, not to be exceeded more than once per year.

In 1976, the EPA decided to revise the existing Criteria Document and scheduled the process to begin in 1979.[68] The agency planned to review and revise the Criteria Document for PM concurrently with that for sulfur oxides.

In March 1984, the EPA proposed changes in the standards based on its review and revision of the criteria. On July 1, 1987, the agency announced final decisions, including (1) a new indicator for PM that includes only those particles with an aerodynamic diameter less than or equal to a nominal 10 micrometers (PM$_{10}$); (2) replacing the twenty-four-hour primary TSP standard with a twenty-four-hour PM$_{10}$ standard of 150 µg/m^3 with no more than one expected exceedance per year; (3) replacing the annual primary TSP standard with a PM$_{10}$ standard of 50 µg/m^3, expected annual arithmetic mean; and (4) replacing the secondary TSP standard with twenty-four-hour and annual PM$_{10}$ standards identical to primary standards.

At the same time that the EPA announced final revisions of primary and secondary NAAQS in terms of PM$_{10}$, the agency published an advance notice of proposed rule making for a new secondary NAAQS for fine particles (less than 2.5 µm in diameter). The principal welfare effect to be addressed by the fine particle standard would be impairment of visibility.[69] The EPA had found that climate and visibility effects were most closely related to regional fine particulate levels.[70] Because such levels were found to be related to sulfur oxide emissions, regulatory options to manage visibility impairment by regulating fine particles overlap with regulatory options for managing the acid deposition. For this reason, the EPA deferred a decision on a fine particle standard to permit development of compatible strategies for these related regional air pollution problems.[71]

Since 1987, the EPA has been accumulating additional information concerning the health and welfare effects of PM. It partially funded a number of studies, including the Harvard "Six Cities Study," to resolve some of the complex scientific issues relating to particulates. The EPA presented its plans for revision of the existing Criteria Document to CASAC.[72] The agency also cosponsored a symposium in January 1994, attended by more than two hundred scientists, to examine new data in the field of particulates. A number of scientific issues were raised concerning recent epidemiological studies, including the Six Cities Study, which reported statistical associations between health effects and particulate pollution levels below the then-existing twenty-four-hour standard. A major issue raised was that no mechanism provides a satisfactory clinical or toxicological explanation for the epidemiological observations of PM effects. Many experts believed that the causal agents are more likely to be fine particles (1 to 2.5 µm) than coarser particles (2.5 to 10 µm). This suggested that the PM_{10} standard might not be sufficient to protect public health. It also had implications for the types of sources that should be regulated, implicating sulfate and nitrate fine particles that are the products of combustion. On April 12, 1994, the EPA published a call for scientific information relevant to updating the PM Criteria Document.[73]

The EPA was sued in 1993 for failing to review and revise the NAAQS for PM as required by the CAA. The complaint was filed by the Arizona Center for Law in the Public Interest on October 18, 1993, on behalf of the American Lung Association, the Arizona Lung Association, and two individuals.[74] The district court ordered the EPA to complete review and revision of its PM air quality criteria and its PM NAAQS by January 31, 1997. The court later extended the deadline to July 1997.[75]

In April, 1995, the EPA made available an external review draft of the Criteria Document and then held a peer review meeting for the document. The agency stated that the accelerated schedule for review of the PM NAAQS meant that review of the draft document would be shortened.[76]

The EPA finally issued a proposed revised PM standard on December 13, 1996 (the same day it proposed tightening the ozone standard). The proposed NAAQS revisions added new standards for $PM_{2.5}$—particles with a diameter of 2.5 microns or less. The proposed agency NAAQS revisions included an annual concentration limit of 15 $µg/m^3$ and a twenty-four-hour limit of 50 $µg/m^3$. The annual standard was to be based on the three-year average of the annual arithmetic mean $PM_{2.5}$ concentrations, spatially averaged across an area. The twenty-four-hour standard would be based on the three-year average of the ninety-eighth percentile of twenty-four-hour $PM_{2.5}$ concentrations at each monitor within an area.[77]

Public interest in the proposed PM standard, as with the ozone NAAQS, was extremely strong. In the preamble to the final rule, the agency noted that it "took extensive and unprecedented steps to facilitate the public comment process," and had received over 14,000 telephone calls, more than 4,000 e-mails, and over 50,000 written and oral comments regarding the PM NAAQS proposal.[78] In addition, the agency held two-day public meetings in Boston, Chicago, Salt Lake City, and Durham, North Carolina.[79] The EPA adopted the revised PM standard at the same time as the revised ozone NAAQS.[80]

The agency cited information in the Criteria Document that PM is associated with "premature mortality, aggravation of respiratory and cardiovascular disease . . . , changes in lung function and increased respiratory symptoms, changes to lung tissues and structure, and altered respiratory defense mechanisms."[81] It noted "significant new evidence on the health effects of PM," particularly from large epidemiological studies, and quoted from the conclusion of the Criteria Document that these provide "evidence that serious health effects (mortality, exacerbation of chronic disease, increased hospital admissions, etc.) are associated with exposures to ambient levels of PM found in contemporary U.S. urban airsheds even at concentrations below current U.S. PM standard."[82]

The new primary $PM_{2.5}$ standard has two parts:

1. A twenty-four-hour standard, "which is met when the three-year average of the 98th percentile of 24 hour $PM_{2.5}$ concentrations at each population-oriented monitor within an area is less than or equal to 65 micrograms/meter^3," and
2. An annual standard, which "is met when the three-year average of the annual arithmetic mean $PM_{2.5}$ concentrations, from single or multiple community-oriented monitors is less than or equal to 15 micrograms/meter^3."[83]

The EPA also retained a "coarse" particle standard, but revised the form to comport with its new objective of "protecting against potential effects associated with coarse fraction particles in the size range of 2.5 to 10 micrograms"—namely, aggravation of asthma and respiratory infections and "symptoms."[84] The new primary coarse particle NAAQS were set as follows:

1. A twenty-four-hour standard, which is met when the three-year average of the 99th percentile of PM_{10} concentrations in an area does not exceed 150 micrograms/meter^3; and
2. An annual standard, which is met when the three-year average of the 99th percentile of PM_{10} concentrations in the area does not exceed 50 micrograms/meter^3.

This revised NAAQS for PM was, of course, the subject of the litigation eventually decided by the Supreme Court in *ATA II*. Subsequent to the promulgation of the new NAAQS for PM, President Clinton issued a memorandum to the Administrator of the EPA that directed that no new emission control measures be implemented under the new PM NAAQS until the completion of a scientific review of the standard and until an air quality monitoring network was put in place across the country.[85]

Sulfur Oxides

Rationale for Control of Sulfur Oxides

In setting primary NAAQS for sulfur oxides (SO_x), the EPA focuses on the health effect of SO_2, alone and in combination with other pollutants.[86] Sulfur oxide gases other than SO_2 are not commonly found in the atmosphere.[87]

SO_2 is emitted principally from combustion or processing of sulfur-containing fuels and ores. SO_2 occurs in the atmosphere with a variety of particles and other gases, and it undergoes chemical and physical interactions with them to form sulfates and other transformation products.

SO_2 can have adverse health effects.[88] Asthmatics who are physically active outdoors are the population segment at most risk for respiratory effects induced by acute exposures to SO_2. The EPA concluded in its 1986 Staff Paper that changes in lung function accompanied by symptoms could be observed at 0.4 ppm in some asthmatics performing "moderate-heavy exercise."[89] As the concentration increases, effects are more pronounced and the fraction of responding asthmatic subjects increases.[90]

Implementation of the existing NAAQS, together with fuel use shifts and siting decisions, has resulted in substantial decreases in SO_2 levels across the country. Ambient air SO_2 concentrations measured from 1983 to 1992 show a downward trend (approximately 2 percent per year), though the rate of decline has slowed over the past few years.[91] Title IV of the CAA, the acid rain program, requires that electric generating facilities reduce annual SO_2 emissions by 9 million metric tons per year from the 1980 baseline of 23.3 million metric tons, resulting in an annual emission rate of 14.22 metric tons in the year 2015.[92]

A History of Sulfur Oxide Regulation

The EPA promulgated primary and secondary NAAQS for sulfur oxides in April 1971.[93] The primary standard, measured as SO_2, was 0.14 ppm, twenty-four-hour average, not to be exceeded more than once per year; and 0.03 ppm, annual arithmetic mean. The secondary standard was 0.5 ppm, three-hour average, not to be exceeded more than once a year. The 1971 rule also included an annual secondary standard. These NAAQS were based on air quality criteria published in January 1969 by the Department of Health, Education, and Welfare, before creation of the EPA.

A court order issued in *Kennecott Copper Corp. v. EPA*[94] remanded the secondary NAAQS rule to the EPA administrator, with instructions to supply an implementing statement that would enlighten the court about the basis for the standard from material in the criteria. The administrator was given freedom to revise the secondary NAAQS if revision seemed appropriate upon reexamination of the available information. Upon remand, the administrator revoked the annual secondary standard.[95]

In 1978, the EPA decided to review the Criteria Document for SO_2 concurrently with that for PM and to produce a combined particulate matter-sulfur dioxide Criteria Document. On October 2, 1979, the agency announced it was in the process of revising the original Criteria Document and reviewing the SO_2 NAAQS.[96]

On January 29, 1982, CASAC issued a closure letter on the Criteria Document. The final Criteria Document was issued on March 20, 1982.

The EPA's Environmental Criteria and Assessment Office (ECAO) prepared an addendum to the Criteria Document on which oral closure was received from CASAC in August 1982. The OAQPS prepared a Staff Paper on which a closure letter was issued by CASAC on August 26, 1983. Subsequently the administrator took no official public action, neither revising nor formally declining to revise the NAAQS.

In 1985, environmental organizations and six states filed suit pursuant to CAA Section 304 to compel the EPA to promulgate revised NAAQS that would include protection against short-term exposure to relatively high concentrations of SO_2.[97] The plaintiffs alleged that the revised air quality Criteria Document indicated (1) that short-term exposure to SO_2 at concentrations allowed by the existing primary NAAQS is harmful to asthmatics and bronchitics; (2) that transformation of SO_2 to sulfates, which return to earth in acid rain or other forms of deposition, causes severe welfare effects through pollution of surface waters, damage to vegetation, and harm to materials; and (3) that these findings were not reflected in the secondary NAAQS. The U.S. District Court for the Southern District of New York held that the EPA administrator's duty to revise the NAAQS was discretionary and dismissed the complaints. On appeal, the Second Circuit Court held that "[a]lthough . . . Administrator has discretion to decide on the precise form and substance of the NAAQS at issue, we believe that under the circumstances the Administrator has a non-discretionary duty to make *some* formal decision whether to revise those NAAQS."[98] By the time that opinion was issued, the administrator had begun the process of decision making,[99] so the appellate court remanded to allow the district court to enter an order that the rule making be continued to final decision. The EPA and the plaintiffs ultimately entered into a consent decree requiring the EPA to take final action on the secondary standard by April 15, 1993. On April 23, 1993, the EPA announced its final decision that revision of the secondary standard was not appropriate.[100]

In 1992, the American Lung Association sued the EPA to compel review of the existing primary standard for sulfur oxides.[101] The court issued an order requiring that the EPA either (1) by November 1, 1994, take final action on the 1988 proposed decision not to revise the primary standards, or (2) propose new standards and take final action on the new proposal within one year after the close of the comment period.

On November 15, 1994, the EPA proposed not to revise the then current twenty-four-hour and annual primary standard.[102] In the same *Federal Register* notice, the agency solicited comment on the need to adopt additional regulatory measures to address short-term peak SO_2 exposures as a means of reducing health risk to exercising asthmatic individuals.

In May, 1996, the EPA issued a final decision not to revise the NAAQS at that time, except for several minor technical changes.[103] This decision was challenged by the American Lung Association and others. In a January 1998 decision, the United States Court of Appeals for the D.C. Circuit vacated and remanded the Administrator's decision.[104] The court held the EPA decision arbitrary because the agency had failed to explain adequately its decision that short-term exposures to high concentrations of sulfur dioxide did not amount to a public health problem within the meaning of Section 108(a)(1) of the Clean Air Act.[105]

The following January the agency proposed rules that would establish a new "intervention level program," rather than a short-term NAAQS, to deal with short-term exposures.[106] Relying on its emergency authority under CAA Section 303, the EPA proposed a novel program to address high five-minute concentrations of SO_2 around stationary sources. The EPA also proposed an implementation strategy for identifying and prioritizing areas with potential five-minute SO_2 peak exposures. Despite the agency's acknowledgement that short-term exposures to SO_2 are a health problem, and despite the court's direction, no program to protect public health has yet been promulgated.

Nitrogen Dioxide

Rationale for Regulation of Nitrogen Dioxide

A variety of nitrogen oxide compounds (NO_x) and their transition products occur naturally and as a result of human activities. These include nitric oxide (NO), nitrogen dioxide (NO_2), and gaseous nitrous oxide (HNO_3), in addition to nitrite and nitrate aerosols. There is little scientific evidence linking most NO_x to specific health or welfare effects at or near ambient concentrations. The one exception is nitrogen dioxide, which at high concentrations can adversely affect human health, vegetation, materials, and visibility. Respiratory effects of nitrogen dioxide in humans were of particular concern in setting primary NAAQS. The EPA identified young children and asthmatics as the groups at greatest risk from exposure to ambient levels of nitrogen dioxide.[107]

In setting secondary standards, the EPA considered reported effects of NO_x on acidic deposition, vegetation effects, materials damage, and visibility impairment.[108] Nitrogen oxides are a precursor to both ozone and acidic precipitation. Atmospheric deposition of NO_x is a potentially significant contributor to ecosystem effects, including algal blooms in certain estuaries such as the Chesapeake Bay.[109]

A History of Nitrogen Dioxide Regulation

On April 30, 1971, the EPA promulgated primary and secondary NAAQS for nitrogen dioxide. Both NAAQS were set at 0.053 ppm (100 µg/m³) averaged over one year.

On December 12, 1978, the EPA announced a review of the 1971 Criteria Document. CASAC endorsed the revised Criteria Document in its June 19, 1981, closure letter. The OAQPS presented a Staff Paper recommending alternative approaches to revising the standards. The EPA administrator concluded that the existing standards adequately protect against adverse health and welfare effects.

On February 23, 1984, the EPA published "Proposed Reaffirmation of the National Ambient Air Quality Standards for Nitrogen Dioxide." In supporting its belief that "it would be prudent public policy to maintain the current annual standard of 0.053 ppm," the EPA noted that (1) the standard was at the lower end of the range cited in the OAQPS Staff Paper to ensure an adequate margin of safety against both long-term and short-term health effects and (2) the standard would keep annual nitrogen dioxide concentrations considerably below the long-term levels for which serious chronic effects have been observed in animals.[110]

In 1993, environmentalists sued the EPA under Section 304 to compel the agency to complete its overdue review of the nitrogen dioxide NAAQS.[111] The OAQPS then issued its Staff Paper; in June 1995 CASAC reviewed it; and in October 1995 the EPA proposed not to revise either the primary or secondary standard.[112] The EPA was placed under court order to issue its final decision by October 1, 1996.[113]

Lead

Rationale for Controlling Lead

Sources

Lead (Pb) is emitted to the atmosphere by vehicles burning leaded fuel and by certain stationary sources. Airborne lead can enter the body directly through inhalation or indirectly through ingestion of lead-contaminated food, water, or nonfood materials such as lead paint, dust, and soil. In developing NAAQS, the EPA was aware that there are multiple sources of lead exposure in addition to airborne lead (e.g., lead paint, drinking water contaminated by lead from plumbing, food contaminated by lead from canning or other processes).

In 1990, Congress added Section 112(b) of the Clean Air Act, designating airborne "lead compounds" as a hazardous air pollutant (HAP). Such HAPs were to be regulated under the technology and air quality requirements of the remainder of Section 112. In the years since, the EPA has promulgated "maximum achievable control technology" (MACT) standards for a variety of sources of lead emissions. See Chapter 8.

Health Effects

Lead accumulates in the body in blood, bone, and soft tissue. Lead is not readily excreted and affects the kidneys, liver, nervous system, and blood formation (the hematopoietic system). Excessive exposure to lead may cause neurological impairments such as seizures, mental retardation, and behavioral disorders.

The EPA considers young children (age one to five years) to be a population group particularly sensitive to lead exposure. The agency based the original primary NAAQS (1.5 micrograms Pb/meter^3) on a belief that a blood lead level of 30 micrograms lead per deciliter of blood (µg Pb/dl) would be associated with impairment of heme synthesis in chronically exposed children.[114] The EPA derived the NAAQS from the administrator's judgment that, applying an appropriate margin of safety, the maximum safe blood lead level for a population of young children was 15 µg Pb/dl, of which 12 µg Pb/dl would be attributable to nonair sources.[115] The EPA considered the difference of 3.0 µg Pb/dl to be the allowable safe contribution to mean population blood level from airborne lead.[116] The latest scientific studies suggest that blood lead levels as low as 10 µm Pb/dl can adversely affect the developing mental abilities of children.[117]

A History of Airborne Lead Regulation

The EPA's initial approach to lead regulation was to limit the lead emissions from automobiles, the principal source of lead emissions, and to require the availability of unleaded gasoline. In 1975, the Natural Resources Defense Council (NRDC) and other plaintiffs brought suit against the EPA to list lead under Section 108. The court ruled in favor of NRDC.[118]

The EPA listed lead on March 31, 1976, and proceeded to develop air quality criteria and a proposed standard. On December 14, 1977, the EPA issued a Criteria Document and proposed a standard of 1.5 µg Pb/m^3, calendar month average, and issued the Criteria Document for lead.

On October 5, 1978, the EPA promulgated a NAAQS for lead at a level of 1.5 µg Pb/m^3 averaged over a calendar quarter. This standard was based on preventing most children in the United States from exceeding a blood lead level of 30 µg Pb/dl.[119] The NAAQS was upheld by the U.S. Court of Appeals for the District of Columbia Circuit in 1980.[120]

The EPA announced it would review the primary and secondary NAAQS in May, 1984. The announcement noted reports published after publication of the 1978 NAAQS suggesting that exposure to lower levels of lead may adversely affect cognitive development and neurobehavioral function in young children.[121] The EPA also noted that lead air quality monitoring performed since promulgation of the 1978 NAAQS showed a significant downward trend in atmospheric lead that correlated closely with the reduction of lead in gasoline.[122] Concentrations of lead in the ambient air of urban areas throughout the country have decreased 89 percent since 1984.[123]

The lead NAAQS is being attained in all areas except those near lead smelters, refineries, and remelters.[124] In these areas, exposures are owing to both current emissions and resuspension of soil contaminated by past emissions.[125]

Carbon Monoxide

Rationale for Regulating Carbon Monoxide

Carbon monoxide is a colorless and odorless gas that is generally unreactive with other constituents of the urban atmosphere.[126] The primary sources of CO emissions are vehicle exhausts.

CO is toxic to mammals because of its strong tendency to combine with hemoglobin to form carboxyhemoglobin.[127] This reduces the oxygen-carrying capacity of the blood, since the hemoglobin that has combined with CO is no longer available to carry oxygen; further, the presence of carboxyhemoglobin inhibits the release of oxygen from the remaining hemoglobin. Relatively low levels of CO exposure have been reported to aggravate cardiovascular disease and to affect the central nervous system. These observations are attributable to the reduced capacity of blood to carry oxygen to these systems. The health threat from CO is most serious for those who suffer from cardiovascular disease.

The primary NAAQS was based on evidence that low levels of carboxyhemoglobin in human blood may be associated with impairment of ability to discriminate time intervals.[128] In 1980, the EPA proposed to base the primary NAAQS on aggravation of cardiovascular disease.[129]

A History of Carbon Monoxide Regulation

On April 30, 1971, the EPA promulgated NAAQS for CO based on a Criteria Document published by the U.S. Department of Health, Education, and Welfare in March 1970. Both primary and secondary standards were set at 9 ppm, eight-hour average, and 35 ppm, one-hour average, neither to be exceeded more than once a year.

On December 1, 1978, the EPA announced review and update of the 1970 Criteria Document. In 1979, CASAC reviewed a revised Criteria Document and Staff Paper. On August 18, 1980, the EPA proposed retaining the existing primary eight-hour standard and lowering the primary one-hour standard to 25 ppm.[130] A secondary-effect standard was not deemed appropriate for CO because its environmental effects have been observed only when its levels reach relatively high concentrations, which are rarely, if ever, reached in the ambient air.[131]

After publishing the 1980 proposal, the EPA became aware of problems with some of the data upon which it had relied and prepared a draft addendum to the 1979 Criteria Document to reevaluate the scientific evidence on the health effects of CO.[132] On June 18, 1982, the EPA announced a second public comment period.[133] During July and August 1982, CASAC met and advised the EPA administrator on key issues. In September 1983, CASAC reviewed a revised Criteria Document prepared by ECAO and a revised staff reassessment prepared by the OAQPS. CASAC sent a closure letter to the administrator on May 17, 1984. On August 9, 1984, the EPA announced availability of the final addendum and staff reassessment.[134] On September 13, 1985, the EPA announced its final decision not to revise the existing primary standards and to revoke the secondary standards for CO.[135]

A draft revised Criteria Document for CO was made available for external review on April 19, 1990,[136] and reviewed by CASAC in April 1991. CASAC sent the administrator a closure letter on July 17, 1991. A revised draft Staff Paper was made available for external review in February 1992 and was reviewed by CASAC in March 1992. CASAC agreed with the Staff Paper's conclusion that a standard of the present form and with a numerical value similar to the present standard was supported by the scientific data.[137]

On August 1, 1994, the EPA announced its final decision not to revise the CO NAAQS.[138] The primary standards for CO remain at 35 ppm averaged over one hour and 9 ppm averaged over eight hours.

Conclusion

With the decision of the Supreme Court in *ATA II*, the battle that has raged for more than three decades over the appropriate basis for NAAQS appears finally to be over. In *ATA II*, the Supreme Court vindicated the concept of the 1970 Clean Air Amendments, the source of the NAAQS program. NAAQS were intended to establish the air quality "requisite to protect public health," unalloyed by reference to cost. The technical and economic difficulties of achieving these goals were to be dealt with elsewhere within the program.

The authors of the 1970 CAA felt that establishing ambitious public health goals would create pressures on government and industry to develop new technologies and practices. To a very considerable extent, this vision has proven prescient. While nonattainment of the ozone and PM NAAQS remains the rule in urban areas, air quality has improved dramatically since 1970, despite continued strong economic growth and more than a doubling of the annual vehicle miles traveled nationally. It is fair to say that without the benchmark of the health standards, this improvement would not have occurred.

Notes

1. *Whitman v. American Trucking Ass'ns, et al.*, 531 U.S. 457 (2001) [hereinafter *ATA II*].
2. CAA § 108(a)(1).
3. 411 F. Supp. 864 (S.D.N.Y.), *aff'd*, 545 F.2d 320 (2d Cir. 1976).
4. S. Rep. No. 91–1196, at 18 (1970).
5. *Id.* at 9, 18.
6. CAA § 108(a)(2).
7. § (3)(c)(2), P.L. 88–206, 77 Stat. 392, 395.
8. CAA § 108(a)(2).
9. CAA §§ 108(a)(2), 109(b)(2).
10. 40 C.F.R. §§ 50.8, 50.6.
11. Section 109(b)(1), 42 U.S.C. § 7409(b)(1).
12. *See, e.g.*, 52 Fed. Reg. 24,634, 24,641 (1987).
13. 59 Fed. Reg. 58,598–59 (1994).
14. S. Rep. No. 91–1196, at 9, 10 (1970). *See also* H.R. Rep. No. 95–294, at 50 (1977).
15. Sen. Comm. on Public Works Rep., National Air Quality Standards Act of 1970 (September 17, 1970), at 10.
16. 647 F.2d 1130 (D.C. Cir.), *cert. denied*, 449 U.S. 1042 (1980) [hereinafter *Lead Industries*].
17. *Id.* at 1154.
18. 598 F.2d 62 (D.C. Cir. 1978).
19. Environmental Defense Fund v. EPA, 598 F.2d 62, 81 (D.C. Cir. 1978).

20. *Lead Industries*, 647 F.2d at 1162.

21. *Id*. at 1148.

22. *Id*. at 1149.

23. 665 F.2d 1176, 1185 (D.C. Cir. 1981).

24. *ATA II, supra*.

25. 42 U.S.C. 7602(h).

26. *American Trucking Ass'ns, et. al., v. EPA*, 175 F.3d 1027 (D.C. Cir. 1999).

27. *See, e.g.*, Justice Scalia's caustic remark that "Were it not for the hundreds of pages of briefing respondents have submitted on the issue, one would have thought it fairly clear that this text does not permit the EPA to consider costs in setting the standards. The language, as one scholar has noted, 'is absolute.'" *ATA II* at 461.

28. *Id*.

29. *Id*. at 464.

30. *Id*. at 477. *See* Chapter 3.

31. *American Trucking Ass'ns v. Environmental Protection Agency*, 283 F.3d 355 (D.C. Cir. 2001) [hereinafter *ATA III*].

32. *ATA III*, at 369.

33. *Id*.

34. *Id*.

35. 68 Fed. Reg. 614 (January 6, 2003).

36. *Id*.

37. CAA § 109(d)(1), 42 U.S.C. 7409(d)(1).

38. American Lung Ass'n, et. al., v. Whitman, C.A. No. 03-778(ESH) before the U.S. District Court for the District of Columbia, Consent Decree.

39. The EPA contracts with many outside scientific experts to author various chapters of the Criteria Document.

40. 59 Fed. Reg. 5164–65 (1994).

41. 57 Fed. Reg. 35,542, 35,544 (1992).

42. 59 Fed. Reg. 5164 (1994).

43. 42 Fed. Reg. 20,493 (1977).

44. 43 Fed. Reg. 16,962 (1978).

45. 40 Fed. Reg. 8,202 (1979).

46. 47 Fed. Reg. 11,561 (1982).

47. American Lung Ass'n v. Reilly, No. 91-CV-4114 (JRB) (E.D.N.Y.).

48. 57 Fed. Reg. 35,542, 35,546 (1992).

49. *Id*. at 35,550.

50. 58 Fed. Reg. 13,008 (1993).

51. The change in the form of the standard represented a fundamental change in the agency's conception of the ozone problem. When the initial standard was set in 1971, the underlying data suggested that excessive public exposure was limited to one-hour peaks that occurred during or after rush hour traffic. Since then, the number of vehicle miles traveled in the U.S. has more than doubled, and it has become apparent that ozone levels of public health concern may extend for many hours during the day.

52. 62 Fed. Reg. 38,863.

53. 61 Fed. Reg. 65,716 (1996).

54. *Id*. at 65,730–31.

55. *Id*. at 65,734.

56. National Ambient Air Quality Standards for Ozone: Final Rule, 62 Fed. Reg. 38,856 (July 18, 1997).

57. 50 C.F.R. § 50.10(b), 62 Fed. Reg. 38,890.

58. *Id.* at 38,858.

59. *Id.* at 38,866.

60. *Id.* at [9].

61. *Id.* at [21–25]. *See also* EPA discussion of cost arguments in the final revised particulate matter NAAQS rule promulgated the same day, 62 Fed. Reg. at 38,683–88.

62. 665 F.2d 1176 (D.C. Cir. 1981), *cert. denied*, 455 U.S. 1034 (1982).

63. 902 F.2d 962 (D.C. Cir. 1990), *vacated in part, dismissed* 921 F.2d 326 (D.C. Cir. 1991), *certs. dismissed*, 498 U.S. 1075, and *cert. denied*, 498 U.S. 1082 (1991).

64. 824 F.2d 1146 (D.C. Cir. 1987)(*en banc*).

65. 52 Fed. Reg. 24,634–35 (1987).

66. 36 Fed. Reg. 8,186 (1971).

67. 40 C.F.R. pt. 50, app. B.

68. 52 Fed. Reg. 24,634–35 (1987).

69. *Id.* at 24,670.

70. *Id.*

71. *Id.*

72. 59 Fed. Reg. 17,375 (1994).

73. *Id.*

74. American Lung Ass'n v. Browner, Civ. No. 93–643 TUC ACM (D. Ariz. Oct. 12, 1993).

75. American Lung Ass'n v. Browner, Civ. No. 93–643 TUC ACM (D. Ariz. Oct. 6, 1994).

76. 60 Fed. Reg. 20,085 (1995).

77. 61 Fed. Reg. 65,638 (1996).

78. National Ambient Air Quality Standards for Particulate Matter: Final Rule, 62 Fed. Reg. 38,652, 38,654 (July 18, 1997).

79. *Id.*

80. 62 Fed. Reg. 38,652 (July 18, 1997).

81. *Id.* at 38,656.

82. *Id.* at 38,655.

83. *Id.* at 38,679.

84. *Id.* at 38,677.

85. The Clinton memo was published at 62 Fed. Reg. 38,421 (July 18, 1997). It was later codified in federal highway legislation.

86. 59 Fed. Reg. 58,958–59 (1994).

87. *Id.* The EPA considered effects of the prinicipal transformation products of sulfur dioxide (i.e., sulfuric acid and sulfates) in the review of the PM NAAQS because they commonly take a particle form in the atmosphere.

88. *Id.* Healthy nonasthmatic individuals are essentially unaffected by acute exposures to SO_2 at concentrations below 2 ppm.

89. *Id.*

90. *Id.*

91. *Id.* at 58,960.

92. *Id.*

93. 36 Fed. Reg. 8186 (1971).

94. 462 F.2d 846, 850 (1972).

95. 38 Fed. Reg. 25,679 (1973).

96. 44 Fed. Reg. 56,731 (1979).

97. Environmental Defense Fund v. Reilly, Civ. No. 85-CV9507 (S.D.N.Y.).

98. Environmental Defense Fund v. Thomas, 870 F.2d 892 (2d Cir. 1989).

99. On April 26, 1988, the EPA administrator published a proposed decision not to revise the NAAQS for sulfur oxides, 53 Fed. Reg. 14,926 (1988).

100. 58 Fed. Reg. 21,351 (1993).

101. American Lung Ass'n v. Browner, Civ. No. 92-CV-5316 (ERK) (E.D.N.Y.).

102. 59 Fed. Reg. 58,958 (1994).

103. 61 Fed. Reg. 25,566 (1996).

104. American Lung Ass'n, et. al., v. EPA, 134 F.3d 388 (D.C. Cir., 1998), *rehearing and suggestion for rehearing en banc denied* (March 3, 1999).

105. *Id*. at 392.

106.

107. 49 Fed. Reg. 6866, 6871 (1984).

108. *Id*. at 6874.

109. EPA, "National Air Quality and Emission Trends Report, 1993 Executive Summary and Selected Graphics" (released Oct. 19, 1994).

110. 49 Fed. Reg. 6,866, 6,872 (1984).

111. Oregon Natural Resources Council v. Browner, No. 91–6529-HO (D. Ore.).

112. 60 Fed. Reg. 52,874, 52,877 (1995).

113. *Id*.

114. 43 Fed. Reg. 46,246 (1978).

115. *Id*.

116. *Id*.

117. These findings were published in the *New England Journal of Medicine* on April 17, 2003.

118. NRDC v. Train, 411 F.Supp. 864 (S.D.N.Y.), *aff'd* 545 F.2d 320 (2d Cir. 1976).

119. *Id*.

120. *Lead Industries*, 647 F.2d at 1130.

121. 49 Fed. Reg. 22,021 (1984).

122. *Id*.

123. EPA, "National Air Quality and Emission Trends Report, 1993 Executive Summary and Selected Graphics" (released Oct. 19, 1994).

124. EPA, "Strategy for Reducing Lead Exposures," Feb. 21, 1991, at 29.

125. *Id*.

126. 45 Fed. Reg. 55,066 (1980).

127. *Id*. at 55,068.

128. 36 Fed. Reg. 8,166 (1971).

129. 45 Fed. Reg. 55,066, 55,073 (1980).

130. *Id*. at 55,066.

131. *Id*.

132. 59 Fed. Reg. 38,906–07 (1994).

133. 47 Fed. Reg. 26,407 (1982).

134. 49 Fed. Reg. 31,923 (1984).

135. 50 Fed. Reg. 38,908 (1985).

136. 55 Fed. Reg. 14,858 (1990).

137. 59 Fed. Reg. 38,906, 38,908 (1994).

138. *Id*. at 38,906.

CHAPTER 3

Meeting Ambient Air Standards: Development of the State Implementation Plans

ROBERT A. WYMAN, JR.
DEAN M. KATO
JEFFREY S. ALEXANDER

Introduction

Under the Clean Air Act (CAA), the Environmental Protection Agency (EPA) must establish the National Ambient Air Quality Standards (NAAQS) and publish a list of airborne pollutants subject to the primary and secondary NAAQS (as discussed in Chapter 2). Once the NAAQS are established, the CAA provides that states have the primary responsibility for achieving and maintaining the NAAQS within each air quality control region (AQCR) within each state.[1] The manner in which the NAAQS will be achieved, maintained, and enforced is to be outlined in a state implementation plan (SIP), prepared and submitted by each state, for each given pollutant. Various SIP requirements and procedures will be triggered depending on the degree of attainment or nonattainment of the NAAQS.

This chapter provides a general overview of SIP contents and other requirements. It begins with a discussion of AQCRs and attainment designations.

Air Quality Control Regions: Classification of Areas

Designation of AQCRs

The CAA identifies three procedures by which AQCRs are designated for the purpose of developing and carrying out the SIPs.[2] First, some AQCRs were designated as such before December 31, 1970, pursuant to the Air Quality Act of 1967. Second, the EPA, in conjunction with appropriate state and local authorities, may designate any interstate or major intrastate area "necessary or appropriate" for the attainment and maintenance of the NAAQS as an

AQCR. Finally, any portion of a state that is not part of any region designated by the first two means is also itself an AQCR. Such a remainder portion may be further subdivided at the state's discretion with the EPA's approval.

Redesignation of AQCRs

Under the CAA, state governors are authorized, with the EPA's approval, to redesignate or reclassify the AQCRs. However, AQCRs, or portions of AQCRs, that "significantly affect" air pollution concentrations in other states may be redesignated within a state only with approval by the EPA and the governors of any states that the EPA determines may be significantly affected by such redesignation.[3]

Interstate Transport Regions and Commissions

In addition to the AQCRs, the EPA may, either at its own discretion or upon petition by a state, establish by rule a special "transport region." To establish such a region, the EPA must determine that the interstate transport of air pollutants contributes significantly to a violation of the NAAQS within the designated region.[4] The EPA may at any time add or remove any state or portion of a state from an interstate transport region.

Each interstate transport region has its own transport commission, which is comprised of, at a minimum, (1) the EPA administrator or his or her designee; (2) the governor of the state or his or her designee; (3) the EPA regional administrator or his or her designee; and (4) a state air pollution control official.[5] Each transport commission assesses the degree of interstate transport of a pollutant, as well as mitigation strategies, and makes recommendations to the EPA to help the affected states meet the requirements of their respective SIPs.[6] Such commissions may also request the EPA to issue a finding, within eighteen months of such a request, that a SIP is "substantially inadequate" with regard to addressing interstate pollution concerns.[7]

One such transport commission, the Northeast States for Coordinated Air Use Management (NESCAUM), petitioned the EPA to allow the region to opt into the California low-emission-vehicles standard, and the EPA approved the petition, although there has been considerable debate concerning the petition. By opting into the California standard, NESCAUM hopes to lower mobile source emissions and use such reductions to help meet attainment as well as provide an offset for less stringent stationary source regulations.

Designation and Redesignation of AQCRs According to Attainment Status

Designation

A state will designate its AQCRs within one of three categories for each listed pollutant.[8] An AQCR is in "attainment" for a particular pollutant if it meets the primary or secondary NAAQS established for such a pollutant.[9]

EXHIBIT 1. National Ambient Air Quality Standards

Pollutant	Standard Value	Standard Type
Carbon Monoxide (CO)		
8-hour Average	9 ppm (10 µg/m³)	Primary
1-hour Average	35 ppm (40 µg/m³)	Primary
Nitrogen Dioxide (NO₂)		
Annual Arithmetic Mean	0.053 ppm (100 µg/m³)	Primary & Secondary
Ozone (O₃)		
1-hour Average	0.12 ppm (235 µg/m³)	Primary & Secondary
8-hour Average	0.08 ppm (157 µg/m³)	Primary & Secondary
Lead (Pb)		
Quarterly Average	1.5 µg/m³	Primary & Secondary
Particulate (PM₁₀)	*Particles with diameters of 10 micrometers or less*	
Annual Arithmetic Mean	50 µg/m³	Primary & Secondary
24-hour Average	150 µg/m³	Primary & Secondary
Particulate (PM₂.₅)	*Particles with diameters of 2.5 micrometers or less*	
Annual Arithmetic Mean	15 µg/m³	Primary & Secondary
24-hour Average	65 µg/m³	Primary & Secondary
Sulfur Dioxide (SO₂)		
Annual Arithmetic Mean	0.03 ppm (80 µg/m³)	Primary
24-hour Average	0.14 ppm (365 µg/m³)	Primary
3-hour Average	0.50 ppm (1300 µg/m³)	Secondary

(See Exhibit 1.) Accordingly, an AQCR is in "nonattainment" for a given pollutant if the "design value" of the pollutant exceeds the applicable primary or secondary NAAQS.[10] For example, the design value for ozone in a given area is the average of the fourth-highest eight-hour ozone measurement in parts per million (ppm) over a three-year period.[11] There has been some debate regarding the need for more representative design values and special intermittent measures. A region can also be in nonattainment as to a pollutant if it "contributes to ambient air quality" in a nearby area that fails to meet the primary or secondary NAAQS for the pollutant.[12] Finally, an area that cannot be classified as either meeting or falling short of the primary or secondary NAAQS for a given pollutant "on the basis of available information" will be deemed "unclassifiable."[13]

Redesignation

Generally, the attainment status of a particular AQCR may be redesignated by one of two methods: (1) The EPA releases a public notice that "available information" indicates that a redesignation would be appropriate and such redesignation is promulgated by the EPA, usually after the state governor submits a list of appropriate areas within the state or interstate area that the governor feels are appropriate for redesignation; or (2) a governor submits a petition requesting that a given area or portion thereof within the state be

EXHIBIT 2. AQCR Attainment Status Redesignation

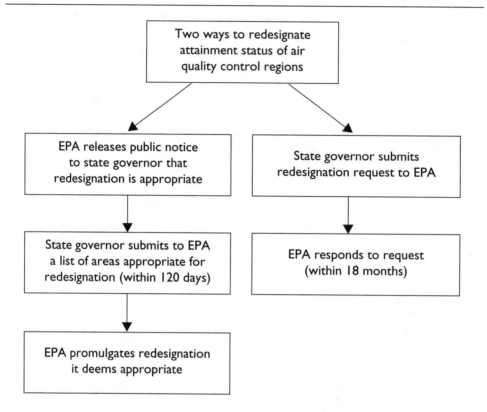

redesignated.[14] The EPA has eighteen months to approve or deny such a request.[15] (See Exhibit 2.)

Such redesignations are subject to other restrictions. First, under the CAA, the EPA may not promulgate redesignations from nonattainment to unclassifiable.[16] Second, a redesignation from nonattainment to attainment will not be granted unless (1) the EPA determines that the area has attained the NAAQS, (2) the state's SIP encompassing the area has met all requirements under the CAA and been fully approved by the EPA, (3) the EPA has fully approved a maintenance plan for the area pursuant to Section 175A of the CAA, and (4) the EPA determines that the improvement in air quality is "due to permanent and enforceable reductions in emissions" resulting from the SIP and applicable federal regulations and any other "permanent and enforceable reductions."[17]

SIP Framework and Procedures

Basic Elements of SIPs

The SIP framework was first established in the 1970 CAA, but it was modified significantly in both the 1977 and the 1990 CAA Amendments. Each SIP

EXHIBIT 3. Basic SIP Elements (CAA Section 110(a)(2))

- Enforceable emissions limitations and other control measures (including economic incentives such as fees, marketable permits, and auctions of emissions rights)
- Schedules and timetables for compliance
- Appropriate plans to monitor, compile, and analyze ambient air quality data (and to make such data available to the EPA)
- Enforcement measures
- Permit program
- Prohibition of significant contributions to nonattainment in other areas and interference with measures of SIPs of other states
- Abatement measures for interstate and international pollution
- Assurances regarding adequate resources (personnel, funding, and authority)
- Requirements regarding monitoring and reports from major stationary sources
- Citizens' suit provisions
- SIP revision provisions
- Contingency plans
- Air quality modeling
- Consultation and participation of local political subdivisions affected by the plan

---

submitted by a state under the CAA must be adopted by the state after reasonable notice and public hearing, and it must include a number of basic elements.[18] (See Exhibit 3 for a summary of the most significant elements.)

First, SIPs must include enforceable emissions limitations and other control measures, means, or techniques "necessary or appropriate" to meet the CAA requirements[19] and include a program for enforcement of such measures.[20] Post-1990 plans now include as appropriate control measures economic incentives such as fees, marketable permits, clean air investment funds, and auctions/trades of emissions rights.

Second, SIPs must also contain specific schedules and timetables for compliance.[21] It is worth noting, however, that the courts and the EPA are very clear that schedules alone are insufficient. For example, in *Natural Resources Defense Council, Inc. v. EPA*,[22] the court held that the EPA could not approve an inspection and maintenance plan of a SIP unless the plan was submitted in "regulatory" (i.e., already implemented) form. While this holding focused on inspection and maintenance plans, the EPA has interpreted it to apply to SIPs generally. However, recognizing that SIPs tend to start out generally and then be modified over the years by the states as more individual rules are adopted, the EPA has stated that SIPs can be deemed complete in this regard if at least 80 percent of the commitments are in regulatory form.

A third general function of SIPs is to provide for the establishment and operation of appropriate means to monitor, compile, and analyze ambient air quality data and to make such data available to the EPA.[23] Fourth, SIPs must provide for the regulation of modifications and construction of any stationary sources within the area.[24] This is achieved by, for example, requiring a new source permitting program as established in Parts C and D of the CAA (discussed in more detail in Chapter 5).[25]

A fifth general function of SIPs is to provide prohibitions against sources or other emissions activity that either contributes significantly to nonattainment or interferes with NAAQS maintenance of another state.[26] Sixth, SIPs must also contain necessary assurances that the state and regional agencies have adequate resources and authority to carry out the SIP.[27]

SIPs must also provide authority for emergency powers (as outlined in Section 303 of the CAA) as well as for adequate contingency plans to implement such authority.[28] In addition to the more specific requirements, outlined in later sections of this chapter, for each particular type of pollutant (e.g., ozone, carbon monoxide, particulate matter), SIPs must contain specific requirements regarding visibility protection and prevention of significant deterioration.[29] (These topics are covered in more detail in Chapter 7 and Chapter 6, respectively.)

Federalism Impact on SIPs

On August 4, 1999, President Clinton issued Executive Order 13132, outlining the fundamental federalism principles and criteria that agencies should take into account when "formulating and implementing policies that have federalism implications."[30] Executive Order 13132 requires the EPA to develop an accountable process to ensure "meaningful and timely input by State and local officials in the development of regulatory policies that have federalism implications," including implementation of SIPs.[31] "Policies that have federalism implications" is defined in the Executive Order to include regulations that have "substantial direct effects on the States, on the relationship between the national government and the States, or on the distribution of power and responsibilities among the various levels of government."[32] Under Executive Order 13132, the EPA can take actions limiting the policy-making discretion of individual states only where there is both constitutional and legislative authority for the actions and where there is a problem of "national significance," such as air pollution.[33] Therefore, states must be consulted when the EPA acts to set national standards and, when implementing the SIPs, states must be given "the maximum administrative discretion possible."[34] This directive is generally consistent with the (at least original) congressional intention that states are the primary authors of their own SIPs and should be afforded considerable deference in interpreting and implementing SIP programs.

Four Approvability Principles of SIPs

The EPA applies four broad principles when testing the approvability of SIPs and their implementing instruments, including permits:

1. Quantifiability
2. Enforceability
3. Replicability
4. Accountability

These four principles are discussed more fully in several guidance documents released by the EPA, but the following is a brief summary.[35] First, since any emissions reductions can be identified only if there is an acknowledged baseline, such baseline emissions from both the source and the control measures must be properly quantified.[36] Furthermore, such emissions must be quantified to best reflect the time period of the inventory.[37] Second, SIP control measures must be enforceable, meaning that they must be "duly adopted, and specify clear, unambiguous, and measurable requirements."[38] "Enforceable" also includes the concept that the SIP is subject to a legal means for ensuring that sources are in compliance with the control measure.[39]

The third fundamental principle for SIPs is that the control measures be replicable, which means that rules must be sufficiently specific and nonsubjective so that two separate entities applying the procedures come to similar results.[40] Finally, SIP control strategies must be accountable. To be accountable, source-specific limits should be permanent and the SIPs must contain means to track emission changes at sources and provide for corrective action if emissions reductions are not achieved.[41]

Nonattainment SIPs—RACT

Section 172 of the CAA provides that nonattainment plans must provide for "implementation of all reasonably available control measures" (RACM) for emissions and emission sources "as expeditiously as practicable."[42] RACM includes reductions from existing sources obtained from "reasonably available control technology" (RACT).[43] Although the CAA does not define RACT, the EPA has defined it elsewhere as the lowest emission limitation that a particular source is capable of meeting by the application of control technology that is reasonably available considering technological and economic feasibility.[44]

A supplement to the Title I preamble[45] provides further guidance. Although this particular supplement focuses on particulate matter (PM) emissions, it discusses technical and economic feasibility and thus may be informative regarding RACT in general. The supplement provides that the feasibility of emission reductions—whether through process changes or add-on control technology—will be analyzed for both technological and economic feasibility, as discussed below.[46] The EPA has also released control technique guidelines for individual air pollutants and some categories, which provide additional data for the states to use in developing RACT.

Technological Feasibility

The EPA identifies four basic factors for determining technological feasibility in identifying RACT measures. First, the feasibility of any process changes or add-on emission control equipment depends on the source's general process and operating procedures as well as the raw materials it uses.[47] Second, the EPA will consider how raw materials and process may affect the operation of and longevity of control equipment.[48] Third, the technological feasibility of any modifications or control equipment is also influenced by the plant's physical layout; that is, space limitations may in turn limit choices as well as the costs of such choices (which goes to economic feasibility, as discussed below).[49]

Lastly, the EPA will analyze the net environmental impact—taking into account water pollution, waste disposal, and energy requirements—of the control measure.[50] While this net impact is an important factor, the EPA suggests that adverse effects to other environmental media can be addressed by alternative means and need not obviate the use of a given control measure.

> In many instances . . . control technologies have known energy penalties and adverse effects on other media, but such effects and the cost of their mitigation are also known and have been borne by owners of existing sources in numerous cases. Such well-established adverse effects and their costs are normal and assumed to be reasonable and should not, in most cases, justify nonuse of the control technology.[51]

While the EPA thus recognizes that effects on other media caused by a given control measure should not be given undue weight in the technological feasibility calculus, the agency does note in this context that the costs of preventing such effects may affect the economic feasibility of the measure.

Economic Feasibility

The economic feasibility of a given control measure is based on a comparison of the costs of the measure to the source in question against the costs that other sources have incurred for similar measures.[52] The individual affordability of a given measure to a given company is therefore to be distinguished from economic feasibility. Rather, economic feasibility for RACT purposes is based on economic practicability, which is "largely determined by evidence that other sources in a source category have in fact applied the control technology in question."[53]

The capital costs, annualized costs, and cost-effectiveness of a control technology should also be considered for all options being debated.[54] Of these factors, cost-effectiveness should be given "substantial weight," according to the EPA, and used to compare the option to other options and other facilities.[55]

> The cost effectiveness of a technology is its annualized cost ($/year) divided by the amount of . . . emission reduction (i.e., tons/year) which yields a cost per amount of emissions reduction ($/ton).[56]

Again, the EPA suggests that economic feasibility rests "very little" on affordability.[57] However, if a company chooses to argue that a given RACT is unaffordable, it must support such a claim with information regarding impacts on (1) variable production costs; (2) production supply and demand elasticity; (3) product prices; (4) costs incurred by competitors; (5) profits; and (6) company employment.[58] Finally, if the RACT is so onerous that it may lead to closure of the facility, the company should also include closure costs in the affordability analysis.[59]

Control Technique Guidelines

The 1977 CAA Amendments required the EPA to issue to the states and appropriate air control agencies information on air pollution control techniques (or, as they are more commonly called, control technique guidelines, or CTGs) for listed pollutants.[60] These CTGs, which are technically not binding on the states, are nevertheless considered strong "presumptive" norms for determining whether a state has adopted RACT.[61] The CTGs may include data relating to the cost of installation and operation of emission control technology, as well as energy requirements, emission reduction benefits, and environmental impact of certain emission control technology.[62] CTGs might also include data on available technology, alternative methods of prevention, and control of air pollution or data on alternative fuels, processes, and operating procedures.[63]

The courts that have addressed the role of CTGs have uniformly concluded that they are not mandatory in nature. In *Citizens for a Better Environment v. Costle*,[64] the U.S. District Court for the Northern District of Illinois stated:

> The RACT limitations [CTGs] are informal suggestions of what EPA considers the state of the art in environmental control technology. *The RACT guidelines are not binding upon the States.* . . . These guidelines are . . . not expressed in mandatory terms. They are not even binding on EPA, no less on the state agencies. Although the guidelines may be consulted by the States . . . to gain a better understanding of the Administrator's views in approving SIP revisions, they do not establish legally enforceable requirements.[65] [emphasis added]

The U.S. District Court for Delaware reached the same conclusions.[66]

The information presented in a CTG pursuant to Section 108 is designed to assist, not to handcuff, state agencies. As acknowledged by the EPA in its RACT guidance,

> the State may develop case-by-case RACT requirements independently of the EPA's recommendation. The EPA will propose to approve any submitted RACT requirement that the State shows will satisfy the requirements of the Act for RACT, *based on the economic and technical circumstances of the particular sources being regulated.*[67] [emphasis added]

Under the 1990 CAA Amendments, Congress required the EPA to review and update CTGs issued before November 15, 1990, by November 15, 1993.

In addition, Section 183 of the 1990 Amendments imposed an additional requirement on the EPA to issue CTGs for eleven categories of stationary sources of volatile organic compound (VOC) emissions by November 15, 1993.

In January 1994, the EPA notified regional air directors that work on remaining CTGs would be halted owing to "substantial budget constraints."[68] While the EPA's work on most of the CTGs, including CTGs for chemical batch processes, was close to completion by January 1994, states have received no CTGs in the areas of auto-body refinishing, industrial wastewater, VOC storage, and industrial cleaning solvents. Instead of CTGs, the EPA will release alternative control techniques (ACTs).

RACM in Addition to RACT

In addition to RACT measures (as defined by CTGs and analogous state technology-oriented control measures), RACM also includes the incorporation of transportation control measures (covered in Chapter 4) as well as more novel alternatives to standard emission control techniques such as market-based emissions trading programs. One example of the latter is the Regional Clean Air Incentives Market (RECLAIM) program adopted in October 1992 in southern California.

The EPA's SIP Review Process

Completeness

Before the EPA begins its formal review of the compliance elements of a SIP submission, it first makes a determination about the SIP's "completeness."[69] (The process is outlined in Exhibit 4.) During this process, the EPA determines whether certain minimum criteria have been met that would trigger the CAA requirement that the EPA review and take action on the submission.

The EPA has proposed and finalized minimum criteria for completeness.[70] Generally speaking, these completeness criteria are divided into two categories: administrative information and technical support information.[71] Administrative information includes the documentation necessary to demonstrate that the state has adhered to basic administrative procedures during the rule adoption process. Technical support information includes documentation that adequately identifies all of the required technical components of the plan submissions. (See Exhibit 5.) Although the EPA will attempt to make its completeness determination within sixty days of submittal, a submission will automatically be deemed complete if the EPA is unable to make such a determination within six months.[72] If complete, the EPA will notify the state by letter and begin its review of the SIP's compliance elements. If the SIP is deemed incomplete, it is returned to the state along with a letter describing its deficiencies.

EXHIBIT 4. SIP Submission Process

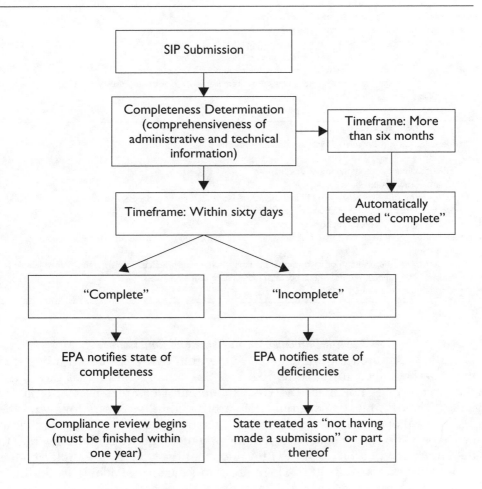

Deadline for Action

Within twelve months after a determination of completeness, the EPA must grant the SIP submission (1) full approval or disapproval based on whether the SIP meets all of the applicable requirements of the CAA, (2) partial approval (subject to full compliance), or (3) conditional approval.[73] Under a conditional approval, the EPA will impose on a state specific enforceable measures that must be completed by a certain date within a year of such conditional approval.[74] The test by which the EPA will grant such conditional approval is unclear. As a practical matter, conditional approvals may be the only way to forestall sanctions and to avoid the imposition of a federal implementation plan (FIP) if the submitted plan cannot otherwise be approved.

EXHIBIT 5. SIP Completeness Determination (40 C.F.R. Part 51, Appendix V)

1. Administrative Materials and Information
- Formal letter of submittal from governor or designee
- Evidence of state adoption of the plan
- Evidence of legal authority of state to adopt and implement the plan
- Copy of the actual state regulation or document submitted for approval
- Evidence that state followed all state procedural requirements in adopting/issuing the plan
- Certification of proper notice for public meetings
- Compilation of public comments regarding the plan

2. Technical Support Information
- Identification of all regulated pollutants affected by the plan
- Locations of affected sources
- EPA attainment or nonattainment designations
- Quantification of emissions change
- Demonstrations that NAAQS, PSD increments, reasonable further progress, and visibility, as applicable, are protected if the plan is approved and implemented
- Modeling information to support the proposed revision
- Evidence, where necessary, that emissions limitations are based on continuous emission reduction technology
- Evidence that the plan conforms to emissions limitations, work practice standards, and record-keeping and reporting requirements, where necessary, to ensure emission levels
- Compliance/enforcement strategies

Federal Implementation Plans and Sanctions

The EPA is required to promulgate a FIP within two years after finding that the state has failed to make its required SIP submission or that the state's submission does not meet the CAA's minimum completeness criteria for SIPs.[75] The EPA must also promulgate a FIP within two years following the disapproval of any or all of a SIP.[76] Additionally, the CAA requires the EPA to impose sanctions on a state after making any of the above findings leading to the imposition of a FIP or if the EPA finds that the state is not implementing a previously approved SIP.[77] There are two sanctions available to the EPA: (1) highway funding sanctions prohibiting the Secretary of Transportation from approving certain projects or awarding certain grants and (2) offset sanctions requiring a ratio of at least 2-to-1 for emissions reductions within nonattainment areas to offset emissions from new or modified major facilities.[78] The EPA must apply one of the two sanctions eighteen months after its finding and both sanctions if the deficiency remains uncorrected twenty-four months after the finding.[79]

EPA Corrections and Calls for Plan Revisions

Should the EPA make an error in its analysis of a SIP submission, the agency itself may "revise such action as appropriate without requiring further submission from the state."[80] In addition, whenever the EPA finds that a SIP is "substantially inadequate" either to attain or maintain the relevant NAAQS, fails to mitigate interstate pollution transport adequately, or otherwise fails to comply with the CAA, the EPA may require the state to revise the plan as necessary to correct such inadequacies.[81]

Economic Incentive Programs

Economic incentive programs (EIP) include a variety of measures designed to increase the flexibility and efficiency, while maintaining accountability and enforceability, of traditional air quality management programs.[82] The EPA has issued nonbinding guidance in order to help states incorporate EIPs into their SIPs. The EPA's guidance provides advice on choosing an appropriate type of incentive program, what emission sources to include in that program, and how to make a program successful.[83] According to the EPA, there are three fundamental principles that apply to all EIPs: integrity, equity, and environmental benefit.[84] The fundamental principles must serve as the foundation for all EIPs and "form the lenses through which all aspects of an EIP must be viewed."[85] Accordingly, the EPA has outlined four main types of economic incentive programs that meet all three fundamental principles:

1. **Emission Trading Programs** create transferable emission reductions. The cost of emission reductions may be relatively low for some sources but may be high for others. In these situations, both types of sources may benefit by trading emission reductions.
2. **Financial Mechanism Programs** include fees paid by emitters for each unit of emissions. A source may decide to reduce emissions in order to avoid paying the fees (usually to a regulatory agency), thereby lowering costs. Financial mechanisms also may include subsidies that promote pollution-reducing activities or products.
3. **Clean Air Investment Funds** provide cost relief for sources when the cost of emission reductions is high. Sources pay into the fund in lieu of reducing emissions; the fund manager procures emission reductions elsewhere.
4. **Public Information Programs** include educational programs such as product certifications, product labels, announcement of "ozone action days," or other information people can consider when making choices that affect air quality.[86]

SIP Requirements for Attainment and Unclassified Areas

The CAA provides that SIPs for areas designated in attainment or unclassifiable must contain emissions limitations and such other measures necessary to "prevent significant deterioration of air quality in each region (or portion thereof)."[87] Briefly, the programs to prevent significant deterioration outlined in Part C of the CAA and the regulations promulgated thereunder are designed to preserve air quality, that is, to regulate regions that have air quality that exceeds the NAAQS. Prevention of significant deterioration (PSD) of air quality is achieved primarily through a permitting program focusing on construction or significant modification of pollution sources. (For a detailed discussion regarding PSD and attainment area plans, refer to Chapter 5.)

Requirements for Ozone Nonattainment SIPs

On July 18, 1997, the EPA, utilizing its authority under Sections 108 and 109 of the CAA, announced a new, stricter eight-hour NAAQS for ozone nonattainment to eventually replace the one-hour scheme contained in Section 181 of the CAA.[88] This revision significantly alters the number of ozone nonattainment areas and the schedules for attainment. While the old CAA standard set the ambient baseline for ozone at 0.12 ppm over a one-hour period, the revised standard measures ozone exposure over an eight-hour time period at a level of 0.08 ppm.[89] The EPA also changed the time period used to evaluate exceedances from a yearly average (based on a one-hour measurement) to a "concentration-based form" three-year average (based upon the annual fourth-highest daily maximum eight-hour concentration).[90] Additionally, the EPA replaced the previous ozone secondary standard, intended to protect vegetation, including agricultural crops, national parks, and forests, with a standard identical to the new primary standard.[91] Ultimately, the EPA announced that the old standard of 0.12 ppm in one hour would not be revoked in a given area until that area had met the standard for three consecutive years.[92]

The American Trucking Decision

Following promulgation of the new eight-hour ozone standard and the revised particulate matter standard (PM) in 1997, numerous lawsuits were filed challenging the EPA's constitutional authority to revise and implement rules originally enacted legislatively by Congress.[93] On February 27, 2001, in *Whitman v. American Trucking Ass'ns,* the Supreme Court held that the section 109(b)(1) of the CAA did not unconstitutionally delegate legislative power when it granted the EPA authority to set or revise NAAQS to levels "requisite to protect the public health" and that the EPA can not consider implementation costs when setting NAAQS.[94] Furthermore, the Court held that the inherent ambiguity within the 1990 amendments to the CAA prevented them from concluding that Congress had intended the CAA ozone standard to be exclusive.[95] As a result of the *American Trucking* decision, the EPA has actively continued to implement the new eight-hour ozone standard, while seeking to phase out the old one-hour standard.

President's Implementation Plan for Revised Ozone and PM Standards

On July 16, 1997, two days prior to the EPA's issuance of its final revised ozone and PM standards, President Clinton issued a memorandum to EPA Administrator Carol M. Browner directing that the revised standards be implemented in a commonsense, flexible, and cost-effective manner and setting out a detailed plan for implementation.[96] To achieve President Clinton's goal of cost-effectiveness and drive the development for new technologies with the potential of greater emission reduction at less cost, the memo determined that the EPA will recommend that states design strategies for attaining the PM and ozone standards that limit the cost of control to under $10,000 per ton of emission reduction for all sources.[97] Additionally, the EPA should support the development of a compliance option for sources who face costs higher than $10,000 per ton (or such lower cost-effectiveness benchmark for the relevant control category) by which the sources would pay into a Clean Air Investment Fund that will fund cost-effective emissions reductions from nontraditional and small sources.[98]

President Clinton's memo described four essential elements necessary to achieving his implementation goals:

1. Implementation of the air quality standards is to be carried out to maximize common sense, flexibility, and cost effectiveness;
2. Implementation shall ensure that the nation continues its progress toward cleaner air by respecting the agreements already made by states, communities, and businesses to clean up the air, and by avoiding additional burdens with respect to the beneficial measures already under way in many areas. Implementation also shall be structured to reward state and local governments that take early action to provide clean air to their residents; and to respond to the fact that pollution travels hundreds of miles and crosses many state lines;
3. Implementation shall ensure that the Environmental Protection Agency ("Agency") completes its next periodic review of particulate matter, including review by the Clean Air Scientific Advisory Committee, within 5 years of issuance of the new standards, as contemplated by the Clean Air Act. Thus, by July 2002, the Agency was to determine, based on data available from its review, whether to revise or maintain the standards. This determination would be made before any areas have been designated as "nonattainment" under the $PM_{2.5}$ standards and before imposition of any new controls related to the $PM_{2.5}$ standards; and
4. Implementation is to be accomplished with the minimum amount of paperwork and shall seek to reduce current paperwork requirements wherever possible.[99]

President Clinton's implementation plan calls for the old one-hour ozone standard to remain in effect until an area attains the standard with three years of air quality data, and it maintains the CAA's one-hour ozone nonattainment classifications and mandatory control measures until an area achieves attainment.[100] (See below for a detailed description of the one-hour ozone nonattainment classifications.) Additionally, the implementation plan creates a "Transitional" classification for those areas that attain the one-hour ozone standard but do not yet meet the eight-hour standards.[101] This classification will require only minor revisions to a state's existing new source review (NSR) and transportation planning programs while allowing the state to achieve attainment through regional reductions in pollutants and early submission of SIPs.[102]

The original implementation plan called for designation of areas as nonattainment for the eight-hour ozone standard by 2000 and required submission of SIPs by 2003.[103] States would then have up to ten years, plus two one-year extensions, to meet the standards.[104] Areas seeking to be designated "Transitional" would be required to submit SIPs addressing transported air pollution prior to receiving the EPA's classification.[105]

EPA Implementation of the Revised Eight-Hour Ozone Standard

As a result of the delay caused by the *American Trucking* litigation, the EPA has not yet designated areas for the eight-hour ozone standard. In May 2003, the EPA proposed a rule containing several options for implementing the eight-hour ozone standard and is currently undertaking a public hearing process to obtain feedback on these various options. The EPA's proposed implementation rule seeks to provide states and local air pollution control agencies with a flexible roadmap describing the requirements needed to prepare SIPs that will allow them to achieve the eight-hour ozone standard. States with areas that are not attaining the eight-hour ozone standard will have to develop emission limits and take other remedial measures, as part of their SIPs, in order to attain the standard within the required time frame. Nonattainment areas will have anywhere from three to seventeen years to achieve the eight-hour ozone standard from the date designations are finalized, depending both on the pollution classification strategy and on the implementation plan formally adopted by the EPA.

As of this printing, the EPA plans to issue its final rule on implementation of the eight-hour ozone standard by December 2003 and to designate eight-hour ozone nonattainment areas by April 2004. In the interim, the EPA is relying solely on continuing implementation of the one-hour ozone standard, which will be revoked at some point following full enforceability of the eight-hour ozone standard. The agency has also encouraged areas to implement voluntary, early emission reductions in anticipation of the fully implemented eight-hour ozone standard. Under the agency's Early Action Compact program, for example, the EPA has offered to defer the effective date of an area's nonattainment designation if the area submits and implements early control programs and meets other milestones.

The Old CAA One-Hour Ozone Standard

Section 181 of the CAA creates a six-category classification structure for ozone nonattainment. (See Exhibit 6 for ozone design values or standards and attainment deadlines.) The categories, in order of severity of nonattainment, are designated Marginal, Moderate, Serious, Severe I, Severe II, and

EXHIBIT 6. Ozone Design Values and Attainment Deadline

OZONE NONATTAINMENT

Area Classification	Design Value (ppm)	Attainment Date
Marginal	0.121 to 0.137	November 15, 1993
Moderate	0.138 to 0.159	November 15, 1996
Serious	0.160 to 0.179	November 15, 1999
Severe I	0.180 to 0.189	November 15, 2005
Severe II	0.190 to 0.279	November 15, 2009
Extreme	0.280 and above	November 15, 2010

Extreme. Some nonattainment areas do not fall within any of these six categories,[106] and the EPA categorizes these areas as transitional, submarginal, or areas with incomplete data.[107]

Marginal Areas

Each state in which a marginal ozone area is located must include the following in the ozone SIP for each marginal area: (1) an inventory of emissions sources, (2) reasonably available control technology corrections, (3) vehicle inspection and maintenance programs, (4) permit programs, (5) periodic inventories, (6) emissions statements, and (7) offset requirements. Most of these items were to be submitted within the two years following the CAA Amendments' enactment date, that is, by November 15, 1992.[108]

SIP requirements are cumulative, meaning that requirements for marginal areas also apply to moderate areas, requirements for moderate areas also apply to serious areas, and so forth. The following marginal area requirements therefore apply to all ozone nonattainment areas.

Inventory

The SIP must include a comprehensive and current inventory of actual peak weekday emissions from all stationary and mobile sources within two years after the enactment date.[109] This inventory, known as the base-year inventory, includes both anthropogenic (i.e., human) as well as biogenic (i.e., non-human living organism) sources of volatile organic compounds (VOCs), nitrogen oxides (NO_x), and carbon monoxide (CO). Emissions from areas within a twenty-five-mile perimeter of the marginal area are also included in the inventory.

Recently, the EPA has questioned the "comprehensiveness" of state inventories. Several studies have concluded that many state inventories are inaccurate and flawed and undercount emissions, particularly from mobile sources.[110] The EPA and local agencies will face difficult questions as they confront the issue of flawed inventories. For example, how will states and the EPA deal with flawed inventories, and what obligations will ensue as a result? Will states be able to wait for the next scheduled SIP submittal date to correct their inventories?

The end result of such corrections and adjustments will likely mean that greater emissions reductions will be required. Local agencies, faced with increasing pressure to improve inventory comprehensiveness and accuracy, will seek new categories of pollutants not previously identified. Such closer examination will no doubt lead to greater regulation, particularly for sources that were previously unregulated.

RACT Corrections

Those areas designated in nonattainment before the CAA must also include in their SIPs RACT rules as well as corrections (known as RACT Fix-ups) to existing VOC RACT rules. RACT Fix-ups are corrections of rules or portions of rules that were adopted by states under the 1977 amendments but that the EPA considered to be less stringent than applicable CTGs or otherwise deficient for one or more reasons.[111] Areas designated in nonattainment under the CAA, however, are not subject to RACT Fix-up requirements.

Requiring the RACT Fix-ups was, in effect, a decision by Congress not to allow states to deviate significantly from CTGs when CTGs applied to regulated sources. One of the main areas of state deviation from the CTGs was the use of "equivalency" provisions, by which state rules would allow a source to comply with a RACT standard by alternate, but equivalent, means. Before the 1990 CAA Amendments, as part of its post-1987 policies, the EPA announced that states would not be allowed to grant such discretion to sources. Subsequent EPA guidelines for demonstrating federally recognized equivalency (denoted alternative emissions control plans, or AECPs) were so strict as to practically eliminate the alternative compliance option.

In many (if not most) cases, the equivalency path allowed by states in the early 1980s was the "bubble." Through its 1986 emissions trading policy statement and subsequent RACT Fix-up requirements, the EPA in essence announced the end of the state equivalency plans and bubbles. Very few post-1987 bubbles or AECPs have been approved owing to the stringent qualifying criteria. Among these stringent criteria are *daily* mass emissions caps, defined as only 80 percent of a facility's historic peak emissions on any given day.

Market-based initiatives such as the South Coast Air Quality Management District's RECLAIM program stand as a refreshing, but ironic, contrast to the congressionally blessed demise of the bubble and state equivalency plans because RECLAIM and other so-called "cap and trade" programs restore the flexibility otherwise removed by the RACT Fix-up provisions. They allow annual, rather than daily, averaging and ensure that facilities will not have to keep daily emissions at a level 20 percent or more below historic levels. This is of fundamental importance to any facility whose emissions may vary from day to day. Cap and trade programs offer the possibility of preserving, and even significantly expanding, important flexibility for regulated sources, while containing accounting assurances of sufficient integrity to ensure environmental performance.

Inspection and Maintenance Program Corrections

States with marginal ozone nonattainment areas must also make corrections to vehicle inspection and maintenance (I/M) programs to meet existing and updated I/M policies and guidance.[112] (For more on the I/M program, refer to Chapter 4.)

New Source Review Permit Programs

Marginal area SIPs must also include provisions to require permits for the construction and operation of new or modified major stationary sources.[113] Major stationary sources in marginal and moderate nonattainment areas are those sources emitting at least 100 tons per year of pollutants. (These permit programs and their respective offset ratios are covered in more detail in Chapter 6.) Major sources are subject to NSR and PSD requirements.

Periodic Inventory

States must also submit inventories every three years, starting in the third year after submission of base-year inventories,[114] until the area is redesignated in attainment. These periodic inventories must meet the same requirements as the base-year inventories and shall likewise cover actual, peak season emissions of VOCs, NO_x, and CO in the area.[115]

Emissions Statements

SIPs for marginal areas must also contain a requirement mandating submission of annual statements from owners and operators of each stationary source of VOC and NO_x that show the actual VOC and NO_x emissions of such sources.[116] States may waive this requirement for certain sources emitting less than 25 tons of NO_x and VOCs per year.[117]

Emissions Offset Ratio

New or modified stationary sources in marginal nonattainment areas must also meet an offset ratio, that is, the ratio of total emissions reductions of VOCs to total net increased emissions of VOCs. In marginal areas, the offset ratio is at least 1.15 to 1. (See Chapter 5 on NSR and PSD/nonattainment analysis for further discussion regarding offsets.)

The marginal area requirements for ozone nonattainment SIPs are summarized in Exhibit 7.

Moderate Areas

As mentioned, moderate areas must meet all of the requirements described for marginal areas, in addition to the requirements outlined in the following paragraphs.

EXHIBIT 7. Ozone Nonattainment SIPs: Requirements for Marginal Areas

- Current inventory of emissions from all sources
- RACT and RACT corrections (Fix-ups)
- I/M program corrections
- New and modified source review permit programs
- "Major source" = emits at least 100 tons per year of pollutants
- Periodic emissions inventories (every three years)
- Emissions statements from NO_x and VOC sources
- Emissions offset requirement (at least 1.1 to 1)

Fifteen Percent Rate of Progress Requirement

To ensure "actual progress" toward attainment in the face of uncertainties inherent in SIP planning,[118] ozone nonattainment areas classified as moderate or above must achieve a total emission reduction of at least 15 percent on an areawide basis from the base-year VOC inventory by the end of the sixth year after enactment (i.e., by November 15, 1996).[119] The 15 percent reduction is calculated based on a 1990 baseline of actual emissions and must reflect reductions that are the net growth in emissions from increased population and economic activity. In other words, the 15 percent must anticipate future growth (or reduction, if the population in an area is decreasing) by taking into account the corresponding change in emissions caused by having more automobiles, more consumer products, and greater industrial activity in general. The inventories used for progress analysis start with current emissions, which are then inflated to take into account anticipated changes in population.

In some cases, the EPA may require emissions reductions greater than 15 percent where modeling shows that such modifications are necessary.[120] Emissions reductions created by the following are explicitly prohibited from inclusion in the 15 percent reduction calculations: (1) tailpipe or evaporation standards promulgated before 1990, (2) Reid vapor pressure (RVP) regulations promulgated before November 15, 1990, (3) SIP corrections of RACT deficiencies, and (4) SIP corrections to correct deficiencies in existing I/M programs or previously required I/M programs.[121]

Predictably, states have experienced much difficulty in meeting the 15 percent reductions. Submittals have been almost uniformly late, and inventories have been deficient and have failed to meet the EPA's expectations, particularly in the area of inspection and maintenance programs and employee commute option (ECO) initiatives to reduce automobile travel and related emissions. States are showing a greater unwillingness to adopt EPA requirements like I/M and ECO initiatives, and given recent political events, the EPA may be more willing to negotiate the details of reduction programs.[122] States have also relied increasingly on organizations like the State and Territorial Air Pollution Program Administrators (STAPPA) and Association of Local Air Pollution Control Officials (ALAPCO), which provide useful "menus" to help states meet the 15 percent reduction requirements.[123]

RACT Catch-Ups

Section 182(b)(2) of the CAA requires moderate areas previously exempted from RACT requirements to "catch up" to nonattainment areas that were subject to such requirements before 1990. States must accomplish these RACT Catch-ups by revising the relevant SIPs to require RACT with respect to the following: (1) categories of VOC sources in areas covered by CTG documents released since November 15, 1990; (2) all VOC sources covered by CTGs released before November 15, 1990; and (3) all other major stationary sources located in the area.[124]

Revisions of RACT requirements for VOC sources covered by post-1990 CTGs must be submitted by the date set forth in the relevant CTG document. VOC sources under CTGs released before November 1990 and all other major stationary sources were to submit revisions by November 15, 1992, with these revised measures to be implemented as expeditiously as practicable, but no later than May 31, 1995.

Gasoline Vapor Recovery

States with moderate or higher ozone nonattainment status were also required to revise their SIPs by November 15, 1992, to require all owners and operators of gasoline dispensing systems to install and operate systems for gasoline vapor recovery of emissions created by the fueling of vehicles.[125]

Inspection and Maintenance

In addition to the I/M requirements previously outlined for marginal areas, moderate areas must also include a specific schedule for implementation of such a program.[126] (See Chapter 4 for further discussion regarding I/M programs.)

Emissions Offset Requirements

Offsets for new emissions in moderate areas must be at a 1.15:1 ratio.[127]

The moderate area requirements for ozone nonattainment SIPs are summarized in Exhibit 8.

Serious Areas

SIPs for serious nonattainment areas must include all of the requirements for moderate areas, in addition to revisions regarding the following requirements.

Enhanced Monitoring

States with serious or greater nonattainment areas must have measures to improve monitoring for ambient concentrations of ozone, NO_x, and VOCs and emissions of NO_x and VOCs.

EXHIBIT 8. Ozone Nonattainment SIPs: Requirements for Moderate Areas

- All requirements for marginal areas
- 15 percent rate-of-progress requirement
- RACT Catch-ups
- Gasoline vapor recovery
- Emissions offset of at least 1.15:1

Attainment and Reasonable Further Progress Demonstrations

SIPs for serious nonattainment areas were to be revised by November 1994 to include modeling-based demonstrations that the plan will attain the ozone NAAQS, as well as a demonstration that the plan, as revised, will result in VOC emissions reductions from the base-year inventory equal to at least 3 percent of baseline emissions for each year following the initial six-year, 15 percent period discussed earlier for moderate areas.[128] This amount may be less than 3 percent if the state can convince the EPA that either (1) the 3 percent rate of progress is not technologically achievable or (2) NO_x control would create an equivalent reduction in ozone concentrations.[129]

Enhanced I/M Program

States with serious (or more severe) nonattainment areas were required to submit SIP revisions by November 1992 to provide for a program to reduce VOC and NO_x emissions from registered motor vehicles in each "urbanized" area within the nonattainment area (urbanized meaning those areas with a population of 200,000 or more according to the 1980 census). The enhanced I/M program for serious areas includes computerized, annual, or biennial emissions testing and centralized operation and administration of the program.[130]

Clean-Fuel Vehicle Programs

Serious areas must also require centrally fueled vehicle fleets to use clean fuels,[131] pursuant to provisions of the clean-fuel vehicle program of Part C of Title II of the CAA.

Transportation Control Measures

States with serious nonattainment areas must also submit demonstrations, starting in 1996 and again each third year thereafter, as to whether aggregate vehicle mileage, aggregate vehicle emissions, and congestion levels are consistent with the area's attainment demonstration. If such predicted levels are exceeded, serious area SIPs must be revised to include transportation control measures to reduce emissions accordingly.[132] (For further discussion regarding transportation control measures, refer to Chapter 4.)

EXHIBIT 9. Ozone Nonattainment SIPs: Requirements for Serious Areas

- All requirements for moderate and marginal areas
- Enhanced monitoring of ambient concentrations of ozone, NO_x, and VOCs and emissions of NO_x and VOCs
- Modeling-based demonstrations of attainment and reasonable further progress
- Enhanced I/M program, including regular emissions testing and centralized administration and operation of I/M program
- Clean fuel vehicle programs
- Transportation control measures
- More stringent new source review
- "Major source" = emits at least 50 tons per year of VOCs
- Emissions offsets of 1.2 to 1

New Source Review: Special Rules for Netting

The CAA created new rules for serious nonattainment areas affecting NSR permit requirements for modifications of major stationary sources. These so-called "netting rules" alter the way proposed modifications will be evaluated to determine whether a modification has occurred and to specify requirements for such sources. (Chapter 5 discusses these rules.) For serious ozone nonattainment areas, major sources are defined as those sources that emit or have the potential to emit at least 50 tons per year of VOCs.

Emissions Offset Ratio

Emissions offset ratios for VOCs for serious nonattainment areas must be at least 1.2 to 1.[133]

The serious area requirements for ozone nonattainment SIPs are summarized in Exhibit 9.

Severe Areas

In addition to the requirements for SIPs and SIP revisions for serious areas, severe areas—both severe I and severe II—must submit the following revisions to each applicable plan covering a severe area.

Vehicle Miles Traveled

Severe area SIPs must include specific enforceable transportation control strategies and measures to "offset any growth in emissions from growth in vehicle miles traveled or number of vehicle trips in such area and to attain reduction in motor vehicle emissions."[134]

Emissions Offset Ratio

For severe ozone nonattainment areas, the emissions offset ratio must be at least 1.3 to 1, unless the SIP requires all existing major sources in the

EXHIBIT 10. Ozone Nonattainment Area SIPs: Requirements for Severe I and II Areas

- All requirements for marginal, moderate, and serious area SIPs
- "Major source" = emits at least 25 tons per year of VOCs
- Transportation control measures to reduce vehicle miles traveled
- Emissions offsets of 1.3 to 1, unless the SIP requires BACT for existing major sources, in which case the ratio is 1.2 to 1

nonattainment area to use best available control technology (BACT), in which case the ratio is 1.2 to 1. Major sources in severe areas are stationary sources, or groups of sources that emit or have the potential to emit at least 25 tons per year.[135]

The serious nonattainment area requirements are summarized in Exhibit 10.

Extreme Areas

Extreme ozone nonattainment areas must meet all requirements for severe areas, in addition to the following significant requirements.

Definition of Major Source and Major Stationary Source

The terms "major source" and "major stationary source" as used with regard to extreme area SIPS include any stationary source or group of sources that emit, or have the potential to emit, at least 10 tons per year of VOCs. In extreme ozone nonattainment areas, major sources face strict modification and offset provisions.

Modifications

In extreme areas, with some exceptions, major stationary sources cannot net out of certain NSR requirements. Any change at a major stationary source that "results in any increase in emissions from any discrete operation, unit, or other pollutant emitting activity at the source" is considered a "modification" for permitting purposes. Such an increase will not be considered a modification if the owner or operator offsets such an increase at a ratio of at least 1.3 to 1 internally (i.e., by achieving offsetting emissions reductions at the same location). This offset requirement as to modification is not applicable to modifications consisting only of installation of required equipment under a SIP, a permit, or the CAA.

It is important to contrast these internal offset requirements (i.e., offsets at a single source) with external emissions offset ratios. For example, external offset ratios for extreme areas are either 1.5 to 1 or 1.2 to 1 depending upon whether the area SIP requires BACT for existing major sources. In addition, note that these offset requirements must be distinguished from lowest achievable emissions rate requirements (discussed in more detail in Chapter 5).

A stationary source may be exempted from internal offset requirements if it is subject to a specific facility compliance plan included in a SIP pursuant to Section 182(e)(2) of the CAA, which addresses extreme ozone nonattainment areas.[136] Local agencies can use Section 182(e)(2) to exempt a given facility from NSR requirements by creating special rules, emissions caps, and other source-specific requirements that are in turn inserted directly into the state's SIP.

Use of Clean Fuels or Advanced Control Technology for Boilers

States containing an extreme area were required to submit a SIP revision in 1993 to require certain boilers emitting more than 25 tons of NO_x per year to use either clean fuels (natural gas, methanol, and ethanol) or advanced control technology, such as catalytic controls, for at least 90 percent of the operating time.[137]

TCMs During Heavy Traffic Hours

Extreme area SIPs must also be revised to include TCMs to reduce the use of high-polluting or heavy-duty vehicles during heavy traffic hours.[138]

New Technologies

Because of the long period between the development of an initial extreme area SIP and the targeted attainment date of the NAAQS, extreme area SIPs and attainment demonstrations that "anticipate development of new control technologies or improvement of existing control technologies"[139] may be approved as part of the SIP as long as the following criteria are met: (1) Such provisions as to new technologies are not necessary to achieve the incremental emissions reductions required from 1990 through 2000 (i.e., the 15 percent reduction required by November 15, 1996, and subsequent 3-plus percent annual reductions through 2000); and (2) the state has submitted commitments to adopt contingency measures if such new technologies do not achieve the planned reductions.

Emissions Offset Ratio

The emissions offset ratio for an extreme area is at least 1.5 to 1, unless all existing major sources are required to use BACT, in which case the ratio must be at least 1.2 to 1.

Extreme area requirements are summarized in Exhibit 11.

Nonattainment Plan Requirements for NO_x Sources

Although both VOCs and NO_x contribute to the formation of ozone, most control measures before the passage of the 1990 CAA Amendments focused on the mitigation of VOC emissions. As a practical matter, however, some areas with higher NO_x levels may find reducing NO_x more cost-effective

EXHIBIT 11. Ozone Nonattainment Area SIPs: Requirements for Extreme Areas

- All requirements for marginal, moderate, serious, and severe area SIPs
- Any increase in emissions at a discrete unit at a major stationary source = modification
- "Major source" = emits at least 10 tons per year of VOCs
- Advanced control technology or clean fuels for boilers emitting more than 25 tons of NO_x per year
- TCMs during heavy traffic hours
- New (anticipated) control technologies may be part of extreme area SIPs
- Emissions offsets of 1.2 to 1 for SIPs with BACT, 1.5 to 1 for SIPs without BACT

than reducing VOCs. In 1990, Congress recognized the importance of NO_x controls to the reduction of ozone, and as a result, explicitly expanded the applicability of the SIP requirements to major stationary sources of NO_x in the CAA.[140] On the other hand, under the CAA, states also have the option not to impose certain NO_x controls if the "net air quality benefits are greater in the absence of NO_x reduction or if additional NO_x reductions would not contribute to attainment of the NAAQS."[141] In October 1998, the EPA issued a NO_x SIP Call that required twenty-two eastern states and the District of Columbia "to revise their SIPs to impose additional controls on NO_x emissions" based upon the finding that these states' NO_x emissions contributed significantly to ozone nonattainment in several "downwind" states.[142] By court order, the deadline for submission of these revisions has recently been extended to May 31, 2004.[143] (Refer to Chapter 5 for a more detailed discussion of the NO_x SIP call.)

Particulate Matter Nonattainment Plan Requirements

Classification and Attainment Dates

The EPA announced a new standard for particulate matter (PM) under the NAAQS in July 1997 at the same time it promulgated the new eight-hour ozone standard.[144] The EPA added a new annual arithmetic mean $PM_{2.5}$ standard set at 15 micrograms per cubic meter ($\mu g/m^3$) and a new twenty-four-hour average $PM_{2.5}$ standard set at 65 $\mu g/m^3$.[145] $PM_{2.5}$ refers to fine particulate matter of a size of 2.5 microns or smaller. The EPA concluded that the new $PM_{2.5}$ standard would better screen those components of PM linked to respiratory illness and mortality and morbidity effects, while the old PM_{10} standard would be retained to continue protecting against problems caused by coarse fraction particles such as aggravation of asthma.[146] As a result, the EPA elected to maintain the current annual PM_{10} standard of 50 $\mu g/m^3$ and only mildly adjusted the PM_{10} twenty-four-hour standard of 150 $\mu g/m^3$ by changing the form of the standard.[147] Additionally, the EPA chose to revise the secondary (welfare-based) PM standards by making them identical to the primary standards.[148]

An area will be in compliance with the annual $PM_{2.5}$ standard when the three-year average of the annual arithmetic mean $PM_{2.5}$ concentrations is less than or equal to 15 $\mu g/m^3$.[149] Attainment of the new twenty-four-hour $PM_{2.5}$ standard requires $PM_{2.5}$ concentrations less than or equal to 65 $\mu g/m^3$ based on the 98th percentile of twenty-four-hour $PM_{2.5}$ concentrations in a year (averaged over three years).[150] An area will be in attainment with the annual PM_{10} standard when the three-year average of the annual arithmetic mean PM_{10} concentrations is less than or equal to 50 $\mu g/m^3$.[151] Attainment of the twenty-four-hour PM_{10} standard will now be met when an area's three-year average of the 99th percentile values at each monitoring site is less than or equal to 150 $\mu g/m^3$.[152]

An area designated in nonattainment for PM_{10} is initially classified as moderate,[153] to be reclassified as serious if the EPA determines that the area cannot attain the NAAQS for PM_{10} by the attainment date for moderate areas.[154] (Refer to Exhibit 12 for attainment dates.) In addition to meeting the PM_{10} NAAQS, an area requesting EPA redesignation from nonattainment to attainment must have a fully approved SIP, must demonstrate that the improvement is due to permanent and enforceable emissions reductions, and must have a fully approved maintenance plan.[155] The maintenance plan should identify the level of air emissions from cars, industry, and other sources of air pollution that is sufficient to maintain the NAAQS and should provide a modeling demonstration that the area will maintain clean air for at least ten years following redesignation.[156]

State Implementation Plan Requirements

As with the revised ozone eight-hour standard, the EPA delayed implementation of the new $PM_{2.5}$ standard pending the *American Trucking* outcome. To date, the EPA is continuing active enforcement of the old PM_{10} annual and twenty-four-hour standards. Now that the Supreme Court has decided the litigation in the EPA's favor, the agency is working quickly to promulgate its $PM_{2.5}$ implementation rule and to finalize area designations, taking into account the requirements contained in President Clinton's memorandum of July 16, 1997.[157] The EPA is hoping to have a final $PM_{2.5}$ implementation rule in place by the fall of 2004 and to make final designations by December 2004. Prior to the development of any control measures to achieve the $PM_{2.5}$

EXHIBIT 12. PM Nonattainment

PM_{10} Nonattainment Areas	Attainment Date
Moderate Areas	
Designated nonattainment under CAA Section 107(d)(4)	December 31, 1994
Other areas	Six years after designation
Serious Areas	
Designated nonattainment under CAA Section 107(d)(4)	December 31, 2001
Other areas	Ten years after designation
$PM_{2.5}$ Nonattainment Areas	**Attainment Date**
Designated nonattainment following EPA review	Ten years after designation (plus two 1-year extensions)

NAAQS, President Clinton's memo called for establishment of a comprehensive monitoring network "to determine ambient fine particle concentrations across the country."[158] In fact, since establishing the $PM_{2.5}$ NAAQS, the EPA has created and deployed a nationwide monitoring network of $PM_{2.5}$ concentrations. Following collection of the data, the EPA will review the standards and designate areas as either in attainment or nonattainment.[159] States will then be required to submit SIPs containing control measures for meeting the $PM_{2.5}$ standard and have ten years (plus two one-year extensions) to meet the standard.[160]

States with moderate PM_{10} areas must submit an implementation plan with the following requirements: (1) a permit program for construction and operation of new and modified major stationary sources of PM_{10} (major sources emit or have the potential to emit 100 tons per year of pollution); (2) a demonstration showing either attainment by the attainment date or that attainment is impracticable; and (3) provisions assuring that RACM for PM_{10} reductions will be in place no later than December 10, 1993, or four years after designation for areas designated as PM_{10} nonattainment after November 15, 1990.[161] Plan submissions for areas designated in nonattainment under Section 7407(d)(4) are due eighteen months after designation of nonattainment.[162]

Serious PM_{10} areas must include all of the moderate area requirements in their SIPs, as well as the following additional requirements. First, the plan must include an attainment demonstration, including air quality modeling, showing how the NAAQS for PM_{10} will be achieved by the attainment date. In the alternative, any state seeking an extension of the attainment date must make a determination showing that the attainment date is impracticable unless revised. The attainment demonstration is due within four years of reclassification to serious; the demonstration showing impracticability is due within eighteen months after reclassification. Second, major sources or major stationary sources in serious PM_{10} areas are defined as those sources that emit or have the potential to emit more than 70 tons per year of PM_{10}. Finally, the PM_{10} SIP must include provisions to assure that BACM for the control of PM_{10} will be implemented no later than four years after the area is classified (or reclassified as a serious area).[163] BACM is defined as "the maximum degree of emissions reduction of PM_{10} and PM_{10} precursors from a source . . . which is determined on a case-by-case basis, taking into account energy, environmental, and economic impacts and other costs, to be achievable for such source through application of production processes and available methods, systems, and techniques for control of each such pollutant."[164]

Waivers for Certain Areas

The EPA may waive, on a case-by-case basis, any SIP requirements for serious areas as well as attainment dates where it determines that anthropogenic sources of PM_{10} do not contribute "significantly" to the violation of the NAAQS.[165]

Regional Haze Regulations

On July 1, 1999, the EPA, in accordance with CAA section 169A, issued its final regional haze regulations to combat visibility impairment caused by air pollution in 156 Class I national parks and wilderness areas, including the Grand Canyon, Great Smokies, Shenandoah, Yellowstone, Mount Rainier, Yosemite, the Everglades, and the Boundary Waters.[166] Fine particles can be a major source of haze when they are directly emitted to the atmosphere and obscure the clarity, color, texture, and form of what people see.[167] Areas that are designated as attainment or unclassifiable for $PM_{2.5}$ will be required to file their initial regional haze SIP no later than one year following the designation.[168] Areas that are designated as nonattainment for $PM_{2.5}$ must file their regional haze SIP at the same time they file their $PM_{2.5}$ SIP (within three years of the nonattainment designation).[169] The Grand Canyon Visibility Transport Commission states (Arizona, California, Colorado, Idaho, Nevada, New Mexico, Oregon, Utah, and Wyoming) must submit their SIPs no later than December 31, 2003, and meet provisions specific to their transport region.[170] There are no "presumptive targets" for showing regional haze progress. Instead, states have flexibility to determine their own reasonable progress goals, taking into consideration the CAA statutory requirements and an ambitious reasonable progress goal of natural background conditions in sixty years.[171] All SIPs are required to be revised to set new progress goals and strategies to meet the goals in 2018, and every ten years thereafter.[172] (Refer to Chapter 7 for a more detailed discussion of the EPA's regional haze regulations.)

Nonattainment Area Plans for Other Pollutants

Carbon Monoxide Nonattainment Areas

Requirements for CO Nonattainment SIPs

Areas designated in nonattainment for CO are categorized as either moderate or serious depending on the severity of the nonattainment.[173] Most of the requirements for SIP revisions for CO moderate nonattainment areas are analogous to those required for ozone areas. These include (1) initial inventory of emissions, (2) periodic inventories (every three years), (3) attainment demonstration, and (4) forecasts of vehicle miles traveled (VMTs) and enhanced vehicle I/M measures for areas with design values greater than 12.7 ppm at the time of classification.[174]

Revisions to SIPs must also include contingency measures in the event that VMT estimates exceed the number predicted in the prior forecast or for failure to attain the NAAQS by the attainment date.[175] (See Exhibit 13.)

EXHIBIT 13. Carbon Monoxide Nonattainment Area Classifications

Area Classification	Design Value (ppm)	Primary NAAQS Attainment Date
Moderate	9.1 to 16.4 ppm	December 31, 1995
Serious	16.5 and above	December 31, 2000

SIP requirements in serious CO areas include those of moderate areas with a design value of 12.7 ppm of CO or greater. In addition, such SIPs must also be revised to include (1) TCMs to reduce CO rather than VOC emissions and clean-fuel programs, as necessary;[176] and (2) requirements for the use and blending of oxygenated gasolines.[177] Also, if the EPA finds that stationary sources "contribute significantly" to the CO problem in the area, the definition for "major stationary sources" will be modified to be those that emit 50 tons or more of CO annually.[178]

States with serious CO areas must also submit emissions reduction demonstrations showing that the area has achieved a reduction in CO emissions equivalent to the total of specific annual emissions reductions required by the attainment date.[179] Failure to submit such a demonstration on time will necessitate SIP implementation measures for economic incentives as well as a transportation control program, as described in Section 187(g) of the CAA.

Nonattainment Areas for Sulfur Oxides, Nitrogen Dioxide, or Lead

States with designated nonattainment areas for sulfur oxides, nitrogen dioxide, or lead must submit an applicable plan within eighteen months of such designation and must meet attainment within five years from the designation date.[180] States lacking fully approved SIPs on November 15, 1990, were to submit revised SIPs by May 15, 1994.[181]

Notes

1. CAA § 107(a).
2. CAA § 107(b), (c).
3. CAA § 107(e).
4. CAA § 176A.
5. CAA § 176A(b)(1).
6. CAA § 176A(b)(2).
7. CAA § 176A(c).
8. CAA § 107(d)(1).
9. CAA § 107(d)(1)(A)(ii).
10. CAA § 107(d)(1)(A)(i).
11. *See* 66 Fed. Reg. 57,269 (2001).
12. CAA § 107(d)(1)(A)(i).
13. CAA § 107(d)(1)(A)(iii).
14. CAA § 107(d)(3).
15. CAA § 107(d)(3)(D).
16. CAA § 107(d)(3)(F).
17. CAA § 107(d)(3)(E). For a more detailed discussion regarding the EPA's approach toward review of a state request to redesignate an area from nonattainment to attainment, and which criteria the EPA uses in determining whether the conditions outlined in this paragraph have been met, refer to General Preamble to Title I of the Clean Air Act; Guidance on Development of State Implementation Plans, 57 Fed. Reg. 13,498 (1992) [hereafter Title I Preamble] at 13,561–65.
18. CAA § 110(a)(1).

19. CAA § 110(a)(2)(A).
20. CAA § 110(a)(2)(C).
21. CAA § 110(2)(2)(A).
22. 22 F.3d 1125 (D.C. Cir. 1994).
23. CAA § 110(a)().
24. CAA § 110(a).
25. *Id.*
26. CAA § 110(a)(2)(D).
27. CAA § 110(a)(2)(E).
28. CAA § 110(a)(2)(G).
29. CAA § 110(a)(2)(J).
30. 64 Fed. Reg. 43,255–59 (1999).
31. *Id.* at 43,255 (1999).
32. *Id.*
33. *Id.* at 43,256.
34. *Id.*
35. *See* Title I Preamble, at 57 Fed. Reg. 13,567–68 (1992) and 51 Fed. Reg. 43,814 (1986).
36. Title I Preamble, at 57 Fed. Reg. 13,567 (1992).
37. Title I Preamble, at 57 Fed. Reg. 13,567–68 (1992).
38. *Id.* at 13,568.
39. *Id.*
40. *Id.*
41. *Id.*
42. CAA § 172(c)(1).
43. *Id.*
44. 44 Fed. Reg. 53,726 (1979).
45. 57 Fed. Reg. 18,070–77 (1992).
46. *Id.* at 18,073–74.
47. *Id.* at 18,073.
48. *Id.*
49. *Id.*
50. *Id.* at 18,073–74.
51. *Id.* at 18,074.
52. *Id.*
53. *Id.*
54. *Id. See* OAQPS CONTROL COST MANUAL, EPA-450/3-90-006 (4th ed., January 1990), for procedures for determining these costs.
55. *Id.*
56. *Id.*
57. *Id.*
58. *Id.*
59. *Id.*
60. CAA § 108(b)(1).
61. 57 Fed. Reg. 18,077 (1992).
62. *Id.*
63. *Id.*
64. 515 F.Supp. 264 (N.D. Ill. 1981).
65. *Id.* at 279.
66. 14 E.R.C. 2108, 2113 (1980).
67. 44 Fed. Reg. 53,762–63 (1979).

68. *See* "Inside EPA's Clean Air Report," February 10, 1994 (Inside Washington Publishers); Memorandum dated January 20, 1994, from John S. Seitz, Director, Office of Air Quality Planning and Standards, to Regional Air Directors.

69. CAA § 110(k).

70. *See* 56 Fed. Reg. 23,826 (1991); 56 Fed. Reg. 42,216 (1991); and 40 C.F.R. pt. 51, app. V.

71. 40 C.F.R. pt. 51, app. V.

72. CAA § 110(k)(1)(B).

73. CAA § 110(k)(2)–(4).

74. CAA § 110(k)(4).

75. CAA § 110(c)(1)(A).

76. CAA § 110(c)(1)(B).

77. CAA § 179(a).

78. CAA § 179(b).

79. CAA § 179(a).

80. CAA § 110(k)(6).

81. CAA § 110(k)(5). Under this authority, the EPA issued the NO_x SIP Call in October 1998, requiring twenty-two states and the District of Columbia "to revise their SIPs to impose additional controls on NO_x emissions." *See* 40 C.F.R. pts. 51, 52, 96, and 97, 67 Fed. Reg. 8,396–8,402 (2002). *See also* Chapter 5.

82. EPA Fact Sheet, "Guidance for Improving Air Quality Using Economic Incentive Programs" (January 19, 2001).

83. *Id.*

84. *Improving Air Quality with Economic Incentive Programs*, EPA-452/r-01-001, p. 33 (January 2001).

85. *Id.*

86. *Improving Air Quality with Economic Incentive Programs*, EPA-452/r-01-001, pp. 18–19 (January 2001).

87. CAA § 161.

88. 62 Fed. Reg. 38,856–75 (1997).

89. *Id.* at 38,858.

90. *Id.*

91. *Id.*

92. *Id.* at 38,863.

93. 66 Fed. Reg. 57,270 (2001).

94. 531 U.S. 457, 486 (2001).

95. *Id.* at 484 (2001).

96. 62 Fed. Reg. 38,421–32 (1997).

97. *Id.* at 38,429.

98. *Id.*

99. *Id.* at 38,421.

100. *Id.* at 38,424.

101. *Id.* at 38,425.

102. *Id.* at 38,425–26.

103. *Id.* at 38,424–25.

104. *Id.*

105. *Id.* at 38,426.

106. CAA Section 181(a)(1) lists five classifications; however, Section 181(a)(2) establishes a seventeen-year attainment date for areas with design values between 0.190 and 0.280 ppm. This is referred to as severe II.

107. Title I Preamble, at 57 Fed. Reg. 13,502–03.

108. CAA § 182(a).

109. CAA § 182(a)(1). *See also* the EPA's "Procedures to the Preparation of Emission Inventories for Carbon Monoxide and Precursors of Ozone," vol. I.

110. Studies have indicated that automobile emissions may be undercounted.

111. *See* CAA § § 108 and 172(b).

112. CAA § 182(a)(2)(B).

113. CAA § 182(a)(2)(C).

114. CAA § 182(a)(3)(A).

115. For further guidance on periodic inventories, refer to the EPA's "Procedures for the Preparation of Emission Inventories for Carbon Monoxide and Procedures of Ozone," vol. 2 (1991).

116. CAA § 182(a)(3)(B).

117. *See* Title I Preamble, at 57 Fed. Reg. 13,505, and the EPA Publication AP-42.

118. Title I Preamble, at 57 Fed. Reg. 13,507.

119. CAA § 182(b)(1).

120. Title I Preamble, at 57 Fed. Reg. 13,507.

121. CAA § 182(b)(1)(D).

122. Recently, the EPA has also shown a greater willingness to negotiate I/M programs. See Chapter 4 for further discussion.

123. *See* STAPPA/ALAPCO, *Meeting the 15-Percent Rate-of-Progress Requirement under the Clean Air Act: A Menu of Options* (1993).

124. CAA § 182(b)(2).

125. CAA § 182(b)(3).

126. CAA § 182(b)(4).

127. CAA § 182(b)(5).

128. CAA § 182(c)(2)(B).

129. *Id.*

130. CAA § 182(c)(3)(C). See Chapter 4 for a discussion of I/M programs.

131. CAA § 182(c)(4).

132. CAA § 182(c)(5).

133. CAA § 182(c)(10).

134. CAA § 182(d)(1).

135. *Id.* Note that "major sources" in marginal and moderate areas are sources that emit 100 tons or more of pollution annually. Major sources in extreme areas are those emitting greater than 10 tons of pollutants annually.

136. CAA Section 182(e)(2) reads in part: "The offset requirements . . . shall not be applicable in Extreme Areas to a modification of an existing source if such modification consists of installation of equipment required to comply with the applicable implementation plan, permit, or this Act."

137. CAA § 182(e)(3).

138. CAA § 182(c)(4).

139. CAA § 182(e)(5).

140. CAA § 182(f)(1).

141. *Id.*

142. 67 Fed. Reg. 8,396–8,402 (2002).

143. *Id.*

144. 62 Fed. Reg. 38,652–38,760 (1997).

145. *Id.* at 38,655.

146. *Id.* at 38,657–58.

147. *Id.* at 38,677–79.

148. *Id.* at 38,683.

149. *Id.* at 38,679.

150. *Id.*

151. *Id.*

152. *Id.*

153. CAA § 188(a).

154. *See* CAA § 189(d) and (e).

155. CAA § 107(d)(3)(E).

156. Memorandum from Lydia Wegman, Director AQSSD (MD-15) re: Limited Maintenance Plan Option for Moderate PM_{10} Nonattainment Areas (August 10, 2001).

157. 62 Fed. Reg. 38,421–32 (1997).

158. *Id.* at 38,427.

159. *Id.* at 38,428.

160. *Id.*

161. CAA § 189(a)(1).

162. CAA § 189(a)(2).

163. CAA § 189(b)(1)(B).

164. General Preamble—PM_{10} Supp., at 59 Fed. Reg. 41,998, Addendum (1994).

165. CAA § 188(f).

166. 64 Fed. Reg. 35,714–74 (1999).

167. *Id.* at 35,715.

168. *Id.* at 35,725.

169. *Id.*

170. *Id.*

171. *Id.* at 35,730–34.

172. *Id.* at 35,746.

173. CAA § 186(a)(1).

174. CAA § 187(a).

175. CAA § 187(a)(3).

176. CAA § 187(b)(2).

177. CAA § 187(b)(3).

178. CAA § 187(c)(1).

179. CAA § 187(d).

180. CAA § 191(a) and § 192(a).

181. CAA § 191(b) and § 192.

CHAPTER 4

Transportation and Conformity Requirements in State Implementation Plans[1]

RICK ZBUR
HAROLD BOO
TROY SAM LEE

Introduction

Before the 1990 amendments to the Clean Air Act (CAA), Congress's mandate to the states to use transportation planning as a weapon against air pollution consisted of the broad requirement that states include "reasonably available transportation controls" in their state implementation plans (SIPs).[1] The 1990 amendments effected dramatic changes in the area of transportation planning in nonattainment areas. New provisions added by the amendments to reduce mobile source emissions[2] included requirements that states revise their SIPs to require certain areas to reduce vehicle miles traveled, to include heightened inspection and maintenance programs for automobiles,[3] and to include measures intended to increase average vehicle occupancy for specified work commute trips.[4]

The CAA amendments also gave new strength to SIPs by amending the act's conformity requirements. Since 1977, federal entities have been required to demonstrate their actions' conformity with the SIPs before undertaking an action. Before the 1990 amendments, this conformity requirement was defined and enforced in such a way as to have little import for federal actions. However, the amendments changed the definition of "conformity" to link it more closely with a state's SIP and to impose specific standards for transportation plans, programs, and projects. The amendments also required the EPA to promulgate regulations for transportation-related actions as well as other federal actions that may have air quality impacts and thus require a conformity determination under the act.

This chapter focuses on the requirements of the transportation-related provisions of the CAA, certain requirements of the Transportation Equity Act for the 21st Century and its impact on the funding of transportation projects,[5] and the conformity provisions of Section 176(c) of the CAA applicable to both transportation and general federal actions.

Transportation-Related SIP Requirements

As discussed in Chapter 3, the CAA requires each state to adopt and submit to the U.S. Environmental Protection Agency (EPA) a SIP that "provides for implementation, maintenance and enforcement of the National Ambient Air Quality Standards (NAAQS) in each air quality region within the states."[6] The SIP must include "enforceable emission limitations and other control measures" that may be necessary to meet the CAA's requirements.[7] Although Section 110 of the CAA gives states broad discretion in fashioning "other control measures" to help attain the NAAQS, there are several other sections in the act that, following the 1990 amendments, require states to include specific transportation control measures (TCMs).

Inspection and Maintenance Programs

Motor vehicle inspection and maintenance (I/M) programs are an integral part of the effort to reduce mobile source air pollution. Despite being subject to the most rigorous motor vehicle air pollution control program in the world, cars and trucks still create about half of the ozone air pollution and nearly all of the carbon monoxide air pollution in United States cities.[8] With the 1990 amendments, the EPA began pursuing a three-point strategy for achieving major emission reductions from transportation sources. This strategy included (1) the development and commercialization of cleaner vehicles, (2) the development and commercialization of cleaner fuels, and (3) in-use controls, primarily I/M programs.[9]

Today's cars are absolutely dependent on properly functioning emission controls to keep pollution levels low. Minor malfunctions in the emission control system can increase emissions significantly; major malfunctions in the emission control system can cause emissions to skyrocket. Unfortunately, it is rarely obvious which cars fall into these categories, as the emissions themselves may not be noticeable and emission control malfunctions do not necessarily affect vehicle driveability. Effective I/M programs can identify these problem cars and ensure their repair.[10]

The CAA requires that most polluted cities adopt either "basic" or "enhanced" I/M programs, depending on the severity of the problem and the population of the area.[11] Under the CAA, the EPA in 1992 published rules related to plans for I/M programs,[12] rules that have since been revised. The following areas must implement basic I/M programs or update existing programs to meet new requirements:[13]

1. Areas classified as marginal ozone nonattainment or moderate carbon monoxide (CO) nonattainment with a design value of 12.7 ppm or less; and

2. Areas with urbanized area populations of 200,000 or more, classified as moderate ozone nonattainment and not required to implement enhanced I/M programs.

Enhanced I/M programs must be implemented in the following areas:[14]

1. Metropolitan statistical areas (MSAs) with populations of 100,000 or more within an ozone transport region (OTR). In the case of a multi-state MSA, enhanced I/M programs must be implemented in all OTR portions if the sum of these portions has a population of 100,000 or more, irrespective of the population of the portion in the individual OTR region area;
2. Areas with urbanized area populations of 200,000 or more, classified as serious or worse ozone nonattainment; and,
3. Areas with urbanized area populations of 200,000 or more, classified as moderate or serious CO nonattainment with a design value greater than 12.7 ppm.

Basic and enhanced I/M programs both achieve their objective by identifying vehicles that have high emissions as a result of one or more malfunctions, and requiring them to be repaired. An "enhanced" program covers more of the vehicles in operation, employs inspection methods that are better at finding high-emitting vehicles, and has additional features to better assure that all vehicles are tested properly and effectively repaired.[15]

The CAA directs the EPA to establish minimum performance standards for both basic and enhanced I/M programs. The standards must be based on the performance achievable by annual inspections in a centralized testing operation. However, neither the CAA's language nor the EPA's performance standards require states to implement annual, centralized testing. States have flexibility to design their own programs if they can show that their program is as effective as the "model" program used in the performance standard.[16]

40 C.F.R. § 51.352 states the performance standard for basic I/M programs; it remains more or less the same as it has been since the initial I/M policy was established in 1978, pursuant to the 1977 amendments to the Clean Air Act. Basic I/M programs were required to meet or exceed the minimum performance standard by 1997 for ozone nonattainment areas and 1996 for CO nonattainment areas; and, for serious or worse ozone nonattainment areas, on each applicable milestone and attainment deadline thereafter.[17]

40 C.F.R. § 51.351 describes the enhanced I/M performance standard. In 1992, as part of the enhanced I/M program, the EPA established high-tech emissions tests for new-technology vehicles (i.e., those with closed-loop control and, especially, fuel-injected engines).[18] In the years since, the EPA has frequently revised the I/M program requirements to provide additional flexibility to state I/M programs. In 1995 the EPA established a new "low" enhanced I/M performance standard, designed for nonattainment areas required to implement enhanced I/M but that could obtain adequate emission reductions

from other sources to meet emission reduction requirements, without the stringency of the normal "high" enhanced I/M performance standard.[19]

The EPA published several amendments to the I/M provisions in 1996. It first established an additional enhanced I/M performance standard for qualified areas in the Northeast OTR; the action also provided more flexibility for non-OTR states in designing quality assurance programs by allowing alternative quality assurance procedures that were as effective as or better than those specified in the original I/M rule.[20] The EPA also effected a rule change allowing states to employ such effective pre-existing motorist compliance enforcement mechanisms as sticker enforcement in any area in the state adopting an I/M program.[21] Finally, the EPA established requirements for the inspection of on-board diagnostic (OBD) systems as part of both basic and enhanced I/M programs.[22]

Initially, OBD testing of all 1996 and newer model year vehicles was required in all I/M programs beginning January 1, 1998 (except that areas in the Northeast OTR eligible to implement an OTR low enhanced I/M program had to begin OBD testing by January 1, 1999). In 1998, however, the EPA amended the OBD rules to delay the deadline by which OBD checks must be implemented.[23] In 2001 the EPA further amended the I/M rule and OBD testing requirements to provide states with greater flexibility, to update requirements based upon technological advances, and to optimize program efficiency and cost effectiveness. This action extended the deadline for mandatory implementation to January 1, 2002, and allows states that show good cause to postpone the program start for up to an additional twelve months (i.e., January 1, 2003).[24]

In 1998 the EPA revised the I/M requirements by replacing the I/M rule requirement that the tailpipe portion of the mandatory program evaluation be performed using only an IM240 exhaust test or equivalent mass emission transient test with a requirement that states use a sound evaluation methodology capable of providing accurate information about the overall effectiveness of an I/M program.[25] The goal of this action was to allow states additional flexibility to use not only IM240 but other approved alternative methodologies for their program evaluation.[26]

Passage of the National Highway System Designation Act of 1995 (NHSDA) as well as the EPA's own amendments providing greater flexibility in 1995 and 1996 contributed to delays by many states required to implement enhanced I/M programs. In response, the EPA in 2000 changed the performance standard modeling requirement from demonstrating that the performance standard is met on January 1, 2000, and each subsequent milestone (including the attainment deadline) to a requirement that the performance standard be met (within +/− 0.02 grams-per-mile) on January 1, 2002, and that the same or better level of emission reduction be demonstrated for the attainment deadline, rounded to the nearest year. This action brought the rule up to date with current policy decisions, technological changes, and statutory requirements, while also providing states the additional flexibility they needed to tailor their I/M programs to better meet their future needs.[27]

Transportation Controls

Section 182 of the CAA details the provisions that states must include in SIP revisions for various categories of ozone nonattainment areas. Where ozone levels have been categorized as severe, Section 182 imposes specific requirements for measuring and reducing emissions related to transportation.

Beginning on November 15, 1996 (and at each third year thereafter), states with areas classified as serious or worse ozone nonattainment were required to submit a demonstration as to whether current aggregate vehicle mileage, aggregate vehicle emissions, congestion levels, and other relevant parameters are consistent with those used for the area's demonstration of attainment. Where such parameters and emissions levels exceed the levels projected for purposes of the area's attainment demonstration, the state must within eighteen months develop and submit a revision of the applicable SIP that includes a TCM program consisting of, but not limited to, measures from Section 108(f) of the CAA that will reduce emissions to levels consistent with emission levels projected in such demonstration.[28] Examples are employer-based transportation management plans, traffic flow improvement programs that achieve emission reductions, and programs to encourage the voluntary removal from use and the marketplace of pre-1980 model year light-duty vehicles.[29]

In considering such TCMs, the CAA directs states to ensure adequate access to downtown and other commercial and residential areas and to avoid measures that increase or relocate emissions and congestion rather than reduce them.[30] The revision must be developed in accordance with guidance issued by the EPA pursuant to Section 108(e) and with the requirements of Section 174(b) and must include implementation and funding schedules that achieve expeditious emissions reductions in accordance with SIP projections.[31] Section 108(e) requires the EPA to periodically update the June 1978 Transportation–Air Quality Planning Guidelines and publish guidance on the development and implementation of transportation and other measures necessary to demonstrate and maintain attainment of NAAQS.[32] In addition, Section 108(f) requires it to from time to time publish and make available to appropriate federal, state, and local environmental and transportation agencies information regarding the formulation and emission reduction potential of TCMs related to criteria pollutants and their precursors.[33] The EPA published this guidance in early 1992, addressing the effectiveness of measures such as programs for improving public transit, ordinances for trip reduction, programs to control extended idling of vehicles, and employer-sponsored programs to permit flexible work schedules.[34]

Section 172(c)(1) of the CAA states that SIPs must include provisions that "provide for the implementation of all reasonably available control measures as expeditiously as practicable (including such reductions in emissions from existing sources in the area as may be obtained through the adoption, at a minimum, of reasonably available control technology)."[35] The EPA initially interpreted this section to require that all of the measures in Section 108(f) be implemented on the theory that these measures were presumed to be reasonably available in all areas; a Ninth Circuit decision bolstered this view.[36] Congress invalidated this view, however, with the enactment of the 1990 amendments and stated in legislative history to Section 176(c) that states were required to implement only those measures necessary to attain the NAAQS.[37] New guidance issued by the EPA in 1992 backed away from this early interpretation and was consistent with the congressional mandate in the CAA amendments. As a result, Section 172(c)(1) requires the implementation of Section 108(f) measures only to the extent that they are deemed "reasonable" for a particular area and necessary to attain the NAAQS.[38]

The Vehicle Miles Traveled Offset Requirement

For severe or extreme ozone nonattainment areas, the CAA imposes an additional requirement relating to SIP revisions. The purpose of the vehicle miles traveled (VMT) offset requirement is to prevent growth in motor vehicle emissions from canceling out the emission reduction benefits of federally mandated programs in the CAA. Sufficient measures must be adopted so that projected motor vehicle volatile organic compound (VOC) emissions will stay beneath a ceiling level established through modeling of mandated transportation-related controls. When growth in VMT and vehicle trips would otherwise cause a motor vehicle emissions upturn, this upturn must be prevented by TCMs. If projected total motor vehicle emissions during the ozone season in one year are not higher than during the previous ozone season due to control measures in the SIP, the VMT offset requirement is satisfied.[39] Again, in considering TCMs, the state should ensure adequate access to downtown and other commercial and residential areas and should avoid measures that increase or relocate emissions and congestion rather than reduce them.[40]

In adopting this interpretation, the EPA rejected comments indicating that Section 182(d)(1)(A) should be interpreted to require areas to offset any growth in VMT above 1990 levels, rather than only when such growth leads to actual emissions increases. Under this rejected approach, areas would have had to offset VMT growth even while vehicle emissions were declining. The EPA stated that, although the CAA requirement that states offset "any growth in emissions from growth in VMT" could be read to support the rejected approach, the agency believed that it was more reasonable to read that provision as requiring the offset of VMT growth only where such growth results in emissions increases from the vehicle fleet in the area.[41] The EPA believed that a contrary position might encourage areas to delay implementation of measures aimed at reducing VMT until the trend in motor vehicle emissions reductions reached a minimum point with emission levels about to turn upward.

Section 182(d)(1)(A) of the CAA sets forth several elements that must be part of a VMT offset SIP:

1. Identification and adoption of specific enforceable transportation control strategies and TCMs to offset any growth in emissions from

growth in vehicle miles traveled or numbers of vehicle trips in such area;[42]

2. Certain reductions in motor vehicle emissions as necessary (in combination with other emission reduction requirements of Section 182) to allow total area emissions to comply with (2a) the CAA's Reasonable Further Progress (RFP) milestones;[43] and (2b) attainment demonstration requirements.[44]

Under the EPA's interpretation, the three required elements are separable and could be divided into three separate submissions that could be submitted on different dates. The first element—the emissions growth offset element—was due on November 15, 1992. The EPA believes this element is not necessarily dependent upon the development of the other elements. The state could submit the emissions growth offset element independent of an analysis of that element's consistency with the RFP or attainment requirements of the Act.[45] (The due dates for the other elements depend on the classification of the area.[46])

The TCM offset provisions apply only to emissions of VOCs. In developing their progress and attainment strategies, however, states may wish to adopt similar offset goals for NO_x emissions from mobile sources, in cases where NO_x reductions are beneficial to attainment.[47]

Reduction of Work-Related Vehicle Trips

The 1990 amendments required employers with 100 or more employees to implement an employee commute options (ECO) program. The employers were required, two years after the SIP revision was submitted to the EPA, to submit employer trip reduction (ETR) compliance plans to the state. These compliance plans were intended to "convincingly demonstrate" that within four years after the SIP was submitted, the employer would achieve an increase in the average passenger occupancy of its employees who commuted to work during the peak period by not less than 25 percent above the average vehicle occupancy of the nonattainment area.[48]

The purpose of the ECO program was to deal directly with the rapid increase in VMT by both automobiles and light trucks, which threatened to supersede any reductions in motor vehicle emissions resulting from cleaner vehicles. Through a guidance document, the EPA clarified for states its expectations regarding ECO SIPs.[49] Subsequent EPA guidance provided flexibility by expanding the choices available for implementation of the ECO program.[50] Congress provided the most significant flexibility, however, in passing Public Law 104-70 in December 1995. Public Law 104-70 allows states that prior to its enactment were required to implement ECO programs to "remove such provisions from the implementation plan, or withdraw its submission, if the state notifies the Administrator, in writing, that the state has undertaken, or will undertake, one or more alternative methods that will achieve emission reductions equivalent to those to be achieved by the removed or withdrawn provisions."[51]

For states with areas classified after the date of the amendment as severe or extreme for ozone nonattainment or serious for CO nonattainment, ECO programs are now voluntary. Equivalent reductions for the purpose of removing ECO programs from SIP submittals may be obtained from measures that are not federally mandated or from surpassing the requirements of federally mandated measures (i.e., by achieving more than federally required emission reductions or by implementing federally required measures at a level beyond federal requirements). These substitutes may be newly identified measures or discretionary measures the state chose to include in its SIP submittals, such as 15 percent plans or attainment demonstrations.[52]

Limits on Land Use Authority

An indirect source review program is "the facility-by-facility review of indirect sources of air pollution, including such measures as are necessary to assure, or assist in assuring, that a new or modified indirect source will not attract mobile sources of air pollution."[53] An indirect source is defined as "a facility, building, structure, installation, real property, road, or highway which attracts, or may attract, mobile sources of pollution."[54]

Section 110(a)(5)(A)(i) leaves within the states' discretion the decision as to whether to include an indirect source review program in their SIPs.[55] Although the EPA is required to approve and enforce these programs if included in the SIPs, this section specifically prohibits the EPA from requiring adoption of such a program as a condition to SIP approval.[56]

This section's precise definitions were added in 1977 with the intent of limiting federal authority to intrude into the area of land use control. In an attempt to remove all doubt about how potentially ambiguous provisions should be interpreted, Congress, with the 1990 CAA Amendments, added Section 131, which states: "Nothing in this Act constitutes an infringement on the existing authority of counties and cities to plan or control land use, and nothing in this Act provides or transfers authority over such land use."[57]

However, when the EPA administrator is required to implement a federal implementation plan (FIP), the general rule against the inclusion of indirect source review programs has a few exceptions.[58] Under these circumstances the administrator does have authority to promulgate, implement, and enforce indirect review programs that apply only to federally assisted highways and airports and other major indirect sources that are federally assisted, owned, or operated.

Funding Transportation Control Measures

One of the main goals behind the 1991 passage of the Intermodal Surface Transportation Efficiency Act (ISTEA) was to provide the funding necessary to implement many of the provisions of the CAA.[59] ISTEA authorized the expenditure of $155 billion for highway, mass transit, highway safety, and other surface transportation programs over six years. Many of the TCMs listed in Section 108(f)(1)(A) of the CAA were specifically eligible for this funding. Section 1008 of the ISTEA established a $6 billion Congestion Mitigation and Air Quality Improvement Program (CMAQ), which was generally restricted to providing funds for programs that contribute to the NAAQS attainment.[60]

The primary purpose of CMAQ is to fund projects and programs that reduce transportation-related emissions in air quality nonattainment and maintenance areas for ozone, CO, and small particulate matter (PM_{10}). Under CMAQ, a transportation program or project is eligible for funding only if the program or project is likely to contribute to the attainment of the NAAQS, is a TCM listed under Section 108(f) of the CAA, or is included in an EPA-approved SIP. Conversely, federal funding under CMAQ is not available for projects that will result in the construction of new highway capacity (which may therefore increase vehicle trips and emissions), except for carpool lanes.[61] States received Section 1008(a) funds based on an apportionment formula that favored states with nonattainment areas. States with CO and extreme ozone nonattainment areas benefited most under ISTEA's allocation scheme.[62]

In 1998 Congress passed the Transportation Equity Act for the 21st Century (TEA-21), reauthorizing ISTEA. TEA-21 continues CMAQ as an independent program, with funding increased by about 35 percent to $8.1 billion.[63] It retains ISTEA's apportionment formula, with the following changes: It includes new weighting factors for ozone and CO maintenance areas, CO nonattainment areas, and ozone submarginal areas; eliminates special treatment for California, New York, and Texas; and eliminates the freeze on the apportionment factors imposed under NHSDA.[64] TEA-21 also expands the areas that are eligible to receive CMAQ funding to include PM_{10} nonattainment and maintenance areas and areas designated as nonattainment under the 1997 revised air quality standards. It limits the eligibility of nonattainment and maintenance areas designated prior to December 31, 1997, to areas classified submarginal through extreme for ozone, and moderate or serious for CO and PM-10.[65]

Section 1221 of the TEA-21 established the $120 million Transportation and Community and System Preservation Pilot Program (TCSP).[66] TCSP provides funding for a comprehensive initiative including planning grants, implementation grants, and research to investigate and address the relationships between transportation and community and system preservation and to identify private sector-based initiatives.[67] Funding for TCMs may be obtained under TCSP if the measures meet the program's criteria, e.g., have preservation or development policies that include a mechanism for reducing potential impacts of transportation activities on the environment.[68]

Conformity under the Clean Air Act: Overview

Because of the ubiquity of federal involvement in all types of actions that can affect air quality, Section 176(c) of the CAA provides a necessary tool for implementing the Act's goals. This section prohibits federal involvement in a variety of actions unless and until the responsible federal entity has made a determination that the action it seeks to undertake or fund conforms to the requirements of the most recently approved implementation plan in the affected state.[69] The statutory language demonstrates the breadth of this conformity requirement:

> No department, agency, or instrumentality of the Federal Government shall engage in, support in any way or provide financial assistance for, license or permit, or approve, any activity which does not conform to an implementation plan after it has been approved or promulgated under section 110.[70]

The statutory language clearly states that this requisite conformity determination is the "affirmative responsibility" of the head of the federal entity.[71] This means that a determination that the intended action complies with the affected state's implementation plan must be performed pursuant to the criteria spelled out in the rules promulgated by the EPA and must be done before the federal entity undertakes the action.

Section 176(c)(1) sets out a two-part definition of conformity that applies to all general federal actions. A proposed federal action will be found to conform to an implementation plan if it meets the following two requirements:

1. The action conforms to the implementation plan's "purpose of eliminating or reducing the severity and number of violations of the national ambient air quality standards and achieving expeditious attainment of such standards."
2. The action will not cause or contribute to any new violation of any standard in any area, will not increase the frequency or severity of any existing violation of any standard in any area, and will not delay timely attainment of any standard or any required interim emission reductions or other milestones in any area.[72]

In addition to this general conformity rule, Sections 176(c)(2) and 176(c)(3) add more specific requirements regarding when a transportation action such as a transportation improvement plan (TIP) drafted by the metropolitan planning organization (MPO) will be found to conform to a SIP.

Although there is no specific exclusion from the conformity requirements for nontransportation actions ("general federal actions") in Section 176(c), the lack of detail in the provisions dealing with these types of actions suggests that Congress may have intended a less rigorous standard of conformity review for these actions. In its draft guidance, the EPA focused on the absence of congressional debate over conformity requirements for general federal actions in finding that Congress intended that it not create "a burdensome set of new rules" for these types of actions.[73] The EPA has continued to maintain this position and, as a result, promulgated separate rules to govern conformity to transportation actions and general federal actions, with the latter having somewhat less rigorous requirements.[74]

The conformity provisions in the CAA illustrate Congress's intent to prevent federal entities from causing a delay in the attainment or maintenance of the NAAQS through their actions. In addition, the requirement that federal entities demonstrate their actions' consistency with a state's implementation plan enables the states to engage in long-term planning by relying on the decisions they made in their SIPs.[75]

Conformity under the 1990 CAA Amendments

In the 1990 amendments, Congress expanded the scope and content of the conformity requirements. First, specific provisions regarding conformity of transportation actions were added to Section 176. In addition, Congress moved away from defining conformity in the context of TCMs and instead tied the definition of conformity to emissions and air quality. The 1990 amendments added the following definition of conformity:

> Conformity to an implementation plan's purpose of eliminating or reducing the severity and number of violations of the national ambient air quality standards and achieving expeditious attainment of such standards; and that such activities will not (i) cause or contribute to any new violations of any standard in any area; (ii) increase the frequency or severity of any existing violation of any standard in any area; or (iii) delay timely attainment of any standard or any required interim emission reductions or other milestones in any area.[76]

The purpose of this new definition was to protect the integrity of the implementation plan by ensuring that its growth projections not be exceeded without measures to counterbalance that growth.[77]

Conformity under the 1997 Transportation Conformity Rule Amendments

On August 15, 1997, the EPA published a final rule amending the transportation conformity rule. This guidance represented the first significant change since the 1990 amendments and a major shift from the 1993 transportation conformity rule.

Under the 1997 final rule, the EPA sought to clarify the transportation conformity rule and to make it more flexible and streamlined. The rule gave state and local governments more authority in selecting the performance measures used as tests of conformity and more discretion when a transportation plan does not conform to a SIP. "For example, the rule allows motor vehicle emissions budgets in a submitted SIP to be used to determine conformity instead of the 'build/no build' test, and rural areas can choose among several conformity tests to address the time period after that covered by the SIP."[78] Another way that the EPA sought to foster creative problem solving was by initiating a pilot program that gives more authority to state and local governments to develop conformity plans.[79]

However, the most significant aspects of the 1997 conformity rule trace their genesis to *Environmental Defense Fund v. Environmental Protection Agency*, the case that successfully challenged it.[80] Specifically, the decision struck down the regulations to the extent that they permitted local authorities to approve transportation projects in the absence of a currently conforming transportation plan and program, that they permitted federal funding of transportation projects in the absence of a currently conforming transportation plan and program, and that they required or permitted conformity determinations to be based on emissions budgets in SIPs that the EPA had disapproved or not yet approved. The EPA has been developing proposals and rules to address the implementation of this decision.[81]

The Transportation Conformity Rule

Scope of the Transportation Conformity Rule

Under the final rule, conformity determinations must be made for any "adoption, acceptance, approval, or support" of transportation plans and TIPs developed pursuant to 23 C.F.R. Part 450 or 49 C.F.R. Part 613 by an MPO or Department of Transportation (DOT).[82] In addition, conformity determinations are required for the "approval, funding, or implementation" of Federal Highway Administration (FHWA) and Federal Transportation Authority (FTA) projects.[83] Projects *exempt* from conformity determinations are listed in Exhibit 1.[84] Projects exempt from regional emissions analyses are listed in Exhibit 2.[85]

EXHIBIT 1. Projects Exempt from Conformity Determinations

Safety
Railroad/highway crossing
Hazard elimination program
Safer non-Federal-aid system roads
Shoulder improvements
Increasing sight distance
Safety improvement program
Traffic control devices and operating assistance other than signalization projects
Railroad/highway-crossing warning devices
Guardrails, median barriers, crash cushions
Pavement resurfacing and/or rehabilitation
Pavement marking demonstration
Emergency relief (23 U.S.C. § 125)
Fencing
Skid treatments
Safety roadside rest areas
Adding medians
Truck climbing lanes outside of urbanized areas
Lighting improvements
Widening narrow pavements or reconstructing bridges (no additional travel lanes)
Emergency truck pullovers

(continued)

EXHIBIT 1. *(continued)*

Mass Transit

Operating assistance to transit agencies

Purchase of support vehicles

Rehabilitation of transit vehicles

Purchase of office, shop, and operating equipment for existing facilities

Purchase of operating equipment for vehicles (e.g., radios, lifts)

Construction or renovation of power, signal, and communications systems

Construction of small passenger shelters and information kiosks

Reconstruction or renovation of transit buildings and structures (e.g., rail or bus buildings, stations, terminals)

Rehabilitation or reconstruction of track structures, track, and track bed in existing rights of way

Purchase of new buses and rail cars to replace existing vehicles or for minor expansions of the fleet

Construction of new bus or rail storage/maintenance facilities categorically excluded in 23 C.F.R. Part 771

Air Quality

Continuance of ride-sharing and van-pooling promotion activities at current levels

Bicycle and pedestrian facilities

Other

Specific activities that do not involve or lead directly to construction, such as:

    Plannings and technical studies

    Grants for training and research programs

    Planning activities conducted pursuant to Titles 23 and 49 U.S.C.

    Federal aid systems revisions

Engineering to assess social, economic, and environmental effects of the proposed action or alternatives to that action

Noise attenuation

Emergency or hardship advance land acquisitions (23 C.F.R. § 712.204(d))

Acquisition of scenic easements

Plantings, landscaping, etc.

Sign removal

Directional and informational signs

Transportation enhancement activities (except rehabilitation and operation of historic transportation buildings, structures, or facilities)

Repair of damage caused by natural disasters, civil unrest, or terrorist acts, except projects involving substantial functional, locational, or capacity changes

EXHIBIT 2. Projects Exempt from Regional Emissions Analyses

Intersection channelization projects

Intersection signalization projects at individual intersections

Interchange reconfiguration projects

Changes in vertical and horizontal alignment

Truck size and weight inspection stations

Bus terminals and transfer points

Conformity determinations are not generally required for "nonfederal projects," projects that receive no federal funding and require no federal approval but are adopted or approved by an entity that receives federal transportation funds for other projects.[86] However, regionally significant projects adopted or approved by these entities must conform under the less stringent requirements of 40 C.F.R. § 93.121.

Recent developments have added force to the requirements. Pursuant to the decision in *EDF v. EPA*,[87] the EPA is developing a proposal to implement the court's ruling that nonfederal projects cannot attain conformity status in the absence of a currently conforming plan. Previously, so long as the nonfederal project was planned for in the first three years of the most recent conforming plan and TIP, the project could proceed even during a conformity lapse.[88] Now the only way that nonfederal projects can be grandfathered-in and thus proceed during a conformity lapse is if they were actually approved under a then conforming plan. Grandfathering, though, is not allowed for federal projects.

The final rule requires that conformity determinations be made for the appropriate transportation actions but only if the transportation action is to be taken in an area that is designated in nonattainment for the transportation-related criteria or precursor pollutants or has a maintenance plan.[89] Under the final rule, conformity determinations are not required for transportation actions taken in areas designated in attainment. During the rule-making process, the EPA stated that Section 176(c) of the CAA was ambiguous as to whether or not it applied in attainment areas but decided to address the issue of conformity in attainment areas in a future rule with a goal of developing flexible and low-resource procedures and criteria requiring conformity determinations only in urban attainment areas that have exceeded 85 percent of the NAAQS of certain criteria pollutants.[90]

Assessing the Conformity of Transportation Actions

To demonstrate the conformity of transportation actions, such actions must meet not only the general criteria set forth in Section 176(c)(1) but also the more specific criteria in Sections 176(c)(2) and 176(c)(3). The requirements and procedures for assessing the conformity of transportation actions in the latter sections differ depending on the type of transportation action at issue. These sections distinguish between three types of transportation actions—plans, programs, and projects—and the EPA's final rule adheres to this distinction.

As used in the rule, the term "transportation plan" refers to the official intermodal metropolitan transportation plan that is developed through the metropolitan planning process for the metropolitan planning area.[91] The plan is generally a long-range (ten to twenty years) plan outlining all proposed transportation projects for the covered area. Lastly, the term "transportation projects" refers to highway projects[92] and transit projects,[93] both of which have broad definitions under the rule.

Section 176(c)(3) applies to transportation actions proposed during the "interim period," that is, the period that runs until the EPA's approval of a state's conformity SIP revisions. The EPA had previously divided up the phases until the state's submission of its control strategy SIP because it would be impossible to apply the new emissions budget test before that time;[94] however, the 1997 rule eliminated references to the Phase II, transitional, and control strategy periods because most states had submitted SIP revisions in the intervening years.[95] Section 176(c)(2) sets forth the final criteria that will be used to assess the transportation actions' conformity after the interim period has ended.

Ultimately, conformity determinations will be made pursuant to the criteria and procedures states have added to SIPs that have been approved by the EPA as consistent with the EPA's regulations.

Transportation Conformity Determinations—General Information

Under the EPA regulations, a conformity determination must generally be made before any transportation action (to which the rule applies) may proceed, and such conformity determination must be updated at least every three years.[96] The frequency of conformity determinations varies with the type of transportation action.

For transportation plans, a new conformity determination must be made before there can be MPO approval and DOT acceptance of a new transportation plan or specified substantive revisions.[97] For existing transportation plans, there must be a redetermination of conformity within eighteen months of when a revision affecting the emissions budget or TCMs or the plan will lapse.[98] In no case, however, can a plan remain intact for more than three years without a redetermination of conformity.[99]

New TIPs and substantive TIP amendments also require conformity determinations before they can be approved or accepted. After an MPO adopts a new or revised transportation plan, there must be a conformity determination of the TIP within six months.[100] In any case, a redetermination of conformity must be done every three years.

New transportation projects must similarly be found to be in conformity before they can be accepted, approved, or funded. Redetermination of conformity, however, is not required if any of the following events occurred within the past three years: NEPA process completion; start of final design; acquisition of a significant portion of the right-of-way; or approval of the plans, specifications, and estimates.[101] This is because the EPA decided that it would not be reasonable to stop projects that had previously undergone a conformity analysis and were proceeding to completion.

Under CAA Section 176(c)(1), the conformity determination is the affirmative responsibility of the federal department, agency, or instrumentality sponsoring the transportation action.[102] In addition, MPOs also must assess the conformity of transportation actions.

Although the EPA's final rule applies only to the FHWA, FTA, and MPOs, other federal agencies that issue ancillary approvals or permits for transportation actions sponsored by one of these listed agencies may be required to issue a conformity determination, but pursuant to the rule on general federal actions rather than the transportation rule.

According to the relevant CAA provision, conformity is demonstrated by determining whether federal actions conform to "a plan approved or promulgated under section 110."[103] The language of this section created a great deal of concern during the rule-making process because the only implementation plans that have been "approved or promulgated" in some states, notably in California, are outdated, although these states may have recent SIP submissions that the EPA has yet to fully approve.[104]

Though the 1997 transportation conformity rule tried to ameliorate the situation, the Court in *EDF v. EPA* decided that only currently conforming plans could be used by local authorities to lawfully approve transportation projects.[105]

Specific Statutory Criteria

As stated previously, transportation actions must conform to the specific requirements in Sections 176(c)(2) and 176(c)(3) as well as to the general requirements set forth in Section 176(c)(1). The requirements of Section 176(c)(3) are intended to apply only during the interim period. Under the provisions of the CAA and the regulations promulgated thereunder, the procedures and criteria for conformity determinations vary by type of transportation action.

For transportation plans and programs to be found in conformity, they must meet the specific statutory requirements listed in Section 176(c)(3)(A). That section states that conformity will be demonstrated only if the transportation plan or program is (1) consistent with the most recent estimates of mobile source emissions, (2) provides for the expeditious implementation of TCMs, and (3) contributes to annual emissions reductions if located in ozone and CO nonattainment areas.[106]

Once the interim period has ended, the specific requirements in Section 176(c)(2) replace those found in Section 176(c)(3).[107] This means that transportation plans and programs established pursuant to U.S.C. Title 23 must implement the SIP's transportation provisions.[108] In addition, a transportation plan will not be found to be in conformity unless the federal entity has demonstrated that (1) emissions expected from implementation of any plan or program are consistent with estimates of emissions from motor vehicles and necessary emissions reductions contained in the implementation plan, and (2) the action will satisfy Section 176(c)(1)(B) requirements, which would prohibit actions that cause or contribute to or increase the frequency or severity of the NAAQS exceedances or delay attainment of the NAAQS.

In developing the specific regulatory criteria to implement these sections, the EPA adhered to the transportation action categories shown in Exhibit 3, which lists the applicable regulations for transportation actions as set out in 40 C.F.R. § 93.109. To further aid practitioners, Exhibit 4 summarizes the regulations by section number.

EXHIBIT 3. Conformity Criteria for Transportation Actions

Relevant Action	Applicable Regulations under 40 C.F.R.	Criteria
All actions at all times	§ 93.110 § 93.111 § 93.112	Latest planning assumptions Latest emissions models Consultation
Transportation Plan	§ 93.113(b) § 93.118 or § 93.119	TCMs Emissions budget or Emissions reduction
TIP	§ 93.113(c) § 93.118 or § 93.119	TCMs Emissions budget or Emissions reduction
Project (From a Conforming Plan and TIP)	§ 93.114 § 93.115 § 93.116 § 93.117	Currently conforming plan and TIP Project from a conforming plan and TIP CO and PM_{10} hot spots PM_{10} control measures
Project (Not from a Conforming Plan and TIP)	§ 93.113(d) § 93.114 § 93.116 § 93.117 § 93.118 or § 93.119	TCMs Currently conforming plan and TIP CO and PM_{10} hot spots PM_{10} control measures Emissions budget or Emission reduction

EXHIBIT 4. Guide to Regulatory Criteria

§ 93.110	The conformity determination must be based on the latest planning assumptions.
§ 93.111	The conformity determination must be based on the latest emission estimation model available.
§ 93.112	The MPO must make the conformity determination according to the consultation procedures of this rule and the implementation plan revision required by Section 51.396.
§ 93.113	The transportation plan, TIP, or FHWA/FTA project that is not from a conforming plan and TIP must provide for the timely implementation of TCMs from the applicable implementation plan.
§ 93.114	There must be a currently conforming transportation plan and currently conforming TIP at the time of project approval.
§ 93.115	The project must come from a conforming transportation plan and program.
§ 93.116	The FHWA/FTA project must not cause or contribute to any new localized CO or PM_{10} violations in CO and PM_{10} nonattainment and maintenance areas.
§ 93.117	The FHWA/FTA project must comply with PM_{10} control measures in the applicable implementation plan.
§ 93.118	The transportation plan must be consistent with the motor vehicle emissions budgets in the applicable implementation plan submission.
§ 93.119	The TIP must be consistent with the motor vehicle emissions budgets in the applicable implementation plan or implementation plan submission.

The new categorization illustrates the EPA's shift away from the multiple phases prior to approval of a SIP. The new regulations focus instead on the overall period prior to SIP approval, and they set forth the different treatment of projects depending on whether or not they come from a conforming plan and TIP.

Regulatory Criteria for All Plans, Programs, and Projects

To meet the conformity requirements under the EPA's final rule, transportation plans and TIPs must contribute to emissions reductions in ozone and CO nonattainment areas[109] and contribute to emissions reductions *or* maintenance of current levels of emissions in PM_{10} and NO_2 nonattainment areas.[110]

Furthermore, conformity determinations must be based on the latest planning assumptions.[111] This means that the assumptions must be derived from the most recent information that the MPO or other relevant agency has on such things as current and future population, employment and congestion, and likely future changes in transit operating policies.[112]

Conformity determinations must also be based on the latest emissions estimation model available.[113] This requirement will be met if the conformity analysis utilizes the most current version of the motor vehicle emissions model approved by the EPA for use in preparing or revising implementation plans.[114]

Neither transportation plans nor TIPs will be found to conform if they fail to provide for specified consultation procedures[115] and the timely implementation of TCMs.[116]

To demonstrate conformity, transportation plans and TIPs must have one additional requirement: they must also be consistent with the motor vehicle emissions budget or budgets in the applicable implementation plan or implementation plan submission.[117] To demonstrate this consistency, a regional emissions analysis of certain pollutants and pollutant precursors must be performed. This analysis must include emissions from the area's entire existing transportation network as well as all proposed regionally significant federal and nonfederal highway and transit projects. This regional emissions analysis must estimate total projected emissions for a specified future period.[118]

After the emissions analysis has been performed, a finding of conformity will be made if the analysis demonstrates that the estimated emissions for each of the pollutants and precursors is less than or equal to the emissions budget as established in the applicable implementation plan or implementation plan submission.[119]

Regulatory Criteria for Projects from a Conforming Plan and TIP

Only one conforming transportation plan or TIP may exist in an area at any time. The criteria for determining whether a project comes from a conforming transportation plan or program are detailed in 40 C.F.R. § 93.115(b) and (c). Provided that these qualifications are met, a demonstration of conformity requires satisfying the criteria applicable to all actions at all times, as set forth in Exhibit 3 above. Additionally, the project must satisfy the special requirements for CO and PM_{10} hot spots[120] and adhere to the PM_{10} control measures in the applicable implementation plan.

Regulatory Criteria for Projects Not from a Conforming Plan and TIP

Should the project be determined to not come from a conforming plan or TIP using the same criteria laid out in 40 C.F.R. § 93.115(b) and (c), it must still conform under the same requirements as a project that did come from a conforming plan and TIP. However, such a project comes under the added scrutiny of the motor vehicle emissions budget,[121] and should the region not have a motor vehicle emissions budget, it must contribute to emissions reductions in some other way.[122]

General Conformity

Overview

Although the latter portion of Section 176(c) focuses solely on determining conformity of federal transportation actions, the first portion of the statute issues a broad mandate that all federal actions conform to the applicable implementation plan. The operative language in that section states that no federal entity "shall engage in, *support in any way* or provide financial assistance for, license or permit, or approve, *any activity* which does not conform to an implementation plan."[123]

If read broadly, the quoted language could subject virtually all federal actions to conformity inquiries. This interpretation not only would increase the costs of federal actions substantially but also would slow government processes dramatically. For these reasons, the EPA has not interpreted the statute as broadly as a literal reading would allow. Rather, with a dearth of legislative history in this area, the EPA has read into the statute several limitations because of practical considerations such as cost and burden to the system.[124]

Scope of the General Conformity Rule

The final rule promulgated by the EPA states that a conformity determination of a federal action is required for "each pollutant where the total of direct and indirect emissions" caused by the action equals or exceeds the emissions limits established in the rule.[125] With respect to "indirect emissions," the EPA decided that because Section 176(c)(1) prohibits federal actions that "support in any way" an activity that does not conform to a SIP, indirect emissions must be included in a conformity determination.[126]

Indirect emissions are defined in the final rule as the emissions of a criteria pollutant or its precursor that meet both of the following two conditions: (1) the emissions are "caused by the federal action, but may occur later in time and/or may be farther removed in distance from the action itself but are reasonably foreseeable";[127] and (2) the federal entity can "practicably control and will maintain control over" the emissions owing to "a continuing program responsibility" of the federal entity.[128]

Throughout the rule making, this definition was referred to as the "exclusive definition,"[129] since the definition excludes from the conformity determination a consideration of all indirect emissions over which the federal entity has no control.

To elaborate on the EPA definition of "caused by," according to the final rule, emissions are "caused by" the federal action if they "would not otherwise occur in the absence of the federal action."[130] This definition includes emissions from any on-site or off-site support facility that would not have been constructed, or would not have increased its emissions, but for the federal action.[131] In addition, emissions resulting from roads, parking, retail, commercial or industrial facilities, or other indirect emissions from mobile sources that are attracted to a facility would be considered in a conformity determination.[132]

With the EPA's expansive definition of "caused by," which requires federal entities to consider such indirect emissions sources as increased traffic resulting from a new facility, critics have contended that this interpretation effectively contradicts the terms of Sections 110(a)(5)(A) and 131 of the CAA.[133] These sections prohibit the EPA administrator from requiring a state to adopt a general indirect source review program and indicate that land use authority resides with the cities and counties, respectively.[134]

The EPA, however, has disputed this reading of the relevant provisions. The agency has stated that Section 176(c) provides it with independent authority for requiring SIP revisions concerning conformity requirements that include provisions addressing indirect emissions.[135] In addition, the EPA believes that the conformity rules regulate emissions by limiting the federal entities' ability to engage in certain actions and, therefore, the rules do not infringe on the land use authority of local governments.[136]

As to the EPA definition of "reasonably foreseeable," the agency has defined "reasonably foreseeable" emissions as "projected future indirect emissions that are identified at the time the conformity determination is made; the location of such emissions is known and the emissions are quantifiable, as described and documented by the Federal agency based on its own information and after reviewing any information presented to the Federal agency."[137] In formulating this definition, the EPA broke from its initial proposal and decided a federal agency is not required to use all emissions scenarios contained in financial documents or environmental analyses.[138] In addition, this definition does not require the use of worst-case assumptions, unlikely growth scenarios, or analyses where it is impossible to assess local air quality impacts.[139]

To assist in the application of this definition, the EPA included in the final rule examples of actions from which the emissions will not be considered reasonably foreseeable.[140] These exempt actions include such things as electric power marketing activities and outer continental shelf lease sales.[141] For both of these examples, the EPA has stated that the reason for the exemption is that the emissions from both actions will be difficult to locate and quantify and, therefore, they are not reasonably foreseeable.[142] The list of actions with emissions considered not foreseeable is not intended to be an exhaustive list, and the EPA has stated that other actions resulting in emissions that are difficult to quantify will similarly be found not reasonably foreseeable.[143]

Lastly, although the phrase "continuing program responsibility" helps delineate the scope of the conformity requirement, it is not specifically defined in the final rule. Rather, the EPA gives some examples intended to illustrate what is meant by this phrase.

Example 1: The United States Army Corps of Engineers (Corps) issues a permit authorizing dredging by a nonfederal entity. If the Corps requires the permittee to transport and dispose of the dredged material at a specific site, the Corps has continuing program responsibility for the air emissions associated with the dredging and for those associated with the disposal activities. However, if the Corps allows the permittee to dispose of the dredged material at a suitable upland disposal site without imposing additional disposal requirements, the Corps has continuing program responsibility for the air emissions associated with the dredging but not for those associated with the disposal.[144]

Example 2: The USDA Forest Service permits a ski resort and imposes conditions regarding the construction and operation of the resort. The resort's housing development will occur nearby but on privately owned land. In this case, the emissions from the construction and operation of the resort are a continuing program responsibility of the Forest Service. However, since the Forest Service did not choose to impose conditions that would result in air pollutant emissions on the housing development, emissions from the housing development are not part of the Forest Service's continuing program responsibility.[145]

A federal agency has no responsibility to attempt to limit emissions that do not meet these tests.[146] Moreover, a federal agency is not required by either the final rule or Section 176(c)(1) to attempt to "leverage" its legal authority to influence or control nonfederal activities that it cannot practicably control or that are not subject to a continuing program responsibility.[147]

Conformity determinations of general federal actions are required only where the total of the direct and indirect emissions of a particular pollutant would equal or exceed the rate specified in the *de minimis* rule.[148] These *de minimis* levels are assigned to each of the criteria pollutants, and several of the pollutants are assigned several rates to be applied according to whether the area is designated as moderate, serious, severe, or extreme.[149]

The levels specified in the final rule generally are based on the CAA's major stationary source definitions for the various pollutants.[150] The EPA rejected the approach in the original proposal of the rule that was to base the *de minimis* levels on the "significance levels" established for preconstruction review of modifications to existing major stationary sources.[151]

Use of *de minimis* emissions levels helps focus conformity requirements on federal actions with potential to cause significant air quality impacts. To help understand how the *de minimis* emissions levels operate, consider this EPA example.

Under the major source definition, the levels for ozone range from 10 tons per year for an extreme ozone nonattainment area to 100 tons per year for marginal and moderate areas. In areas that are close to attainment, smaller projects, like strip shopping centers with small emissions levels, would not be subject to conformity review. However, in areas with more severe air quality problems, such projects are more likely to be subject to review. Large projects, such as an airport expansion, would likely require a conformity review as it probably would not meet any of the *de minimis* levels.[152]

Federal actions that are presumed by the agency not to cause an increase in emissions do not require an applicability analysis or a positive conformity determination.[153] Rather, these types of actions are exempt from the requirements of the rule and the federal agency is not required to document emissions levels.[154] This section does not create a rebuttable presumption for these types of actions but an outright exemption.[155] This exemption is intended to ensure that the conformity rules do not overly burden federal agencies by requiring them to spend undue time assessing actions that have little or no effect on air quality.[156]

Many of the types of actions that fall into this category are listed in the final rule.[157] The list includes such actions as administrative proceedings, routine maintenance activities, maintenance dredging, and the granting of licenses for export and is intended to be illustrative rather than exhaustive.[158]

Federal actions that do not cause direct and indirect emissions in excess of the allowable levels may still be required to have a conformity determination prepared if the action is considered "regionally significant."[159] Under the final rule, an action is regionally significant if the total direct and indirect emissions represent 10 percent or more of a nonattainment area's total emissions for that pollutant.[160] If an action is found to be regionally significant, a full conformity analysis must be prepared by the federal agency.

In addition to the exemptions in 40 C.F.R. § 51.853(c) for federal actions presumed to be below *de minimis* levels and those actions determined to be without reasonably foreseeable emissions, 40 C.F.R. § 51.583(d) provides an outright exemption for other types of federal actions that do not necessarily meet the other exemption criteria.[161] This subsection states that generally a conformity determination is not required for actions such as those requiring a permit under the new source review (NSR) program, those in response to emergencies or natural disasters, and those altering or adding to existing structures as required by new environmental legislation.[162]

Although many of the listed activities receive a complete exemption from the conformity requirements, other types of actions receive only a presumption that they are exempt under specified circumstances. For example, although generally a conformity determination is not required for federal actions in response to emergencies, if the federal action is part of a continuing response and it occurs more than six months after the commencement of the response, the action will be exempt only if the agency makes a written determination that a conformity analysis is impractical and that the federal action cannot be delayed because of concerns about the public welfare.[163] The actions and rules related to these exemptions, conditional exemptions, and presumptions are set out in Exhibit 5.

EXHIBIT 5. Exemptions, Conditional Exemptions, and Presumptions of Exemption from Conformity Requirements

EXEMPTIONS

Type of Federal Action	Applicable Rule
Actions in which the total of direct and indirect emissions are below the level specified for the pollutant in § 51.853(b).	§ 51.853(c) (1)
Actions that the EPA and federal agencies have determined result in no emissions increase or one that is clearly *de minimis*. The rule lists twenty-one categories (such as judicial and legislative proceedings and rule making and policy development) of actions that fall within the exemption, but it also notes that this list is intended to be exhaustive and agencies will be permitted to add to this list.	§ 51.853(c) (2)
Initial outer continental shelf lease sales made on a broad scale and electric power marketing activities that involve the acquisition, sale, and transmission of electric energy, if the emissions from these activities are not reasonably foreseeable.	§ 51.853(c) (3)
Actions that implement a decision to conduct or carry out a conforming program that is consistent with a conforming land management plan.	§ 51.853(c) (4)
The portion of an action including major new or modified stationary sources that requires a permit under the NSR or prevention of significant deterioration (PSD) programs of the CAA.	§ 51.853(d) (1)
Actions taken in response to emergencies or natural disasters and commenced within hours or days of the emergency or disaster.	§ 51.853(d) (2)
Research, investigations, studies, demonstrations, or training to further air quality if such an action does not cause environmental detriment.	§ 51.853(d) (3)
The alteration or addition of existing structures already determined in compliance with environmental laws or regulations.	§ 51.853(d) (4)
Direct emissions from remedial or removal actions under the Comprehensive Environmental Response, Compensation, and Liability Act (CERCLA).	§ 51.853(d) (5)

CONDITIONAL EXEMPTIONS

Type of Federal Action	Applicable Rule
Federal actions that are part of a continuing response to an emergency or natural disaster more than six months after the emergency or natural disaster. These actions are exempt if the agency makes a written determination that it is not practical to prepare a conformity determination for an additional six months owing to overriding concerns about public health. This must be done every six months to continue the exemption.	§ 51.853(e)

(continued)

EXHIBIT 5. *(continued)*

PRESUMPTIONS	
Type of Federal Action	**Applicable Rule**
Actions specified by an agency for which it claims (based on documentation from similar actions taken over recent years) that the total of direct and indirect emissions would (1) not cause or contribute to any new violation of any standard in the area; (2) not interfere with provisions in the applicable SIP for the maintenance of any standard; (3) not increase the severity or frequency of any violation; and (4) not delay the timely attainment of any standard or milestone. This presumption can be rebutted with a showing that one of the above four criteria is not met or with a showing that the action is "regionally significant."	§ 51.853(g)

Conformity determinations for general federal projects need be made only if the projects are proposed in nonattainment or maintenance areas.[164] As discussed earlier with respect to the transportation conformity rule, the EPA believes that Section 176(c) of the CAA is ambiguous with respect to whether conformity determinations are required in attainment areas. Despite this, the EPA has stated that it will likely require conformity determinations to be made in attainment areas at 85 percent of nonattainment levels, although it will address attainment areas in a separate rule.[165]

General Conformity Determinations—Procedures

The general conformity rules establish a specific set of procedural requirements in making conformity determinations. These rules cover notice and public participation requirements, frequency of the determinations, and a set of technical procedures. The federal agency making the conformity determination must provide a thirty-day notice describing the proposed action and its draft conformity determination to the appropriate EPA regional office and to state and local air quality agencies.[166] The final rule requires notice to these agencies because their expertise should be sought by the federal entity when interpretation of the SIP is needed.[167] In addition, notice must be given to an MPO when planning assumptions are at issue in a conformity determination of the project, and notice must be given to the applicable federal land manager (FLM) when the proposed federal action is within 100 kilometers of a Class I area.[168]

Under the final rule, federal agencies undertaking conformity determinations must adhere to specific requirements that enable the public to participate in the conformity determination process.[169] The federal agency must make its draft conformity determination public by publishing a notice in a newspaper of general circulation.[170] To enable the public to submit written comments on the draft, the notice must be published at least thirty days before the agency takes any formal action.[171] The agency must also make the draft available upon request to any person in a timely manner.[172]

The federal agency must respond to all written comments on the draft determination, and it must document those responses and make them publicly available.[173] Finally, the agency is required to make public its final conformity determination by placing a notice in a newspaper of general circulation.[174]

Generally conformity determinations for general federal actions made by federal agencies will be good for five years, as opposed to only three years for conformity determinations for transportation actions.[175] After that time, a determination automatically lapses unless the federal action has been completed or a continuous program has been commenced to implement the action within a reasonable time.[176] This rule ensures that conformity determinations will not be valid indefinitely, since the environment surrounding the proposed action will change over time.[177]

Federal activities that are ongoing and continue beyond the five-year mark will not be considered new actions requiring new conformity determinations as long as the activities are within the scope of the original conformity determination.[178] If, however, at any time after a conformity determination is made, there is a change in the federal action that increases emissions above *de minimis* levels, a new conformity determination will be required.[179]

Conformity determinations must be based on the latest planning assumptions, which, in turn, must be derived from the estimates of population, employment, travel, and congestion most recently approved by the appropriate agency authorized to make such estimates.[180] In addition, conformity determinations must rely on the applicable air quality models, databases, and other requirements specified in the most recent version of the "Guideline on Air Quality Models" and on the latest and most accurate emissions estimation techniques available.[181] For motor vehicle emissions, this means that the agency must use the most current version of the motor vehicle emissions model as specified by the EPA.[182] With respect to non-motor-vehicle emissions sources, the agency must use the latest emissions factors specified by the EPA in the "Compilation of Air Pollutant Emission Factors (AP-42)."[183]

Finally, the estimation of the total direct and indirect emissions used by the federal agency in making the conformity determination must reflect the following three emissions scenarios: (1) the mandated attainment year under the CAA; (2) the year during which emissions are expected to be the greatest; and (3) any year for which the SIP specifies an emissions budget.[184] This provision essentially links emissions from the action to the emissions reduction targets required by the act to ensure that the action would not "delay timely attainment" of any standard or milestone. For an action to conform to the applicable SIP, it must conform at all three times.[185]

General Conformity Determinations—Analysis

A federal action subject to the general conformity rule will be determined to conform to the applicable SIP if the total emissions are consistent with all relevant requirements, assumptions, and milestones in that SIP *and* the action meets *one* of the five air quality criteria discussed in the following paragraphs.[186]

If the total emissions for any criteria pollutant from the federal action are already specifically identified and accounted for in the SIP's attainment and maintenance demonstration, the project will be found to be conforming.[187] In a case such as this, the emissions attributable to such a project would have been taken into account in making the required demonstrations of attainment and reasonable further progress (RFP) and, therefore, should not interfere with attainment or maintenance of standards as projected by the SIP.

If the total emissions of ozone and NO_2 are fully offset within the attainment or maintenance area through a revision to the applicable SIP, or a similarly enforceable measure, that creates emission reductions, the federal project will be found to conform. However, there must be no net increase in emissions of that pollutant, taking into account the reductions necessary to meet attainment and demonstrate RFP.[188]

For projects causing emissions of lead, CO, PM_{10}, and SO_2, if the total emissions meet either the areawide or local air quality modeling requirements or the requirement for local air quality modeling analysis and the requirements for meeting conformity for actions emitting ozone or nitrogen dioxide (NO_2), as described later, the project will be found to conform.[189]

There are two additional ways in which federal actions causing CO or PM_{10} emissions can demonstrate conformity. First, if the state agency responsible for the applicable SIP determines that an areawide modeling analysis is not needed and the total emissions meet the local air quality modeling analysis requirements, the project will be found to conform. Second, when the state agency responsible for the applicable SIP determines that an areawide modeling analysis is appropriate and a local air quality analysis is not needed and the total emissions meet the areawide modeling requirements or meet the requirements discussed in the following subsection, the project will be found to conform.[190]

The NO_x and VOC emissions that precede ozone or NO_2 violations generally occur over a large area, and thus a regional analysis is more appropriate than a local, scale analysis.[191] Traditional air quality analysis for the purpose of determining the impacts on ozone and NO_2 concentrations from a single federal action has also been found inadequate because of the complex interactions of ozone precursors and the regional nature of ozone and NO_2 problems.[192] For these reasons the EPA has included five alternative analyses that can be used to determine the conformity of actions emitting ozone or NO_2, or other pollutants under appropriate circumstances. Therefore, the action will be found in conformity if it fully meets *any* of the five requirements enumerated in 40 C.F.R. § 51.858(a)(5).

Enforcement and Sanctions

Challenging SIP Revisions

Under the CAA, it generally is the EPA that is vested with the authority to ensure that states comply with the act, and the regulations promulgated under the act, when the states revise their SIPs to meet the new conformity requirements.[193] However, as discussed below, the act gives citizens indirect enforcement authority in this area because a citizens' suit can be brought to force the EPA to take required nondiscretionary actions if it has failed to do so.[194]

Two CAA provisions give the EPA authority to impose sanctions against states that fail to revise their SIPs in compliance with the CAA's conformity requirements. One section *requires* the EPA to impose sanctions under specified circumstances and the other section *allows* the EPA to impose sanctions under other circumstances.

Section 179 is the mandatory sanctions provision and requires the EPA to impose sanctions against a state if (1) the EPA finds that the state failed to submit a plan for a nonattainment area or submitted a plan for such an area that did not contain all the requisite components, (2) the EPA disapproves a submission for a nonattainment area because it does not meet all of the requirements of the act, or (3) the EPA determines that the state failed to make any other submission required under the act.[195]

Whenever one of these three conditions occurs, the EPA must impose sanctions on the state by prohibiting new highway projects or grants if the state has not corrected the deficiency within eighteen months of the finding, disapproval, or determination.[196] There is a statutory exception for projects or grants necessary to ensure safety, and there are many discretionary exceptions to this complete ban that the EPA can apply in its discretion.[197] The sanction will apply until the EPA administrator determines that the state has come into compliance.[198]

Because sanctions under Section 179 are mandatory, the CAA allows a citizens' suit to be brought to force the EPA to impose such sanctions against a state that fails to complete its conformity SIP revisions in such a way as not to violate one of the conditions listed in that section.[199] However, because sanctions under Section 110 are discretionary only, a citizens' suit cannot be brought to require the EPA to impose sanctions under that section.[200]

Challenging Conformity Determinations

When there is doubt whether an agency making a conformity determination of either a transportation or general federal action has satisfied the criteria in an applicable implementation plan, the CAA gives enforcement power to both the EPA and citizens. However, when the requisite conformity criteria has not yet become part of the SIP, it is unclear whether citizens can challenge conformity determinations made on that basis.

Under CAA Section 113, the EPA administrator can challenge a conformity determination's sufficiency regardless of whether the determination was based on criteria in an applicable SIP or on interim period or transitional period criteria.[201] Section 113(a)(1) states that whenever the EPA administrator finds that "any person . . . has violated or is in violation . . . of an applicable implementation plan," the agency can issue an order requiring that person to comply, issue an administrative penalty order, or bring a civil action against that person. Section 113(a)(3) makes conformity criteria not yet adopted into a SIP enforceable by allowing the administrator to issue an order or administrative penalty order, or to bring a civil or criminal suit, against any person who violates "any other requirement or prohibition of this subchapter."

It seems clear that a citizens' suit can be brought against an acting agency when a citizen claims that the agency's conformity determination was inconsistent with the conformity requirements in the revised implementation plan. Under CAA Section 304, any person can commence an action against a governmental entity that "is alleged to have violated or be in violation of an emission standard or limitation."[202] An "emission standard or limitation," which is defined quite specifically, includes "any condition or requirement under an applicable implementation plan."[203]

Although a citizen can sue to enforce a SIP's conformity requirements, it is unclear whether a citizen can sue an agency claiming that the agency's conformity determination of its action did not comply with criteria not yet contained in the state's applicable implementation plan. The majority of cases addressing this issue in broad terms have held that a citizens' suit can be brought only to enforce specific SIP requirements.[204] In *Wilder v. Thomas*,[205] for example, the court stated that "[C]ongress carefully circumscribed the scope of the provision by authorizing citizens to bring suit only for violations of the specific provisions of the act or specific provisions of an applicable implementation plan."[206]

One recent case, however, decided the issue the other way. In *Conservation Law Foundation v. Federal Highway Administration*,[207] the court held that citizens can sue under Section 304 to challenge an agency's conformity determination that is based on criteria not contained in the SIP. The court stated that Section 304 allows a citizen to sue to enforce any "emission standard or limitation" that the court said was defined in the CAA as a "standard of performance . . . which is in effect *under this chapter . . . or* under the applicable implementation plan."[208] The court acknowledged that most other courts have stated that citizens' suits can be brought to enforce only specific SIP requirements rather than general statutory directives. However, the court stated that the non-SIP criteria used to judge conformity in this case were so specific as to make it more similar to a SIP requirement than a general statutory directive.[209]

Notes

1. *See generally* CAA § 172.
2. *See* CAA § 182(c)(5), (d)(1).
3. CAA § 182(a)(2)(B), (b)(4), (c)(3), (d), (e).
4. *See* CAA § 182(d)(1)(B).
5. Transportation Equity Act for the 21st Century, Pub. L. No. 105-178, 112 Stat. 107 (1998).
6. CAA § 110(a)(1). *See* Chapter 2 for further details on the NAAQS.
7. CAA § 110(a)(2)(A).
8. 57 Fed. Reg. 52,950 (1992) (Inspection and Maintenance Program Requirements).

9. *Id.*

10. *Id.*

11. CAA § 182(a)(2)(B), (b)(4), (c)(3), (d), (e).

12. *See* 57 Fed. Reg. 52,950.

13. 40 C.F.R. § 51.350(a)(3), (4).

14. 40 C.F.R. § 51.350(a)(1), (2).

15. 57 Fed. Reg. 52,950, 52,951.

16. *Id.*

17. 40 C.F.R. § 51.352(a)(12).

18. 57 Fed. Reg. 52,950, 52,952.

19. 60 Fed. Reg. 48,029, 48,030 (1995); 40 C.F.R. § 51.351(g).

20. 61 Fed. Reg. 39,032–34 (1996); 40 C.F.R. § 51.351(h).

21. 61 Fed. Reg. 49,680 (1996); 40 C.F.R. § 51.361.

22. 61 Fed. Reg. 40,940 (1996); 40 C.F.R. §§ 51.351(c), 51.352(c).

23. 63 Fed. Reg. 24,429 (1998).

24. 66 Fed. Reg. 18,156 (2001); 40 C.F.R. § 51.373(g). The action also allows I/M programs a one-test-cycle phase-in period for the OBD-I/M check during which OBD-failing vehicles will be required to be repaired only if the vehicle also fails a tailpipe emission test.

25. 63 Fed. Reg. 1,362 (1998); 40 C.F.R. § 51.353(c). The IM240 involves a brief driving cycle that is based upon the Federal Test Procedure (FTP), the driving cycle by which new vehicles are certified. Emissions are measured during acceleration and deceleration of the vehicle. 57 Fed. Reg. 52,950, 52,954.

26. 63 Fed. Reg. 1,362 (1998); 40 C.F.R. § 51.353(c).

27. 65 Fed. Reg. 45,526, 45,527 (2000); 40 C.F.R. § 51.351(f)(13), (g)(13), (h)(11). The action also expanded the options for complying with the on-road testing requirement at 40 C.F.R. § 51.371 by (a) removing language suggesting that such testing must be tailpipe-based and (b) inserting language making the out-of-cycle repair requirement optional where on-road testing is used as a clean-screen approach.

28. CAA § 182(c)(5).

29. CAA § 108(f)(1)(A)(iii), (v), (xvi).

30. CAA § 182(c)(5).

31. *Id.*

32. CAA § 108(e).

33. CAA § 108(f)(1)(A).

34. U.S. EPA, Transportation Control Measure Information Documents (March 1992).

35. CAA § 172(c)(1).

36. *See Delaney v. EPA*, 898 F.2d 687 (9th. Cir.), *cert. denied*, 111 S. Ct. 556, 112 L. Ed. 2d 563 (1990).

37. 136 CONG. REC. S16933, S16971 (daily ed. Oct. 17, 1990) (Chafee-Baucus Statement of Senate Managers).

38. 57 Fed. Reg. 13,498, 13,560–61 (1992) (General Preamble to Title I of the Clean Air Act; Guidance on Development of State Implementation Plans).

39. 57 Fed. Reg. 13,498, 13,521–23.

40. CAA § 182(d)(1)(A).

41. 57 Fed. Reg. 13,498, 13,521–22.

42. *Id.*

43. CAA § 182(b)(1), (c)(2)(B).

44. CAA § 182(c)(2)(A).

45. 66 Fed. Reg. 57,247, 52,429 (2001).

46. *See* CAA § 182(b)(1), (c)(2)(B), (c)(2)(A).

47. 57 Fed. Reg. 13,498, 13,521.

48. 62 Fed. Reg. 49,152, 49,153 (1997).

49. U.S. EPA, "Final Guidance for the Employee Commute Options (ECO) Program."

50. *See* EPA, *Transportation Control Measures, available at* http://www.epa.gov/otaq/transp/traqtcms.htm (visited Dec. 6, 2001).

51. Employer Trip Reduction Program Revision, Pub. L. No. 104-70, § 1, 109 Stat. 773 (1995).

52. Marge T. Oge, *Guidance on Implementation of the Recent Employee Commute Options Legislation, available at* http://www.epa.gov/otaq/transp/commute/ecoguidf.txt (visited Dec. 6, 2001).

53. CAA § 110(a)(5)(D).

54. CAA § 110(a)(5)(C).

55. CAA § 110(a)(5)(A)(i).

56. *Id.*

57. CAA § 131.

58. CAA § 110(a)(5)(A)(ii), (B).

59. Intermodal Surface Transportation Efficiency Act of 1991, Pub. L. No. 102-240, 105 Stat. 1914 (1991).

60. ISTEA §§ 1008(a), 1003(a)(4).

61. ISTEA § 1008(a).

62. ISTEA § 1008(b).

63. TEA-21 §§ 1110(a), 1101(a)(5).

64. TEA-21 § 1103.

65. TEA-21 § 1110(b).

66. TEA-21 § 1221(a), (e).

67. TEA-21 § 1221(a).

68. TEA-21 § 1221(d)(2).

69. CAA § 176(c).

70. CAA § 176(c)(1).

71. *Id.*

72. *Id.*

73. U.S. EPA, "Determining Conformity to State Implementation Plans" (Draft) 15 (Sept. 26, 1991).

74. *See* 58 Fed. Reg. 62,188 (1993) and 58 Fed. Reg. 63,214 (1993).

75. *See* H.R. REP. No. 101-490(I), at 222 (1990).

76. CAA § 176(c)(1); 42 U.S.C. § 7506(c)(1).

77. 58 Fed. Reg. 62,188, 62,190 (1993).

78. 62 Fed. Reg. 43,780 (1997).

79. 40 C.F.R. §§ 51.390, 93.129.

80. 167 F.3d 641 (D.C. Cir., 1999).

81. *See* U.S. EPA, "Conformity Guidance on Implementation of March 2, 1999 Conformity Court Decision" (May 14, 1999).

82. 40 C.F.R. § 93.102(a)(1)(i)–(ii).

83. 40 C.F.R. § 93.102(a)(1)(iii).

84. 62 Fed. Reg. at 43,816–18; 40 C.F.R. § 93.126.

85. 40 C.F.R. § 93.127.

86. 40 C.F.R. § 93.102(a)(2).

87. *Environmental Defense Fund v. EPA,* 167 F.3d 641 (D.C. Cir. 1999).

88. 62 Fed. Reg. at 43,788 (1997).

89. 40 C.F.R. § 93.102(b).

90. *Id.*

91. 40 C.F.R. § 93.101.

92. A highway project is "an undertaking to implement or modify a highway facility or highway-related program. Such an undertaking consists of all required phases necessary for implementation." 40 C.F.R. § 93.101.

93. A transit project is "an undertaking to implement or modify a transit facility or transit-related project; purchase transit vehicles or equipment; or provide financial assistance for transit operations. It does not include actions that are solely within the jurisdiction of local transit agencies, such as changes in routes, schedules or fares." 40 C.F.R. § 93.101.

94. 58 Fed. Reg. at 62,191.

95. 62 Fed. Reg. at 43,800.

96. 40 C.F.R. § 93.104(b).

97. 40 C.F.R. § 93.104(b)(1), (2).

98. 40 C.F.R. § 93.104(b)(3).

99. 40 C.F.R. § 93.104(b)(4).

100. 40 C.F.R. § 93.104(c)(3).

101. 40 C.F.R. § 93.104(d).

102. CAA § 176(c)(1).

103. CAA § 176(c).

104. 58 Fed. Reg. at 62,208.

105. 167 F.3d 641.

106. CAA § 176(c)(3)(A).

107. CAA § 176(c)(2).

108. *Id.*

109. 40 C.F.R. § 93.109(c), (d).

110. 40 C.F.R. § 93.109(e), (f).

111. 40 C.F.R. § 93.110.

112. *Id.*

113. 40 C.F.R. § 93.111.

114. *Id.*

115. 40 C.F.R. § 93.112.

116. 40 C.F.R. § 93.113.

117. 40 C.F.R. § 93.118(a).

118. 58 Fed. Reg. at 62,195.

119. 40 C.F.R. § 93.118(c).

120. 40 C.F.R. § 93.116.

121. 40 C.F.R. § 93.118.

122. 40 C.F.R. § 93.119.

123. CAA § 176(c)(1).

124. *See* General Federal Action Rule, 58 Fed. Reg. 63,214, 63,219 (1993).

125. 58 Fed. Reg. at 63,249; 40 C.F.R. § 51.853(b).

126. 58 Fed. Reg. at 63,218.

127. *Id.* at 63,247; 40 C.F.R. § 51.852.

128. 58 Fed. Reg. at 63,247.

129. *Id.* at 63,218.

130. *Id.* at 63,248; 40 C.F.R. § 51.852.

131. 58 Fed. Reg. at 63,224.

132. *Id.*

133. *Id.*

134. CAA §§ 110(a)(5)(A), 131.
135. 58 Fed. Reg. at 63,225.
136. *Id.*
137. 58 Fed. Reg. at 63,247; 40 C.F.R. § 51.852.
138. 58 Fed. Reg. at 63,226.
139. *Id.*
140. 58 Fed. Reg. at 63,249; 40 C.F.R. § 51.853(c)(3).
141. 58 Fed. Reg. at 63,249.
142. 58 Fed. Reg. at 63,226.
143. *Id.*
144. 58 Fed. Reg. at 63,220.
145. 58 Fed. Reg. at 63,221.
146. *Id.*
147. *Id.*
148. 58 Fed. Reg. at 63,249; 40 C.F.R. § 51.853(b), (c)(1).
149. 58 Fed. Reg. at 63,249.
150. 58 Fed. Reg. at 63,228.
151. *Id.*
152. *Id.*
153. 58 Fed. Reg. at 63,229, 63,232–33.
154. 58 Fed. Reg. at 63,249; 40 C.F.R. § 51.853(c)(1).
155. 58 Fed. Reg. at 63,229.
156. 58 Fed. Reg. at 63,228.
157. 58 Fed. Reg. at 63,249; 40 C.F.R. § 51.853(c)(2).
158. 58 Fed. Reg. at 63,249.
159. 58 Fed. Reg. at 63,250; 40 C.F.R. §§ 51.853(i), (j).
160. 58 Fed. Reg. at 63,247; 40 C.F.R. § 51.852.
161. 58 Fed. Reg. at 63,250; 40 C.F.R. § 51.853(d).
162. 58 Fed. Reg. at 63,250.
163. 58 Fed. Reg. at 63,250; 40 C.F.R. § 51.853(e).
164. 58 Fed. Reg. at 63,249; 40 C.F.R. § 51.853(b).
165. 58 Fed. Reg. at 63,227–28.
166. 58 Fed. Reg. at 63,250; 40 C.F.R. § 51.855(a).
167. 58 Fed. Reg. at 63,233.
168. *Id.*
169. 58 Fed. Reg. at 63,251; 40 C.F.R. § 51.856.
170. 58 Fed. Reg. at 63,251; 40 C.F.R. § 51.856(b).
171. 58 Fed. Reg. at 63,251.
172. 58 Fed. Reg. at 63,251; 40 C.F.R. § 51.856(a).
173. 58 Fed. Reg. at 63,251; 40 C.F.R. § 51.856(c).
174. 58 Fed. Reg. at 63,251; 40 C.F.R. § 51.856(d).
175. 58 Fed. Reg. at 63,251; 40 C.F.R. § 51.857(a).
176. 58 Fed. Reg. at 63,251.
177. 58 Fed. Reg. at 63,239.
178. 58 Fed. Reg. at 63,251; 40 C.F.R. § 51.857(b).
179. 58 Fed. Reg. at 63,251; 40 C.F.R. § 51.857(c).
180. 58 Fed. Reg. at 63,252; 40 C.F.R. § 51.859(a)(1), (2).
181. 58 Fed. Reg. at 63,252; 40 C.F.R. § 51.859(b), (c).
182. 58 Fed. Reg. at 63,252; 40 C.F.R. § 51.859(b)(1).
183. 58 Fed. Reg. at 63,252; 40 C.F.R. § 51.859(b)(2).

184. 58 Fed. Reg. at 63,252; 40 C.F.R. § 51.859(d).

185. 58 Fed. Reg. at 63,243.

186. 58 Fed. Reg. at 63,251; 40 C.F.R. § 51.858.

187. 58 Fed. Reg. at 63,251; 40 C.F.R. § 51.858(a)(1).

188. 58 Fed. Reg. at 63,251; 40 C.F.R. § 51.858(a)(2).

189. 58 Fed. Reg. at 63,251; 40 C.F.R. § 51.858(a)(3).

190. 58 Fed. Reg. at 63,251; 40 C.F.R. § 51.858(a)(4).

191. 58 Fed. Reg. 13,836, 13,845 (1993).

192. *Id.*

193. CAA § 110(m).

194. CAA § 304(a)(2).

195. CAA § 179(a).

196. *Id.*

197. CAA § 179(b).

198. *Id.*

199. CAA § 304(a)(2).

200. *Id.*

201. CAA § 113(a)(1), (3).

202. CAA § 304(a)(1).

203. CAA § 304(f).

204. *See* Council of Commuter Orgs. v. Metropolitan Transp. Authority, 683 F.2d 663, 670 (2d Cir. 1982), which stated that plaintiffs seeking to bring a citizens' suit "for violation of an emission standard or limitation contained in an applicable plan . . . must allege a violation of a specific strategy or commitment in the SIP and describe, with some particularity, the respects in which the compliance is deficient."

205. 854 F.2d 605 (2d Cir. 1988), *cert. denied*, 489 U.S. 1053, 109 S. Ct. 1314, 103 L.Ed. 2d 583 (1989).

206. *Id.* at 613.

207. 24 F.3d 1465 (1st Cir. 1994).

208. *Id.* at 1477.

209. *Id.* at 1478.

CHAPTER 5

Regional SIP Issues

ROBERT A. WYMAN, JR.
JANDA D. R. KUHNERT

Introduction

Although Congress addressed the problem of ozone transport in a limited fashion in the 1990 Clean Air Act (CAA) Amendments, during the 1990s the U.S. Environmental Protection Agency (EPA) and numerous states grappled further with ozone transport and ultimately established a much more ambitious regional program than Congress envisioned. The EPA and the states are likely to rely on this experience as they address transport issues associated with the recently implemented national ambient air quality standard (NAAQS) for fine particulates ($PM_{2.5}$).

The 1990 Amendments to the CAA contemplated the need to address transport across state boundaries.[1] The CAA requires that a state implementation plan (SIP) contain provisions to prevent a state's facilities or sources from contributing significantly to air pollution problems downwind, specifically in those areas that fail to meet the national air quality standards for ozone.[2] As discussed in Chapters 2 and 3, under the CAA the EPA promulgates NAAQS for air pollutants. States must then adopt SIPs providing for the implementation, maintenance, and enforcement of the NAAQS for each air quality control region. The SIP is then submitted to the EPA for approval.[3] The EPA may later call for SIP revisions if the Administrator finds a SIP inadequate to attain or maintain the NAAQS, to meet the dictates of pollution transport commissions, or to otherwise comply with the CAA.[4]

In 1997, the EPA proposed to require twenty-two states and the District of Colombia to submit SIPs addressing the regional transport of ground-level ozone.[5] At the same time that the EPA proposed what it called the "NO_x SIP call," it also proposed to adopt a federal implementation plan (FIP) under Section 110(c) of the CAA for those states that did not respond adequately to the SIP call. Meanwhile, to ensure the EPA took action to address the regional transport of ozone, several states petitioned the EPA under Section 126 of the CAA and the EPA prepared to grant a number of the petitions. The EPA later took final actions on these proposals and, for the most part, these actions survived strong judicial challenges brought by opponents.

This chapter provides a general overview of the NO$_x$ SIP call, the proposed FIP, a state petition process under Section 126 for addressing interstate transport, and other regional attempts to improve air quality.

The Need for Regional Planning

Effects of Ozone

The atmospheric characteristics and adverse health effects of ozone have been widely studied. Ozone is formed when emissions of nitrogen oxide (NO$_x$) and volatile organic compounds (VOCs) react in the presence of sunlight. While ozone is beneficial in the upper atmosphere by protecting the earth from solar radiation, it is harmful at ground level. At ground level, it can cause a variety of health problems, especially among sensitive populations, such as children. Ozone also interferes with a plant's ability to produce and store food. Ground-level ozone has been shown to reduce agricultural yields for many economically vital crops. Nitrogen oxides also contribute to airborne particulate matter, regional haze problems, and global warming.[6]

Transport of Ozone and Its Effect on Attainment

As described in Chapter 3, the CAA requires states in each air quality control region to demonstrate attainment of the NAAQS for ozone. Ozone modeling conducted during the 1990s, however, demonstrated the difficulty of addressing ozone by focusing exclusively on control strategies within a single state. The chemical reactions that create ozone take place while the pollutants are being blown through the air by the wind, which means that ozone can be more severe many miles away from the source of emissions than it is at the source.[7] Many downwind states found it difficult to demonstrate attainment of the one-hour ozone NAAQS due to the widespread regional transport of ozone, NO$_x$, and VOCs.[8]

The contribution of upwind sources outside of nonattainment areas became a source of significant controversy among states seeking to reach air quality goals.[9] Some argued that states should develop local ozone mitigation strategies adequate to address the effect of both local emissions and transported ozone. Other states argued that undue reliance on strictly local measures would be ineffective and harmful to the local economy. The EPA ultimately resolved this dispute by finding that upwind sources significantly contributed to ozone nonattainment and by requiring upwind states to implement more aggressive NO$_x$ controls.

Development of Regional Plans Covering Multiple States

Interstate Transport Commissions

The CAA includes general provisions addressing the interstate transport of ozone. For example, Section 176A grants the EPA the authority to establish by rule interstate air pollution transport regions whenever the EPA believes "that the interstate transport of air pollutants from one or more States contributes significantly to a violation of national ambient air quality standards in one or more other States."[10] Whenever the EPA establishes an air transport region, it must create an interstate transport commission comprised of the EPA and state officials.[11] The interstate transport commission's responsibilities include: assessing the degree of interstate transport in the designated region, assessing strategies for mitigating interstate pollution, and recommending to the EPA measures it "determines to be necessary to ensure that the plans for the relevant States meet the requirements of Section 110(a)(2)(D)."[12] Finally, the interstate transport commission may request that the EPA issue a "finding under Section 110(k)(5) that the implementation plan . . . is substantially inadequate to meet the requirements of Section 110(a)(2)(D)."[13] The EPA has the authority to approve, disapprove, or partially approve and partially disapprove the request.[14]

Ozone Transport Commission

Additionally, the 1990 CAA Amendments included a specific provision focusing on the interstate transport of ozone in the Northeast. Section 184 delineates a multistate transport region in the Northeast, requires specific additional controls for that region,[15] and establishes the Ozone Transport Commission (OTC) for the purpose of recommending to the EPA regionwide controls affecting all areas in that region. The OTC comprises the states of Maine, New Hampshire, Vermont, Massachusetts, Connecticut, Rhode Island, New York, New Jersey, Pennsylvania, Maryland, Delaware, the northern counties of Virginia, and the District of Columbia.

In addition to creating the OTC, Section 184(c) created a mechanism for states within a transport region to petition the commission to develop recommendations for additional control measures to bring any area in the region into attainment. The commission must inform the EPA of the states' recommended additional control measures.[16] The EPA is then required to review the commission's recommendations and conduct a public hearing.[17] In approving or disapproving the recommendations, the EPA's discretion is somewhat limited. The EPA must consult with the commission and the affected states and take into account public comments, data, and views.[18] The EPA then has nine months to approve, disapprove, or partially approve and partially disapprove the recommendations. Upon approval or partial approval of the commission's recommendations, the EPA must make a finding under Section 110(k)(5) that the affected state's SIP is inadequate and require the state to revise its SIP within one year.[19]

Rather than relying exclusively on the Section 184(c) recommendation process, the OTC encouraged member states to adopt measures on their own. In 1994, the OTC states, except Virginia, adopted a memorandum of understanding (MOU)[20] to achieve regional emission reductions of NO_x.[21] In signing the MOU, states committed to developing and adopting regulations that would reduce regionwide NO_x emissions. To reflect the differences in conditions in the OTC, the states divided the OTC into three regions: (1) the "Northern Zone," consisting of the northern portion of the OTC; (2) the "Inner Zone," consisting of the central eastern portion of the OTC; and (3) the "Outer Zone," consisting of the remainder of the OTC. In the MOU, the OTC committed to reductions for NO_x emissions, with the level of emissions reductions and deadlines for those deductions determined by zone.[22] Finally, the states agreed to develop a regionwide trading mechanism to reduce and cap regional NO_x emissions.

Two years later, the OTC states developed a model rule (the NO_x Budget Program) as part of the regional effort to attain and maintain the one-hour ozone NAAQS. The model rule identified key elements that should be consistent among the regulations in all participating states so that an integrated interstate emissions trading program is created. The elements determined in the model rule include program applicability, control period, NO_x emissions limitations, emissions monitoring, recordkeeping of emissions and allowances, and electronic reporting requirements. Each state is responsible for developing and adopting state rules consistent with the model rule in order to achieve the regionwide NO_x reductions in a consistent and enforceable manner. Each state is also responsible for identifying its sources and allocating its allotment of NO_x allowances. The states are responsible for ensuring that sources comply with all of the program's requirements, including both the monitoring and reporting of actual emissions and the compliance demonstration process. Consistent with the model rule, each state determines the baseline of any source wishing to opt in to the program and the early reduction allowances to be awarded sources for reductions undertaken prior to the beginning of the program in 1999. In 2001, OTC promulgated another model rule for additional NO_x control measures.

Through the regional NO_x Budget Program, the OTC hoped to reduce ozone transport throughout the Northeast. Nevertheless, notwithstanding the program, many northeastern states argued they would still be unable to meet the statutory deadline for attainment of the one-hour ozone NAAQS because they could not address transport from upwind areas outside of the Northeast. They urged the EPA to consider a broader regional program, which would lead to NO_x reductions from the midwestern states and further assist the OTC states in attaining the NAAQS.[23]

Ozone Transport Assessment Group[24]

The control decisions contained in the EPA's NO_x SIP call were based in significant part on technical work conducted by the Ozone Transport Assessment Group (OTAG). OTAG was a partnership among the EPA, thirty-seven easternmost states and the District of Columbia, industry representatives, and environmental groups who were assembled to evaluate the degree of ozone transport. For two years, OTAG held meetings to identify and evaluate flexible and cost-effective strategies for reducing long-range transport of ozone and ozone precursors. This collaboration resulted in the most comprehensive analysis of ozone transport ever conducted.[25] OTAG conducted air quality modeling runs to determine the level of contribution from emissions in upwind areas to ozone nonattainment downwind.[26] OTAG issued its final recommendations to the EPA in July 1997. Although the OTAG participants did not reach final consensus, the EPA relied on much of the OTAG work product to propose that twenty-two states and the District of Columbia should submit SIPs to reduce NO$_x$ emissions as the primary tool to address the regional transport of ground-level ozone.[27]

NO$_x$ SIP Call

In October 1998, the EPA announced its final SIP call to address the regional transport of NO$_x$ and its contribution to ozone nonattainment in downwind areas.[28] The final rule was intended to assist downwind states in achieving compliance with both the one-hour and new eight-hour ozone NAAQS. In addition to its reliance on the OTAG work product, the EPA also based its decision on information resulting from its own analysis and on extensive public input generated through notice and comment rulemaking.[29] This final rule found that NO$_x$ emissions from sources and emitting activities in twenty-three jurisdictions significantly contribute to nonattainment, or potential nonattainment, of the one-hour and eight-hour ozone NAAQS, or will inter-fere with the maintenance of the eight-hour NAAQS, in one or more down-wind states throughout the eastern United States. The final SIP call targets emissions reductions from utilities and other large stationary sources, speci-fies overall NO$_x$ budgets that states are required to meet for their SIPs to be approvable, and creates a model NO$_x$ trading rule for the entire region. Following a court challenge mounted by midwestern states, electric utilities, and industry groups, the U.S. Court of Appeals for the D.C. Circuit upheld the principal aspects of the NO$_x$ SIP call.[30] See further discussion of the litiga-tion below.

Section 110 Provisions

The EPA claimed its authority under CAA Sections 110(a)(1), 110(a)(2)(D), and 110(k)(5).[31] CAA Section 110(a)(1) provides the framework for SIPs. Each state must adopt a plan that provides for implementation, maintenance, and enforcement of the NAAQS.[32] Section 110(a)(2)(D) provides one of the most important tools for addressing the problem of transport. This section applies to every SIP submitted for each pollutant covered by a NAAQS and for all areas regardless of their attainment designation.[33] Under this section, each SIP must contain adequate provisions

> prohibiting . . . any source or other type of emissions activity within the State from emitting any air pollutant in amounts which will (I) contribute significantly to nonattainment in, or interfere with maintenance by, any other State with respect to any such national primary or secondary

ambient air quality standard, or (II) interfere with measures required to be included in the applicable implementation plan for any other State under part C to prevent significant deterioration of air quality or to protect visibility.[34]

Section 110(k) grants the EPA power to find that a SIP is substantially inadequate to attain or maintain CAA requirements.[35] If the EPA makes such a finding, it can require the state to revise the plan to meet CAA requirements.[36] Section 110(m) further grants the EPA the ability to impose sanctions on any state that does not meet the Act's requirements.[37]

Jurisdictions Included in the NO_x SIP Call

The EPA determined that twenty-three jurisdictions are "significant contributors" to downwind nonattainment. This determination was made by evaluating the relative magnitude, frequency, and amount of each state's ozone contribution to nonattainment.[38]

States Included in the Original NO_x SIP Call[39]

Alabama	Massachusetts	Pennsylvania
Connecticut	Maryland	Rhode Island
Delaware	Michigan	South Carolina
District of Colombia	Missouri	Tennessee
Georgia	North Carolina	Virginia
Illinois	New Jersey	West Virginia
Indiana	New York	Wisconsin
Kentucky	Ohio	

Not every state of the OTAG region was included in the NO_x SIP call.[40] However, the EPA does expect them to work together when necessary to address local ozone problems. Furthermore, the EPA did not exclude those states based on a finding of absence of contribution to downwind nonattainment. Instead, it decided to conduct further analysis to characterize transport from those states.

NO_x Budget

The EPA NO_x SIP call establishes a NO_x budget for each identified state to determine whether it meets its NO_x reduction obligation. The budgets are seasonal, reflecting emissions in the summer ozone season from May 1 through September 30 of each year. The EPA determined the budgets by projecting the total amount of NO_x that sources in each state were projected to emit in 2007 without SIP call controls. It then determined the amount of NO_x emissions that would remain after application of the EPA's suggested control measures to utilities and other sources of NO_x.[41] Each state was required to reduce NO_x by an amount reflecting the use of "highly cost-effective controls." Such controls were those that the EPA found capable of removing

NO_x at a cost of \$2000 or less per ton.[42] For example, the EPA chose a control level (0.15 lb/mmBtu) for electricity-generating units that it determined could be achieved by using available, cost-effective technology[43] and that corresponded to the most protective level recommended by OTAG. The EPA did not require additional local controls on area, small point, and mobile sources.[44]

A state's NO_x budget represents the maximum allowable level of NO_x emissions. However, a state is allowed to determine the best mix of controls necessary to meet the NO_x budget. Under the original timeline, states had until September 1999 to submit a SIP in response to the NO_x SIP call, and they were required to implement the controls by May 1, 2003. Due to litigation, the deadline for implementation has been extended to May 31, 2004.[45] If a state fails to adopt adequate measures to achieve required reductions, then the EPA will not approve the state's SIP. The state would then be subject to a FIP and possibly sanctions.[46] As a practical matter, few, if any, states are likely to have the administrative resources necessary to develop an alternative control strategy for submittal to the EPA nor are they likely to be prepared to incur the time delays or sanctions risk associated with an alternative approach.

The EPA claims that the overall budget number is not enforceable against the states. It serves only as a method of projecting in advance whether a state has adopted adequate measures to produce the required amounts of emissions reductions. The budgets are also a way to determine from 2003 to 2007 whether states are fully implementing those measures.[47] According to the EPA, the budgets themselves are really an accounting mechanism to ensure that upwind states have adopted and implemented control measures that sufficiently control NO_x emissions targeted by the SIP call.

NO_x Budget Trading Program

A cornerstone of the NO_x SIP call is the NO_x budget and trading program. It is a voluntary, market-based program established as one possible means for a state to meet its NO_x emissions reduction obligations. The EPA developed a model NO_x budget trading rule, which established a "cap-and-trade" program for certain large combustion sources. The program employs a cap on total emissions to ensure environmental performance while providing the flexibility and cost-effectiveness of a market-based system.[48] The EPA recommends the cap-and-trade program because, by limiting total NO_x emissions to the "level determined to address the interstate transport problem, a cap better ensures achievement and maintenance of the environmental goal articulated in the NO_x SIP call."[49] While implementation of the NO_x trading program is voluntary, the EPA will grant streamlined SIP approval to states that adopt its model rule.[50]

The model rule also allows for banking of unused allocations.[51] To address concerns about the potential use of a large volume of banked NO_x allowances in a single year, the EPA adopted a flow control mechanism. This mechanism discounts allowances if the total number of allowances used exceeds a predetermined level. If the total number of banked allowances is less than or equal to ten percent of the NO_x budget for that year, then banked allowances may be used on a one-to-one ratio. If, however, the total amount of banked allowances exceeds ten percent, then banked allowances will be recalculated through a withdrawal ratio.[52] Banked allowances in an amount exceeding the withdrawal ratio would be used on a two-for-one basis, while banked allowances not exceeding the ratio would be used on a one-to-one basis.

Emissions Reporting Requirements

There are three important reporting requirements in the NO_x SIP call. States are required to report annually on all regulated sources and source categories. Triennially, a state must report on emissions from all NO_x sources, even if they are not regulated by the NO_x SIP call. Finally, in 2007, all states must submit to the EPA a special onetime statewide inventory from all NO_x sources within the state.[53]

Early Reduction Credits (ERCs)

Under the NO_x SIP call, to a limited extent, a source can generate early reduction credits (ERCs) if it reduces its NO_x emissions before May 1, 2003, to a level below that which is required by any regulatory scheme. ERCs are designed to be an incentive for sources to reduce NO_x emissions prior to the 2003 ozone season. They can then be used to offset emissions above required levels in a later time period. This will extend the timeframe for achieving actual emissions reductions at specific sources that may require additional time.[54] The EPA limited the amount of available ERCs for each state to the size of each state's compliance supplemental pool (CSP).[55] The CSP is an additional allowance of emissions that allows the twenty-three jurisdictions to emit 200,000 tons of NO_x in the 2003–2004 ozone seasons over the state emissions budgets. The 200,000 tons are spread among the states in proportion to the reduction needed. The CSP was created in response to concerns that compliance with the May 1, 2003, deadline could cause unacceptable risks for a source and its associated industry. Commentators were particularly concerned about disruptions to the electric industry.[56] If a state chooses to use the CSP, it can either provide ERCs or distribute the allowances to sources that demonstrate a need for the compliance supplement.[57]

EXHIBIT 1. NO_x SIP Call

NO_x Budget	• Sets maximum allowable NO_x emissions for state. • Reflects emissions in summer ozone season May 1–September 30. • States must reduce NO_x by amount accomplished using highly cost-effective controls (controls the EPA found capable of removing NO_x at a cost of $2000 or less per ton). • Individual states select the control measures to reduce NO_x levels.

(continued)

EXHIBIT 1. (*continued*)

State NO$_x$ Budget Trading Program	• States may choose to implement NO$_x$ market-based program. • Model NO$_x$ trading rulecap-and-trade programs. • Program employs a cap on total emissions and banking of unused allocations. • Streamlined SIP approval to states that adopt the model rule.
Emissions Reporting Requirements	• Annually, states must report on all sources and source categories regulated by the NO$_x$ SIP call. • Triennially, states must report on emissions from all NO$_x$ sources, even if they are not regulated by the NO$_x$ SIP call. • In 2007, all states must submit a special statewide inventory from all NO$_x$ emissions sources within the state.
Early Reduction Credits (ERCs)	• Available if a source reduces its NO$_x$ emissions before May 1, 2003, to a level below that which is required by any regulatory scheme. • Used to offset emissions above required levels in a later time period. • Amount of available ERCs is limited to the size of each state's compliance supplemental pool.

Federal Implementation Plan

To ensure state compliance with the NO$_x$ SIP call, the EPA simultaneously proposed a federal implementation plan (FIP) under CAA Section 110(c) that would take effect upon a state's failure to implement the necessary SIP revisions.[58] The NO$_x$ FIP would apply to the same jurisdictions governed by the NO$_x$ SIP call.[59] Under the CAA, a FIP is designed to "fill a gap or correct all or a portion of an inadequacy in a state implementation plan."[60] The EPA has wide-ranging authority under Section 110(c) to correct inadequacies in the SIP.

Under a FIP, the EPA, not the state, selects the control measures for each source sector and ensures compliance with those measures. Accordingly, a state may be subject to specific control measures that are different from what the state may choose.[61] Not surprisingly, given its intended purpose as a backstop for the NO$_x$ SIP call, the FIP uses the same method as in the NO$_x$ SIP call to calculate required emissions reductions and would require the same amount of emissions reductions from the source categories to which the EPA found highly cost-effective measures can be applied.[62]

Under the FIP, the EPA proposed a Federal NO$_x$ Budget Trading Program, a cap-and-trade program to control NO$_x$ emissions. Sources would trade NO$_x$ allowances representing a limited authorization to emit one ton of NO$_x$. As in the state plan, banking is permitted. This program would coincide with the State NO$_x$ Budget Trading Program and is very similar to the state program. States subject to FIPs and sources for which the EPA makes a significant contribution finding under Section 126 would be included in the federal program. The EPA would administer this common program. The EPA would determine the NO$_x$ allowance allocations for each unit in the program, rather than provide a recommended methodology for the states to determine allocations in the state trading program.[63]

EXHIBIT 2. Federal Implementation Plan

Elements	• Takes effect upon a state's failure to implement the necessary SIP revisions. • EPA selects the control measures for each source sector and ensures compliance with those measures. • Uses the NO_x SIP call methods to calculate required emissions reductions.
Federal NO_x Budget Trading Program	• Cap-and-trade program to control NO_x emissions. • States trade NO_x allowances representing a limited authorization to emit one ton of NO_x. • Banking is permitted. • Includes states subject to FIPs and sources in states for which the EPA makes a significant contribution finding under Section 126. • EPA determines the NO_x allowance allocations for each unit in the program.

Sanctions	• Imposed in addition to a FIP on any state that fails to submit a SIP or for which the submitted SIP is incomplete.
	• One of two sanctions will apply 18 months after the EPA determines the SIP is incomplete and the state fails to submit a complete SIP.
	  1. new or modified sources subject to a § 173 new source review program must offset their new emissions at a 2:1 ratio; and
	  2. withholding of certain federal highway funds.
	• If a state does not make a complete submission 6 months after the 1st sanction is imposed, then a 2nd sanction will apply.

Sanctions

In addition to the FIP, the EPA is prepared to impose sanctions under Section 179 on any state that fails to submit a SIP or for which the SIP submitted is incomplete. Once the EPA finds that the SIP is incomplete, an 18-month sanctions clock begins. If the state fails to submit a complete SIP, then one of two sanctions will apply: (1) new or modified sources subject to a Section 173 new source review (NSR) program must offset their new emissions at a 2:1 ratio, or (2) the withholding of certain federal highway funds. If the state still has not made a complete submission six months after the first sanction is imposed, then a second sanction will apply.[64]

Section 126 Petitions

Another method for combating cross-boundary transport of ozone is through a CAA Section 126 petition.[65] Section 126(a) requires states to provide written notice to other affected states identifying new or existing major sources that may significantly contribute to levels of air pollution in excess of NAAQS. Additionally, Section 126(b) provides that any state or political subdivision may petition the EPA for a finding that any major source emits or would emit air pollution in violation of Section 110(a)(2)(D)(ii). The EPA can then require the offending upwind state to take appropriate measures to reduce emissions at the offending source. Any control remedy must be implemented within three years from the date of the finding that major sources or a group of sources would emit in violation of Section 110(a)(2)(D).[66]

This mechanism is distinct from the NO_x SIP call and proposed FIP in certain important respects. First, a state must initiate the Section 126 process, while the EPA initiates the SIP call and the proposed FIP. Second, the Section 126 petition applies only to contributions from one or more major stationary sources in other states. Therefore, it is not an appropriate tool for addressing minor stationary sources or mobile sources.

The EPA took the position, ultimately upheld by the courts, that once it makes the necessary finding of a significant contribution, it is authorized to establish federal emissions limits for major stationary sources that significantly contribute to ozone nonattainment in petitioning states. As noted above, the Section 126 proposed action is limited to major stationary sources or groups of stationary sources that are named in the petition. Under the EPA's interpretation of Section 126, a source or group of sources are subject to CAA Section 110(a)(2)(D)(i) when the applicable SIP does not adequately address emissions from a source that the EPA determines significantly contributes to nonattainment or interferes with maintenance in a downwind state.[67]

In August 1997, eight northeastern states filed petitions under Section 126 requesting a finding that certain upwind sources significantly contribute to nonattainment of ozone NAAQS.[68] These filings were made as a further encouragement to the EPA to issue the NO_x SIP call (and proposed FIP) and to provide a backup should the EPA not act. The petitions varied in geographic scope covered, types of sources identified, and recommended control measures. All eight of the states requested findings under the one-hour ozone standard, while five states also requested Section 126 findings under the eight-hour standard.[69] A final decision on these petitions was delayed by litigation. In April through June of 1999, the EPA received four new ozone-related Section 126 petitions.[70] The four new petitions all requested a finding that NO_x emissions in upwind states significantly contribute to nonattainment and maintenance problems of the one-hour and eight-hour standards. These petitions recommended that the EPA establish an interstate trading program for sources that would receive a Section 126 finding.

In a rule published on May 25, 1999, the EPA had determined that NO_x emissions in twelve states and the District of Columbia contribute significantly to nonattainment of one-hour ozone NAAQS in Connecticut, Massachusetts, New York, and Pennsylvania.[71] The EPA did not make Section 126 findings at that time. It postponed making findings until the NO_x SIP call process was resolved. The EPA issued a rule stating that the findings would automatically be deemed made with regard to sources from a given state should that state fail to comply with the NO_x SIP call deadline. This decision was based upon the belief that full compliance with the NO_x SIP call would obviate the need for Section 126 findings.[72] Once made, Section 126 findings would require covered sources to come into compliance no later than May 31, 2004.[73] Sources that failed to comply by that date would be required to cease operations.

On January 18, 2000, the EPA issued its final rule to control emissions of NO_x under Section 126. The EPA made final its findings that stationary sources of NO_x in twelve upwind states and the District of Columbia contribute significantly to ozone nonattainment in northeastern states. This finding triggered direct federal regulation of stationary sources of NO_x in the upwind states. This rule further established a "cap-and-trade" system for NO_x emissions within each upwind jurisdiction. Covered sources must obtain NO_x emissions allowances to offset their emissions, adopt emission controls, or cease operations. Numerous petitions for review (discussed below) challenged the final rule.[74]

Because a Section 126 petition is a separate statutory mechanism from the Section 110 NO_x SIP call, some groups have argued that sources could be subject to two contemporaneous, potentially conflicting, regulatory regimes. They argued that states would be pressured to adopt SIP controls identical to the Section 126 controls because the states might conclude that only by adopting identical controls could they minimize the overall administrative burden of meeting the EPA's demands. The EPA rejected this argument. It argued that the two systems are separate. While it may be more attractive for a state to obtain emissions reduction from the Section 126 sources, this does not "impermissibly pressure the States to adopt any particular control measure."[75] To further separate the NO_x SIP call process from the Section 126 petitions, the EPA did not include a provision to automatically withdraw the Section 126 findings upon the EPA approval of a later SIP revision that complies with the NO_x SIP call.[76]

The EPA's rulemaking authority under Section 126 was addressed by two decisions of the U.S. Court of Appeals for District of Columbia Circuit. In *American Trucking Ass'ns v. EPA*, the court remanded the eight-hour NAAQS for ozone, which formed part of the underlying technical basis for certain of the EPA's determinations under Section 126.[77] Additionally, the D.C. Circuit in *Michigan v. EPA* granted a motion to stay the SIP submission deadlines established in the NO_x SIP call.[78] To address issues raised by the rulings, the EPA proposed to stay indefinitely the portion of the rule based on the eight-hour standard and proposed to make Section 126 findings solely under the one-hour standard. Sources subject to findings under the one-hour standard will be required to implement controls beginning in May 2004. The EPA also proposed to detach the mechanism for making Section 126 findings from state compliance with NO_x SIP call deadlines.[79]

EXHIBIT 3. Section 126 Petition

CAA § 126(a)	Requires states to provide written notice to other affected states of new or existing major sources that may significantly contribute to levels of air pollution in excess of NAAQS.
CAA § 126(b)	Any state or political subdivision may petition the EPA for a finding of significant contribution for any major source.

(continued)

EXHIBIT 3. (*continued*)

Finding of Significant Contribution	EPA is authorized to establish federal emissions limits for major stationary sources.
Differences from NO$_x$ SIP call and FIP	1. State must initiate the § 126 process. 2. § 126 applies only to contribution from one or more major stationary sources in other states.

The NO$_x$ SIP call, proposed FIP, and Section 126 petitions overlap significantly. They all address NO$_x$ transport in the eastern United States and are aimed at reducing the transport of ozone by controlling NO$_x$ emissions from sources that are found to be contributing significantly to nonattainment or maintenance problems in another state. Given this obvious overlap, the EPA attempted to coordinate its actions. As stated above, the proposed FIP would be implemented only to the extent that a state fails to submit an adequate SIP revision. Likewise, the enforceable remedies under a Section 126 petition would be exercised only to the extent that a state failed to timely submit a complete and approvable SIP or the EPA failed to promulgate a FIP.

Litigation Concerning Regional Planning

NO$_x$ SIP Call

After the EPA published the final NO$_x$ SIP call, numerous states,[80] industry associations, and environmental groups filed suit in the D.C. Circuit[81] challenging the EPA's final SIP call. On March 3, 2000, the D.C. Circuit Court of Appeals substantially upheld the NO$_x$ SIP call in its ruling in *Michigan v. EPA*.[82] The opinion was based only on the EPA's authority to implement the one-hour ozone NAAQS. The EPA moved to stay consideration of the issues involving the eight-hour NAAQS because it had stayed the eight-hour findings contained in the SIP call.[83]

The EPA requested a stay of the eight-hour NAAQS because of the D.C. Circuit Court of Appeals holding in *American Trucking Ass'ns, Inc. v. EPA*.[84] In July 1997, the EPA promulgated a new, more stringent eight-hour NAAQS, which limited ozone levels to 0.08 ppm averaged over an eight-hour period. The EPA did this pursuant to its statutory authority to review and revise NAAQS as appropriate.[85] In *American Trucking*, the D.C. Circuit found that the construction on which the EPA relied in creating the new NAAQS was an unconstitutional delegation of legislative power.[86] (As is discussed in Chapter 2, the Supreme Court later overturned this decision.) After promulgating the new standards, the EPA began phasing out the one-hour standard on an area-by-area basis. The SIP call mandated SIP revisions pursuant to the eight-hour standard even though the EPA did not designate eight-hour nonattainment areas before 1999. Therefore the *American Trucking* ruling stayed the eight-hour findings.

In *Michigan v. EPA,* petitioners challenged the NO$_x$ SIP call on several grounds. These arguments and the courts' holdings will have an impact on future attempts at regional planning. First, the petitioners argued that CAA Sections 176A and 184[87] required the EPA to convene a transport commission prior to issuing the NO$_x$ SIP call.[88] The court held that the EPA is not required to establish a transport region and that a transport commission must be established only when the EPA creates a transport region.[89] This finding will enable the EPA to enact further transport regulations without necessarily undertaking the formal process of creating a regional planning organization; however, the EPA is likely to consult with affected states in any such situation.

The court also upheld the SIP call against a multifaceted challenge to the EPA's determination that NO$_x$ emissions from upwind SIP call states make a "significant contribution" to elevated ozone levels in downstream states within the meaning of Section 110(a)(2)(D)(i)(I). Specifically, the court rejected claims (1) that the EPA acted contrary to precedent;[90] (2) that the EPA improperly considered the factor of cost in determining significance; (3) that the EPA irrationally imposed uniform controls;[91] and (4) that the EPA's determination was so devoid of intelligible principles as to violate the nondelegation doctrine.[92] Perhaps the most important of these challenges was petitioners' argument that Section 110(a)(2)(D)(i)(I) does not permit the EPA to take cost into account in determining what sources or emissions activities contribute significantly to downwind nonattainment. After selecting non–*de minimis* contributing states based on modeling, the EPA then defined the "significant" emissions contributed by those states as the amount that could be reduced with "highly cost-effective controls." The majority held that it was permissible for the EPA to consider costs in such a determination because (1) the term "significant" encompasses the consideration of costs; and (2) the D.C. Circuit has historically held that an agency's consideration of cost is permissible in the absence of clear congressional intent to the contrary. The court could find no such contrary congressional intent with respect to Section 110(a)(2)(D)(i)(I).[93]

Petitioners also challenged the sufficiency of the EPA's analysis of each state's contribution to downwind ozone formation. The EPA relied upon regional and multistate data collected by OTAG.[94] However, the CAA requires that the relevant emissions be "emissions activity within the state."[95] The court upheld the NO$_x$ SIP call against this challenge because the EPA performed state-specific modeling that confirmed the regional model results.

The EPA initially included twenty-three jurisdictions in the NO$_x$ SIP call. The court removed three states from the NO$_x$ SIP call: Wisconsin, Missouri, and Georgia. Wisconsin industry petitioners separately challenged Wisconsin's inclusion in the NO$_x$ SIP call. They argued that Wisconsin emissions do not contribute significantly to nonattainment in another state as would be required by Section 110(a)(2)(D)(i)(1) for Wisconsin to be included in the SIP call. The EPA contended that Wisconsin contributed significantly to nonattainment because the state significantly contributes ozone over Lake Michigan. The EPA conceded that there was no evidence that Wisconsin's contributions to ozone formation actually affected onshore attainment. The court held that the "EPA acted unlawfully by including Wisconsin in a SIP call limited by statute to states contributing significantly to nonattainment in any other state."[96]

The court vacated the application of the EPA's final rule to Missouri and Georgia and remanded this portion of the rule to the EPA. For Missouri and Georgia, NO_x budgets were calculated using all NO_x emissions in the state. However, only the eastern one-half of Missouri and the northern two-thirds of Georgia were found to contribute to downwind nonattainment. Portions of the states were in OTAG's "coarse grid," which OTAG analyses indicated do not contribute measurably to nonattainment. The court rejected the EPA's arguments that those regions should be included and also rejected the EPA's claim of administrative convenience. Administrative convenience was the EPA's only real defense, but the court ruled that it was not a valid basis for imposing controls.[97] The court left open the possibility for the EPA to impose SIP controls only on those portions of the two states within the "fine grid" region.[98]

Finally, petitioners challenged the NO_x SIP call on federalism grounds. They argued that the NO_x SIP call was an impermissible intrusion on the statutory right of states to fashion their own SIP submissions.[99] But the *Michigan* court agreed "with EPA that the NO_x budget plan does no more than project whether states have reduced emissions sufficiently to mitigate interstate transport."[100] The court found that the EPA reasonably concluded that long-range ozone transport can adequately be addressed only through NO_x reductions. There was sufficient scientific evidence that VOC controls alone would not effectively address interstate ozone transport.[101] Furthermore, the court concluded that the EPA's action did not impermissibly direct the states on how to achieve SIP compliance. The EPA merely provides the levels to be achieved by state-determined compliance mechanisms. The budgets are based on "highly cost-effective control measures," but the states are free to implement other "cost-effective" or "reasonably cost-effective" measures. States are able to focus reduction efforts based on local needs or preferences.[102] The court held that the EPA's NO_x budget established reduction levels, but left the selection of control measures to the individual states. As a practical matter, given both limited state resources and the difficulties of obtaining, and delays associated with, the EPA approval of alternative measures, it is questionable whether the states will really be able to select their own control measures.

In addition to the particular state findings discussed above, some portions of the final NO_x SIP call were struck down. The Council of Industrial Boiler Owners challenged the NO_x SIP call as arbitrary and capricious, alleging that (1) the EPA failed to determine whether non-electric generating units (EGUs) are significant contributors; (2) the EPA used flawed cost assumptions in its determination of cost-effective control measures for non-EGUs; (3) the EPA erroneously calculated non-EGU budgets; and (4) the EPA arbitrarily defined the term EGU.[103] The court agreed that the EPA's definition of EGUs was arbitrary and capricious, and that the EPA did not provide sufficient notice and opportunity to comment on the change in the definition of EGU. Although throughout the rule making, the EPA had defined EGU as it was defined under the acid rain program, two months after the rule's promulgation, the EPA redefined EGU as a unit that serves a "large" generator (greater than 25 megawatts) that sells electricity.[104] The court therefore remanded the rule making to the EPA.

Section 126 Petitions

After the EPA published the final Section 126 rule, numerous groups petitioned for review.[105] The court's decision in *Appalachian Power v. EPA* affirms the EPA's authority to impose direct federal controls on individual sources found to contribute significantly to nonattainment downwind, irrespective of the requirements of the SIP call.[106] In the holding, the court resolved many important issues regarding the EPA's authority to impose limits directly upon the states.

The court resolved in the EPA's favor the threshold question of whether Section 126 authorizes the EPA to impose federal controls on sources found to contribute significantly to downwind nonattainment. The EPA derives its authority to impose direct controls on a state from CAA Section 126(c), notwithstanding the Section's cross-reference to Section 110(a)(2)(D)(ii).[107]

Midwestern and southeastern states argued that the relationship between Sections 110 and 126 required the EPA to refrain from making any Section 126 findings while the NO_x SIP call is ongoing. They also argued that a similar constraint was imposed by the doctrine of cooperative federalism that is embodied in the CAA.[108] They argued that, to preserve primary state authorship of control strategies, a SIP call must be considered the preferred remedy to the federal imposition of controls under Section 126. According to the court, three critical provisions of Section 126 would lose their force if the lengthened timetable of the NO_x SIP call were to suspend the Section 126 process.[109] First, Section 126 requires that any contributing source cannot operate for more than three years after a finding of contribution to downwind nonattainment.[110] Second, unlike a SIP revision, relief under Section 126 does not depend upon any action of the upwind states.[111] Third, relief under Section 126 is independent of the discretionary policy preferences of the EPA. The EPA must act upon a request for a finding within sixty days.[112] The court's ruling thus strongly implies that the EPA must require implementation of emission controls within three years after making a finding.[113]

The court also rejected petitioners' challenge to the methodology used by the EPA to make findings of "significant contribution" to nonattainment of the one-hour ozone standard. The EPA began with the two-step method it had used in issuing the SIP call. The EPA first performed computer modeling to determine whether a state's man-made NO_x emissions perceptibly hindered a downwind state's attainment.[114] The EPA then defined as significant those emissions that could be eliminated through the application of "highly cost-effective" controls—measures that cost no more than $2000 per ton of

NO$_x$ removal. The EPA relied upon the threshold statewide findings made in the SIP call and then applied the same cost-effectiveness criterion to determine which sources to include.[115]

Furthermore, the court upheld the EPA's authority to regulate future sources under Section 126. Under the EPA's Section 126 plan, the NO$_x$ budget for upwind states is allocated 95 percent to existing sources and 5 percent to future sources. Once a plant is proposed, it becomes part of the regulated class. The court rejected the argument that Section 126 applied only to sources existing at the time of the rule's promulgation.[116] Finally, the court remanded the EPA's EGU growth factor determinations. The court questioned the reliability of the EPA's growth factor projections. In some instances, actual utilizations in 1998 exceeded the EPA's projected levels for 2007.[117] The EPA has since responded to the court's remand on the growth factors issue, and a number of petitions for review were promptly filed.[118] As of early 2003, these cases have not been decided.

Other Regional Planning Efforts

Other regions have begun to address cross-state pollutant transport issues. In the southeast, the Southeast States Air Resource Managers (SESARM) is working to develop a regional strategy to address visibility impairment, ground-level ozone, and acid deposition effects on water bodies and vegetation. Additionally, western states have collaborated to address regional haze and visibility through a regional commission, the Western Regional Air Partnership (WRAP).

The WRAP follows the work of the Grand Canyon Visibility Transport Commission. It is a voluntary organization of western states, tribes, and federal agencies. The WRAP will address not only visibility and regional haze, but other air quality objectives. Although the WRAP has not yet developed specific plans to address NO$_x$ emissions, it is beginning a process to develop such proposals. WRAP focuses on finding regional solutions, instead of a federal solution, to Western air quality problems. See Chapter 7 for more details.

Conclusion

Although the 1990 CAA Amendments attempted to address transborder pollution by, among other strategies, the creation of transport commissions, the Amendments did not entirely address a variety of regional air quality challenges. The EPA responded to the problem of ozone transport in the eastern U.S. by implementing the NO$_x$ SIP call, proposing the FIP, and approving several state Section 126 petitions. To date these three tools have in prominent part withstood legal challenge. They will almost certainly provide a future means for the EPA to address other air quality challenges that are regional in nature. The next likely subject for the EPA's regional powers will be a SIP call to address the precursors to fine particulate formation, as individual state efforts prove insufficient to attain the new PM$_{2.5}$ NAAQS.

Notes

1. When emitted, nitrogen oxides (NO_x) react in the atmosphere to form compounds that, together with other pollutants, contribute to the formation of ozone. These compounds and ozone can travel hundreds of miles across state boundaries to affect air quality in areas far from the source of the pollution. Thus, while one city or area may have relatively clean air, its activities may be contributing to a downwind city's ozone problem.

2. Clean Air Act § 110, 42 U.S.C. § 7410 (2001).

3. *See* Clean Air Act § 110(a)(1).

4. *See id.* § 110(k)(5).

5. The so-called NO_x SIP call.

6. *EPA: Latest Findings on National Air Quality: 1999 Status and Trends* (Aug. 2000), pp. 6–8.

7. Finding of Significant Contribution and Rulemaking for Certain States in the Ozone Transport Assessment Group Region for Purpose of Reducing Regional Transport of Ozone, 63 Fed. Reg 57,356, 57,359 (Oct. 27, 1998) (to be codified at 40 C.F.R. pts. 51, 72, & 96).

8. Regulatory Impact Analysis for the Final Section 126 Petition Rule, p. 1-1.

9. *See id.* at 1-13.

10. Clean Air Act § 176A(a), 42 U.S.C. § 7506(a) (2001).

11. *See* Clean Air Act § 176A(b).

12. *Id.*

13. *Id.*

14. *Id.*

15. Clean Air Act § 184(b)(1) requires each state included within a transport region to submit a SIP or revised SIP that requires each metropolitan area or part thereof with a population of 100,000 or more in the state to (1) comply with the provisions of Section 182(c)(2)(A) (pertaining to enhanced vehicle inspection and maintenance programs) and (2) implement reasonably available control technology for all sources of VOCs covered by a control techniques guideline issued before or after the date of the enactment of the CAA amendments of 1990. Additionally, EPA has three years to identify control measures capable of achieving emissions reductions comparable to those achievable through vehicle refueling controls contained in Section 182(b)(3). Within one year of the completion of the study, EPA shall revise the applicable implementation plan to reflect such measures. Any stationary source that emits, or potentially could emit, at least 50 tons per year of VOCs is considered a major stationary source and is subject to the requirements applicable to major stationary sources if the area were classified as a moderate nonattainment area [Section 184(b)(2)].

16. Clean Air Act § 184(c)(1), 42 U.S.C. § 7511c(c)(1) (2001).

17. *See* Clean Air Act § 184(c)(2).

18. *See id.* § 184(c)(3).

19. *See id.* § 184(c)(5).

20. *Memorandum of Understanding Among the States of the Ozone Transport Commission on Development of a Regional Strategy Concerning the Control of Stationary Source Nitrogen Oxide Emissions, 9/27/94.*

21. These reductions are in addition to previous OTC state efforts to control NO_x emissions, which included the installation of reasonably available control technology.

22. By May 1, 1999, sources in the Inner Zone were to reduce NO_x emissions by 65 percent from base year levels or to emit NO_x at a rate no greater than 0.2 pounds per million BTU. Additionally, by May 1, 1999, sources in the Outer Zone were to reduce NO_x

emissions by 55 percent from base year levels or to emit NO_x at a rate no greater than 0.2 pounds per million BTU. The states also agreed to require sources in the Inner Zone and the Outer Zone to reduce their NO_x emissions by 75 percent by May 1, 2003, or to emit NO_x at a rate no greater than 0.15 pounds per million. The states also agreed that sources in the Northern Zone should reduce their rate of NO_x emissions by 55 percent from base year levels by May 1, 2003, or to emit NO_x at a rate no greater than 0.2 pounds per million BTU. *See supra* note 20.

23. EPA, Ozone Transport Commission (OTC) NO_x Budget Program, *available at* http://www.epa.gov/airmarkets/otc/overview.html.

24. The OTAG states are Alabama, Arkansas, Connecticut, Delaware, District of Colombia, Florida, Georgia, Illinois, Indiana, Iowa, Kansas, Kentucky, Louisiana, Maine, Maryland, Massachusetts, Michigan, Minnesota, Missouri, Mississippi, Nebraska, New Hampshire, North Carolina, North Dakota, New Jersey, New York, Ohio, Oklahoma, Pennsylvania, Rhode Island, South Carolina, South Dakota, Tennessee, Texas, Vermont, West Virginia, and Wisconsin.

25. 63 Fed. Reg. 57,361–62.

26. *Id.* at 57,364.

27. *Id.* at 57,356.

28. *Id.*

29. *Id.* at 57,358.

30. *See Michigan v. EPA*, 213 F.3d 663 (D.C. Cir. 2000) (upholding the EPA's ability to address transport without first convening a transport commission and the EPA's methodology for determining significant contribution; vacating the EPA's determinations regarding Wisconsin, Missouri, and Georgia, but upholding the EPA's determination regarding South Carolina; rejecting the EPA's change in the definition of electricity generating units; and upholding the agency's limits on early reduction credits).

31. 63 Fed. Reg. 57,358.

32. Clean Air Act § 110(a)(1), 42 U.S.C. § 7410(a)(1) (2001).

33. 63 Fed. Reg. 57,360.

34. Clean Air Act § 110(a)(2)(D), 42 U.S.C. § 7410(a)(2)(D) (2001).

35. *See* Clean Air Act § 110(k).

36. *Id.*

37. Clean Air Act § 110(m), 42 U.S.C. § 7410(m) (2001).

38. 63 Fed. Reg. 57,359.

39. Georgia, Missouri, and Wisconsin were ultimately removed from the NO_x SIP call due to the Court's ruling in *Michigan v. EPA*, 213 F.3d 663 (D.C. Cir. 2000).

40. OTAG states not included in the NO_x SIP call: Arkansas, Florida, Iowa, Kansas, Louisiana, Maine, Minnesota, Mississippi, North Dakota, New Hampshire, Oklahoma, South Dakota, Texas, and Vermont.

41. 63 Fed Reg. 57,405.

42. *Id.* at 57,399.

43. E.g., selective catalytic reduction (SCR).

44. 63 Fed. Reg. 57,402.

45. *Michigan v. EPA*, No. 98-1497, 2000 WL 1341477 (D.C. Cir. Aug. 30, 2000) (order extending the deadline for full implementation of SIP provisions).

46. 63 Fed. Reg. 57,426.

47. *Id.*

48. *Id.* at 57,457.

49. *Id.* at 57,458.

50. *Id.*

51. *Id.* at 57,472.

52. The ratio is calculated as follows (0.10 × total trading program / total # of banked allowances.) 63 Fed. Reg. 57,473.

53. 63 Fed. Reg. 57,455.

54. *Id.* at 57,429.

55. *Id.* at 57,474.

56. *Id.* at 57,428.

57. *Id.* at 57,429–30.

58. Federal Implementation Plan to Reduce the Regional Transport of Ozone, 63 Fed. Reg. 56,394 (proposed Oct. 21, 1998) (to be codified at 40 C.F.R. pts. 52 & 98).

59. 63 Fed. Reg. 56,396.

60. Clean Air Act § 302(y), 42 U.S.C. 7602(y) (2001).

61. 63 Fed. Reg. 56,399.

62. *Id.*

63. *Id.* at 56,405–06.

64. *Id.* at 56,400.

65. Clean Air Act § 126, 42 U.S.C. § 7426 (2001).

66. *See* Clean Air Act § 126(c).

67. Findings of Significant Contribution and Rulemaking of Section 126 Petitions for Purposes of Reducing Interstate Ozone Transport, 64 Fed. Reg. 33,962, 33,963 (proposed June 6, 1999) (to be codified at 40 C.F.R. pt. 52).

68. The eight states that filed petitions were Connecticut, Maine, Massachusetts, New Hampshire, New York, Rhode Island, Pennsylvania, and Vermont. These petitions were filed regarding both the one-hour and eight-hour NAAQS.

69. The five states were Maine, Massachusetts, New Hampshire, Pennsylvania, and Vermont. Findings of Significant Contribution and Rulemaking on Section 126 Petitions for Purpose of Reduction Interstate Ozone Transport, 65 Fed. Reg. 2673, 2675 (Jan. 18, 2000) (to be codified at 40 C.F.R. pts. 52 & 97).

70. These petitions were submitted individually by the District of Columbia, Delaware, Maryland, and New Jersey. 65 Fed. Reg. 2679.

71. The twelve states were Delaware, Indiana, Kentucky, Maryland, Michigan, New Jersey, New York, North Carolina, Ohio, Pennsylvania, Virginia, and West Virginia. Findings of Significant Contribution and Rulemaking on Section 126 Petitions for Purposes of Reducing Interstate Ozone Transport; Final Rule, 64 Fed. Reg. 28,249, 28,250 (May 25, 1999) (to be codified at 40 C.F.R. pt. 52).

72. 64 Fed. Reg. 28,250.

73. Originally, the deadlines for the NO$_x$ SIP call and the Section 126 Rule shared the same compliance deadline of May 1, 2003. However, the D.C. Circuit Court's order in *Michigan v. EPA* subsequently extended the NO$_x$ SIP call compliance date to May 31, 2004. As a result of this order, the NO$_x$ SIP call had a later compliance date than the Section 126 Rule. Furthermore, the D.C. Circuit Court tolled the compliance period for EGUs under the Section 126 Rule pending the EPA's response to the growth factor remand. (*Appalachian Power v. EPA*, 249 F.3d 1032 (Order Aug. 24, 2001)). The tolling of the compliance period resulted in a delay in the implementation of the Section 126 Rule until the 2004 ozone season. Thus, the EPA had to extend the deadline to May 31, 2004, which corresponds with the NO$_x$ SIP call deadline. [Section 126 Rule: Revised Deadlines, 67 Fed. Reg. 21,522, 25,123–25 (Apr. 30, 2002) (to be codified at 40 C.F.R. pt. 97).]

74. 65 Fed. Reg. 2674.

75. *Id.* at 2683.

76. *Id.*

77. 175 F.3d 1027 (D.C. Cir. 1999).

78. No. 98-1497 (D.C. Cir. 1999).

79. 65 Fed. Reg. 2679.

80. The states involved were Michigan, West Virginia, Alabama, South Carolina, Virginia, Indiana, Ohio, and North Carolina.

81. The EPA claimed that NO$_x$ SIP call constituted a nationally applicable rule, so that suit may be brought only in D.C. Circuit. 42 U.S.C. 7609(b)(i).

82. *Michigan v. EPA*, 213 F.3d 663 (D.C. Cir. 2000).

83. *Michigan v. EPA*, 213 F.3d at 671.

84. *American Trucking Ass'ns v. EPA*, 175 F. 3d 1027 (D.C. Cir. 1998).

85. Clean Air Act §§ 108–09.

86. *American Trucking Ass'ns v. EPA*, 175 F.3d at 1033.

87. Section 184 established an ozone transport region in the Northeastern United States and set a deadline for convening a transport commission required as a result of its establishment. Under Section 176A(a) the EPA may establish an interstate air pollution transport region. Under (b) it must set up a commission if it creates a region.

88. *Michigan v. EPA*, 213 F.3d at 672.

89. Clean Air Act § 176A(b)(1), 42 U.S.C. § 7506(a) (2001).

90. Petitioners argued that the EPA, under pre-1990 language of the CAA, on several occasions rejected calls to control interstate pollution transport even in light of downwind contributions greater than those addressed by the SIP call. By extension, petitioners argued that the EPA was thereby prevented from lowering the bar on the amount of downwind contribution for which to require controls. The court rejected this argument, noting that neither the 1990 amendments to the CAA nor the EPA's implementation of the statute binds the agency to any fixed concept of "how much [contribution] was too much." *Michigan v. EPA*, 213 F.3d at 674.

91. Petitioners challenged the EPA's imposition of uniform controls on all SIP call states on two grounds: (1) that SIP call states that make only small contributions to downwind nonattainment must impose on their sources the same level of control that states making large contributions must install; and (2) that because of distance and the vagaries of pollutant migration and ozone formation, emissions further from nonattainment areas may cause less of an air quality impact than nearby emissions. The Court rejected both of these contentions. It noted that the EPA's uniform control targets flow from its decision to determine "significant contribution" among the twenty-three selected states on the basis of control costs. In upholding the EPA's cost-based approach to "significant contribution," the court of necessity also upheld the EPA's imposition of uniform controls. As to the second contention, the court accepted the EPA's explanation that a nonuniform tiered control approach based on downwind distance to nonattainment areas would not provide a significant improvement either in terms of air quality or in reducing compliance costs. *Michigan v. EPA*, 213 F.3d at 679–680.

92. State petitioners argued that in issuing the SIP call, the EPA had not determined "significant contribution" based on any intelligible principles. The court, however, upheld the EPA's "essentially unbounded" reading of the CAA in this instance, resting its conclusion on a line of cases upholding agencies' exercise of "essentially standardless discretion" in instances where they could deploy that discretion only within a relatively narrow scope of regulated activities. In this case, the court distinguished the SIP call from the ozone NAAQS on the grounds that, in imposing controls on regional transport, the EPA must make a number of threshold determinations relating to emissions activity, evidence of pollution transport, and the contribution of these emissions to nonattainment. *Michigan v. EPA*, 213 F.3d at 680–81.

93. *Michigan v. EPA*, 213 F.3d at 674–79.

94. *Id.* at 673.

95. Clean Air Act § 110(a)(2)(D)(i)(1), 42 U.S.C. § 7410(a)(2)(D)(i)(1) (2001).

96. *Id.*

97. *Michigan v. EPA*, 213 F.3d at 684.

98. *Id.*

99. *Id.* at 686.

100. *Id.* at 687.

101. *Id.* at 688.

102. *Id.*

103. *Id.* at 690.

104. *Id.* at 691–92.

105. Upwind states from the midwestern and southeastern United States, utilities of other electric generating industrial facilities, and several individual companies that have facility specific concerns.

106. *Appalachian Power v. EPA*, 249 F.3d 1032 (D.C. Cir. 2001).

107. The EPA claimed that this cross-reference was an inadvertent mistake. The Clean Air Act Amendments of 1990 eliminated a subsection of Section 110 of the CAA causing § 110(a)(2)(E) to be renumbered as Section 110(a)(2)(D). Several references to § 110(a)(2)(E)(i) were updated to correspond with the CAA Amendments. The 1990 Amendments substitute (D) for (E) in Section 125 and also substituted (ii) for (i). The EPA claimed that Congress amended Section 126 only in order to update the cross-references and inadvertently substituted (ii) for (i). The EPA ignored this scrivener's error and construed Section 126 as though it had never occurred. Although the Court found this evidence alone to be unconvincing, it was ultimately persuaded that Congress intended to allow the EPA to impose federal controls. The petition process existed before the amendments. Congress did not intend to withdraw the mechanism whereby a state could compel the EPA to control emissions from sources in a neighboring state that contributed to nonattainment of NAAQS. *Appalachian Power v. EPA*, 249 F.3d at 1040–43.

108. *Appalachian Power v. EPA*, 249 F.3d at 1045.

109. *Id.* at 1047.

110. Clean Air Act § 126(c), 42 U.S.C. § 7426(c) (2001).

111. 64 Fed. Reg. 28,264.

112. Clean Air Act § 126(b), 42 U.S.C. § 7426(b) (2001).

113. *Appalachian Power v. EPA*, 249 F.3d at 1047.

114. Rather than relying on individual state projections, the EPA projected 2007 emissions based on its integrated planning model (IPM), which used historic heat input and projected growth rates. The Court upheld the agency's reliance on the IPM. Nevertheless, the Court remanded the EPA's determination of electric generating units (EGU) growth rates recognizing that in some instances actual rates had already exceeded projected rates. *Appalachian Power v. EPA*, 249 F.3d at 1051–52.

115. *Appalachian Power v. EPA*, 249 F.3d at 1049.

116. *Id.* at 1058.

117. *Id.* at 1054–55.

118. *See* Response to Court Remand on NO$_x$ SIP Call and Section 126 Rule, 67 Fed. Reg. 21,868 (May 1, 2002) (to be codified at 40 C.F.R. pts. 51, 52 et al.). *See also, Appalachian Power v. EPA*, 2002 U.S. App. LEXIS 16412 (D.C. Cir. Aug. 12, 2002) consolidating many of the states' petitions for review.

CHAPTER 6

The New Source Review Program: Prevention of Significant Deterioration and Nonattainment New Source Review

BERNARD F. HAWKINS, JR.
MARY ELLEN TERNES

Introduction

The Clean Air Act (CAA) requires promulgation of National Ambient Air Quality Standards (NAAQS) for criteria pollutants (as described in Chapter 2).[1] These criteria pollutants currently include lead, sulfur dioxide (SO_2), nitrogen dioxide (NO_2), carbon monoxide (CO), particulate matter (PM), and ozone, which is regulated by its precursors, nitrogen oxide (NO_x) and volatile organic compounds (VOCs).[2] NAAQS requirements were established to protect human health and the environment and to serve as ceilings for acceptable maximum air quality concentrations.

The goals of the CAA include attaining and protecting air quality to satisfy all NAAQS requirements.[3] A primary means of achieving this is through placing preconstruction review and permitting requirements on certain new and modified sources of air pollution to require control technology and to protect against degradation of air quality. These requirements are implemented through the new source review (NSR) program.[4] The program has three subparts. The first two, which apply to large or "major" sources of air pollution, are the prevention of significant deterioration (PSD) program under Part C of Title I[5] and the nonattainment area (NAA) program under CAA Section 173 and other provisions contained in Part D of Title I.[6] A third component of the NSR program is the individual state "minor new source review programs" that apply to smaller sources of air pollution.[7] Because minor new source review programs vary widely from state to state, they are not covered in this chapter.

Significant development of what is now the NSR program occurred in the 1970s. The 1970 CAA Amendments required the states to develop procedures in state implementation plans (SIPs) for preventing the construction of sources that would prevent the state from satisfying NAAQS requirements.[8] These SIPs would then be federally approved. The U.S. Environmental Protection Agency (EPA) provided details on the elements needed for the SIPs to be approved.[9] Each state's NSR program is federally approved into its SIP under these EPA requirements.[10] In 1972, the decision in *Sierra Club v. Ruckelshaus*[11] created a requirement that states include in their SIPs preconstruction review requirements (for new and modified sources) that would prevent the significant deterioration of air quality in areas that had already satisfied NAAQS mandates. The EPA again responded by promulgating PSD regulations indicating what must be included in SIPs for federal approval.[12] States submitted and obtained SIP-approved PSD programs.

In 1976, attention turned to permits being issued in areas that did not satisfy the air quality standards established under the NAAQS program. The EPA issued an "offset ruling," which provided minimum preconstruction requirements for new and modified sources locating in these areas. These requirements included more stringent control technologies, certifying that other owned sources were in compliance with SIP provisions and reducing other similar emissions to "offset" any emissions that resulted from the new or modified source.[13]

The NSR program was further defined by the 1977 CAA Amendments.[14] The EPA and the states determined which areas of the country satisfied NAAQS requirements. Areas with ambient air quality levels satisfying the standards were designated as "attainment" areas while those with levels exceeding these standards were designated as "nonattainment" areas. Areas not classified for meeting a NAAQS were treated for review purposes as being in attainment for that pollutant.[15] States were then required to revise their SIPs further to provide ways they would achieve attainment status for all areas.[16] Limitations on construction of new or modified sources continued as part of this control strategy. The 1977 amendments also mandated PSD-specific requirements with express statutory requirements.[17]

PSD "increments" established the maximum amount of increases in ambient pollution levels for specified criteria pollutants that can result from all sources within the area after certain dates, which, as discussed later, is referred to as the baseline. The key requirement is that no increment be completely consumed (or exceeded) by the combination of the emissions from specified existing sources and the emissions associated with the new or modified source covered by the PSD program.[18] Associated with NAAQS and PSD increments, Congress provided special protection for air quality (including visibility) in specified areas (e.g., national parks, forests, wilderness areas). In these areas, known as Class I areas, PSD increments allow the least amount of impact from new or modified growth. Other areas allowing more growth are qualified as Class II and III areas.[19] SIP-approved NSR programs also address these issues.

After the 1977 amendments, the EPA implemented new and revised NSR regulations.[20] Significant litigation questioning the application of the

NSR program and its regulations also followed.[21] Further regulatory changes and guidance for the NSR program followed that litigation.[22]

In 1990, Congress once again amended the NSR program.[23] Because many areas of the country still did not meet attainment status for all NAAQS requirements, Congress further classified specific nonattainment areas by the extent to which they were out of attainment. Requirements were then assigned for these designated nonattainment areas to bring them into attainment within specified time periods. For example, the thresholds at which sources were covered under the NSR program were lowered and greater emissions offsets were required. The farther out of compliance the area was from NAAQS requirements, the more stringent the new requirements would be.[24] The regulations previously discussed also implement these new changes.

Amendments to the NSR Program

As a result of the complex and time-consuming nature of NSR, various groups appealed to the EPA to simplify the NSR program. In 1992, groups representing industry, environmentalists, and state and federal government began meeting to discuss possible revisions to the NSR program.

Proposed changes involved simplifying and providing more certainty to the process for selecting appropriate emissions control technology, such as by limiting the number of sources a permit applicant must investigate in selecting control technologies; providing exemptions from NSR for certain environmentally beneficial programs; extending the time period for determining a source's baseline; allowing states to issue source-specific, plant-wide applicability limits; facilitating use of undemonstrated and innovative technologies such as pollution prevention efforts; and improving coordination among the federal land managers (FLMs), permitting authorities, and permit applicants. The purpose of bringing together various representatives to discuss proposed changes to the NSR program was the hope that these groups could develop a consensus on needed changes to the program acceptable to the various group interests. The process, however, has not been completely successful, and there is not a complete consensus on proposed or final revisions.

The EPA published a draft version of the proposed revisions on July 11, 1994. A formal notice of proposed rule making was issued on July 23, 1996.[25] The proposed regulations were the subject of discussions among stakeholders for several years. Finally, on December 31, 2002, the EPA promulgated revisions to the NSR rules adopting many of the revisions proposed in 1996,[26] followed by a notice of reconsideration on July 30, 2003,[27] and clarifying amendments on November 7, 2003.[28] On December 31, 2002, the EPA issued a proposed rule regarding NSR's controversial routine maintenance, repair, and replacement (RMRR) exemption,[29] and on October 27, 2003, promulgated the equipment replacement provisions (ERP) of the RMRR exemption.[30] A complete discussion of these promulgated revisions is beyond the scope of this chapter. However, the primary changes are summarized briefly below, and incorporated into the body of the following discussion.

The EPA's 2002 revisions included five methods of enhancing flexibility in the NSR permitting process: revised baseline actual emission calculations, actual-to-projected-actual emissions methodology, plant-wide applicability limits (PALs), Clean Units, and pollution control projects (PCPs).[31] With these revisions, the EPA also codified its long-standing Wisconsin Electric Power Company (WEPCO) policy regarding the method of calculating baseline emissions for electric utility steam generating units (EUSGUs). Additionally, the EPA codified a new definition of "regulated NSR pollutant" for evaluating which pollutants are regulated for purposes of major NSR. The EPA did not address the remaining issues included in its 1996 proposed rule.[32] The EPA did, however, require states to adopt the 2002 NSR revisions as minimum requirements for state air regulatory programs.

The EPA's first method of enhancing flexibility was to revise the method for calculating emissions increases to determine whether physical changes or changes in the method of operation trigger major NSR requirements. Specifically, the EPA adopted a new procedure for calculating the pre-change emissions, or the "baseline actual emissions." With this new procedure, any consecutive twenty-four-month period in the ten years prior to the change may be used to determine the actual baseline emission rate of a non-electric utility steam generating unit (non-EUSGU) source. The original baseline calculation generally allowed consideration of only the actual emission rate over the past two years of operation prior to the change. With this rule, the EPA also promulgated its WEPCO policy, pursuant to which EUSGUs calculated baseline actual emissions as the average emissions during any two-year period within the five-year period preceding the change.

Second, the EPA added a new method for calculating whether a physical or operational change at an existing emission unit will result in an emissions increase. This new method, the actual-to-projected-actual applicability test, is applicable to both non-EUSGUs and EUSGUs alike, while non-EUSGUs still have the option of using the actual-to-potential test. Operators availing themselves of this new method will need to keep records for five to ten years depending upon the nature of the change to demonstrate that actual emissions after the change are consistent with the actual emissions projected for the emissions resulting from the change.

Third, the EPA promulgated into the NSR rules plant-wide applicability limits, or PALs, which is essentially a facility-wide emissions cap. This emissions cap provides a relatively simple method for determining whether changes at a facility trigger NSR. A facility operating under a PAL can make changes to its processes without triggering NSR as long as its emissions remain below the cap. PALs are not entirely new. Consistent with the EPA's 1996 proposal, several PALs have been implemented successfully. Thus, with the experience of the past several years, the EPA addressed in its revisions issues such as PAL duration and modification, as well as several specific questions that have arisen in the PAL implementation process.

Fourth, the EPA included a new applicability test for units that have already gone through the major NSR process deemed Clean Units. With this new test, facilities are allowed to make changes to units that have already installed best available control technology (BACT) or lowest achievable emissions rate (LAER) without triggering additional major NSR review if the project, first, does not alter emissions in a way that requires a change to existing permitted emissions limitations or work practice requirements for the unit that were adopted with the BACT or LAER, and second, the project does not change any physical or operational characteristics upon which the BACT or LAER relied.

Finally, to supplement the existing pollution control project provisions the EPA included a new list of environmentally beneficial technologies that qualify as PCPs. This list allows owners or operators installing a listed PCP to automatically qualify for the PCP exclusion, if there is no adverse air quality impact. PCPs that are not listed may also qualify on a case-by-case basis depending upon whether the project is environmentally beneficial when used for the proposed application.

The EPA's Equipment Replacement Provision final rule allows the RMRR exemption for activities that involve identical replacements where the costs do not exceed 20 percent of the replacement cost of the unit, and the replacement doesn't alter the basic design parameters or cause the unit to exceed any emissions limitation.[33]

The EPA's 2002 NSR revisions were met with disagreement by many state agencies. Ten northeastern and mid-Atlantic states joined to file a petition with the EPA's Administrator Whitman alleging that the rule violated the CAA and the Administrative Procedure Act.[34] The states argued that PALs, Clean Units, and the changes to calculations for significant emissions increases were not logical outgrowths of the proposed rules. The states also argued that the EPA's requirement that the states adopt the EPA's NSR rules as minimum requirements is not a logical outgrowth of the proposed rules, and that the EPA had no authority to require states to adopt the NSR revisions because such a requirement was inconsistent with each state's right to promulgate regulations more stringent than federal requirements.[35] Operators should be aware of their state's approach to adopting the final revisions, and realize that their state may elect to adopt only portions of the final revisions, resulting in state NSR rules that vary across the board.[36] At time of publication, all aspects of both the December 2002 rule and the 2003 equipment replacement rule are being litigated before the U.S. Court of Appeals for the District of Columbia Circuit.

In addition to the question of precisely what provisions states must adopt in response to the 2002 NSR revisions, there is the question of when states must adopt the reforms. The 2002 revisions were effective March 3, 2003. States in attainment with the NAAQS and delegated with authority to implement the NSR PSD program may be required to implement the program immediately.[37] States with approved PSD SIPs are required to promulgate SIP revisions consistent with the NSR revisions. These states have three years to revise their SIPs.[38] Operators should be aware of their resident state's delegation status and consider timing of implementation of the revisions in evaluating whether to undertake changes that may require NSR review.

General Framework of the NSR Program

The NSR Program's General Focus

To achieve and maintain desired air quality goals, the NSR program focuses on controlling and limiting the emissions of criteria pollutants from certain "major stationary sources" of air pollution that have a "potential to emit" specified significant levels of any pollutants regulated under the CAA.[39] NSR analysis is required before a new major stationary source is constructed or before an existing major stationary source undertakes a major modification as defined in the regulations.[40]

NSR analysis is very complex. It requires the operator of the source to review and analyze the potential impact that emissions from the new or modified source will have on ambient air quality. The operator must demonstrate that the source will not violate any NAAQS for covered criteria pollutants and will not exceed any applicable PSD increments. In nonattainment areas, regulated emission increases for various pollutants that are in nonattainment generally must be offset by other sources.[41]

Pathways for NSR Permit Review

New or modified major stationary sources that have the potential to emit one or more regulated pollutants at specified thresholds must undergo the review required to obtain a construction permit. There are two permit review pathways.

PSD Analysis

Covered major stationary sources located or to be constructed in attainment areas for one or more criteria pollutants (or one or more unclassified criteria pollutants) must undergo analysis under the PSD pathway of NSR.[42]

Nonattainment Analysis

Covered sources that are major sources for any criteria pollutant that is in nonattainment for a designated area (or covered sources located in specified ozone transport regions) must follow a nonattainment analysis pathway for that criteria pollutant if the source has the potential to emit that pollutant in major amounts.[43]

Overlapping Pathways

A source may have to undergo review under both pathways. If a covered major source has a potential to emit significant amounts of one or more pollutants for which the area is in attainment (or unclassified) and has a potential to emit in major amounts one or more pollutants for which the area is in nonattainment, the operator of the source would have to conduct a PSD analysis for attainment (or unclassified) criteria pollutants and conduct a nonattainment analysis for covered nonattainment criteria pollutants.

For example, if a designated area (often classified by county or municipality) was in attainment for one criteria pollutant (e.g., NO_2 or CO) and in nonattainment for another criteria pollutant (e.g., ozone), a covered major source locating in that area would undergo PSD analysis for the attainment criteria pollutant and nonattainment analysis for the nonattainment pollutant.

In addition, there are circumstances in which a source locating in an attainment area (or an area that has been unclassified for a criteria pollutant) could have a significant impact on a nonattainment area. Under these circumstances (defined at 40 C.F.R. § 51.165(b)), the source could be required to undergo a nonattainment analysis even though it is locating in an attainment area. As subsequently discussed, additional analysis of other regulated pollutants emitted in significant amounts may also be required under the PSD pathway.

Permits Required

Construction

Construction permits must be obtained before constructing or making major modifications to major sources of air pollution subject to NSR.[44] Construction permits specify the terms and conditions under which emissions units must be constructed and must operate to be in compliance. These permits document the technology and operating scenarios proposed and selected during the NSR process to control emissions and may include emissions limitations for each unit. Specific limits on operating conditions may also be included.

Operation

Construction permits are eventually "rolled over" into complex and comprehensive operating permits. These permits generally include the same terms and conditions as construction permits. PSD operating permits have been incorporated into Title V comprehensive permits for a facility. (See Chapters 15 and 16.)

Overview of the Application and Permit Process

Obtaining a NSR permit is an involved process. Exact requirements vary depending on which pathway the applicant follows, PSD or nonattainment analysis or both. Each pathway requires the applicant to determine whether the covered source is in an attainment area, a nonattainment area, or both and then whether it is a major source as defined for that area. The applicant must then determine what covered pollutants the source will emit and must evaluate further. Methods for controlling these emissions must then be considered. BACT is required for PSD and LAER is generally required for nonattainment analysis.

The applicant must then evaluate what impact the source's emissions will have on the ambient air quality of the surrounding area (including Class I areas). This impact analysis often includes consideration of certain incremental increases and limits. Determining the impact of potential emissions from the facility involves, among other things, assessing existing ambient air quality and predicting what impact the proposed new or modified source will have on air quality, including the impact from growth that may occur as a result of the construction or modification of the covered source. These demonstrations typically involve complex modeling procedures. They may also require gathering existing ambient air quality and meteorological data before conducting any modeling.[45]

This evaluation, as well as anything the permittee concludes it must do in response to the evaluation to reduce emissions to acceptable levels (including obtaining emission offsets under nonattainment analysis), must be included in the permit application. The construction permit application may ultimately be reviewed by the state, the EPA, affected FLMs (i.e., those that are responsible for protecting the air quality of protected Class I areas), and the general public.

Existing Guidance on the NSR Process

Despite the controversy surrounding the 2002 NSR revisions, most of the basic program elements remain the same. A great deal of guidance exists on how to conduct an NSR analysis under the current program. Perhaps the most important guidance document on the existing NSR program is the "Draft New Source Review Workshop Manual" (NSRWM), released by the EPA in 1990. Although this manual was never promulgated as a rule or as a formal regulation, or even issued in final form, state agencies often refer to it religiously in implementing NSR programs. The guidance has not been modified to incorporate the 2002 revisions. However, the guidance continues to provide the best illustration of the practical aspects of NSR implementation and thus, this chapter continues to refer to this manual extensively and, to some extent, follows its outline. In addition, many other EPA guidance documents on NSR exist.[46] These documents are referenced throughout this chapter when relevant. Fortunately, the EPA has posted most, if not all, of its NSR guidance, including the NSRWM, on its Web site.[47]

In addition to seeking federal guidance, any operator contemplating construction or modification of a stationary source of air emissions that may be subject to NSR should obtain and review state NSR regulations and requirements. It should also contact the state permitting agency to obtain any state guidance documents on conducting a review. As indicated, state programs may differ from the federal program, and the state programs are the primary law involved in the permitting process, although all state programs must meet basic federal standards to obtain EPA approval.

If the permittee and an agency, whether it be the state or the EPA, disagree over an NSR element, the permittee should consult decisions from the state, regional administrators, the environmental appeals board, and the courts for further guidance. State permitting agencies that have processed NSR permit applications for similar sources are often invaluable resources for information and precedent. Of the two possible NSR pathways, the PSD pathway normally involves more pollutants and currently applies to more areas of the country. As a result, there is perhaps more guidance on this pathway than on the nonattainment pathway. There is, however, overlap between the programs, and some of the subsequent discussions on PSD analysis can be applied to nonattainment analysis.

Prevention of Significant Deterioration Review Pathway

Introduction

Major steps in the PSD review pathway include conducting the source applicability determination; identifying pollutants emitted in "significant amounts" that must be evaluated; selecting BACT emission control methods for covered pollutants; evaluating ambient air quality impacts through NAAQS and PSD increment analysis; considering additional impacts, including those from associated growth and those on local air quality, soils, vegetation, and visibility; and evaluating impacts on potentially affected Class I areas.[48]

Timing of Permitting Analysis

The PSD pathway applies to construction of new major stationary sources[49] and to major modifications[50] of existing sources located in areas that are in attainment or are unclassified for one or more criteria pollutants that will emit or have the potential to emit defined significant[51] amounts of at least one pollutant regulated under the CAA.[52] As indicated, operators of sources that may be subject to the permitting requirement must evaluate applicability before "beginning actual construction" of any new or modified source because PSD requirements must be satisfied before the actual construction is begun. Construction is defined as "any physical change or change in the method of operation (including fabrication, erection, installation, demolition, or modification of an emissions unit) which would result in a change in emissions."[53] The phrase "begin actual construction" is defined as follows:

> [I]n general, initiation of physical on-site construction activities on an emissions unit which are of a permanent nature. Such activities include, but are not limited to, installation of building supports and foundations, laying underground pipework and construction of permanent storage structures. With respect to change in method of operations, this term refers to those on-site activities other than preparatory activities which mark the initiation of the change.[54]

Again, most PSD programs apply to sources before actual construction is begun, as defined.

Certain exemptions from the PSD program apply to "grandfather" sources that "commenced construction" before specified dates, presumably to avoid penalizing operators that entered into contracts to construct facilities prior to the promulgation of the NSR regulations.[55] A source may be considered to have commenced construction when the owner or operator has all necessary preconstruction approvals on permits and has either

(i) Begun, or caused to begin, a continuous program of actual on-site construction of the source, to be completed within a reasonable time; or

(ii) Entered into binding agreements or contractual obligations, which cannot be cancelled or modified without substantial loss to the owner or operator, to undertake a program of actual construction of the source to be completed within a reasonable time.[56]

Though the term "commence construction" appears merely to set the "grandfathering" date for older facilities, and "beginning actual construction" clearly applies to the present construction of new facilities, over time, these definitions (and significance) have become confused in practice with regard to how these terms apply to dictate when a preconstruction permit review is required and what can be done before that time. Under some views, operators of potentially covered sources must be careful not to begin "breaking ground" for new covered sources before they complete a PSD review. Some advise these operators to avoid entering into contracts that cannot be easily broken.[57] Other interpretations of the PSD regulations allow the permittee to enter into contracts and even perhaps break ground for a building that will house the source, as long as actual emission units are not constructed or installed.[58]

The permittee should consult the individual state and the EPA for guidance on what can be done before PSD permit reviews. Some state interpretations could be unique and confusing to applicants, especially those accustomed to dealing with other environmental laws under which preconstruction review is not normally required.

The EPA has indicated that it will accept comments on whether there should be any change in the federal NSR program, allowing more site preparation work or other preconstruction activities before issuance of an NSR construction permit. However, the agency has also indicated that there will be a reluctance to relax preconstruction prohibitions.[59]

Applicability to New Sources

Whether a new stationary source must undergo PSD analysis is determined by the designation of the area in which it will be located and by whether it will be considered a major stationary source. [60]

Attainment Area Determination

The operator may check with the applicable state permitting agency to determine whether the area in which the source will be located is designated as an attainment, an unclassified, or a nonattainment area (or possibly an ozone transport region requiring nonattainment analysis) for the various criteria pollutants. Air quality designations are also listed in 40 C.F.R. Part 81. Attainment or nonattainment designations are normally made according to the county or municipality in which the source will locate. The source's status as attainment or nonattainment is resolved by determining the areas upon which the new source will have a significant impact. If any of those areas are attainment or unclassified, then the covered source must undergo PSD analysis.[61]

Identifying the Stationary Source and Emissions Units

An initial step in the PSD analysis for a new source is to identify the stationary source and the emissions units that will be located at the source. A stationary source is "any building, structure, facility or installation which emits or may emit any air pollutant subject to regulation under the Clean Air Act."[62] Building, structure, facility, or installation is defined as "all the pollutant emitting activities which belong to the same industrial grouping,[63] are located on one or more contiguous or adjacent properties," and are under common ownership or control.[64] An emissions unit is "any part of a stationary source that emits or has the potential to emit any regulated NSR pollutant."[65] Based on these definitions, the applicant can identify each proposed emissions unit at the stationary source. However, there can be significant disagreement over the scope of the definition and resulting coverage for these terms.

Determining the Stationary Source's Potential to Emit

The next step is to determine each emissions unit's "potential to emit" (PTE) for all regulated pollutants under the CAA. PTE is defined as "the maximum capacity of a stationary source to emit a pollutant under its physical operation design."[66] It is the emissions unit's potential to emit a given pollutant at the maximum design capacity or operational capability for the unit, whichever is higher. Except in the limited circumstances discussed later in this section, to determine PTE it should be assumed that a given emissions unit will operate continuously, 24 hours a day, 365 days per year (8,760 hours per year).[67]

Numerous methods may be used to estimate potential emissions. However, the applicant should select the method or methods that produce the "most representative data available" to determine potential emissions from each emissions unit. The applicant should discuss the selected method with the permitting agency to ensure the agency's acceptance. Available methods include obtaining data from equipment vendors, actual operating data from similar sources (including permit applications for these sources), emissions data from the EPA or state agencies, AP-42 emissions estimate factors,[68] and data contained in trade and technical journals.[69] Once the applicant determines the potential emissions that will result from emissions units, often referred to as point sources, the applicant should determine whether or not it must account for fugitive emissions.

Fugitive emissions can be defined as emissions "which could not reasonably pass through a stack, chimney, vent, or other functionally equivalent opening,"[70] but that result from the construction or operation of the stationary source. These emissions could include such sources as leaks from flanges and valves, dust created from loading and unloading coal, fumes from an open paint-mixing container, and many other things. Determining what constitutes a fugitive emission is often the subject of tremendous debate and disagreement in NSR applicability analysis. This results because fugitive emissions do not have to be considered in calculating the PTE in some NSR applicability determinations.

Fugitive emissions are normally considered in the calculation of PTE for the following:

1. Any stationary source belonging to one of twenty-eight listed stationary source categories listed in Section 169 of the CAA;[71]
2. Any stationary source belonging to a stationary source category regulated under the new source performance standards (NSPS) of Section 111 of the CAA as of August 7, 1980;
3. Any stationary source belonging to a stationary source category that was regulated under the National Emissions Standards for Hazardous Air Pollutants (NESHAP) program of Section 112 of the CAA as of August 7, 1980.[72]

For sources falling into any of these three categories, "quantifiable" fugitive emissions must be considered in determining the PTE for a given pollutant.[73] Adding the total PTE from each emissions unit to any quantifiable fugitive emissions that must be considered, the applicant can determine the "maximum" PTE for each regulated pollutant. If that maximum PTE is in excess of "major source thresholds" that would subject the source to NSR, the applicant may want to consider limiting the source's PTE in order to opt out of NSR analysis.

PTE is based on maximum design or operating capacity. This capacity can be limited by certain design restrictions. The definition of PTE indicates that "[a]ny physical or operational limitation on the capacity of a source to emit a pollutant, including air pollution control equipment and restrictions on hours of operation or on the type or amount of material combusted, stored or processed, shall be treated as part of its design if the limitation or the effect it would have on emissions is federally enforceable."[74]

Historically, a key provision of the preceding passage was that any design limitation on PTE must be "federally enforceable."[75] To be federally enforceable, a term or condition must be included in a permit issued under a federally approved program. Federally enforceable permit programs include the Title I NSR program (major and minor source review), the Section 111 NSPS program, the Title IV acid rain program, the National Emissions Standards for Hazardous Air Pollutants (NESHAPs) program, the Section 112 air toxics program, the Title V program's operating permit requirements, and state permit programs federally approved under SIPs. Significantly, federally approved state permit programs also often include minor new source review construction permit programs. Such construction permits often can be used as a federally enforceable means to limit PTE and thus avoid NSR.[76] As long as states consider federal enforceability as a prerequisite for determining NSR applicability, limits on PTE must be included in one of the listed types of permits.

The requirement of federal enforceability was thrown out for purposes of calculating potential to emit in 1995, when in *Chemical Manufacturers Association v. EPA* the U.S. Court of Appeals for the District of Columbia Circuit, without an opinion, vacated the requirement that limits on PTE be "federal enforceability" and remanded to the EPA for justification of the requirement.[77] In the 2002 NSR revisions, the EPA explained that, despite the NSR rules continued use of "federal enforceability" in the definition of "potential to emit," the EPA now simply requires that the limit be "enforceable as a practical matter," which requires that the limit be both legally enforceable and practicably enforceable.[78] That is, the permitting agency must be able to determine that the source is actually complying with the restriction to which it was committed on a measurable basis. This often requires record-keeping, monitoring, and reporting requirements verifying any self-imposed limitations on emissions. Also, restrictions on potential emissions normally must be such that they are permanent without requiring a permit modification.

In any case, some state SIP permit programs may still require sources' PTE to be limited by federally enforceable limits.[79] In these states, federally enforceable restrictions on design capacity for emissions units may still be required for a source to avoid exceeding the PTE threshold that would force it to undergo NSR. However, a permittee should consider all potentially troubling aspects of accepting federally enforceable restrictions to avoid NSR. In any event, once federally enforceable emissions limits have been established and approved by the state permitting agency, the limits may be considered in calculating the total PTE for a stationary source for each regulated pollutant the source will emit. The applicant may calculate the total PTE by adding the potential emissions (considering any limitations) for each emissions unit for the entire stationary source.

Major Source Determination

Once a facility's total PTE is known, the next step is to determine whether the facility will be a "major stationary source." The PSD pathway applies only to stationary sources that have the potential to emit at least one regulated NSR pollutant in amounts that exceed major source thresholds. Sources exceeding these thresholds are referred to as major stationary sources, which the PSD program defines as follows:

a. Any of the following stationary sources of air pollutants which emit, or has the potential to emit, 100 tons per year or more of any pollutant subject to regulation under the [federal Clean Air] Act: Fossil fuel-fired steam electric plants of more than 250 million British thermal units per hour heat input, coal cleaning plants (with thermal dryers), kraft pulp mills, portland cement plants, primary zinc smelters, iron and steel mill plants, primary aluminum ore reduction plants, primary copper smelters, municipal incinerators capable of charging more than 250 tons of refuse per day, hydrofluoric, sulfuric and nitric acid plants, petroleum refineries, lime plants, phosphate rock processing plants, coke oven batteries, sulfur recovery plants, carbon black plants (furnace process), primary lead smelters, fuel conversion plants, sintering plants, secondary metal production plants, chemical process plants, fossil fuel boilers (or combinations thereof) totaling more than 250 million British thermal units per hour heat input, petroleum storage and transfer units with a total storage capacity exceeding 300,000 barrels, taconite ore processing plants, glass fiber processing plants and charcoal production plants;

b. Notwithstanding the stationary source size specified in paragraph [a] . . . of this section, any stationary source which emits, or has the potential to emit, 250 tons per year or more of any air pollutant subject to regulation under the [federal Clean Air] Act; or

c. Any physical change that would occur at a stationary source not otherwise qualifying under paragraph [a] . . . of this section, as a major stationary source, if the changes would constitute a major stationary source by itself.[80]

As explained by these definitions, existing minor sources can become major stationary sources if modifications at the facility, taken alone or in conjunction, push the source above emissions thresholds described for major source status.

Using the facility's calculated PTE, the applicant may determine whether it will be a major stationary source subject to PSD review by comparing the total PTE for each regulated pollutant to the major source threshold. If the PTE for any regulated pollutant equals or exceeds a major source threshold, the source must undergo PSD review, unless the operator can find ways to further limit the PTE and thus bring the source below the major source threshold.

Exemptions

As noted, by accepting limits on PTE that are enforceable as a practical matter or operating restrictions to reduce potential emissions below PSD thresholds, a new source can avoid the PSD program.[81] The applicant, however, should consider several factors before accepting such restrictions.

First, future emissions needs should be evaluated. If the operator knows that it will likely need to expand production or emissions in the near future, it may be wise to undergo PSD review now rather than later. It is easier to incorporate emissions control technology while a facility is being built than after it is built. In addition, as sources continue to undergo change and as new sources locate in areas where available air quality may change, it could become more difficult to obtain a PSD permit for a major modification. The same concern would be true if an area currently in attainment is likely to be redesignated for nonattainment. Redesignation is likely to occur with the revisions to the ozone and particulate NAAQS and, under these circumstances, it may be less costly to undergo PSD review as a source locating in an attainment area than nonattainment review as a source locating in an area not satisfying the NAAQS requirements.

Further, if an operator reasonably believes that it will change in the near future and that the change would cause it to exceed applicable PSD thresholds and the operator avoids PSD analysis by asking for less capacity than it reasonably believes it needs, then the application for this capacity could be viewed as a "sham application." Sham applications can result in revocation of existing permits as well as civil and even criminal penalties.[82]

Applicability to Major Modifications

General Applicability

An existing source is subject to PSD review under the following four circumstances:

1. The source is a major stationary source that proposes to undergo a modification (i.e., a physical change or change in method of operation)[83] that will result in both (1) a defined "significant emissions increase" of a regulated NSR pollutant (unless all of those pollutants that will be emitted in significant amounts are pollutants for which the area is nonattainment, in which case the source will be subject to nonattainment analysis) and (2) a significant "net emissions increase" of that pollutant from the major stationary source;[84] or

2. The source is a major stationary source located within ten kilometers of a Class I area and proposes to undergo a modification that will result in an increase of 1 microgram per cubic meter ($\mu g/m^3$) or more (for a twenty-four-hour average) in the ambient concentration of a regulated pollutant within the Class I area;[85] or

3. The source is a minor source and proposes to undergo a modification that would *by itself* have a PTE that would satisfy the definition of major stationary source;[86] or

4. The source is a minor source and becomes a major source as a result of a change in the SIP standards for the area.[87]

The last three definitions are fairly self-explanatory or will follow the applicability determinations discussed for new sources. The first definition, however, requires an explanation of how the operator of a major stationary source determines whether a proposed modification will lead to a "significant emissions increase" and a "significant net emissions increase" requiring PSD review. In the following sections, which explain how to make this determination, it is assumed that the source is a major stationary source[88] and that air quality in the area where the source is locating is designated in attainment or unclassified for at least one criteria pollutant.

General Steps for Determining the Whether the Emissions Change and Net
Emissions Change Resulting from Proposed Modification Are Significant
Modifications that do not result in emissions increases above established significance levels for a given pollutant normally do not have to undergo
NSR.[89] Thus, if the modification results in an emissions increase that is
below significance levels, then the analysis is generally complete. However,
if the modification results in a significant increase of a regulated NSR pollutant, then the next step is determining the net emissions change resulting
from the proposed modification. The EPA has recommended the following
steps for calculating whether a source will undergo a significant net emissions
increase as a result of an emissions change associated with a modification:

1. Determine the emissions increases (but not any decreases) from the
   proposed project. If any increases are significant, proceed; if not, the
   source is not subject to review.
2. Determine the beginning and ending dates of the contemporaneous
   period as it relates to the proposed modification.
3. Determine which emissions units at the source experienced (or will
   experience, including any proposed decreases resulting from the proposed project) a credible increase or decrease in emissions during the
   contemporaneous period.
4. Determine which emissions changes are credible.
5. Determine, on a pollutant-by-pollutant basis, the amount of each contemporaneous and credible emissions increase or decrease.
6. Sum all contemporaneous and credible increases and decreases with
   the increase from the proposed modification to determine if a significant net emissions increase will occur.[90]

These steps can also be summarized in a simplified formula as follows:
   Net emissions change
      equals
   Emissions increases associated with the proposed modification
      minus
   Sourcewide creditable contemporaneous emissions *decreases*[91]
      plus
   Sourcewide credible contemporaneous emissions *increases*

These steps are discussed further in the following paragraphs.

Determination of Whether the Proposed Modification Will Result
in a Significant Emissions Increase
The first step in evaluating major modification status is to determine what
emissions increases, without considering any decreases, will be associated with
the proposed modification of the existing major stationary source. If a proposed
change will not result in an increase or potential increase in emissions[92] that

triggers the significant emissions increase thresholds for regulated pollutants, then no net emissions changes need be considered and no further analysis is needed. However, a net emissions change must be calculated for any regulated pollutant for which a proposed modification will result in a potential significant emissions increase.[93]

As with new source evaluation, operators of modified sources may seek to keep emissions below review thresholds by applying emissions control technology or by making other operational changes that will reduce emissions below the significant threshold level. Some agencies, however, indicate that if the operator proposes to take credit for any emissions decrease, including one associated with the proposed modification itself, "all source-wide creditable and contemporaneous emissions increases and decreases of the pollutant subject to netting must be included in the PSD applicability determination."[94]

State regulations should be consulted to determine how "significant emission thresholds" are defined. Under federal regulations, "significant" can be defined in three ways:

1. *"Significant"* means, in reference to a net emissions increase or the potential of a source to emit any of the following pollutants, a rate of emissions that would equal or exceed any of the following rates:

   Pollutant and emission rates
   Carbon monoxide: 100 tons per year (tpy)
   Nitrogen oxides: 40 tpy
   Sulfur dioxide: 40 tpy
   Particulate matter
   25 tpy of particulate matter emissions; 15 tpy of PM_{10} emissions
   Ozone: 40 tpy of volatile organic compounds
   Lead: 0.6 tpy
   Asbestos: 0.007 tpy
   Beryllium: 0.0004 tpy
   Mercury: 0.1 tpy
   Vinyl chloride: 1 tpy
   Fluorides: 3 tpy
   Sulfuric acid mist: 7 tpy
   Hydrogen sulfide (H_2S): 10 tpy
   Total reduced sulfur (including H_2S): 10 tpy
   Reduced sulfur compounds (including H_2S): 10 tpy
   Municipal waste combustor organics (measured as total tetra-through octa-chlorinated dibenzo-p-dioxins and dibenzofurans): 3.2×10^{-6} megagrams per year (3.5×10^{-6} tpy). Municipal waste combustor metals (measured as particulate matter): 14 megagrams per year (15 tpy).
   Municipal waste combustor acid gases (measured as sulfur dioxide and hydrogen chloride): 36 megagrams per year (40 tpy).
   Municipal solid waste landfills emissions (measured as nonmethane organic compounds): 45 megagrams per year (50 tpy).

2. *"Significant" means*, in reference to a net emissions increase or the potential of a source to emit a pollutant regulated under the Clean Air Act that paragraph (1) above does not list, *any* emissions rate.[95]
3. Notwithstanding paragraph (1) of this subsection, *"significant" means* any emissions rate of any new major stationary source or major modification, which would construct within 10 kilometers of a Class I area, and have an impact on such area equal to or greater than 1 $\mu g/m^3$ (twenty-four-hour average).[96]

Any projected or potential emissions increase from the modification will be compared to these significant thresholds. If the number is equal to or greater than the threshold value, further emission netting must be performed (unless, as discussed below, the applicant proceeds to the actual-to-projected-actual test instead of evaluating potential emissions).[97]

Under revisions to the NSR program, increases in emissions resulting from modifications can also be measured by changes in actual emissions. The EPA allows operators of existing sources to project anticipated emissions resulting from modifications using either the "actual-to-projected-actual"[98] applicability test or the "actual-to-potential" test.[99] An emission increase for a modified unit is determined as follows:

New emission rate = (1) If using the actual-to-projected-actual test, the new emission rate is the projected actual emission rate expected in any one of the five years post modification, or ten, if the modification increases the unit's design capacity or PTE;[100] (2) If using the actual-to-potential test, the new emission rate is the PTE (or an emission rate that is enforceable as a practical matter, whichever is lower) for the unit expected after the proposed modification.[101]

minus

Old emission rate = The old emission rate is the "baseline" actual emission rate for the unit. The baseline for existing non-EUSGUs is the average rate at which the emissions unit actually emitted the pollutant during any consecutive twenty-four-month period within the ten-year period immediately preceding construction or submittal of a complete permit application.[102] The baseline for existing EUSGUs is the average rate at which the unit actually emitted the pollutant during any consecutive twenty-four-month period within the five-year period immediately preceding actual construction (based on actual hours of operation, use of raw materials, etc., unless the applicant shows and the EPA and/or a delegated state accepts a demonstration that emissions from some other period are more representative).[103] However, the old emission rate cannot exceed the legally enforceable emission limits for the unit existing at the time of the change.

The actual-to-projected-actual emission test and new baseline definition are the EPA's response to criticism of the actual-to-potential test and are intended to enhance the efficiency of the NSR permit process. Projected actual emissions are the maximum annual rate at which an existing emissions unit is projected to emit a regulated NSR pollutant in any one of the five years following the date the unit resumes normal operation after the project is complete.[104] If an applicant chooses to use this applicability test, it must track emissions from the modified unit for five years, or ten years if the modification increases the unit's design capacity or potential to emit the regulated NSR pollutant.[105] At the end of each year, if post-change annual emissions exceed the baseline actual emissions by a significant amount and differ from projections, the applicant must submit a report to the reviewing authority within sixty days after the end of the year.[106]

Operators can continue to use the actual-to-potential emission test and avoid tracking emissions after the change. However, this test can produce surprising results. For example, suppose an emission unit has a PTE (as well as an allowable emission limit) before modification of 150 VOC tpy. Assume this source has an actual emission rate of 50 tpy for the designated two-year period preceding the change. This means that there is a 100 tpy buffer between the PTE (which is also the allowable emission rate) for the source and the average actual emissions for the source over the past two years. This unit is modified. As a result of the modification, the actual (or "real") emissions for the unit are expected to decrease from 50 to 45 tpy. However, unless the operator takes a limit that is practically enforceable on its PTE (i.e., creates an allowable limit) of no greater than 89 tpy, this change could result in a significant modification because of the method for calculating the difference between the new emission rate and the old emission rate. That is, the emission increase calculation would be as follows:

> *New emission rate* = lower of PTE or allowable emission, which is 150 tpy
> *Old emission rate* = 50 tpy
> *Emission increase* = 100 tpy

Again, one way to keep this change below the 40-tpy significant level for VOCs would be to take an allowable emission limit on the modified source of no greater than 89 tpy, adjusting the calculation as follows:

> *New emission rate* = lower of PTE or allowable emission, which is 89 tpy
> *Old emission rate* = 50 tpy
> *Emission increase* = 39 tpy

This procedure (i.e., comparing projected actual or PTE to baseline actual emissions for the two designated representative years) is the same method by which the "net emissions increase" is determined for netting purposes (i.e., for determining the emissions increase during the contemporaneous period).[107] However, as discussed below, in netting emissions, the period contemporaneous with the modification remains five years prior to the change.

The EPA has indicated that in determining emission increases from modifications, separate modifications need not be added to determine whether a significant net emissions increase threshold has been reached.[108] For example, assume an operator modifies one emission unit and this results in an emissions increase of 20 tpy of VOCs. Eighteen months later the operator modifies a second unit that will result in a VOC emissions increase of

25 tpy. As long as these are separate and unrelated projects, the operator normally does not have to add the two increases. Thus, both would be considered minor modifications and would not be covered under major source NSR.[109]

However, an operator may not avoid major source NSR by artificially breaking a single project into smaller minor projects to avoid significant emissions thresholds for PSD review.[110] Such an attempt to circumvent the NSR process could be considered a sham application and could result in civil and criminal penalties. A key factor in evaluating whether a modification is a sham attempt to avoid PSD review appears to be determining how "related" the projects are (i.e., whether it appears that they could (or should) have been proposed as part of the same project) and over what time period they are being conducted (i.e., the closer in time, the more suspicious the need to break up the proposals).[111]

Determining the Contemporaneous Period for Additional Netting Analysis
If the calculated emissions increase for a proposed modification exceeds a significant emissions threshold, other emissions increases and decreases that have occurred during the "contemporaneous" (or five-year) period must be considered to determine what net emissions change will result from the modification.[112] The next step in this process is to determine the contemporaneous period for the proposed change.

To be considered in the netting process, an emissions change must have occurred within a contemporaneous time period before the start date for the proposed modification.[113] This means that the modification that resulted in the emissions change must have occurred "within a period beginning five years before the date construction is expected to commence on the proposed modification[114] and ending when the emissions increase from the modification occurs."[115]

However, in calculating baseline actual emissions for each contemporaneous change, non-EUSGUs may use the full ten-year look-back period relevant to that change, and with multiunit changes, may select separate two-year periods for each part of the multiunit change, if these changes to the NSR program have been adopted for that state.[116]

Identifying Emission Units That Have Undergone Changes
during the Contemporaneous Period
Actual increases or decreases in emissions for a specific pollutant should be identified on a sourcewide basis. Therefore, all changes in emissions from all sources, including fugitive sources, that have occurred during the contemporaneous period should be identified and quantified.[117]

Determining Which Emissions Changes Are Creditable
To be "creditable" (i.e., to be acceptable for use in the netting process), a contemporaneous emissions[118] reduction currently must be enforceable as a

practical matter.[119] This generally means that a proposed emissions reduction must be verifiable or enforceable on and after the date construction is scheduled to begin on any proposed modification the emissions are used to offset. Emissions decreases claimed from past reductions must also be verifiable and enforceable. Reductions cannot be counted from sources that were never constructed or operated, or from a "Clean Unit."[120]

Creditable contemporaneous emissions increases occur as a result of construction or changes in methods of operation at a facility that increase emissions levels for a given pollutant above the baseline emissions level for that pollutant during the contemporaneous (i.e., five-year) period.[121] The baseline emissions level is determined by calculating actual average emissions using, for non-EUSGUs, any two-year period ten years prior to the change, or for EUSGUs, any two-year period five years prior to the change.[122] For EUSGUs, if there are no representative two-year periods in the five years prior to the change, alternative emissions averaging periods may be proposed.[123]

In addition to the preceding requirements, to be creditable, a permitting agency cannot have "relied upon" an emissions change in issuing a prior PSD permit still in effect at the time of the proposed modification under consideration. That is, if the emissions increase or decrease was considered when issuing an effective PSD permit, those emissions changes have been accounted for once and cannot be relied on again.[124]

Determining the Amount of Contemporaneous Creditable Emissions Changes
As previously explained in calculating the emission change from the modification under review, calculating contemporaneous emission increases and decreases involves comparing the differences between "old" and "new" actual emission rates for the effected emissions unit.

Emission increases are calculated in the same manner as explained earlier. This calculation would be conducted for each emission unit that had undergone some emissions increase within the contemporaneous period under review.[125]

Emission decreases are determined as follows:

Old emission rate = the lower of the old level of actual emissions or the old level of allowable emissions[126]

minus

New emission rate = projected actual or PTE as limited by the allowable emission level for the modified unit[127]

For example, suppose that a source has an allowable emission rate of 100 tpy, actual emissions of 110 tpy (average of two consecutive years from previous ten-year period), and a PTE of 140 tpy, and that after the modification, allowable emissions will be limited (in a practically enforceable permit) to 70 tpy. The credible emissions reduction from this modification would be calculated as follows:

Old emission rate = 100 tpy (this is the lower of actual and allowable emission rates; note that one cannot take advantage of emissions that exceed an allowable rate and that the PTE for the source is not relevant to the calculation)

minus

New emission rate = 70 tpy

equals

Emission decrease = 30 tpy

Again, note that an emissions decrease cannot be credited from a unit that has not been constructed or operated.[128]

Once all contemporaneous increases and decreases have been calculated for the contemporaneous period, they are netted together with any emission increases or decreases, or both, from the modification under consideration. If the net result is greater than a significant threshold, the PSD analysis applies.

Common Problems in Performing Netting Calculations

The EPA indicates that the following are common errors that applicants make in conducting the emissions netting determinations:

- Failing to include contemporaneous emissions increases when considering decreases.
- Improperly using the allowable emissions instead of actual emissions level for the old emissions level for existing units.
- Using prospective (i.e., proposed) unrelated emissions decreases to counterbalance proposed emissions increases without also examining all previous contemporaneous emissions changes.
- Failing to consider a contemporaneous increase creditable because the increase previously netted out of review by relying on a past decrease that was, but is no longer, contemporaneous. If contemporaneous and otherwise creditable, the increase must be considered in the netting calculus.
- Failing to document properly all contemporaneous emissions changes.
- Failing to ensure that emissions decreases are covered by federally or practically enforceable restrictions, which may be a requirement for credibility in some states (see prior discussion of requirement for federal enforceability).[129]

Permittees should carefully evaluate and avoid these errors in calculating PSD applicability to modifications.

Exemptions from Major Modification Status

Certain activities may not be considered to be modifications (i.e., they may not be considered to be "physical changes or changes in methods of operation") covered by the NSR major modification analysis.[130] Examples include the following:

- Routine maintenance, repair, and replacement[131]
- Use of alternate fuels or raw materials under various federal acts[132]

- An increase in hours of operation or in production rate, unless such change would be prohibited under certain practically enforceable permit conditions[133]
- Any change of ownership[134]
- Use of certain pollution control projects[135]
- Clean Units[136]
- Plantwide Applicability Limits, or PALs[137]

These exemptions can exclude from NSR those projects that would otherwise be significant. In recent years, the EPA has undertaken much greater scrutiny of these exemptions, to many of which the EPA applies a case-by-case analysis.

ROUTINE MAINTENANCE, REPAIR AND REPLACEMENT   The most scrutinized exemption has been the "routine maintenance, repair, and replacement" (RMRR). In 1999 and 2000, the EPA initiated NSR enforcement actions against a large number of electric utilities, alleging failure to obtain NSR permits required due to physical changes that constituted major modifications.[138]

Initially, the most publicized case, *In re Tennessee Valley Authority*, involved TVA's replacement of certain equipment which the EPA alleged were clearly physical changes and not "routine maintenance, repair, and replacement."[139] Factors identified in evaluating whether a project can be considered exempt routine maintenance include (1) the nature and extent of the project, (2) the purpose, (3) the frequency, and (4) the cost.[140] The EPA EAB evaluated these factors against the equipment changes TVA had made, including replacement or upgrade of boiler components such as horizontal reheaters, superheaters, economizers, furnaces, waterwalls, and cyclones. The EAB also considered the fact that TVA had classified these projects as capital projects, and that many cost more than any plant's operations and maintenance budget. TVA argued that such changes were standard in the industry; however, the EAB's definition of "routine" requires more than the fact that the changes are simply standard in the industry.

TVA petitioned the Eleventh Circuit for review of the EAB Order. After first holding that the EAB Order was a reviewable final order,[141] the court reconsidered, and surprisingly, on June 24, 2003, held the CAA unconstitutional to the extent that mere noncompliance with the terms of an administrative compliance order (ACO) could be the sole basis for the imposition of severe civil and criminal penalties. The court then held that the ACOs lacked finality, that the court thus lacked jurisdiction to review their validity, and that the EPA was required to prove the existence of a CAA violation in district court, including the alleged violation that caused the EPA to issue the ACO in the first place.[142]

Two subsequent cases reached the merits of the EPA's RMRR allegations. On August 7, 2003, an Ohio district court supported the EPA's enforcement positions in *United States v. Ohio Edison Company*, holding that "routine" maintenance repair and replacement are evaluated on a facility-specific basis rather than across an industry. The Court also held that projections of future emission increases post-production must consider increased utilization.[143] Then, on August 26, 2003, another court reached an almost opposite holding. In *United States v. Duke Energy Corporation*, a North Carolina district court issued orders holding that "routine" maintenance repair and replacement are evaluated on an industry basis, and that NSR is not triggered without an increase in the maximum hourly rate of emissions.[144]

Finally, on November 5, 2003, the day before EPA Administrator Leavitt's swearing in, it appeared that the EPA was dropping all NSR enforcement actions that had not yet been filed as of that date. With this action, the EPA was reported to have dropped complaints not yet filed against approximately fifty facilities already determined to be in noncompliance, and pending investigations of over seventy power companies.[145] The EPA had previously initiated a wide-scale enforcement initiative against petroleum refineries, wood products facilities, and other industries alleging violations of the PSD/NSR rules.

With the EPA's October 27, 2003, promulgation of the RMRR equipment replacement provisions (ERP), operators should find greater certainty when implementing this exemption. The ERP rule exempts from NSR an activity, or aggregations of activities, if (1) the activity involves replacement of any existing component(s) of a process unit with component(s) that are identical or that serve the same purpose as the replaced components(s); (2) the fixed capital cost of the replaced component(s), plus costs of any activities that are part of the replacement activity, does not exceed 20 percent of the current replacement value of the process unit; and (3) the replacement(s) does not alter the basic design parameters of the process unit or cause the process unit to exceed any emission limitation or operational limitation that applies to any component of the process unit and that is legally enforceable.[146] Note that these regulations are being challenged. In addition, they may have to be adopted on a state-by-state basis before becoming applicable.

POLLUTION CONTROL PROJECTS   Before the 2002 NSR revisions, the pollution control project (PCP) exemption from the definition of "major modification" or "WEPCO rule"[147] allowed electric utilities to undertake certain facility modifications involving implementation of pollution control projects without a permit, even if those changes could result in significant increases of other pollutants. This same type of exemption was theoretically allowed for nonutility sources on a case-by-case basis consistent with EPA guidance, but the availability of this exemption was uncertain.[148] With the 2002 revisions, the EPA promulgated a single comprehensive exemption applicable to all sources, covering a variety of defined pollution control projects. These revisions provide greater certainty in obtaining exclusions, and should minimize procedural delays for many projects.[149] A PCP can be any activity, set of work practices, or project undertaken at an existing emissions unit that reduces emissions of air pollutants from such a unit.[150] The PCP definition lists specific types of projects such as the addition of pollution control systems or technologies and projects undertaken to accommodate switching to less polluting fuels or from the use of an ozone-depleting substance to one with a lower ozone depletion potential. This list of potential PCPs is not exclusive, but can be expanded as long as the project can be shown to be environmentally beneficial.[151] Significantly, however, changes to the source that are not necessary to reduce emissions through the PCP are not considered part of the PCP.[152]

CLEAN UNIT EXCLUSION   With the 2002 NSR revisions, the EPA promulgated provisions allowing certain changes to emission units that have undergone emission control satisfying major NSR control requirements (i.e., BACT or LAER), or equivalent emission control requirements, within the past ten years.[153] With these revisions, emission increases at units that have applied BACT or equivalent within the past ten years would not trigger the definition of "major modification" as long as the change does not void the unit's Clean Unit designation.[154] Clean unit status is automatic for sources that have already gone through the major NSR modification process and have accepted BACT or LAER and resulting emission limits. Other units can apply for clean unit status and demonstrate the installation of BACT or LAER equivalent controls. The "clean unit" determination is valid for ten years from the date of the construction of the BACT or equivalent project.[155] Sources may requalify for Clean Unit status even after it has expired by obtaining either a new major NSR permit with current BACT or LAER, or a permit with BACT-equivalent controls.[156] Significantly, emission changes at qualified clean units must not be included in netting analyses unless the changes occur before the clean unit designation, except if the changes are reductions below the emissions level that qualified the unit as a clean unit.[157]

PLANTWIDE APPLICABILITY LIMITS   With the 2002 NSR revisions, the EPA promulgated provisions allowing for Plantwide Applicability Limits (PALs). PALs are a voluntary alternative for determining NSR applicability. PALs are rolling twelve-month, pollutant-specific emission caps that include all conditions necessary to make the limitation enforceable as a practical matter.[158] The PAL levels for each regulated NSR pollutant may be calculated by summing the baseline actual emissions of the PAL pollutant for each emissions unit at an existing major stationary source, and then adding an amount equal to the applicable significant level for the PAL pollutant under the NSR regulations or under the CAA, whichever is lower.[159] The term of a PAL is ten years, and renewal requests must be submitted six months prior to the expiration date of the PAL. The details of the PAL provisions are complicated and beyond the scope of this chapter. However, such a mechanism has already been used by various facilities to achieve greater operating flexibility and is recognized as one of the more beneficial and less controversial of the 2002 NSR revisions.

Determining What Pollutants Must Be Analyzed
under the PSD Pathway

Once it is determined that a project, either a new construction or a major modification, triggers any PSD review applicability threshold, the applicant must perform an emissions impact analysis for all pollutants regulated under the CAA that the source will have the potential to emit in significant amounts and that have not been otherwise exempted from NSR analysis.[160] Significant amounts are defined as discussed in earlier sections.

Preparing the Permit Application

The Process

Once a source has been determined to be subject to PSD analysis, the next step is to prepare a PSD permit application that includes all of the required demonstrations under the program. Preparing a proper construction permit application, one containing all required determinations and demonstrations, is difficult, but it is perhaps the most important step in the PSD process. If prepared correctly, this step can save many headaches, delays, and unnecessary costs.

One of the best ways to avoid substantial delay is to involve—from the outset—all parties that the permittee knows will be commenting on the permit application after its submission. Parties that could need to be involved include the state agency, the EPA, FLMs, local government, and, in some instances, citizens and citizens' groups. If everyone can understand and feel that they are a part of the process that results in the permit application and resulting permit, it is less likely that an involved party will delay or appeal the permit once issued.

A PSD permit application will routinely contain the following major components:

- A determination of BACT to control emissions
- An analysis of any required ambient air quality
- A determination of whether the proposed covered new or modified source will adversely affect ambient air quality, including NAAQS or PSD increments
- An analysis of what impact associated growth will have on the local environment, if applicable
- An analysis of what impact emissions will have on any potentially affected Class I areas, if applicable

BACT Determination

General Principles

A major source subject to PSD review, either as a new source or as a major modification, must determine that BACT will be applied to each emissions unit or other pollutant emitting activity from which there will be any net increase in a pollutant that the facility will emit or have the potential to emit in significant amounts. The BACT determination is required for each pollutant emitted by the source for which there will be a significant increase in emissions.[161]

BACT is defined as

> an emissions limitation (including a visible emission standard) based on the maximum degree of reduction for each pollutant subject to regulation under the Clean Air Act which would be emitted from any proposed major stationary source or major modification which the Administrator, on a case-by-case basis, taking into account energy, environmental, and economic impacts and other costs, determines is achievable for such source or modification through application of production processes or available methods, systems, and techniques, including fuel cleaning or treatment or innovative fuel combustion techniques for control of such pollutant. In no event shall application of best available control technology result in emissions of any pollutant which would exceed the emissions allowed by any applicable standard under 40 CFR Parts 60 [NSPS] and 61 [NESHAP]. If the Administrator determines that technological or economic limitations on the application of measurement methodology to a particular emissions unit would make the imposition of an emissions standard infeasible, a design, equipment, work practice, operational standard, or combination thereof, may be prescribed instead to satisfy the requirement for the application of best available control technology. Such standard shall, to the degree possible, set forth the emissions reduction achievable by implementation of such design, equipment, work practice, or operation, and shall provide compliance by means which achieve equivalent results.[162]

It is the BACT determination that will ultimately allow the reviewing agency to assign emissions limits on the facility. These emissions limits reflect the degree of BACT emissions control applied to the facility, and thus this selection is very important.

The recommended steps for making the BACT determination are as follows:

Step 1: Identify available pollution control options.
Step 2: Eliminate technically infeasible options.
Step 3: Rank remaining control technologies by control effectiveness.
Step 4: Evaluate the most effective controls (considering energy, environmental, and economic impacts) and document the results.
Step 5: Make the BACT selection.[163]

The following paragraphs discuss these steps in more detail.

Identifying Available Pollution Control Options

The first step in the so-called "top-down" BACT analysis[164] is to identify, for each emissions unit, any process or activity emitting a regulated pollutant and, for each regulated pollutant, the potentially available emissions control options. There are two basic types of pollution control technologies: emissions control technologies and emissions control techniques. Potentially available control options are those "air pollution technologies or techniques with a practical potential for application to the emissions unit and the regulated pollutant under evaluation."[165]

To identify these potential control options, the applicant can consult a number of information resources, including the EPA's RACT/BACT/LAER Clearinghouse and Control Technology Center available on the EPA's Web site; technology vendors; federal, state, and local NSR permits and associated inspection and performance test reports; technology or emissions control practices required under other CAA programs; environmental consultants; technical journals, reports, and newsletters; and air pollution control seminars.[166]

This review could include the possibility of "transferring technologies" from other industries to the source, including technologies applied outside of the United States.[167] However, technologies that have not been applied to or permitted for full-scale operations do not necessarily have to be considered because these technologies are not available (i.e., the applicant should be able to purchase or construct a technology or control device that has already been demonstrated in practice).[168] The applicant may also consider technologies still under development, if desirable and appropriate.[169] As a result of this analysis, the applicant can generate a list of potential control options.

Eliminating Technically Infeasible Options

Control options that have been applied or been demonstrated as practical for use with an identical source or with a similar source ordinarily cannot be eliminated unless there are special circumstances that would differentiate use of the option from use at other, similar sources and would make application impracticable. Sources that have not been demonstrated as being practical to use for a source, or pollutant, at a similar source can be eliminated from further consideration if they are not "technically feasible."[170]

The key to determining whether a control option is technically feasible is to evaluate its availability and applicability. An "available technology" is one that has been licensed and can be obtained through ordinary commercial channels, as opposed to a concept or experimental technology.[171] Available technologies should also be "applicable" to be technically feasible.[172]

A technology is applicable if its emissions control qualities or characteristics are physically or chemically compatible with the emissions stream being evaluated, taking into consideration the chemical and physical characteristics of the emissions stream.[173] Again, if the technology has been applied to control analogous emissions, it will generally be considered "applicable."[174] If the technology under consideration is being transferred from one type of source to another or has not previously been demonstrated as being an effective emissions control technology for the source being reviewed, applicability must be determined.[175]

Applicability determinations for transferred or partially demonstrated (i.e., not fully demonstrated on a source identical to the source under review) technologies are normally made by comparing the conditions under which a technology has been successfully applied to those conditions existing for the source being considered. Emissions streams, physical and chemical characteristics, engineering principles, and empirical data should be evaluated in making applicability comparisons. A technology successfully applied or demonstrated at one source may not be applicable at another source because of different circumstances. For example, a water-based scrubber system may be applicable at many sources where water is plentiful, but it may not be applicable where water is a scarce resource. Ultimately, applicability must be determined in conjunction with the reviewing agency.[176] Generally, costs should not be considered in making technical feasibility determinations. Cost is considered later, under the economic impacts analysis step of the BACT determination.

The applicant must clearly identify those sources that are technically infeasible. The applicant is responsible for providing a basis on which the reviewing agency can confirm decisions on technical infeasibility for control options. Control technologies that are not eliminated as technically infeasible remain for further review.[177]

Ranking Remaining Technically Feasible Alternatives by Emissions Control Effectiveness

Control options that are not eliminated are ranked from best to worst according to their emissions reduction potential.[178] Emissions control factors must be identified and quantified in terms (e.g., tons of pollutant eliminated per year) that can then be compared with other potential control options. Source performance levels for technologies with wide ranges of control potentials must be determined (e.g., at what degree of efficiency a particular control technology will be proposed to operate) before comparison and ranking can take place. The applicant should review the most recent regulatory decisions and determinations to establish what the performance levels for a control technology should be.[179] Manufacturing data, engineering estimates, and determinations for other permits should be considered in determining achievable emissions control.[180]

The applicant should prepare a chart with a listing and analysis summary for each feasible technology for each pollutant at each emissions unit.[181] Technologies should be ranked from those achieving the greatest or best emissions reduction to those achieving the least. This chart should also include information on the expected emission rate (e.g., tons per year); emissions performance level (e.g., pollutant removal efficiency); emissions per unit product (e.g., parts per million, lbs/mmBtu); expected emissions reduction (e.g., tons per year); economic impacts of technology (e.g., total annualized costs, cost-effectiveness, incremental costs); environmental impacts resulting from application of technology (e.g., impacts on other media such as soil and water); and energy impacts (e.g., significant energy use or conservation).[182] The information included in the chart will allow the applicant to make a BACT determination.

Evaluating the Most Effective Controls Considering Energy, Environmental, and Economic Impacts and Documenting the Results

The applicant must consider beneficial and adverse energy-consumption, economic, and incidental environmental impacts for possible BACT selections before making a final selection.[183] The applicant should start with the top emissions control option. If the evaluation of this option leads to acceptance as BACT and there are no significant collateral environmental impacts associated with the option (e.g., groundwater or soil contamination), subsequent analysis probably will not be required. If, however, the top emissions control option is rejected, the analysis must be repeated for the next best option and so on until an acceptable option appears. The applicant must then document the basis for the decision to the permitting agency.[184]

In considering energy impacts, the applicant should determine the amount of energy that must be expended to obtain incremental emissions reductions. The key to this analysis is to determine whether there is a significant difference, either positive or negative, in the use of energy associated with the operation of the top emissions control option in comparison to the operation of other, similar, but less effective, control options.[185] Most of the energy considerations involve costs and thus can be factored into the economic impacts analysis. In this analysis, the applicant may consider the scarcity or availability of fuels on a local or regional basis.[186]

The EPA has prepared detailed guidance on how to conduct cost analysis and comparisons between possible emissions control options. Much of this discussion is beyond the scope of this chapter. As an overview, the key steps in the cost-analysis comparison involve identifying and ensuring that design parameters are properly evaluated in light of emissions estimates used in the application; determining and documenting the costs for each element of the control equipment being considered; determining and documenting capital and annual costs of implementing the control option; and comparing incremental costs of certain "dominant emissions control options."[187]

Before an applicant can compare average and incremental cost considerations for control technologies, it must identify and estimate the cost of the control design parameters of the various technologies (e.g., scrubbers, incinerators) being considered and calculate the estimated emissions reduction capability or efficiencies for the various control technologies.[188] Reduction control options may need to be considered at different efficiency levels (e.g., a scrubber operating at 75 percent removal efficiency versus 98 percent removal efficiency). Emissions reduction estimates must not be overestimated or underestimated or the comparison of cost-per-pollution-reduction capability will be skewed. Estimated costs to operate a technology under specific design parameters and at specified control efficiencies must be calculated. This should be done on a per ton basis and a yearly basis.[189]

After design parameters, control efficiencies, and costs are computed, applicants must consider the average and incremental cost-effectiveness for control technologies. "Cost effectiveness" is the economic criterion used to assess the potential for achieving an objective at the least cost.[190] Effectiveness is measured in terms of tons of pollutant removed. Cost is measured in terms of annualized costs.[191] Cost effectiveness can be calculated on an average or incremental basis. Average costs are calculated in terms of the total annual cost for the control option divided by the annual expected emissions reduction for the source. Stated differently, it is the difference between the costs of the uncontrolled (baseline) emission rate and the controlled emission rate.[192]

Incremental cost is the cost per ton reduced and should be considered in conjunction with total average effectiveness. It is an incremental cost comparison of the technology under review to the next most effective control technology being considered.[193] Incremental cost comparisons should be conducted for the "dominant" alternative technologies, those technologies that provide varying degrees of emissions control at different costs. For example, if technologies have vastly different costs and provide the same emissions control and have similar consequential environmental impacts, the more expensive control option could be eliminated without any incremental analysis.[194] Incremental cost analysis can also be used to evaluate control options that can be operated with varying costs over a variety of efficiency ranges (e.g., the cost of operating at 75 percent emissions reduction versus 98 percent reduction).[195]

Ultimately, the primary focus of the economic analysis, from the agency perspective, is comparing costs of control options as an element of their efficiencies to various technologies, not determining whether the total cost is prohibitive to the applicant. This means that when a technology has been successfully applied to a similar source, only significant cost differences (i.e., in average cost-effectiveness or incremental cost) between that source and the applicant's situation will normally justify rejection of the control option.[196]

Finally environmental impacts associated with a particular control technology must be identified in evaluating its control effectiveness. This analysis includes considering any secondary or collateral effects that the use of a control technology might have on the environment. Collateral impacts that should be considered include any waste products or by-products from emissions control equipment that affect water or groundwater; affect soil or air quality (specifically including production of hazardous or toxic air pollutants[197] or other pollutants such as ozone-forming pollutants that affect visibility); result in production of secondary wastes (such as solid or hazardous waste); generate heat; or generate noise.[198] These secondary impacts should be identified for each emissions control technology considered.

Examples of secondary impacts are the production of NO_x from a burner used to control VOC emissions, PM residue (dust) from a filter, or wastewater residual from a wet scrubber.[199] These by-products of emissions control may present particular environmental problems. For example, the dust from the filter may need to be disposed of as hazardous waste, the wastewater may need to be treated before discharge, and the NO_x air emissions may need to be controlled to prevent ozone degradation. These secondary effects may present special problems in particular areas of the country (e.g., where there is limited wastewater discharge capacity, or where ozone formation is driven primarily by NO_x as opposed to VOCs being controlled by the incinerator, or where there is no hazardous waste disposal capacity).

If one control technology provides only slightly better emission controls than the next-best technology, then the less effective technology might be selected over the more efficient one if the more efficient technology has significant secondary environmental impacts associated with its use. In addition, if one technology would produce secondary environmental impacts in an area or region that would be particularly sensitive to them, then this impact may warrant discarding this option in favor of a less effective technology that would not result in the same detrimental consequential impacts.

The BACT Selections

The applicant will continue to evaluate emissions control options until it has selected BACT alternatives for each pollutant subject to PSD evaluation as well as for each emissions unit. Again, if the best pollution control option is not selected, because of economic analysis, energy analysis, or consequential environmental impacts analysis, the reasons must be clearly documented.[200]

The applicant must then propose its BACT selections to the state permitting agency, which makes the final selection. The applicant's primary goal in the top-down analysis is to provide the reviewing agency with sufficient information to verify and accept proposed control options. The more data and verification that the applicant provides (e.g., acceptance at other, similar sources), the easier it will be to have selections approved.[201]

Selection of BACT does not mean that the applicant will be able to demonstrate compliance with applicable state and federal ambient air quality standards, with PSD increments, or with both. Once this evaluation is made, if the source fails to meet these standards, more stringent emissions control measures must be proposed. In addition, states may have individual emissions control requirements that require sources in attainment areas to apply LAER control technology instead of BACT.

Further, BACT selection is routinely treated as an ongoing process until the final permit is issued. If changes in technology occur during the permitting process, the reviewing agency may require the applicant to consider the new controls.[202]

The final result of the BACT process is an enforceable BACT emissions limits and control standard or practice for each pollutant subject to PSD review and for all affected emissions units for which control options must be applied. These BACT emissions limits must be written so that they are verifiable and must allow the operator to determine whether the source is affecting any applicable air quality standard.[203]

Potential Impact of the 1996 Proposed NSR Amendments

As explained, the top-down BACT process involves evaluating and selecting emission control methods by ranking available controls in descending order of effectiveness. The regulated community has experienced significant problems with this process. Under the current system, the scope of what is required to select BACT (i.e., including where the applicant must look) has not been clearly defined. Finding and evaluating the "available" emission control technologies is the applicant's primary responsibility and can be difficult. Another problem has been requiring an applicant to consider new or developing technologies even after its application is completed. On the other hand, operators have not always been allowed to propose and use innovative emission control technologies. In addition, there is no exemption to account for the fact that a covered source may have recently undergone a BACT review or similar emission control process.

The EPA's 1996 proposed NSR amendments would have codified the top-down BACT process with some improvements and allowed the states, under limited circumstances, to use alternative emission control evaluation programs.[204] As described below, the 1996 proposed NSR amendments also sought to clarify some of the points that have previously caused confusion about the BACT selection process.

The RACT/BACT/LAER Clearinghouse (RBLC) is a database of prior RACT/BACT/LAER determinations established to promote the sharing of information about available control options. This is a good place to start in trying to find the right emission control method. With the 1996 proposed NSR revisions, the EPA proposed to modify the RBLC by:

- Requiring states to submit final BACT determinations upon the issuance of a permit[205]
- Focusing resources on categorizing complete and correct information about new permit determinations as opposed to focusing on filling in gaps in former decisions[206]
- Simplifying the selection reporting form to reduce the burden on permitting agencies[207]
- Standardizing emissions units to allow comparison and ranking of emissions control options[208]
- Establishing technical support to identify the most stringent RBLC determinations and follow-up on verification of installation and compliance[209]
- Providing guidance from the EPA on rankings of certain technologies for particular processes and pollutants[210]

Improvements to the RBLC should make it easier for the applicant to identify demonstrated available emission controls that could satisfy NSR (PSD and nonattainment) review requirements.

In addition, to reduce the applicant's burden to investigate new technologies, the EPA proposed to limit the number of sources an applicant must investigate regarding control technologies. The five required source groups are as follows:

1. The EPA's RBLC
2. Major source construction permits issued pursuant to Parts C (PSD) and D (nonattainment) of Title I of the CAA

3. Emission limits contained in federally approved implementation plans, excluding emission limitations established by permits issued pursuant to programs for nonmajor sources
4. Permits and standards developed under Sections 111 and 112 of the CAA
5. All control technology documents and control technology guidelines issued by the EPA[211]

Of greatest importance to regulated sources, this proposed revision authorizes the permitting authority, in most cases, to end consideration of new and evolving control technologies when the permittee submits a complete application. However, those commenting on the permit application could identify technologies that have not been evaluated.[212]

The proposed NSR revisions were intended to facilitate pollution prevention efforts by limiting the risks incurred by applicants listing undemonstrated technologies as BACT. If a waiver is granted, the operator would have had two to five years to demonstrate successful implementation of the control technology.[213]

Finally, with the 1996 proposed NSR revisions, the EPA proposed guidance on what constitutes a complete permit application. This guidance should make it easier to prepare a satisfactory application, and thus to begin the cutoff date from which additional technology review should not be required.[214] These proposals have yet to be acted upon.

Ambient Air Quality Impacts Analysis

Required Demonstration
Each applicant must demonstrate that the new emissions from its proposed new source or regulated modification, plus any emissions resulting from associated growth from the project, and emissions from existing sources will not have an unacceptable impact on ambient air quality.[215] At a minimum, the applicant must analyze each regulated pollutant that will be emitted in significant amounts.[216]

For criteria pollutants, this analysis involves demonstrating that emissions from the source considered with existing emissions will not exceed any primary or secondary NAAQS or PSD increments.[217] For noncriteria pollutants, including air toxics, this involves considering what impact these emissions might have on other air quality standards (e.g., air toxics, NSPS, NESHAP) and demonstrating that the emissions will not otherwise have a negative impact on sensitive receptors.[218]

The required analysis must be conducted in accordance with 40 C.F.R. § 52.21 or with any state-approved PSD program requirements. Each analysis must consider such unique factors as ambient air quality standards, meteorological conditions, sensitive receptors (including those in Class I areas), and area topography. Analysis will involve assessment of existing air quality and prediction of the expected impact of new emissions (i.e., through dispersion modeling).[219] Before analyzing criteria pollutants, the applicant must understand NAAQS and PSD increments and how impacts on these standards are considered.

NAAQS

As indicated, NAAQS are "ceilings" on maximum allowable concentrations for criteria pollutants. NAAQS are measured in terms of the total concentration of the pollutant in the atmosphere. An applicant determines a new source's impact by (1) modeling for the predicted impact from that source for each covered criteria pollutant; (2) adding this concentration to the background concentration for the pollutant; and (3) adding this total to any secondary emissions for the pollutant that are expected as a result of the modification.[220]

PSD Increments

PSD increments specify the maximum allowable ambient air quality concentration increases that may occur for a given criteria pollutant above a "floor" concentration level known as the baseline concentration level. Baseline concentration levels are specified for specific "baseline areas," and they are usually calculated by intrastate areas (i.e., by county or municipality).[221] Baseline concentrations are defined for various criteria pollutants over different average time periods. Once the entire increment has been "consumed," no more major sources or major modifications may be constructed.

There are three types of PSD increments, established according to the degree of growth or protection desired for the area of concern. Class I areas (national parks, forests, landmarks, etc.) have the smallest increments and thus permit the least amount of air quality degradation.[222] Class II areas have the next smallest increments and Class III areas have the largest increments.[223] No source or combination of sources can increase pollution for a covered criteria pollutant in a manner that would exceed the increment established for that pollutant above its baseline concentration level.

When evaluating any available PSD increment, the applicant must determine the baseline concentration, if one exists, for that pollutant in the area that the new or modified source will affect. To complete this rather complicated analysis, the applicant must consider three dates: the major source baseline date, the trigger date, and the minor source baseline date.

The major source baseline date is a predetermined date "after which actual emissions associated with construction (i.e., physical changes or changes in method of operation) at a major stationary source affect the available PSD increment."[224] Other changes in actual emissions "occurring at any source after the major source baseline date do not affect the increment, but instead (until after the minor source baseline date is established) contribute to the baseline concentration."[225] The trigger date is a preset date after which the minor source baseline date may first be established.[226] The minor source baseline date is "the earliest date after the trigger date on which a complete PSD application is *received* by the permit reviewing agency."[227]

Any pollutant that will be emitted at significant thresholds by the first complete PSD application triggers the minor source baseline for that pollutant. After the minor source baseline date is triggered for a pollutant, emissions from any source for that pollutant affect the available PSD increment. Thus, the minor source baseline date is considered the "baseline date" for a criteria pollutant.[228]

The ambient air concentration for a covered criteria pollutant (NO_2, SO_2, and PM_{10}) at the baseline date sets the floor for increment calculations. From this floor concentration, the applicant, as explained later, must calculate whether emissions from the proposed new or modified source combined with emissions from existing minor and major sources will exceed the allowed ambient concentration increase (i.e., the allowed increment) for the pollutant being evaluated.

Any emissions for a given covered criteria pollutant that occur before the major source baseline date simply add to the "background concentration" level for that pollutant. Any increase in the covered criteria pollutant that occurs from a new or modified source and that occurs after the major source baseline date consumes some increment, but that is not calculated until after a source triggers the minor source baseline date. After this later date, any new or modified sources, either minor or major, emitting the covered criteria pollutant will affect the available increments. If these sources increase emissions for the covered pollutant, the available increment will shrink; if they decrease emissions for the pollutant, the increment may increase (i.e., if they are enforceable and verifiable).[229]

Procedure for Determining Ambient Impact

The following discussion provides an outline of how an applicant evaluates existing ambient air quality and then demonstrates whether or not the proposed new or modified emissions source will have any adverse impacts on air quality.

The applicant must consider any pollutants that the covered new or modified facility will have the potential to emit. Evaluating possible impacts of emissions the source will have the potential to emit in significant amounts will be particularly important. This includes criteria and noncriteria pollutants. The applicant should identify dispersion modeling protocols that will allow it to determine what impact potential emissions will have on air quality in the area surrounding the facility. The applicant should consult with state agencies and the EPA to determine the proper modeling protocols. Part of the modeling process requires the applicant to input meteorological data. At the screening stage, the applicant will probably be able to use existing data to satisfy this input requirement. This issue should be discussed with the state and the EPA to determine whether sufficient relevant and reliable data exists to conduct the initial modeling. Typically, the initial modeling will be a screening model, which is more basic than models used in a full impacts analysis. However, these models can provide sufficient data to eliminate sources and pollutants that need no further evaluation.

The initial analysis for air quality impacts from the proposed new or modified covered facility will consider the potential impact the source will have on air quality without considering impacts from other sources. For any pollutant the source will emit (or have the potential to emit) in significant amounts, the facility will most likely be required to conduct initial dispersion modeling. This is done to determine whether emissions from the source by itself have the potential to exceed certain specified significance levels for air quality impacts. The values exist for criteria pollutants and are calculated over various averaging periods.

If a source alone will not emit any covered pollutant in concentrations that will cause exceedance in any averaging period for significance levels, then no further evaluation of air quality may be required. For pollutants modeled as potentially exceeding significance values, a full impacts analysis will likely be required.

There are four general steps to a full impacts analysis. The first step is to determine whether there is a need to perform any preapplication ambient air quality monitoring. That is, part of the full impacts analysis involves considering impacts on existing air quality; models require input on existing conditions, including meteorological conditions.[230] As indicated, if existing data on ambient air quality is relevant and reliable, it can be used in lieu of additional monitoring. Whether the existing data will be sufficient will depend in large part on how current it is and how close existing monitoring stations are to the proposed location.[231] A sufficiency determination must ultimately be made in conjunction with state and federal authorities.

If existing data is not adequate for impacts analysis, the applicant must conduct preapplication ambient air quality monitoring. Monitoring is typically required for a period of at least twelve months.[232] The permitting agency, however, has discretion to accept data collected over shorter time periods, although no time period may be less than four months.[233] In addition, under certain circumstances postconstruction monitoring may be substituted for preapplication monitoring.[234] Valid circumstances could include threatened NAAQS or PSD increment violations and uncertain modeling databases.[235]

The second general step in the analysis is to determine the impact area. Initial screening modeling allows the applicant to determine the "area of impact" for the facility. This is the area that must be evaluated further in the full impacts analysis and is the perimeter in which the source will have a potential to affect ambient air quality in a manner that will exceed designated significance levels for air quality impacts.[236] The impacts area may be limited to state boundaries.

The third general step in the analysis is to develop emissions inventories. Before emissions impacts can be analyzed, the applicant must develop and consider an inventory of those sources that emit the same pollutants the applicant is evaluating. The applicant must consider emissions from these other sources in determining the total impact the new emissions from the applicant's project will have on air quality.[237]

When preparing the NAAQS inventory, the applicant must consider nearby major sources and various other background sources that will affect air quality for the pollutant being evaluated.[238] The two source groups should be considered as follows:

- For a NAAQS demonstration, all existing and proposed "nearby sources" must be identified and accounted for in the modeling analysis. Nearby sources are those point sources "expected to cause a significant concentration gradient in the vicinity of the proposed new source or modification." Vicinity may be defined as the "impact area."[239] Collecting information on nearby sources ordinarily begins by identifying nearby major sources. For such sources, emissions data must be collected so that the impact from these facilities can be considered when determining the emissions impact from the proposed new or modified facility. The data collected for these facilities can be the "actual operating data" or can be based on the "maximum potential to emit" for the sources. Obviously, it will take more time to collect actual data for each nearby major source, but this may be necessary if the emissions impact from the proposed project will approach exceeding NAAQS or PSD increment limits.[240]
- Other background sources must be considered in completing the NAAQS inventory, if such sources are "expected to cause a significant concentration gradient in the vicinity of the proposed new source or modification." Detailed modeling information may not be required for these sources, and these sources may be adequately accounted for in the background ambient air quality data existing for the impact area.[241] In addition, screening models may be used to estimate impacts from these background sources.

As for the PSD inventory, there are two primary aspects to consider:

- The PSD inventory must identify the emissions impact from all relevant and applicable sources that could consume increment for the pollutant being evaluated within the impact area.[242]
- Increment-consuming sources located outside of the impact area must be considered if it can reasonably be determined that they will affect the increment consumption within the impact area. The applicant should work with local, state, and federal agencies to identify other increment consuming sources for which data must be gathered.[243]

Finally, the fourth general step in the full impacts analysis is to conduct the required air quality compliance demonstrations. Dispersion modeling runs are conducted for each covered pollutant for which a NAAQS exists. Modeling takes into account the proposed emissions impact developed from the inventory data for nearby major and background sources.[244] Once this step is completed, the estimated emissions concentration impact can be compared to allowable NAAQS requirements. No estimated impact can exceed any NAAQS. If it would, the applicant must determine a way to reduce the proposed emissions impact (e.g., through more stringent controls or through offsets).[245]

In addition, dispersion modeling runs are conducted for each covered pollutant for which a PSD increment exists. Modeling takes into account the proposed emissions impact developed from the PSD inventory for PSD increment-consuming sources. From these dispersion models, the applicant can determine whether the total impact from the new or modified source and existing sources will consume the available PSD increment. If so, additional analysis is required (i.e., going back and using actual modeling data for sources versus using maximum potential to emit) or the applicant must determine a way to reduce the source's proposed emissions impact to bring it within the allowable PSD increment. Even if a source meets PSD increment requirements, it cannot under any circumstances exceed a NAAQS limitation.[246]

Additional Impacts Analysis

The applicant may be required to prepare an additional impacts analysis for each pollutant regulated under the CAA that the new or modified source will emit.[247] This analysis considers the impact that emissions from the facility and emissions expected from "associated growth"[248] will have on air, soils, vegetation, and visibility.[249] "Although each applicant for a PSD permit is required to perform an additional impacts analysis, the depth of analysis will generally depend on existing air quality, the quantity of emissions, and the sensitivity of local soils, vegetation, and visibility in the source's impact area."[250] General elements of the additional impacts analysis are discussed in the following paragraphs.

Associated Growth Analysis

The associated growth analysis considers emissions impacts expected from reasonably foreseeable residential, commercial, or industrial growth associated with the proposed new or modified facility.[251] This determination involves considering factors such as whether the new or modified source will require an additional workforce that will in turn require new housing and commercial stores to service them and whether it is reasonably foreseeable that satellite or support facilities will locate within the impact area as a result of the new or modified source.[252] An emissions inventory is developed for expected associated growth.[253]

Associated growth impact analysis is often uncertain when a major new facility is locating in an area. It is often difficult to predict what impact the source will ultimately have. The applicant should not, however, need to be a fortune-teller. Associated growth impacts, like secondary impacts, should have some degree of specificity, capable of being defined and quantified and having an expected impact in the same general area as the source under consideration.[254]

Air Quality Impact Analysis

The applicant should evaluate the total air quality impact that will result from the new or modified source in the area in which the source will be located. This involves consideration of the combined emissions impact from the new or modified source, any associated growth connected with the new or modified source, any nonrelated proposed new or modified source that has been permitted but is not yet in operation, and consideration of background emissions resulting from existing sources. Modeling of the above information is often required to demonstrate that total emissions from the new or modified source, combined with emissions from associated growth and existing sources, will not adversely impact the air quality of the area.[255]

Note that the impacts analysis here is not limited to pollutants that the source emits in significant amounts.[256] Thus, the applicant may have to consider potential impacts from pollutants that it has not previously modeled. This may include potential impacts from air toxic compounds that, although not emitted in significant amounts, could have an adverse impact. The requirements of a "no impact" determination are largely left to state and federal permit agencies and the applicant should work with these agencies to develop the requirements. Existing air quality standards provide a good guideline for demonstration. For example, for air toxic compounds, the applicant should be able to demonstrate that emissions from the new or modified covered source will satisfy state or federal air toxic program requirements, or both.

Soils and Vegetation Analysis

The applicant may be required to assess whether any emissions of regulated pollutants from the facility will have an adverse impact on the soil and vegetation in the area surrounding the facility. This usually involves determining whether there are any particularly sensitive receptors in the impact area surrounding the facility that would be adversely affected by the total expected emissions from the new or modified covered facility plus any emissions from associated growth.[257] Sensitive receptors may include local crops, parks, and the like. An inventory of potential sensitive receptors may need to be developed in cooperation with appropriate state agencies.[258]

Visibility Impairment Analysis

The applicant should consider whether the emissions from the new or modified source, combined with existing emissions and emissions expected from associated growth, will have an adverse impact on visibility in the area surrounding the project. The primary emphasis of this analysis should be the impacts area. The EPA has set out a screening process for visual impacts impairment, which essentially involves determining the area's existing visual quality and then screening for potential impacts.[259] This demonstration is separate and distinct from the Class I area visibility impacts analysis discussed in the next section.[260]

Class I Area Impacts Analysis

In completing the PSD analysis, the applicant should evaluate what analysis it may (or will) need to prepare to demonstrate that the proposed new or modified source will not have any unacceptable negative impact on Class I areas.[261] Before the applicant begins preparing a PSD application, it should attempt to verify what type of impact its proposed project might have on Class I areas. Initial steps involve determining that the projected emissions should not violate a Class I increment and could also involve discussions with the state and FLMs about potentially affected Class I areas.

Once it is determined that a permit will not violate a Class I increment, the federal PSD regulations may not be read to require the applicant specifically to conduct any further Class I impacts analysis.[262] The applicable state permitting agency, however, can require that this additional analysis be completed before it will consider the application "complete." If the applicant does not prepare a Class I area impacts analysis for potentially affected areas, the state will need to prepare it for these areas.[263] Thus, when applicable, it is in the applicant's best interest to complete this analysis.

Determining additional Class I area impacts (i.e., beyond Class I increment violations) has proven increasingly controversial in recent years, as FLMs have begun to play a more active role in the PSD review process and have tried to block construction of a number of projects. The first part of this analysis is to identify the Class I areas that must be considered.

Identifying Potentially Affected Class I Areas

The applicant should consult with the local permitting agency to identify all Class I areas located within a one-hundred-kilometer radius of the new or modified facility (and sometimes farther).[264] Any Class I areas located within this radius are potentially affected areas and may need further evaluation. In addition, some FLMs have taken the position that projects within two hundred kilometers of Class I areas should be considered for impacts.[265]

Identifying Air Quality–Related Values for Potentially Affected Class I Areas

The applicant should contact FLMs for each potentially affected Class I area to identify any air quality–related values (AQRVs) for these areas.[266] AQRVs are specific attributes of Class I areas that deterioration of air quality may negatively impact.[267] Examples of AQRVs are specific types of plants or animals that may be particularly sensitive to increased emissions of certain pollutants.[268]

Assessing Possible Adverse Impacts on Class I Areas

Recall that there are special increments for Class I areas that are more stringent than those for Class II or III areas.[269] Of course, a source must not violate any of the Class I increments.

The applicant should consider, through dispersion modeling or other means, the potential impact of the emissions that the new or modified source will make on each identified AQRV in the potentially affected Class I area. This may involve demonstrating what the change in air quality impact for each pollutant of concern is expected to be in the Class I area as a result of emissions from the new or modified source.[270] This could also involve a commitment to conduct biological studies, either pre- or post-application, and to gather and submit information from other sources on the expected impact from predicted emissions levels.

One specific AQRV that demands special attention is determining what impact emissions from the new or modified source might have on visibility in the potentially affected Class I area. The visibility in national parks and forests has been impaired from ozone formation associated with increased emissions of VOCs and NO_x.[271] The applicant may be required to analyze whether emissions from its covered facility are expected to have an adverse impact on visibility of the Class I area.[272] An adverse impact on visibility occurs when emissions interfere with the "management, protection, preservation, or enjoyment of a visitor's visual experience of a Class I area."[273]

The FLM makes recommendations on adverse impact on a case-by-case basis, "taking into account the geographic extent, duration, intensity, frequency, and time of visibility impairment, and how these factors correlate with (1) times of visitor use of the Class I area, and (2) the frequency and timing of natural conditions that reduce visibility."[274]

Undergoing FLM Review

When the state agency receives notice that an operator intends to submit a PSD application with the potential to impact a Class I area adversely, the agency will contact the FLM for the Class I area within thirty days of receiving notice. After receiving a complete application, the reviewing agency will provide written notice to the FLM within thirty days and within sixty days of any public hearing on the permit determination.[275] For this reason, it is often prudent to involve FLMs in affected PSD projects from the outset. They are thus made "part of the process" and can provide valuable insight on how to avoid problems later in the application process.

After reviewing a PSD application, the FLM may determine that the proposed project will have no adverse impact on potentially affected Class I areas or may recommend that the project may not be permitted or that it may be permitted only after certain changes are made that will lessen the potential impact on Class I areas.[276] If the reviewing agency does not follow the FLM's recommendations, the permitting agency may be required to provide a public hearing, during which it would explain its decision or inform the public of where the relevant information may be obtained regarding the agency's decision. In addition, the FLM may appeal the permit.[277] To resolve potential conflicts with FLMs, the applicant can offer to negotiate. Possible areas of negotiation could include commitments to install more stringent control technology, performance of postconstruction monitoring in Class I areas, and commitments to obtain offsets for certain pollutants. An applicant may favor these approaches rather than having the final construction permit delayed by appeals.

Effect of the 1996 Proposed NSR Amendments on Review of Class I Area Impacts
The 1996 proposed NSR amendments involved extensive changes to the regulation of air quality in Class I areas, including a focus on better defining the role of the FLM. The full extent of these proposed changes goes beyond the scope of this chapter. However, some of the highlights of these amendments are addressed here, pending possible future agency action on these proposed revisions.

The 1996 proposed NSR amendments gave basic definitions to the terms "AQRV" and "adverse impact," which are currently undefined. The proposed definitions could prove to be too general to provide any real restriction or insight into what these terms may include. However, the proposed amendments clearly identified the need for FLMs to attempt to define more precisely what AQRVs are and what adversely affects them.[278]

The 1996 proposed NSR amendments recognized the role of FLMs as having the primary responsibility for protecting the air quality in Class I areas by identifying adequate AQRVs. Not all NSR applications should trigger Class I analysis. The proposed amendments provided that Class I analysis will be triggered when FLMs (or certain other government officials) file a notice alleging that emissions from a proposed permit may cause or contribute to changes in air quality for a Class I area and also identify the potential adverse impact.[279] FLMs must provide certain minimum information about Class I areas and potential adverse impacts to affected permit applicants. In addition, the proposed NSR revisions attempted to coordinate action better between the FLMs and permitting authorities. The proposed regulations may codify the requirement that permitting authorities provide notice of major NSR permit applications to FLMs responsible for Class I areas within one hundred kilometers of the proposed NSR project. The proposal also indicated that sources locating beyond the one-hundred-kilometer radius may still be required to conduct a Class I impacts analysis.[280]

The 1996 proposed NSR revisions also proposed significant and *de minimis* levels for better determining when a Class I analysis should be required.[281] The revisions also provided that when a proposed major NSR permit application may negatively affect a Class I area, certain offsets could be needed to mitigate that impact while still allowing the project. Offsets have commonly been requested by FLMs for PSD permits locating near Class I areas—even though offsets would not normally be required in attainment areas. This presents a problem in attainment areas where offsets are commonly unavailable. Under the 1996 proposed revisions, FLMs could also require post-modification verification (i.e., emission monitoring) on the effect of mitigating emission offsets.[282]

Processing the Permit Application

Once the permit application is submitted to the state review agency,[283] there are a number of general steps to the review.[284]

The Completeness Determination

Once the reviewing agency receives the permit application, it must determine that all required information is included and that all required air quality demonstrations, modeling, preapplication monitoring, and the like have been completed.[285] This stage of the process can cause much delay because the state agency may need to contact the applicant repeatedly to obtain all of the needed information. Typically, agency review time frames do not begin until the application is complete.[286] This required "completeness" determination is the reason that detailed up-front work on the application is necessary to avoid subsequent delays.

Review by State and Federal Agencies

After receiving a complete application, the state agency must review all of the applicant's determinations and make its own assessment of those determinations. The critical reviews usually focus on selection of BACT and the adequacy of demonstrations regarding the potential impact on air quality.

The state will forward the complete application to the appropriate regional EPA office, and the regional office, with guidance from headquarters when necessary, will independently review the permit. If the EPA has been involved from the outset, there should be no major surprises. The EPA is usually interested in BACT determinations and the adequacy of potential impacts demonstrations. The agency is also interested in ensuring that requirements under the NSR program are uniformly enforced across the country. As explained earlier, the FLMs for potentially affected Class I areas must also complete their review during this time period.

Issuance of Draft Permits

Once the state agency is satisfied with the permit application, it may issue draft PSD construction permits.[287] These construction permits contain items such as BACT commitments, emissions limits, emissions monitoring, and record-keeping and reporting requirements. These construction permits usually constitute a "full permit" that can be rolled over into an operating permit when construction is complete.[288]

Public Comment Period

Once the draft permits are issued, the state agency must provide an opportunity for public review and comment.[289] The review period must be no less than thirty days.[290] The state agency must make a copy of the application and draft permits available to any interested parties.[291]

The review period must also afford an opportunity for a public hearing. One mechanism that can avoid delay is to give notice of the public comment period and the date for a public hearing, if one is requested, at the same time so that the periods will run consecutively. Public notice is normally placed in the local or regional newspaper for the area in which the new or modified covered source will be located.[292] As indicated, affected FLMs and the EPA must have an opportunity to comment during the public notice period and must be given notice of the comment period.

The applicant may also want to use the public comment period to review the draft construction permits in detail and to request any desired changes. These changes might include considerations of start-up requirements, emissions monitoring requirements, and other factors that the operator may have to face as operating requirements. In addition, considerations for "ramp-up" periods (e.g., testing requirements that require the source to be at maximum production capacity within short time periods) may have to be analyzed.

Response to Comments

If comments are submitted, the applicant's response is often crucial. The state agency issuing the permit must respond to the comments, but no one understands the detailed analysis in the permit application better than the applicant.[293] Therefore, the applicant should do everything possible to answer comments that are submitted. These comments provide support to the state's decision to issue the permit and provide the state with a starting point to make its own response to comments. Ultimately, the state will respond to most comments. As part of this process, the state agency may seek additional information from the applicant.[294]

Final Construction Permits

When the reviewing agency has responded to comments, it will be in a position to issue final PSD construction permits. These permits normally will not be effective until after the time for potential appeals has run and after any administrative appeals are resolved.[295] Therefore, construction of the new or modified covered source normally cannot begin until the administrative appeals time frame runs or until any administrative appeals are resolved. The time in which to request an administrative appeal may vary, but it is normally fifteen to thirty days.[296] In addition, a state may mandate that those who do not submit comments during the public comment period are barred from raising issues on appeal. If there is an appeal, the applicant should determine whether this requirement exists in its state.

Impact of Administrative Appeals

The process for administrative appeals varies from state to state, but appeals involving complex determinations such as PSD decisions often take six months to a year, or even longer, to resolve. The appeal provides an administrative level of review for a final agency decision. An administrative judge, hearing officer, or board for the state agency issuing the permit usually hears the appeal. Until administrative appeals are resolved, the applicant normally cannot begin actual construction of the covered source.

Impact of Judicial Appeals

When administrative appeals are resolved, the losing party may normally appeal to the state court system for further review. The standard for reviewing agency decisions at the judicial level varies from state to state, but it is usually a strict standard—a court will not generally overturn a reviewing agency's determination unless there is a lack of substantive evidence to support the agency's decision to issue or deny a permit.

In addition, once administrative appeals are exhausted, construction permits normally become effective and construction can begin on the new or modified source unless the party appealing to the courts seeks an injunction. Injunctive relief normally requires a demonstration that the appealing party is likely to succeed on the merits of the appeal and that irreparable harm is likely to result if the injunction is not granted. This is a difficult standard to meet.

Operating Permits

Once the new or modified covered source is constructed, the construction permits for that source are typically "rolled over" into operating permits. The original construction permits may need to be altered to become operating permits. Sources subject to PSD will need to obtain Title V permits. (See Chapters 15 and 16 for further guidance on Title V.)

Nonattainment Area Applicability Program

Differences between the PSD and Nonattainment Area Applicability Permit Review Pathways

This chapter does not fully discuss the nonattainment analysis permit review pathway because this pathway is similar to the PSD permit review process. The applicant must go through most of the stages previously discussed for PSD pathways, and, thus, the reader should refer to the earlier sections of this chapter.

The main differences in the nonattainment analysis process center on the fact that the applicant must demonstrate that the emissions from a new or modified source locating in a nonattainment area will not make the nonattainment condition worse or prevent the area from complying with NAAQS requirements. This section focuses on some of the key differences between the nonattainment analysis and PSD review pathways:

1. The definition of stationary source
2. Applicability thresholds
3. Applicability to criteria pollutants
4. Applicability to major modifications
5. LAER versus BACT review
6. Emissions offsets
7. Certification of compliance for other sources within the state

Definition of Stationary Source

There are two ways in which an applicant can evaluate emissions from a new or modified stationary source. These are the "plantwide stationary source" definition and the now rare "dual source" definition. The option of using a plantwide definition was added in October 1981. The definition the plant must use depends on the definition used to define the source in the applicable SIP.[297]

The definition of "plantwide" is the same as that discussed earlier to define PSD stationary sources. Essentially, this definition requires analysis of physical or operational changes that result in a significant net emissions increase at the entire plant. Thus, if the operator of an existing source plans to add a new source of emissions and also plans to reduce an existing source of emissions, these changes can cancel each other to avoid review. Thus, the source nets out of NSR.[298]

As to the "dual source" definition,[299] "The dual source definition of stationary source treats each emissions unit as (1) a separate, independent stationary source, and (2) a component of the entire stationary source."[300] Thus, a stationary source is both a building, structure, or facility and an installation (i.e., individual piece of equipment). Consequently, "emissions from each physical or operational change at a plant are reviewed both with and without regard to reductions elsewhere at the plant."[301] The NSRWM gives the following as an example:

> For example, a power plant is an existing major SO_2 source in an SO_2 nonattainment area. The power plant proposes to 1) install SO_2 scrubbers on an existing boiler and 2) construct a new boiler at the same facility. Under the "plantwide" definition, the SO_2 reductions from the scrubber installation could be considered, along with other contemporaneous emissions changes at the plant and the new emissions increase of the new boiler to arrive at the source's net emission increase. This might result in a net emissions change which would be below the SO_2 significance level and the new boiler would "net" out of review as [a] major modification. Under the dual source definition, however, the new boiler would be regarded as a[n] individual source and would be subject to nonattainment NSR requirements if its potential emissions exceed the 100 tpy threshold. The emissions reduction from the scrubber could not be used to reduce net source emissions, but would instead be regarded as an SO_2 emissions reduction from a separate source.[302]

Major Source Thresholds

Like PSD review, nonattainment analysis review applies only to new "major stationary sources" or "major modifications" to existing sources that would emit "major" amounts of pollutants for which the area is designated in nonattainment.[303] For purposes of the nonattainment analysis pathway, major stationary source thresholds vary depending on the severity of the nonattainment for the area. The definition of "major source" also varies.[304] First, it applies to stationary sources that emit or have the potential to emit the following pollutants in the specified quantities:

- **Ozone:**[305] (1) in "marginal" and "moderate" nonattainment areas, stationary sources that emit or have the potential to emit 100 tpy of VOCs or NO_x;[306] (2) in "serious" nonattainment areas, stationary sources that emit or have the potential to emit 50 tpy of VOCs or NO_x; (3) in "severe" nonattainment areas, stationary sources that emit or have the potential to emit 25 tpy of VOCs or NO_x; (4) in "extreme" nonattainment areas, stationary sources that emit or have the potential to emit 10 tpy of VOCs or NO_x; and (5) in "transport regions" (not classified as severe or extreme), stationary sources that emit or have the potential to emit 50 tpy of VOCs and 100 tpy of NO_x.
- **Carbon monoxide:** In serious nonattainment areas, stationary sources that emit or have the potential to emit 50 tpy of carbon monoxide.[307]
- **PM_{10}:** In serious nonattainment areas, stationary sources that emit or have the potential to emit 70 tpy of PM_{10}.[308]

Second, "major source" relates to any physical change or change in method of operation at an existing nonmajor source that constitutes a major stationary source by itself.[309] Note that states may set lower thresholds in their NSR programs[310] and that, unlike PSD, there is no 250-tpy category in nonattainment analysis review. Modifications to existing "major stationary" sources are covered if they exceed certain "significant net increase" values, discussed earlier in the section on PSD analysis, for pollutants for which the area is designated in nonattainment and for which the source is a major source.[311] Similarly, changes to nonmajor sources are covered only if emissions or potential emissions resulting from the modification will, by themselves, meet or exceed major source thresholds for the nonattainment analysis pathway.

Applicability to Pollutants

Nonattainment analysis review applies to emissions of any criteria pollutant for which the area is designated in nonattainment and for which the new or modified covered source is major and will cause a significant increase (and significant net emissions increase under the plantwide source definition).[312] With limited exceptions, such as discussed in the following paragraphs, significant emissions thresholds are identical to those discussed in the PSD pathway. Note the specificity of the nonattainment analysis program. Unlike the PSD program, the nonattainment analysis program does not require the covered source to evaluate all pollutants regulated under the federal CAA. Nonattainment analysis is specific to criteria pollutants for which the source is major and for which the area is in nonattainment.

Applicability to Major Modifications

The 1990 CAA Amendments made certain modifications to the procedures for determining applicability of nonattainment NSR to major modifications that occur in certain designated areas, such as serious, severe, and extreme ozone nonattainment areas.[313] Differences include lowering the emission threshold numbers for significant emission rates triggering the nonattainment area program process and placing more stringent limitations on how modifications must be evaluated.[314]

The 1996 proposed NSR amendments would have implemented the effect of the 1990 CAA Amendments for serious, severe, and extreme ozone nonattainment areas by revising the existing NSR regulations.[315] These proposed amendments have not been acted upon to date.

Lowest Achievable Emission Rate Determination

The technology selection under nonattainment analysis review differs from the BACT selection. Operators of sources subject to nonattainment analysis review must select technology that satisfies the more stringent LAER standard for covered pollutants.[316] LAER is defined as

> the most stringent emission limitation which is contained in the implementation plan of any State for such class or category of source, unless the owner or operator of the proposed source demonstrates that such limitations are not achievable; *or* the most stringent emission limitation which is achieved in practice by such class or category of source.[317]

Therefore, the operator of a source undergoing nonattainment analysis review must consider LAER to be the most stringent emissions limit found in a SIP for its class or source category unless (1) a more stringent limit has been shown to be achievable in practice or (2) the SIP limit has been shown to be unachievable by the applicant.[318]

Applicants select LAER technology in a similar manner as BACT, except that there is no consideration of economic, energy, or environmental factors. The only cost consideration is whether the cost of a proposed emissions control is so prohibitive that it has never been applied at any other source because it would have been too expensive to build the source.[319] Even then, cost alone may not be a valid justification for declining to use an otherwise available emissions control technique or technology.[320]

After choosing a LAER limit, the limit is, if possible, expressed as a numerical emissions limit (lb/mmBtu) and as an emission rate (lb/hr). If these expressions are "technically infeasible," the EPA may draft the permit to contain a "design, operational, or equipment standard; however, such standards must be clearly enforceable, and the reviewing agency must still make an estimate of the resulting emissions for offset purposes."[321]

Emissions Offsets: Process and Goals

Unless a source subject to nonattainment analysis review is located in an area where specified growth allowances are permitted, the applicant will have to obtain emissions offsets for new emissions of nonattainment criteria pollutants. Emissions offsets can be greater than a one-to-one ratio. The 1990 CAA Amendments classified certain nonattainment areas on the basis of how near to compliance an area was. Offset requirements can depend on the classification of the nonattainment area for these pollutants—the farther out of compliance, the higher the offset that can be required. The purpose of requiring emissions offsets is to help improve air quality in nonattainment areas, while allowing mechanisms for continued economic development in those areas.[322]

Emissions offsets can often be obtained from other sources located in the same general area. States may create banks within the area to stockpile these offsets.[323] The EPA has given some indication that facilities locating in certain nonattainment areas may be able to obtain offset credits from attainment areas.[324] The EPA may allow new and modified sources in this category to use emissions offset credits from other stationary, mobile, and area sources if the source can meet EPA restrictions.[325] Finally, the operator of the source may be able to reduce emissions at its own facility, depending on whether the plantwide or dual source definition of stationary source is applied. Normally, emissions reductions that are required under other regulatory programs cannot be considered offsets.

Emissions offsets must achieve two important objectives: (1) ensuring progress toward satisfying attainment goals and (2) providing a positive net air quality benefit in the affected area.[326] Several factors must be considered in reviewing proposed emissions offsets, including the pollutants requiring offsets and the amount of offset required; the location of offsets relative to the proposed source; the allowable sources for offsets; the baseline for calculating emissions reduction credits;[327] and the enforceability[328] of proposed offsets.[329]

When determining the offset ratios that must be used, a facility must consider actual, not potential, emissions. Where required, offset ratios for PM_{10}, CO, SO_2, NO_2, and lead are generally 1 to 1. However, the offset ratios for ozone—regulated through VOCs and NO_x—depend on the area's ozone nonattainment classification, as follows:

- **Marginal areas:** The offset ratio is 1.1 to 1.
- **Moderate areas:** The offset ratio is 1.15 to 1.
- **Serious areas:** The offset ratio is 1.2 to 1.
- **Severe areas:** The offset ratio is 1.3 to 1.
- **Extreme areas:** The offset ratio is 1.5 to 1.
- **Transport region areas:** The offset ratio is dependent on classification.

A facility modification that would increase, for example, VOC emissions and is located in a severe nonattainment area would need to decrease its VOC emissions by 1.3 tons for each ton by which it increases VOC emissions.

Compliance Certification for Other Sources Operating in the Permit State

Operators of sources subject to nonattainment analysis review must certify that all other sources operating in the state are in compliance with CAA and SIP requirements.[330]

Conclusion

This chapter provides an overview of the current major NSR process (i.e., the PSD and nonattainment analysis pathways). NSR is a complex preconstruction review process requiring covered new or modified sources to undergo detailed and involved analysis of the potential impact any emissions from the new or modified covered facility will have on ambient air quality values created and designated for protection under the program. Applicants must demonstrate that the covered source will not adversely affect these protected air quality values. In addition, applicants must identify and select emissions control techniques required under the program and commit to emissions limitations that will result from using the required degree of control.

The NSR program is designed to bring air quality into compliance for all areas of the country. The nonattainment analysis and PSD pathways together require progress toward satisfying NAAQS for all areas and ensure that these air quality standards will be maintained. The program recently underwent revisions intended to simplify the process. Anyone affected by the NSR program should carefully review the 2002 and 2003 NSR revisions and determine how to take advantage of the flexibility provided by the revisions to their fullest extent.

Notes

1. *See* CAA § 109; 40 C.F.R. pt. 50 (2002).

2. Certain organic compounds are normally exempted from the definition of VOCs. A list of these exempted compounds is found at 40 C.F.R. § 51.100(s). Exempted compounds normally need not be considered in the evaluation of the potential to emit for a source. Specific state rules may need to be consulted on this issue.

3. *See* CAA § 110.

4. *See* 2 Law of Environmental Protection, Environmental Law Institute, Clark, Boardman, Callaghan § 11.05 (1994); Theodore L. Garrett & Sonya D. Winner, "A Clean Air Act Primer," ch. 1, 5–6, Clean Air Deskbook, Environmental Law Reporter, Environmental Law Institute (1992) (providing excellent discussions of the historical development of the new source review program); Arnold W. Reitze, Jr., Air Pollution Control Law: Compliance & Enforcement, Environmental Law Institute (2001), ch. 7: Preconstruction Permits.

5. *See* CAA §§ 160–69B (also referred to as Part C—Prevention of Significant Deterioration of Air Quality); 40 C.F.R. § 51.160 (2002); 40 C.F.R. § 52.21 (2002).

6. *See* CAA §§ 171–93 (also referred to as Part D of Title I—Plan Requirements for Nonattainment Areas).

7. These preconstruction state permit programs (required under CAA § 110(a)(2)(C)) apply to sources that do not meet or exceed certain "major source thresholds" that will be discussed in following sections. There is tremendous variation among these state programs, and individual state requirements must be consulted.

8. *See* Law of Environmental Protection, *supra* note 4, § 11.05 at 138–39.

9. *Id.; supra* note 8. These regulatory requirements are currently found at 40 C.F.R. § 51.160.

10. States obtain authority to implement the federal NSR program by approval through their SIPs. Although these state programs are normally very similar to the federal program discussed in this chapter, individual differences can exist. The state program should always be consulted first.

11. 344 F. Supp. 253 (D.C. Cir. 1972), *aff'd per curiam,* 2 Envtl. L Rep. 20656 (D.C. Cir. 1972), *aff'd by equally divided court mem. sub nom.* Fri v. Sierra Club, 412 U.S. 541 (1973). There was little justification for this requirement other than generic "protect and enhance" language included in Section 101 of the CAA.

12. *See* 39 Fed. Reg. 42,510 (1974). The current federal PSD regulations are promulgated at 40 C.F.R. § 52.21. *See also* Law of Environmental Protection, *supra* note 4, § 11.05[2][a] at 139–40; Clean Air Deskbook, *supra* note 4, ch. 5 at 39.

13. *See* Law of Environmental Protection, *supra* note 4, § 11.05[2][a] at 141–42 & fn. 29; 41 Fed. Reg. 55,524, 55,528 (1976). This provision has been revised and the current version of the offset ruling appears at 40 C.F.R. pt. 51, app. S.

14. EPA New Source Review Workshop Manual (draft) [hereinafter NSRWM], at 4–6; Law of Environmental Protection, *supra* note 4, 11.05[2][b] at 142; Clean Air Deskbook, *supra* note 4, at ch. 6; *see also* Law of Environmental Protection, *supra* note 4, § 11.05[3][a] at 154–55; Air Pollution Control Law, *supra* note 4, § 4.1.

15. *See* CAA § 107(d); Law of Environmental Protection, *supra* note 4, § 11.05[2][b] at 142–43; *see also* Law of Environmental Protection, *supra* note 4, § 11.05[3][a] at 154–55; Air Pollution Control Law, *supra* note 4, § 4.1 at 79–80.

16. *See* CAA §§ 172–73.

17. *See* 42 U.S.C. §§ 7407, 7410 (CAA §§ 107, 110); NSRWM, Introduction at 4; Law of Environmental Protection, *supra* note 4, § 11.05[2][b]; Clean Air Deskbook, *supra* note 4, chs. 5 and 6; *see also* Law of Environmental Protection, *supra* note 4, § 11.05[3][a] at 154–55; Air Pollution Control Law, *supra* note 4, § 4.1, and ch. 5.

18. *See* 42 U.S.C. §§ 7407, 7410 (CAA §§ 107, 110); NSRWM, Introduction at 4; Law of Environmental Protection, *supra* note 4, § 11.05[2][b]; Clean Air Deskbook, *supra* note 4, chs. 5 and 6; *see also* Law of Environmental Protection, *supra* note 4, § 11.05[3][a] at 154–55; Air Pollution Control Law, *supra* note 4, at ch. 5.

19. *See* 42 U.S.C. §§ 7472–76 (CAA §§ 162–66); 40 C.F.R. § 52.21(c); Clean Air Deskbook, *supra* note 4, at ch. 5.

20. *See, e.g.,* 43 Fed. Reg. 26,382 (1978). Current regulations appear at 40 C.F.R. § 51.166 (minimum requirements that PSD air permits must satisfy); 40 C.F.R. § 52.21 (federal PSD program); 40 C.F.R. § 51.165 (a)–(b) (elements of approvable state permit program for preconstruction review); 40 C.F.R. pt. 51, App. S (offset ruling); and 40 C.F.R. § 52.24 (construction moratorium for certain sources in nonattainment areas). *See* Law of Environmental Protection, *supra* note 4, § 11.05[2][b] at 145; *see also* Law of Environmental Protection, *supra*

note 4, § 11.05[3][a] at 154–55; AIR POLLUTION CONTROL LAW, *supra* note 4, § 5-1(b), at 105–106.

21. *See* Alabama Power Co. v. Costle, 606 F.2d 1068 (D.C. Cir. 1979), *modified*, 636 F.2d 323 (D.C. Cir. 1979); Citizens to Save Spencer County v. EPA, 600 F.2d 844 (D.C. Cir. 1979); LAW OF ENVIRONMENTAL PROTECTION, *supra* note 4, § 11.05[2][b] at 145–52.

22. *See, e.g.,* 45 Fed. Reg. 52,676 (1980) (responding to the decision in *Alabama Power Co. v. Costle, supra* note 21); CLEAN AIR DESKBOOK, *supra* note 4, ch. 5 at 39; *see also* LAW OF ENVIRONMENTAL PROTECTION, *supra* note 4, § 11.05[3][a] at 154–55; AIR POLLUTION CONTROL LAW, *supra* note 4, § 5-1(c) at 106.

23. 42 U.S.C. §§ 7470–71 (CAA §§ 160–169).

24. *See* CAA §§ 171–93; LAW OF ENVIRONMENTAL PROTECTION, *supra* note 4, § 11.05[3]; CLEAN AIR DESKBOOK, *supra* note 4, ch. 4 at 22–37; *see also* LAW OF ENVIRONMENTAL PROTECTION, *supra* note 4, § 11.05[3][a] at 154–55; AIR POLLUTION CONTROL LAW, *supra* note 4, ch. 4 and § 5-1(d) at 107.

25. *See* 61 Fed. Reg. 38,250 (1996).

26. 67 Fed. Reg. 80,186 (2002) (to be codified at 40 C.F.R. pts. 51 and 52).

27. 68 Fed. Reg. 44,620 (2003).

28. 68 Fed. Reg. 63,021 (2003) (to be codified at 40 C.F.R. pts. 51 and 52) (adding definitions of "replacement unit" and specifying that the PAL baseline calculation procedure for newly constructed units do not apply to modified units).

29. 67 Fed. Reg. 80,290 (2002).

30. 68 Fed. Reg. 61,248 (2003) (to be codified at 40 C.F.R. pts. 51 and 52).

31. 67 Fed. Reg. 80,187, at 80,189 (2002).

32. Compare outline of proposed rulemaking for complete list of proposed changes. 61 Fed. Reg. 38,250 (1996).

33. 68 Fed. Reg. 61,248, at 61,252.

34. These states include Connecticut, Maine, Maryland, Massachusetts, New Hampshire, New Jersey, New York, Pennsylvania, Rhode Island, and Vermont. Inside EPA Clean Air Report, Vol. XIV, No. 4, at 5 (Feb. 13, 2003).

35. *Id.*

36. The State and Territorial Air Pollution Program Administrators and Association of Local Air Pollution Control Officials (STAPPA/ALAPCO) developed a Menu of Options for states to use in developing their own rules from the EPA's NSR revisions. This outline is available at http://www.cleanairworld.org/newsourcemenu.html.

37. 46 Fed. Reg. 11,316 (2003) (to be codified at 40 C.F.R. pt. 52). *See also* 67 Fed. Reg. 80,187, at 80,240. Attainment states delegated with authority to implement the NSR PSD program include Hawaii, Illinois, Indiana, Massachusetts, Michigan, Minnesota, Nevada, New Hampshire, New Jersey, New York, South Dakota, and Washington. See http://www.epa.gov/ttnnsr01/gen/psd_status_june02.pdf.

38. *See* 67 Fed. Reg. 80,187, at 80,240 (requiring SIP states to include changes as minimum program elements by January 2, 2006).

39. 40 C.F.R. § 52.21(b)(1)(i), (b)(23).

40. 40 C.F.R. § 52.21(b)(1)(i); *see* CAA §§ 165, 173.

41. *See* CAA § 173(c); 40 C.F.R. pt. 51, app. S (offset ruling); *In re* Keystone Cogeneration Syst., PSD Appeal (App.) No. 91-42, 1992 WL 26,862 (EPA Jan. 7, 1992).

42. CAA §§ 160–69 (Part C of Title I—Prevention of Significant Deterioration of Air Quality); 40 C.F.R. § 52.21.

43. *See* CAA §§ 171–93 (Part D—Plans and Requirements for Nonattainment Areas); 40 C.F.R. § 52.24; 61 Fed. Reg. at 38,252.

44. *See* CAA §§ 165, 173; *see also In re Hudson Power* 14—Buena Vista, PSD App. No. 92-3, 92-4, 92-5, 1992 WL 345661 (EPA Oct. 5, 1992); AIR POLLUTION CONTROL LAW, *supra* note 4, chs. 5 and 7.

45. *See, e.g.*, NSRWM, C.16–23 (October 1990); *In re Hudson Power* 14—Buena Vista, PSD App. No. 92-3, 92-4, 92-5, 1992 WL 345661 (EPA Oct. 5, 1992).

46. The EPA and the Air and Waste Management Association have published a multivolume set of these documents. *See* NEW SOURCE REVIEW, PREVENTION OF SIGNIFI-CANT DETERIORATION AND NONATTAINMENT AREA GUIDANCE NOTEBOOK, volumes I–III, Update, and Update I and II. Many NSR decisions have also been made by regional EPA administrators and the Environmental Appeals Board that provide NSR precedent.

47. These Web pages can be found by browsing the EPA's Web site under the topic "air" at http://www.epa.gov. More specifically, the top four NSR Web pages are (1) the EPA's "What's New" NSR Web page, http://www.epa.gov/ttnnsr01/whatsnew.html, (2) the EPA's uncategorized NSR guidance documents, http://www.epa.gov/ttnnsr01/poly_gui.html; (3) the EPA's compendia of NSR regulation and guidance, http://www.epa.gov/ttn/nsr/ and (4) the EPA Region VII's Web page from which one can download the contents of the NSR guidance notebooks, http://www.epa.gov/region07/programs/artd/air/policy/search.htm.

48. AIR POLLUTION CONTROL LAW, *supra* note 4, ch. 5.

49. *See* 40 C.F.R. § 52.21(b)(1).

50. 40 C.F.R. § 52.21(b)(2).

51. 40 C.F.R. § 52.21(b)(23).

52. *See* CAA § 165; 40 C.F.R. § 52.21.

53. 40 C.F.R. § 52.21(b)(8).

54. 40 C.F.R. at § 52.21(b)(11).

55. *See* CAA § 165(a) (applying PSD preconstruction requirements to major emitting facilities for which construction is "commenced after August 7, 1977").

56. 40 C.F.R. § 52.21(b)(9).

57. This view is really confusing the distinction between "beginning actual construction" and "commencing construction."

58. *See* 40 C.F.R. § 52.21 (b)(11) and 40 C.F.R. § 51.166(b)(11) (definition of "[b]egin actual construction"); *but cf. In re Virginia Power*, PSD App. No. 88-2, 1988 WL 249042 (EPA Feb. 1, 1988) ("Clean Air Act . . . which forbids construction of a facility before the emissions limitations in the permit have been established").

59. *See* 61 Fed. Reg. at 38,270–71.

60. *See, e.g.*, 42 U.S.C.A. §§ 7470–76 (CAA §§ 160–66); NSRWM, ch. A; *In re Hibbing Taconite Co.*, PSD App. No. 87-3, 1989 WL 266359 (EPA July 19, 1989).

61. *See* 40 C.F.R. § 51.165(b); *see, e.g.*, NSRWM at ch. A. As noted, the primary exception to this result would be if the source locating in an attainment area would have a significant impact on a nearby nonattainment area, in which case NAA analysis could be required—even though the source was locating in an attainment area. *See* 40 C.F.R. § 51.165(b).

62. 40 C.F.R. § 52.21(b)(5); NSRWM at A.3. "Regulated pollutants under the Act" include all criteria pollutants and any noncriteria pollutants regulated under the requirements for New Source Performance standards (40 C.F.R. pt. 60), the National Emissions Standards for Hazardous Air Pollutants (40 C.F.R. pt. 61), the air toxics program (42 U.S.C. § 112), and any other pollutant designated for regulation.

63. "Same industrial grouping" means the groups identified by the same two-digit codes in the *Standard Industrial Classification (SIC) Manual*, published by the Office of Management and Budget. *See* 40 C.F.R. § 52.21(b)(6); NSRWM at A.3.

64. 40 C.F.R. § 52.21(b)(6); NSRWM at A.3.

65. 40 C.F.R. § 52.21(b)(7) (this definition distinguishes between new emissions units and existing emissions units, and includes an electric utility steam generating unit as defined by 40 C.F.R. § 52.21(b)(31)).

66. 40 C.F.R. §§ 51.165(a)(1)(iii), 52.21(b)(4).

67. NSRWM, app. C, at c.1.

68. AP-42 emission estimate factors are published by the EPA and provide a basis for estimating what the potential emissions would be for a particular source operating under certain conditions. These estimates tend to be conservative, though there are some notable exceptions, thus sources should be careful when using these factors to ascertain the accuracy of these factors to preempt the possibility of later noncompliance demonstrated by any credible evidence.

69. NSRWM, app. C, at c.2.

70. 40 C.F.R. § 52.21(b)(20).

71. *See* 40 C.F.R. § 52.21 (b)(1)(iii)(a)–(aa).

72. NSRWM at A.9–A.16.

73. *See* 40 C.F.R. 52.21(b)(1)(iii); NSRWM at A.9–A.16; 66 Fed. Reg. 59,161 (2001).

74. *See* 40 C.F.R. 51.165(a)(1)(iii); 52.21(b)(4).

75. Chemical Mfrs. Ass'n v. EPA, No. 89–1514 (D.C. Cir. 1995) (Sept. 15, 1995); National Mining Ass'n v. EPA, 59 F.3d 1351 (D.C. Cir. 1995). Air Pollution Control Law, *supra* note 4, § 7-3(d) at 186–87.

76. 59 F.3d 1351 (D.C. Cir. 1995).

77. Chemical Mfs. Ass'n v. EPA, No. 89–1514 (D.C. Cir. 1995) (basing its decision on *National Mining Association v. EPA*, 59 F.3d 1351 (D.C. Cir. 1995) in which the court had just remanded the requirement of federal enforceability in the air toxics program). *See* Release of Interim Policy on Federal Enforceability of Limitations on Potential to Emit, EPA Memorandum from John Seitz (Jan. 22, 1996) (EPA response to litigation challenging federal enforceability); "Effective" Limits on Potential to Emit: Issues and Options, EPA Letter from Steven A. Herman and Mary D. Nichols (Jan. 31, 1996); *see also* Second Extension of January 25, 1995 Potential to Emit Transition Policy and Clarification of Interim Policy, EPA Memorandum from John Seitz (July 10, 1998).

78. 67 Fed. Reg. at 80,190–91 (providing specific elements of permit provisions that satisfy the requirements for both legal and practical enforceability). *See also* Options for Limiting Potential to Emit (PTE) of a Stationary Source under 112 and Title V of the Clean Air Act (Act), EPA Memorandum from John Seitz, at 4 (Jan. 25, 1995) (extended via EPA memorandum on August 27, 1996, until July 1, 1998, and then again on July 10, 1998, until December 31, 1999); Approaches to Creating Federally-Enforceable Emissions Limits, EPA Memorandum from John Seitz (Nov. 3, 1993). *But cf.* EPA Memorandum from John Seitz (Nov. 2, 1994) (discussing possible restrictions for using construction permits to limit PTE when they do not undergo sufficient public notice and/or comment).

79. Options for Limiting Potential to Emit (PTE) of a Stationary Source under 112 and Title V of the Clean Air Act, EPA Memorandum from John Seitz, at 2, 5 (Jan. 25, 1995); NSRWM at A.5–A.9.

80. 40 C.F.R. § 52.21(b)(1); NSRWM, app. A, at a.4.

81. *See* NSRWM at A.5–A.9.

82. *See* Limiting Potential to Emit in New Source Permitting, EPA Memorandum from Office of Air Quality Planning and Standards, at 6–9 (June 13, 1989).

83. *See* 40 C.F.R. § 51.21(b)(2)(iii) (providing several exclusions such as routine maintenance, repair, and replacement; use of alternative fuels; emission increases resulting solely from increase in the hours of operation or production rate; pollution control projects; and PALs).

84. *See* 40 C.F.R. §§ 52.21(b)(2), (b)(3), (b)(23), (b)(40), and (b)(50).

85. *See id. See also* 40 C.F.R. § 52.21 (b)(23)(iii). This is also considered a "significant modification."

86. *See* NSRWM at A.33.

87. In this event, the agency might attempt to treat the source as if it were not existing and could try to require it to go through the NSR process as if it were a new source. *See* NSRWM at A.33.

88. Defined in previous sections of this chapter and at 40 C.F.R. § 52.21(b)(1).

89. *See, e.g.,* 40 C.F.R. § 51.165(a)(1)(x); NSRWM at 33.

90. NSRWM at A.45.

91. NSRWM at A.35.

92. Future emissions for proposed modifications of existing sources can be calculated using either the "actual-to-projected-actual" applicability test or the same "actual-to-potential" applicability test used for proposed new sources. *See* 67 Fed. Reg. 80,187 (2002) (to be codified at 40 C.F.R. pts. 51 and 52); 40 C.F.R. § 52.21(a)(2)(iv)(b) through (f).

93. NSRWM at A.36; *see In re Hibbing Taconite Co.,* PSD App. No. 87-3, 1989 WL 266359 (EPA July 19, 1989).

94. NSRWM at A.36. Note that other EPA regions, and some states, may take the position that if the "project" itself has increases and decreases that stay below the significant threshold, no other contemporaneous emission changes need be considered. That is, if the source does not need to go outside the "project" being considered to take advantage of other emission decreases, then no emission increases outside the "project" need be considered. The applicability of this position should be verified.

95. *Air Toxic Compounds:* The 1990 CAA Amendments exempt Section 112 air toxic compounds from coverage under the PSD program. The EPA has interpreted this exemption to mean that a source would not be required to independently evaluate air toxic compounds to determine whether they were emitted in "significant" amounts (i.e., anything above zero). Air toxic compounds that were covered under PSD review but are now exempted from individual consideration include arsenic, benzene, radionuclides, asbestos, beryllium, mercury, and vinyl chloride. 67 Fed. Reg. 80,186, at 80,239; 40 C.F.R. § 51.21(b)(50). However, the exclusion from individual consideration does not exempt a compound if it is otherwise covered under a generic category. For example, although benzene is a regulated air toxic (and would not have to be evaluated individually), it would have to be evaluated in the generic category as a nonexempt VOC compound. *See* CAA § 112(b)(6). This exemption has not been uniformly applied, and the state regulations may require additional coverage. The applicability of NSR to Section 112 pollutants should always be discussed with the permitting authority.

Chlorofluorocarbons (CFCs): CFCs regulated under Title VI of the CAA currently have no assigned significant level and thus their significant threshold could be considered zero. 40 C.F.R. § 52.21(b)(23)(ii).

96. 40 C.F.R. § 52.21(b)(23)(iii).

97. NSRWM at A.36.

98. 40 C.F.R. § 51.21(a)(2)(iv)(*c*).

99. 40 C.F.R. § 52.21(b)(21)(iv). Prior to the promulgation of the "actual-to-projected actual test," the actual emissions for sources that had "not begun normal operations," were equal to the potential to emit for the unit. In adopting the new test, EPA eliminated the term "begun normal operations" from the determination of whether a change results in a significant emissions increase. 67 Fed. Reg. 80,187, at 80,195. However, if using the "actual-to-potential" test, note that the EPA or the delegated state can consider "actual emissions" to equal the allowable emissions rate for the unit if the allowable emissions rate is enforceable as a practical matter. *Id.* § 52.21(b)(21)(iii). *See also* 67 Fed. Reg. at

80,191. Thus, if a modification resulted in a PTE of 100 tpy, but the source agreed to accept an emission rate that was enforceable as a practical matter on the unit of 50 tpy, this lower allowable emission rate could be approved as the "actual emission rate."

100. *See* 40 C.F.R. § 51.21(b)(41).

101. *See* 40 C.F.R. § 51.21(b)(4).

102. *See* 40 C.F.R. § 52.21(b)(48)(ii). The baseline calculation for non-EUSGUs is one of the controversial changes promulgated in the December 2002 NSR revisions. See 67 Fed. Reg. at 80,191 to 80,204. Note that non-EUSGUs are not allowed to request a different, more representative period demonstrating baseline actual emissions than the ten years preceding the modification.

103. *See* 40 C.F.R. § 52.21(b)(48)(i). This is the *WEPCO* rule, which EPA promulgated into the NSR rules with its December 2002 NSR revisions.

104. *See* 40 C.F.R. § 52.21(b)(41).

105. *See* 40 C.F.R. § 51.165(a)(6)(iii). *See also* 67 Fed. Reg. at 80,197.

106. *Id.*

107. *See* 40 C.F.R. § 52.21(b)(3)(i)*(b)*.

108. *See* NSRWM at A.36; Request for Clarification of Policy Regarding the Net Emission Increase, EPA Memorandum from John Calcagni (September 18, 1989); Review of De Minimis Emissions—Sanctions, EPA Guidance Memorandum from Ronald Shafer (October 28, 1988).

109. The projects would be covered under the applicable state's minor NSR program and the modifications would most likely require minor NSR construction permits.

110. *See* NSRWM at A.36.

111. NSRWM at A.36–A.37. Other factors to consider in determining whether a minor modification should be considered together with a previously conducted minor modification include the following: (1) filing of more than one minor source or minor modification application associated with emissions increases at a single plant within a "short period of time"—most likely a *"planning period"*; (2) application of funding; (3) reports of consumer demand and projected production; (4) statements of authorized representatives of the source regarding plans for operation; and (5) the EPA's (or the state's) analysis of the economic realities of the projects being considered together. *See* Applicability of New Source Review Circumvention Guidance to 3M—Maplewood, Minnesota, EPA Memorandum from John B. Rasnic (no date); Applicability of PSD to Portions of Plant Constructed in Phases without Permits, EPA Memorandum from Darryl Tyler (Oct. 21, 1986).

112. *See* 40 C.F.R. § 52.21(b)(3)(i); NSRWM at A.37.

113. NSRWM at A.37.

114. Reviewing agencies may use the date construction is *scheduled* to commence provided that it is reasonable considering the time needed to issue a final permit. NSRWM at A.37–38.

115. NSRWM at A.38; *see* 40 C.F.R. § 52.21 (b)(3)(ii).

116. *Id. See also* 67 Fed. Reg. at 80,197.

117. NSRWM at A.38–A.39.

118. This term is discussed in preceding sections.

119. NSRWM at A.38; *see* 40 C.F.R. § 52.21(b)(3)(vi)*(b)*, (b)(17). *See also* 67 Fed. Reg. at 80,190–91 (providing components of "enforceable as a practical matter"). Requirements should be reviewed on a state-by-state basis.

120. *See* 40 C.F.R. § 52.21(b)(3); NSRWM at A.38–A.44.

121. 40 C.F.R. § 52.21(b)(3) and (48).

122. *Id.* NSRWM at A.39.

123. *Id.*

124. 40 C.F.R. § 52.21(b)(3)(iii); NSRWM at A.40. Although, note that some agencies may continue to consider impacts on existing emissions that have been previously addressed by a NSR permit (i.e., those emissions are still evaluated in the NSR process). This again is a question that needs to be reviewed with the state permitting agency.

125. *See id.;* 40 C.F.R. § 52.21(b)(3).

126. NSRWM at A. 41; 40 C.F.R. § 52.21(b)(3)(vi). A source cannot receive emissions reduction credit for reducing any portion of emissions that resulted because the source was operating out of compliance. *See* NSRWM at 41.

127. *See* 40 C.F.R. § 52.21(b)(21).

128. NSRWM at A.41.

129. NSRWM at A.44.

130. Exceptions covered in this section are often subject to widely differing interpretations. For example, an activity that might otherwise be excluded from NSR, such as routine maintenance, repair, or replacement, might still be covered if it results in "debottlenecking" a process. Thus, prudence dictates conferring with the state and federal permitting agencies before relying on one of these exceptions.

131. 40 C.F.R. § 52.21(b)(2)(iii)(a). There has been considerable confusion concerning what this term means and when this exemption should be used to describe certain anticipated activities most often associated with and performed during regularly scheduled equipment outages to maintain a plant and its equipment in good operating condition. To resolve years of controversy, EPA proposed NSR revisions addressing the scope of the routine maintenance, repair, and replacement exemption on December 31, 2002, 67 Fed. Reg. 80,290 (2002), and promulgated its Equipment Replacement Provisions on October 27, 2003. 68 Fed. Reg. 61,248 (2003) (to be codified at 40 C.F.R. pts. 51 and 52).

132. 40 C.F.R. § 52.21(b)(2)(iii)(b)–(e), (i)–(j).

133. 40 C.F.R. § 52.21(b)(2)(iii)(f).

134. 40 C.F.R. § 52.21(b)(2)(iii)(g).

135. 40 C.F.R. § 52.21(b)(2)(iii)(h), (b)(32).

136. 40 C.F.R. § 52.21(a)(2)*(e)*.

137. 40 C.F.R. § 52.21(b)(2)(iv) (exempting sources accepting Plantwide Applicability Limits from the definition of "major modification" as long as the source is complying with 40 C.F.R. § 52.21(aa)(2)(viii)).

138. *See* Tennessee Valley Authority v. EPA, 278 F.3d 1185 (11th Cir. 2002).

139. *See In re* Tennessee Valley Authority, No. CAA-2000-04-008, 2000 EPA App. LEXIS 25 (Sept. 15, 2000).

140. *Id.*

141. Tennessee Valley Authority v. Whitman, 278 F.3d 1185 (11th Cir. 2002).

142. Tennessee Valley Authority v. Whitman, 336 F.3d 1236 (11th Cir. 2003).

143. United States v. Ohio Edison Co., 276 F. Supp. 2d 829 (S. D. 2003).

144. United States v. Duke Energy Corp., No. 1:00-CV-01262 (M.D.N.C. orders issued August 26, 2003).

145. Environmental Integrity Project, "Administration Pulls Plug on Enforcement Cases" (available at http://environmentalintegrity.org/pub117.cfm).

146. 68 Fed. Reg. 61,248, at 61,252.

147. *See* Wisconsin Elec. Power Co. v. Reilly (WEPCO), 893 F.2d 901 (7th Cir. 1990); 57 Fed. Reg. 32,314 (1992).

148. Pollution Control Projects and New Source Review (NSR) Applicability, EPA Memorandum from John Seitz (July 1, 1994).

149. *See* 40 C.F.R. § 52.21(b)(32). *See also* 67 Fed. Reg. at 80,232–40.

150. Including pollution prevention projects, defined at 40 C.F.R. § 52.21(b)(39). *Id.*

151. *See* 40 C.F.R. § 52.21(b)(32), (z)(2) through (z)(5).

152. *Id.*

153. *See* 40 C.F.R. § 52.21(b)(42).

154. *See* 40 C.F.R. § 52.21(a)(2)*(e)* (stating that such projects are deemed to have occurred with no emissions increase).

155. *See* 40 C.F.R. § 52.21(x), (y)(3)(i); 40 C.F.R. §§ 51.165(c), 51.166(t). *See also* 67 Fed. Reg. at 80,222–32.

156. *Id.*

157. *See* 40 C.F.R. § 52.21(b)(2)*(x)*(8).

158. *See* 67 Fed. Reg. at 80,208; 40 C.F.R. § 52.21(aa).

159. *Id.*; 40 C.F.R. § 52.21(b)(23).

160. *See* NSRWM at A.24.

161. CAA § 165(a)(4); 40 C.F.R. § 52.21(j)(2); NSRWM at B.1–B.4.

162. 40 C.F.R. § 52.21(b)(12).

163. *See* NSRWM at B.6; *see also In re* Brooklyn Navy Yard Resource Recovery Facility, PSD App. No. 88-10, 1992 WL 80946 (EPA Feb. 28, 1992).

164. *See* 61 Fed. Reg. at 38,272–73; *In re* World Color Press, Inc., PSD App. No. 88-4, 1990 WL 324095 n.20 (EPA Dec. 13, 1990) (general definition of the "top-down" method).

165. NSRWM at B.5; *see, e.g., In re* Spokane Regional Waste-to-Energy, PSD App. No. 88-12, 1989 WL 266360 (EPA June 9, 1989).

166. NSRWM at B.11. EPA's BACT, LAER Clearinghouse can be accessed through EPA's TTN Web site, at www.epa.gov/ttn/ttn_search.html and conducting a search with these terms.

167. *See, e.g., In re Mecklenburg Cogeneration Ltd.*, PSD App. No. 90-7, 1990 WL 324094 n.3 (EPA Dec. 21, 1990).

168. NSRWM at B.12.

169. *See* 40 C.F.R. §§ 52.21(b)(19), .21(v); *see also In re Brooklyn Navy Yard Resource Recovery Facility*, PSD App. No. 88-10, 1992 WL 80946 (EPA Feb. 28, 1992).

170. NSRWM at B.17.

171. NSRWM at B.18; *see In re* Hawaiian Comm. & Sugar Co., PSD App. No. 92-1, 1992 WL 191948 n.17 (EPA July 20, 1992).

172. NSRWM at B.18.

173. *Id.*

174. *Id.*

175. NSRWM at B.19.

176. *See* NSRWM at B.21.–B.22.

177. *Id.*; *see In re* Spokane Regional Waste-to-Energy, PSD App. No. 88-12, 1989 WL 266360 (EPA June 9, 1989).

178. *See In re* Robbins Resource Recovery Co., PSD App. No. 90-8, 1991 WL 311862 (EPA July 30, 1991); *In re* Mecklenburg Cogeneration Ltd. Partnership, PSD App. No. 90-7, 1990 WL 324094 (EPA Dec. 21, 1990).

179. NSRWM at B.23–B.24.

180. NSRWM at B.24.

181. NSRWM at B.25–B.26.

182. NSRWM at B.25.

183. *See In re* Brooklyn Navy Yard Resource Recovery Facility, PSD App. No. 88-10, 1992 WL 80946 (EPA Feb. 28, 1992); *In re* World Color Press, Inc., PSD App. No. 88-4, 1990 WL 324095 (EPA Dec. 13, 1990).

184. NSRWM at B.26–B.29.

185. NSRWM at B.29–B.30.

186. NSRWM at B.30–B.31.
187. *See* NSRWM at B.31–B.46.
188. NSRWM at B.32–B.35.
189. *Id.*
190. NSRWM at B.36–B.37.
191. *Id.*
192. NSRWM at B.36–B.41. The formula is

Average cost-effectiveness (dollars per ton removed)
  equals
Control option annualized cost
  divided by
Baseline emission rate
  minus
Control option emission rate

Baseline emission rate is the realistic (or actual) upper bound of the uncontrolled emission rate. If baseline emissions are reduced by limits on operations (e.g., reduced hours, low pollutant containing fuels), then these limitations must be enforceable as part of a permit condition. *Id.* at B.37–B.41.

193. NSRWM at B.41. The formula for calculating incremental cost (dollars per incremental ton removed) is

Total costs (annualized) of control option
  minus
Total costs (annualized) of the next control option
  divided by
Next control option emission rate
  minus
Control option emissions rate
Id.

194. NSRWM at B.41–B.44.
195. NSRWM at 43.
196. NSRWM at B.31, B.44–B.46.
197. The applicant will need to evaluate any duty to identify and analyze the risk associated with any toxic or hazardous compound. This may need to be done in light of any Section 112 MACT requirements or state air toxic requirements.
198. NSRWM at B.49–B.50.
199. NSRWM at B.47.
200. NSRWM at B.53–B.54.
201. *Id.*
202. NSRWM at B.54–B.55.
203. NSRWM at B.56.
204. *See* 61. Fed. Reg. at 38,271–72.
205. *See* 61 Fed. Reg. at 38,274.
206. *Id.*
207. *Id.*
208. *Id.*
209. *Id.*
210. *Id.*
211. *See* 61 Fed. Reg. at 38,274–75.
212. *See* 61 Fed. Reg. at 38,276–78.
213. *See* 61 Fed. Reg. at 38,278.

214. *See* 61 Fed. Reg. at 38,277.

215. Ambient air has been interpreted as: "that portion of the atmosphere, external to buildings, to which the general public has access." *In re* Hibbing Taconite Co., PSD App. No. 87-3, 1989 WL 266359 (EPA July 19, 1989).

216. *See id.*; NSRWM at ch. C ("The Air Quality Analysis").

217. NSRWM at ch. C.

218. NSRWM at C.1.

219. NSRWM at C.1–C.2.

220. NSRWM at C.3.

221. Specifically, the baseline area includes all portions of an attainment or unclassified area in which the PSD applicant will locate and includes any attainment or unclassified area in which proposed emissions from the new or modified covered source will have a "significant impact"—causing at least a 1 $\mu g/m^3$ annual increase in the average ambient concentration for a covered criteria pollutant. NSRWM at C.9.

222. CAA §§ 160–65; 40 C.F.R. § 52.21(c); *In re Hudson Power* 14—Buena Vista, PSD App. No. 92-3, 92-4, 92-5, 1992 WL 345661 (EPA Oct. 5, 1992).

223. 40 C.F.R. 52.21(c)–(g); NSRWM at C.3–C.5. Note that there are no existing Class III areas. Class I and II areas may be redesignated under limited circumstances. This would be a very difficult process. *See* 40 C.F.R. 52.21(e) and (g).

224. NSRWM at C.6. Major source baseline dates are as follows: PM—January 6, 1975; SO_2—January 6, 1975; and NO_2—February 8, 1988. NSRWM at C.8.

225. NSRWM at C.6.

226. NSRWM at C.6–C.8. Trigger dates are as follows: PM—August 7, 1977; SO_2—August 7, 1977; NO_2—February 8, 1988. NSRWM at C.8.

227. NSRWM at C.8.

228. *Id.*

229. NSRWM at C.10.

230. NSRWM at C.16.

231. NSRWM at C.18–C.19 ("To be acceptable, such data must be judged by the permitting agency to be representative of the air quality for the area in which the proposed project would construct and operate"). *Id.* at C.18.

232. 40 C.F.R. § 52.21(m)(1)(iv).

233. *Id.* § 52.21(m)(1)(v)(b).

234. For instance, this might be done for VOC monitoring. The commitment to conduct the postconstruction monitoring currently must be federally enforceable. *See* 40 C.F.R. § 52.21(m)(1)(vi).

235. *See* 40 C.F.R. § 52.21(m)(2).

236. NSRWM at C.26–C.31.

237. NSRWM at C.31.

238. 40 C.F.R. § 52.21(n); *see* NSRWM at C.32.

239. NSRWM at C.32. "[N]earby sources could be anywhere within the impact area or an annular area extending 50 kilometers beyond the impact area." *Id.*

240. *See* C.31–C.34.

241. NSRWM at C.32–C.34.

242. NSRWM at C.35.

243. *Id.*

244. NSRWM at C.37. If the source is not using a model found in the modeling guideline, state and EPA preapproval should be sought. It is prudent to consult with the state (and possibly the EPA and any involved FLMs) before making any final decisions on modeling. *See* NSRWM at C.38.

245. NSRWM at C.51–C.53.

246. *Id.*

247. NSRWM at D.1.

248. Associated growth may be defined as "the growth (and emissions) that come about as the result of the construction or modification of a source (including secondary emissions), but which are not a part of that source. It does not include growth which has already occurred." NSRWM at D.3. and n.1.

249. 40 C.F.R. § 52.21(o); *see also* NSRWM at D.3.

250. NSRWM at D.1.

251. NSRWM at D.3.

252. *See* NSRWM at D.9.–D.10.

253. 40 C.F.R. § 52.21(o)(2).

254. *See* NSRWM at A.16–A.18 and D.3–D.4.

255. NSRWM at D.4.

256. *See* 40 C.F.R. § 52.21(o).

257. NSRWM at D.4–D.5.

258. NSRWM at D.5.

259. 40 C.F.R. § 52.21(o)(3); *see also* NSRWM at D.5–D.7.

260. NSRWM at D.5.

261. Recall that Class I areas are those "areas of special national or regional value from a natural, scenic, recreational, or historic perspective." NSRWM at E.1.

262. *See* 40 C.F.R. § 52.21(p). However, under Section 52.21(o), the EPA administrator may require sufficient monitoring to verify that visibility is not adversely impacted in Class I areas. 40 C.F.R. § 52.21(o)(3).

263. *See* 40 C.F.R. § 52.21(p).

264. There is no specific regulatory requirement as to how far away an applicant must consider Class I area impacts. Local and state requirements should be consulted. Also, state guidance should be sought as to what types of permits and at what distances from Class I areas FLMs have shown past interest. The goal here is to make the best effort to avoid a situation in which a PSD analysis is completed (i.e., without input from FLMs) only to have that analysis challenged and perhaps even appealed by the FLM once a draft permit is issued. The proposed amendments to the NSR program would provide more guidance for when a source must evaluate impacts on Class I areas and concerning what notice must be provided to involved FLMs (and when it must be provided). *See* 61 Fed. Reg. at 38,282–95.

265. *See* 40 C.F.R. pt. 81, subpt. D; *see also* NSRWM at E.2–E.8 (mandatory federal Class I areas).

266. 40 C.F.R. § 52.21(p) (giving FLMs the primary responsibility for protecting AQRVs).

267. NSRWM at E.10; *see generally,* USDI, *Permit Application Guidance for New Air Pollution Sources,* Natural Resources Report NPS/NRAQD/NRR-93/09 (March 1993).

268. NSRWM at E.10–E.11.

269. *See* 40 C.F.R. § 52.21(c); NSRWM at E.17.

270. NSRWM at E.10–E.17.

271. *See* Chapter 6 for a general discussion of CAA regulation to preserve visibility.

272. 40 C.F.R. § 52.21(o)(3).

273. NSRWM at E.22.

274. NSRWM at E.22; *see generally,* USDI, *Permit Application Guidance for New Air Pollution Sources,* Natural Resources Report NPS/NRAQD/NRR-93/09 (March, 1993); Workbook for Plume Visual Impact Screening and Analysis, EPA-450/4-88-015 (EPA Sept. 1988).

275. 40 C.F.R. § 52.21(p)(1).

276. *See id.* § 52.21(p)(2), (p)(4).

277. *Id.*

278. *See* 61 Fed. Reg. at 38,283–84.

279. *Id.*

280. *See* 61 Fed. Reg. at 38,286–87.

281. *See* 61 Fed. Reg. at 38,291–92.

282. *See* 61 Fed. Reg. at 38,290–91.

283. In some states, sources will submit the permit application directly to an EPA regional office. However, this section assumes that the state has an approved or delegated program.

284. 40 C.F.R. § 52.21 (referring to 40 C.F.R. pt. 124 for further provisions).

285. 40 C.F.R. § 124.3(c).

286. 40 C.F.R. § 124.3(f).

287. 40 C.F.R. § 124.6.

288. 40 C.F.R. § 124.6(d)(4)(iii).

289. *See* 40 C.F.R. § 52.21(q); 40 C.F.R. § 124.10.

290. 40 C.F.R. § 124.10(b).

291. 40 C.F.R. § 124.10(d)(iv).

292. 40 C.F.R. § 124.10(c)(4); *see also* 40 C.F.R. § 124.10(c)(1)(vii).

293. 40 C.F.R. § 124.13; *see* § 124.17(a).

294. *See* 40 C.F.R. § 124.17(b).

295. *See* 40 C.F.R. § 124.15.

296. *See* 40 C.F.R. § 124.19 (thirty-day period).

297. NSRWM at F.2.

298. NSRWM at F.2–F.3.

299. The EPA no longer uses the "dual source" definition. The definition may be used by some states, but its use is rare. Applicants need to check with local and state agencies to determine whether the definition is still in use in that particular locality or state.

300. NSRWM at F.3.

301. *Id.*

302. NSRWM at F.3–F.4.

303. *See* CAA § 173.

304. The Section 302(j) 100 tpy threshold applies unless there is a lower threshold. CAA § 302(j).

305. The major source threshold applies to VOC or NO_x, not to combined emissions. CAA §§ 181–85(B).

306. Pursuant to CAA Section 182(f), the EPA can exempt certain major sources of NO_x where increasing such emissions would not contribute to NAAQS nonattainment status.

307. Note that the stationary source must significantly contribute to ambient carbon monoxide levels. Nonattainment for carbon monoxide cannot result from only mobile source carbon monoxide emissions. CAA §§ 186–87.

308. CAA §§ 188–90.

309. NSRWM at F.7.

310. CAA § 116.

311. NSRWM at F.7.

312. *Id.*

313. *See* CAA §§ 182(c)–(e).

314. *Id.; see* 61 Fed. Reg. at 38,298.

315. *See* 61 Fed. Reg. at 38,298.

316. CAA § 173(a)(2).

317. *Id.;* NSRWM at G.2.

318. NSRWM at G.2. LAER may never be less stringent than an applicable new source performance standard.

319. If a facility in the same or similar industry employs a control technology, the EPA will likely consider that use as evidence that the cost of the control technology is not prohibitive.

320. NSRWM at G.4.

321. NSRWM at G.4.

322. NSRWM at G.5.

323. NSRWM at G.5.

324. Inside EPA's Clean Air Report, vol. VI, no. 20, at 30 (EPA Oct. 5, 1995) (citing memorandum from John Seitz dated Sept. 12, 1995).

325. *Id.*

326. NSRWM at G.5.–G.6.

327. To determine how much of an offset is available from a source, the baseline concentration for that source must be determined. In most cases, the SIP emissions limit for the source under consideration in effect at the time the nonattainment permit application is filed may be used to set the baseline concentration. Where there is no meaningful SIP or permitted emission limit, actual emissions for the source must be used for baseline calculations. *See* NSRWM at G.7.

328. All offsets currently must be included in federally enforceable permit conditions or in a modified SIP establishing new emission limits for the source providing the offset. *See* NSRWM at G.8. As discussed in the section on PSD analysis, the requirement for federal enforceability has been significantly challenged and eliminated in many circumstances—although state regulations may continue to require "federal enforceability" in some instances.

329. NSRWM at G.4–G.8.

330. NSRWM at G.9.

CHAPTER 7

The Visibility Protection Program

VICKIE L. PATTON

Overview

Since 1977 the Clean Air Act (CAA) has included a visibility program specially designed to protect scenic vistas in the country's premier national parks and wilderness areas.[1] To guide the administration of the visibility protection program, Congress declared and codified a national visibility goal that calls for "the prevention of any future, and the remedying of any existing, impairment of visibility in mandatory Class I Federal areas which impairment results from manmade air pollution."[2]

The national goal delineates several key elements of the visibility protection program. First, the areas protected under the program are mandatory Class I federal areas where visibility has been determined to be an important value. Second, the program is both preventive and remedial, designed to prevent prospective impairment and redress existing visibility impairment. Third, man-made sources of visibility impairment are targeted. At the same time, "any" man-made impairment is of concern. "Man-made air pollution" is also defined broadly to include air pollution that results directly or indirectly from human activities.[3] And "visibility impairment" includes reduction in visual range and atmospheric discoloration.[4]

Congress adopted the visibility program to protect the "intrinsic beauty and historical and archeological treasures" of certain federal lands, observing that "areas such as the Grand Canyon and Yellowstone Park are areas of breathtaking panorama; millions of tourists each year are attracted to enjoy the scenic vistas."[5]

The average visual range in most of the eastern United States is less than 30 kilometers (approximately 20 miles), about one-fifth of the visual range that could be perceived absent man-made air pollution.[6] In the West, visual range averages about 100–150 kilometers (60–100 miles), about one-half to two-thirds of the range that could be perceived in the absence of anthropogenic air pollution.[7]

Visibility impairment is caused by small particles that scatter and absorb sunlight, diminishing or altogether eliminating the color, clarity, and perception of a scenic vista.[8] Fine particles are discharged directly into the atmosphere and as gaseous precursors, such as sulfur dioxide and oxides of nitrogen, that transform into fine particles. These fine particles are buoyant, can remain in the atmosphere for several days, and can be transported hundreds of kilometers from their origin by prevailing winds.[9]

Regional haze is formed when fine particles from a variety of sources across a broad area are transported, mix together, and cause a widespread haze.[10] Recent activity under the CAA's visibility protection program has concentrated on initial steps to develop and carry out air quality management plans to abate this regionwide or regional haze.

The National Park Service analyzed visibility trends in Class I areas from 1990 to 1999 to assess where progress is being made and where conditions are worsening. This period corresponds with the implementation of the 1990 CAA Amendments, including the far-reaching reductions in sulfur dioxide required under the law's acid rain control program. The trends indicate that visibility conditions have improved or held steady in a number of Class I areas and that the reductions in sulfur dioxide air pollution have led to improved visibility conditions. There are also, however, a number of areas where visibility on the haziest days has significantly worsened, especially in the western United States, including in Bryce Canyon, Crater Lake, Grand Canyon, and Yosemite national parks.[11] And during the 1990s visibility worsened even on the clearest days in some areas, including Mesa Verde, Big Bend, and Great Smoky Mountains national parks.[12] The EPA's Web site has visibility trend data for a number of Class I areas.[13] While some areas show improvement and some indicate degradation, the scenic vistas in all of our protected national parks and wilderness areas continue to be adversely impacted by visibility-impairing air pollution.

Areas Protected under the Visibility Program: Mandatory Class I Federal Areas

The mandatory Class I Federal areas granted special protection under the visibility program are the federal Class I areas specified in Section 162(a) of the CAA, 42 U.S.C. § 7472(a). These areas may not be designated other than Class I and include international parks, national wilderness areas and national memorial parks larger than five thousand acres, and national parks larger than six thousand acres.[14] The areas must have been in existence on August 7, 1977.[15] The scope of a mandatory Class I area includes any subsequent changes in boundaries, such as park expansions.[16]

Each mandatory Class I Federal area is the responsibility of a federal land manager (FLM), namely the secretary of the federal department with authority over such lands (e.g., the secretary of agriculture for U.S. Forest Service lands and the secretary of the interior for National Park Service and U.S. Fish and Wildlife Service lands).[17] Under internal agency procedures, the departmental secretaries have delegated FLM authority to surrogate officials.

The statute further refines the Class I mandatory areas of concern to include those where visibility is identified as an important value.[18] Soon after the adoption of the 1977 CAA Amendments, the secretary of the interior identified, in consultation with other FLMs, those mandatory Class I areas where visibility is an important value.[19] The U.S. Environmental Protection Agency (EPA) considered the FLMs' analysis and concluded that visibility is an important value for 156 of the eligible 158 mandatory Class I areas.[20] Two wildernesses, Rainbow Lake (in Wisconsin) and Bradwell Bay (in Florida), were excluded. The list of mandatory Class I Federal areas where visibility is an important value is codified at 40 C.F.R. Part 81, Subpart D.

The visibility regulations implemented by the EPA also provided for the protection of integral vistas, views perceived from within a mandatory Class I area of a specific landmark or panorama located outside of the boundary.[21] The FLM must identify an integral vista according to specified criteria, including whether the vista is important to the visitor's visual experience of the mandatory Class I area. The Roosevelt Campobello International Park (in Maine and Canada) is the only area for which integral vista protection is required under the federal visibility protection program.[22] States may identify and protect additional integral vistas under their own authority,[23] and some states have done so.

Section 169A of the Clean Air Act: Statutory Framework for Implementation of Visibility Protection

The legal centerpiece of the Section 169A visibility protection provisions is the mandate for the EPA to promulgate regulations to ensure "reasonable progress" toward meeting the national visibility goal.[24] The regulations must require that each state containing a mandatory Class I area where visibility is an important value, and states with emissions that may reasonably be anticipated to cause or contribute to visibility impairment in a mandatory Class I area, develop and submit SIPs containing "emission limits, schedules of compliance and other measures as may be necessary to make reasonable progress toward meeting the national goal."

Section 169A specifically requires visibility SIPs to include (1) best available retrofit technology (BART) for certain existing stationary sources that emit pollutants that "may reasonably be anticipated to cause or contribute" to visibility impairment in a mandatory Class I area for the purpose of eliminating or reducing any such impairment, and (2) a long-term (ten to fifteen years) strategy for making reasonable progress toward meeting the national goal.[25]

The state and federal roles in protecting visibility are similar to the state and federal air quality management partnership envisioned for protection of the national ambient air quality standards. The EPA establishes guidelines and overarching regulatory requirements, and the states, in turn, have the primary role in implementing the visibility protection requirements through SIPs.[26] The EPA has the responsibility to provide visibility protection through federal implementation plans (FIPs) when a state fails to submit an approvable visibility plan.[27]

The FLMs are given a unique role in the development of visibility SIPs because federal lands, the mandatory Class I federal areas, are the focus of visibility protection. States are required to consult in person with FLMs in developing visibility SIPs and to include the FLMs' recommendations in the public notice announcing the proposed SIP revision.[28]

The EPA's 1980 Visibility Protection Regulations: A Phased Approach

In 1980, the EPA issued regulations intended to ensure reasonable progress toward the national visibility protection goal.[29] These regulations were originally codified at 40 C.F.R. §§ 51.300 to 307 and, at the time, represented the existing core requirements for visibility protection. The rules required the thirty-six states[30] containing mandatory Class I areas where visibility is an important value to submit SIP revisions by September 2, 1981. In broad overview, the SIP revisions were to include the following:

- Emission limitations representing BART for certain existing stationary sources (Section 51.302(c)(2)(iii))
- A monitoring strategy for evaluating visibility and considering available data in state regulatory decisions (Section 51.305)
- A long-term (ten to fifteen years) strategy for making reasonable progress toward the national goal and provision for periodic review and revision, as appropriate, of the strategy at least every three years (Section 51.306)
- A program to review the potential visibility impacts from new or modified major stationary sources (Section 51.307)

The EPA's 1980 regulations adopted a phased approach to visibility protection. The agency segregated visibility impairment into two general types: (1) smoke, dust, colored gas plumes, or layered haze emitted from stacks that obscure the sky or horizon and are relatable to a single source or a small group of sources; and (2) widespread, regionally homogeneous haze from a multitude of sources that impairs visibility in every direction over a large area.[31]

The 1980 rules addressed the first type of impairment, requiring remediation of impairment that is relatable or "reasonably attributable" to a single existing stationary facility or small group of facilities.[32] The EPA indicated that future regulatory initiatives would address regional haze, the second type of impairment, when regional scale models were refined and scientific knowledge about the relationships between emitted air pollutants and visibility impairment improved.[33]

The EPA finalized regional haze rules in 1999, nearly two decades after it proposed this regulatory program. The rules resulted from concerted state and congressional pressure on the agency, landmark recommendations from the National Academy of Sciences' National Research Council, and the broad-based policy efforts of an interstate visibility transport commission established under the 1990 CAA Amendments.

Unsuccessful Attempts to Compel the EPA to Address Regional Haze

After waiting several years for the EPA to develop a regional haze program, New England states and environmental organizations attempted to advance EPA action. To address summertime haze in the Lye Brook National Wilderness Area, Vermont submitted to the EPA a long-term strategy containing a summertime ambient sulfate standard and an associated forty-eight-state emissions reduction plan to achieve the standard. Vermont also requested EPA disapproval and revision of the SIPs of eight upwind states allegedly responsible for the haze at Lye Brook Wilderness Area, which included requiring four of the states not containing Class I areas to be added to the list of states required to submit visibility SIPs.[34] The EPA declined to approve the elements of the Vermont SIP addressing regional haze or the request for EPA action against the eight upwind states.[35] The EPA reasoned that Vermont's regional haze measures exceeded the scope of the EPA's existing regulatory authority and could not be federally approved, and become federally enforceable, until the EPA issued regional haze regulations.[36]

The state of Vermont, the Conservation Law Foundation of New England, and Vermont Natural Resources Council challenged the EPA's decision not to take action on the regional haze portions of the SIP, contending that the EPA's 1980 regulations encompassed measures to address regional haze and, alternatively, that the CAA imposes on the states an independent duty to provide for visibility protection to ensure "reasonable progress" toward the national goal.[37] The U.S. Court of Appeals for the Second Circuit upheld the EPA's decision, reasoning that the EPA's 1980 regulations do not on their face address regional haze and that the preamble accompanying the regulations expressly deferred action on regional haze.[38] The court nevertheless admonished the EPA for failing to address regional haze:

> [M]ore than ten years after the enactment of section 169A, there still is no national program addressing regional haze. We are sympathetic to petitioners' argument that something must be done soon. EPA's assurances of future action on regional haze are little comfort to Vermont and visitors to Lye Brook. We can only hope that EPA will act quickly in furtherance of the national visibility goal.[39]

In a more direct attempt to engender EPA action, seven northeastern states and several environmental groups initiated a citizens' suit under Section 304 of the CAA, 42 U.S.C. § 7604, to compel the EPA to carry out an alleged mandatory duty to address regional haze.[40] The U.S. Court of Appeals for the First Circuit affirmed a district court decision dismissing the action for lack of jurisdiction.

The court reasoned that the EPA's decision to defer action on regional haze at the time the EPA issued its 1980 rules constituted final action judicially reviewable under CAA Section 307(b), 42 U.S.C. § 7607(b). Section 307(b) provides that a petition for review must be filed in the court of appeals within sixty days after final agency action is published in the *Federal Register*. The court held that the EPA's action was not judicially reviewable in district court through a citizens' suit to compel the EPA to fulfill a mandatory statutory duty.[41] In essence, the court concluded that the EPA's mandatory statutory duty under Section 169A(a)(4) to issue regulations to ensure reasonable progress toward the national visibility goal was fulfilled by its final 1980 regulations addressing "reasonably attributable" impairment and a final, judicially reviewable, agency decision deferring action to address regional haze.[42]

The court observed that the appellants were not without some administrative and potential judicial recourse to pursue the EPA fulfillment of its regional haze promise. The court explained that the appellants could petition the EPA for rule-making action to address regional haze, demonstrating that the conditions by which the EPA committed to take eventual regulatory action are satisfied. If the EPA denied the request, the appellants could seek judicial review in the court of appeals.[43]

Clean Air Act Amendments of 1990 Propel Regional Haze Regulations: Overview of Section 169B and Its Relation to Section 169A

In the 1990 CAA Amendments, Congress added visibility protection provisions in Section 169B that placed the EPA on a path to address regional haze.[44] In overview, Section 169B provided for the following:

1. Research identifying the sources and source regions of visibility impairment and clean air, including the adaptation of regional models
2. Periodic assessments of visibility improvement from the implementation of the 1990 amendments, other than the visibility protection provisions
3. Establishment of interstate visibility transport regions and associated commissions for Class I areas experiencing visibility impairment, which commissions are to report to the EPA on the promulgation of regulations addressing regional haze

Section 169B, therefore, spurred action to abate regional haze by providing for improved technical tools including regional modeling techniques, an assessment of the benefits of the other clean air programs under the 1990 amendments, and the establishment of an interstate effort to recommend federal policy solutions.

At the same time, section 169A remained the core statutory authority for addressing regional haze. Congress indicated that the advent of Section 169B did not affect the EPA's preexisting authority, or responsibility, to address regional haze under Section 169A.[45] Indeed, Section 169A was not revised in the 1990 amendments, and the EPA retained broad delegated rule-making authority under Section 169A(a)(4) to promulgate regulations to ensure reasonable progress toward meeting the national visibility goal. The national goal in turn calls for remedying "any existing" visibility impairment including regional haze.[46] And in adopting Section 169A, Congress evinced its intent to address impairment caused by "hazes" and the potential corresponding need to control a "variety of sources" and "regionally distributed sources."[47] Section 169B also referred to Section 169A as the source of authority for regulating regional haze.[48]

The Grand Canyon Visibility Transport Commission

The requirement to establish an interstate commission to evaluate regional haze problems and recommend policy solutions was one of the pivotal provisions of Section 169B. Section 169B directed the EPA to establish, by November 15, 1991, a visibility transport commission for the region affecting the visibility of the Grand Canyon National Park.[49] The EPA established the Grand Canyon visibility transport commission on November 13, 1991.[50] Based on the EPA's "broad discretionary authority under Section 169B(c) . . . to establish visibility transport regions and commissions," it expanded the scope of the Grand Canyon Commission "to include additional class I areas in the vicinity of the Grand Canyon National park, what is sometimes referred to as the 'Golden Circle' of parks and wilderness areas. This includes most of the national parks and national wilderness areas on the Colorado Plateau."[51]

The governors of Arizona, California, Colorado, New Mexico, Nevada, Oregon, and Utah were initially invited to participate on the commission. The EPA administrator also invited the governor of Idaho, who declined to participate.[52] Representatives of the EPA, U.S. Forest Service, U.S. Bureau of Land Management, U.S. Fish and Wildlife Service, and National Park Service also were commissioners, but were nonvoting members.[53] The EPA subsequently added the governor of Wyoming to the commission "based on, among other things, [the] State's assessment that activities in the Green River Basin may significantly contribute to visibility impairment in the 'Golden Circle.' "[54] All governors were voting members. The EPA also added the Hopi Tribe, Navajo Nation, and Pueblo of Acoma as voting commission members in 1994. The EPA subsequently added the Hualapai Tribe as a voting commission member and the Columbia River Inter-Tribal Fish Commission as a nonvoting member.[55]

The Grand Canyon Commission was directed to report to the EPA on "the promulgation of regulations under Section 169A to address long range strategies for addressing regional haze which impairs visibility in affected class I areas."[56] The Commission issued a report in June 1996 that recommended a number of strategies to abate regional haze.[57]

This report, in turn, triggered an eighteen-month statutory deadline for the EPA to carry out its regulatory responsibilities under Section 169A, including criteria for measuring reasonable progress toward the national visibility protection goal.[58] The statute also directed the resulting EPA regulations to require SIP revisions within twelve months.[59]

The Grand Canyon Commission, therefore, provided key technical and policy foundation for a national regional haze program as well as political support. And it established a new, legally enforceable deadline for the EPA to promulgate a regional haze program.

1993 National Research Council Report

In 1993, the National Research Council's Committee on Haze in National Parks and Wilderness Areas completed a review of the state of visibility science.[60] The findings informed the EPA's development of a regional haze program. The report was particularly important because the EPA deferred action on a regional haze program in its 1980 regulations reasoning that its technical tools were inadequate.

The Committee recommended, for example, regional air pollution abatement programs: "Progress toward the national goal of remedying and preventing man-made visibility impairment in Class I areas (Clean Air Act, Section 169A(a)) will require regional programs that operate over large geographic areas and limit emissions of pollutants that can cause regional haze."[61] Conversely, the Committee found that strategies targeting individual pollution sources, the focus of the 1980 visibility regulations, would remain important only in limited circumstances: "[S]trategies should be adopted that consider many sources simultaneously on a regional basis, although assessment of the effect of individual sources will remain important in some situations."[62]

The Committee also provided pivotal technical findings, concluding that current scientific knowledge is adequate to support a regulatory regional haze program, recommending regional modeling analysis and methods, and suggesting priorities for future research and analysis.[63]

Inhofe Amendment to TEA-21: $PM_{2.5}$ National Ambient Air Quality Standards and Regional Haze

In 1998, President Clinton signed into law the Transportation Equity Act for the 21st Century (dubbed "TEA-21").[64] Title VI of the law, advanced as a rider by Senator James Inhofe, established a schedule for carrying out the monitoring and air quality designations for the 1997 fine particle ($PM_{2.5}$) national ambient air quality standards. And, it addressed the interplay between the fine particle standards and the regional haze program.

Section 6102(c)(2) of TEA-21 provides:

> For any area designated as nonattainment for the July 1997 PM national ambient air quality standard in accordance with the schedule set forth in this section, notwithstanding the time limit prescribed in paragraph (2) of section 169B(e) of the Clean Air Act, the Administrator shall require State implementation plan revisions referred to in such paragraph (2)

to be submitted at the same time as State implementation plan revisions referred to in section 172 of the Clean Air Act implementing the revised national ambient air quality standard for fine particulate matter are required to be submitted. For any area designated as attainment or unclassifiable for such standard, the Administrator shall require the State implementation plan revisions referred to in such paragraph (2) to be submitted 1 year after the area has been so designated. The preceding provisions of this paragraph shall not preclude the implementation of the agreements and recommendations set forth in the Grand Canyon Visibility Transport Commission Report dated June 1996.

This statutory language has several implications. First, it allows $PM_{2.5}$ nonattainment areas to submit their regional haze plans at the same time their $PM_{2.5}$ nonattainment plans are due under Section 172(b) of the CAA, which requires the submittal of nonattainment plans no later than three years from the date of the nonattainment designation. This schedule for $PM_{2.5}$ nonattainment areas to submit regional haze SIPs expressly supersedes the schedule in section 169B(e)(2), which required SIP revisions within twelve months of EPA's final regional haze rules.

The statutory language also requires $PM_{2.5}$ unclassifiable and attainment areas to submit their regional haze SIPs within one year of the $PM_{2.5}$ air quality designation. And, the language expressly preserves implementation of the Grand Canyon Visibility Transport Commission agreements and recommendations, which are on a more advanced schedule. The EPA interpreted the Inhofe amendment to TEA-21 in its final regional haze rules, promulgated in 1999.

The EPA's 1999 Regional Haze Regulations and Implementation Program

Reasonable Progress Goals

The EPA published final regional haze regu-lations on July 1, 1999.[65] The rules apply to all states and the District of Columbia, but not to the territories of Guam, Puerto Rico, American Samoa, and the Mariana Islands, which are included in the definition of "state" in section 302(d) of the CAA.[66] The overarching framework of the rule is the requirement that states develop plans for each of their Class I areas that establish dual "reasonable progress goals": "providing for an improvement in visibility for the most impaired days over the period of the implementation plan and ensuring no degradation in visibility for the least impaired days over the same period."[67] The "most impaired days" are, in turn, defined to mean the average visibility impairment for the twenty percent of monitored days in a calendar year with the highest amount of visibility impairment.[68] Conversely, the "least impaired days" are the twenty percent of monitored days with the lowest amount of visibility impairment.[69] And the period that the plan must cover is generally a ten-year long-term strategy period beginning from the deadline that the original regional haze SIPs are due. So, states must adopt ten-year-long plans that prohibit deterioration of visibility for the cleanest days and establish a goal for improving visibility on the dirtiest days.

The rules pointedly elaborate on the prong of the "reasonable progress goals" requiring states to improve visibility in the dirtiest 20 percent of days. First, the affected states are required to establish a projected glide path based on the rate of uniform progress that would be needed to restore visibility to natural conditions by 2064.[70] If an affected state establishes a reasonable progress goal that is slower than the projected rate of progress to restore natural conditions by 2064, the state must demonstrate, consistent with a number of factors, why the goal of attaining natural conditions by 2064 is not reasonable.[71] To provide public transparency for an alternative decision by the state, the rule requires the state to "provide to the public for review as part of its implementation plan an assessment of the number of years it would take to attain natural conditions if visibility improvement continues at the rate of progress selected by the State as reasonable."[72]

There are also a number of key technical issues governing affected states' determination of the baseline visibility conditions for the most and least impaired days and in turn for determining what constitutes natural visibility conditions for a given area.[73]

Best Available Retrofit Technology and Other Control Measures

The CAA requirement for certain major stationary sources to install best available retrofit technology (BART) is one of the core control strategies under the regional haze rule for states to achieve the reasonable progress goals.[74] By statute, BART applies to twenty-six listed source categories of industrial facilities constructed between 1962 and 1977 that emit "any air pollutant which may reasonably be anticipated to cause or contribute to any impairment of visibility in any" Class I area.[75] The CAA also delineates the factors that govern the states' determination of BART, including "the costs of compliance, the energy and nonair quality environmental impacts of compliance, any existing pollution control technology in use at the source, the remaining useful life of the source, and the degree of improvement in visibility which may reasonably be anticipated to result from the use of such technology."[76]

Congress provided at least limited immunity for sources more than fifteen years old at the time of the 1977 amendments. The EPA "may not require States to apply the best retrofit technology to sources which have been in existence more than 15 years. States may do so if they choose but could not be required by the administrator."[77] Accordingly, sources operating before August 7, 1962, are excluded from the BART requirement. BART must be installed and operated no later than five years after SIP approval.[78]

As noted, "major stationary source" is defined to include the following twenty-six stationary sources in existence on August 7, 1977, with the potential to emit at least 250 tons per year of any pollutant: fossil-fuel-fired steam electric plants of more than 250 million BTUs-per-hour heat input; coal cleaning plants (thermal dryers); kraft pulp mills; portland cement plants; primary zinc smelters; iron and steel mill plants; primary aluminum ore reduction plants; primary copper smelters; municipal incinerators capable of charging more than 250 tons of refuse per day; hydrofluoric, sulfuric, and nitric acid plants; petroleum refineries; lime plants; phosphate rock processing plants; coke oven batteries; sulfur recovery plants; carbon black plants (furnace process); primary lead smelters; fuel conversion plants; sintering plants; secondary metal production facilities; chemical process plants; fossil fuel boilers of more than 250 million BTUs-per-hour heat input; petroleum storage and transfer facilities with a capacity exceeding 300,000 barrels; taconite ore processing facilities; glass fiber processing plants; and charcoal production facilities.[79]

The EPA may exempt a source from BART, but only upon the concurrence of the affected FLMs. [80] To qualify for an exemption, the source must demonstrate that it does not, by itself or *in combination with* other sources, emit any air pollutant that may be reasonably anticipated to cause or contribute to a significant impairment of visibility in a mandatory Class I area.[81] Any fossil fuel-fired power plant with a total generating capacity of 750 megawatts or greater must demonstrate that it is located at such a distance from all mandatory Class I areas that it similarly could not cause or contribute to significant impairment.[82]

The EPA has relied on the exemption provision as evidence of very broad authority to remedy visibility impairment. The EPA reasoned that the discretionary authority to exempt a source that does not by itself or in combination with other sources cause or contribute to significant impairment presupposes that the agency may remedy virtually "any" amount of visibility impairment attributable to a particular source.[83]

The regional haze rule provides that states "must submit an implementation plan containing emission limitations representing BART and schedules for compliance with BART for each BART-eligible source that may reasonably be anticipated to cause or contribute to any impairment of visibility in any Class I Federal area."[84] The rule goes on to lay out specific procedures and considerations that govern the states' BART determination.

The rule also provides states with the option of administering a declining air pollution cap and emissions trading program as an alternative to BART.[85] States pursuing this alternative compliance option must demonstrate that the emissions trading program or other alternative measure "will achieve greater reasonable progress than would be achieved through the installation and operation of BART."[86] The rule specifies the procedures and methodologies by which states must make such a demonstration.

A haze abatement strategy is not, however, limited to BART. BART is only one specific element of a visibility protection program that includes emission limitations, schedules of compliance, and other measures that are necessary to make reasonable progress toward the national goal.[87] States must, therefore, consider the full suite of anthropogenic sources of visibility impairment in designing a long-term strategy including "major and minor stationary sources, mobile sources and area sources."[88]

Technical Foundation for Haze Abatement Plans

The regional haze rule also calls on states to establish the technical foundation for regional haze programs including the collection and reporting of monitoring and emissions inventory data.[89] For example, state plans are required to include a monitoring strategy for "measuring, characterizing, and reporting . . . regional haze visibility impairment that is representative of all mandatory Class I Federal areas within the State."[90] State plans must also provide for a "statewide inventory of emissions of pollutants that are reasonably anticipated to cause or contribute to visibility impairment in any mandatory Class I Federal area" and must commit to periodically update the inventory.[91]

The Dynamic Planning Horizon

The extraordinarily long-range planning horizon for the regional haze rule is delineated by the establishment of a presumptive glidepath to restore natural visibility conditions by 2064. For the states, more immediate planning obligations are divided into ten-year increments. After the first plan submittal, which is to cover the period of time from the SIP submittal due date through 2018, states must overhaul their regional haze SIPs every ten years thereafter.[92] This includes reassessing all basic planning obligations and establishing additional control measures to ensure that the reasonable progress goals are achieved.

States are also required to conduct periodic assessments and make appropriate mid-course adjustments every five years.[93] The mid-course evaluation includes a review of the status of control measure implementation, emission reductions achieved, changes in visibility conditions, and an analysis of emissions trends.[94]

Interstate Cooperation and Coordination

The challenge of addressing an interstate air pollution problem through an individual state air quality management plan places a premium on interstate consultation and coordination. The EPA's regional haze program encourages such interstate efforts through the combination of incentives, cooperation, and accountability. The EPA has helped establish and support five regional planning organizations across the country that provide the forum for affected states to coordinate in the research, analysis, and development of haze air pollution abatement strategies.[95]

The regional haze rule requires states to address their share of regional haze problems in affected Class I areas by expressly providing that "[w]here other States cause or contribute to impairment in a mandatory Class I Federal area, the State must demonstrate that it has included in its implementation plan all measures necessary to obtain its share of the emission reductions needed to meet the progress goal for the area."[96] The EPA also recognizes the emission reduction apportionment efforts under the auspices of regional planning organizations: "If the State has participated in a regional planning process, the State must ensure it has included all measures needed to achieve its apportionment of emission reduction obligations agreed upon through that process."[97] And the rule establishes a mechanism by which a state can redress plan inadequacies that are due to sources located in another state.[98]

Grand Canyon Visibility Transport Commission Program

The regional haze rule also incorporated a distinct implementation pathway for the nine western states in the Grand Canyon transport region: Arizona, California, Colorado, Idaho, Nevada, New Mexico, Oregon, Utah, and Wyoming.[99] The rule incorporates, in 40 C.F.R. § 51.309, the Grand Canyon Visibility Transport Commission recommendations. The transport region states are given the choice of implementing the general haze program planning requirements, codified at 40 C.F.R. § 51.308, or the commission's recommendations. This option of administering a western haze program under 40 C.F.R. § 51.309 applies for the first long-term strategy planning period, through 2018.[100] After 2018, all states will administer their regional haze programs under 40 C.F.R. § 51.308.

The Grand Canyon regional haze program incorporated into the final regional haze rule addresses a variety of emission sources. It includes a market-based program that is an alternative to BART and that requires a decline in emissions from stationary sources. If the reductions are not achieved, a backstop market-based program is automatically triggered to ensure that the reductions are realized and to impose penalties for emissions discharges in excess of allowances.[101] Some of the key elements of the stationary source pollution reduction program were addressed in a separate EPA rulemaking.[102] The program would cap haze-forming sulfur dioxide emissions on all sources, in participating states, discharging 100 tons or more and was derived assuming an 85 percent reduction from uncontrolled power plants as well as a number of countervailing assumptions regarding growth and uncertainty.[103]

The western component of the regional haze rule also requires a steady decline in emissions from mobile sources, and an enhanced smoke management program to address pollution from prescribed fire.[104] Additional technical assessment and, if necessary, policy responses are required for emissions sources in clean air corridors and area sources of dust emissions.[105] And there are provisions requiring programs to prevent pollution through expanded reliance on renewable energy resources, energy conservation, and energy efficiency. Participating states must demonstrate efforts to meet their contribution toward the region's goal of ten percent renewable energy by 2005 and twenty percent by 2015.[106]

Because the Commission's recommendations focused on the "golden circle" of Class I areas on the Colorado Plateau, the haze rule also establishes requirements for the Commission states implementing the western program to address other Class I areas within their state or impacted by emissions from their state.[107] States also must address other pollutants from stationary sources, including PM and nitrogen oxides, since the market-based alternative to BART is focused on sulfur dioxide.[108]

Tribal Program Implementation

The CAA and implementing rules authorize tribes to implement programs in the same manner as states.[109] Federally recognized Indian tribes may, therefore, also seek authorization to implement the regional haze rule. Indeed, Indian tribes had a central role in the development of the Grand Canyon Visibility Transport Commission recommendations, and tribes within the transport region may also choose to implement the western program.[110]

SIP Submittal Deadlines

The EPA interpreted the SIP submittal schedule under TEA-21, above, in promulgating the regional haze rule. The rule requires states to submit regional haze SIPs for areas designated in attainment or unclassifiable for the $PM_{2.5}$ NAAQS, within one year of the air quality designation.[111] For any area designated in nonattainment for the $PM_{2.5}$ NAAQS, states are given three years from the designation and no later than December 31, 2008, to submit regional haze SIPs. The regional haze rule provides that those states engaged in a regional planning process with other states may defer core aspects of the regional haze plans, regardless of their $PM_{2.5}$ NAAQS air quality status, until the latest date by which any area in the planning process would be required to submit, provided a committal SIP is submitted.[112]

Legal Challenges to the Regional Haze Rule

A number of industrial interests challenged the final regional haze rule including an association of electric utilities, coal interests, and mining interests.[113] The State of Michigan also challenged the final rule. The Sierra Club filed a petition for judicial review challenging certain aspects of the rule. A number of states and environmental and conservation organizations intervened in defense of the EPA's rule. The legal actions were reviewed in the D.C. Circuit, which has exclusive jurisdiction over nationally applicable regulations under the CAA.[114]

In a May 24, 2002 opinion, a three judge panel voted 2-1 to affirm the rule in part and to remand and vacate aspects of the rule.[115] The court rejected industry's claim that the no-degradation requirement was impermissibly more rigorous than the statutorily authorized prohibitions on deterioration under the CAA's prevention of significant deterioration (PSD) of air quality program, and that the EPA had unlawfully imposed the natural visibility goal on the states. The court also determined that the Sierra Club's challenge to the leniency of the reasonable progress goal was unripe. So the dual overarching programmatic requirements of the regional haze program were left intact.

At the same time, two significant elements of the rule were remanded. The court remanded and vacated aspects of the BART provisions of the rule, in response to industry's challenge. As noted, the statute delineates several factors for determining BART. In the final haze rule, the EPA interpreted one of these factors "the degree of improvement in visibility which may reasonably be anticipated to result from the use of such technology" to require states to consider the visibility improvement benefits due to the emission reductions achievable from all sources subject to BART located within the region that contributes to visibility impairment in the Class I area.[116] The court held that the EPA's interpretation of this factor was unlawful, vacated the provision, and remanded it to the EPA. The court likewise overturned the EPA's approach for determining which sources are subject to the BART requirement.

The Sierra Club also successfully challenged the EPA's interpretation of TEA-21. In particular, it challenged the EPA's rules giving states participating in regional planning organizations three years from a $PM_{2.5}$ designation to submit a SIP for areas declared unclassifiable or attainment. The court reasoned that the EPA effectively extended the SIP submittal deadline for $PM_{2.5}$ unclassifiable and attainment areas from one year to three based on a committal SIP, and remanded this to the agency for further consideration.

BART Guidelines

The CAA directs the EPA regulations required under Section 169A to contain guidelines for the states on methods for implementing the visibility protection program.[117] And the statute pointedly mandates that the BART emission limitations for fossil-fuel-fired generating power plants having a total generating capacity in excess of 750 megawatts be determined pursuant to such guidelines.

In the final regional haze rule, the EPA indicated it would issue BART guidelines separately, within a year of promulgation of the regional haze rule.[118] The EPA published proposed BART guidelines on July 20, 2001. The guidelines proposed a "top-down" methodology for determining BART, similar to the methodology for determining BACT. The guidelines examine, in some detail, how each of the BART factors would be considered in a BART analysis. And the guidelines proposed to establish a presumptive 90 percent to 95 percent control as BART for sulfur dioxide from uncontrolled power plants.[119] After the D.C. Circuit declared part of the BART rules unlawful, however, the EPA held further action on the BART guidelines in abeyance.

Status of the EPA's Response to BART Remand

The EPA has publicly announced its schedule for responding to the court's remand. The agency has indicated that it intends to concurrently address both the aspects of the BART rule remanded by the D.C. Circuit and the

BART guidelines. The EPA's schedule is to publish a proposal for both by April 2004 and publish a final rule-making package by April 2005.[120]

The EPA has also identified some of the key issues that will be addressed in the rule making. The EPA indicated that it will address "the concerns that the Court raised about the criteria we provided for determining which sources should be subject to BART, and the appropriate standard for evaluating the degree of visibility improvement that BART will provide. It will also consider whether to provide a mechanism by which states may exempt sources from BART determinations."[121]

The EPA's Continued Administration of its 1980 Visibility Program

While considerable attention has been focused on the EPA's regional haze program, the EPA's long-standing 1980 visibility protection program remains intact. The 1980 rules provided for remedial action where visibility impairment in a Class I area could be relatable or attributable to pollution from a stationary source or small group of sources.[122] States and the EPA continue to administer these program requirements although there have been few significant developments in recent years.

A source is identified by determining whether visibility impairment in a mandatory Class I area is "reasonably attributable" to a facility. This attribution determination is a prerequisite or corequisite to conducting a BART analysis for a facility under the 1980 visibility regulations. "Visibility impairment" under the regulations means "any humanly perceptible change in visibility (visual range, contrast, coloration) from that which would have existed under natural conditions."[123] To be remedial under the 1980 program, such impairment may be reasonably attributable "by visual observation or any other technique the State deems appropriate."[124] Thus, states are given broad discretion in selecting the techniques used to attribute impairment to a particular facility.

There are specific BART guidelines for "reasonably attributable" impairment. The EPA proposed to update these guidelines as part of its proposed BART guidelines for regional haze.[125] The pre-existing guidelines provide that the level of control necessary to meet the new source performance standard (NSPS) for power plants is generally available for large power plants. If BART is equivalent to the NSPS level of control, no detailed analysis of BART factors is required. The guidelines allow an emission limit other than the NSPS if it reflects a reasonable balance of the BART factors.[126] The EPA observed some time ago that these BART guidelines were "outdated in certain respects."[127]

Visibility New Source Review

The CAA's PSD program provides for preconstruction review of the air quality impacts associated with new or modified major stationary sources.[128] The PSD program applies to areas of the country designated as "attainment" or "unclassifiable" for the NAAQS pursuant to Section 107 of the CAA. These areas are generally referred to as PSD areas.[129]

The PSD program protects Class I areas by allowing only a small increment of air quality deterioration in these areas and by providing for assessment of the potential impacts on the air quality-related values (AQRVs) of Class I areas.[130] AQRVs include visibility and the other fundamental purposes for which such lands have been established and preserved by Congress.[131] The PSD program places an "affirmative responsibility" on FLMs to protect the AQRVs of Class I areas.[132] (The PSD program is detailed in Chapter 6.)

The visibility goal of the Section 169A visibility protection program includes preventing any future visibility impairment in mandatory Class I areas. The EPA's visibility regulations therefore provide for review of the visibility impacts associated with proposed new and modified sources.[133] The visibility NSR requirements specifically apply to "any new major stationary source or major modification."[134] The visibility rules define the terms "major stationary source" and "major modification" to have the same meanings as defined under the PSD permit program.[135]

The visibility new source review (NSR) provisions are broader in applicability than those protecting federal Class I areas under the PSD program in that they apply to proposed new or modified stationary sources in both PSD and nonattainment areas. The net effect for a PSD source locating near a mandatory Class I area is that it must consider both the PSD provisions (which include BACT, Class I increments, and protection of AQRVs) and the NSR provisions related exclusively to visibility protection. Similarly, a new or modified major stationary source proposing to locate in a nonattainment area must meet the nonattainment NSR permit requirements in addition to the visibility NSR requirements.[136] The dual requirements, however, may be addressed in a single "one stop" permit proceeding.[137]

The EPA's visibility NSR regulations specifically provide for implementation in conjunction with and through the PSD permitting requirements at 40 C.F.R. §51.166 (formerly codified at Section 51.24).[138] The visibility NSR regulations require state PSD programs to provide for special coordination with FLMs. If the state requires or receives advance notification of a permit application for a source that may affect visibility, the state must notify affected FLMs within thirty days of the early notice.[139]

In addition to any advance notification of a potential permit application, the state must provide written notification to the FLMs within thirty days of receipt of a permit application for a source that may affect visibility. The notification must include all information relevant to the application and an analysis of the anticipated impacts on visibility and must be provided at least sixty days before the state's public hearing on the permit.[140] The state must consider any analysis performed by the FLM within thirty days after notification of the permit application. If the state disagrees with the FLM about the proposed source's visibility impacts, it must explain its decision or indicate where to obtain such an explanation in the notice of public hearing on the proposed permit.[141]

The same protections apply to new or modified major stationary sources proposing to locate in nonattainment areas that may affect visibility in a mandatory Class I area. In addition, visibility NSR in nonattainment areas requires compliance with the following PSD provisions:

- The requirement that the owner or operator analyze the impairment to visibility, soils, and vegetation that would occur as a result of the source and general commercial, residential, industrial, and other growth associated with the source and the air quality impact projected for the area as a result of other growth (Section 51.166(o))
- The requirement that the reviewing authority provide the EPA with a copy of the permit application and notice of actions related to consideration of the permit (Section 51.166(p)(1))
- Recognition of the FLMs' affirmative responsibility to protect visibility (Section 51.166(p)(2))
- The public participation requirements specified in Section 51.166(q), including the requirement to send the FLM a notice of public comment on the proposed permit[142]

In the preamble to the adoption of the EPA's visibility NSR regulations, the agency suggested several options available to a state and source to mitigate the potential visibility impacts.

> The State could (1) require the source to analyze alternative sites, (2) impose additional control requirements, (3) limit the source's capability to emit the pollutant which is expected to cause the impairment by limiting the source's operating conditions, or (4) deny the source permission to construct. Among the options available to the source are modifying its proposed operating conditions to reduce its potential impact and locating at other sites where the potential impact on the area is expected to be less.[143]

The EPA has also endorsed the use of offsetting emissions reductions from existing sources to mitigate the potential impact of a proposed source on visibility impairment in a Class I area.[144]

The NSR provisions also give states broad authority to require monitoring in a Class I area near a proposed source.[145]

States' Failure to Submit Approvable Programs and Federal Implementation of the 1980 Regulations

Virtually all of the affected thirty-six states failed to timely submit SIPs in response to the EPA's 1980 visibility rules. Environmental groups sued the EPA to issue FIPs.[146] The parties agreed to a settlement that established a sequential rule-making schedule for the EPA to issue FIPs containing elements of the visibility program for states with outstanding planning deficiencies.[147]

Through the series of rule makings, the EPA issued federal visibility programs and inserted them into the SIPs of the deficient states.

Pervasive state failure to make the required submittals and the resulting prominent federal role in directly administering the visibility protection program is unusual. For the practitioner, it creates an additional layer of complexity in determining the applicable law and administering government entity. Over the past years, some states have addressed these deficiencies. The state-by-state status of SIP programs in 40 C.F.R. Part 52 provides a good starting point in determining whether the state is administering its own federally approved visibility protection program under the 1980 rules, the EPA administers the program, or some combination of the two implements specific program elements.

Federal Visibility New Source Review

The EPA established visibility preconstruction review programs, including requirements for both PSD and nonattainment areas, for states failing to submit programs meeting the visibility NSR requirements of 40 C.F.R. § 51.307.[148]

The EPA adopted visibility NSR revisions to the federal PSD regulations at 40 C.F.R. § 52.21 applying to states that do not have an approved PSD program. The federal regulations provide that the EPA or a delegated state[149] may require a proposed source to conduct visibility monitoring, including preapplication monitoring.[150] The regulations implement the FLM notice and coordination provided for in 40 C.F.R. § 51.307(a)(1), (2), and (3).[151] In addition, the EPA or a delegated state must provide the FLM with a copy of its preliminary determination on the permit application, indicating whether construction should be approved, approved with conditions, or disapproved.[152]

The EPA promulgated and applied 40 C.F.R. § 52.27 to those states having approved PSD programs but not meeting the specific visibility NSR requirements. The regulations require the state's permit reviewing authority to adhere to the FLM notice and coordination provided for in 40 C.F.R. § 51.307(a)(1), (2), and (3).[153] The regulations clarify that the permit will not be issued where the permitting authority determines that a proposed source will have an adverse impact on visibility.[154] If the state fails to provide the required FLM notice and coordination, the public may request, within sixty days of the notice seeking public comment on the draft permit, that the EPA assume responsibility for reviewing the visibility impacts of the proposed source.[155] If the state consistently fails to provide the required coordination, then the EPA must require prospective permit applicants to apply directly to the EPA so that it may conduct the visibility review. The regulations establish the procedures that the EPA must follow in reviewing the visibility impacts.[156]

The EPA promulgated and applied 40 C.F.R. § 52.28 to those states failing to adopt the visibility NSR program for nonattainment areas, as required by 40 C.F.R. § 51.307. The regulations require the permit applicant to provide an analysis of the visibility impairment that would occur as a result of the source and growth associated with the source, provide for FLM notification and coordination, recognize that the FLM has an affirmative responsibility to protect the AQRVs (including visibility) of Class I areas, and grant the EPA broad authority to require preconstruction and postconstruction visibility monitoring.[157] The regulations specify that the EPA may issue permits only to sources whose emissions will be consistent with making reasonable progress toward the national visibility goal.[158] The agency may delegate this authority to states without their own approvable programs.[159]

Periodic SIP Reviews

The EPA's 1980 visibility protection rules require states and the federal government, for states without approved programs, to review the adequacy of the plans adopted under those rules every three years and, as appropriate, to revise the programs. The state must consult with the FLM during the periodic review, and it must report to the public and the EPA its progress toward the national visibility goal evaluating, for example, additional measures, including SIP revisions, that may be necessary to ensure reasonable progress toward the national visibility goal.

The EPA adopted 40 C.F.R. § 52.29 for those states failing to implement programs requiring periodic assessments under the 1980 rules and incorporated it into the plans for the deficient states.[160] The regulations call for the EPA to review, and revise if appropriate, the strategy for all affected Class I areas at least every three years from November 24, 1987, and to report on any progress made toward the national visibility goal.[161]

The triennnial assessments provide an important checkpoint for a state to determine whether visibility problems are being adequately evaluated and addressed. The final regional haze rule merges the five-year reviews under that program with the triennial reviews under the 1980 regulations by putting states on a consolidated five-year review cycle once the state's first regional haze SIP is adopted.[162]

Reasonably Attributable Visibility Impairment at Grand Canyon National Park

In the most significant regulatory action to date under its 1980 visibility regulations, the EPA required a 90 percent reduction in sulfur dioxide (SO_2) emissions at the Navajo Generating Station (NGS) to remedy attributable visibility impairment at Grand Canyon National Park (Grand Canyon). The rule-making process was controversial and involved informal regulatory negotiations, with subsequent litigation.

The Rule-Making Process

The Interior Department certified the existence of visibility impairment at the Grand Canyon and identified NGS as a probable source of impairment.[163] NGS is a 2,250-megawatt coal-fired power plant consisting of three 750-megawatt units. It is located near Page, in northern Arizona, approximately fifteen miles from the Grand Canyon boundary.[164] At the time, NGS emitted more than 70,000 tons of uncontrolled SO_2 per year.

The EPA preliminarily attributed visibility impairment at the Grand Canyon to NGS based on the "collection of analyses" in the final draft report of a six-week field study conducted by the National Park Service.[165] The study included the release of a unique tracer from the NGS stacks that was detected at a monitoring site sixty-five miles away at the south rim of the Grand Canyon. Among other analyses, the study also included an emissions inventory assessment, meteorological analysis, time-lapse photography, and statistical regression analysis. The study estimated that NGS was the most substantial contributor to winter visibility impairment episodes. The EPA requested comment on its preliminary decision.

The agency proposed further action based on the final National Park Service field study report, the National Academy of Sciences (NAS) review of the study, the preliminary results of a National Park Service analysis documenting more intense wintertime impairment episodes below the canyon's rim, and the preliminary results of a field study by the NGS's owners that showed a much smaller NGS contribution to impairment.[166] The NAS review of the Park Service field study concluded that the study did not provide a basis for quantifying the fraction of impairment attributable to NGS but did establish, qualitatively, that NGS is a significant contributor to impairment at the Grand Canyon.[167]

The EPA proposed to find that certain winter visibility impairment episodes at the Grand Canyon were reasonably attributable to NGS and again requested comment.[168] In the same *Federal Register* notice, the EPA proposed a BART emission limitation representing a 70 percent reduction in SO_2 emissions, determined on a thirty-day rolling average, to be phased in at all three units between 1995 and 1999.[169] The EPA proposed three other control options, including 50 percent and 90 percent emission reductions and a seasonal option based on experimental technology, with a 70 percent emission reduction backstop if the technology failed.[170] The agency conducted a detailed BART analysis based on the BART guidelines applicable to large power plants.[171]

After the public comment period, in a series of meetings facilitated by the EPA, the owners and interested environmental groups reached an agreement on a recommended control strategy for NGS.[172] The agreement, set out in a memorandum of understanding (MOU), recommended a 90 percent SO_2 emission reduction based on an annual average and phased in by unit between November 1997 and August 1999, along with scheduled wintertime maintenance. The EPA reopened the comment period to request the public's views on the recommendation.[173]

In its final rule-making action, the EPA finalized its attribution determination.[174] The EPA concluded that the techniques used in the National Park Service field study, the field study conducted by the owners-operators, and other data and analyses in the administrative record employed appropriate techniques for determining reasonably attributable visibility impairment. The agency determined that the data and analyses showed that impairment at the Grand Canyon was reasonably attributable to NGS for the following reasons: (1) the unique tracers used in the two field studies were observed in substantial quantities at the Grand Canyon during impairment episodes; (2) NGS is the predominant source of SO_2 in the region; (3) SO_2 converts to visibility-impairing sulfates through transformation in the atmosphere; (4) meteorological data show that the NGS plume easily can and frequently does travel to the Grand Canyon; and (5) sulfates are the major contributor to visibility impairment at the Grand Canyon.

The EPA expressly recognized that NGS is not the only source of impairment at the Grand Canyon. The agency concluded that NGS is nevertheless a dominant source of visibility impairment episodes at the Grand Canyon and that "the addition of emissions controls at NGS alone will result in a significant improvement in visibility" at the Grand Canyon.

The EPA's final action adopted a control strategy consistent with the recommendations in the MOU. The EPA determined that the MOU control strategy provided a greater degree of visibility improvement at lower cost than the EPA's proposed strategy.[175] The cost savings were realized from two elements of the MOU control strategy. First, the 90 percent reduction control strategy utilized a longer averaging period than that proposed by the EPA— an annual average compared with a thirty-day rolling average. The annual average obviated the need for backup scrubbers in the event of intermittent malfunction. Second, the control strategy provided a longer period to phase in the emission limitation, spreading the costs over a longer time.

The EPA predicted the resulting visibility improvement based on the two field studies assessing impacts at the canyon rim and monitoring data collected below the rim.[176] The agency estimated that the 90 percent reduction in SO_2 would improve winter seasonal average visibility above the rim by approximately seven percent. The EPA estimated that more dramatic improvements were expected to occur during peak winter episodes monitored in the canyon and that reducing NGS emissions could result in increases in standard visual range of up to 300 percent during such episodes.

The CAA calls for BART to be procured, installed, and operated "as expeditiously as practicable" and "in no event later than five years" after the date of the EPA's issuance of a plan revision.[177] The EPA's 1991 final rule called for the emission limitation to be phased in by unit in 1997, 1998, and 1999, more than five years later. Therefore, instead of BART, the EPA's final emission limitation was based on the overarching requirement to adopt "emission limits, schedules of compliance, and other measures as may be necessary to make reasonable progress toward meeting the national goal."[178] The EPA concluded, based on the relevant "reasonable progress" factors, that the 90 percent SO_2 reduction control strategy would provide for greater reasonable progress toward the national goal by providing more visibility protection at less cost than the EPA's proposal, which was based on BART.[179]

Legal Challenge

Several irrigation districts in Arizona that receive electricity from NGS to pump water challenged the EPA's final rule. The petitioners' central claim was that the EPA exceeded its regulatory authority by remedying regional haze visibility impairment. The petitioners argued that under the 1980 regulations the "EPA is limited to addressing visibility impairment caused by a noticeable plume that is directly traceable to a given source through the use of visual observation or simple monitoring techniques."[180]

The court construed the EPA's 1980 rules as conferring broad authority to regulate visibility impairment that is reasonably attributable to a source.[181] The court observed that the EPA acknowledged that NGS is not the only source of impairment and that regional haze affects visibility at the Grand Canyon.[182] Nevertheless, the court reasoned,

> Even if the Final Rule addresses only a small fraction of the visibility impairment at the Grand Canyon, EPA still has the statutory authority to address that portion of the visibility impairment problem which is, in fact "reasonably attributable" to NGS. Congress mandated an extremely low triggering threshold, requiring the installment of stringent emission controls when an individual source "emits any air pollutant which may reasonably be anticipated to cause or contribute to any impairment of visibility."[183]

Further, the court reasoned that the CAA does not require "ironclad scientific certainty establishing the precise relationship between a source's emission and resulting visibility impairment."[184] It also reasoned that the EPA had broad discretion in the methods it used to determine whether visibility impairment at the Grand Canyon is "reasonably attributable" to NGS because the EPA's 1980 regulations define "reasonably attributable" as attributable by visual observation or any other technique deemed appropriate.

The court held that "the technical, scientific record more than adequately supports the EPA's reasonable conclusion that visibility impairment in the Grand Canyon is 'reasonably attributable' to NGS."[185] The court also concluded that the EPA acted within its discretion in relying on the overarching requirement of achieving reasonable progress toward the national goal instead of the more specific BART requirement in the circumstances of this case, since the resulting emission limit "would produce greater visibility improvement at a lower cost" and "more 'reasonable progress' will thereby be attained."[186]

Recent Issues under the 1980 Regulations

Since the Navajo Generating Station rule-making, there have been several circumstances where documented concerns about visibility impairment at a Class I area were in whole or part responsible for pollution abatement at an existing power plant. The Class I areas affected and the power plants implicated include

- Mount Zirkel Wilderness Area in Colorado (Craig and Hayden power plants)
- Mount Rainier National Park in Washington (Centralia power plant)
- Grand Canyon National Park (Mohave power plant)

The prior edition of this Handbook examined some of these issues. The Western States Air Resources Council, an association of western state air directors, recently issued recommendations for making attribution determinations under the 1980 visibility protection rules.[187]

Notes

1. *See* Pub. L. No. 95-95, 91 Stat. 685, 742–45 (1977). For a detailed examination of the programs in the 1977 amendments affecting visibility protection, with a focus on visual air quality in the southwestern United States, *see* Jerome Ostrov, *Visibility Protection under the Clean Air Act: Preserving Scenic and Parkland Areas in the Southwest,* 10 Ecology L.Q. 397 (1982).

2. CAA § 169A(a)(1).

3. CAA § 169A(g)(3).

4. CAA § 169A(g)(6).

5. *See* H.R. Rep. No. 95-294, at 203–04 (1977).

6. Committee on Haze in National Parks and Wilderness Areas, National Research Council, Protecting Visibility in National Parks and Wilderness Areas, vol. 1 at 1 (National Academy Press, 1993).

7. *Id.*

8. EPA, *Protecting Visibility: An EPA Report to Congress* (EPA 450/5-79-008 Oct. 1979).

9. EPA, *Air Quality Criteria for Particulate Matter,* vol. 1 at 3-99 (EPA/600/P-95/001aF April 1996).

10. *See* 1993 National Academy of Sciences Report, *supra* note 6, at 2.

11. National Park Service, Air Quality in the National Parks, 2d. ed. (Sept. 2002) at 14–15.

12. *Id.*

13. EPA, *Visibility in Our Nation's Parks and Wilderness Areas, available at* http://www.epa.gov/oar/visibility/monitor.html.

14. *See* CAA § 169A(g)(5). By contrast, Section 169B of the CAA, 42 U.S.C. § 7492, containing companion visibility protection provisions added in the 1990 CAA amendments and discussed in a later section, refers to "class I area." If not limited to "Federal" and "mandatory" Class I areas, then the term could encompass any state, tribal, and federal lands initially designated as Class II areas under Section 162(a) of the CAA but subsequently redesignated as Class I under Section 164 of the CAA. Several American Indian reservations have been redesignated Class I areas pursuant to CAA Section 164(c). *See* 40 C.F.R. §§ 52.1382(c) (Class I redesignations for the Northern Cheyenne, Flathead, and Fort Peck Indian Reservations) & 52.2497(c) (Class I redesignation for Spokane Indian Reservation); *see also* 59 Fed. Reg. 18,346 (1994) (The EPA proposal to approve Class I redesignation for Yavapai-Apache Reservation) & 60 Fed. Reg. 33,779 (1995) (The EPA proposal to approve Class I redesignation for lands within the Forest County Potawatomi Reservation). Thus, Section 169B is potentially broader in scope. At the same time, there is a strong counterargument that the scope of the related provisions, Sections 169A and 169B, should be the same. The EPA has not indicated whether the two provisions should be interpreted differently.

15. Congress may always specifically designate newly created parks and wilderness areas or other federal lands as mandatory Class I federal areas.

16. CAA § 162(a).

17. CAA § 302(i).

18. CAA § 169A(a)(2), (b)(2).

19. *See* 43 Fed. Reg. 7721 (1978).

20. *See* 44 Fed. Reg. 69,122 (1979).

21. 40 C.F.R. § 51.301(n).

22. The EPA codified the integral vistas associated with Roosevelt Campobello. *See* 40 C.F.R. § 81.437. Because Maine was deficient in implementing visibility requirements, the EPA also adopted a federal visibility new source review program that included protection of integral vistas (40 C.F.R. § 52.27) and applied it to Maine. *See* 52 Fed. Reg. 45,132, 45,136–37 (1987) and 54 Fed. Reg. 21,904 (1989) (clarifying revision to § 81.437).

23. *See* 45 Fed. Reg. 80,084, 80,095 (1980); CAA § 116.

24. CAA § 169A(a)(4).

25. CAA § 169A(b)(2).

26. The general SIP requirements under the CAA direct that SIPs meet the requirements of the visibility protection provisions in Section 169A of the CAA. *See* CAA § 110(a)(2)(J), 42 U.S.C. § 7410(a)(2)(J).

27. Section 110(c)(1) of the CAA calls for the EPA to promulgate a FIP within two years of finding that a state has failed to submit an approvable visibility plan. *See* CAA § 169A(b)(2)(A) (BART is determined by the state "or the Administrator in the case of a plan promulgated under section 110(c)"). The legislative history suggests that Congress deliberately conferred on the EPA the FIP authority for visibility:

> The conferees . . . rejected a motion to delete EPA's supervisory role under section 110 to assure that the required progress toward [the national visibility goal] will be achieved by the revised State plan. If a State visibility protection plan is not adequate to assure such progress, then the Administrator must disapprove that portion of the SIP and promulgate a visibility protection plan under section 110(c).

See SENATE COMM. ON ENVIRONMENT AND PUBLIC WORKS, 95th Cong., 2d Sess., A LEGISLATIVE HISTORY OF THE CLEAN AIR ACT AMENDMENTS OF 1977, vol. 3 at 320–21 (Comm. Print 1978) (Statement of Congressman Rogers during House consideration of Conference Committee Report, Aug. 4, 1977). The EPA has additional supervisory authority under the CAA. If the EPA determines that a SIP is substantially inadequate to comply with a requirement of the CAA, including the visibility protection provisions, then the EPA may require the state to revise the SIP to correct the inadequacies. *See* CAA § 110(k)(5).

28. CAA § 169A(d).

29. *See* 45 Fed. Reg. at 80,084.

30. Affected states are listed at 40 C.F.R. Section 51.300(b)(2).

31. *See* 45 Fed. Reg. at 80,085.

32. *See* 45 Fed. Reg. at 80,085–86.

33. *See* 45 Fed. Reg. at 80,086.

34. Vermont v. Thomas, 850 F.2d 99, 101 (2d Cir. 1988).

35. *See* 51 Fed. Reg. 43,389 (1986) (The EPA's proposed action on Vermont's visibility SIP); *see also* 52 Fed. Reg. 26,973 (1987) (The EPA's final action on Vermont's visibility SIP).

36. *Vermont*, 850 F.2d at 102.

37. *Vermont*, 850 F.2d at 102–03.

38. *Vermont*, 850 F.2d at 103.

39. *Vermont*, 850 F.2d at 104.

40. Maine v. Thomas, 874 F.2d 883 (1st Cir. 1989).

41. *Maine*, 874 F.2d at 886–88 & 891.

42. The EPA's ability to elude judicial review of its failure to issue regional haze regulations in the *Maine* decision was at least in part the impetus for the adoption of 1990 revisions to the CAA citizens' suit provisions: "The amendments to section[] 304 . . . of the act address the specific circumstances raised by [the *Maine*] case. These amendments should clarify the jurisdiction of the district court to provide relief when The EPA defers final action, and then fails to complete the action deferred." *See* 136 Cong. Rec. S2877 (daily ed. March 21, 1990) (statement of Senator Adams). The CAA now authorizes citizens' suits in district court to compel agency action that has been unreasonably delayed. *See* CAA § 304(a), 42 U.S.C. § 7604(a).

43. *Maine*, 874 F.2d at 889–91.

44. Section 816 of the 1990 CAA Amendments added Section 169B to the act. *See* Pub. L. No. 101–549, 104 Stat. 2399, 2695–97 (1990).

45. *See* 136 Cong. Rec. S2878 (daily ed. March 21, 1990) (statement of Senator Adams) ("[t]he authority to establish visibility transport regions and commissions is a supplement to the administrators [sic] obligation under current law" and "[t]he Administrator may not delay requirements under section 169A because of the appointment of a commission for a region under section 169B"); *id.* at S2887 (statement of Senator Wirth); *see also* 136 Cong. Rec. H12883 (daily ed. Oct. 26, 1990) (statement of Rep. Wyden) ("[n]either the original House language nor the Senate language adopted in conference repealed or lessened the EPA's obligations under the 1977 law"). If the EPA does not address regional haze through the commission process or otherwise, it may face renewed legal challenge from citizens or states concerned about regional haze. The EPA's ability to elude judicial review of its failure to issue regional haze regulations in the *Maine* decision was at least in part the impetus for the adoption of 1990 revisions to the CAA citizens' suit provisions: "The amendments to section[] 304 . . . of the act address the specific circumstances raised by [the *Maine*] case. These amendments should clarify the jurisdiction of the district court to provide relief when the EPA defers final action, and then fails to complete the action deferred." *See* 136 Cong. Rec. S2877 (daily ed. March 21, 1990) (statement of Senator Adams).

The CAA now authorizes citizens' suits in district court to compel agency action that has been unreasonably delayed. *See* CAA § 304(a), 42 U.S.C. § 7604(a). During the final congressional debate on the bill that was adopted as the 1990 CAA Amendments, Congressman Wyden, a sponsor of park protection amendments defeated earlier in the session, opined that the EPA had unreasonably delayed adoption of regional haze regulations:

> [T]he amendments to section 304 in the enforcement title of these amendments should make EPA's failure to complete regulations after the 13 years [counting from the adoption of the 1977 amendments to the adoption of the 1990 amendments] actionable as unreasonable delay. If missing a 2-year deadline by 11 years is not unreasonable, I'm not sure what is.

136 Cong. Rec. H12883.

46. *See Maine*, 874 F.2d at 885 ("EPA's mandate to control the vexing problem of regional haze emanates directly from the Clean Air Act, which 'declares as a national goal the prevention of any future, and the remedying of any existing, [anthropogenic] impairment of visibility in mandatory class I Federal areas'") (citation omitted).

47. *See* H.R. Rep. No. 294, 95th Cong., 1st Sess., at 204.

48. *See* CAA § 169B(d)(2)(C), (e)(1), & (e)(2).

49. CAA § 169B(f). Section 169B also grants the EPA administrator general discretionary authority to establish a visibility transport region whenever he or she has reason to believe that the current or projected interstate transport of air pollutants from one or more states contributes significantly to visibility impairment in Class I areas in affected states. The administrator may establish a region on his or her initiative or by petition from the governors of two affected states. The administrator also has authority to add a state that significantly contributes to interstate visibility impairment in a Class I area in the region or to remove a state if emission controls will not significantly contribute to visibility protection in such a Class I area. CAA § 169B(c)(1).

50. *See* 56 Fed. Reg. 57,522 (1991).

51. *See* 56 Fed. Reg. at 57,523.

52. *See* 56 Fed. Reg. at 57,523; 57 Fed. Reg. 5447, n.1 (1992).

53. *See* 56 Fed. Reg. at 57,523.

54. *See* Letter from Carol M. Browner, EPA Administrator, to the Honorable Mike Sullivan, Governor of Wyoming (April 19, 1993).

55. *See* Letter from Carol M. Browner, EPA Administrator, to Ted Strong, Executive Director, Columbia River Inter-Tribal Fish Commission, and Delbert Havatone, Chairman, Hualapai Tribal Council (June 27, 1995).

56. CAA § 169B(d)(2)(C).

57. Grand Canyon Visibility Transport Commission, *Recommendations for Improving Western Vistas*, June 10, 1996.

58. CAA § 169B(e)(1).

59. CAA § 169B(e)(2).

60. *See* NAS National Research Council Committee on Haze in National Parks and Wilderness Areas, Protecting Visibility in National Parks and Wilderness Areas (1993).

61. *Id.* at 6.

62. *Id.* at 7.

63. *Id.* at 7–8 and 11–15.

64. Pub. L. No. 105-178 (1998).

65. 64 Fed. Reg. 35,714 (1999).

66. 40 C.F.R. § 51.300(b)(3); *see also* 64 Fed. Reg. at 35,720–22.

67. 40 C.F.R. § 51.308(d)(1).

68. 40 C.F.R. § 51.301.

69. *Id.*

70. 40 C.F.R. § 51.308(d)(1)(i)(B).

71. 40 C.F.R. § 51.308(d)(1)(ii).

72. *Id.*

73. 40 C.F.R. § 51.308(d)(2).

74. 40 C.F.R. § 51.308(e).

75. CAA § 169A(b)(2)(A) & (g)(7).

76. CAA § 169A(g)(2).

77. *See* H.R. Rep. No. 294, at 206.

78. 40 C.F.R. § 51.302(c)(4)(iv).

79. CAA § 169A(g)(7). Potential to emit is the maximum capacity of a source to emit a pollutant under its physical and operational design, including consideration of federally enforceable emission limitations. Secondary emissions, emissions that occur as a result of the construction or operation of a facility, but not from the facility itself, are not counted. *See* 40 C.F.R. § 51.301(r), (u). Fugitive emissions (emissions that could not reasonably pass through a stack, chimney, vent, or other functionally equivalent opening) must

be counted, to the extent quantifiable, in determining potential to emit. *See* 40 C.F.R. § 51.301(e), (j).

80. CAA § 169A(c). *See also* 40 C.F.R. § 51.303(h).

81. 40 C.F.R. § 51.303(a)(2) (emphasis added).

82. 40 C.F.R. § 51.303(b).

83. *See* 56 Fed. Reg. 50,172, 50,177, n.16 (1991).

84. 40 C.F.R. § 51.308(e).

85. 40 C.F.R. § 51.308(e), (e)(2).

86. 40 C.F.R. § 51.308(e)(2).

87. CAA § 169A(b)(2); 40 C.F.R. §§ 51.302(c)(2)(i) & 51.306(c)(4).

88. 40 C.F.R. § 51.308(d)(3)(iv).

89. 40 C.F.R. § 51.308(d)(4).

90. *Id.*

91. 40 C.F.R. § 51.308(d)(4)(v).

92. 40 C.F.R. § 51.308(f).

93. 40 C.F.R. § 51.308(g).

94. *Id.*

95. *See* EPA, *Regional Planning Organizations, available at* http://www.epa.gov/air/visibility/regional.html.

96. 40 C.F.R. § 51.308(d)(3)(ii).

97. *Id.*

98. 40 C.F.R. § 51.308(h)(2).

99. 40 C.F.R. § 51.309(b)(2).

100. 40 C.F.R. § 51.309(d)(1).

101. 40 C.F.R. § 51.309(d)(4).

102. 68 Fed. Reg. 33,764 (2003).

103. *Id.*

104. 40 C.F.R. § 51.309(d)(5)–(d)(6).

105. 40 C.F.R. § 51.309(d)(3), (d)(7).

106. 40 C.F.R. § 51.309(d)(8).

107. 40 C.F.R. § 51.309(g).

108. 40 C.F.R. § 51.309(d)(4)(v).

109. 40 C.F.R. part 49.

110. 40 C.F.R. § 51.309(d)(12).

111. 40 C.F.R. § 51.308(b)(1).

112. 40 C.F.R. § 51.308(c).

113. The industry petitioners included the American Corn Growers Association, Appalachian Power Company, et al., the National Mining Association, West Virginia Chamber of Commerce, Midwest Ozone Group, Western Fuels Association, the Center for Energy and Economic Development, and the Utility Air Regulatory Group.

114. CAA § 307(b), 42 U.S.C. § 7607(b).

115. American Corn Growers, et al., v. EPA, 291 F.3d 1 (D.C. Cir. 2002).

116. 40 C.F.R. § 51.308(e)(1)(ii)(B).

117. CAA § 169A(b)(1).

118. *See* 64 Fed. Reg. at 35,740.

119. *See* 66 Fed. Reg. 38,108, 38,130 (2001).

120. *See* Letter from Christine Todd Whitman, EPA Administrator, to Michael Leavitt, Governor of Utah (April 1, 2003).

121. *Id.*

122. 40 C.F.R. § 51.302(c)(4).

123. 40 C.F.R. § 51.301.

124. *Id.*

125. *See* 66 Fed. Reg. at 38,109.

126. *See* 56 Fed. Reg. 5173, 5177 (1991).

127. *See* 56 Fed. Reg. at 5177–79.

128. CAA § 165(a), 42 U.S.C. § 7475(a).

129. CAA § 161, 42 U.S.C. § 7471.

130. CAA §§ 163(b), 165(a)(3), (a)(5), & (d), 42 U.S.C. §§ 7473(b), 7475(a)(3), (a)(5), & (d). For a detailed analysis of the PSD permit requirements to protect federal Class I areas, *see* Craig N. Oren, *The Protection of Parklands from Air Pollution: A Look at Current Policy*, 13 HARV. ENVTL. L. REV. 313 (1989).

131. Section 165(d) of the CAA expressly provides that AQRVs include visibility. The CAA does not identify or define AQRVs other than visibility. The legislative history of the 1977 amendments provides further guidance:

> [T]he term "air quality related values" of Federal lands designated as Class I includes the fundamental purposes for which such lands have been established and preserved by the Congress and the responsible Federal agency. For example, under the 1916 Organic Act to establish the National Park Service (16 U.S.C. § 1), the purpose of such national park lands "is to conserve the scenery and the natural and historic objects and the wildlife therein and to provide for the enjoyment of the same in such manner and by such means as will leave them unimpaired for the enjoyment of future generations."

See S. REP. No. 127, 95th Cong., 1st Sess. 36 (1977).

132. CAA § 165(d)(2)(B).

133. For an examination of the visibility NSR, *see* Ostrov, *supra* note 1, at 440–45, and Oren, *supra* note 130, at 389–98. Prevention of additional emission increases in clean air areas is particularly important for visibility protection because "[t]he introduction of a small amount of pollutant into clean air is likely to be much more perceptible than a similar amount introduced into an already polluted environment." *See* Ostrov, *supra* note 1, at 403.

134. 40 C.F.R. § 51.307.

135. 40 C.F.R. § 51.301(p).

136. The nonattainment NSR permit requirements are generally set out at CAA Section 173 and 40 C.F.R. Section 51.165.

137. *See, e.g.*, Oren, *supra* note 130, at 394 (footnotes omitted):

> Under [EPA's] view . . . section 169A and the rest of the PSD provisions would be administered within a common set of procedures that would require only one permit for a proposed source. This view has some basis; the language of the conference report [for the 1977 amendments] . . . declares that visibility concerns are to be considered within the PSD permit procedures, and similarly the statement of intent emphasizes the desire of the conferees for a "one-stop" permitting process.

138. For a detailed description of the coordinated implementation of the PSD and visibility NSR provisions, *see* 45 Fed. Reg. at 80,087–89. As of October 31, 1995, the EPA was expected to issue proposed changes to its PSD rules, including substantial revisions to the provisions related to protection of Class I areas. If adopted, these changes will likely necessitate conforming changes to the EPA's visibility NSR regulations.

139. 40 C.F.R. § 51.307(a)(2).

140. 40 C.F.R. § 51.307(a)(1).

141. 40 C.F.R. § 51.307(a)(3). The requirement for indicating the state's disagreement in the public notice "ensures that the public has access before the hearing to the State's reasons for not being satisfied with any demonstration by the Federal Land Manager that an adverse impact on visibility would result. This will aid the public's ability to comment meaningfully at the hearing." *See* 45 Fed. Reg. at 80,095.

142. 40 C.F.R. § 51.307(c).

143. *See* 45 Fed. Reg. at 80,089.

144. *See Multitrade Limited Partnership*, PSD Appeal Nos. 91-2 *et al.* at n.5 (Jan. 21, 1992).

145. 40 C.F.R. § 51.307(d).

146. *EDF v. Reilly*, No. C82-6850 (N.D. Cal. filed December 1982).

147. *See* 49 Fed. Reg. 20,647 (1984).

148. *See generally* 50 Fed. Reg. 28,544 (1985).

149. The provisions at 40 C.F.R. Section 52.21 are either administered directly by the EPA or by a state delegated authority under 40 C.F.R. Section 52.21(u). In either instance, the permit is ultimately an EPA permit under the law and may be reviewed by the EPA's Environmental Appeals Board pursuant to 40 C.F.R. Part 124.

150. *See* 40 C.F.R. § 52.21(o)(3); *see also* 50 Fed. Reg. at 28,548.

151. 40 C.F.R. § 52.21(p)(1) & (3).

152. 40 C.F.R. § 52.21(p)(1).

153. 40 C.F.R. § 52.27(d).

154. 40 C.F.R. § 52.27(d)(2).

155. 40 C.F.R. § 52.27(c).

156. 40 C.F.R. § 52.27(e), (f), & (g).

157. 40 C.F.R. § 52.28(d), (e), & (h).

158. 40 C.F.R. § 52.28(g).

159. 40 C.F.R. § 52.28(c)(1) & (i).

160. 40 C.F.R. Section 51.306(e) sets out criteria that states must consider in developing strategies, including smoke management techniques for agricultural and forestry management. In adopting the federal strategy for deficient states, the EPA indicated that it needed to gain a better understanding of smoke management issues and to coordinate with affected agencies before it could develop a federal smoke management program for incorporation into SIPs. *See* 52 Fed. Reg. at 45,135.

161. 40 C.F.R. § 52.29(c)(2) & (c)(4).

162. 40 C.F.R. § 51.306(c).

163. *See* 56 Fed. Reg. 5173, 5175 (1991).

164. *See* 56 Fed. Reg. 50,172, 50,174 (1991). NGS is jointly owned by the U.S. Bureau of Reclamation, Salt River Project Agricultural Improvement and Power District, Los Angeles Department of Water and Power, the Arizona Public Service Company, the Nevada Power Company, and the Tucson Electric Power Company.

165. *See* 54 Fed. Reg. 36,948, 36,949 (1989).

166. *See* 56 Fed. Reg. at 5179–80.

167. *See* NAS National Research Council Committee on Haze in the National Parks and Wilderness Areas, *Haze in the Grand Canyon: An Evaluation of the Winter Haze Intensive Tracer Experiment*, at 3–5 (1990). *See also* 56 Fed. Reg. at 5179.

168. *See* 56 Fed. Reg. at 5176–77, 5178–80.

169. The EPA simultaneously proposed its attribution decision and a remedial emission limitation for NGS. Commenters had argued that the EPA's 1980 regulations should be

read to require sequential decision making: that the EPA must finalize its attribution decision before it is authorized to undertake a BART analysis. The EPA responded that its regulations at 40 CFR Section 51.302(c)(4) speak to a single requirement—to "identify and analyze for BART"—and that while the agency may make these decisions sequentially, it was not compelled to do so. *See* 54 Fed. Reg. at 36,952.

170. *See* 56 Fed. Reg. at 5178.

171. *See* 56 Fed. Reg. at 5180–84.

172. Based on the informal regulatory negotiations, representatives of the power plant owners generally addressed the utility of regulatory negotiation. They were highly critical of the EPA's scientific integrity and raised concerns about the legal risks of sharing information with potentially adversarial parties. They nevertheless concluded that "in situations where some form of regulations is inevitable, negotiations may offer substantial opportunities to devise and obtain policy consensus for innovative solutions that protect the environment at reduced costs to industry." *See* D. Michael Rappoport and John F. Cooney, *Visibility at the Grand Canyon: Regulatory Negotiations under the Clean Air Act*, 24 Ariz. St. L.J. 627, 628 (1992).

173. *See* 56 Fed. Reg. 38,399 (1991).

174. *See* 56 Fed. Reg. 50,172, 50,177–79 (1991).

175. *See* 56 Fed. Reg. at 50,177–78. The EPA's proposed 70 percent SO_2 reduction control strategy was estimated to have a capital cost of $510 million and a total levelized annual cost of $106 million. The 90 percent SO_2 reduction control strategy adopted was estimated to have a capital cost of $430 million and a total levelized annual cost of $89.6 million. *Id.* at 50,177.

176. *See* 56 Fed. Reg. at 50,180–81.

177. CAA § 169A(b)(2)(A) & (g)(4). *See also* 56 Fed. Reg. at 5184.

178. CAA § 169A(b)(2). *See also* 56 Fed. Reg. at 38,401–03 & 50,177.

179. CAA § 169A(g)(1). *See also* 56 Fed. Reg. at 50,177.

180. *See Central Arizona Water Conservation Dist. v. EPA*, 990 F.2d 1531, 1540–41 (9th Cir.), *cert. denied*, 114 S. Ct. 94 (1993).

181. For an examination of the Central Arizona Water Conservation Dist. decision, see R. Nicole Cordan, Lost in the Haze? Central Arizona Fulfills Congress's Promise to Protect Visibility in the National Parks, 24 Envtl. L. 1371 (1994). Cordan concludes that "[t]he Ninth Circuit's decision promises that visibility in the nation's most pristine areas will be protected from impairment by readily identifiable sources." *Id.* at 1393. Cordan reasons that "[b]oth Central Arizona and the [EPA] visibility regulations state that as long as the appropriate regulatory agency can attribute impairment to any given source, that agency can require emission control technology at that specific source." *Id.* at 1392 (footnote omitted).

182. *See Central Arizona Water Conservation Dist.*, 990 F.2d at 1540–41.

183. *Id.* at 1541 (citation omitted).

184. *Id.* (citation omitted).

185. *Id.*

186. *Id.* at 1543.

187. Western State Air Resources Council, *Recommendations for Making Attribution Determinations in the Context of Reasonable Attributable BART* (May 2003).

CHAPTER 8

Hazardous Air Pollutants

ROBERT J. MARTINEAU, JR.[1]

Introduction

The regulation of air toxics, or hazardous air pollutants (HAPs), under the Clean Air Act (CAA) has undergone tremendous change since 1970. The wholesale revisions to the air toxics program that occurred in the 1990 CAA Amendments significantly expand those toxics regulated under Section 112. This chapter examines the development of the air toxics program and focuses on the basic statutory and regulatory changes in the 1990 CAA Amendments. Particular focus is given to the process for developing the technology-based standards for industrial source categories. The chapter will also address, namely, the preconstruction review provisions of Section 112(g), case-by-case permitting under Section 112(j), delegation to states under Section 112(1), and the accidental release provisions of Section 112(r). The chapter will also provide an overview of the risk-based provisions of Section 112 and other mechanisms to address hazardous air pollutants.

Historical Background

Since 1970 the CAA has distinguished between two categories of pollutants: criteria pollutants and hazardous air pollutants. Criteria pollutants are conventional pollutants that come from diverse mobile or stationary sources, and they are characterized as endangering public health or welfare.[2] Since they represent pollutants for which the Environmental Protection Agency (EPA) establishes the National Ambient Air Quality Standards (NAAQS), criteria pollutants are also known as NAAQS pollutants. Such pollutants tend to be more pervasive, but less toxic, than HAPs. The EPA currently establishes NAAQS for six criteria pollutants (as discussed in Chapter 3): ozone, carbon monoxide, particulate matter, sulfur dioxide, nitrogen dioxide, and lead.

Under CAA Section 112, "hazardous air pollutants" are pollutants that theoretically pose especially serious health risks. Section 112 of the 1970 CAA defined these as pollutants that "cause or contribute to an increase in mortality or an increase in serious irreversible, or incapacitating, reversible, illness."[3] These HAPs could cause cancer, neurological disorders, reproductive dysfunctions, other chronic health effects, or adverse acute human health effects. The 1970 and 1977 versions of the CAA directed the EPA to list those air pollutants that the EPA believed caused or contributed to death or serious illness. Before 1990, Section 112 required the EPA to establish health-based emission limits for hazardous pollutants at a level that provided "an ample margin of safety to protect the public health."[4] These emission standards were named the National Emission Standards for Hazardous Air Pollutants (NESHAPs).

The EPA's attempt to regulate HAPs under the 1970 and 1977 versions of the CAA met with little success. During the nineteen years before the 1990 amendments, the agency listed only eight substances as HAPs: beryllium, mercury, vinyl chloride, asbestos, benzene, radionuclides, arsenic, and coke oven emissions. In that time, the EPA issued standards for only seven of the eight pollutants; standards for coke ovens were not issued before the 1990 amendments. In addition, most of the standards that the EPA did issue covered only a limited number of emission sources of those pollutants."[5]

Perhaps the greatest problem in listing and subsequently establishing emissions standards for HAPs was the difficulty in conducting the necessary risk analysis and ambient air quality analysis to determine at what level the emission limits would provide for "an ample margin of safety to protect the public health," as required by the statute. Indeed, it was particularly difficult to set standards to provide an ample margin of safety for nonthreshold carcinogens. The EPA's position was that, in the absence of strong evidence to the contrary, it would assume that for a carcinogen there was no atmospheric concentration that would pose absolutely no health risk.[6]

Based on this assumption, the EPA's view was that Section 112 could be interpreted in one of two ways. The first would require a complete prohibition of emissions because a zero emission limitation would be the only emission standard that would be completely safe.[7] If the EPA prohibited certain emissions, it could force the closure of the operations that emitted the pollutant. This could result in the shutdown of whole or parts of many businesses. Faced with the political and practical difficulty of establishing standards that would shut down manufacturing operations, the EPA concluded that such an alternative was undesirable and had too high a cost for "elimination of a risk to health that is of unknown dimensions."[8] Under the second approach, the EPA would consider process cost and technical feasibility in developing lowest achievable emission standards where a "complete emission prohibition would result in widespread industry closure" and the agency determined that the cost of closure significantly outweighed the remaining risk after installation of best available technology.[9]

The EPA adopted its vinyl chloride NESHAP using this second approach. The Natural Resources Defense Council (NRDC) challenged the standard, contending that the EPA was not allowed to consider cost and technology in setting health-based standards.[10] The collapse of the risk-based program to regulate air toxics under Section 112 came in 1987 as a result of the U.S. Circuit Court of Appeals for the District of Columbia's decision in the vinyl chloride case. In *Natural Resources Defense Council v. EPA,* the court reviewed the EPA's decision to withdraw the vinyl chloride standards that had been proposed during the late 1970s. The court rejected NRDC's position that the EPA was not allowed to consider cost at all in setting standards that provided for an "ample margin of safety."[11] The court found that cost could not be considered when establishing a "safe" level of exposure to toxic air pollutants under the dictates of Section 112 but that safe did not mean risk free.[12] The court stated that

> the congressional mandate to provide an ample margin of safety "to protect public health" requires the Administrator to make an initial determination of what is "safe." This determination must be based exclusively upon the Administrator's determination of the risk to health at a particular emission level.[13]

The court concluded that it is only in establishing the second step—the "ample margin of safety" step—that the EPA is authorized to consider cost and technological feasibility. This decision led the way for the wholesale revision of Section 112, which occurred in the 1990 amendments.

Congressional Reaction

In deciding to revamp the air toxics program completely, Congress concluded that (1) routine and episodic releases of HAPs posed a significant threat to public health; (2) the risk of adverse health effects, particularly cancer, was significant, particularly for those Americans living in areas of concentrated industrial activity; (3) air toxic emissions may be causing significant environmental damage; and (4) the EPA had failed to implement an air toxics program successfully under its current authority.[14]

As a result of Congress's conclusion that the CAA's air toxics program was fundamentally flawed, Congress, with the EPA's support, dramatically restructured Section 112 in the 1990 amendments. The first and most dramatic restructuring was to move, at least in the initial phase of regulation, from a risk-based ambient air quality standards approach to technology-based standards. In addition, under the CAA, the EPA was directed to develop standards by industrial source category rather than focusing on individual pollutants. This approach to regulating HAPs follows the general model employed under the Clean Water Act to control toxic effluent discharges by major industrial point sources.[15] Further, because of the controversy in determining which pollutants should be deemed hazardous, Congress included an initial list of HAPs in the statute. This new statutory scheme, however, does not altogether abandon risk under Section 112. The EPA is to develop risk-based standards where necessary, *following* implementation of the technology-based program.

The attempt to restructure the program to regulate HAPs also coincided with the EPA's April 1989 issuance of its first Toxic Release Inventory (TRI), which was compiled from reports required by the Emergency Planning and Community Right-to-Know Act of 1986 (EPCRA). The initial TRI report indicated that in 1987 toxic releases to the air from major manufacturing facilities were approximately 2.7 billion pounds. This report brought renewed public attention to the fact that substantial amounts of HAPs were being emitted into the atmosphere, particularly in industrial centers and where chemical manufacturing facilities were located, such as in Louisiana, Ohio, Texas, Tennessee, and Virginia.[16]

Likewise, in 1989 the EPA released a study examining potential cancer-causing effects of exposure to air toxics. In that study, the EPA estimated that approximately 2,700 cancer cases occur annually in the United States as a result of exposure to toxic air pollutants. Extrapolating that data to the public at large could lead one to conclude that approximately 190,000 Americans would be expected to contract cancer from exposure to air toxics during the course of an average lifetime of seventy years.[17] While there is much controversy surrounding the methodology for estimating cancer and the likelihood of cancer incidences from exposure to air toxics emissions, the report again drew attention to the substantial releases of HAPs into the atmosphere and provided further support for a whole restructuring of the regulation of air toxics emissions.

The MACT Standards—Applicability

Overview

The goal of the Section 112 revisions set forth in the 1990 CAA Amendments was to set a course for the rapid development of technology-based standards for all major and industrial source categories that emit HAPs. The statute directed that by November 2000 (i.e., ten years after enactment) the EPA was to establish technology-based standards for all major industrial source categories and for such smaller sources as is deemed warranted. These technology-based standards are known as maximum achievable control technology, or MACT, standards.

Years after an initial technology-based standard is in place, the agency, where necessary for public health, is to go back and conduct a risk analysis and promulgate any additional controls that may be necessary to assure adequate protection of public health. This second step is referred to as the residual-risk analysis. Congress's belief was that by the time the agency would be in a position to conduct the residual-risk analysis and promulgate risk-based standards, the methodology for conducting risk analysis would be substantially more refined; thus, appropriate risk analysis could take place. Further, the assumption was that a residual-risk analysis would be necessary for only a relatively few number of pollutants and industrial source categories. The risk-based standards would be necessary only in those instances in which the technology-based standards are not adequate to protect public health and the environment. The move from risk-based to technology-based standards in Section 112 actually runs counter to the EPA's emerging theme that the agency's efforts should be focused on those areas of the most significant public health and environmental concerns and that it should not impose technology control merely for the sake of control, or to address newspaper headlines.

Indeed, many of the criticisms of the early technology-based standards proposed or promulgated by the EPA were that the costs of control were excessive given the minimal health risks at issue. As the saying goes, "The grass is always greener on the other side of the fence."

The statute lists 189 HAPs, removing from the EPA's discretion the ability to determine which pollutants should be listed, at least initially.[18] The statute did, however, direct the EPA to develop an initial list of all "major sources" of HAPs and such "area sources" as the EPA administrator determined warranted regulation.[19] The term "major source" under Section 112 is defined as "any stationary source or group of stationary sources located within a contiguous area and under common control that emits or has the potential to emit considering controls" 10 tons per year of any one hazardous air pollutant or 25 tons per year of any combination thereof.[20]

Technology-based MACT standards are to be based on the "maximum degree of reductions and emissions deemed achievable for the category or subcategory, the EPA administrator, taking into consideration the cost of achieving the reduction, any non-air-quality health and environmental impacts and energy requirements, determines is achievable for new or existing sources."[21] The CAA requires certain "floor" requirements for new and existing sources. Standards for categories or subcategories cannot be less stringent than the floor levels.[22] Under Section 112(i), new sources are to be in compliance with the performance standards upon commencement of operations; existing sources may have up to three years after the rule's promulgation to comply.

This section focuses on the basic statutory and regulatory framework for developing the first phase technology-based MACT standards for industrial source categories. One of the key generic regulations promulgated by the EPA to implement the Section 112 standards is the "General Provisions" rule. The General Provisions rule was promulgated by the EPA in 1994 to "eliminate the need to repeat general information and requirements for each [emission] standard."[23] The general provisions are designed to provide a comprehensive codification of general rules necessary to implement the Section 112 emission standards. The general provisions cover general definitions, the process for obtaining applicability determinations, compliance extensions, performance testing requirements, monitoring requirements, and general record keeping and reporting requirements. Throughout this chapter, and whenever any air toxics problems are presented, the practitioner should always refer to the general provisions as part of the analysis, as well as any specific emission standard to which a source might be subject. The EPA's interpretation of the key statutory provisions are embodied in those regulations.

Where a specific standard and a general provision conflict, the specific standard will govern.

There are several critical questions one must ask in determining whether a stationary source will be subject to a Section 112 standard.

- Does the source emit one of the listed pollutants?
- Does it emit HAPs in an amount significant enough to be covered by the standard?
- Is it a source category listed for regulation?
- Is the emission point subject to control in the standard promulgated for that source category?

The following sections look at the basic statutory and regulatory framework developed to answer these questions.

Listing of Hazardous Air Pollutants

Statutory Framework

To avoid controversy over which pollutants would be listed as HAPs and a lengthy delay in making that determination, Congress wrote an initial list of 189 HAPs directly into the statute.[24] The list of pollutants is supposed to represent those pollutants on which there was at least some agreement that, when emitted into the atmosphere, the pollutants were harmful to public health or the environment. The list of 189 pollutants includes numerous volatile organic chemical compounds and metals. The list also includes a series of compounds, such as coke oven emissions, chromium compounds, and other metals. Thus, the list actually contains more than 189 individual pollutants. The complete list is set forth in Section 112(b)(1) of the CAA.

Changing the Listed HAPs

Congress recognized that the list of HAPs would not remain static and that in some instances pollutants should be deleted from the list or others should be added. Thus, the CAA includes provisions to authorize the EPA to amend the list on its own or in response to a petition to modify the list. The act requires the EPA to review periodically the list established in the statute and publish the results thereof.[25] When appropriate, the EPA is to revise the list by adding pollutants "which present, or may present, through inhalation or other routes of exposure, a threat of adverse human health effects . . . or adverse environmental effects, whether through ambient concentrations, bioaccumulation, deposition, or otherwise," but not including releases subject to the regulation under Section 112(r). Criteria pollutants may not be added to the list, except for any pollutant that independently meets the listing criteria under Section 112 and is also a precursor to a criteria pollutant. Likewise, no substance, practice, process, or activity regulated under Title VI of the CAA ("Protection of Stratospheric Ozone") is subject to regulation solely because of its adverse effects on the environment.[26]

Any person may petition the EPA administrator to modify the list of hazardous pollutants to add or delete a substance.[27] The EPA is directed to respond to the petition within eighteen months and to grant or deny the petition and publish a written explanation of the reasons for its decision. The EPA may not deny a petition solely on the basis of inadequate time or resources for review. The petitioner has the burden of showing in the petition that there is adequate data on the health and environmental effects of the pollutant or other evidence to support the petition. To add a substance to the list, a petitioner must show (or the EPA administrator may determine independently) that "emissions, ambient concentrations, bioaccumulation, or deposition of the air pollutant are known to cause, or may reasonably be anticipated to cause, adverse effects to human health or adverse environmental effects."[28]

The administrator shall delete a substance on the list upon a showing that there is adequate data to support the conclusion that the substance may not reasonably be anticipated to cause *any* adverse effects to human health or the environment.[29] Obviously, the "any adverse effects" standard is a very high threshold to meet.

In the twelve years since the passage of the 1990 CAA Amendments, the EPA has delisted only caprolactam and redefined the definition of glycol ethers.[30] It is currently in the process of evaluating methyl ethyl ketone (MEK) and methanol.[31] The controversy surrounding any delisting petition has made any such undertaking extremely difficult.

Although the EPA administrator may add or delete a substance on his or her own initiative, the burden is on a petitioner to include sufficient information to support the requested addition or deletion under the substantive criteria set forth in Section 112(b)(3)(B) and (C). As noted, the EPA administrator must either grant or deny a petition within eighteen months of receipt. If the administrator decides to grant a petition, the agency publishes a written explanation of the administrator's decision, along with a proposed rule to add or delete the substance. If the administrator decides to deny the petition, the agency publishes a written explanation of the basis for denial. A decision to deny a petition is a final agency action subject to review in the D.C. Circuit Court of Appeals under CAA Section 307(b).

To delete a substance from the HAPs list, Section 112(b)(3)(C) provides that the EPA administrator must determine that

> there is adequate data on the health and environmental effects of the substance to determine that emissions, ambient concentrations, bioaccumulation, or deposition of the substance may not reasonably be anticipated to cause any adverse effects to the human health or adverse environmental effects.

The EPA has stated that, for a petition to be complete, the petition must consider all available health and environmental effects data; provide comprehensive emissions data for each source; estimate exposures from the emissions;

and address the environmental impacts associated with the emissions to ambient air and impacts associated with the subsequent cross-media transport of those emissions.[32] In proposing to delist caprolactam, the EPA made clear that delisting requests would be given serious consideration, and it showed signs of openness to make the possibility of delisting real. For example, the EPA indicated that it did not interpret Section 112(b)(3)(C) to require *absolute* certainty that a pollutant will not cause adverse effects on human health.[33] Thus, the EPA stated:

> Uncertainties concerning the risk of adverse health or environmental effects may be mitigated if EPA can determine that projected exposures are sufficiently low to provide reasonable assurance that such adverse effects will not occur. Similarly, uncertainties concerning the magnitude of projected exposures may be mitigated if EPA can determine that the levels which might cause adverse health or environmental effects are sufficiently high to provide reasonable assurance that exposures will not reach harmful levels.[34]

In its proposal, however, the EPA made clear that the burden remains on a petitioner to resolve any critical uncertainties associated with missing information. The EPA indicated that it would not grant a petition to delete a substance if there are major uncertainties that need to be addressed before the EPA would have sufficient information to make the requisite determination.

The petition to delist caprolactam was submitted by various companies, including 100 percent of the U.S. caprolactam producers.[35] The petition contained extensive information about caprolactam. Based on the submission, the EPA reviewed the petitioners' data and proposed to delete caprolactam from the Section 112 list of HAPs and solicited comments thereon, even though the data did not answer every possible uncertainty. Indeed, the EPA even afforded some interim relief in immediately suspending caprolactam for purposes of determining the applicability of Title V permitting requirements.[36]

The EPA ultimately granted the petition to delist caprolactam in 1996.[37] Before delisting, however, the EPA responded to concerns. The EPA entered into agreements with one manufacturer to install certain emission controls in two of its facilities once caprolactam was delisted.

The EPA also modified the definition of glycol ethers to exclude surfactant alcohol ethoxylates and their derivatives (SAED).[38] The EPA exercised this authority under Section 112(b)(3)(D) in response to an analysis of potential exposure prepared by the Soap and Detergent Association. The EPA concluded that sufficient data existed to determine that these emissions would not reasonably be anticipated to cause adverse human health or environmental impacts.

A third substance, methylethyl ketone (MEK) (CAS. No. 78-93-3), is under EPA review in response to a petition from the American Chemistry Council. Following the receipt of the petition, the EPA conducted a preliminary evaluation to determine that the petition presented considered all relevant health and environmental effects data, a comprehensive emissions data, potential exposure information and information impacts and cross media transport. In 1999, the EPA determined the petition was complete and published notice of receipt and request for information.[39] The EPA proposed delisting of MEK in May 2003.[40] As noted, the EPA is also evaluating the chemical methanol in response to a petition from the American Forest & Paper Association.

The EPA's willingness to implement provisions to delete hazardous substances from the list of 189 pollutants is an acknowledgment that the list was developed through a negotiation process and was not always based on clear and convincing science. Further, while it is often difficult to prove a negative, which, in effect, is what a proponent of delisting must do, the EPA's statements that every uncertainty need not be answered definitively provides some comfort that the delisting process may be more than an illusory possibility.

Definition of Major Source and Area Source

The 1990 amendments to Section 112 require the EPA to regulate air toxics emissions from all major stationary sources and from such area sources as are deemed appropriate. The term "major source" is used throughout various parts of the CAA. The definition for Section 112 purposes, however, is different from the definition contained in Section 302 or in other provisions of Title I. (Indeed, the major source definition in Section 112(a) is not even applicable to the accidental release provisions contained within Section 112.)

The act defines "major source" *under Section 112* as:

> [A]ny stationary source or group of stationary sources located within a contiguous area and under common control that emits or has the potential to emit considering controls, in the aggregate, 10 tons per year or more of any hazardous air pollutant or 25 tons per year or more of any combination of hazardous air pollutants.[41]

An area source is defined as "any stationary source of hazardous air pollutants that is not a major source."[42] The term "area source" does not include motor vehicles or nonroad vehicles subject to regulation under Title II of the CAA. The term "stationary source" in Section 112 is the same as under Section 111, which defines stationary source as "any building, structure, facility, or installation which emits or may emit any air pollutant."[43]

Collocation of Sources

There are several important aspects to the EPA's definition of a major source. First, a major source can be an individual stationary source or a group of stationary sources *located within a contiguous area and under common control*. The issue of what constitutes a contiguous area under common control is not as simple as one might suspect. There has been substantial controversy in development of particular source category standards about what this phrase means.

Several industry groups argued that the EPA's definition in the General Provisions rule was unlawful because a major source should be defined by reference to a Standard Industrial Classification (SIC) code for business, which focuses on product produced. Under that industry argument, fewer facilities would be considered major sources under the HAP-program when they are located at the same location as other HAP-emitting units because the 10/25-ton limits could be segregated by SIC code activity. The EPA rejected this position in the General Provisions rule.[44] Other industry representatives argued that the major source should include only units within one source category, even if multiple operations were at the same location. The EPA rejected industry's arguments, stating that separation of sources by SIC codes "would be an artificial division of sources that, in reality, all contribute to public exposure around a plant site."[45] In rejecting the source category definition approach urged by industry, the EPA contended that all portions of a major source be subject to MACT emission standards regardless of the number of source categories into which a facility is divided.[46] On review, the D.C. Circuit rejected both arguments by industry, stating that it essentially read out of the definition the "contiguous" language in the definition. The court stated that the EPA's reading of the term "is nearly compelled by the statutory language."[47] Thus, practitioners should be careful to note that the SIC-code-based definition often relied on in prevention of significant deterioration (PSD) program review does not apply to the definition of major source under Section 112.

Similarly, unlike under the other provisions of Title 1, when the EPA must conduct a rule making to include a source's fugitive emissions in calculating major source status, under Section 112 the EPA concluded that fugitives are included in the major source definition.[48] The court upheld the EPA's position in response to arguments that CAA Section 302 requires the EPA to conduct a rule making to include fugitive emissions.[49]

Potential to Emit

Perhaps the most controversial phrase in the definition of major source is the phrase "potential to emit considering controls." This language is similar to language contained in the PSD and new source review (NSR) programs (which are described in Chapter 6). The EPA's interpretation of this phrase in the general provisions was the subject of litigation by a cross section of industry groups as part of a challenge to the General Provisions rule.[50] In the General Provisions rule, the EPA reiterated its long-standing position under the PSD rules that "potential to emit considering controls" requires a demonstration that a limit on potential to emit be "federally enforceable." The EPA defines potential to emit as "the maximum capacity of a stationary source to emit a pollutant under its physical and operational design."[51] The agency has taken the position that a physical or operational limitation may include pollution control equipment and restrictions on hours of operations or on the type and amount of material combusted, stored, or processed, if those limitations are federally enforceable.[52]

In the General Provisions rule, the EPA adopted its definition of federally enforceable for PSD programs and reiterated its June 28, 1989, position that the emission limitations for the source must be "practicably enforceable" as well.[53] To be a federally enforceable limit on the potential to emit, the EPA must be able to enforce the provisions, which means that the limit must effectively be approved in a state implementation plan (SIP). The EPA has construed the term "practicably enforceable" to mean written in such a manner as to provide for effective operational controls. Thus, for example, the EPA takes the position that *annual* emissions caps are not practicably enforceable. In addition, to be practicably enforceable, the EPA stated that appropriate record-keeping, monitoring, and reporting provisions must be required.[54]

The EPA was widely criticized for its broad definition of "potential to emit" as set forth in the General Provisions rule. There was significant concern that many sources that actually emitted less than the major source thresholds of HAPs would be caught in the regulatory web of Section 112, as well as the Title V permit program, when in fact those hazardous air emissions were relatively minor. Industry sources contended that such a result was not Congress's intent. Moreover, industry has always objected to the EPA's definition of potential to emit as requiring federally enforceable measures and disregarding state emission limits or other voluntary measures. This continuing disagreement was the basis of the challenge by the Chemical Manufacturers Association (CMA) to this portion of the General Provisions rule.[55]

Before the case was decided—and as a result of the 1994 elections coupled with the overwhelming concern about the burden of the Title V permitting process on the EPA, the states, and industry sources—the EPA agreed to an interim relaxation of its strict adherence to the requirements for federal enforceability. This interim relief was seen as a way of providing sources with an opportunity to limit their emissions and avoid major source applicability and the Title V permit program. In early 1995 the EPA issued a guidance memorandum setting out options for limiting a stationary source's potential to emit under Section 112 and Title V.[56] In that memorandum, the EPA outlined several options for creating federally enforceable limits on potential to emit, including federally enforceable state operating permits (FESOPs); limitations by rule in state rules, which are often referred to as exclusionary or prohibitory rules; general permits; and construction permits. In addition, Title V permits for other purposes may be used as a readily available mechanism to create an enforceable limit. During the transition period, the EPA agreed to accept certain other types of state permits as avowed limits on potential to emit even though they do not meet the requirements of federal enforceability. The initial transition period was to last two years.

In the midst of this voluntary transition policy, on July 21, 1995, the D.C. Circuit, in *National Mining Association v. EPA,* granted the CMA's petition for review and ruled that the EPA had not justified its determination that only federally enforceable emission limits would be recognized within the term "potential to emit considering controls." The court found that the EPA's regulations "proposed conditions for achieving 'federal enforceability' that go beyond the mere effectiveness of particular constraint as a practical matter."[57] The court noted that there may be techniques in addition to those that the EPA deems acceptable that are equally effective and yet are foreclosed as mechanisms because of the EPA's approach. Thus, the court concluded, "What EPA has not explained is how its refusal to consider limitations other than those that are 'federally enforceable' serves the statute's directive to 'consider controls' when it results in a refusal to credit controls imposed by a state or locality even if they are unquestionably effective."[58]

After years of debate on this issue in other contexts, industry finally won its long-sought position, and the EPA was reeling from a setback of one of its most fundamental policy positions concerning state emission limits. The agency was left to attempt to justify its position and is still trying to do so. In an era of federalism, the argument that a state emission limit—for which a source may be subject to strict enforcement penalties—is not an effective limit on a source's potential to emit was simply untenable to the court and unexplained by the EPA.

This decision opens a brand-new debate between the EPA, sources, and the states on how to define whether a source is major under the air toxics program, as well as under other provisions of Title 1.[59] The EPA has thrice extended its "transition policy" for potential to emit relative to MACT standards but has not taken any further regulatory action.[60] Given the EPA's long-held belief that "federal enforceability" is a critical component of any valid limit on potential to emit, the EPA policy makers will face a difficult decision on whether to attempt to justify a similar rule following the remand or whether to move in the direction of flexibility as set out in the "transition policy."

Lesser Quantity Cutoffs

The CAA allows the EPA to set a lower threshold than the 10/25-ton major source threshold for any individual source category.[61] This lower threshold is known as a lesser quantity cutoff. A lesser quantity cutoff for a major source may be established on the basis of the air pollutant's potency, persistence, and potential for bioaccumulation, other characteristics of the air pollutant, or other relevant factors. Although this is a broad set of criteria that the EPA could use at its discretion, the agency has indicated that at this time it does not plan to use the lesser quantity cutoff mechanism. Rather, where appropriate, it will regulate area sources. As noted previously, Section 112(d) requires the EPA to promulgate regulations for each category or subcategory of major sources and area sources of hazardous pollutants listed for regulation under the source category list issued pursuant to Section 112(c). An area source is any source that has the potential to emit less than 10 tons per year of any hazardous pollutant or 25 tons per year of any combination of HAPs.

Having answered the question of which pollutants Section 112 applies to and how big a source must be to be considered a major source, this chapter now turns to the EPA's basis for setting particular standards—the source category.

Source Category Listings

Under Section 112(c) of the CAA, the EPA was required to publish by November 15, 1991, an initial list including all categories of major sources that emitted one or more of the HAPs listed in Section 112(b). In addition, the EPA administrator was to list each category of area sources that presented a threat of adverse effects to human health or the environment (by such sources individually or in the aggregate) warranting regulation under Section 112.[62] The EPA was also directed to list those categories of area sources that address 90 percent of the aggregate emissions of the thirty most significant HAPs found in urban areas.[63] The act also includes requirements providing for the listing of research facilities, boat manufacturing, and oil and gas wells and pipeline facilities.[64]

No less often than every eight years, in response to public comment or new information, the EPA is directed to revise, if appropriate, the list of source categories. The agency may, at any time, designate additional categories of sources to be listed according to the same criteria that were applied to the initial list.

The CAA also provides a mechanism whereby source categories may be delisted, based on a petition by any person or on the EPA administrator's initiative. In the case of carcinogenic HAPs, the EPA may delete a category if it is determined that no source in the category (or group of sources in the case of area sources) emits such HAPs in quantities that may cause a lifetime risk of cancer greater than one in a million to the most exposed individual.[65] For noncarcinogenic HAPs, the EPA may delete a category if no source in the category (or group of sources in the case of area sources) emits such HAPs in quantities that exceed a level adequate to protect public health with an ample margin of safety and no adverse environmental effect will result from emissions from any source (or group of area sources).[66] The EPA is required to grant or deny a petition to delete a category within one year after a petition is filed. The agency has indicated that if data suggest that a source category does not warrant regulation, it will delete the source category. It has already proposed deleting asbestos processing as an area source category. The proposal was at the administration's initiative, not in response to a petition, due to information that the initial listing was based on incorrect data.[67] The CAA does not distinguish between the terms "category" and "subcategory," directing only that the EPA list such categories or subcategories as meet the specified conditions. Once the categories are initially listed, the EPA administrator must establish emissions standards under Section 112(d) for all categories on the initial list in accordance with the schedule the EPA is required to establish under Section 112(e). For source categories and subcategories listed after publication of the initial list, the administrator shall establish technology-based emissions standards by the year 2000 or within two years after the date on which the category or subcategory is listed, whichever is later.[68] Section 112(c)(5) authorizes the administrator to add additional categories or subcategories.

The EPA's Initial Listing Decisions

The EPA's initial listing of source categories was neither subject to notice and comment rule making under CAA Section 307 nor subject to judicial review.[69] Nevertheless, the EPA did promulgate an initial *draft* source category list for public comment.[70] The draft list included approximately 800 categories, broken down by industrial group. The list included hundreds of source categories under the industrial grouping "production and use of inorganic chemicals."[71] Most of these categories were to be included in the rule that the EPA was developing for the chemical manufacturing industry, known as the Hazardous Organics NESHAP (HON) or the Synthetic Organic Chemical Manufacturing Industry (SOCMI) rule. Because of emissions averaging concerns, when the EPA issued the "final" initial source category list, it consolidated several hundred inorganic chemical categories into fewer than ten categories. Thus, in contrast to the initial list, the final source category list includes only about 160 major source categories and eight area source categories.[72]

The source categories on the list are grouped by industrial production process type. For example, some of the general groupings include ferrous and nonferrous metal processing, mineral products processing, petroleum and natural gas production and refining, agricultural chemicals production, fibers production processes, inorganic chemicals production, and polymers and resins production.[73] Within each industrial process group are several individual source categories. Again, the EPA chose to list only source categories, not subcategories. In November 1993 the EPA amended the initial list to add marine vessel loading operations.[74] During the last decade the EPA has periodically updated the list of major and area source categories as it has obtained new information or regrouped categories.[75]

In addition to industrial process type categories such as petroleum and natural gas production, there were a number of source categories the EPA identified that could be found at a wide variety of industrial or manufacturing facilities. For example, source categories on the list include industrial boilers, process heaters, institutional and commercial boilers, and halogenated solvent cleaning operations.[76] The EPA also included such categories as hazardous waste incinerators, municipal landfills, and industrial cooling towers, among others.

The source category list includes production process units as well as generic units such as industrial boilers or degreasing operations. Therefore, in determining whether a source has an emission point that may be subject to a MACT standard, an owner or operator of a facility that emits HAPs must not only look at its basic production process, it must also consider whether it has an emission point that is subject to any one of the more generic source category listings. It is also important to note that, under the EPA's interpretation, if a contiguous facility is a major source, each source category unit subject to standards will also be considered a major source, even if that source category emits less than the 10 tons per year of any one HAP or 25 tons per year of any combination. That is, if an industrial boiler has the potential to emit only 5 tons of a HAP at a facility but the facility is a major source under another source category, it will be considered a major source for the industrial boiler category when such category is promulgated.

In the EPA's initial listing notice, it made the adverse effects findings under Section 112(c)(3) for eight categories of area sources as required by the section.[77] The agency recognized that the CAA did not establish a bright-line test for the agency's use in making its area source findings when determining what source categories to list. The EPA indicated that it would consider the risk criteria used for developing the benzene NESHAP following the D.C. Circuit's decision in the vinyl chloride case.[78] Under that analysis, the EPA articulated a two-step policy for providing for protecting public health with an ample margin of safety under Section 112. The first step is to protect the greatest number of persons possible to an individual lifetime-risk level no greater than one in a million (1×10^{-6}). The second step is to limit to no higher than approximately one in a thousand (1×10^{-3}) the estimated risk a person living near a plant would have if he or she were exposed to the maximum pollutant concentrations for seven years. In addition, the agency considered the weight of evidence with respect to potential carcinogenicity or other health effects of pollutants, gaps in data, and science policy assumptions associated with any risk measures. In other words, the agency indicated that it would look at a number of parameters and measures involving emissions, toxicities, numbers of facilities, reasonableness of control measures, population exposures to HAP emissions, individual risk, and population incidents in determining what constitutes a significant threat for the purpose of listing a category of area sources.

Based on this methodology, the EPA initially listed seven area source categories: commercial ethylene oxide sterilizers, perchloroethylene dry cleaners, degreasing operations using halogenated solvents, asbestos processing, and three different types of chromium electroplating operations.[79] Not coincidentally, these were each categories for which the EPA was developing risk analysis data under the pre-1990 Section 112 air toxics regime.

Priority Schedule for Issuance of MACT Standards

The CAA directs that the EPA is to promulgate regulations for all source categories on the initial list. Under Section 112(e), the EPA was to issue standards for forty source categories (not counting coke oven batteries) by November 1992, for 25 percent of the source categories by November 1994, and for 50 percent of the categories by November 1997, with standards for the remainder of the categories to be issued not later than November 15, 2000. Beyond establishing the schedule for issuance of particular source categories, the source category list is important because it relates to the date for establishing equivalent emission limits by permit under Section 112(j). As discussed in more detail later, if the EPA administrator fails to meet the schedule for establishing regulations for any listed category of sources by more than eighteen months, under Section 112(j), a source within that source category must submit a permit application to the permitting authority in compliance with the Title V rules. Section 112(j) specifies how the state (assuming it is the permitting authority) is to determine on a case-by-case basis what the MACT standard would require had it been promulgated.

The EPA was directed to develop priorities for promulgating the Section 112(d) standards and to publish a schedule of when it intended to promulgate particular standards. The agency promulgated that schedule in late 1993.[80] In issuing the schedule of time frames for promulgating emissions standards for the initial list of source categories, Section 112(e) prescribed three criteria the EPA was to use in terms of setting priorities: (1) the known or anticipated effects of HAPs from the source category on public health and the environment; (2) the quantity and location of emissions; and (3) the efficiency of grouping categories according to process or similarities of pollutants. The EPA established a source category ranking system (SCRS) to address the first two criteria.[81]

As noted, the CAA required promulgation of forty source categories by November 1992. However, when the EPA promulgated its schedule, it included only five dry-cleaner categories and the HON source categories as well as the equipment leak portions of twenty non-HON source categories in the two-year bin. The EPA's position was that it would satisfy the requirement to issue standards for forty source categories by promulgating the HON and dry-cleaner rules, even though those standards added up to fewer than forty source categories as currently defined by the EPA. The agency's position was based on its belief that, at the time the statute was written, the intent was for the EPA to issue the HON within the first two years. At that time, the HON included hundreds of source categories.

The four-year schedule included forty-five source categories. Included in that list were several projects already under way by the EPA; categories already under investigation for control technique guideline projects; and others selected because of efficiency grouping, a level of knowledge, and potential for completion by November 1994. The remaining 129 source categories were then grouped in the seven- and ten-year schedules.

In response to the EPA's position that the HON satisfied the two-year deadline requirement for issuing MACT standards, the Sierra Club and NRDC brought a citizens' suit under Section 304 to require the EPA to issue standards for the forty source categories as required in Section 112(e)(1). To settle the lawsuit, the EPA entered into a consent decree that included a number of the categories listed under the four-year schedule.[82] Without conceding the legal issue with respect to whether the HON satisfied the forty-source-category requirement, the EPA entered into a consent decree including the source categories, but the deadline stretched from mid-July 1994 into 1995. Thus, the EPA effectively entered into court-ordered deadlines to satisfy both the two-year and most of the four-year requirements.

After a variety of revisions and reprioritizations, the EPA embarked on this ambitious program to promulgate technology-based standards for this long list of source categories. Given the limited success in issuing standards under the pre-1990 version of Section 112, whether the EPA could meet such a challenge was open to question. While there are a number of standards that fell somewhat behind, the EPA was able to issue the vast majority of standards. Prior to the ten-year standards, the EPA did not trigger the provisions under Section 112(j) discussed below.

Technology-Based MACT Standards

The fundamental change central to the 1990 amendments to Section 112 is the movement away from a risk-based standards-setting process to a technology-based program to be followed by risk-based standards when warranted. Congress directed that the level of control to be achieved by HAP sources should be very high. During the debate on the 1990 CAA Amendments, Congress expressed some frustration that for new source performance standards (NSPS) under Section 111 and for best available control technology (BACT) determinations under the PSD program, the level of control required was not sufficiently stringent.[83] Thus, rather than borrowing a well-known technology-based term from another provision of the act, Congress developed a new, technology-based limitation, which has become known as the MACT standards.

All major sources subject to emission standards under Section 112(d) are required to meet MACT. Listed area sources are required to meet MACT or, if the EPA administrator so chooses, a less stringent requirement known as generally available control technology (GACT). Unlike the NSPS program, which applies to only new or modified sources, or the NSR program, which applies to new sources and modifications of existing sources that increase emissions, the MACT technology standards apply to both new and existing sources.

The Standards-Setting Process

Defining the Source

Under Section 112, the term "stationary source" is to have the same meaning that it has under Section 111 (new source performance standards). That section of the Act defines the term "stationary source" as "any building, structure, facility, or installation which emits or may emit any air pollutant."[84] Section 112 then defines "major source" as

any stationary source or group of stationary sources located within a contiguous area and under common control that emits or has the potential to emit considering controls, in the aggregate, 10 tons per year or more of any hazardous air pollutant or 25 tons per year or more of any combination of hazardous air pollutants.[85]

As discussed earlier, in the general provisions to Section 112, the EPA took an expansive view of this definition. Unlike the definitions under the SIP program for MACT sources and under Title V, the EPA concluded that for purposes of Section 112 all sources of emissions within a contiguous facility should be included. It did not limit source groupings to the two-digit SIC code or to single source categories. The EPA concluded that in Section 112 Congress included a definition of major source that does not include reference to SIC codes or limit the definition to source categories.[86] This position was upheld by the D.C. Circuit on review of the General Provision's rule making.

An area source is any source of HAP emissions that is not a major source.[87] The EPA's regulatory definition of area source tracks the statutory definition.[88] Nonetheless, for the purposes of implementing Section 112, area sources may be further divided into affected area sources and unaffected area sources. An affected area source would be a plant site that is not a major source but is subject to a relevant emission standard that regulates major sources in that source category.

In distinguishing between area and major sources, it is important to note that a new area source that increases its emissions of (or its potential to emit) HAPs such that it becomes a major source must comply with the relevant emission standard immediately upon becoming a major source.[89] An unaffected existing area source that increases its emissions (or its potential to emit) such that it becomes a major source must comply by the date specified in the standard for such a source. If such a date is not specified, the source's period of time to comply would be equivalent to the period specified in the standard for other existing sources. If, however, the existing area source becomes a major source by the addition of a new affected source, or by reconstruction, the portion of the source that is new or reconstructed must comply with the standard's requirements for new sources. These compliance periods apply to area sources that become affected major sources regardless of whether the new or existing area source was previously affected by that standard.[90]

Determining Which Units Fall under a Source Category

In addition to determining whether the source is a major or area source, individual source categories will define what units are subject to the rules for that source category. As noted, a stationary source may be any building, structure, facility, or installation. Obviously these terms are broad and can include an entire facility such that the major source is equivalent to the stationary source that defines the source category. In other cases, the stationary source may be an individual installation or structure, such as an industrial boiler or incinerator.

The next important issue in developing the standard is to identify and understand the source category that will be subject to the standard. At the time the EPA issued the source category list, it recognized that the categories on the list sometimes encompass several industry sectors, operations, or types of equipment. The agency recognized the importance of describing what was included under each listed category. Hence, included in the record and the docket for the new source category list is a description of the category. The purpose of the information is to delineate as much as possible the potential coverage of each category. The EPA, however, made the caveat that the description itself could be revised from time to time, as the agency learned more about each category. The ultimate category description will be set forth in the proposed rule for that source category. Moreover, the agency made it explicit that the documentation accompanying the source category list would not limit what might be included in the category for purposes of establishing Section 112(d) standards or for making case-by-case MACT determinations under Section 112(j). Nevertheless, for a company trying to assess whether it might be covered by a particular source category in advance of the proposal, the background documentation on the source category listing notice should provide some insight into what emission units the EPA was focusing on when it defined a particular source category.

The determination of whether a piece of process equipment falls within a particular source category is often a discussion that occurs with a state or local permitting authority and is tantamount to an applicability determination. Where the EPA is consulted by the permitting authority, the EPA often takes an expansive view of the scope of the rule.

The Affected Source

The general provisions also include the term "affected source," which should not be confused with major or area source. The EPA uses the term "affected source" to designate the specific source or group of emission units that are subject to a particular Section 112 standard. The term is analogous to the term "affected facility" under Section 111. The particular affected source for each standard will be defined in that standard.[91] Practitioners should carefully examine the definition of affected source in a particular source because, in many cases, not all possible emission units within a broad industrial source category will be covered by that standard.

Setting the Standard: Defining MACT and the MACT Floor

Because of Congress's concern over how the EPA had previously interpreted such provisions as the best demonstrated technology (BDT) provision in Section 111[92] and the BACT provision in Section 169,[93] Congress sought to provide more explicit direction to the EPA in defining what constituted the technology control levels required for standards under Section 112. In addition, unlike the limitations on considering costs under the old risk-based program, Congress did allow the EPA to consider costs in setting MACT standards, subject to some very important caveats.

The CAA provides that the EPA administrator shall set emissions standards for new or existing sources of HAPs, which shall require

> the maximum degree of reduction in emissions of [HAPs] subject to this section (including a prohibition on such emissions, where achievable) that the Administrator, taking into consideration the cost of achieving such emission reduction, and any non-air quality health and environmental impacts and energy requirements, determines is achievable for new or existing sources in the category or subcategory to which such emission standard applies.[94]

It is worth noting that in the 1990 CAA Amendments Congress did not use the words "maximum achievable control technology" in Section 112 in defining the standard of control, although this is what the Section 112 standard has popularly been referred to since enactment. The act authorizes the EPA administrator, in establishing MACT standards for source categories, to consider application of measures that reduce or eliminate emissions through substitution of materials; that enclose systems or processes to eliminate emissions; that collect, capture, or treat such pollutants; that are design, equipment, or work practice standards; or any combination thereof.[95]

The foregoing sounds like a straightforward technology-based standard, not unlike the BDT language of Section 111. Congress, however, placed a most significant and—as the rule makings have played out—controversial limitation on the EPA administrator's discretion to define what standard constitutes MACT for a particular source category. Section 112(d)(3) sets minimum levels of control, or what have come to be known as "MACT floors," that significantly limit the administrator's discretion in defining MACT for a particular source. The floor is different for new and existing sources. For new sources, the EPA may not set a standard for a category or subcategory that is "less stringent than the emission control that is achieved in practice by the best controlled similar source, as determined by the Administrator."[96] Thus, the EPA's discretion in defining the MACT standard is very limited. If any existing source is achieving a certain level of reduction, that source determines the floor for the entire source category. The EPA takes the position that it may not consider costs in this step of the standard-setting process.

The agency has never taken a formal position on what constitutes a "similar source," but the language is typically interpreted to mean a best-controlled similar source *within* the same source category or subcategory. One could argue, however, that similar source does not necessarily have to be a source within the same source category, particularly if the emissions point is similar to or identical to emissions points in other source categories.

Congress gave the EPA somewhat more flexibility in setting MACT standards for existing sources. The MACT floor for existing sources is defined as the "average emission limitation achieved by the best performing

12 percent of the existing sources (for which the Administrator has emissions information)."[97] The CAA excludes from the floor analysis sources that within eighteen months of proposal or thirty months of promulgation had achieved an emission rate constituting the lowest achievable emission rate under the NSR program.[98] For source categories with fewer than thirty sources, a MACT floor is defined as the average emission limitation achieved by the best performing five sources for which the EPA administrator has or can reasonably obtain information.[99] While this statutory numerical formula approach may seem a straightforward means for determining minimum technology standards, significant controversy has surrounded the MACT floor analysis.

For the EPA, one of the most controversial aspects of the entire MACT development process has been determining the MACT floor for existing sources. The first controversy was over whether the MACT floor for existing sources should be set at the level of emissions reduction by a source at the eighty-eighth or ninety-fourth percentile of sources in the source category. The EPA takes the position that the phrase "the average emission limitation achieved by the best performing 12 percent of the existing sources" requires that the EPA look at the top 12 percent of sources in a source category in terms of emissions control and take the average of the maximum emission reduction limit achieved by those sources. In other words, the agency's position is that the MACT floor for existing sources is the emission reductions actually achieved by the ninety-fourth percentile of the source category. In contrast, industry sources, as well as the Office of Management and Budget during the first Bush administration, argue that the MACT floor language for existing sources should be interpreted as requiring a MACT floor that reflects the eighty-eighth percentile. Proponents of this interpretation argue that the floor language requires that all sources within the top 12 percent be able to achieve the emission limit that would serve as the MACT floor. In other words, to determine the floor one looks at the emission level achieved by the source at the eighty-eighth percentile in terms of control.

The EPA initially set forth a discussion of this issue in the chromium electroplating MACT standard and the proposed pulp and paper MACT standard.[100] In addition, because of the controversy and its potential impact on the development of all MACT standards, the EPA issued a separate notice on this issue for generic comment applicable to all source categories.[101] The agency announced its position on the floor language in the context of issuing the MACT standard for a certain portion of the HON, although it said it could revisit the issue in later MACT standards.[102] One interpretation groups the words "average emission limitation achieved by" together in a single phrase and asks what is the average emission limitation achieved by this best performing 12 percent. This interpretation places the emphasis on the word "average." A second interpretation groups the words "average emission limitation" into a single phrase and asks what average emission limitation is "achieved by all members of the best performing 12 percent." In the latter case, the average emission limitation might be interpreted as the average reduction across the HAPs emitted by emission at a point and over time. Thus, as noted under this approach, the EPA would take the lowest emission limit achieved by each of the best performing 12 percent.[103]

After taking comment on this issue, the agency reaffirmed its position that the ninety-fourth-percentile interpretation would guide the EPA standard development.[104] Industry did not challenge the position at that time. This has been dubbed the "Higher Floor Interpretation" by the EPA. The controversy over this issue has faded. The focus of the debate on determining floors, and thereby typically defining the actual MACT standard, has shifted to how to subcategorize sources to achieve desired results.

Defining the Category or Subcategory

Another critical step in establishing a MACT floor is deciding whether or not to subcategorize the source category, since each category or subcategory can have its own floor. Subcategorization of a particular source category might be appropriate if some segments of the industry are significantly different from others even though they may fall into the same source category. In several rule makings, the EPA has subcategorized within a particular source category in developing standards. In the wood furniture MACT standard, for example, the EPA subcategorized on the basis of the type of furniture being produced (e.g., residential home furniture manufacturers are treated differently from commercial office furniture makers).[105] In that case, the type of process and level of quality control necessary for the different furniture sectors suggested that it was inappropriate to consider the wood furniture industry as one source category. The EPA concluded that it would be appropriate to subcategorize by furniture type. In the proposed MACT standard for the pulp and paper industry, the EPA initially rejected subcategorizing according to the pulping process, such as kraft, sulfite, soda and semichemical, or end-product subcategorizations. However, in a recent supplemental proposal conducting that analysis, the EPA decided to subcategorize the source category according to pulping process.[106]

The importance of subcategorization cannot be underestimated. The way the EPA subcategorizes, if it does at all, can significantly affect the floor determination for the source category, and thereby dramatically affect the ultimate MACT standard's degree of stringency. If one sector of a particular industry segment has better pollution control equipment than another segment in the same source category, the highly controlled units will drive the floor determination and thus set a minimum standard for the rest of the source category. If, however, the source category is subcategorized into two industry segments, one that is heavily controlled and one that is not (for whatever reason), the MACT floor for the less-controlled subcategory would be substantially different. If the floor is less control, the EPA has the discretion to set less stringent standards. Given the political climate, and the difficulties in the EPA's ability to set standards "above the floor," the floor analysis will often dictate the standard.

Obviously, in looking at a proposed standard to which a source may become subject, it will be critical to look at how the EPA has subcategorized the source category, if at all, or whether there is a subcategorization that the EPA did not utilize that may be advantageous to a given portion of the industry. In contrast, environmental groups will often try to force the most stringent floor in as broad a category of sources as possible. Where there is little discretion to maneuver, the more stringent the controls likely will be. Likewise, environmental groups will argue for technology forcing across source categories. For example, if one source category has stringent control mechanisms for VOC coatings and other source categories have similar coating devices, then, so the environmentalists argue, the standard for the second category should be based on the first even if no one in the second category is using the control methodology, because the source is a "similar" source.

Miscellaneous Floor Issues

Another issue in the development of particular MACT standards is how to analyze the applicable data as well as how representative the database is of the industry in general. In some instances, the EPA has looked at a select group of data, perhaps emissions information on only a small percentage of the sources in the source category, and extrapolated that data to the entire industry. The statute specifies that the EPA administrator can make floor determinations based on available information. Some, however, have questioned whether that data is representative of an entire source category. In some instances, the industry has attempted to show that the data the EPA had available was not representative and tended to include information on the most well-controlled sources. (This debate, in fact, took place during the development of the MACT standard for the wood furniture industry.)

Whether the floor should be determined by actual emission rates or permit limits is also a subject of some controversy.[107] In many cases, if one looks at permit limits, the emission limits will be substantially higher (less restrictive) than the emission reductions that could be achieved in practice. This is not surprising given the natural tendency of a permittee and permit writer to want emission limits in permits that provide ample cushion room. Similarly, the agency may use short-term emissions data in determining a floor number as opposed to an emissions level that can be achieved on a continuous basis. In looking at any proposed MACT standard for an industry, a company should look carefully at whether the emission limits can be achieved on a continuous basis. At times this issue has been a controversy in development of standards under Section 112, but it becomes more critical as the EPA moves toward continuous compliance demonstrations, enhanced monitoring protocols, Title V permitting requirements, and the corresponding compliance certification requirements. The issue of variability of performance also is an important, and sometimes contentious, factor in developing the floor. Courts have determined that the EPA may account for variability by setting floors at a level that reasonably estimates the performance of the best controlled similar unit under the "worst reasonably foreseeable circumstances."[108]

Going Beyond the Floor

Under Section 112(d), once the EPA defines the floor for the proposed MACT standard, it examines possible standards that are more stringent than the floor. In evaluating these options, the statute provides that the EPA administrator shall determine what reduction in emissions constitutes MACT, taking into account the cost of achieving the reductions, any non-air-quality health and environmental impacts, and energy requirements.[109] These factors parrot the consideration to be used in defining "best demonstrated technology" under Section 111, although Section 112(d) expressly authorizes the EPA administrator to set a zero emission limit.

Thus, the MACT floor issue is important for several reasons. As many of the first-phase standards were being developed, the EPA took the position that it had no discretion to propose standards that did not meet the MACT floor, notwithstanding any considerations of the reasonableness of costs. Where the floor would lead to a stringent but costly standard, the EPA could rely on the floor requirements as being driven by congressional directive, rather than engaging in a lengthy dispute over whether the costs were justified in a particular standard. In addition, in those instances where the floor level of control was less stringent than what the EPA wanted to propose, other factors in Section 112(b), such as the cost of achieving such reductions, became of paramount importance.

Where the EPA uses the MACT floor as the basis for the standards, it takes the cost argument out of the debate. If industry or, in some instances, the EPA perceives that the costs of a particular floor were too harsh, it could look for creative ways to redefine the floor through subcategorization or one of the other factors described earlier. At this point, the debate on the relative merits of various proposed levels of control is similar to that for the cost analysis undertaken in the Section 111 program. The EPA has undertaken its data analysis in a variety of different ways. For example, in the HON it established reference control technologies, not on actual emissions collected from individual plants, but on model chemical manufacturing plants. In a standard developed under Section 129, but using the same MACT floor analysis, the EPA looked at individual permit limits in municipal waste combustors rather than actual emission limits achieved. The agency took the position that the emission limits were not representative enough of long-term continuous emissions and that the permit limits were more reflective for purposes of determining the floor. In other instances, the EPA may discount or exclude certain data points for a variety of reasons. A facility looking at a proposed MACT standard to which it is subject should carefully examine the EPA's database and calculations therefrom to determine the basis on which the MACT floor was set, particularly when the MACT floor is equivalent to the proposed standard.

In looking at standards beyond the floor, the EPA typically has used the same kind of dollar-per-ton-of-pollutant-removed cost analysis that it does under the NSPS program. In those instances in which the EPA has gone beyond the MACT floor, the costs of control have driven the decision. If the costs are deemed reasonable for the particular source category, the EPA might be able to adopt a standard that goes beyond the floor. Since the 1994 elections, however, the EPA has generally been reluctant to adopt many standards that go beyond the minimum floor requirements. Thus, as noted, defining the "floor" often defines the standard.

Exhibit 1 lists all of the MACT standards issued by early 2003, their compliance date, and their citation to the promulgation date in the *Federal Register*.

EXHIBIT 1.

MACT Standard Source Categories Affected	C.F.R. Subparts	Final *Federal Register* Citation	Compliance Date for Existing Sources
Two-Year Final MACT Standards			
Dry Cleaning • Commercial dry cleaning dry-to-dry • Commercial dry cleaning transfer machines • Industrial dry cleaning dry-to-dry • Industrial dry cleaning transfer machines	M	58 Fed. Reg. 49,354 (Sept. 22, 1993)	09/23/96
Hazardous Organic NESHAP	F, G, H, I	59 Fed. Reg. 19,402 (Apr. 22, 1994)	F/G-05/14/01 H-05/12/99 New Sources 05/12/98
Four-Year Final MACT Standards			
Aerospace Industry	GG	60 Fed. Reg. 45,948 (Sept. 1, 1995)	09/01/98
Asbestos Processing	—	DELISTED 60 Fed. Reg. 61,550 (Nov. 30, 1995)	—
Chromium Electroplating Chromic Acid Anodizing	N	60 Fed. Reg. 4,948 (Jan. 25, 1995)	decorative 01/25/96; others 01/25/97
Decorative Chromium Electroplating Hard Chromium Electroplating			

(continued)

EXHIBIT I (*continued*)

MACT Standard Source Categories Affected	C.F.R. Subparts	Final *Federal Register* Citation	Compliance Date for Existing Sources
Coke Ovens Charging, Top Side and Door Leaks	L	58 Fed. Reg. 57,898 (Oct. 27, 1993)	Contact Project Lead
Commercial Sterilizers Commercial Sterilization Facilities	O	59 Fed. Reg. 62,585 (Dec. 6, 1994)	12/06/98
Degreasing Organic Cleaners Halogenated Solvent Cleaners	T	59 Fed. Reg. 61,801 (Dec. 2, 1994)	12/02/97
Gasoline Distribution (Stage 1)	R	59 Fed. Reg. 64,303 (Dec. 14, 1994)	12/15/97
Hazardous Waste Combustion	Parts 63, 261 and 270	65 Fed. Reg. 52,827 (Sept. 30, 1999)	09/30/02
Industrial Cooling Towers	Q	59 Fed. Reg. 46,339 (Sept. 8, 1994)	03/08/95
Magnetic Tape	EE	59 Fed. Reg. 64,580 (Dec. 15, 1994)	without new control devices 12/15/96; with new control devices 12/15/97
Marine Vessel Loading Operations	Y	60 Fed. Reg. 48,388 (Sept. 19, 1995)	RACT 09/19/98; MACT 09/19/99
Off-Site Waste Recovery Operations	DD	61 Fed. Reg. 34,140 (July 1, 1996)	02/01/00
Petroleum Refineries	CC	60 Fed. Reg. 43,244 (Aug. 18, 1995)	08/18/98
Polymers and Resins I Butyl Rubber Epichlorohydrin Elastomers Ethylene Propylene Rubber Hypalon (TM) Production Neoprene Production Nitrile Butadiene Rubber Polybutadiene Rubber Polysulfide Rubber Styrene-Butadiene Rubber and Latex	U	61 Fed. Reg. 46,906 (Sept. 5, 1996)	07/31/97

EXHIBIT 1 (*continued*)

MACT Standard Source Categories Affected	C.F.R. Subparts	Final *Federal Register* Citation	Compliance Date for Existing Sources
Polymers and Resins II Epoxy Resins Production Non-Nylon Polyamides Production	W	60 Fed. Reg. 12,670 (Mar. 8, 1995)	03/03/98
Polymers and Resins IV • Acrylonitrile-Butadiene-Styrene • Methyl Methacrylonitrile+ Methyl Methacrylate-Butadiene++ • Polystrene Styrene Acrylonitrile Polyethylene Terephthalate	JJJ	61 Fed. Reg. 48,208 (Sept. 12, 1996)	07/31/97
Printing/Publishing	KK	61 Fed. Reg. 27,132 (May 30, 1996)	05/30/99
Secondary Lead Smelters	X	60 Fed. Reg. 32,587 (June 23, 1995)	06/23/97
Shipbuilding and Ship Repair	II	60 Fed. Reg. 64,330 (Dec. 15, 1995)	12/06/96
Wood Furniture	JJ	60 Fed. Reg. 62,930 (Dec. 7, 1995)	11/21/97

Seven-Year Final MACT Standards

MACT Standard Source Categories Affected	C.F.R. Subparts	Final *Federal Register* Citation	Compliance Date for Existing Sources
Chromium Chemical Manufacturing	—	DELISTED 61 Fed. Reg. 28,197 (June 4, 1996)	—
Electric Arc Furnace: Stainless and Non-Stainless Steel	—	DELISTED 61 Fed. Reg. 28,197 (June 4, 1996)	—
Ferroalloys Production	XXX	64 Fed. Reg. 27,450 (May 20, 1999)	05/20/01
Flexible Polyurethane Foam Production	III	63 Fed. Reg. 53,980 (Oct. 7, 1998)	10/08/01
Generic MACT, plus: Acetal Resins Hydrogen Fluoride Polycarbonates Production Acrylic/Modacrylic Fibers	YY	64 Fed. Reg. 34,853 (June 29, 1999)	06/29/02
Mineral Wool Production	DDD	64 Fed. Reg. 29,489 (June 1, 1999)	06/01/02

(*continued*)

EXHIBIT 1 (*continued*)

MACT Standard Source Categories Affected	C.F.R. Subparts	Final *Federal Register* Citation	Compliance Date for Existing Sources
Nylon 6 Production	—	DELISTED 63 Fed. Reg. 7,155 (Feb. 12, 1998)	—
Oil and Natural Gas Production	HH	64 Fed. Reg. 32,609 (June 17, 1999)	06/17/02
Pesticide Active Ingredient Production 4-Chlror-2-Methyl Acid 2, 4 Salts and Esters Production 4, 6-dinitro-o-cresol Production Butadiene Furfural Cotrimer Captafol Production Captan Production Chloroneb Production Chlorothalonil Production Dacthal (tm) Production Sodium Pentachlorophenate Production Tordon (tm) Acid Production	MMM	64 Fed. Reg. 33,549 (June 23, 1999)	06/30/02
Pharmaceuticals Production	GGG	63 Fed. Reg. 50,280 (Sept. 21, 1998)	09/21/01
Phosphoric Acid/Phosphate Fertilizers	AA BB	64 Fed. Reg. 31,358 (June 1, 1999)	06/10/02
Polyether Polyols Production	PPP	64 Fed. Reg. 29,419 (June 1, 1999)	06/01/02
Polymers and Resins III Amino Resins Phenolic Resins	OOO	65 Fed. Reg. 3,275 (Jan. 20, 2000)	01/20/03
Portland Cement Manufacturing	LLL	64 Fed. Reg. 31,898 (June 14, 1999)	06/10/02
Primary Aluminum Production	LL	62 Fed. Reg. 52,384 (Oct. 7, 1997)	10/07/99
Primary Lead Smelting	TTT	64 Fed. Reg. 30,194 (June 4, 1999)	05/04/01
Publicly Owned Treatment Works (POTW)	VVV	64 Fed. Reg. 57,572 (Oct. 26, 1999)	10/26/02
Pulp and Paper (noncombustible) MACT I	S	63 Fed. Reg. 18,504 (April 15, 1998)	04/15/01

EXHIBIT I (*continued*)

MACT Standard Source Categories Affected	C.F.R. Subparts	Final *Federal Register* Citation	Compliance Date for Existing Sources
Pulp and Paper (nonchemical) MACT III	S	61 Fed. Reg. 9,383 (Mar. 8, 1996)	04/16/01
Secondary Aluminum	RRR	65 Fed. Reg. 15,689 (Mar. 23, 2000)	03/24/03
Steel Pickling—HCL Process	CCC	64 Fed. Reg. 33,202 (June 22, 1999)	06/22/01
Tetrahydrobenzaldehyde Manufacturer (Formerly Butadiene Dimers Production)	F	63 Fed. Reg. 26,078 (May 12, 1998)	05/12/01
Wet Formed Fiberglass Mat Production	HHHH	67 Fed. Reg. 17,823 (April 11, 2002)	04/11/05
Wood Treatment MACT	—	DELISTED 61 Fed. Reg. 28,197 (June 4, 1996)	—
Wool Fiberglass Manufacturing	NNN	64 Fed. Reg. 31,695 (June 14, 1999)	06/14/02

Ten-Year Final MACT Standards

Aerosol Can-Filling Facilities	—	DELISTED 64 Fed. Reg. 63,025 (Nov. 18, 1999)	—
Alumina Processing	—	DELISTED 66 Fed. Reg. 8,220 (Jan. 30, 2001)	—
Antimony Oxides Manufacturing	—	DELISTED 64 Fed. Reg. 63,025 (Nov. 18, 1999)	—
Asphalt Concrete Manufacturing	—	DELISTED 67 Fed. Reg. 6,521 (Feb. 12, 2002)	—
Asphalt Roofing Asphalt Processing	LLL	68 Fed. Reg. 22,975 (April 29, 2003)	05/01/06

(*continued*)

EXHIBIT I (*continued*)

MACT Standard Source Categories Affected	C.F.R. Subparts	Final *Federal Register* Citation	Compliance Date for Existing Sources
Boat Manufacturing	VVVV	66 Fed. Reg. 44,217 (Aug. 22, 2001)	08/22/04
Brick and Structural Clay Products Manufacturing Clay Ceramics Manufacturing	JJJJ and KKKKK	68 Fed. Reg. 26,689 (May 16, 2003)	05/16/06
Cellulose Production Manufacturing Caroxymethylcellulous Production Cellulose Ethers Production Cellulose Food Casing Manufacturing Cellophane Production Methylcellulose Production Rayon Production	UUUU	67 Fed. Reg. 40,043 (June 11, 2002)	06/11/05
Coke By-Product Plants	—	DELISTED 66 Fed. Reg. 8,220 (Jan. 30, 2001)	—
Coke Oven: Pushing, Quenching, and Battery Stacks	CCCCC	66 Fed. Reg. 8,220 (Jan. 30, 2001)	—
Combustion Sources at Kraft, Soda and Sulfite Pulp, and Paper Mills	MM	68 Fed. Reg. 18,007 (April 14, 2003)	
Cyanuric Chloride Production	—	DELISTED 63 Fed. Reg. 7,155 (Feb. 12, 1998)	—
Engine Test Cells/Stands (Combined with Rocket Testing Facilities)*	PPPPP	68 Fed. Reg. 28,774 (May 27, 2003)	—
Fabric Printing, Coating, and Dyeing	OOOO	68 Fed. Reg. 32,171 (May 29, 2003)	05/29/06
Flexible Polyurethane Foam Fabrication Operation	MMMMM	68 Fed. Reg. 18,061 (April 14, 2003)	—
Generic MACT, plus: Carbon black production Cyanide chemicals mfg. Ethylene processes Spandex production	YY	64 Fed. Reg. 34,853 (June 29, 1999)	06/29/02
Integrated Iron and Steel*	FFFFF	68 Fed. Reg. 27,645 (May 20, 2003)	05/20/06
Large Application (surface coating)	NNNN	67 Fed. Reg. 48,253 (July 23, 2002)	07/23/05

EXHIBIT 1 *(continued)*

MACT Standard Source Categories Affected	C.F.R. Subparts	Final *Federal Register* Citation	Compliance Date for Existing Sources
Lead Acid Battery Manufacturing	—	DELISTED (May 17, 1996)	—
Leather Finishing Operations	TTTT	67 Fed. Reg. 915,510 (Feb. 27, 2002)	02/27/05
Lightweight Aggregate (Being addressed in the Brick, Structural Clay Products, and Clay Ceramics Manufacturing rule making)	—	DELISTED (July 22, 2002)	
Manufacturing Nutritional Yeast (formerly Bakers Yeast)	CCCC	66 Fed. Reg. 27,876 (May 21, 2001)	05/21/04
Metal Coil (Surface Coating) Industry	SSSS	67 Fed. Reg. 39,793 (June 10, 2002)	06/10/05
Metal Furniture (Surface Coating)	RRRR	68 Fed. Reg. 28,605 (May 23, 2003)	05/23/06
Municipal Solid Waste Landfills	AAAA	68 Fed. Reg. 2,227 (Jan. 16, 2003)	01/16/04
Natural Gas Transmission and Storage	HHH	64 Fed. Reg. 32,610 (June 17, 1999)	06/17/02
Petroleum Dry Cleaners	—	DELISTED 66 Fed. Reg. 8,820 (Jan. 30, 2001)	—
Petroleum Refineries Catalytic Cracking, Catalytic Reforming, and Sulfur Plant Units	UUU	67 Fed. Reg. 17,761 (April 11, 2002)	04/11/05
Polyvinyl Chloride and Copolymers Production	J	67 Fed. Reg. 45,885 (July 10, 2002)	07/10/05
Paper and Other Web (Surface Coating)	JJJJ	65 Fed. Reg. 72,341 (Dec. 4, 2002)	12/04/05
Primary Copper	QQQ	67 Fed. Reg. 40,477 (June 12, 2002)	06/12/05
Refractory Products Manufacturing	SSSSS	68 Fed. Reg. 18,729 (April 16, 2003)	04/16/05
Reinforced Plastic Composites Production	WWWW	68 Fed. Reg. 19,375 (April 21, 2003)	04/21/05
Semiconductor Manufacturing	BBBBB	68 Fed. Reg. 30,848 (May 22, 2003)	05/22/05
Sewage Sludge Incinerators	—	DELISTED 67 Fed. Reg. 6,521 (Feb. 12, 2002)	

(continued)

EXHIBIT 1 (*continued*)

MACT Standard Source Categories Affected	C.F.R. Subparts	Final *Federal Register* Citation	Compliance Date for Existing Sources
Solvent Extraction for Vegetable Oil Productions	GGGG	66 Fed. Reg. 19,006 (April 12, 2001)	04/12/04
Tire Manufacturing	XXXX	67 Fed. Reg. 45,598 (July 9, 2002)	07/11/05
Uranium Hexafluoride Production	—	DELISTED 67 Fed. Reg. 6,521 (Feb. 12, 2002)	—

Area Source Standards

Congress recognized that the very high level of controls required under the MACT definition required for major sources might cause the EPA to shy away from developing any standards for area sources. Therefore, to give the EPA additional flexibility with respect to the area source standards, Congress provided an alternative technology-based standard for area sources. CAA Section 112(d)(5) authorizes the administrator to establish standards "which provide for the use of generally available control technologies or management practices." This less stringent standard has come to be known as GACT. As the plain language of the statute indicates, there is no floor analysis or minimum control requirement. Indeed, the EPA has very broad flexibility to determine what constitutes GACT. The agency has already used this control option in some of the early area source standards, such as the perchloroethylene dry cleaners standard.[110] Lastly, another important factor, and another incentive for deeming an area source standard to be GACT, is that the administrator does not have to issue residual risk standards for such source categories.

The development of area source standards also led directly to the EPA's efforts in addressing urban air toxics as required by Section 112(c), which is discussed later in this chapter. As of early 2003, the EPA had established area source standards for several source categories and was evaluating potential regulation of many additional area source categories. Exhibits 2 and 3 set forth a list of those source categories.

EXHIBIT 2. Area Source Categories for which the EPA Has Promulgated a New Source Standard[111]

Chromic Acid Anodizing	Hazardous Waste Incineration
Commercial Sterilization Facilities	Medical Waste Incinerators
Decorative Chromium Electroplating	Portland Cement Manufacturing
Dry Cleaning Facilities	Secondary Aluminum Production
Halogenated Solvent Cleaners	Secondary Lead Smelting
Hard Chromium Electroplating	Municipal Landfills
Publicly Owned Treatment Works	Municipal Waste Combustors

EXHIBIT 3. Area Source Categories the EPA Has Indicated Will Be Subject to Standards

Acrylic Fibers/Modacrylic Fibers Production	Lead Acid Battery Manufacturing
Agricultural Chemicals and Pesticides Manufacturing	Mercury Cell Chlor-Alkali Plants
Asphalt Processing and Asphalt Roofing Manufacturing	Miscellaneous Organic Chemical Manufacturing (MON)
Auto-Body Refinishing Paint Shops	Nonferrous Foundries
Brick and Structural Clay	Oil & Natural Gas Production
Carbon Black Production	Clay Ceramics
Chemical Manufacturing: Chromium Compounds	Other Solid Waste Incinerators (Human/Animal Cremation)
Chemical Preparations	Paint Stripping Operations
Copper Foundries	Paints & Allied Products Manufacturing
Cyclic Crude & Intermediate Production	Pharmaceutical Production
Electrical & Electronic Equipment: Finishing Operations	Plastic Parts & Products (surface coatings)
Fabricated Metal Products	Plastic Materials and Resins Manufacturing
Fabricated Structural Metal Manufacturing	Plating & Polishing
Ferroalloys Production: Ferromanganese & Silicomanganese	Polyvinyl Chloride & Copolymers Production
Flexible Polyurethane Foam Fabrication Operations	Prepared Feeds Manufacturing
Flexible Polyurethane Foam Production	Primary Copper (not subject to Primary Copper Smelting MACT)
Fabricated Plate Work	Primary Metals Products Manufacturing
Gasoline Distribution (Stage I)	Primary Nonferrous Metals: Zinc, Cadmium, and Beryllium
Heating Equipment, except electric	Pressed and Blown Glass and Glassware Manufacturing
Hospital Sterilizers	Secondary Copper Smelting
Industrial Boilers	Secondary Nonferrous Metals
Industrial Inorganic Chemical Manufacturing	Sewage Sludge Incineration
Industrial Organic Chemical Manufacturing	Stationary Internal Combustion Engines
Industrial Machinery & Equipment: Finishing Operations	Synthetic Rubber Manufacturing
Inorganic Pigments Manufacturing	Stainless & Non-Stainless Steel Manufacturing: Electric Arc Furnaces (EAF)
Institutional/Commercial Boilers	Steel Foundries
Iron Foundries	Valves & Pipe Fittings
Iron & Steel Forging	Wood Preserving

Revisions to Technology-Based Standards

In addition to the residual risk standards for certain source categories for which significant risk remains after implementation of the MACT standards, the EPA is directed to review and revise as necessary emissions standards promulgated under Section 112(d) no less often than every eight years. This provision is similar to the review provisions under Section 111. In implementing Section 112(d)(6), the EPA administrator is directed to take into account developments in practices, processes, and control technologies. If the Section 111 experience is any guide, the EPA will undertake revisions of Section 112 emission standards in few instances and then only in response to pressure from environmental groups.

Case-by-Case Decision Making

Section 112(g) Requirements

Section 112(g)(2) of the CAA provides that

> After the effective date of a permit program under [Title] V in any State, no person may construct or reconstruct any major source of hazardous air pollutants unless the Administrator (or the State) determines that the maximum achievable control technology emission limitation under this section for new sources will be met. Such determination shall be made on a case-by-case basis where no applicable emissions limitations have been established by the Administrator.[112]

Section 112(g) also prohibits the modification of a major HAP source in a state with an approved Title V program unless the EPA or the state determines that the MACT for existing sources will be met. However, as discussed below, the EPA chose not to implement these statutory provisions.[113]

The CAA envisions that Section 112(g) will be implemented by the states, given that the subsection's requirements are triggered by the establishment of a Title V program in a state. The statute required the EPA to publish guidance by May 15, 1992, to assist the states in implementing Section 112(g), which the agency did not do until late 1996.[114] The EPA initially took the position that Section 112(g) was self-implementing and its effective date in a state would be the date that state's Title V program received approval (or, in the case of a state that did not submit a Title V program, the date that a federal Title V program became effective in that state). Under such an interpretation, states were required to implement Section 112(g) upon approval of their Title V programs, regardless of whether the EPA had published final Section 112(g) guidance by that time.[115] The agency threatened to withhold approval or interim approval from state Title V programs unless the state had adequate authority to enforce Section 112(g). Under the agency's policy, most existing state preconstruction review programs gave states sufficient authority to implement Section 112(g).[116]

The agency subsequently reversed this policy because of state and industry concerns. The agency stated in an interpretive notice published in the *Federal Register* that Section 112(g) would not take effect—and states therefore would not be required to implement it—until *after* the EPA had published a final Section 112(g) rule.[117] In the final rule, the EPA further delayed the effective date for a period of up to eighteen months (to June 1998) to allow states sufficient lead time to ensure that they had adequate authority to implement Section 112(g).[118]

The Section 112(g) Rule

As stated, Section 112(g) had directed the EPA to publish guidance by May 15, 1992.[119] The final rule was not issued until December 1996.[120]

In the final rule, the EPA did not adopt provisions relating to modifications of existing units in response to overwhelming criticism of the provisions contained in its proposed rule. The EPA rationalized its decision by stating that it concluded that the "greatest benefits to be derived from Section 112(g) would be from the control of major source construction and reconstruction before the MACT standards go into effect."[121] It went on to say that its decision was premised on the agency's ability to issue the Section 112(d) MACT standards in a timely manner and on the assumption that many states already operate state air toxics programs.[122] The EPA reserved the right to reconsider whether to issue regulations to cover Section 112(g) modifications if substantial future delays occurred, but it has never done so.[123]

Constructions and Reconstructions

The Section 112(g) rule requires that major HAP sources that are constructed or reconstructed must install new-source MACT[124] immediately upon startup.[125] The definition of construction refers to two types of constructions. The first "construction" occurs where an entirely new facility (that is a major HAP source) is built on a greenfield site. The other is any construction of a new "process or production unit" at an existing site where the process or production unit itself is a major source, unless the process or production unit satisfies certain criteria for exclusion.[126] An existing facility has been "reconstructed" only when there has been a replacement of components at an existing process or production unit that, in and of itself, is a major HAP source of such a magnitude that the fixed capital costs would exceed 50 percent of the cost of constructing an entirely new comparable facility and where it is technically and economically feasible to meet MACT.[127]

Thus, a "reconstruction" includes not only a replacement that exceeds 50 percent of the cost of a new *facility* but also the replacement of components at an existing *emissions unit* that exceeds 50 percent of the cost of constructing a new *emissions unit*, where the emissions unit is a major HAP source.

The primary purpose of the 112(g) rule is to serve as a case-by-case permit program for "new" sources where that source is in a listed source category for which the EPA has not issued a MACT standard. The EPA also takes the position that a new major HAP source or major new unit is subject to 112(g) even if the EPA has not yet listed the source category for regulation under Section 112(d).[128]

MACT Determinations

Once Section 112(g) review has been triggered, a determination must be made regarding the level of HAP emission controls that constitute MACT for that source,[129] and the source's Title V permit must be modified to reflect this new applicable requirement.[130] The Section 112(g) rule requires the source to make an initial determination regarding what level of emission control should constitute new-source MACT for that source and to submit that determination to the permitting authority for approval.[131] The Section 112(g) rule and preamble contain guidance for making this determination.[132] The EPA has also published a guidance document titled "Guidelines for MACT Determinations under Section 112(g)," which contains information to help sources and permitting authorities make these determinations.[133] The final rule also contains administrative procedures for submitting and obtaining approval for the MACT determination and for incorporating the MACT requirements into the source's Title V permit. Once a Section 112(d) standard is promulgated for a source category, a major source regulated under Section 112(g) may be granted up to eight years of extra time to comply with the subsequently promulgated MACT standard.[134] The EPA may specify the length of time on a standard or allow permitting authorities to grant case-by-case extensions.[135]

The MACT Hammer

Under Section 112(j) of the CAA, if the EPA fails to promulgate a section 112(d) MACT standard within eighteen months of the scheduled regulatory deadline, owners and operators of major sources of hazardous air pollutant emissions are required to obtain an equivalent emission limitation by permit.[136] "Equivalent emission limitation means an emission limitation, established under section 112(j) of the [CAA], which is at least as stringent as the MACT standard that the EPA would have promulgated under section 112(d) of the [CAA]."[137] The date on which the EPA should have certain standards promulgated has been referred to as the "MACT Hammer" or "Hammer date."[138]

The "Hammer date" for source categories in the ten-year MACT bin was May 15, 2002.[139] Although the EPA could have prevented the MACT hammer from falling on this date by issuing the Section 112 MACT standards, the agency did not meet this deadline; thus numerous source categories must apply for an equivalent emission limitation by permit.[140]

As a result of the hammer falling on many of the ten-year source categories, the burden shifted to states to develop plans to reduce adverse effects of air toxics.[141] On May 15, 2002, states were required to begin making case-by-case determinations of the MACT standards for thirty-two air pollutants in sixty different source categories.[142] As the EPA was moving rapidly to issue standards, states sought relief from having to write individual MACT standards for sources. To minimize the burden on states and sources, however, the EPA developed a two-part application process.

Section 112(j) shifts the burden to each owner and operator "of a major source in a source category or subcategory for which the statutory deadline for a section 112(d) emission standard is missed by 18 months" to comply with requirements of 112(j).[143] Pursuant to this provision, all affected industries were required to complete Part 1 of a permit application containing detailed information on air toxic emissions by May 15, 2002, "to allow state permitting agencies to determine MACT standards for each individual facility."[144] Part 1 of the two-part permit process was intended to be "brief so that completing it [would] not be a complicated, burdensome requirement."[145] The test for whether a source should submit a Part 1 application is based on a reasonableness standard.[146] The EPA directed that the application should be completed "if the source can reasonably determine it is in one of the source categories or subcategories subject to the section 112(j) requirements."[147]

Part 1 of the permit application must contain the following information: (1) the name and address of the source; (2) a brief description of the major source and an identification of the relevant source category; (3) an identification of the types of emission points belonging to the relevant source category; and (4) an identification of any affected sources for which a section 112(g) MACT determination has been made.[148] If a source has not submitted a "Part 1 MACT application and the permitting authority notifies [the source that it is] subject to section 112(j), [the source] must submit an application for a title V permit or for a revision to an existing title V permit [within thirty days] of being notified."[149] "Under the revised 112(j) rule Part 2 of the application was due by May 15, 2004, and [*must*] contain more detailed, comprehensive information about the source."[150] For instance, the Part 2 submission should include the following: (1) "[f]or new affected sources, the anticipated date of startup of operation"; (2) "[t]he HAP emitted by each affected source in the relevant source category and an estimated total uncontrolled and controlled emission rate for HAP from the affected source"; (3) "[a]ny existing Federal, State, or local limitations or requirements applicable to the affected source"; (4) "[f]or each affected emission point or group of affected emission points, an identification of control technology in place"; (5) "[i]nformation relevant to establishing the MACT floor, and, at the option of the owner or operator, a recommended MACT floor"; and (6) "[a]ny other information reasonably needed by the permitting authority including, at the discretion of the permitting authority, information required pursuant to subpart A of 40 C.F.R. part 63."[151] Furthermore, Part 2 of the application *may* also, "but is not required to, include the following": (1) "[r]ecommended emission limitations for the affected source and support information consistent with 40 C.F.R. 63.52(f)";[152] (2) "[a] description of the control technologies that [the source] would apply to meet the emission limitation including technical information on the design, operation, size, estimated control efficiency and any other information deemed appropriate by the permitting authority, and identification of the affected sources to which the control technologies shall be applied"; and (3) "[r]elevant parameters to be monitored and frequency of monitoring to demonstrate continuous compliance with the MACT emission limitation over the applicable reporting period."[153] Upon submission of the application, the permitting authority has up to eighteen months "to prepare and issue a title V permit containing terms and conditions of case-by-case MACT."[154]

Although the EPA has established the criteria that must be included in Part 2 of the permit application, the agency expects to promulgate all remaining air toxic standards before any facility would be required to submit this portion of the application.[155] For this reason, the EPA has provided the procedure to be used when a standard is promulgated between submission of Part 1 and Part 2.[156] "If a MACT standard is promulgated *during* this permit development process, the case-by-case MACT development [will be] discontinued and the permit would ultimately incorporate the MACT standard" (emphasis added).[157] Thus, a facility need not submit Part 2 of the application if the EPA issues a standard before the Part 2 application is due.

Sierra Club challenged the two-year delay in requiring complete case-by-case MACT submissions where the EPA had not yet promulgated a MACT standard by the May 2002 deadline (eighteen months after the deadline for issuance of the ten-year MACT standard).[158] The group also filed a citizens' suit against the EPA for failing to issue the MACT standards in a timely manner.[159] As a result of negotiation between the EPA and litigants, the parties agreed to a schedule for issuance of the remaining MACT standards. In addition, in the settlement the obligation to file a Part 2 application under Section 112(j) was changed from a uniform date to dates tied to the deadlines for issuance of a particular standard. Thus, Part 2 is due sixty days after the EPA issues a deadline for issuance of a MACT standard as required by the consent decree in the deadline suit for issuing the underlying MACT standards. Depending on the standard, Part 2 application due dates will be April 28, 2004; August 13, 2005; and October 30, 2007.[160]

Delegation of the MACT Program to States

In revising the federal air toxics program in 1990, Congress favorably viewed the "aggressive air toxics programs" being developed by many state and local air pollution control agencies "to fill the void left by Federal inaction."[161] Hence, while it sought to avoid compromising those programs, it also sought to enhance states' ability to expand and enforce them. The amended Section 112 "significantly expands the statutory role for State and local air pollution control agencies" through the delegation program contained in the new subsection (*l*).[162]

Section 112(l) provides:

Each State[163] may develop and submit to the Administrator for approval a program for the implementation and enforcement (including a review of enforcement delegations previously granted) of emission standards and other requirements for [HAPs] subject to this section or requirements for prevention and mitigation of accidental releases pursuant to subsection (r) of this section.[164]

States that submit such HAP programs to the EPA may obtain partial or complete delegation of the EPA's Section 112 authority, but they may not set standards less stringent than those promulgated by the EPA.[165]

Section 112(l) further provides that the EPA must approve or disapprove state programs within 180 days of receipt and after giving notice and opportunity for public comment. The EPA must disapprove a program if

(A) the authorities contained in the program are not adequate to assure compliance by all sources within the State with each applicable [section 112] standard . . . established by [the EPA];

(B) adequate authority [or resources] do not exist . . . to implement the program;

(C) the schedule of implementing the program and assuring compliance . . . is not sufficiently expeditious; or

(D) the program is otherwise not in compliance with the guidance issued by [EPA under this subsection] or is not likely to satisfy . . . the objectives of this chapter.[166]

This Section 112(l) rules are set out in 40 C.F.R. Part 63, Subpart E.[167] The rules were issued by the EPA on September 14, 2000, replacing earlier provisions.[168] The regulations establish procedures for approval of state rules, programs, and other requirements necessary to implement a state program in place of the federal provisions.

The rules set out the procedures for simple delegations as well as the procedures for state requirements that adjust a Section 112 rule.[169] The provisions also establish how a state can seek to substitute state requirements which defer to a federal rule and a mechanism to utilize permit terms and conditions in lieu of the standards.[170]

New Directions in MACT Standards: Emissions Averaging, Pollution Prevention, and Work Practice Standards

Since the tragic chemical release in Bhopal, India, as well as the release of TRI data by the EPA and the focus on significant health risk from air toxics emissions, the EPA, states, and industry have been looking for more creative, nontraditional ways of reducing air toxics emissions. The traditional "end of the stack" controls can do only so much to limit HAP emissions. Moreover, if the pollutant is not emitted into the air, it often ends up in some other medium such as solid waste or water discharges.

The 1990 CAA Amendments, therefore, directed the EPA to look at a wide variety of emission reduction mechanisms in determining what should be included in a MACT standard. Indeed, the act specifically provides that MACT may include a prohibition of any emissions of a particular type from a source category.[171] Heretofore, this concept was relatively unknown in pollution control programs. The long-standing premise of regulatory programs is that "you take the source as you find it" and simply require controlled emission reductions from that type of source. Neither the EPA nor other regulatory agencies have often dictated what kinds of raw material products a source may use at the front end of the production process or how the actual production unit should be designed to minimize emissions. In this new era of environmental regulation, however, such is not the case. In developing standards under Section 112, the EPA is looking at inherently less-polluting production systems in developing MACT standards. For example, in the dry cleaner rule, the EPA looked at the two basic types of process systems to dry clean clothes. One mechanism was essentially a closed system and produced substantially fewer emissions per pound of clothing. The other, transfer machines, required a transfer of the clothes from one piece of equipment to the other, thereby creating substantially higher emissions for the same amount of clothes. In the final rule, the EPA set a rule that effectively banned new transfer machines because the standard was below what transfer machines could achieve.[172]

The EPA and states have also begun to look for ways to give industry more flexibility in meeting targeted emissions reductions. These are often referred to as performance-based systems, with an overall emissions reduction target. Likewise, flexible control programs such as emissions averaging have taken hold. For example, in the HON the reference level of control technology, defined as MACT, for the different types of emission points is established in a rule. However, if a source is able to "overcontrol" one set of emission points, it can take credit for that and "undercontrol" another set of emission points covered by the standard. The EPA's process for making that balance determination between the overcontrolled and undercontrolled emission points in the HON is extremely complicated; in fact, a number of sources probably chose not to do emissions averaging simply because the record keeping is so difficult. The precedent is set and future MACT standards may focus more on emissions averaging provisions to encourage flexible control measures. The EPA typically has taken the position that the emissions averaging can be done only within a source category and will not average across source categories. For those facilities that include only one source category, this is not a big issue. For a number of complex industrial facilities with multiple categorical standards, this could severely limit emissions averaging potential.

More recently, however, the EPA has espoused interest in a "predominant MACT" concept, whereby a facility covered by multiple categorical standards for a similar process might choose to comply with the "predominant" MACT across all units. For example, a plant that has process equipment subject to multiple coating standards (e.g., miscellaneous metal, plastics, and automobile topcoat) could choose the predominant MACT.

Some MACT standards also incorporated pollution prevention concepts in a number of different ways. For example, in the industrial cooling towers MACT standard, the EPA prohibited the use of chromium in the cooling tower process.[173] In doing so, the EPA determined that there were methodologies for accomplishing the same process without the use of a hazardous air pollutant.[174] The pollution prevention practice is written into the standard as a work practice under Section 112(h). Thus, the MACT standard for cooling towers prohibits emissions of chromium from major source industrial process cooling towers by prohibiting the use of chromium-based water treatment chemicals in those industrial process cooling towers.[175]

In the halogenated solvents (degreasers) MACT standard, the EPA also specifically incorporated the concept of pollution prevention into its standards. The agency stated in its proposal that the degreaser standards would encourage source reduction by (1) encouraging elimination or reduction and the need to clean wherever feasible; (2) increasing efficiency of cleaning operations and thereby reducing overall use of solvents; (3) improving house-keeping measures, work practices, and equipment maintenance; and (4) discouraging use of end-of-the-pipe treatment technologies, such as carbon absorbers, that may have multimedia impacts.[176] This standard also incorporated multiple options for meeting the standard's requirements. For example, the final rule has an equipment standard, in conjunction with work practice requirements and an alternative overall solvent emissions standard.[177] Once again, these multiple compliance options reflect the EPA's attempts to focus on results, and less on command-and-control method requirements for sources.

Compliance Issues

Before the 1990 amendments, the Section 112 standards were, in effect, freestanding requirements. In other words, there was no requirement that the standards be incorporated into a federal or state permit. Under Section 112 the states were typically delegated implementation authority and folded those requirements into state regulations, similar to the process for implementation of Section 111 standards. In many instances, compliance requirements in the old Section 112 standards required only an initial compliance demonstration and then, at best, a periodic compliance determination. There was only a limited focus on "continuous compliance."

With the advent of Title V permit requirements, major sources subject to Section 112 standards will be required to obtain a Title V permit. Section 112 contains several special provisions that relate to compliance with the MACT standards. Traditionally these requirements were freestanding. However, the relationship to the Title V permitting process also becomes important in the post-1990 era. Sources subject to Section 112 standards must also have an understanding of how these limits will become federally enforceable conditions in a Title V permit. (The Title V permitting process is detailed in Chapters 15 and 16.)

The CAA sets forth specific requirements for when a MACT source must comply with the standard. In addition, the source category-specific standards will often contain initial notification requirements or other interim requirements that may be imposed before the ultimate compliance date. Practitioners should not assume that an existing source will have three years to comply with a newly issued standard, even if the final compliance date is that far off.

Compliance Deadlines

As a general rule, a new or reconstructed source subject to a standard promulgated under Section 112(d), 112(f), or 112(h) shall comply with such standard upon start-up.[178] If, however, a source commences construction after proposal of a standard, but before the effective date of the standard, it may have three years to comply with the promulgated standard if (1) the final standard is more stringent than the proposal and (2) the source complies with the standard as proposed during the three-year period.[179] An owner or operator of a source that intends to comply with the proposed rule for three years must so notify the EPA administrator.

If an unaffected area source (that is, an area source that commences construction or reconstruction after the proposed date of an applicable standard) increases its HAP emissions (or potential emissions) such that it becomes a major source, that source is subject to the new source standard immediately upon becoming a major source.[180]

The CAA provides that the EPA administrator shall establish a compliance date for each category or subcategory of existing sources subject to a standard that shall provide for compliance as "expeditiously as practicable" but not later than three years after the standard is promulgated, with limited exceptions.[181] In general, the EPA has typically provided the full three years for full compliance with the existing source standards, although a source may have to undertake interim steps toward control.

As with most programs, the CAA also affords the administrator several statutory mechanisms whereby sources may extend compliance beyond the specific compliance stated in the regulation. The EPA administrator, or a state with an approved Title V program, may issue a permit that grants the existing source an extension of up to one additional year to comply with the Section 112(b) standard "if such additional period is necessary for the installation of controls."[182] A source wishing to request an additional year for installation of controls must submit to the appropriate permitting authority a written request for extension not later than twelve months before the affected source's compliance date for those sources that are not including emission points and emissions averaging schemes.[183] The precise requirements for justifying an extension of compliance are set forth in the General Provisions.

The statute and regulations also provide for a source's obtaining a compliance extension if the owner or operator of an existing source has installed BACT, as defined in CAA Section 169(3), or technology required to meet the lowest achievable emission rate (LAER), as defined in Section 171. To qualify for the extension, BACT or LAER must be installed before the promulgation of an emission standard for such source category for the same pollutant or stream of pollutants controlled pursuant to the BACT or LAER determination for five years after the date on which such installation was achieved, as determined by the EPA administrator.[184] The request for an extension must be submitted in writing to the administrator not later than 120 days after the promulgation date of the standard.[185] The general provisions also provide extensive regulations concerning the process for obtaining a compliance extension, the agency's review thereof, and demonstration required by the source applicant consultation, including notice to the source's owner or operator of the administrator's intent to grant or deny the extension and the basis for any proposed denial of the standards.[186]

There is also an exemption for national security purposes. Under this provision, the president of the United States may exempt the stationary source from compliance for up to two years "if the president determines that the technology to implement such standard is not available and that it is in the national security interests of the United States" to grant the extension.[187] Further extensions of up to two years may be granted by the president.[188]

The Early Reductions Program

In addition to the specific time extensions under Section 112, Congress created an early compliance extension program to encourage sources to make reductions well in advance of when otherwise required. In exchange for substantial early reduction of HAPs, the facility gains an additional six years to achieve compliance with the actual MACT standard. Section 112(1)(5) of the CAA sets forth the basic statutory parameters of the early reductions program, and the implementing regulations are set forth in 40 C.F.R. Section 63.70, *et seq*. Congress included the early reductions program as an incentive to encourage companies to reduce emissions quickly in the most cost-effective manner. It was included at the encouragement of several chemical companies, including Monsanto, which had made significant reductions in HAP emissions in anticipation of future air toxics controls under the CAA and for various other programs such as the voluntary 33/50 program designed to reduce emissions. Congress viewed the early reductions program as a mechanism to reduce HAPs quickly, without waiting for the EPA regulatory process. In essence, it was a program designed to reduce emissions and an acknowledgment of the length of time needed to issue and implement technically sound standards under Section 112.

The early reductions program provides two mechanisms by which sources can apply for an extension from a subsequently promulgated Section 112(d) standard. The first way to earn the six-year extension is to achieve the reductions before the otherwise applicable standard is first proposed.[189] Alternatively, if the standard was proposed but the reduction was achieved before January 1, 1994, the source may also apply for an extension.[190] The source must achieve in excess of 90 percent reduction of HAPs and 95 percent control of particulate HAPs as a condition of obtaining the six-year extension. The reductions must be over a baseline set of emissions. The early reductions may be made for other purposes, such as to comply with a state air toxics program, provided that they are not otherwise required under a federal Section 112 standard. The source will be granted a six-year extension from the MACT standard if it successfully demonstrates that it has achieved the 90 percent reduction within the appropriate time frame. Section 63.74 of the implementing regulations sets forth the basic requirements that must be included in the reduction demonstration.[191]

One complicating aspect of the 90 percent reduction requirement is the CAA's restriction on limiting the use of offsetting reductions of high-risk pollutants, as set forth in Section 112(i)(5)(E). The rationale for this provision is that a source emitting extremely toxic pollutants should not be able to defer compliance with the MACT standard to reduce those toxic pollutants by reducing less dangerous emissions, albeit HAPs. This provision is implemented through 40 C.F.R. Section 63.74(e)(1).

Although the early reductions program was seen as a great incentive program to encourage facilities to reduce hazardous air emissions well before implementation of the MACT standards, the program has met with very limited success. Initially only some sixty or seventy companies filed enforceable commitments to make the early reductions. The cumbersomeness and complexity of establishing base-year emissions and the difficulty of making the appropriate demonstrations has dissuaded some from participating in the program. In addition, as the MACT standards have developed, in many instances they have not been significantly more stringent than the 90 percent reduction required by the early reductions compliance program, and in some cases have been less stringent. Thus, the incentive to make the early reductions to gain a six-year compliance extension has been minimized.

Preconstruction Review Provisions

Section 112(1)(1) provides that, after the effective date of a MACT standard promulgated under Section 112(d), (f), or (h), no person may construct a new major source or reconstruct an existing major source subject to the standard unless the EPA administrator (or a state with an approved Title V permit program) determines that the major source, if properly constructed, reconstructed, and operated, will comply with the required standard. The EPA's regulations to implement this preconstruction review requirement are set forth at 40 C.F.R. Section 63.5.[192] The preconstruction review requirements generally require the administrator's advance written approval for new major sources or reconstructed major sources. Applicants are required to submit a preconstruction or reconstruction application for approval before the construction or reconstruction commences. If construction has commenced at the time a standard becomes effective but start-up has not occurred, the applicant shall submit an application not later than sixty days after the effective date of the relevant standard. The application must include the basic information about the source, expected commencement and completion dates of construction, and anticipated start-up date of the source. The application must also include by type and quantity the HAPs emitted by the source and other information such that the source can demonstrate it will be able to comply with the MACT standard.[193] In addition to general application requirements, there are specific information requirements for new sources and for reconstructed sources.[194]

Applications for approval of construction must also include basic technical information describing the nature, size, design, operating design capacity, and method of operation of the source, as well as information about the emissions and planned pollution control equipment. The reconstruction application must include a description of the current source and components that are to be replaced and information on the control equipment and emissions control efficiency. The basis for the EPA administrator's review of the application for construction or reconstruction is set forth at 40 C.F.R. Section 63.5(e). The regulations require the administrator to notify the applicant of the agency's intent to approve or deny approval of the application within sixty calendar days after receipt of the complete application.[195] The administrator has thirty days from receipt of the original application to determine if the application is complete or if supplementary information is needed.[196] If the state has subjected the source to a state preconstruction review that substantially satisfies the requirements for the administrator's review, the administrator may approve the request.[197]

Malfunction Provisions

The general provisions also include basic requirements for start-up, shutdown, and malfunction. 40 C.F.R. Section 63.6(e) requires a source to operate at all times, including periods of start-up, shutdown, and malfunction, in a manner consistent with good air pollution control practices for minimizing emissions to the environment at least to the levels required by applicable standards. The owner or operator of an affected source is required to develop and implement a written start-up, shutdown, and malfunction plan, which, among other things, describes in detail procedures for operating and maintaining the source during periods of start-up, shutdown, and malfunction and a program for corrective action for malfunctioning process and air pollution control equipment used to comply with any relevant standard. As with the previous Section 112 standards, the purpose of a malfunction plan is to minimize emissions to the atmosphere. The facility must keep records to demonstrate that procedures specified in the malfunction plan are adhered to, and start-up, shutdown, and malfunction plans must be kept available for inspection for the life of the affected source.[198] The general MACT provisions and a number of MACT source specific standards provide that the standard is not violated if a malfunction occurs and the source follows its plan and minimizes emissions.[199] Practitioners must be cautious that start-up, shutdown, and malfunction provisions are specifically considered in the source's Title V operating permit.

Beyond the MACT Standards

Congress set forth several other provisions requiring the EPA to continue to look at how to reduce hazardous air pollutants in the environment. By far, the bulk of the reduction is likely to occur as a result of the implementation of the MACT standards provided for in the ten-year implementation schedule discussed above. The act does, however, provide several additional mechanisms for the EPA to evaluate the need for further programs. These include looking at specific HAP pollutants, urban air toxics, and risk. These provisions are reviewed below.

Residual Risk

Although Congress moved the EPA away from risk-based analysis in the initial phase of setting air toxic standards under Section 112, it did not altogether abandon the risk program. Instead, Congress directed the EPA to conduct a risk-based standard-setting process in the second step of the HAP control program. This process is referred to as the residual risk analysis.

In the absence of any new legislation, the CAA directs the EPA to promulgate risk-based standards for each category or subcategory of sources for which MACT technology-based standards were established within eight years after promulgation of such technology-based standards, if the promulgation of risk-based rules is required "in order to provide an ample margin of safety to protect public health" in the same manner as was previously done under the old Section 112.[200] Residual risk standards are also promulgated if necessary to prevent an adverse environmental effect, taking into account cost, energy, safety, and other relevant factors. In the absence of new legislation, the risk-based emission standards under Section 112(f) are to be promulgated in a manner consistent with the two-step, risk-based approach used by the EPA before the 1990 CAA Amendments, unless the EPA administrator determines that a more stringent standard is necessary.[201]

The threshold inquiry for determining whether to promulgate risk-based standards for a particular source category is set out in the statute. The CAA provides that the EPA administrator shall issue residual risk standards for a particular source category if the standards promulgated under Section 112(d) applicable to sources emitting a pollutant or pollutants classified as known, probable, or possible human carcinogens do not reduce lifetime excess cancer risk to most exposed individuals in the source category to less than one in a million.[202]

The EPA administrator is to determine whether to promulgate such risk standards, and if the decision is that the standards are necessary, the administrator shall promulgate the standards eight years after the promulgation of the standards under Section 112(d). In other words, if a source category has three years to comply with a Section 112(d) MACT standard, the EPA must make a determination and issue standards within five years after implementation of the MACT standard. This will leave little time to determine whether or not the standard will provide for the ample margin of safety to protect public health. For those standards that were required to be promulgated within the first two years after enactment, the EPA administrator has nine years after promulgation of the standards under Section 112(d) to determine whether residual risk standards are necessary and, if required, to promulgate the standards.[203] As the EPA is still scrambling to issue the final technology-based standards, it has only just seriously begun the process of looking at residual risk standards except in the most broad terms. Much of the risk work has been done in the context of the urban air toxic studies.

Thus, although Congress deferred consideration of risk-based standards under Section 112, it did not abandon the concept. Given the difficulty the EPA has had in promulgating technology-based standards for the more than 170 source categories and the continuing budget crisis, it is very unlikely that the EPA will be able to promulgate risk-based standards until well into the next decade.

Finally, if a residual risk standard is promulgated, new sources must comply upon start-up. Existing sources would have ninety days to comply, although the EPA administrator may grant a waiver for up to two years if necessary for installation of such controls, if steps are taken during the waiver period to ensure persons' protection from any imminent endangerment.[204]

Residual Risk Report

The Residual Risk Report to Congress ("Risk Report") is a response to a congressional directive in Section 112(f)(1), in which Congress determined that the EPA administrator should report on the method of calculating the risk remaining after the imposition of Section 112(d) technical standards.[205] The Risk Report describes the origins of the current system as well as describing the process used for risk assessment. Its stated goal is to "address the legislative requirements of section 112(f)(1) and to provide the reader with a basic understanding of the methods and process the Agency plans to follow" in risk analyses for air toxics.[206]

Background

Prior to the 1990 amendments, air toxics were dealt with on a toxic-by-toxic basis. The EPA was to list HAPS based on health risks; then emissions standards were set for individual pollutants. The result of this process was found to be highly inefficient. By 1990 standards had been established for only eight HAPs. Moreover, hard limits on pollutants were found to be very costly to address by industry.

The 1990 CAA Amendments developed a new, two-step paradigm. The concept was to use existing or available technologies and work practices in order to get immediate gains in emissions limitations. Hence, the first step involves the imposition of technology-based standards under Section 112(d) as discussed above. The second step, residual risk assessment, is an added layer added on top of these technical requirements. This step requires a level of protection to be established that provides "an ample margin of safety" to protect public health and the environment while at the same time "taking into consideration costs, energy, safety, and other relevant factors."[207] Essentially the goal is greater protection of the populace through more flexible, but immediate, application of the CAA.

The Risk Report itself references the creation of the benzene NESHAP as an example of this newer approach.[208] In analyzing the human health risk, the benzene process took two steps. Initially "acceptable" risk or exposure was established (it was determined that benzene was a linear carcinogen with a maximum individual risk for exposure of one in ten thousand).[209] The second step determined the "ample margin of safety" (determined to be one in one million). Thus, the EPA would balance practical concerns with absolute protection by "protecting the greatest number of persons possible to an individual lifetime risk level" no higher than one in one million while limiting exposure of individuals near sources to one in ten thousand.

Process

The current risk assessment methodology evolved from the approaches outlined in three influential studies: the 1983 National Research Council (NRC) report on risk assessment and its 1994 follow-up as well as the 1997 Presidential/Congressional Commission on Risk Assessment and Risk Management (CRARM). From these approaches two frameworks for risk analysis are described. The traditional approach is an extension of the NRC recommendation, a four-step process involving hazard identification, dose-response analysis, exposure assessment, and risk characterization. More recently the EPA identified a three-phase framework for ecological assessments, but which is consistent with human risk assessment as well: problem formulation, analysis, and risk characterization.[210] This methodology is inclusive of the NRC's four-step approach, but includes the problem formulation phase.

The EPA's hope is that risk assessment under the current regime will be more efficient than in the past. Efficiencies are expected to come from several areas. First, tiered analysis will be used where appropriate. The initial step will be screening analysis. The aim here is to identify situations in which no further action is needed and those for which further analysis is needed through simple, inexpensive analyses. More involved analysis is reserved for the refined tier. The Risk Report also makes better management and use of existing data a goal. For example, human health risk assessments are expected to be based on data from the EPA's Integrated Risk Information Center. Other sources will be consulted only as needed. It is also hoped that this will help provide for more consistent and predictable assessment.

Urban Air Toxics

The concern for harmful effects of air toxics in urban areas is the particular focus of the residual risk program because of the "large number of people and the variety of sources of toxic air pollutants, such as cars, trucks, large factories, gasoline stations, and dry cleaners" in these settings.[211] Although individually these sources do not emit large amounts of air toxics, collectively they pose significant threats to urban residents and to the environment.[212] In fact, "approximately 75 percent of the total HAP emissions of all 188 HAPS from all sources" are in urban areas.[213] For this reason, Congress, through the 1990 CAA Amendments, prompted the EPA to develop a plan to address this growing problem.[214] Section 112(k)(3)(B)(ii) of the amendments provides the following guidance to the EPA:

> (B) The strategy shall:
>
> (i) identify not less than 30 hazardous air pollutants which, as the result of emissions from area sources, present the greatest threat to public health in the largest number of urban areas and that are or will be listed pursuant to subsection (b) of this section, and
> (ii) identify the source categories or subcategories emitting such pollutants that are or will be listed pursuant to subsection (c) of this section. When identifying categories and subcategories of sources under this subparagraph, the Administrator shall assure that sources accounting for 90 per centum or more of the aggregate emissions of each of the 30 identified hazardous air pollutants are subject to standards pursuant to subsection (d) of this section.

In July of 1999, the EPA released its plan, the Integrated Urban Air Toxics Strategy, to address threats of air pollutants in urban settings by looking at major, mobile, and indoor source emissions.[215] The plan was designed to complement the existing efforts to reduce air toxics while building on the reductions already achieved from vehicles, fuels, and industries such as chemical plants and oil refineries.[216] In developing the strategy, a county was considered to be urban if (1) it included a "metropolitan statistical area with a population greater than 250,000" or (2) "the U.S. Census Bureau designate[d] more than 50 percent of the population as urban."[217] When this program is fully implemented, almost all major metropolitan cities will be affected.[218]

The Integrated Urban Air Toxics Strategy cites thirty-three[219] air toxics that pose the greatest threat to the health of people living in urban areas. In compiling this list, the EPA conducted three separate analyses, relying on emissions estimates, ambient monitoring, and air quality modeling.[220] Furthermore, twenty-nine area source categories, which release a significant percentage of these air toxics, were initially identified in the plan.[221] Of the area source categories listed, the EPA had already issued or was working on a number of the standards. Exhibits 2 and 3 set out those categories being addressed by the EPA.[222] The EPA added to these initial listings in 2001 and 2002, bringing the total to 70 area source categories.[223] With the additional listings, the EPA has stated that it met the required 90 percent of the thirty listed toxics.[224] Furthermore, the agency is scheduled to have all of the area source standards necessary to meet the 90 percent requirement of Section 112(d)(3)(B)(ii) of the 1990 CAA Amendments in place by 2009.[225] Full compliance under these standards is expected by 2012.[226]

The EPA has identified the following three goals for the Integrated Urban Air Toxics Strategy:

1) attain a 75% reduction in incidence of cancer attributable to exposure to HAPs emitted by large and small stationary sources nationwide; 2) attain a substantial reduction in public health risks (such as birth defects and reproduction effects) posed by HAP emissions from small industrial/commercial sources[; and] 3) address disproportionate impacts of air toxics hazards across urban areas, such as geographic "hot spots," highly exposed population subgroups, and predominantly minority and low-income communities.[227]

In order to accomplish these objectives, the EPA will continue to "develop regulations addressing source of air toxics at both the national and local levels."[228] Second, the agency will initiate both national- and local-level projects in order to "address specific pollutants (such as mercury) and to identify and address specific community risks (through pilot projects)."[229] Third, the EPA will conduct assessment activities, which are designed to enhance the EPA's understanding of the risks associated with air toxics in urban areas.[230] These assessment activities "include expanding air toxics monitoring, improving and periodically updating emissions inventories, and air quality and exposure modeling."[231] Finally, education and outreach programs will be conducted in order to inform stakeholders about the Integrated Urban Air Toxics Strategy and to get their input.[232]

Furthermore, continual advances in the broader air toxics program will play a vital role in implementing the urban air toxics strategy. For instance, the "EPA is currently developing an indoor air toxics strategy which will assess indoor air exposures and present next steps in [the] strategic approach, building upon the current information and relying heavily on voluntary, nonregulatory efforts to reduce risks from air toxics indoors."[233] This indoor environments program is particularly relevant to the Integrated Urban Air Toxics Strategy because people living in urban areas spend as much as 80 percent of their time indoors.[234] In addition to the indoor air toxics exposure, outside air is brought indoors through infiltration and mechanical ventilation, posing even greater risks.[235] Moreover, through the Great Waters Program, the EPA is focusing on reducing adverse effects of contaminated ecosystems and fish.[236] The information obtained through this program will be helpful in determining the potential dangers to urban residents living in coastal areas "from both inhalation of [hazardous air pollutants (HAPs)] and consumption of fish contaminated by deposition of HAPs to waterways."[237]

The agency is also making efforts to "address the unique perspectives of state, local, and tribal governments, public health groups, environmental justice communities, small business communities, and environmental interest groups."[238] The EPA has become involved in "community assessment and risk reduction projects by providing technical support, risk assessment tools, and supplemental funding to several existing, regionally led, community projects."[239] One case example is a project involving the City of Cleveland, Ohio, and the EPA.[240] These two entities are working together "to develop methods to characterize local risks (including indoor, stationary, and mobile sources) and to implement risk reduction measures."[241] The EPA anticipates that this project will provide a framework for implementing various other urban air toxics programs across the nation.[242]

Section 112(c)(6) of the CAA directed the EPA to list categories and sub-categories of sources of seven specific HAPs to ensure control of at least 90 percent of the emissions of each compound. These HAPs include alkylated lead compounds, polycyclic organic matter (POM), hexachlorobenzene (HCB), mercury, polychlorinated biphenyls (PCBs), and 2, 3, 7, 8 - tetrachlorodibenzo-p-dioxin (TCDD).[243] The EPA published its initial list of categories on April 10, 1998.[244] In that notice the EPA evaluated emissions inventory data. The EPA found that the bulk of the emissions inventory of sources potentially subject to regulation were already listed.[245] The EPA added only two new source categories: open burning of scrap tire and Gasoline Distribution (Aviation Fuel). The EPA revised that list in November 2002 deleting several area source categories,[246] including the scrap tire category. The November 2002 notice also deleted the scrap tire area source category under Section 112(k).

Mercury Study

The Mercury Study is a report to Congress mandated by Section 112(n)(1)(B) of the CAA.[247] It assesses the extent of mercury emissions by source, the health and environmental impact of these emissions, and the availability of cost control technologies today. It recognizes that the science surrounding mercury is continually evolving, and so postures itself as a snapshot of the understanding of mercury. The report recognizes that mercury sources are varied. Mercury exists naturally in trace amounts, but is also cycled through the environment as a result of weather patterns and anthropogenic activities. It may exist as a gas or in particles that may be airborne or deposited on land.

One principal danger of mercury is its bioaccumulation. For this reason certain populations see greater exposure. For example, mercury accumulates most efficiently, and in its most toxic form, at the top of the aquatic food chain. For this reason human populations that eat large amounts of fish at the top of the chain tend to have the greatest exposure to mercury. Studies of these populations, in Japan and in Iraq, have demonstrated that mercury's most devastating effect comes with fetal exposure. Bioaccumulation has a similar impact on the environment. Fish-eating birds and mammals face high exposures to mercury. The resulting adverse effects include death, reduced reproductive success, and behavioral abnormalities. Some reports suggest that airborne mercury emissions may also be leading to adverse effects.

Despite wide use in industry, mercury emissions have fallen some 75 percent due to the elimination of mercury as an additive in certain products.

Most of the remaining emissions come through the burning of waste or fuel that contains mercury, primarily from the emissions of coal-fired utility boilers. Emissions from mercury sources have been difficult to control, as control technologies remain in the research stage. Estimates of the cost of implementing such technologies reach into the billions of dollars. Moreover, their development is complicated by the varied species of mercury emitted from different plants. Consequently, the most cost-effective means of dealing with mercury emissions remains through removal from the product cycle.

Based on the Mercury Study and a 1998 Utility Air Toxics Report to Congress the EPA found in late 2000 that regulation of coal-fired utilities under Section 112 was warranted.[248] The EPA proposed such standards in early 2004.[249] The EPA found, however, that regulation of HAP emissions from natural gas fuel units was not necessary.

Great Waters Study

The Great Waters Study deals with the impact of atmospheric deposition of air pollutants on the Great Waters, which include the Great Lakes, Lake Champlain, the Chesapeake Bay, and many U.S. coastal estuaries.[250] The study is primarily concerned with the effects of fifteen toxics associated with damage to certain organs, the endocrine system, and the immune system.[251] Because many of these toxins are bioaccumulators, like mercury, the greatest health risk in these waters comes to risk groups with above average consumption of fish. As with mercury, young children and pregnant women—as well as those who eat large amounts of fish—are particularly at risk. Certain nitrogen compounds are also a concern because they facilitate excessive algal growth, which may lead to eutrophication.[252]

The Great Waters Study suggests that pollutant deposition is generally constant or declining. Lead and cadmium deposition in the Great Lakes has fallen, while nitrogen deposition has remained constant. However, the EPA cautions that limited monitoring and other technological barriers makes such trend information uncertain. Moreover, while conditions may be improving, existing concentrations continue to have an effect on the ecological health of the Great Waters. And because these pollutants may travel long distances in the atmosphere, it is difficult to determine the emissions source.

The Great Waters Study also addresses efforts to reduce atmospheric deposition. Because the link to sources is attenuated, these efforts have been broad-based. The EPA is involved with many programs, frequently multimedia or "cross-programs," that in some way contribute to the reduction of this deposition. The EPA is also trying to formalize its efforts administratively through the introduction of regional work plans, and through six recommendations put forward in the study. These include continued and expanding support of research and monitoring; continued development and implementation of regional, national, and international programs; better definition of baselines; and efforts to increase public awareness.

The Section 112(r) Accidental Release Program

Section 112(r) is in some ways the most unusual part of the 1990 CAA Amendments, for it does not aim to limit normal air emissions. Instead, it is designed to prevent disastrous *accidental* releases of hazardous substances. Hence, Section 112(r) imposes requirements on many facilities that previously never needed to worry about CAA mandates. Many of these regulated facilities usually only store or handle chemicals; they do not emit them under normal conditions. Therefore, such facilities are often not otherwise regulated under the CAA. Before 1990, the act focused almost entirely on normal emissions from stationary and mobile sources of air pollution.

Thus, numerous facilities that neither manufacture goods nor normally emit air pollutants are covered by the CAA for the first time. For example, public drinking water systems, chemical wholesalers, and propane retailers must prepare and file a risk management plan (RMP) showing how they are complying with Section 112(r). Sources already regulated under the CAA also face these new requirements, which bear more resemblance to Occupational Safety and Health Administration (OSHA) rules than to CAA regulations.

The prevention of accidental releases provisions in Section 112(r) are part of the mosaic of federal environmental and occupational health and safety programs developed over the past decade to prevent and minimize the consequences of unintended releases. Several states—including New Jersey, California, Nevada, and Delaware—have developed their own regulations to prevent accidental chemical releases. The tragic chemical release that killed thousands of people in Bhopal, India, in 1984 served as the primary impetus for these various programs.

The EPA issued final rules implementing the Section 112(r) accidental release provisions in June 1996.[253] In addition, in January 1994, the EPA issued a list of substances to be regulated under Section 112(r), along with quantity thresholds for these substances.[254] The agency has also issued several guidance documents elaborating on various aspects of the accidental release program.

The EPA's rules implement CAA Section 112(r)(7)—the core of Section 112(r)—and are codified at 40 C.F.R. Part 68. The regulations probably affect more plants than any other rule issued under the 1990 CAA Amendments. The EPA estimates that its accidental release rules could affect over 66,000 facilities, with many of these being nonmanufacturing facilities.[255] Related accidental release regulations that affect many facilities were adopted by OSHA in February 1992.[256] Section 304 of the 1990 CAA Amendments required that OSHA, in coordination with the EPA, issue a chemical process safety management standard under authority of the Occupational Safety and Health Act (OSH Act). Given the focus of the OSH Act, these rules are designed to protect *workers* at facilities using highly hazardous materials, not the general public or the environment. The OSHA standard is briefly discussed in a later section.

Overview of CAA Section 112(r)

As with much of the 1990 CAA Amendments, Congress wrote many particulars of the accidental release program into the statute itself rather than drafting a broad outline and having the EPA fill in the details. The new Section 112(r) takes up nearly twelve pages of the House of Representatives Energy and Commerce Committee print of the CAA and other environmental statutes. That makes Subsection (r) more than four times longer than the entire pre-1990 Section 112, which governed all aspects of air toxics control.

The General Duty Provision

Paragraph (1) of Section 112(r) is known as the "general duty" provision. It states in part:

> The owners and operators of stationary sources producing, processing, handling, or storing [certain listed and other extremely hazardous] substances have a general duty . . . to identify hazards which may result from [accidental] releases using appropriate hazard assessment techniques, to design and maintain a safe facility taking such steps as are necessary to prevent releases, and to minimize the consequences of accidental releases which do occur.

The statute specifies that companies have this general duty in the same manner and to the same extent as under an OSH Act provision that says employers have a general duty to maintain a safe workplace.[257] In a not particularly helpful comment on how the CAA and OSH Act provisions relate to each other, the EPA has simply said that it "is investigating the relationship between requirements under section 112(r) and OSHA's general duty provisions."[258] Elsewhere, however, the EPA has stated, "The plain language of section 112(r)(1) applies not only to the regulated substances listed [by the EPA] but also to 'any other extremely hazardous substance.'"[259]

The Section 112(r)(1) general duty also does not appear to be qualified by the quantity of listed and other extremely hazardous substances that a facility uses or stores; the *de minimis* threshold quantities, discussed in subsequent sections of this chapter, seem not to apply to this provision. The general duty provision is self-implementing and facility owners must comply regardless of whether they need to file an RMP under Section 112(r).[260]

Companies may fear that the EPA could allege a violation of the general duty clause even though a facility uses or stores only minute amounts of the relevant materials and is also in compliance with all of the agency's Section 112(r) rules. However, the Environment and Public Works Committee report accompanying the Senate CAA Amendments bill suggests that this will not be the case. The report states that OSHA cites the OSH Act's general duty clause "for enforcement purposes when a hazard is found in the workplace for which there is no specific OSHA regulation or standard, and when the employer is aware that the hazard exists."[261]

The Senate report also cites an OSHA administrative decision on the OSH Act's general duty clause "to indicate that a similar standard is an appropriate application of the general duty to operate a facility free from accidents established by the proposed [accident release section of the Senate bill]."[262] The quoted section of that decision sets forth the elements of an OSH Act general duty clause violation:

> In order to establish a . . . violation, the Secretary [of Labor] must prove: (1) the employer failed to render its workplace free of a hazard, (2) the hazard was recognized either by the cited employer or generally within the employer's industry, (3) the hazard was causing or was likely to cause death or serious harm, and (4) there was a feasible means by which the employer could have eliminated or materially reduced the hazard.[263]

List of Substances and Threshold Quantities

Section 112(r)(3) directs the EPA to promulgate a list of at least one hundred substances "which, in the case of an accidental release, are known to cause or may reasonably be anticipated to cause death, injury, or serious adverse effects to human health or the environment." Congress itself wrote sixteen substances into the list. As described later, the EPA issued its list of such substances in January 1994, but in 1996 it proposed to amend the list and stayed the effectiveness of certain provisions.[264]

Paragraph (4) specifies the factors that the EPA must consider in listing the substances. Under paragraph (5), the EPA must establish a "threshold quantity" for each substance, meaning the amount that may cause death, injury, or serious adverse effects to health or the environment. These threshold quantities were also set in the January 1994 rule.

The Chemical Safety Board and Other Provisions

Paragraph (6) creates a five-member independent Chemical Safety Board, which is charged with the following duties:

- Investigating the cause of serious accidental releases
- Recommending ways to reduce the likelihood or consequences of accidental releases
- Issuing regulations that establish requirements for reporting accidental releases.

Under the statute the Chemical Safety Board also has a number of other duties and authorities. It appears, however, that Section 112(r)(6) will essentially be ignored. In 1994 the Clinton administration nominated five members for the board, three of whom were confirmed. To save costs, however, funding for the board was rescinded and none of the members received appointments. The administration explained that the board's responsibilities could be fulfilled by the EPA and OSHA under these agencies' existing authorities.

Under paragraph (9), the EPA may issue an order to prevent imminent and substantial endangerment from an actual or threatened accidental release. Paragraph (11) allows states to adopt more stringent laws on accidental releases. Paragraph (7) is the real core of Section 112(r).

Section 112(r)(7) Risk Management Programs

Paragraph (7) is the heart of CAA Section 112(r), both in terms of reflecting the congressional goal of avoiding accidental releases and in adding new regulatory requirements for tens of thousands of sources. Subparagraph (A) of this provision grants the EPA broad authority "to promulgate release prevention, detection, and correction requirements which may include monitoring, record keeping, reporting, training, vapor recovery, secondary containment, and other design, equipment, work practice, and operational requirements." Some of these requirements will be familiar to those who handle compliance with other environmental laws. Secondary containment, for example, often is required for storage of hazardous waste under the Resource Conservation and Recovery Act (RCRA).

Subsection (B) of Section 112(r)(7) sets out the real obligations for accidental release programs as well as the EPA's mandate for issuing rules governing these requirements. Under Subsection (B), the owner or operator of a facility that has more than a specified threshold amount of an EPA-listed substance must prepare and implement an accidental release risk management plan. Although the EPA was required to promulgate rules (described later) stating what these plans (and the broader programs) are to contain,[265] Congress itself specified a number of details. Section 112(r)(7)(B) provides that the plan must include

> "a hazard assessment to assess the potential effects of an accidental release . . . includ[ing] an estimate of potential release quantities and a determination of downwind effects";
> "a program for preventing accidental releases of regulated substances, including safety precautions and maintenance, monitoring and employee measures to be used at the source"; and
> "a response program providing for specific actions to be taken . . . including procedures for informing the public and local agencies responsible for responding to accidental releases, emergency health care, and employee training measures."[266]

Thus, the RMP is to contain three main elements: (1) a hazard assessment, (2) a prevention program, and (3) a response program. The OSHA process safety management standard, in contrast, focuses on *prevention* of accidental releases. The detailed RMPs obviously will require careful preparation. Companies that wait until shortly before the due date before beginning work may find themselves without enough time to design an adequate plan that meets the EPA's requirements.

A facility must submit its plan to the Chemical Safety Board (assuming the positions for that body are filled), the state emergency response commission, and any local emergency planning committee that has responsibility for planning and responding to accidental releases in the area. The facility must also register with the EPA. The RMP will be available to the public.[267]

The EPA's List of Regulated Substances and Thresholds

The EPA has issued two major rules to carry out Section 112(r): (1) the list of "regulated substances" and their threshold quantities under Section 112(r)(3)–(5); and (2) requirements for accidental release RMPs under Section 112(r)(7)(B). The rules build on related requirements of the Emergency Planning and Community Right-to-Know Act of 1986 (EPCRA), also known as Title III of the Superfund Amendments and Reauthorization Act of 1986 (SARA). The EPA's Chemical Emergency Preparedness and Prevention Office, in the Office of Solid Waste and Emergency Response (OSWER), administers the rules under those other statutes. The agency therefore gave the lead for developing the Section 112(r) program to this office rather than to the Office of Air and Radiation even though the rules implement the CAA.

In January 1994 the EPA issued its list of regulated substances under Section 112(r), along with the threshold quantities for these substances.[268] The list is codified at 40 C.F.R. Section 68.130.

The EPA selected the regulated substances based on the three statutory criteria: (1) the severity of acute adverse health effects associated with accidental releases of the substance; (2) the likelihood of a release; and (3) the potential magnitude of human exposure.[269] As it currently stands, the EPA's list (before proposed changes) includes (1) seventy-seven substances that the agency considers to be acutely toxic; (2) sixty-three flammable gases and volatile flammable liquids; and (3) explosives that the Department of Transportation designates as "high explosives." The threshold quantities for the various substances range from 500 to 20,000 pounds. For explosives, the threshold quantity for all substances is 5,000 pounds; for toxic and flammable substances, the quantities are listed in tables.[270]

Several industry groups challenged various aspects of the list.[271] Following negotiations with the parties, the agency changed the list in several respects by deleting explosives from the list, modifying threshold provisions to exclude flammable substances in gasoline and other mixtures before entry into a processing unit or plant, changing the threshold provisions for other flammable mixtures, and clarifying the definition of "stationary source" in several respects.[272]

CAA Section 112(r)(3) requires the EPA to review the list at least every five years. In its January 1994 listing notice, the agency also issued rules for adding and deleting substances from the Section 11.2(r) list. The rules specify the criteria that the EPA will apply in acting on petitions to add or delete substance.[273]

The EPA's Risk Management Plan Rules

The risk management program is the center of the Section 112(r) program to avoid Bhopal-type accidental chemical releases. The EPA issued its final rules in June 1996.[274] These rules significantly changed many aspects of the EPA's original proposal, particularly by creating a "tiering system" under which the stringency of requirements for the RMP is related to the perceived risk of accidental releases and resulting harm posed by different types of facility processes. Under this tiering system, processes are placed in Program 1, 2, or 3, with Program 3 being the most rigorous. A source can have processes in one or more of the three programs.[275]

The EPA made several changes to the list.[276] The most significant were amendments adopted in 2000 to the Section 112(r) regulations, promulgated to conform to the fuel provisions of the Chemical Safety Information, Site Security and Fuels Regulatory Relief Act signed into law in 1999.[277] The rule change excluded from the list of substances covered under the program those flammable substances used for fuel or held for sale at a retail facility.[278] As a result of this action the EPA took no further action on previous proposals concerning flammable substances.[279]

The preamble to the final rules summarizes applicability criteria for Programs 1, 2, and 3:

> Program 1 is available to any process that has not had an accidental release with off-site consequences in the five years prior to the submission date of the RMP and has no public receptors within the distance to a specified toxic or flammable endpoint associated with a worst-case release scenario. Program 3 applies to processes in Standard Industrial Classification (SIC) codes 2611 (pulp mills), 2812 (chlor-alkali), 2819 (industrial inorganics), 2821 (plastics and resins), 2865 (cyclic crudes), 2869 (industrial organics), 2873 (nitrogen fertilizers), 2879 (agricultural chemicals), and 2911 (petroleum refineries). Program 3 also applies to all processes subject to the OSHA Process Safety Management (PSM) standard (29 C.F.R. 1910.119), unless the process is eligible for Program 1. Owners or operators will need to determine individual SIC codes for each covered process to determine whether Program 3 applies. All other covered processes must satisfy Program 2 requirements.[280]

For the three main elements of the RMP—the hazard assessment, the prevention program, and the emergency response component—the requirements depend on whether a facility's particular process falls under Program 1, 2, or 3.

The Section 112(r) rules were revised in 1997 to add certain program elements to the RMP plans and to switch from the SIC code basis of grouping industry categories to the more broadly based North American Industry Classification System (NAICS),[281] as well as to add or modify certain substances on the list.

Accidental Release Rules under EPCRA and OSHA

The EPA's RMP rules build on similar requirements under the OSHA process safety management standard (codified at 29 C.F.R. Part 1910) and EPCRA. Therefore, this section provides a quick overview of those requirements, and how they differ from the CAA mandates, before examining the EPA's rules to implement Section 112(r)(7).

Of the more than 66,000 facilities that the EPA believes will be subject to Section 112(r)(7), many are covered by the OSHA process safety management standard. The EPA predicts that facilities in compliance with the OSHA rule also will be in compliance with the release *prevention* aspects of the EPA's proposed rules. The OSHA standard, however, is designed to protect workers and therefore requires only an analysis of potential impacts on workers.[282] The EPA's rules, on the other hand, include significant requirements for *off-site* assessment and response as well as for process hazard analysis elements similar to those found in the OSHA rule.

The Section 112(r)(7) rules also include other important requirements not covered by the OSHA standard. For many sources, the emergency response plan will have to be more extensive (e.g., facilities will have to conduct drills and exercises). In addition, unlike the EPA's proposed Section 112(r)(7) rules, the OSHA standard does not require registration, submission, and auditing of the RMPs. Thus, many facilities will be subject to significant new obligations even if they have complied with the OSHA standard.

The differences between EPCRA requirements and the Section 112(r)(7) plan rules are even greater. While EPCRA requires companies to report the existence of extremely hazardous substances at their plants, it does not require them to establish accident prevention programs. But the state emergency response commissions and local planning committees established under EPCRA also will be a part of the RMP process. Under EPCRA, the local committees are responsible for developing emergency response plans for districts. A facility must notify both the committee and the state commission if it releases a specified amount of an extremely hazardous substance.

Hazard Assessment

The first main part of the full RMP is the hazard assessment. Subpart B of the EPA's Part 68 rules sets forth the requirements for these assessments.[283] Although all processes are subject to hazardous assessment mandates, the provisions for Program 2 and 3 processes are the most stringent.

Perhaps the most controversial aspect of the EPA's rules has been the requirement—applicable to all processes—to conduct a "worst-case release scenario." The EPA's original proposed definition of the term "worst-case release" caused an uproar in the regulated community because of its breadth. Under the EPA's October 1993 proposal, worst-case release was defined as "the loss of all of the regulated substance from the process in an accidental release that leads to the worst off-site consequences."[284] The preamble to the October 1993 proposal stated that the facility would need to estimate, "using models or other approaches specific to each substance, the possible rate of release, quantity released, and duration of the release, and the distances in any direction that the substance could travel before it dispersed enough to no longer pose a hazard to the public health or environment.[285]

The EPA essentially withdrew this broad definition of the term after industry sharply attacked it as unrealistic. Thus, the final rule defines worst-case release as "the release of the largest quantity of a regulated substance from a vessel or process line failure that results in the greatest distance to an endpoint defined in Section 68.22(a)."[286] Section 68.22(a), in turn, contains a number of technical descriptions of various endpoints. The net result is that the off-site consequence analysis will not be as stringent as originally proposed.

The regulations require that one worst-case scenario be included for each Program 1 process.[287] For Program 2 and 3 processes, the rules are more complicated. A company needs to conduct separate worst-case scenarios for (1) all toxic substances and (2) all flammable substances, although these exercises generally do not have to be conducted for each individual process. Furthermore, additional scenarios must be analyzed if a worst-case release from another covered process at the source could affect "public receptors" differently than those potentially affected by the general analyses.[288] In addition, companies with Program 2 and 3 processes must conduct alternative release scenarios (those more likely to occur) for toxic and flammable substances.[289]

The requirements to prepare an off-site consequence analysis (OCA) and its public availability have been the subject of great controversy since the promulgation of these rules. In 1999, the EPA amended the RMP rule to modify the rule for conducting worst-case scenario analyses for flammable substances and to clarify its interpretation of how the requirements of Section 112(l) relate to DOT requirements.[290]

The most significant changes to the OCA provision came in 2000. In recent years, with heightened concern over international terrorism and the aftermath of September 11, 2001, the EPA's initial strong reluctance to protecting the public release of worst-case scenarios has waned somewhat. Indeed in 1999, Congress passed the Chemical Safety Information, Site Security, and Fuels Regulatory Relief Act to restrict access by the public to certain OCA information.[291] That law delayed release until August 2000. On August 4, 2000, the EPA (and Department of Justice) issued a final rule establishing the procedures for public access to the OCA analysis of hypothetical releases from industrial factories, implementing the provisions of the Site Security Relief Act.[292] Under the rule, the public and government officials such as local agencies may obtain access to certain material, but the rule is designed to reduce the risk to national security associated with the posting of the information on the Internet.

Another component of the hazard assessment is a five-year accident history. This aspect, which is required for all processes, includes all releases during the previous five years that "resulted in deaths, injuries, or significant property damage on site, or known off-site deaths, injuries, evacuations, sheltering in place, property damage, or environmental damage."[293] The rules specify the data that must be supplied for each of these accidental releases.[294]

Prevention Program and Management System

The EPA's proposed rules would have required all sources to put in place a comprehensive "prevention program" to evaluate potential hazards and determine the best way to control them. In the final rule, the agency essentially dropped the requirement for Program 1. For these processes, the company need only certify that no such measures "are necessary to prevent off-site impacts from accidental releases."[295] Moreover, companies need not comply with management system requirements under Program 1.

Programs 2 and 3 include different accident prevention mandates. Subpart C of the rules governs the Program 2 prevention program.[296] There are detailed requirements for the following:

- Compiling and maintaining safety information and ensuring that the process is designed in compliance with recognized and generally accepted good engineering practices (Section 68.48)
- Conducting a review of hazards associated with the process and regulated substances (Section 68.50)
- Preparing written procedures for safely operating the process (Section 68.52)
- Instituting training programs (Section 68.54)
- Preparing and implementing maintenance procedures (Section 68.56)
- Conducting compliance audits (Section 68.58)
- Carrying out and documenting incidents that resulted in (or could reasonably have resulted in) a catastrophic release (Section 68.60).

The EPA stated that it "expects that many Program 2 processes will already be in compliance with most of the requirements through compliance with other Federal regulations, state laws, industry standards and codes, and good engineering practices."[297]

The prevention program under Program 3, found in Subpart D of the rules,[298] is more extensive. It is very similar to the OSHA process safety management standard described earlier.[299] Owing to differences in CAA Section 112(r)(7) and OSHA, however, the two rules are different in several respects. The EPA predicts that sources already in compliance with the OSHA standard will not need to take additional steps to comply with the CAA accidental release requirements,[300] although industry has been wary of such claims.

Related to the prevention program is a requirement to develop and maintain a management system to oversee implementation of RMP requirements. As noted, there is no such requirement under Program 1. For Program 2 and 3 processes, however, the owner or operator must put the system in place and designate a qualified person to assume overall responsibility.[301]

Emergency Response

As with the prevention program, the emergency response part of the EPA's rules applies only to Programs 2 and 3.[302] Unlike the prevention program regulations, however, the rules governing emergency response plans are fairly brief and general in nature. Section 68.95 sets forth required plan elements, such as procedures for notifying the public and local emergency response agencies; documentation of emergency treatment that may prove necessary; procedures for the use, inspection, and maintenance of response equipment; and training for employees.[303]

Moreover, a source with Program 2 or 3 processes often will not need to prepare a special CAA emergency response plan if the source's own employees will not address accidental releases. A facility with toxic substances above the threshold quantities does not have to prepare a special plan if (1) the source already is addressed in the community emergency response plan developed under EPCRA and (2) appropriate mechanisms for notifying response officials are in place. For sources subject to Section 112(r)(7) only because flammable substances are held in sufficient quantities, coordinating with the local fire department and putting notification mechanisms in place obviates the need to meet the specific plan requirements found in Section 68.95.[304] The EPA also predicts that "plans developed to comply with other EPA contingency planning requirements and the OSHA Hazardous Waste and Emergency Operations (HAZWOPER) rule (29 C.F.R. 1910.120) will meet most of the requirements for the emergency response program."[305]

The Risk Management Plan Submittal

All sources with more than the threshold quantity of a regulated substance must prepare and submit an RMP containing the required elements by dates specified in Sections 68.10 and 68.150. These provisions specify that the plan shall be submitted and the source must be in compliance with it by "no later than the latest of the following dates: (1) June 21, 1999; (2) Three years after the date on which a regulated substance is first listed under Section 68.130; or (3) The date on which a regulated substance is first present above a threshold quantity in a process." The third of these deadlines could pose serious hardships for sources that quickly decide to change operations and surpass the applicability threshold sometime after June 1999—under the rules, the company would be out of compliance unless it submitted the RMP at the same time it brought the substance to the facility. As a general matter, sources must also update their RMP every five years, although under certain circumstances a quicker revision is required.[306]

In addition to the program elements described in the preceding paragraphs, the RMP must include an executive summary and a registration covering all affected processes and substances. The owner or operator also needs to sign a certification, the language for which is specified in the rules.[307] Providing false or misleading information could be grounds for criminal liability.

Relationship to Title V Permits

The preamble to the CAA Title V permit rules issued in 1992 states that the plan need not be included in the source's operating permit. Rather, the permit could simply note the company's obligation to prepare a plan and refer to the plan's existence.[308] The EPA maintained this position in the final accidental release rules. The agency reasoned that the plan should not be included as part of the permit conditions "because the RMP and part 68 elements will be highly source-specific and subject to frequent change introducing unnecessary complexity and delaying permit implementation."[309]

In the March 1995 supplemental proposal on Section 112(r)(7) and the final rules, however, the EPA added several permit content requirements not found in the original proposal. Section 68.215 specifies that a Title V permit must contain a statement listing 40 C.F.R. Part 68 as an applicable requirement as well as conditions requiring the source to submit a compliance schedule and a compliance certification attesting that the source is in compliance with Part 68. If a facility receives its Title V permit before the deadline for submitting the RMP, the permit must be revised or reopened to incorporate the necessary terms and conditions.[310]

Notes

1. This chapter was presented as three separate chapters in the first edition. In the first edition, the section on case-by-case MACT was written by Robert J. Mueller, and the sections on risk management plans and accidental releases were written by David P. Novello. The author also gratefully acknowledges the assistance of Nate Gilmer, Jennifer Brundige, and Brandi Wilson in preparation of this chapter.

2. *See* CAA §§ 107, 109. For a full discussion of the NAAQS pollutants, *see* Chapter 2.

3. *See* 42 U.S.C. § 7412(a) (1982); *see also* H.R. Conf. Rep. No. 101-490, pt. 1, at 315–16 (1990) (Conference Report of the Committee on Energy and Commerce, House of Representatives, on H.R. 3030).

4. 42 U.S.C. § 7412(b)(1)(B) (1982).

5. 40 C.F.R. pt. 61 contains the regulations implementing the NESHAPS program under the pre-1990 CAA. For a congressional perspective on that program's failure, *see* H.R. Conf. Rep. No. 101-490, *supra* note 2, at 315–16.

6. 40 Fed. Reg. 59,532, 59,534 (1975) (proposed NESHAP for vinyl chloride).

7. *Id.*

8. *Id.*

9. *Id.*

10. For a more complete procedural history of the EPA's rule making on the vinyl chloride standard and challenges thereto, *see* the court's discussion in the vinyl chloride decision, Natural Resources Defense Council v. EPA, 824 F.2d 1146 (D.C. Cir. 1987) (en banc).

11. *Id.* at 1152–55.

12. *Id.*

13. *Id.* at 1164.

14. *See* S. Comm. Rep. No. 101-228, at 132 (Report on S. 1630, Clean Air Amendments of 1989).

15. For an excellent discussion of the Clean Water Act's program, see Chapter 2, titled *Water Pollution Control under the National Pollutant Elimination System*, in The Clean Water Act Handbook (Evans, ed.; American Bar Association, 1993).

16. S. Comm Rep. No. 101-228, *supra note* 14, at 128.

17. *Id.* at 128–129.

18. The list was developed in cooperation with the EPA and there was substantial agreement as to the list of HAPs.

19. CAA § 112(c)(1).

20. *Id.*

21. CAA § 112(d)(2).

22. CAA § 112(d)(3).

23. 59 Fed. Reg. 12,408 (1994) (codified at 40 C.F.R. pt. 63, subpt. A).

24. CAA § 112(b)(1).

25. CAA § 112(b)(2).

26. *Id.*

27 CAA § 112(b)(3).

28. CAA § 112(b)(3)(B).

29. CAA § 112(b)(3)(C).

30. *See* 40 C.F.R. pt. 63, subpt. C (2002).

31. 64 Fed. Reg. 33,453 (1999) (MEK); 64 Fed. Reg. 38,668 (1999) (Methanol).

32. *See* the discussion in the proposed delisting for caprolactam. 60 Fed. Reg. 48,081–82 (1995).

33. *Id.*

34. *Id.*

35. *Id.*

36. 60 Fed. Reg. at 48,085.

37. 61 Fed. Reg. 30,816 (1996).

38. 65 Fed. Reg. 47,342.

39. 64 Fed. Reg. 33,453 (1999).

40. 68 Fed. Reg. 32,606 (2003).

41. CAA § 112(a)(1).

42. CAA § 112(a)(2).

43. CAA § 111(a)(3).

44. National Mining Ass'n v. Browner, 59 F.3d 1351 (D.C. Cir. 1995).

45. 59 Fed. Reg. 12,408, 12,412 (1994).

46. *Id.* at 12,411.

47. *National Mining Ass'n*, 59 F.3d at 1356.

48. 40 C.F.R. § 63.2 (1995); *see also* 59 Fed. Reg. at 12,433.

49. *National Mining Ass'n*, 59 F.3d at 1361 ("We conclude that EPA may require the inclusion of fugitive emissions in the site's aggregate emissions without conducting any special rulemaking").

50. 59 Fed. Reg. 12,408 (1994).

51. *Id.* at 12,408, 12,433–34 (codified at 40 C.F.R. pt. 63, subpt. A).

52. *Id.*

53. 59 Fed. Reg. at 12,414.

54. *Id.*

55. *National Mining Ass'n*, 59 F.3d at 1351. The CMA also challenged the 1989 notice, but the litigation was stayed pending passage of the 1990 CAA Amendments.

56. Memorandum from John Seitz and Robert Van Heuvelen to Regional Air Directors on Options for Limiting the Potential to Emit (PTE) of a Stationary Source Under Section 112 and Title V of the Clean Air Act (Jan. 25, 1995).

57. 59 F.3d at 1363.

58. *Id.* at 1364.

59. Following the decision in the *National Mining Association* case, the court also upheld industry's challenge to the June 1989 notice defining the term "potential to emit" in the NSR context.

60. *See* "Third Extension of January 25, 1995, Potential to Emit Transition Policy" December 20, 1999, by J. Sentza E. Schaeffer.

61. CAA § 112(a)(1).

62. CAA § 112(c)(1), (3).

63. *Id.*

64. CAA § 112(c)(7), (c)(8), (n)(4).

65. CAA § 112(c)(9).

66. *Id.*

67. 60 Fed. Reg. 4624 (1995).

68. CAA § 112(c)(5).

69. *See* CAA § 112(e)(4).

70. 56 Fed. Reg. 28,548 (1991).

71. *Id.* at 28,554–57.

72. 57 Fed. Reg. 31,576 (1992).

73. *Id.*

74. 58 Fed. Reg. 60,021 (1993).

75. *See* 67 Fed. Reg. 6521 (2002); 66 Fed. Reg. 8,220 (2001); 64 Fed. Reg. 63,025 (1999); 64 Fed. Reg. 26,743; 63 Fed. Reg. 7155 (1999).

76. *Id.*

77. 57 Fed. Reg. at 31,587.

78. Natural Resources Defense Council v. EPA, 824 F.2d 1146 (D.C. Cir. 1987).

79. *See* 57 Fed. Reg. at 31,592.

80. 58 Fed. Reg. at 63,941 (1993).

81. The SCRS is discussed in detail in the final listing notice at 58 Fed. Reg. at 63,941, 63,943.

82. Sierra Club v. Browner, 93-0124 (D.D.C.).

83. *See* S. Comm. Rep. No. 101-228, *supra* note 14, at 166.

84. CAA § 111(a)(2).

85. CAA § 112(a)(1).

86. *Id.*

87. CAA § 112(a)(2).

88. 40 C.F.R. § 63.2.

89. *Id.* § 63.6(b)(7).

90. *Id.* § 63.6(c)(5).

91. For more discussion on the definition of the term "affected source" and its relationship to "major source," see the discussion in the preamble to the general provisions rule making. 59 Fed. Reg. 12,408, 12,412–13 (1994).

92. *See* Chapter 9 for a discussion of CAA Section 111 and new source performance standards.

93. *See* Chapter 5 for a discussion of the NSR program under Section 169.

94. CAA § 112(d)(2).

95. *Id.*

96. CAA § 112(d)(3).

97. CAA § 112(d)(3)(A).

98. *Id.*

99. CAA § 112(d)(3)(B).

100. 58 Fed. Reg. 65,768, 65,770 (Dec. 16, 1993) (chromium electroplating); 58 Fed. Reg. 66,078, 66,136 (1993).

101. 59 Fed. Reg. 11,018 (1994).

102. *Id.* at 29,196.

103. *See* 58 Fed. Reg. at 66,078, 66,136–37.

104. 59 Fed. Reg. at 29,199.

105. *Id.* at 62,652.

106. 58 Fed. Reg. 66,137 (1993).

107. *See, e.g.,* Cement Kiln Recycling Coalition v. EPA, 255 F.3d 855, 860–61 (D.C. Cir. 2001) (refusing to reach issue of whether statute requires consideration of permit limits rather than performance of best performance sources because issue not properly raised during rule making).

108. *Id.* at 863.

109. CAA § 112(d)(2).

110. 58 Fed. Reg. 49,354 (1993).

111. Information taken from the EPA Air Toxics Website—Urban Air Toxics Strategy, *available at* http://www.epa.gov/ttn/atw/urban/arearules.html.

112. CAA § 112(g)(2)(B).

113. CAA § 112(g)(2)(A).

114. 61 Fed. Reg. at 68,384 (1996).

115. Memorandum from John Seitz, Director, Office of Air Quality Planning and Standards (OAQPS), to the EPA Regional Air Division Directors on Guidance for the Initial Implementation of Section 112(g) (June 28,1994).

116. *Id.* at 2–4; *see e.g.,* 59 Fed. Reg. 61,820, 61,823–24 (1994) (final approval of the Oregon Title V program).

117. 60 Fed. Reg. 8333 (1995).

118. Attachment to letter from Mary Nichols, Assistant Administrator for Air and Radiation, to William Lewis, Morgan, Lewis & Bockius, on the EPA Response to Issues Raised by Industry on Clean Air Act Implementation Reform 36 (May 31, 1995).

119. Despite the use of the word "guidance" in the statute, the EPA undertook a full notice and comment rule-making proceeding.

120. 61 Fed. Reg. at 68,384.

121. *Id.* at 68,386.

122. *Id.*

123. *Id.*

124. In most cases, new-source MACT will be more stringent than existing-source MACT. 40 C.F.R. Proposed § 63.41; *see supra* note 37.

125. 40 C.F.R. Proposed §§ 63.42, 63.45(l)(1).

126. 40 C.F.R. § 63.41; *see* 61 Fed. Reg. at 68,388.

127. 40 C.F.R. § 63.41; *see* 61 Fed. Reg. at 68,388.

128. 61 Fed. Reg. at 68,385.

129. For new sources, MACT can be no less stringent than the emission control that is achieved in practice by the best controlled similar source. CAA § 112(d)(3).

130. CAA § 112(g)(2)(3).

131. 40 C.F.R. § 63.43.

132. *Id.;* 61 Fed. Reg. at 68,392–94.

133. OAQPS, EPA 450/3-92/007b, PB94-156684, Mar. 1994.

134. 61 Fed. Reg. at 68,385.

135. *Id.*

136. EPA, *Direct Final Notice for Hazardous Air Pollutants: Amendments to Regulations Governing Equivalent Emission Limitations by Permit,* Fact Sheet (May 7, 1996), *available at* http://www.epa.gov/ttn/oarpg/t3/fact_sheets/112jfact.txt.

137. *Id.; see* 42 U.S.C. § 7412(j)(5) (2002).

138. EPA, *Technology Transfer Information for Equivalent Emission Limitations by Permit 112(j),* Air Toxics Website (June 3, 2002), *available at* http://www.epa.gov/ttn/atw/112j/112jaypg.html.

139. *Id.*

140. *Agency Prepares to Issue Rule to Prevent "MACT Hammer" from Hitting Industry in May*, Env't. Reporter, Mar. 1, 2002, *available at* http://pubs.bna.com.

141. *Id.*

142. *Id.*

143. 67 Fed. Reg. 16,591 (Apr. 5, 2002) (to be codified at 40 C.F.R. pt. 63).

144. *Agency Prepares to Issue Rule to Prevent "MACT Hammer" from Hitting Industry in May*, Env't. Reporter, Mar. 1, 2002, *available at* http://pubs.bna.com.

145. 67 Fed. Reg. 16,590 (Apr. 5, 2002) (to be codified at 40 C.F.R. pt. 63).

146. *Id.*

147. *Id.* The EPA estimated that "approximately 84,000 affected sources [would likely have] to prepare and submit a Part 1 permit application." *Id.* at 16,593. "The total estimated cost of this 1-time event [was estimated at] about $9,000,000." *Id.* However, no additional costs are anticipated since the agency plans to develop the remaining standards before Part 2 of the permit application is due. *Id.*

148. *Id.* at 16,592.

149. *Id.*

150. EPA, *Rule and Implementation Information for Equivalent Emission Limitations by Permit 112(j)*, Air Toxics Website (June 3, 2002), *available at* http://www.epa.gov/ttn/atw/112j/112jaypg.html.

151. 67 Fed. Reg. 16,592 (Apr. 5, 2002) (to be codified at 40 C.F.R. pt. 63).

152. *Id.* A source may recommend "a specific design, equipment, work practice, or operation standard, or combination thereof, as an emission limitation." *Id.*

153. *Id.*

154. EPA, *Rule and Implementation Information for Equivalent Emission Limitations by Permit 112(j)*, Air Toxics Website (June 3, 2002), *available at* http://www.epa.gov/ttn/atw/112j/112jaypg.html.

155. EPA, *Final Amendments to the Clean Air Act's "Section 112(j) Rule,"* Fact Sheet (Mar. 5, 2002), *available at* http://www.epa.gov/ttn/atw/112j/112jaypg.html.

156. EPA, *Rule and Implementation Information for Equivalent Emission Limitations by Permit 112(j)*, Air Toxics Website (June 3, 2002), *available at* http://www.epa.gov/ttn/atw/112j/112jaypg.html.

157. *Id.*

158. Sierra Club v. EPA, Civ. No. 02-1135 (D.C. Cir. 2002).

159. Sierra Club v. Whitman, Civ. No. 01-1337 (D.D.C. 2001).

160. *See* 67 Fed. Reg. at 72,882, to be codified as Table 1 to 40 C.F.R. pt. 67, subpt. B.

161. S. Comm. Rep. No. 101-228, at 149 (1989) (Report on S. 1630, Clean Air Amendments of 1989).

162. *Id.* at 149, 192–93; CAA § 112(l).

163. Section 112(l) also applies to HAP programs developed and implemented by local air pollution agencies. CAA § 112(l)(8).

164. CAA § 112(l)(1). The act requires the EPA to publish guidance by November 1991 to assist the states in developing and submitting their HAP programs. CAA § 112(l)(2). The EPA complied with this mandate, albeit over one year late. *See supra* notes 68–75 and accompanying text.

165. CAA § 112(l)(1). The EPA stated in a recent policy memorandum that the regional offices have the authority to determine whether a state HAP provision is as stringent as its federal counterpart. Memorandum from John Seitz, Director OAQPS, to the EPA Region IX (June 26, 1995).

166. CAA § 112(l)(5). States may revise and resubmit previously disapproved programs. Additionally, the EPA may withdraw its approval from a state program if it

determines, after a public hearing, that the state is not adequately administering and enforcing the program pursuant to EPA guidance or the four statutory criteria listed in text. CAA § 112(l)(5), (6).

167. 40 C.F.R. §§ 63.90–63.99 (2002).

168. 65 Fed. Reg. 55,809 (2000).

169. *See* 40 C.F.R. §§ 63.91 and 63.92.

170. 40 C.F.R. § 63.94.

171. CAA § 112(d)(2)(A).

172. 58 Fed. Reg. at 49,354.

173. 59 Fed. Reg. 46,339 (1994).

174. *See* 58 Fed. Reg. 43,028 (1993) (proposed chromium standard). The final rule is at 59 Fed. Reg. 46,339 (1994) (codified at 40 C.F.R. § 63.340 *et seq.* (subpart N)).

175. 59 Fed. Reg. at 46,339.

176. *See* 58 Fed. Reg. 62,566, 62,572 (1993). The final rule is set forth at 59 Fed. Reg. 61,801 (1994).

177. 59 Fed. Reg. at 61,802.

178. 40 C.F.R. § 63.6(b)(1).

179. *Id.* § 603(b)(3). The general provisions also contain an exception in the event standards are proposed under Section 112(f).

180. 40 C.F.R. § 63.6(b)(7).

181. CAA § 112(i)(3)(A).

182. CAA § 112(i)(3)(B). There is an additional extension available for mining-waste operations of up to three years if the initial four-year compliance time is insufficient to "dry and cover mining waste in order to reduce emissions of any [hazardous air] pollutant listed."

183. 40 C.F.R. § 63.6(i)(4)(B).

184. *Id.* § 63.6(i)(2)(ii).

185. *Id.* § 63.6(1)(5).

186. *See id.* § 63.6(1)(9)–(1)(14).

187. CAA § 112(1)(4).

188. *Id.*

189. CAA § 112(i)(5)(A).

190. 40 C.F.R. § 63.72(b)(c).

191. *Id.* § 63.74.

192. *See also* 57 Fed. Reg. at 61,992.

193. *See* 40 C.F.R. § 63.5(d)(1) for a detailed discussion of the general application requirements.

194. The additional application requirements for new sources are set forth at 40 C.F.R. § 63.5(d)(2) and the requirements for reconstructed sources are at 40 C.F.R. § 63.5(d)(3).

195. 40 C.F.R. § 635(e)(2).

196. *Id.*

197. *Id.* § 635(f).

198. *See id.* § 63.6(e).

199. *See* 40 C.F.R. § 63.6(e).

200. CAA § 112(f)(2)(A).

201. *Id.*

202. *Id.*

203. *Id.* § 112(f)(2)(C).

204. *Id.* § 112(f)(4).

205. EPA, *Residual Risk Report to Congress* (March 1999) (hereafter *Residual Risk*), *available at* http://www.epa.gov/ttn/oarpg/t3/reports/risk_rep.pdf. In addition to this

report, section 112 has spawned the Mercury, Great Waters, Utilities, and Urban Air Toxics reports. CAA § 112.

206. *Residual Risk, supra* note 205, at 2.

207. CAA § 112(f)(2)(A).

208. *Residual Risk, supra* note 205, at ES-11. Note that the benzene risk assessment process took place in 1989. This process became the model for the 1990 CAA Amendments.

209. *Id.* at ES-11.

210. *See id.* at ES-5.

211. OAQPS, EPA, *National Air Toxics Program: Integrated Urban Strategy*, Fact Sheet (Nov. 5, 2001), *available at* http://www.epa.gov/ttn/atw/urban/urbanfs.html.

212. *Id.*

213. Robert Perciasepe, EPA, EPA *Policy on National Air Toxics Program: The Integrated Urban Strategy*, Policy Statements (July 6, 1999), available at http://esweb.bna.com.

214. *Id.*

215. OAQPS, EPA, *Taking Toxics Out of the Air* (Sept. 5, 2001), *available at* http://www.epa.gov/oar/oaqps/takingtoxics/; *see* Final Air Toxics Strategy, 64 Fed. Reg. 38,705 (1999).

216. OAQPS, EPA, *National Air Toxics Program: Integrated Urban Strategy*, Fact Sheet (Nov. 5, 2001), *available at* http://www.epa.gov/ttn/atw/urban/urbanfs.html.

217. OAQPS, EPA, *Air Toxics Strategy: Overview* (Aug. 9, 2001), *available at* http://www.epa.gov/ttnatw01/urban/urbanpg.html.

218. OAQPS, EPA, *National Air Toxics Program: Integrated Urban Strategy*, Fact Sheet (Nov. 5, 2001), *available at* http://www.epa.gov/ttn/atw/urban/urbanfs.html.

219. The thirty-three air toxics included in the Integrated Urban Air Toxics Strategy are acetaldehyde, acrolein, acrylonitrile, arsenic compounds, benzene, beryllium compounds, 3-butadiene, cadmium compounds, carbon tetrachloride, chloroform, chromium compounds, coke oven emissions, dioxin, ethylene dibromide, propylene dichloride, 1, 3-dichloropropene, ethylene dichloride, ethylene oxide, formaldehyde, hexachlorbenzene, hydrazine, lead compounds, manganese compounds, mercury compounds, methylene chloride, nickel compounds, polychlorinated biphenyls, polycyclic organic matter, quinoline, 1, 1, 2, 2-tetrachloroethane, perchloroethylene, trichloroethylene, and vinyl chloride. OAQPS, EPA, *Air Toxics Strategy: Overview* (Aug. 9, 2001), *available at* http://www.epa.gov/ttnatw01/urban/urbanpg.html. These thirty-three pollutants emit an estimated 38 percent of all emissions of air toxics. OAQPS, EPA, *National Air Toxics Program: Integrated Urban Strategy*, Fact Sheet (Nov. 5, 2001), *available at* http://www.epa.gov/ttn/atw/urban/urbanfs.html.

220. Robert Perciasepe, EPA, *EPA Policy on National Air Toxics Program: The Integrated Urban Strategy*, Policy Statements (July 6, 1999), *available at* http://esweb.bna.com. A complete summary of the methodology is provided in "Ranking and Selection of Hazardous Air Pollutants," which is available on the EPA's Web site. *Id.*

221. OAQPS, EPA, *National Air Toxics Program: Integrated Urban Strategy*, Fact Sheet (Nov. 5, 2001), *available at* http://www.epa.gov/ttn/atw/urban/urbanfs.html.

222. Robert Perciasepe, EPA, *EPA Policy on National Air Toxics Program: The Integrated Urban Strategy*, Policy Statements (July 6, 1999), *available at* http://esweb.bna.com.

223. *See* 67 Fed. Reg. 43,112 (2002); 66 Fed. Reg. 8270 (2001).

224. 67 Fed. Reg. at 43,113.

225. *Id.* The EPA will prioritize the order in which standards will be promulgated in accordance with those posing the greatest risks first. *Id.*

226. *Id.*

227. OAQPS, EPA, *National Air Toxics Program: Integrated Urban Strategy*, Fact Sheet (Nov. 5, 2001), *available at* http://www.epa.gov/ttn/atw/urban/urbanfs.html.

228. *Id.*

229. *Id.* Studies that have already been completed include the following: (1) Utility study; (2) Great Waters program; (3) Mercury study. Robert Perciasepe, EPA, *EPA Policy on National Air Toxics Program: The Integrated Urban Strategy,* Policy Statements (July 6, 1999), *available at* http://esweb.bna.com.

230. OAQPS, EPA, *National Air Toxics Program: Integrated Urban Strategy,* Update (Aug. 9, 2001), *available at* http://www.epa.gov/ttn/atw/urban/urbanfs.html.

231. *Id.; see also* Robert Perciasepe, EPA, *EPA Policy on National Air Toxics Program: The Integrated Urban Strategy,* Policy Statements (July 6, 1999), *available at* http://esweb .bna.com.

232. OAQPS, EPA, Fact Sheet (Nov. 5, 2001), *available at* http://www.epa.gov/ttn/ atw/urban/urbanfs.html.

233. *Id.*

234. *Id.*

235. Robert Perciasepe, EPA, *EPA Policy on National Air Toxics Program: The Integrated Urban Strategy,* Policy Statements (July 6, 1999), *available at* http://esweb.bna.com.

236. *Id.*

237. *Id.*

238. OAQPS, EPA, Fact Sheet (Nov. 5, 2001), *available at* http://www.epa.gov/ttn/ atw/urban/urbanfs.html.

239. *Id.*

240. *Id.*

241. *Id.*

242. *Id.*

243. CAA § 112(c)(6).

244. 63 Fed. Reg. 17,838 (1998).

245. *Id.*

246. 67 Fed. Reg. 68,124 (2002).

247. Clean Air Act § 112; EPA, *Mercury Study Report to Congress* (December 1997) *available at* http://www.epa.gov/oar/mercury.html.

248. 65 Fed. Reg. 79,825 (2000).

249. 69 Fed. Reg. 4652 (Jan. 30, 2004). *See also* "Study of Hazardous Air Pollutants Emissions from Electric Utility Steam Generation Units—Final Report to Congress," February 24, 1998. The report is available at http://www.epa.gov/ttn/oarpg/tc3.htm.

250. *See generally* EPA, *Deposition of Air Pollutants to the Great Waters* (June 2000) *available at* http://www.epa.gov/ttn/oarpg/t3/reports/head_2kf.pdf.

251. Mercury; cadmium and lead; dioxins; furans; organic matter; polychlorinated biphenyls (PCBs); chlordane, DDT/DDE, dieldrin, hexachlorobenzene, alphahexachloro-cyclohexane, lindane, and toxaphene.

252. Eutrophication is the reduction of oxygen levels in water, which may harm fish and other aquatic life.

253. 61 Fed. Reg. 31,668 (1996).

254. 59 Fed. Reg. 4478 (1994). For the EPA's proposed list and thresholds, *see* 58 Fed. Reg. 5102 (1993).

255. 61 Fed. Reg. at 31,715.

256. 57 Fed. Reg. 6356 (1992). The rules are codified at 29 C.F.R. § 1910.

257. The specified OSH Act provision is 29 U.S.C. § 654.

258. 59 Fed. Reg. at 4491.

259. *Id.* at 4481.

260. *See* 60 Fed. Reg. at 13,529 ("EPA emphasizes that, under CAA § 112(r)(1), all sources are required to identify their hazards and design and maintain a safe facility and/or would continue to be subject to this general duty under today's proposed rule"). For a more thorough discussion of the "General Duty" clause, *see* David P. Novello & Keith W. Holman, "Understanding the Clean Air Act Section 112 General Duty Clause," 6 *Envtl. Law & Practice* 26 (Winter 1999).

261. S. Comm. Rep. No. 101-228, at 209 (1989).

262. *Id.*

263. *Id.*, quoting Secretary of Labor v. Duriron Company, Inc., 11 OSHC 1405, 1407.

264. 59 Fed. Reg. 4478 (1994) (final rule); 61 Fed. Reg. 16,598 (1996) (proposed changes); 61 Fed. Reg. 31,730 (1996) (stay).

265. The EPA has at times used the terms "risk management plan" and "risk management program" interchangeably. Most recently, however, the agency has referred to the "plan" as the document summarizing the activities required by the EPA's rules. The plan will be submitted to authorities and be made available to the public. The "program" must address all of the Section 112(r)(7) requirements and will contain more detail. *See* 60 Fed. Reg. at 13,526–27.

266. CAA § 112(r)(7)(B)(ii).

267. *Id.* § 112(r)(7)(B)(iii).

268. 59 Fed. Reg. 4478 (1994).

269. CAA § 112(r)(4); *see also* 58 Fed. Reg. at 5104–09 (proposal) and 59 Fed. Reg. at 4481–87 (preamble to final rule).

270. 40 C.F.R. § 68.130; *see also* discussion in preamble at 58 Fed. Reg. at 51,915, and in preamble to final rule at 59 Fed. Reg. at 4481–89.

271. American Petroleum Institute v. EPA, No. 94-1293 (D.C. Cir.); General Electric Co. v. EPA, No. 94-1294 (D.C. Cir.); and Institute of Makers of Explosives v. EPA, No. 94-1296 (D.C. Cir.).

272. 61 Fed. Reg. 16,598 (1996).

273. 40 C.F.R. § 68,120; *see also* 59 Fed. Reg. at 4489–90.

274. 61 Fed. Reg. 31,668 (1996).

275. *See id.* at 31,670.

276. *See* 62 Fed. Reg. 45,132 (1997) (change HCl concentration); 63 Fed. Reg. 640 (1998) (delist certain explosives; clarify transportation exemption and address flammable substances).

277. Pub. L. 106-40.

278. 65 Fed. Reg. 13,243 (2000).

279. *Id.*

280. 61 Fed. Reg. at 31,670. The eligibility criteria are stated in the rules at 40 C.F.R. § 68.10.

281. 64 Fed. Reg. 964 (1999) (NAICS changes and change in required RMP data elements); 64 Fed. Reg. 28,696 (1999) (change to worst-case-scenario analysis for flammable substances); 62 Fed. Reg. 45,132 (1997) (change to concentration of hydrochloric acid); 63 Fed. Reg. 640 (1998) (delist certain explosives).

282. 29 C.F.R. § 1910.119(e).

283. Subpart B encompasses 40 C.F.R. §§ 68.20–68.42.

284. Proposed 40 C.F.R. §§ 68.50 and 68.15, 58 Fed. Reg. at 54,218–19 and 54,213–14; definition at proposed § 68.3, 58 Fed. Reg. at 54,213.

285. 58 Fed. Reg. at 54,194.

286. 40 C.F.R. § 68.3.

287. *Id.* § 68.25(a)(1).
288. *Id.* § 68.25(a)(2).
289. *Id.* § 68.28.
290. 64 Fed. Reg. 28,696 (1999).
291. 65 Fed. Reg. 48,107 (2000).
292. 65 Fed. Reg. 13,243 (2000).
293. 40 C.F.R. § 68.42(a).
294. *Id.* § 68.42(b).
295. *Id.* § 68.12(b)(4).
296. *Id.* §§ 68.48–68.60.
297. 61 Fed. Reg. at 31,672.
298. 40 C.F.R. §§ 68.65–68.87.
299. *Id.*
300. 61 Fed. Reg. at 31,673.
301. 40 C.F.R. § 68.15.
302. *Id.* § 68.90(a).
303. *Id.* § 68.95(a).
304. *Id.* § 68.90(b).
305. 61 Fed. Reg. at 31,673.
306. 40 C.F.R. § 68.190(b).
307. *Id.* §§ 68.12, 68.155, and 68.160.
308. 57 Fed. Reg. 32,250, 32,275–76 (1992).
309. 61 Fed. Reg. at 31,690.
310. 40 C.F.R. § 68.215(a)–(c).

CHAPTER 9

New Source Performance Standards

ROBERT J. MARTINEAU, JR.
MICHAEL K. STAGG[1]

Introduction

Section 111 was included in the Clean Air Act (CAA) in 1970.[2] For the first time, Congress directed the EPA to establish nationwide uniform emission standards for new or modified stationary sources. Section 111 was designed to complement the National Ambient Air Quality Standards (NAAQS) under Sections 108 through 110. In contrast to the *ambient* air standards, Section 111 establishes technology-based emission standards for industrial source categories. Implementation of Section 111 standards is not dependent on the ambient air quality of a particular region. Rather, the main purpose of Section 111 is to prevent new pollution problems.

One of the reasons for the development of these national performance standards for new or modified sources was the desire to level the playing field for states competing for new industrial growth. Under the NAAQS standards, as implemented through the state implementation plans (SIPs), cleaner areas might gain an economic advantage, since those areas could set less stringent pollution control requirements. The new source performance standards (NSPS) under Section 111 apply without regard to the actual ambient air quality in a particular area. Section 111's scheme to impose emissions control technology at the time a source is built, regardless of an area's particular air quality level at a given time, also reflects the basic notion that it is cheaper and easier to design emissions control equipment into production equipment at the time of initial construction than it is to engage in costly retrofits, which are required when controls are imposed on existing sources under SIP attainment plans.[3]

> The standards under Section 111 are to reflect the degree of emission limitation achievable through the application of the best system of emission reduction which (taking into account the cost of achieving such reduction and any nonair quality health and environmental impact and energy requirements) the Administrator determines has been adequately demonstrated.[4]

This technology standard has come to be known as "best demonstrated technology" (BDT).[5]

Section 111 of the CAA directs the EPA administrator to develop a list and set standards for source categories of stationary sources that cause or contribute significantly to "air pollution which may reasonably be anticipated to endanger public health or welfare."[6] The EPA's first list of source categories was published in 1971.[7] The EPA's first sets of standards were issued in the early 1970s and focused on large emitting source categories such as utility boilers. By 2002, the agency had established NSPS for more than seventy industrial source categories, ranging from petroleum dry cleaners to large utility boilers. In some cases, the EPA has issued one or more revisions to the NSPS for a particular source category.

As the implementation of the CAA has developed, the perceived importance of Section 111 has diminished. Major new sources or major modifications of existing sources require permitting through the new source review (NSR) program, either through prevention of significant deterioration (PSD) NSR or through nonattainment NSR. These programs require case-by-case technology determinations in permitting for individual sources. The NSPS, however, play an important role in these permitting programs because they create the "floor" for the case-by-case technical analysis. The NSPS also play an important role for two additional reasons.

First, they do not apply only to "new" sources. As discussed later, modifications and reconstructions are also subject to the NSPS in many instances. Indeed, the modification provisions have been the subject of the most controversy over the past five to ten years of the NSPS program. Second, despite Section 111's commonly being referred to as the NSPS section, Section 111(d) provides a mechanism for regulating existing source emissions of certain pollutants not regulated under Section 108 or 112. Unlike the PSD program, the NSPS program itself is not a permitting program under the CAA. Thus, before the passage of the 1990 amendments and the Title V permit program, the NSPS were not necessarily incorporated into any operating permit.

In addition to NSPS and Section 111, this chapter discusses Section 129 of the CAA, which addresses regulation of emissions from solid waste combustion units. Section 129 was added in the 1990 amendments as a provision separate from Section 111 or Section 112 because of a particular concern in Congress—air emissions from new and existing solid waste incinerators.

Applicability of the NSPS Program

Stationary Source and Affected Facility

Section 111 defines a stationary source as any "building, structure, facility, or installation which emits or may emit any air pollutant."[8] The EPA has used this term both broadly and narrowly to define a source or source category.

For purposes of Section 111, and to further the goal of bringing the most emission units into the regulatory scheme, the EPA typically defines a stationary source under Section 111 for applicability purposes as the smallest discrete emissions unit possible. Such a unit is then referred to as the "affected facility."[9] The term "affected facility" does not appear in the CAA. The EPA uses the term, however, in the NSPS regulations (and the National Emissions Standards for Hazardous Air Pollutants rules as well) to identify the particular pieces of equipment or the process to which a performance standard applies. Affected facilities run a broad range, from a piece of process equipment to an entire plant. For example, in the NSPS for utility boilers, each individual utility boiler unit is considered an affected facility.[10] In the standard for lead acid battery plants, the standard lists six individual types of operations used at the plant as affected facilities.[11] Thus, the source category or stationary source category is a broad industrial unit covered by a standard, and the affected facility identifies the specific emission units subject to a standard. The EPA uses the broad flexibility to pick and choose those emission units that it believes warrant control. The affected facilities for a particular standard are typically defined in the first section of the regulation.

Listing of Source Categories

Following passage of the Clean Air Act of 1970, the EPA began listing those source categories the EPA administrator determined may "reasonably be anticipated to endanger public health or welfare."[12] These source categories were typically sources of NAAQS criteria pollutants that presented a significant enough number of sources that together their impact on overall air quality warranted regulation under Section 111.

Following the 1977 CAA Amendments, the EPA added fifty-nine new source categories to the list and prioritized them.[13] The 1977 amendments established a schedule to issue standards for a certain percentage of the source categories each year. The EPA was to complete issuance of all standards by 1982. To date, the EPA has promulgated NSPS for more than seventy source categories, including such sources as large utility boilers, industrial boilers, automobile painting operations, petroleum dry cleaners, magnetic tape coating, rubber manufacturing, and many others. The EPA has promulgated most of the source categories it identified and listed as meriting standards,[14] and with the new technology-based approach to Section 112, it no longer puts an emphasis on developing standards under Section 111. Indeed, with the maximum achievable control technology (MACT) standards for the same source category, compliance with NSPS may be an afterthought for the source owner.

Regulation of New Sources

Section 111 defines a new source as "any stationary source, the construction or modification of which is commenced" after proposal of regulation.[15] Thus, a new source is subject to a NSPS requirement upon proposal, even if the regulation is not final at the time the source is built. This is contrary to the typical regulatory approach with respect to grandfathering sources before issuance of a final rule. Congress chose this approach to prevent a flurry of activity to grandfather sources just shortly after proposal of a rule as a means to avoid being subject to a new standard. In other words, under Section 111, a regulated entity that commences construction of a source after proposal of a NSPS is on notice that it must comply with the NSPS once that rule is final and the source commences operation.

The term "commence construction" is one of importance in many applicability determinations and enforcement actions under the NSPS program. Under Section 111, if an owner or operator "commences construction" before proposal of an applicable standard, the source will not be considered a new source under Section 111.

The question is at what point does one "commence construction" for the purposes of triggering applicability.[16] For purposes of Section 111, "commencing" may occur one of two ways: (1) when an owner or operator has undertaken a continuous program of construction or modification so that modification of existing physical construction would be required to meet the NSPS; or (2) when an owner or operator has entered into a contractual obligation to undertake and complete, within a reasonable time, a continuous program of construction or modification.[17] Construction is defined as "fabrication, erection, or installation of an affected facility."[18] If redesign work is necessary, as opposed to actual physical modification, it will not preclude NSPS applicability.[19]

Under the second test, if there is a binding contractual obligation to undertake the project and adverse consequences should arise from breaching the contract, one need not have moved any dirt or poured the first footing to have "commenced construction" under the NSPS program. The EPA limits the ability to circumvent applicability through the use of open-ended contractual obligations, however, by requiring the construction to commence within a reasonable time and for it to be continuous. Thus, contractual obligations that remain open into the indefinite future will not create a way around the "commence construction" provision.

It is important to note the practical difference of the "commence construction" test here as compared with the PSD-NSR program (discussed in Chapter 6). Here, if the owner or operator commences construction after proposal of a NSPS requirement, the source must comply with the NSPS upon completion of construction and start-up, or upon promulgation of a final NSPS (whichever is later). Under the PSD and NSR requirements, an owner or operator may not commence construction without first obtaining a permit.

Control of Existing Sources

Modifications

Section 111 of the CAA also subjects existing sources to NSPS if they are "modified." Modification is defined in the statute as "any physical change in, or change in the method of operation of, a stationary source which increases the amount of any air pollutant emitted by such source or which results in the emission of any air pollutant not previously emitted."[20] As defined in the statute, numerous minor physical or operational changes could subject an existing unit to NSPS. To prevent every change at a facility from triggering NSPS requirements, the EPA adopted a more pragmatic approach. The EPA's regulatory definition, although still very expansive, provides some exclusions so that routine activities do not trigger NSPS applicability.

As a threshold matter, in order for a modification to occur, emissions must first increase as a result of the physical or operational change. This sounds simple, but it is often difficult to determine. For NSPS purposes, however, determining whether an increase occurs is far less cumbersome than it is under the NSR program. Under Section 111, the modification test requires the owner or operator to determine if there is an increase in the "emission rate" of any pollutant.[21] The emission rate is determined using the hourly emission rate, not annual emissions as is the case for the PSD program. Section 111 does not look at annual actual versus potential emissions. In determining whether there is an emissions increase, the EPA compares the maximum hourly emissions rate just before and just after the change. If the rate increases, there is a modification. In some cases, if the source can demonstrate that the actual maximum capacity rate before the change is inappropriate, the EPA allows the use of a different rate.[22]

If there is an increase, the owner or operator must determine whether one of the exemptions applies. Under the EPA's regulations, routine "maintenance, repair, and replacement" is not by itself considered a modification.[23] Determining what constitutes routine maintenance, repair, or replacement is a difficult and fact-specific analysis. Using an automobile for analogy, it is easy to say that changing the oil, air filter, or spark plugs is routine maintenance, but what about rebuilding an engine or replacing a transmission? Is replacing an engine or transmission beyond "routine" replacement for a car? Obviously, practitioners must be ready to address the specific factual circumstances surrounding the equipment in question. Information about industry standards and practices, replacement costs, and the like will be important information.[24]

Increases in the production rate at a facility are not modifications, provided the increase can occur without a capital expenditure.[25] Similarly, an increase in the hours of operation is not a modification.[26] Fuel switching is not a modification if the existing facility was designed to accommodate the alternative fuel under the facility's original construction specifications.[27] There are also special exemptions crafted for utilities, known as the WEPCO (for Wisconsin Electric Power Company) rule, which was adopted in 1992.[28]

The "routine maintenance, repair, and replacement" exclusion under both the NSPS and NSR regulations has been the subject of the EPA's recent NSR enforcement initiative against the electric utility industry as well as several other industrial source categories. This initiative is discussed in Chapter 17, "Civil Enforcement." The "routine maintenance" exemption under the NSR rules is discussed in Chapter 6. In December 2002, the EPA proposed changes to the "routine maintenance" provisions for the NSR program but did not address the applicability of such changes to the NSPS analysis.[29]

Owners or operators of existing sources undergoing "process improvements"—physical or operational changes—should be cautious of the modification provisions. It is easy for an "existing" source to become "new" without being new. These changes can have unintended, and expensive, consequences. The EPA's regulations provide a mechanism whereby the EPA will, upon request, determine whether an intended action constitutes a modification or construction or reconstruction.[30] The agency is supposed to respond to such a request within thirty days.[31] Many states will provide similar applicability determinations upon request. The failure to obtain an up-front determination may increase the risk of later enforcement action if the state or the EPA disagrees after the fact. Typically, the BDT for particular NSPS was developed focusing only on the technical feasibility and costs for truly new sources. Thus, control costs for existing sources to meet NSPS can far exceed what the EPA deemed acceptable for determining BDT on new sources.

Reconstruction

Reconstruction is another mechanism by which an existing source can become subject to NSPS. The term "reconstruction" is not defined in the statute; it is solely a regulatory creation of the EPA. The policy behind the reconstruction provision is to discourage the perpetuation of a facility, instead of replacing it at the end of its useful life with a newly constructed facility without regard to emissions.[32]

Practitioners should remember that, unlike the modification requirements, reconstruction rules apply regardless of whether the emission rate of the unit increases.[33] Reconstruction is defined as the replacement of components at an existing facility such that (1) the fixed capital cost of the new components exceeds 50 percent of the fixed capital cost that would be required to construct a comparable entirely new facility and (2) it is technologically and economically feasible.[34]

If an owner or operator of an existing unit plans to replace significant components of an existing facility exceeding the 50 percent threshold, the owner or operator must notify the EPA administrator of the proposed replacements before construction is commenced.[35] The notice must include an estimate of the fixed capital cost of the replacement and the cost of constructing a comparable entirely new facility, information about the remaining useful life of the facility after the replacements, and information on any technical or economic limitations on complying with the NSPS.[36] Within thirty days of the notification, the EPA administrator must determine whether the proposed replacement constitutes a reconstruction.[37]

NSPS applicability will typically apply to a reconstruction unless the source is able to demonstrate that it is technically infeasible to incorporate the NSPS requirements into the entire existing facility even after the capital project, or that the cost of requiring the performance standard to be met is much higher in terms of dollars per ton of pollutant removed than is deemed reasonable considering the particular NSPS at issue.

Setting the Performance Standard

Best Demonstrated Technology Standards

Section 111 of the CAA defines the standard of performance for which the EPA administrator is to set NSPS as the

> degree of emission limitation achievable through the application of the best system of emission reduction which (taking into account the cost of achieving such reduction and any nonair quality health and environmental impact and energy requirements) the Administrator determines has been adequately demonstrated.[38]

This is the BDT standard, which is yet another of the many technology measures found in the environmental statutes. There are several key terms that clarify how BDT is defined under the CAA.

First, the phrase "degree of emission limitation" refers to the maximum quantity of pollutant that may be emitted. The drafters of Section 111 wanted to ensure that the owner or operator was required only to meet a specific performance level, not to impose the ways of achieving it. In theory, this gives the owner or operator significant flexibility. In practice, the standards are based on a particular technology, and there may be few, if any, other means for achieving them.

Second, in determining BDT, the EPA is allowed to consider costs, but how it does so is not specified. The courts have afforded the EPA significant discretion in taking costs into account in determining BDT. The EPA is not required to conduct a true cost-benefit analysis to measure the economic benefit of the lower emission (such as saving lives or reducing risks of some disease) against the cost of the control devices.[39] One factor that the EPA assesses in evaluating costs is the economic costs to the industry and the ability to pass those costs along to the consumer without affecting demand.[40] In establishing which costs are reasonable, the agency does not have to equate the costs to one industry in one NSPS with those for other standards.[41]

In the 1980s the EPA, at the urging (or demand) of the Office of Management and Budget (OMB) under Executive Order 12291, centered its cost analysis on an incremental cost-effectiveness approach. Cost-effectiveness is not a cost-benefit analysis. Under the cost-effectiveness approach, the EPA evaluated the costs of achieving the incremental additional pollution reduction associated with increasing the stringency of a control requirement. For example, in evaluating two control options where Control A reduced emissions of a pollutant by 80 percent and Control B reduced emissions of the same pollutant by 90 percent, the EPA evaluated the incremental cost of achieving the additional 10 percent control. The EPA and OMB "agreed" on acceptable incremental cost ranges for particular pollutants. If the incremental costs exceeded the range, the EPA would either reject the more stringent option or attempt to justify the additional costs. For example, additional costs might be deemed acceptable if the control device also achieved reductions in a toxic air pollutant. The cost analysis is typically one of the most controversial aspects of any NSPS rulemaking. Although cost-effectiveness does not equal cost-benefit in determining what incremental cost is acceptable for a particular pollutant, one must, to some degree, measure the benefits that accrue from the removal of that pollutant from the atmosphere. Although Executive Order 12291 is no longer in effect, Executive Order 12866 provides the mechanism for undertaking a cost-benefit analysis.[42]

The EPA must also consider other non-air-quality environmental impacts of a standard, and thus BDT may not always equal the lowest air emission standard achievable if it creates other negative consequences. As one court stated, "The standard of the best system is comprehensive, and we cannot imagine that Congress intended that the best system could apply to a system which did more damage to water than it prevented to air."[43] Thus, in evaluating two different control systems, the EPA must not simply choose the most cost-effective air pollution control system if there are environmental impacts on other media. To the extent that the EPA is aware of adverse environmental consequences, it must address those in the rule making, although the EPA is not required to conduct a formal environmental impact assessment.[44] Similarly, the agency is to evaluate the energy impacts associated with a particular system.

Section 111 also requires that the standard be adequately demonstrated. To be adequately demonstrated, it need not have been used in the regulated source category or in any commercial scale operation. Instead, the EPA administrator may rely on pilot scale operations or ones used in other industries or other countries.[45]

Courts have stated that a demonstrated standard need not be one already routinely achieved in the industry, but to be achievable, "a uniform standard must be capable of being met under most adverse conditions which can reasonably be expected to recur and which are not or cannot be taken into account in determining the 'costs' of compliance."[46] By including start-up, shutdown, and malfunction provisions in standards, the EPA recognized that the standards are not always achievable. The flexibility is really in the enforcement of the standards and may not be sufficient to sustain a standard not achievable on a consistent basis.[47] Thus, the EPA must do more than show that the standard was achieved at a model plant for a short period of time. It has the burden of showing how the standard is achievable under the range of relevant conditions that may affect the emissions to be regulated anywhere in the country.[48]

In sum, the technology may not be one that is purely theoretical, but it can be a result of technology forcing. The EPA "may make a projection based on existing technology, though that projection is subject to the restraints of reasonableness and cannot be based on crystal ball inquiry."[49]

Work Practice Standards

Section 111(h) allows the EPA administrator to establish design, equipment, work practice, or operational standards. Equipment or work practice standards run counter to Section 111's concept of setting a performance standard. Thus, Section 111(h) standards are permissible only if the administrator determines that "it is not feasible to prescribe or enforce a standard of performance."[50] In setting a standard under Section 111(h), the administrator analyzes the standard using the same criteria used for setting a performance standard.

There are two basic types of situations in which performance standards are deemed not feasible. The first is when the pollutants cannot be captured and conveyed through a pollution control device, such as fugitive emissions.[51] The second is when the application of a measurement methodology to a particular class of sources is impractical owing to technological or economic reasons.[52]

Innovative-Technology Waivers

The statute also provides for innovative-technology waivers for new sources for technology not yet demonstrated.[53] This provision encourages continued technology-forcing activities. The waivers were designed to allow testing of control systems that might prove to achieve greater reductions than the NSPS, or achieve equivalent reductions in a more cost-effective manner.[54] The waiver may be issued only after notice and comment, is limited in duration, and terminates if the EPA administrator determines that the system has failed.[55]

Guidelines for Existing Sources under Section 111

Despite the common assumption that Section 111 relates only to new sources, Section 111 also provides mechanisms for the EPA to control emissions from existing sources. As previously discussed, the modification or reconstruction of an existing source may subject an existing facility to NSPS. In addition, Section 111(d) provides a mechanism whereby, under certain circumstances, the EPA may control new *and* existing sources in an industrial source category. Unlike Section 112, however, the EPA does not directly set regulations. Instead, it establishes "emission guidelines" for existing sources, which must be implemented by states. The EPA has used Section 111(d) on several occasions to require emissions controls of existing sources; however, the EPA's authority to regulate existing sources is limited. Further, with the adoption of technology-based emissions standards for hazardous air pollutants (HAPs) under Section 112, with the exception of waste incineration units, the EPA is not likely to pursue additional regulatory initiatives for existing sources under Section 111.

Scope of Regulatory Authority

Under Section 111(d), the EPA may establish emissions guidelines for existing sources in a source category when the EPA has promulgated NSPS for that category; the pollutant regulated is not a criteria pollutant (i.e., nitrogen oxides, ozone, volatile organic compounds, particulate matter, sulfur dioxide, carbon monoxide, lead); and the category is not subject to regulation under Section 112. These pollutants are referred to as "designated pollutants."[56]

The EPA has issued Section 111(d) guidelines for sulfuric acid mist from sulfuric acid plants, fluoride emissions from phosphate fertilizer plants, total reduced sulfur (TRS) emissions from kraft pulp mills, fluoride emissions from primary aluminum plants, municipal waste combustion (MWC) emissions from solid waste incinerators, and nonmethane organic emissions from landfills, among other pollutants.[57]

As the foregoing list suggests, Section 111(d) guidelines are developed for specialized types of emission sources that emit discrete types of pollutants. In the case of municipal waste combustor emissions, before the 1990 CAA Amendments, the enactment of Section 129 specifically addressing incineration units, and the revisions to Section 112 to make it a technology-based program, the EPA was under pressure to control MWC emissions from new and existing sources. The agency did not want to develop risk-based standards for MWC emissions, so it designated "MWC organics," "MWC metals," and "MWC gases" as pollutants of concern.

Implementation Mechanism to Control Existing Sources

As noted, under Section 111(d), the EPA issues guidelines that must then be used by states in developing regulations to control existing sources. The guidelines provide the same type of information found in the NSPS and include the following:

- Information on the known or suspected health or welfare concerns of the pollutant
- Information on control systems that the administrator believes reflect BDT
- Information on costs
- Information on the time necessary for design, installation, and start-up of the control systems[58]

Within nine months of the EPA's publication of a final guideline document, a state must adopt and submit a plan to the EPA for the control of the designated pollutant to which the guideline applies.[59] If there are no facilities within the state, the state must submit a negative declaration to the EPA.[60]

If the designated pollutant is a concern to public health, the state plan must establish emission standards at least as stringent as the EPA's guidelines, unless on a case-by-case basis for a facility or type of facility the state demonstrates that the guidelines are unreasonably expensive given the control, age of the plant, or basic process design.[61] The requirements may also be less stringent if related to physical impossibility or other factors.[62] If the designated pollutant is only a welfare-based concern, states have greater flexibility to adopt standards that deviate from the EPA's guidelines.[63] Similar to SIP requirements, the plans must also provide mechanisms to implement and enforce the standards adopted.[64]

Implementation of Section 111

Notification of Construction and Start-up

Before the passage of the Title V permitting program, NSPS sources were not subject to any specific permit program, unless states incorporated the NSPS requirements into state operating permits or unless the source triggered PSD-NSR review. The general NSPS provisions are found in 40 C.F.R. Part 60, Subpart A. These general provisions, however, can be overridden by contradictory provisions found in the source specific standards.

Sources subject to NSPS are required to notify the EPA administrator, or the delegated state program (as discussed later), of the commencement of construction within thirty days after such date.[65] The owner or operator must also notify the EPA of the anticipated date of start-up at thirty days and not more than sixty days before such date.[66] Once start-up occurs, the owner or operator has fifteen days to provide notification.[67]

Likewise, the owner or operator must provide notification of any modification sixty days in advance, or as soon as practicable before the change is made.[68] The notification must include information describing the precise nature of the change, the pre- and post-change emission controls, and the production capacity of the facility before and after the change.[69]

Within sixty days of achieving maximum production rate, but not later than 180 days after start-up, the owner or operator is required to conduct a performance test to demonstrate compliance with the applicable standard.[70] Performance tests must be conducted in accordance with the reference test methods, unless the EPA administrator approves an alternative method.[71] Performance tests are to be conducted under "representative" conditions.[72] The owner or operator must provide thirty days' notice to the regulating entity of a scheduled performance test and afford the opportunity to have an observer present.[73]

The NSPS general provisions state that compliance with the standard (other than opacity limits) shall be determined only by the established reference test methods.[74] This provision is at the heart of the controversy between the EPA and industry over the proposed compliance assurance monitoring (CAM) rules and the "any credible evidence" provisions. The EPA takes the position that all relevant evidence can be used to determine both the existence and duration of a violation. Industry argues that the language in the NSPS makes clear that only the performance tests can determine noncompliance and that use of other monitoring data to show a violation is tantamount to increasing the standard's stringency. In response to the issuance of the "any credible evidence" rule, industry is seeking to revisit many of the program's standards. The CAM and credible evidence rules are discussed further in Chapter 17.

Delegation of Authority to Implement the Program

Section 111(c) of the CAA provides for delegating to the states the implementation and enforcement of the NSPS program. A state must develop and submit a plan to the EPA for implementing and enforcing the standards. If the EPA finds the state program adequate, the NSPS program is delegated to the state under a delegation agreement. Most states have been delegated the authority to implement and enforce the program. Some states receive wholesale delegations, while others receive partial delegations, or delegation on a source category-by-source category basis. Typically, however, the EPA will retain authority to approve alternative test methods. Once a program is delegated, all reports and notifications are sent to the delegated authority and not the EPA. Although the program is delegated, the standards remain federally enforceable and may be enforced at any time by the EPA.[75]

Solid Waste Combustion and Section 129

In addition to the EPA's general authority to establish NSPS and emission guidelines for source categories that the EPA administrator determines may adversely affect public health or welfare, Congress directed the EPA to address solid waste incineration units by adding Section 129 to the CAA in the 1990 CAA Amendments. The MWC emissions of primary concern are organics (dioxins and furans), metals (cadmium, lead, mercury, particulate matter, and opacity), acid gases (hydrogen chloride and sulfur dioxide), and nitrogen oxides (NO_x).[76]

Background

Authority to regulate emissions from MWCs is granted to the EPA under CAA Sections 111 and 129. MWCs were first regulated under Section 111(b) of the CAA when, in the early 1970s, NSPS were developed for particulate matter (PM) emissions from MWCs with a capacity of greater than 50 tons per day.[77] In 1986, the EPA promulgated a PM standard that applied to industrial, commercial, and institutional steam generating units that burned certain fuels, including municipal solid waste, if the units had a heat input capacity larger than 29 megawatts, or 100 million Btu per hour.[78] However, these Subpart Db and E standards were aimed at the control of PM, not toxic organics.[79]

In the 1984 Hazardous and Solid Waste Amendments to the Resource Conservation and Recovery Act, Congress directed the EPA to study the risks from dioxin emissions from MWCs and to explore ways to reduce dioxin emissions.[80] In 1985, the EPA announced the National Air Toxics Strategy, which included the EPA's commitment to study MWCs as one of the group of source categories that emit multiple pollutants.[81] The following year, the Natural Resources Defense Council (NRDC) and a handful of states petitioned the EPA to regulate MWC air emissions under Sections 111 and 112 of the CAA.[82] In 1987, the EPA released its report to Congress on MWCs,[83] responded to the NRDC petition, and issued an advance notice of proposed rule making regarding MWC air emissions.[84] The notice announced the EPA's intention to regulate new and existing MWCs under Section 111(b) and (d).[85]

In 1989, the EPA proposed guidelines to control emissions from existing MWCs,[86] under the authority of CAA Section 111(d), and NSPS to control emissions from new MWCs,[87] under the authority of Section 111(b)(1)(B). The EPA was under a court-imposed December 31, 1990, deadline to promulgate final rules governing MWC air emissions when, on November 15, 1990, the CAA was amended.[88] A new section specifically addressing solid waste combustion, Section 129, was added to the CAA in response to public concerns regarding solid waste incineration. Section 129 requires the EPA to promulgate regulations containing standards and guidelines that reflect the MACT for MWCs.[89] Although Section 129 requires the EPA to issue performance standards based on MACT, it also contains a savings clause preventing Section 129 from altering any schedule for the promulgation of standards applicable to MWCs under any consent decree entered into before November 15, 1990.[90] Thus, the EPA subsequently issued guidelines and standards for MWCs reflecting BDT, required by CAA Section 111, under a consent decree issued in *New York v. Reilly.*[91]

Section 129 limited coverage of the 1991 regulations to MWCs with capacities greater than 250 tons per day of municipal waste.[92] Both the guidelines for these large existing units and the standards for large new units were promulgated as final rules on February 11, 1991.[93] The emission guidelines for existing MWCs (constructed before December 20, 1989) are codified at 40 C.F.R. Part 60, Subpart Ca. Subpart Ea governs MWCs constructed after December 20, 1989.

The 1990 CAA Amendments and 1995 MWC Regulations

As discussed previously, Section 111 requires the EPA to develop performance standards and guidelines for new and existing sources that cause or contribute to "air pollution which may reasonably be anticipated to endanger public health or welfare."[94] Section 129, added by the 1990 amendments, requires that the MWC standards and guidelines represent MACT.[95] The 1990 CAA Amendments required the EPA to review the 1991 regulations to determine whether they were consistent with Section 129. The EPA performed this review, concluded the 1991 regulations were not consistent, and proposed new regulations on September 20, 1994.[96] The agency issued its final rule setting forth MACT standards and guidelines for MWCs under Section 129 on December 19, 1995.[97] This final rule replaced the 1991 regulations and created a new framework for control of MWC air emissions.

Applicability
Under the new regulatory structure, a source is regulated based on when construction of the source began. Three classes of MWCs were created by the 1995 final rule, and the regulations are organized by subparts in 40 C.F.R.

Part 60. First, existing sources are governed by Subpart Cb, and were defined as MWC plants "for which construction was commenced on or before September 20, 1994."[98] Second, new sources are regulated by Subpart Eb and were defined as MWC plants "for which construction is commenced after September 20, 1994 or for which modification or reconstruction is commenced after June 19, 1996."[99] Lastly, plants constructed during a roughly five-year period during the early 1990s are governed by Subpart Ea and were defined as MWC plants for which "(1) Construction is commenced after December 20, 1989 and on or before September 20, 1994 [or] (2) Modification or reconstruction is commenced after December 20, 1989, and on or before June 19, 1996."[100] Subpart Ea, which was first created by the 1991 regulations and contained the new source standards,[101] was revised in 1995 to be consistent with Subparts Eb and Cb.[102] If an MWC is subject to Subpart Ea, it will also be subject to Subpart Cb. Subpart Ca, which contained the guidelines for existing sources under the 1991 regulations, was reserved and removed by the 1995 regulations.[103]

The 1995 regulations also classified plants by size, and only MWC plants with a capacity to burn more than 35 megagrams per day of municipal solid waste were regulated. MWC plants that had the capacity to combust more than 225 megagrams per day of municipal solid waste were classified as large MWC plants.[104] MWC plants that had the capacity to burn greater than 35 megagrams per day but equal to or less than 225 megagrams per day of municipal solid waste were classified as small MWC plants.[105] More stringent standards were placed on the large plants.

On April 8, 1997, the D.C. Circuit Court vacated Subparts Cb and Eb as they applied to MWC units with the capacity to combust less than or equal to 250 tons per day of municipal solid waste and all cement kilns combusting municipal solid waste.[106] As a result, Subparts Cb and Eb as they previously existed apply only to MWC units with the capacity to combust more than 250 tons per day of municipal solid waste per unit and thus changed the definition of large MWC. The EPA amended Subparts Cb and Eb to reflect this change.[107] The amendments also added supplemental emission limits for four pollutants: hydrogen chloride, sulfur dioxide, NO_x, and lead. As will be discussed below, the EPA also promulgated limits that apply to small MWCs.

There are numerous exemptions from the standards. Certain MWC plants that are capable of combusting more than 250 tons per day of municipal solid waste and are subject to a federally enforceable permit limiting the maximum amount of municipal solid waste combusted to less than or equal to 11 tons per day are exempt.[108] In addition, the following may be exempt:

- Certain small power production facilities
- Qualifying cogeneration facilities
- Units combusting a single-item waste stream of tires
- Units permitted under the Solid Waste Disposal Act
- Materials recovery facilities used to recover metals

- Cofired combustors
- Air curtain incinerators
- Pyrolysis or combustion units that are an integrated part of a plastics or rubber recycling unit[109]

Schedule for Release of Standards and Guidelines

Under Section 129, by November 15, 1991, the EPA was to promulgate MACT standards and guidelines for large MWCs (greater than 250 tons per day, or tpd) to modify the 1991 standards and guidelines, which were issued under Section 111 and reflected BDT.[110] Section 129 also required the EPA to promulgate standards and guidelines for small MWCs (equal to or less than 250 tpd) by November 15, 1992.[111] The EPA did not comply with the Section 129 schedule, and the Sierra Club, NRDC, and Integrated Waste Services Association sued the EPA. Under the resulting consent decree, the EPA agreed to propose standards and guidelines no later than September 1, 1994, and to promulgate a final rule by October 31, 1995.[112] The agency issued the proposal on September 20, 1994,[113] and promulgated the final rule on December 19,1995.[114]

The MACT Standards

Section 129 requires that the revised standards for new MWCs and the revised guidelines for existing MWCs promulgated under the Section be based on MACT, regardless of whether the MWCs are existing or new.[115] MACT is defined as "the maximum degree of reductions in emissions of air pollutants . . . that the Administrator, taking into consideration the cost of achieving such emission reduction, and any non-air quality health and environmental impacts and energy requirements, determines is achievable for new or existing units in each category."[116] The process for developing the MWC standards is similar to that used under Section 112(d). Section 112(d) is discussed in Chapter 8, "Hazardous Air Pollutants." The MACT NSPS promulgated under Sections 111 and 129, covering both new and existing sources, may focus on the removal of pollutants before, during, or after combustion.[117] The EPA must specify numerical emission limitations for certain pollutants: "particulate matter (total and fine), opacity (as appropriate), sulfur dioxide, hydrogen chloride, oxides of nitrogen, carbon monoxide, lead, cadmium, mercury, and dioxins and dibenzofurans."[118] The EPA is required to review, and if appropriate revise, standards promulgated under Sections 111 and 129 every five years after initial promulgation.[119]

As noted, the 1995 regulations created two new subparts under 40 C.F.R. Part 60: Subpart Cb, which established guidelines for existing MWCs, and Subpart Eb, which set standards for new MWCs. In addition, Subpart Ea was revised in 1995 and applies to sources for which construction was commenced between the time the 1991 regulations were proposed and the 1995 regulations were proposed.[120] The guidelines under Subpart Cb also apply to any MWC subject to Subpart Ea.

Large Municipal Waste Combusters

Existing Units

Subpart Cb applies to any MWC plant with a capacity to combust greater than 250 tons per day of municipal solid waste for which construction was commenced on or before September 20, 1994.[121] The guidelines established by the EPA for these existing MWCs "shall not be less stringent than the average emissions limitation achieved by the best performing 12 percent of units in the category."[122] This standard is known as the MACT floor. The 1995 regulations established emission guidelines for metals,[123] acid gases,[124] organics,[125] NO_x,[126] carbon monoxide (CO),[127] and fugitive ash.[128] As mentioned above, the 1997 amendments added supplemental limits for hydrogen chloride, sulfur dioxide, nitrogen oxides, and lead.

On November 12, 1998, the EPA promulgated federal plan requirements for large MWCs constructed on or before September 20, 1994.[129] The federal plan implements emission guidelines for MWC units located in areas not covered by an approved and effective state plan, and will apply until the state has an approved plan in effect.

For new sources, the 1995 final rule established Subpart Eb.[130] MWC units with the capacity to burn 250 tons per day of municipal solid waste for which construction was commenced on or before September 20, 1994, are regulated by Subpart Eb.[131] The MACT floor for these new units states that emissions standards "shall not be less stringent than the emissions control that is achieved in practice by the best controlled similar unit."[132] Thus, the MACT standards established in Subpart Eb are more stringent than those established for existing sources in Subpart Cb. However, Subpart Eb regulates the same categories of pollutants: metals,[133] acid gases,[134] organics,[135] NO_x,[136] CO,[137] fugitive ash, hydrogen chloride, sulfur dioxide, and lead.[138]

In July 2001, the EPA amended the standards of performance for large MWCs by expanding the definition of mass burn rotary waterwall MWCs to include mass burn tumbling-tile grate waterwall MWCs.[139] In November 2001, the EPA revised the large MWC rules to extend the time during which large MWCs would be excused from compliance with the emission limits for carbon monoxide due to certain malfunctions.[140]

Units Constructed between December 20, 1989, and September 20, 1994

The 1991 regulations placed the guidelines for existing MWCs in Subpart Ca and the standards for new MWCs in Subpart Ea.[141] The 1995 regulations removed and reserved the Subpart Ca regulations for existing MWCs and replaced them with Subpart Cb. However, the 1995 regulations established standards for new MWCs in Subpart Eb but retained, albeit with modifications, Subpart Ea. The Subpart Ea standards apply to MWC units at MWC plants capable of combusting 250 tons per day of municipal solid waste if construction was commenced after December 20, 1989, and on or before September 20, 1994, or if modification or reconstruction was commenced after December 20, 1989, and on or before June 19, 1996.[142] The EPA selected these dates to avoid overlap with the Subpart Eb NSPS.[143] The Subpart Ea standards are not as strict as the Subpart Eb standards and do not set standards for fugitive ash emissions, although Subpart Ea does set limitations on the other emission categories covered by Subparts Cb and Eb: metals,[144] acid gases,[145] organics,[146] NO_x,[147] and CO.[148]

Small Municipal Waste Combusters

In 2000, the EPA promulgated small MWC rules.[149] A small MWC is a unit with an individual MWC capacity of 35 to 250 tons per day. The NSPS for small MWCs list emission limits for dioxins/furans, cadmium, lead, mercury, particulate matter, hydrogen chloride, sulfur dioxide, and nitrogen oxides. The NSPS of the small MWC rule are the same as the 1995 NSPS for small MWC units. 40 C.F.R. Part 60, Subpart BBBB lists NSPS for small MWC units that commenced construction on or before August 30, 1999. The NSPS for new, modified, or reconstructed small MWC units are found at 40 C.F.R. Part 60, Subpart AAAA.

The EPA promulgated a federal plan for small MWC units constructed on or before August 30, 1999, in 2003.[150] The plan applies in areas not covered by an approved state or tribal plan and will cease to apply on the effective date of an approved state or tribal plan.

Non-MWC Solid Waste Combustion

In addition to MWCs, under Section 129 the EPA must regulate three other types of solid waste incinerators: (1) units combusting hospital waste, medical waste, and infectious waste;[151] (2) units combusting commercial or industrial waste;[152] and (3) other categories of solid waste incineration units.[153]

Medical Waste Incineration

The EPA promulgated standards for new and existing units that combust hospital waste, medical waste, and infectious waste on September 15, 1997.[154] Subpart Ec to the Part 60 regulations contains standards of performance for new hospital/medical/infectious waste incinerators (HMIWIs) that became effective on March 16, 1998. Subpart Ce contains emissions guidelines for existing HMIWIs that became effective on November 14, 1997. This rule places emissions limits on particulate matter, opacity, sulfur dioxide, hydrogen chloride, oxides of nitrogen, carbon monoxide, lead, cadmium, mercury, dioxins and dibenzofurans, and fugitive ash emissions. In addition, it establishes requirements for operator training and qualification, waste management plans, and testing and monitoring of pollutants and operations. Furthermore, the rule lists equipment inspection requirements and the standards for new HMIWIs.

In *Sierra Club v. EPA*,[155] the D.C. Circuit reviewed the HMIWI rule and held that the EPA's use of state permit and regulatory data, rather than performance data, in setting MACT limits for existing HMIWIs was not prohibited by the CAA.[156] The court specifically rejected the Sierra Club's arguments that the CAA forbids the use of permit and regulatory data, and held that the use of such information is acceptable if "it allows for a reasonable inference as to the performance of the top 12 percent of units."[157] The D.C. Circuit remanded the case because the EPA did not adequately explain its reasoning in determining the floors for new and existing HMIWIs.[158]

On August 15, 2000, the EPA promulgated federal plan requirements for HMIWIs constructed on or before June 20, 1996.[159] The federal plan applies to incinerators used by hospitals and health care facilities, as well as to incinerators used by commercial disposal companies to burn hospital waste and/or medical/infectious waste. The federal plan became effective on September 14, 2000, and appears at 40 C.F.R. Part 62, Subpart HHH. The federal plan for HMIWIs implements emission guidelines for HMIWIs located in states or Indian territories without effective state or tribal plans and will apply until the state or tribe has an approved plan in effect.

Industrial and Commercial Waste Incineration

The EPA promulgated standards for units combusting commercial or industrial solid waste on December 1, 2000.[160] 40 C.F.R. Part 60, Subpart CCCC applies to commercial and industrial solid waste incinerators (CISWIs) where construction commenced after November 30, 1999, or where modification or reconstruction commenced on or after June 1, 2001. 40 C.F.R. Part 60, Subpart DDDD applies to CISWIs where construction commenced on or before November 30, 1999. These standards became effective on January 30, 2001, and apply to owners and/or operators of combustion devices that combust commercial and industrial waste. Commercial and industrial waste is "solid waste combined in an enclosed device using controlled flame combustion without energy recovery that is a distinct operating unit of any commercial or industrial facility" or "solid waste combusted in an air curtain incinerator without energy recovery that is a distinct operating unit of any commercial or industrial facility."[161] Fifteen types of combustion units are exempt from these standards.[162]

In late 2002, the EPA issued a proposed rule containing a federal plan for CISWIs constructed on or before November 30, 1999.[163] The proposed federal plan would serve to implement emission guidelines for CISWI units located in states or Indian territories without effective state or tribal plans and would apply until the state or tribe has an approved state plan in effect.

Other Solid Waste Incineration

In addition to the specific categories of solid waste incineration units specified in the statute, the EPA was required to publish a schedule for promulgating standards for "other solid waste incinerators" (OSWIs) by no later than eighteen months after November 15, 1990.[164] On November 2, 1993, the EPA published a final list of types of incinerators to be included in this category and a regulatory schedule.[165] The list included the following seven types of incinerators:

1. Small MWCs, being those MWC plants with capacities of 35 megagrams per day or less
2. Residential incinerators
3. Agricultural waste incinerators
4. Wood waste incinerators
5. Construction and demolition waste incinerators
6. Crematories
7. Contaminated soil treatment facilities

As discussed above, the EPA promulgated small MWC rules. On November 9, 2000, the EPA extended its deadline for the promulgation of rules for other solid waste incinerators.[166] The new deadline is November 15, 2005.

Requirements Applicable to All Solid Waste Incineration Units

Permits

A solid waste incineration unit must have a permit within thirty-six months after the promulgation of standards for its category or after the effective date of the Title V program to which it is subject, whichever is later.[167] The permit must be issued under Section 129 and Title V and can be renewed under the provisions of Title V. MWC permits may be issued for a period not to exceed twelve years and must be reviewed by the issuing agency, including public comment and hearing, at least every five years. Under Section 129(e), the permitting authority has the discretion to place emission limitations or other requirements on an operator or owner of a solid waste incineration unit if emissions without such limitations or measures may endanger public health or the environment.[168]

Operator Training

The EPA is required to develop and promote a model state program for the training and certification of operators of solid waste incineration units and high-capacity fossil fuel plants.[169] States may implement their own training program, if the EPA approves the program as being at least as effective as the EPA program. Thirty-six months after performance standards are final for a category of solid waste incineration units, it is unlawful under the CAA for a unit in that category to operate unless each person controlling processes that affect emissions has completed an approved training program.[170]

Monitoring, Reporting, and Record Keeping

Section 129 requires the EPA to promulgate regulations, along with each performance standard promulgated under Sections 111 and 129, that require the owner or operator of a solid waste incineration unit to monitor emissions to the ambient air, monitor other operational parameters that affect pollution control, and report the monitoring results.[171] The regulations must include requirements relating to frequency of monitoring, test methods and procedures, and form and frequency of reports. Exceedances discovered during monitoring must be reported separately. The results of monitoring must be maintained at the regulated facility and must be available to the public for inspecting and copying.[172]

Residual Risk Analysis

Solid waste incineration units subject to Section 111 and Section 129 NSPS are not subject to regulation under Section 112(d)(2), which authorizes the establishment of MACT standards for HAPs.[173] Solid waste incineration units may, however, become subject to Section 112 HAPs regulation under one scenario. Section 112(f) requires the EPA to investigate and report to Congress on any risk to the public health that may remain after Section 112(d) HAP standards are established and to include recommendations on legislation to address any remaining risks.[174]

If Congress fails to act on the EPA's recommendations, the EPA is to promulgate standards for any source category it deems necessary, and the agency shall promulgate standards for a source category "if promulgation of such standards is required to provide an ample margin of safety to protect public health . . . or to prevent . . . an adverse environmental effect."[175] If the EPA promulgates standards under Section 112(f) for any category of solid waste incineration units, Sections 111 and 129 NSPS are deemed to be Section 112(d) HAP standards for purposes of Section 112(f) analysis, and the EPA is restricted to regulating under Section 112(f) only those pollutants listed under Section 129(a)(4).[176]

Notes

1. The authors gratefully acknowledge this assistance of Caroline Strickland in the preparation of this chapter.
2. 42 U.S.C. § 1857c-6 (1970) (codified at 42 U.S.C. § 7411).
3. *See* National Asphalt Pavement Ass'n v. Train, 539 F.2d 775, 783 (D.C. Cir. 1976); United States v. City of Painesville, 431 F. Supp. 496, 500, n.6 (N.D. Ohio 1977) (citing Legislative History of 1970 Amendments), *aff'd*, 644 F.2d 1186 (6th Cir. 1977).
4. CAA § 111(a)(1).
5. The 1990 CAA Amendments amended the definition of BDT to remove the word "technological" from the definition in Section 111(a)(1) to repeal the percent reduction requirements for utility boilers. *See* Pub. L. No. 101-549, § 403(a), 104 Stat. 2399, 2589–92 (1990). The word "technological" was added to the definition of BDT in the 1977 amendments for the purpose of forcing the EPA to revise the NSPS for utilities, to force the use of SO_2 scrubbers, and to preclude the use of low-sulfur coal or oil as BDT for utility boilers. For a discussion of the NSPS for utilities issued after the 1977 amendments, *see* Sierra Club v. Costle, 657 F.2d 298, 315–20 (D.C. Cir. 1981).
6. CAA § 111(b)(1)(A).

7. 36 Fed. Reg. 5931 (1971).

8. CAA § 111(a)(3).

9. *See* the definition of the term "affected facility" at 40 C.F.R. § 60.2.

10. 40 C.F.R. § 60.40a(a).

11. *See id.* § 60.370(a).

12. CAA § 111(b)(1)(A).

13. 44 Fed. Reg. 49,222 (1979).

14. *See* 40 C.F.R. § 60.1.

15. CAA § 111(a)(2).

16. This term is also important in the PSD and NSR context, as discussed in Chapter 6, because one may not commence construction without having obtained a permit.

17. 40 C.F.R. § 60.2; *See City of Painesville,* 431 F. Supp. at 500–01.

18. 40 C.F.R. § 60.2.

19. *City of Painesville,* 431 F. Supp. at 501, n.8.

20. CAA § 111(a)(1).

21. *See* 40 C.F.R. § 60.14(a).

22. For an extensive discussion of the emissions increase issue, *see* Wisconsin Electric Power Co. v. Reilly, 893 F.2d 901 (7th Cir. 1990).

23. 40. C.F.R. § 60.14(e)(1).

24. For an extensive discussion of the routine replacement test, *see Wisconsin Electric Power Co.,* 893 F.2d at 910–13.

25. 40 C.F.R. § 60.14(e)(2).

26. *Id.* § 60.14(e)(3).

27. *Id.*

28. *Id.* § 60.14(h)–(l). *See* 57 Fed. Reg. 32,339 (1992).

29. 67 Fed. Reg. 80,290 (2002).

30. 40 C.F.R. § 60.5(a).

31. *Id.* § 60.5(b).

32. 39 Fed. Reg. 36,946, 36,948 (1974).

33. 40 C.F.R. § 60.15(a).

34. *Id.* § 60.15(b).

35. *Id.* § 60.15(d).

36. *Id.*

37. *Id.* § 60.15(e).

38. CAA § 111(a)(1).

39. Portland Cement Ass'n v. Ruckelshaus, 486 F.2d 375, 387 (D.C. Cir. 1973), *cert. denied,* 417 U.S. 921 (1974).

40. *Id.* at 387–88.

41. *Id.*

42. President Clinton issued Executive Order 12866 on September 30, 1993. 58 Fed. Reg. 51,735 (1993). President Bush amended the Executive Order on February 28, 2002. 67 Fed. Reg. 9385 (2002).

43. *Portland Cement Ass'n,* 486 F.2d at 386.

44. *Id.*

45. *See* Sierra Club v. Costle, 657 F.2d 298, 374 (D.C. Cir. 1981); American Iron & Steel Inst. v. EPA, 526 F.2d 1027, 1057–61 (3rd Cir. 1975); Essex Chemical v. Ruckelshaus, 486 F.2d 427, 440 (D.C. Cir. 1973); Portland Cement Ass'n v. Ruckelshaus, 486 F.2d 375, 391 (D.C. Cir. 1973).

46. National Lime Ass'n v. EPA, 627 F.2d 416, 431, n. 46 (D.C. Cir. 1980).

47. *Id.*

48. *Id.* at 433.

49. *Portland Cement Ass'n,* 486 F.2d at 391.

50. CAA § 111(h)(1).

51. CAA § 111(h)(2).

52. *Id.*

53. CAA § 111(j).

54. CAA § 111(j)(1)(A).

55. CAA § 111(j)(1)(D).

56. 40 C.F.R. § 60.21(a).

57. *See generally* 40 C.F.R. pt. 62 (approval of various state plans to incorporate these guidelines into state regulations); 40 C.F.R. pt. 60, subpt. C.

58. 40 C.F.R. § 60.22(b).

59. *Id.* § 60.23(a).

60. *Id.* § 60.23(b).

61. *Id.* § 60.24(f).

62. *Id.*

63. 40 C.F.R. § 60.24(d).

64. *Id.* § 60.25.

65. *Id.* § 60.7(a)(1).

66. *Id.* § 60.7(a)(2).

67. *Id.* § 60.7(a)(3).

68. *Id.* § 601(a)(4).

69. *Id.*

70. *Id.* § 60.8(a).

71. *Id.* § 60.8(b).

72. *Id.* § 60.8(c).

73. *Id.* § 60.8(d).

74. *Id.* § 60.11(a).

75. CAA § 111(c)(2).

76. 60 Fed. Reg. 65,387, 65,390 (1995).

77. *See* 40 C.F.R. pt. 60, subpt. E; 56 Fed. Reg. 5488 (1991).

78. *See* 40 C.F.R. pt. 60, subpt. Db; 56 Fed. Reg. at 5488.

79. *See* 56 Fed. Reg. at 5488.

80. *See id.*

81. *See id.*

82. *See id.*

83. U.S. EPA, Municipal Waste Combustion Study, EPA/530-SW-87-121A (June 1987).

84. Response to Petition for Rulemaking and Advance Notice of Proposed Rule-making, 52 Fed. Reg. 25,399 (1987).

85. *Id.*

86. 54 Fed. Reg. 52,209 (1989).

87. 54 Fed. Reg. 52,251 (1989).

88. Pub. L. No. 101-549, 104 Stat. 2399 (1990) (codified as amended throughout Title 42).

89. CAA § 129(a)(2).

90. CAA § 129(a)(1)(B).

91. No. 89-1729 (D.D.C.).

92. *Id.*

93. Standards of Performance for New Stationary Sources: Municipal Waste Combustors, 56 Fed. Reg. 5488 (1991); Emission Guidelines; Municipal Waste Combustors, 56 Fed. Reg. 5514 (1991).

94. CAA § 111(b)(1)(A).

95. CAA § 129(a)(2).

96. Standards of Performance for New Stationary Sources: Municipal Waste Combustors, 59 Fed. Reg. 48,198 (1994); Emission Guidelines: Municipal Waste Combustors, 59 Fed. Reg. 48,228 (1994).

97. 60 Fed. Reg. 65,387 (1995).

98. 40 C.F.R. § 60.32b(a).

99. *Id.* § 60.50b(a).

100. *Id.* § 60.50a(a).

101. 56 Fed. Reg. at 5488.

102. 60 Fed. Reg. 65,382 (1995).

103. *See id.* at 65,414.

104. 40 C.F.R. §§ 60.51a, 60.51b.

105. *Id.* § 60.51b.

106. Davis County Solid Waste Management and Recovery District v. EPA, 101 F.3d 1395 (D.C. Cir. 1996), *amended by* 108 F.3d 1454 (D.C. Cir. 1997).

107. 62 Fed. Reg. 45,116 (1997). Technical amendments appear at 62 Fed. Reg. 45,124 (1997).

108. 40 C.F.R. § 60.32b(b).

109. *See id.* §§ 60.32b(d)-(1), 60.50a(c)–(k), 60.50b(b)–(m).

110. CAA § 129(a)(1)(B).

111. *Id.*

112. *See* 60 Fed. Reg. at 65,390.

113. 59 Fed. Reg. at 48,198, 48,228.

114. 60 Fed. Reg. at 65,387.

115. CAA § 129(a)(2).

116. *Id.*

117. CAA § 129(a)(3).

118. CAA § 129(a)(4).

119. CAA § 129(a)(5).

120. 60 Fed. Reg. at 65,382.

121. 40 C.F.R. § 60.32b.

122. CAA § 129(a)(2).

123. 40 C.F.R. § 60.33b(a).

124. *Id.* § 60.33b(b).

125. *Id.* § 60.33b(c).

126. *Id.* § 60.33b(d).

127. *Id.* § 60.34b(a).

128. *Id.* § 60.34b.

129. 63 Fed. Reg. 63,191 (1998), *corrected in* 64 Fed. Reg. 17,219 (1999), *amended by* 65 Fed. Reg. 33,461 (2000).

130. 60 Fed. Reg. at 65,391, 65,419.

131. 40 C.F.R. § 60.52b(a).

132. CAA § 129(a)(2).

133. 40 C.F.R. § 60.52b(a).

134. *Id.* § 60.52b(b).

135. *Id.* § 60.52b(c).

136. *Id.* § 60.52b(d).

137. *Id.* § 60.53b(a).

138. *Id.* § 60.55b.

139. 40 C.F.R. § 60,586; 66 Fed. Reg. 36,473 (2001).

140. 40 C.F.R. § 60,586; 66 Fed. Reg. 57,824 (2001).

141. *See* 56 Fed Reg. at 5,514, 5,488.

142. 40 C.F.R. § 60.50a(a).

143. 60 Fed. Reg. at 65,382.

144. 40 C.F.R. § 60.52a.

145. *Id.* § 60.54a.

146. *Id.* § 60.53a.

147. *Id.* § 60.55a.

148. *Id.* § 60.56a.

149. 65 Fed. Reg. 76,350 (2000).

150. 68 Fed. Reg. 5,144 (2003).

151. CAA § 129(a)(1)(C).

152. CAA § 129(a)(1)(D).

153. CAA § 129(a)(1)(E).

154. 62 Fed. Reg. 48,348 (1997).

155. 167 F.3d 658 (D.C. Cir. 1999).

156. 167 F.3d at 633.

157. *Id.* at 663.

158. *Id.* at 666.

159. 65 Fed. Reg. 49,868 (2000).

160. 65 Fed. Reg. 75,338 (2000). Subpart CCCC, Table 1 was corrected on March 27, 2001 in 66 Fed. Reg. 16,605 (2001).

161. 65 Fed. Reg. at 75,340.

162. *Id.*

163. 67 Fed. Reg. 70,640 (2002).

164. CAA § 129(a)(1)(E).

165. 58 Fed. Reg. 58,498 (1993).

166. 65 Fed. Reg. 67,357 (2000).

167. CAA § 129(e).

168. *Id.*

169. CAA § 129(d).

170. *Id.*

171. CAA § 129(c).

172. *Id.*

173. CAA § 129(h)(2).

174. CAA § 112(f)(1).

175. CAA § 112(f)(2)(A).

176. CAA § 129(h)(3). The pollutants listed under Section 129(a)(4) are particulate matter (total and fine), opacity (as appropriate), sulfur oxide, hydrogen chloride, oxides of nitrogen, carbon monoxide, lead, cadmium, mercury, and dioxins and dibenzofurans.

CHAPTER 10

Regulation of Mobile Sources: Motor Vehicles, Nonroad Engines, and Aircraft

MICHAEL J. HOROWITZ

Introduction

The Clean Air Act (CAA) divides mobile sources into three categories: on-highway motor vehicles, like cars, trucks, and buses; aircraft; and nonroad vehicles and engines, which is a catch-all category for vehicles and equipment that are not generally used on the highways but are self-propelled or portable or transportable, including cranes and other construction equipment, tractors, lawnmowers, chainsaws, all-terrain vehicles, portable generators, motorboats and ships, locomotives, snowmobiles, forklifts, mining trucks, and airport ground service equipment.

Emissions from motor vehicles and other mobile sources have been linked to increased concentrations of ozone, the main component of smog, as well as the other criteria pollutants: carbon monoxide (CO), particulate matter (PM), nitrogen dioxide, sulfur dioxide, and, historically, lead. Mobile sources also emit hazardous air pollutants (HAPs), including benzene, formaldehyde, and dioxins. Additionally, a recent U.S. Environmental Protection Agency (EPA) study has concluded that exhaust from diesel engines is a likely human carcinogen.[1]

Regulation of mobile sources has generally been run on a parallel but separate track from regulation of stationary sources. The provisions of the CAA relating to regulation of new vehicles and engines are found in Title II. Title I of the CAA contains certain provisions providing for state regulation of vehicles and engines, for example, through inspection and maintenance programs and vehicles control measures. This chapter will concentrate on Title II. Unlike regulation of stationary sources, where states and local governments have considerable power to regulate, regulation of new mobile sources under Title II of the CAA has been dominated by two programs: the EPA's national program and California's state program. While other states can enact their own programs, these programs must for the most part match California's.

Title II also authorizes the EPA regulation of mobile source fuels. These provisions are discussed separately in Chapter 11. Though the program for regulation of vehicles has generally been distinct from the regulation of fuels, recent EPA regulations have emphasized the interaction between vehicle emission control systems and the need for cleaner fuels that ensure that these systems work in use.

Historical Development

Early Motor Vehicle Control Legislation

In the early 1950s, studies performed by the California Air Resources Board linked emissions from automobiles to air pollution. Shortly thereafter, California initiated the first regulatory regime for air pollutants from automobiles.

The authority to set federal standards was provided for the first time in 1965 in the Motor Vehicle Air Pollution Control Act.[2] Under the Act, the Department of Health, Education, and Welfare (HEW) could set emission standards for new vehicles with "appropriate consideration to technological feasibility and economic costs." The first federal emission standards were promulgated in 1966 and became effective in the 1968 model year.[3] The 1965 Act also contained enforcement provisions, including a prohibition on the manufacture or sale of nonconforming vehicles and on the rendering inoperative of any pollution control device before sale to the ultimate purchaser.

The 1965 Act was amended by the Air Quality Act of 1967.[4] The most critical provision of the 1967 Act was the provision relating to federal preemption. Under the 1967 Act, no state was permitted "to adopt or attempt to enforce any standard relating to the control of emissions from new motor vehicles or new motor vehicle engines."[5] However, the Act provided that HEW could waive the preemption for any state that had adopted standards for the control of emissions on new vehicles before March 30, 1966 (the only state meeting the condition for the preemption waiver was California), unless HEW found that more stringent state standards were not required to meet "compelling and extraordinary conditions" or that the standards were inconsistent with Section 202(a) of the Act, which provided HEW's own standard-setting authority.

This preemption provision, which has survived with little change, was a compromise. The automobile industry was becoming increasingly concerned that, without preemption, each state could promulgate its own set of standards, which could potentially subject manufacturers to up to fifty-one separate sets of standards for all of their vehicle models. On the other hand, California was concerned that if it were not allowed to continue its separate program, its unique and severe air quality problems would not be addressed adequately at the federal level. Congress decided that there was substantial benefit in allowing California to continue its lead in setting standards for motor vehicle emissions. This provision in effect established the state as a laboratory for emission control technology and regulation that could be applied later at the federal level.

The preemption provision also made clear that states were not preempted from establishing controls on the "use, operation, or movement of licensed motor vehicles," thus allowing states and local authorities to continue regulating the way vehicles are used in local areas.

The 1970 Clean Air Act

After passage of the 1967 Air Quality Act, congressional committees held hearings to consider the efficacy of further motor vehicle controls. In the course of those hearings, Congress collected information on the feasibility of alternatives to the internal combustion engine.[6]

The new congressional attitude was based, in part, on a report published by HEW's National Air Pollution Control Administration (NAPCA), "Federal Motor Vehicle Emission Goals for Carbon Monoxide, Hydrocarbons, and Nitrogen Oxides, Based on Desired Air Quality Levels." The report determined that to reach ambient air quality levels that were protective of public health, significant reductions from levels of uncontrolled motor vehicles emissions would be required. Specifically, the report called for reductions of 92.7 percent for CO, 99 percent for hydrocarbons (HC, an ozone precursor), and 93.6 percent for oxides of nitrogen (NO_x, also an ozone precursor) by 1980. Other NAPCA research indicated that advanced internal combustion engines, as well as unconventional engines such as the steam engine and hybrid turbine, could meet the percentage reductions by 1975.

The 1970 CAA was more prescriptive than previous legislation regarding the regulatory requirements on motor vehicles to be promulgated by the EPA, which had replaced HEW as the government entity authorized to implement the CAA.[7] Congress required a 90 percent reduction of HC and CO from a baseline of emissions allowed for light-duty vehicles (e.g., automobiles and small trucks) produced in the 1970 model year and a 90 percent reduction of NO_x from light-duty vehicles produced in the 1971 model year.[8] The HC and CO standards were required to be met in the 1975 model year, and the NO_x standard was required to be met in the 1976 model year. Congress allowed the EPA administrator to suspend the standards for a year if the agency determined, after a public hearing, that the technology required to meet the standards was not available.

The 1970 CAA also established the modern framework for motor vehicle emissions regulation that has been preserved in later amendments. In addition to the standard-setting provisions contained in Section 202,[9] Section 206 now made mandatory the certification program that had previously been voluntary under the 1965 Motor Vehicle Air Pollution Control Act. Under the certification program, specially built prototypes of production-line cars are tested to determine whether the emissions comply with the standards. If the emissions conform to the standards, the EPA issues a certificate of conformity. This certificate allows the manufacturer to demonstrate compliance with the standards as long as the production line cars are "in all material respects substantially the same construction as the test vehicle or engine." The testing of vehicles in use is provided under Section 207 of the CAA. Section 207 also contains the requirement that a manufacturer warrant the design and performance of the emission control equipment to the vehicle's ultimate purchaser.

The standards set under the 1970 CAA were immediately challenged by the automotive industry. As permitted under the CAA, the manufacturers applied to the EPA for a suspension of the standards for the 1975 model year. The EPA considered a substantial amount of technical evidence and ruled against the manufacturers, finding that they had failed to prove that the required technology would not be available. The agency then denied the requested one-year suspension, and the manufacturers promptly filed suit in *International Harvester v. Ruckleshaus*.[10]

The court reexamined the technical and policy arguments that had been presented to the agency and held that the EPA had not adequately supported its decision that the standards could be met. The court found in particular that the EPA had not supported its decision that the technology would be available in time and that there would be enough catalytic converters available to supply the 1975 model-year automotive fleet. In accordance with the decision, the EPA held new hearings and granted the suspension.

International Harvester showed that there were clearly limits to what technology-forcing standards could accomplish. Although the manufacturers had to show that they had made good-faith efforts to meet the standards by the required deadlines, the court found that the EPA was required to produce "a reasoned presentation of the reliability of a prediction and methodology that is relied upon to overcome a conclusion, of lack of available technology, supported . . . by the only actual and observed data available, the manufacturers' testing."[11]

However, the court also found that "as long as feasible technology permits the demand for new passenger automobiles to be generally met, the basic requirements of the [CAA] would be satisfied, even though this might occasion fewer models and a more limited choice of engine types."[12] A later court opinion in *Natural Resources Defense Council v. EPA* found that

EPA will have demonstrated the reasonableness of its basis for prediction [that standards are feasible] if it answers any theoretical objections . . . , identifies the major steps necessary in refinement of the [technology], and offers plausible reasons for believing that each of those steps can be completed in the time available.[13]

The 1977 CAA Amendments

In 1977, Congress passed further amendments to the CAA. Congress again reviewed the stringency of the motor vehicle standards and the schedule imposed on the manufacturers[14] and in effect decided that its 1970 timetable had been too ambitious. The 1977 CAA Amendments postponed what had originally been the 1975 standards. The HC standard was set for the 1980 model year, the CO standard was extended to 1981 (with authority provided for further waivers), and the NO$_x$ standard was significantly relaxed. The 90 percent reduction of NO$_x$ was no longer a requirement but a "research objective"; the NO$_x$ standard of 0.4 grams per mile (gpm) was relaxed to 1.0 gpm, with a new extended deadline of 1981.

In the 1977 amendments, Congress directed the EPA to establish standards for heavy-duty vehicles and engines (e.g., large trucks and buses) using a technology-forcing standard. Because manufacturers were not as far along in controlling emissions from heavy-duty engines, Congress provided separate and unique flexibility for manufacturers of such engines. Congress added Section 206(g), which allowed manufacturers whose engines were not able to meet the model-year standards to receive certificates of conformity upon payment of a "nonconformance penalty."

In the 1977 amendments, Congress also granted increased flexibility to California in setting state motor vehicle standards, and it allowed other states to duplicate California's standards. This was reflected in two important provisions. Prior to 1977, California was permitted under CAA Section 209(b) to regulate motor vehicle emissions if they were at least as protective of public health and welfare as applicable federal standards. In the 1977 amendments, Congress required only that the standards be as stringent "in the aggregate" as the federal standards.

In addition, the 1977 amendments added Section 177 to the CAA, which provided that states that contain nonattainment areas could adopt California's motor vehicle standards under two conditions: (1) The state standards had to be identical to California standards (for which the EPA has granted a waiver), and (2) California and the state were required to provide two years of lead time before the standards would go into effect. Before 1977, no state, other than California, could promulgate standards for new motor vehicles. Section 177 was designed to make the California standards directly available to other states that might benefit from the more stringent California standards while ensuring that motor vehicle manufacturers would not have to produce a "third car" (in addition to the federal model and California model). The section initially was little used; however, since the early 1990s, several states have promulgated motor vehicle regulations pursuant to this section, and these state regulations have been the subject of several rounds of litigation, discussed below.

The 1990 CAA Amendments

In 1990, Congress passed a comprehensive set of revisions to the CAA.[15] Though the 1990 amendments did not fundamentally change Title II's motor vehicle regulatory program, Congress did add several new provisions designed to deal with specific emission and enforcement concerns. It specified new standards for light-duty cars and trucks and provided authority for a second tier of new standards. It revamped the provisions for regul-ating heavy-duty trucks. It required regulation of emissions previously given little attention by the EPA, including vehicle evaporative and refueling emissions, cold temperature CO emissions, and toxic air emissions. It instituted new programs for regulating rebuilt urban bus engines and requiring clean fuel vehicles for certain centrally fueled fleets. It also authorized the promulgation of emission standards for nonroad engines. Finally, it added several provisions to ensure that vehicle and engine emissions are controlled in use, including increasing the regulatory life of the vehicles, requiring vehicle onboard emission monitoring equipment, and requiring that vehicle test procedures accurately reflect actual in-use conditions.

Regulatory Programs

Light-Duty Vehicles and Light-Duty Trucks

Tier 1 and Tier 2 Exhaust Emission Standards

In 1990, Congress set up a detailed set of requirements for light-duty vehicles (LDVs, i.e., passenger cars) and light-duty trucks (LDTs). Light-duty trucks are defined under the CAA, by reference to the pre-existing EPA regulations, as motor vehicles that have a gross vehicle weight rating (GVWR) of 8,500 lbs. or less and that have one of the following features: designed primarily for transportation of property, or derived from such a vehicle; designed for transportation of more than twelve persons; or with special features enabling off-street use.[16]

Congress specified a set of tailpipe standards to be phased in beginning in model year 1994. These standards are generally referred to as the Tier 1 standards. Under Section 206(g), Congress set forth standards for nonmethane hydrocarbons (NMHC—methane has been excluded from the measurements because it is not considered a significant ozone precursor), CO, and NO_x from light-duty vehicles and light-duty trucks up to 6,000 lbs. GVWR. Larger LDTs in this category were provided a less stringent standard. All vehicles are required to meet two sets of standards, one for five years or 50,000 miles, whichever comes first, and one for ten years or 100,000 miles, whichever comes first. The required standards are shown in Exhibit 1.

Congress also required LDVs and LDTs up to 6,000 lbs. GVWR to meet PM standards of 0.08 gpm for five years or 50,000 miles and 0.10 gpm for ten years or 100,000 miles. Because gasoline-fueled vehicles can easily meet these standards without emission control devices, the PM standards are primarily aimed at diesel-fueled vehicles.

Section 202(h) mandated, beginning in the 1996 model year, LDTs over 6,000 lbs. GVWR to meet revised standards on a phased schedule. These standards are set forth in Exhibit 2.

Because diesel-fueled vehicles have traditionally had a more difficult time meeting NO_x requirements, Section 202(g) and (h) provide some relief for diesel-fueled vehicles from the Tier 1 NO_x standards, either by requiring a less stringent standard or, in the case of the larger LDTs, requiring no five-year standard. This relief lasts only until the 2003 model year.

EXHIBIT 1. Emission Standards for Light-Duty Vehicles and Trucks up to 6,000 lbs. GVWR (in gpm)

Vehicle Type	Column A 5 years/50,000 miles			Column B 10 years/100,000 miles		
	NMHC	CO	NO$_x$	NMHC	CO	NO$_x$
LDVs/LDTs (up to 3,750 lbs. LVW)	0.25	3.4	0.4*	0.31	4.2	0.6*
LDTs (3,751–5,750 lbs. LVW)	0.32	4.4	0.7**	0.40	5.5	0.97

Standards are expressed in grams per mile.
Column A standards, for purposes of vehicle certification under Section 206, shall apply to a useful life of five years or 50,000 miles. Column B standards, for purposes of vehicle certification under Section 206, shall apply to a useful life of ten years.
*In the case of diesel-fueled light-duty trucks (0–3,750 LVW) and light-duty vehicles, before the model year 2004, in lieu of the 0.4 and 0.6 standards for NO$_x$ the applicable standards for NO$_x$, shall be 1.0 gpm for a useful life of five years or 50,000 miles (or the equivalent), whichever first occurs, and 1.25 gpm for a useful life of ten years or 100,000 miles (or the equivalent), whichever first occurs.
**This standard does not apply to diesel-fueled, light-duty trucks (3,751 to 5,750 lbs. LVW).

EXHIBIT 2. Emission Standards for Light-Duty Trucks over 6,000 lbs. GVWR (in gpm)

Light-Duty Truck Test Weight	Column A 5 years/50,000 miles			Column B 11 years/120,000 miles			
	NMHC	CO	NO$_x$	NMHC	CO	NO$_x$	PM
3,751–5,750 lbs. TW	0.32	4.4	0.7*	0.46	6.4	0.98	0.10
Over 5,750 lbs. TW	0.39	5.0	1.1*	0.56	7.3	1.53	0.12

Standards are expressed in grams per mile.
Column A standards, for purposes of vehicle certification under Section 206, shall apply to a useful life of five years or 50,000 miles. Column B standards, for purposes of vehicle certification under Section 206, shall apply to a useful life of ten years.
*Not applicable to diesel-fueled light-duty trucks.

Congress specifically mandated, in Section 202(b)(1)(C), that the EPA could not revise the Tier 1 standards prior to model year 2004. However, Congress set in place the mechanism for EPA promulgation of standards thereafter. Under Section 202(i), the EPA and the Office of Technology Assessment[17] are required to perform a study designed to determine whether Phase II standards requiring even further emission reductions are needed for light-duty vehicles and light-duty trucks with a test weight below 3,750 lbs. Congress established as a benchmark for further requirements the following standards: 0.125 gpm for NMHC, 0.2 gpm for NO$_x$, and 1.7 gpm for CO. The benchmark useful life was ten years or 100,000 miles.

Congress required the EPA to determine, based on the study, whether (1) there is a need for further emission reductions; (2) the technology for meeting more stringent emission standards will be available (taking into account cost, lead time, energy, and safety impacts); and (3) it will be cost-effective to obtain further emission reductions. If any one of these criteria are not met, the EPA is not to issue more stringent standards under this subsection. If all three criteria are met, then the EPA must promulgate the benchmark standards, or alternative standards, to take effect beginning in model year 2004, 2005, or 2006.

The EPA submitted its final study in a report to Congress dated July 31, 1998.[18] The study indicated that in the 2004 time frame, there will be a need for emission reductions to aid in meeting and maintaining several National Ambient Air Quality Standards (NAAQS), particularly those for ozone and PM. The study found ample evidence that technologies will be available in that time frame for light-duty vehicles and trucks to meet standards more stringent than the existing Tier 1 standards. In addition, the study provided evidence that such standards could be implemented at a similar cost per ton of pollutants reduced as other programs aimed at similar air quality problems.

Based on this study, the EPA promulgated Tier 2 standards for light-duty vehicles and trucks, to be phased in beginning in model year 2004.[19] The final Tier 2 rule created a comprehensive program that is far more ambitious than was initially contemplated in Section 202(i). First, the standards promulgated are substantially more stringent than the benchmark standards provided in Section 202(i). Following passage of the 1990 amendments, emission control technologies developed that allowed emissions to be reduced to levels well below the conservative predictions provided in 1990.

The second comprehensive element of the program is the range of vehicles covered by the program. Section 202(i) refers only to light-duty vehicles and the lightest light-duty trucks. However, the final Tier 2 regulations apply not only to those vehicles, but to all light-duty trucks and also to medium-duty passenger vehicles (MDPVs), which are defined as vehicles with GVWR between 8,500 and 10,000 lbs. that are designed primarily for the transportation of persons. The EPA relied on its authority under Subsections (a) and (b) of Section 202 to regulate these vehicles. The main purpose for including these vehicles in the program was to cover emissions from minivans and sport-utility vehicles (SUVs), some of which come under the EPA definitions of heavy light-duty truck and MDPV. These vehicles had greatly increased in popularity in the 1990s and had been subject to standards that were much less stringent than those for automobiles. It was a stated goal of the Tier 2 rule to ensure that larger passenger vehicles were subject to the same standards as passenger cars.[20]

The third comprehensive element of the program is a requirement that gasoline refiners lower the sulfur in gasoline to 30 parts per million (ppm) on average. This requirement, promulgated under Section 211 of the CAA, will be discussed in more detail in Chapter 11. It is important to note here that the sulfur limitation was a critical element in ensuring that light-duty vehicles and trucks could meet the stringent Tier 2 standards throughout the

EXHIBIT 3. Tier 2 Emission Standards for Light-Duty Vehicles and Trucks (in gpm)

Column A: 50,000 miles				Column B: 10 years (11 years for LDTS > 6,000 lb. GVWR)/120,000 miles				
NMOG	CO	NO$_x$	HCHO	NMOG	CO	NO$_x$	PM	HCHO
0.075	3.4	0.05	0.015	0.090	4.2	0.07	0.01	0.018

useful life of the vehicles. The advanced emission controls that would be used to meet the stringent Tier 2 standards are sensitive to sulfur in gasoline, and would deteriorate significantly if sulfur in gasoline were not lowered to the levels in the final Tier 2 rule. The EPA has said that this approach of lowering emission levels from vehicles simultaneously with requiring cleaner fuels in such vehicles treats the vehicle and fuel as a single "system."[21] This "system" approach has been a hallmark of the EPA's recent rules regulating motor vehicles and will likely continue.

The Tier 2 program allows manufacturers to certify each of their vehicle families to one of several different bins, each with its own set of emission requirements.[22] The program initially contains eleven bins, but the three top bins with the highest emission levels are eliminated after the Tier 2 program is fully phased in. In addition, each manufacturer must ensure that its fleet average NO$_x$ emissions are no higher than 0.07 gpm, which equates to the fifth bin in the Tier 2 bin table.[23] Because manufacturers' average NO$_x$ levels must match the NO$_x$ levels in bin 5, levels of other pollutants—PM, CO, nonmethane organic gas, or "NMOG" (similar to NMHC), and formaldehyde (HCHO)—will likely also be approximately at bin 5 levels, which are shown in Exhibit 3.

The National Low Emission Vehicle Program

The National Low Emission Vehicle (NLEV) program is a voluntary emissions control program that manufacturers, the EPA, and several states negotiated in the late 1990s.[24] It resulted from several events not contemplated in the 1990 amendments.

As noted above, the 1990 amendments prevented the EPA from mandating standards more stringent than Tier 1 standards prior to the 2004 model year. Manufacturers had wanted this provision to allow a period of stability between Phase I and Phase II standards. However, emission control technology continued to improve in the 1990s, due in part to California's separate low emission vehicle (LEV) program, under which manufacturers were required to meet more stringent standards that were phased in gradually over several years beginning in 1994. As discussed below in the section on preemption, many states, particularly those in the northeast, who were faced with the need to find major reductions in ozone concentrations to meet the ozone NAAQS, decided to implement California's LEV program using the authority granted them under Section 177.

Thus, automakers, having successfully prevented the EPA from promulgating new standards to be applicable between 1994 and 2004, were faced with the potential of fifty-one [per Historical Standards section] separate programs implementing new standards during that time frame. Automobile manufacturers strongly opposed these state measures. One reason for the opposition was the fact that manufacturers would be faced with a patchwork of emission control programs in different states, each with potential differences in implementation and enforcement. Another major obstacle for manufacturers was the requirement in California, and other states, that a certain percentage of each manufacturer's vehicles must be zero emission vehicles (ZEVs). Under California's initial regulations, the percentage of ZEVs (which at the time was recognized to mean electric vehicles) required in manufacturer fleets started at two percent in 1998 and rose to ten percent by 2003. Manufacturers believed that ZEVs could not be manufactured in a manner that could make them economically competitive with conventional vehicles, and that they would not be able to sell them in the volumes contemplated by the mandate.

Manufacturers were therefore eager for the EPA to implement a national program that avoided the patchwork of programs feared by manufacturers and that did not require ZEVs. The EPA agreed to work with manufacturers and states to craft such a program, but only if all manufacturers agreed to be bound by the program's provisions and only if the emission reductions from the program were comparable to those from the California LEV program. In return, manufacturers wanted states to promise not to implement their own vehicle emission programs until 2004.

After several years of negotiations, the EPA promulgated a series of rules laying out the requirements of the NLEV program.[25] The NLEV program would be implemented in thirteen northeastern states beginning in 1999 and would be a nationwide program by 2001. Under the NLEV program, manufacturers would have to meet emission standards similar to those for the California LEV program, including a fleet average NMOG standard that would be made more stringent over time and would eventually match the NMOG standard for the LEV vehicle category. The NLEV program did not include any requirements to manufacture ZEVs. The EPA believed that the ZEV requirement was more designed to spur technology than to affect emissions directly, and the EPA believed that the California LEV program, which was not affected by the NLEV program, would be sufficient to spur the appropriate technology.

Manufacturers subsequently opted into the program, despite the fact that some of the northeastern states decided not to eliminate their state LEV programs,[26] and manufacturers have met the NLEV standards as required under the program. The NLEV program stands out as an example of how cooperative efforts between federal and state governments and industry can lead to substantial emission reductions implemented in an efficient and cost-effective manner.

Supplemental Emission Standards

One of the most important elements of a motor vehicle emissions control program is the need to ensure that the test for determining emissions levels is rigorous and reflects the conditions that the motor vehicle is expected to see in actual use. Emission standards for light-duty vehicles and trucks have traditionally been measured over a federal test procedure (FTP) that was developed in the 1960 and early 1970s and that was intended to simulate urban driving.

By 1990, however, many believed that the FTP was out of date and did not include important elements of normal driving; in particular, high speed and rapid accelerations. In the 1990 amendments, Congress specifically revised Section 206 to require that the EPA review and revise as necessary its test procedures to ensure that vehicles will be tested under circumstances reflecting actual current driving conditions.[27]

In October 1996, following an extensive study of driving patterns and the representativeness of the existing FTP, the EPA published revisions to the FTP for light-duty vehicles and light-duty trucks designed to address some of the weaknesses of the existing procedure.[28] The new test procedure adds two new supplemental test cycles that are designed to be more realistic in its representation of aggressive driving behavior (high speed and rapid acceleration), rapid speed fluctuations, driving behavior following start-up, and use of air conditioning. The EPA also published revisions designed to reflect real road forces on the test dynamometer more accurately. Accompanying these revisions were supplemental emission standards for the new test cycles, which are referred to as SFTP (Supplemental FTP) standards. These standards were supplemented in the NLEV rule by new standards, which applied only for the first 4,000 miles of vehicle life.[29] These standards were then incorporated and slightly modified in the Tier 2 rule.[30]

Controls on Evaporative Emissions, Including Refueling Emissions

In addition to emitting pollution from their tailpipes, many motor vehicles emit "evaporative emissions"; that is, emissions caused by fuel evaporation. Gasoline-fueled vehicles, including virtually all light-duty vehicles and trucks, have particularly high evaporative emissions. These emissions are all hydrocarbons and include HAPs, particularly benzene. Evaporative emissions tend to occur in one of three ways: (1) during motor vehicle refueling; (2) during operation, also referred to as "running losses"; and (3) during periods of nonoperation when the vehicle is exposed to high ambient temperatures. Regulation of these emissions had traditionally taken a backseat to regulation of exhaust emissions, but in the 1990 amendments, Congress added several provisions to ensure that these emissions were regulated.

CAA Section 202(a)(6) relates to regulation of refueling emissions, also referred to as onboard refueling vapor recovery. Under that section, the EPA was directed to work with the Department of Transportation to promulgate standards requiring that onboard vapor recovery systems be installed on light-duty vehicles, which would meet an emissions capture efficiency of 95 percent.

On April 15, 1992, the EPA issued a decision not to require onboard canisters but instead to rely on Stage II gasoline fuel pump recovery systems.[31] The Department of Transportation's National Highway Traffic Safety Administration had questioned the safety of onboard canisters even before the 1990 amendments and prevailed on the EPA to drop the vehicle controls.

This decision was challenged in *Natural Resources Defense Council v. Reilly,* in which the D.C. Circuit rejected the EPA's decision to rely on gasoline fuel pump controls.[32] The EPA argued that the statutory requirement to consult with the Department of Transportation gave it the discretion to defer onboard controls in light of safety concerns. The court found that the requirement to promulgate vehicle controls was unambiguous and that the agency decision was not entitled to deference under *Chevron USA, Inc. v. Natural Resources Defense Council.*[33] The court rejected the EPA's position that it could substitute Stage II controls for onboard controls, set aside the EPA decision, and ordered the agency to adopt onboard control regulations.

In April of the following year, the EPA promulgated a final rule requiring the onboard refueling equipment.[34] The rule phases in the requirements for light-duty vehicles over a three-year period beginning in the 1998 model year, with a later phase-in period for light-duty trucks. Test procedures, a specific refueling emission standard, certification requirements, and enforcement provisions are also included in the rules.

Regarding evaporative running loss emissions and emissions during nonoperation, the 1990 amendments added Section 202(k), which required the EPA to promulgate regulations covering evaporative emissions during operation and during two or more days of nonuse. The EPA responded by issuing regulations tightening its test procedures.[35] The procedures are essentially designed to present a more challenging set of test conditions to promote more effective evaporative emission control technology. The rule also limits fuel pump dispensing rates to ten gallons per minute for most facilities.

The Tier 2 rule subsequently promulgated more stringent standards for LDVs, LDTs, and MDPVs. The standards essentially cut in half the emissions permitted for nonoperation evaporative emissions.[36] These new standards will be phased on the same schedule as the Tier 2 exhaust standards, from model year 2004 to 2009.

Onboard Diagnostics and Service Information

Another control measure required by the 1990 CAA Amendments is onboard diagnostics. A vehicle's onboard diagnostics system is designed to check whether the vehicle's emission control systems are working properly. If an emission control system is not working properly, the onboard diagnostics system alerts the vehicle driver that a malfunction exists and places a code in the vehicle's computer memory identifying the particular malfunction for the mechanic who services the vehicle. The 1990 amendments added Section

202(m), which requires the EPA to promulgate a rule mandating the installation of diagnostics equipment on light-duty vehicles and light-duty trucks. The section requires the onboard equipment to identify emission-related systems deterioration or malfunction (including the oxygen sensor and catalytic converter); to alert the vehicle operator to the likely need for system maintenance or repair; to provide for the storage and retrieval of fault codes; and to provide access to the stored information.

The EPA published final regulations implementing these requirements in 1993.[37] Pursuant to these regulations, vehicles manufactured beginning in model year 1994 must detect emission-related malfunctions including catalyst deterioration, evaporative emission control deterioration, misfire, and oxygen sensor deterioration.[38] Once the malfunction is detected and confirmed, vehicle dashboards must illuminate with a message such as "Service Engine Soon," and the message must stay illuminated until the malfunction is fixed. The vehicle computer also stores an error code that provides information to repair personnel regarding the likely malfunction. The most recent revision of these requirements was promulgated in 1998.[39] The EPA has also promulgated regulations requiring checks of onboard diagnostics malfunction-indicator lights in certain state inspection and maintenance programs.[40]

Section 202(m)(5) requires that the EPA promulgate regulations requiring manufacturers to provide the service and repair industry with information necessary to make use of the onboard diagnostics systems and any other information needed to make emission-related diagnoses and repairs. The EPA published final regulations implementing this requirement in 1995.[41] The regulations required that manufacturers provide all service manuals and other materials that they give to their dealerships to unaffiliated "aftermarket" service and repair personnel, for a reasonable cost.[42] The regulations also require that manufacturers provide further information and access to equipment that would allow aftermarket technicians to communicate with the vehicle computer to better determine how to repair the vehicle.

Several associations representing the aftermarket parts industry sued the EPA in 1996. The associations claimed that the EPA violated the CAA by permitting California to enforce its regulations requiring that vehicle onboard computers be resistant to tampering.[43] The parts manufacturers claimed that this "anti-tampering" provision violated Section 202(m)(5) because it prevented aftermarket parts manufacturers from extracting information they needed from vehicle computers to build their parts. The D.C. Circuit ruled against the parts manufacturers, agreeing with the EPA and vehicle manufacturers that information needed to manufacture aftermarket parts was not information needed to repair vehicles, and was potentially protected by Section 202(m)(5)'s language protecting trade secrets.[44]

Cold CO Standards

An additional issue for light-duty vehicles and trucks is the cold CO standard, one of the regulatory initiatives that the EPA had been working on at the time of the 1990 amendments. The EPA research had indicated that at very cold temperatures CO emissions could be significantly higher than when the same engine was operating at warmer temperatures. In addition, the EPA was concerned because of data showing that the major source of the problem for most CO nonattainment areas was motor vehicle emissions. This regulatory initiative was adopted in the 1990 amendments.

Under Section 202(j), the EPA was required to promulgate regulations to control CO emissions from light-duty vehicles and trucks when operated at 20 degrees Fahrenheit. On July 17, 1992, the EPA published a rule limiting CO emissions at 20 degrees Fahrenheit from light-duty vehicles and trucks to 10.0 gpm.[45] Under the phase-in schedule established in the statute, 40 percent of the vehicles must comply by the 1994 model year, 80 percent by 1995, and 100 percent by the 1996 and later model years. The statute also authorized the EPA to promulgate cold temperature CO regulations for heavy-duty vehicles and engines.[46] Finally, the statute provides for Phase II standards if, by June 1, 1997, six or more nonattainment areas have a CO design value of 9.5 ppm or greater. In such a case, the CO standard at 20 degrees Fahrenheit may not exceed 3.4 gpm for light-duty vehicles or 4.4 gpm for light-duty trucks up to 6,000 lbs. GVWR.

Emission Standards for Heavy-Duty Vehicles and Engines

New Emission Standards Since 1990 Amendments

Though the EPA initially focused its attention on reducing emissions from passenger cars, in recent years the agency has directed considerable energy towards reducing emissions from large trucks and buses, which the CAA calls heavy-duty vehicles and engines. Under Section 202(a)(3) of the CAA, as amended in 1990, the EPA must set heavy-duty engine standards reflecting the "greatest degree of emission reduction achievable" from available technology giving appropriate consideration to "cost, energy, and safety factors" associated with such technology. The agency is allowed to establish different standards for different classes based on gross vehicle weight, horsepower, type of fuel used, or other factors deemed appropriate. Manufacturers may comply with heavy-duty engine standards by averaging the emissions of their different engine families, or by banking emissions credits in one year for use in a later year.[47] Manufacturers may also trade emission credits among themselves, but this flexibility is rarely used.

The 1990 amendments included a provision requiring the EPA to reduce NO_x emissions from new heavy-duty trucks to 4.0 grams per brake horsepower hour (g/bhp-hr) by model year 1998.[48] In 1993, the agency published the 4.0 g/bhp-hr standard for 1998 and later model years.[49] In 1997, the EPA promulgated new regulations further reducing NO_x and NMHC emission levels for heavy-duty diesel engines, beginning in model year 2004.[50] Beginning that year, the combined level of NO_x and NMHC can be no higher than 2.5 g/bhp-hr. Standards for heavy-duty gasoline engines were later reduced to 1.0 g/bhp-hr, beginning in model year 2005, though manufacturers could meet a less stringent level of 1.5 g/bhp-hr if they agreed to meet the standard beginning in either 2003 or 2004.[51]

EXHIBIT 4. Emission Standards for Heavy-Duty Engines (in g/bhp-hr)[54]

NMHC	NO_x	PM	CO
0.14	0.20	0.01	15.5 (14.4 for gasoline)

In the 1997 rule, the EPA indicated that it believed substantial further reductions in emissions from diesel engines would not be possible without a reduction in sulfur levels from diesel fuel.[52] However, there were advanced emission controls being developed that could meet substantially more stringent standards if fuel sulfur levels were also reduced. As a result, the EPA began to review the possibility of reducing diesel engine emission levels while at the same time reducing sulfur levels in diesel fuel. This process culminated in the publication of a rule (called the Phase 2 rule) drastically reducing emissions from heavy-duty engines and vehicles and at the same time reducing sulfur levels from diesel fuel.[53] As with the Tier 2 light-duty vehicle rule discussed above, the EPA treated the engine and fuel as a single "system," with the fuel sulfur limitation as a critical element in ensuring that engine standards could be met throughout the engines' useful life. The standards for heavy-duty engines are shown in Exhibit 4.

These standards will be phased in beginning in model year 2007 for diesel engines and 2008 for gasoline engines. Standards that are similar in stringency were also promulgated for heavy-duty vehicles with vehicle weight at or below 14,000 lbs. GVWR. Heavy-duty vehicles are tested as complete vehicles rather than as loose engines.

Accompanying these new standards will be new fuel specifications that lower sulfur levels in diesel fuel by 97 percent compared with current levels. This rule was challenged by several parties in the Court of Appeals for the District of Columbia Circuit. The court upheld the rule, noting that the EPA's judgment on technological issues is entitled to deference and that the EPA need show only that technology will be available in the lead time provided, not that the technology is currently available.[55]

Supplemental Emission Standards

As noted above, one of the most important elements of a strong motor vehicle emissions control program is a test procedure that reflects the conditions that the motor vehicle is expected to see in actual use. As with emission standards for light-duty vehicles and trucks, emission standards for heavy-duty engines had for many years been measured over an FTP that was intended to simulate urban driving, and contained a substantial amount of transient (i.e., acceleration and deceleration) operation. However, in the late 1990s, the EPA began to find evidence that heavy-duty engines produced since the late 1980s were emitting pollutants, particularly NO_x, at levels well above the federal standard when those engines were operating over conditions not well tested on the existing FTP. In particular, the EPA found that NO_x emissions in many engines were increasing when the engines were run over extended "steady state" conditions, for example, extended highway driving with few starts and stops. This type of driving constituted a great deal of the operations of heavy-duty engines, particularly the largest engines. The EPA estimated that there would be excess emissions totaling 15 million excess tons of NO_x over the life of the engines.[56]

As a result, the EPA brought civil challenges against seven heavy-duty engine manufacturers, alleging that the manufacturers programmed their onboard computers to reduce the emission controls on the engines (e.g., through fuel injection timing adjustments) under conditions reasonably expected to occur in normal operations and use but not substantially covered by the FTP.[57] This would constitute a "defeat device" under the EPA's regulations and is forbidden under the CAA.[58] The EPA and the manufacturers subsequently entered into consent decrees, in which the manufacturers agreed to take certain actions with regard to existing and future engines, including a "pull-ahead" of the 2.5 g/bhp-hr standard from model year 2004 to October 2002, and to pay civil penalties.[59]

The EPA also embarked on a regulatory program to make it more difficult for manufacturers to use such strategies in the future. In particular, in 2000, the EPA promulgated two new test procedures, the supplemental steady state (SSS) test and the not-to-exceed (NTE) test.[60] The SSS test, later renamed the supplemental emission test (SET), is a traditional test procedure that tests emissions at specific steady-state operating points for a specific periods of time. The NTE test is a more wide-ranging and flexible procedure. Under the NTE test, an engine can be tested at any operating point or points within the normal operation of the engine and the engine must not exceed a specific level of emissions at those points over a thirty-second (or longer) period. The NTE test approach allows engines to be tested on the road, which is substantially more convenient, and more realistic, than having to test engines by taking them out of their cabs.[61]

Each test was accompanied by numerical standards. The standards for the SSS test were the same as those for the FTP. The standards for the NTE test were the FTP standards multiplied by 1.25, to allow sufficient room given the wide range of the test. In the Phase 2 rule, discussed above, the EPA increased the multiplier to 1.5 to account for the increased stringency of the FTP standards.[62]

The NTE procedure has been challenged by engine manufacturers in the Court of Appeals for the District of Columbia Circuit, and the parties are currently engaged in negotiations that are still in progress at the time of the writing of this chapter.[63]

Other Requirements for Heavy-Duty Engines and Vehicles

The recent regulations of heavy-duty engines have additionally extended several of the regulations on light-duty vehicles to some of the heavy-duty fleet. In particular, the October 6, 2000, rule discussed above extended the requirement for onboard diagnostics systems to heavy-duty vehicles and engines below 14,000 lbs. GVWR and also required onboard refueling vapor recovery systems in gasoline-fueled heavy-duty vehicles up to 10,000 lbs. GVWR.[64] Evaporative emission standards similar to those for light-duty vehicles and engines also apply to heavy-duty vehicles and engines.[65]

Special Requirements for Urban Buses

Under Section 219 of the CAA, the EPA was required to issue standards applicable to urban bus emissions for the 1994 and later model years. Although urban buses use heavy-duty engines, and are generally regulated similarly to heavy-duty trucks, the two types of vehicles are operated differently. Unlike long-haul trucks, urban buses spend much more of their time at lower speeds and accelerating and decelerating in urban traffic. In addition, they are subject to much more frequent maintenance intervals and generally have a shorter service life.

On March 24, 1993, the EPA published a rule establishing more stringent PM standards for urban buses than for other heavy-duty engines.[66] The rule established a PM standard for 1994 and 1995 model-year urban buses of 0.07 g/bhp-hr, which is further reduced to 0.05 g/bhp-hr for 1996 and later model years. The rule also extended from eight years to ten years the useful life for buses regulated under the standards. Under the Phase 2 rule discussed above, the PM standards for all heavy-duty engines, including urban bus engines, is reduced to 0.01 ppm beginning in model year 2007.

Under authority provided in Section 219(d), the EPA has also established provisions for an urban bus rebuild/retrofit program. The program affects 1993 and earlier model-year urban buses (operating in metropolitan areas with a population of 750,000 or more) whose engines are rebuilt or replaced after January 1, 1995.[67] Under the rebuild/retrofit program, affected urban bus companies rebuilding their engines after January 1, 1995, must use an engine retrofit kit that has been certified by the EPA as having low PM emissions. This program is the first of its kind to use a certification program to reduce emissions from engines already in use, and the EPA and states may use similar approaches in the future to deal with in-use emissions from mobile sources.

Clean-Fuel Vehicle Programs

Although the 1990 CAA Amendments scaled back the ambitious program for clean-fuel vehicles proposed by the first Bush administration, two significant programs remain relating to vehicle fleets and the California Pilot Test Program. In Sections 241 *et seq.*, Congress established standards for vehicles operated on "clean alternative fuel," defined as methanol, ethanol, 85 percent mixture of alcohol-based fuel with gasoline, reformulated gasoline, diesel, natural gas, liquefied petroleum gas, hydrogen, or electricity.[68] Congress established clean-fuel vehicle standards in two phases: Phase I begins with the 1996 model year and Phase II takes effect beginning with the 2001 model year.[69] Under the program, these requirements apply to "covered fleets" of more than ten vehicles in defined ozone and CO nonattainment areas.[70] The program does not apply to certain exempt fleets such as rental cars, dealer demonstration vehicles, law enforcement and other emergency vehicles, and nonroad vehicles (including farm and construction vehicles).

The EPA promulgated implementing regulations for the clean-fuel fleet program in late 1993.[71] Under the CAA, areas classified as serious, severe, and extreme nonattainment areas for ozone and areas with a CO design value at or above 16.0 ppm must revise their SIPs to incorporate a clean-fuel fleet program. Under the program, specified percentages of new vehicles acquired in 1998 and later model years by certain fleet owners are required to meet clean-fuel fleet vehicle emission standards. The rule provides that the requirement could be met by the purchase of new clean-fuel fleet vehicles, the conversion of conventional vehicles to clean-fuel fleet vehicles, or the purchase of credits under a credit program. The revised SIPs for affected states are required to include a credit program and to exempt clean-fuel fleet vehicles from certain transportation control measures. Emission standards and regulations for the conversion of conventional vehicles to clean-fuel fleet vehicles were issued by the agency in 1994.[72]

Under Section 249 of the CAA, the EPA is required to establish a separate California pilot program to study the operation of clean-fuel light-duty vehicles and light-duty trucks by the public.[73] Under the pilot program, at least 150,000 vehicles for the 1996 to 1998 model years, and 300,000 vehicles for every year thereafter, are to be produced and sold in the state. The program also requires the EPA to establish a voluntary "opt-in" program for other states, which allows other states to adopt the pilot program in their implementation plans. The EPA adopted regulations applicable to the California pilot program in 1994.[74] The EPA has also adopted emissions credit programs for the California pilot program and the clean-fuel fleet program.[75]

Given that the EPA has promulgated standards that essentially match the clean-fuel fleet standards nationwide beginning in 2001 and are more stringent than them beginning in 2004, it is doubtful whether this program will have much use in the future.

Emission Standards for Nonroad Sources

As noted above, the term nonroad engine is a catch-all category for internal combustion engines in vehicles and equipment that are not generally used on the highways but are self-propelled or portable or transportable, including cranes and other construction equipment, tractors, lawnmowers, chainsaws, all-terrain vehicles, portable generators, motorboats and ships, locomotives, snowmobiles, forklifts, mining trucks, and airport ground service equipment.

Prior to 1990, the EPA did not have explicit authority under Title II of the CAA to regulate nonroad engines. However, as regulation of on-highway motor vehicles and stationary sources of pollutants was requiring more and more stringent standards for these sources, emissions from nonroad engines were growing as a percentage of the overall emissions inventory. Congress therefore decided that the EPA should place particular attention on regulating nonroad sources. In the 1990 CAA Amendments, Congress added Section

213, which requires the EPA to study emissions from nonroad vehicles and engines to determine whether emissions from these sources are significant contributors to ozone and CO concentrations in more than one nonattainment area. If the EPA concludes that nonroad sources are significant contributors to CO or ozone concentrations in more than one nonattainment area, it must issue standards requiring the "greatest degree of emission reduction achievable," giving appropriate consideration to cost, noise, energy, and safety factors, for those classes or categories of nonroad engines that contribute to such pollution. Section 213 also provides the EPA with authority to issue standards controlling other pollutants, such as PM, emitted by nonroad engines. Lastly, the EPA must promulgate standards for emissions from locomotives and engines used in locomotives.

The EPA released its study of emissions from nonroad engines in November 1991.[76] The study revealed that emissions from nonroad engines accounted for more than 10 percent of the total VOCs emitted in at least twelve of the nineteen ozone nonattainment areas studied, more than 10 percent of the total NO_x emitted in at least sixteen of the nineteen ozone nonattainment areas studied, and more than 10 percent of the total CO emitted in at least six of the fourteen CO nonattainment areas studied. Based on the study, the EPA determined that emissions from nonroad sources are significant contributors to ozone and CO concentrations in more than one nonattainment area.[77]

In the same rule, the EPA promulgated its first set of emission standards for nonroad engines. The EPA promulgated CO, HC, PM, NO_x, and smoke standards for nonroad compression-ignition (CI) (i.e., diesel cycle) engines at or above 50 horsepower (37 kilowatts). These standards were upheld by the D.C. Circuit after a challenge by the National Mining Association.[78] The court found, among other things, that the EPA did not act arbitrarily by classifying engines in large mining equipment with other large CI engines in making the finding that such engines "cause or contribute" to ozone or CO pollution.

Since 1995, the EPA has also promulgated a series of rules regulating various categories of nonroad engines. The EPA has promulgated standards regulating emissions from the following: (1) spark-ignition (SI) (e.g., gasoline fueled) engines at or below 25 horsepower (19 kilowatts), excluding recreational vehicles;[79] (2) SI marine engines;[80] (3) locomotives;[81] (4) CI engines, both marine and land-based, below 50 horsepower;[82] (5) marine CI engines above 50 horsepower, excluding recreational engines and large oceangoing (Category 3) engines;[83] (6) SI engines above 25 horsepower;[84] (7) recreational SI land-based and CI marine engines;[85] and (8) engines in oceangoing Category 3 vessels.[86] As a result, no category of nonroad engines remains unregulated. In addition, the EPA promulgated a second phase of emission standards for large CI engines[87] and for small SI engines. The second phase of standards for small SI engines was divided between engines for non-handheld equipment, like lawnmowers, and engines for handheld equipment, like chainsaws and leaf blowers.[88]

The EPA was challenged on one of its recent nonroad rules, the rule promulgating Phase 2 standards for handheld small SI engines. In that case, Husqvarna, an engine manufacturer, claimed that the standards promulgated by the EPA were arbitrary and capricious and not supported by the record. The D.C. Circuit found in favor of the agency.[89] The court noted that it grants significant deference to the agency on issues within the EPA's expertise. The court also noted that the statute required standards that achieve the greatest degree of emission reduction achievable through available technology, taking into account factors such as cost, thus putting air quality as a overriding goal of Section 213, with cost being an important but subordinate secondary factor.

Enforcement Programs

The standards and emission reduction goals adopted by the EPA would be meaningless without a comprehensive program to show compliance with the standards. Congress provided the EPA with several tools to ensure that standards regulating emissions from motor vehicles and nonroad engines would be backed up with a vigorous enforcement program. These provisions were initially enacted in Sections 203 through 207 for enforcement of motor vehicle emission standards. When Congress extended Title II's authority to include nonroad engines, it added Section 213(d) to the CAA, which requires that standards for nonroad engines be subject to the same enforcement regime as motor vehicles, "with such modifications of the applicable regulations . . . as the Administrator deems appropriate."

Certification

The first step in the compliance process is certification. Under Section 203 of the CAA, manufacturers may not introduce new vehicles into commerce unless the vehicles are covered by a certificate of conformity demonstrating compliance with the appropriate standards. To obtain a certificate of conformity, the manufacturer must perform its own testing, usually on prototype vehicles, prior to introducing the vehicles into commerce. These prototypes are generally tested by the manufacturer and the data is supplied to the EPA. In some cases, however, the EPA will perform its own confirmatory testing.

Once the manufacturer has successfully completed the testing and the results are approved by the EPA, the agency issues a certificate of conformity. It allows the manufacturer to produce engines and vehicles built to the same specifications as the prototype. Although this has been an accepted form of testing for some time, some have asserted that the certification process was faulty because it uses custom-built prototypes that may operate quite differently from the mass-produced vehicles; because projected deterioration rate for the vehicles is often optimistic; and because vibration, heat, and other problems encountered in actual use are minimized.

In part as a response to this criticism, the EPA has recently put more emphasis on its "in use" testing program as a key element of its enforcement program. For example, the EPA recently promulgated revisions to its light-duty vehicle enforcement program, under the name Compliance Assurance Program (CAP) 2000.[90] The program simplifies the procedures for granting certifications, but requires manufacturers to test in-use vehicles to monitor in-use compliance with emission standards. A similar program has also been promulgated as a voluntary measure for nonroad small spark-ignited engines.[91]

Selective Enforcement Audits

The certificate of conformity, of course, demonstrates only that the prototype was able to comply with the standards. To determine whether the vehicles as built comply with the standards, the EPA performs assembly-line tests. Section 206(b) authorizes the EPA to perform tests on a sample of new vehicles or engines coming off of the assembly line.

The EPA has implemented this requirement in its selective enforcement audit (SEA) program. Under the SEA program, the EPA inspectors order a manufacturer to perform the FTP on a relatively small number of vehicles or engines randomly selected from those on the assembly line. If the vehicle or engines pass the test, the audit is complete. If the first tests indicate a compliance problem, a larger number is tested to determine whether the class passes or whether the certificate should be suspended or revoked. As initially promulgated in 1976, manufacturers were permitted only a 10 percent failure rate.[92] That acceptable failure rate, described as the "acceptable quality level," is now set at 40 percent.[93]

Recall Program

Under Section 207(c), if the EPA determines that a substantial number of vehicles or engines, though properly maintained and used, do not comply with the standards when in actual use throughout their useful life, the agency may order the manufacturer to recall and repair the class of vehicles or engines.

Predictably, the EPA and auto manufacturers have disagreed on what constitutes a "substantial number" and whether vehicles have been "properly maintained and used." With respect to a "substantial number" of failing vehicles, the courts have required "any number large enough to show that a 'systematic or pervasive problem in a particular class or category of vehicles' exists."[94] The "proper maintenance" issue is often raised by manufacturers fighting a recall order. The D.C. Circuit has recognized that the qualifier is "an acknowledgment of the limited ability of manufacturers to prevent those nonconformities primarily caused by intentional or negligent faulty maintenance by owners and mechanics."[95] However, the court also noted that reading the defense too broadly in favor of the manufacturers would remove "a large part of the incentive to design emission systems that would operate effectively while in actual use." The court held that the EPA was not restricted to using vehicles in the recall testing that were "laboratory-pure" and followed the manufacturer's maintenance instructions in every last detail.[96] In practice, the EPA tries to screen out vehicles that have not been properly maintained in accordance with the manufacturer's instructions so as to deprive the manufacturer of the defense if the recall order is contested.

As noted above, the EPA has increasingly been emphasizing in-use testing in its enforcement of its standards. Its CAP 2000 program for light-duty vehicles is designed to place additional emphasis on manufacturer testing of engines after they are in operation. Similarly, a key reason for the EPA's promulgation of NTE standards for heavy-duty on-highway engines was the ability to test compliance with NTE standards using on-road testing in trucks, rather than having to remove engines from trucks prior to testing, which has been an impediment to having a vigorous in-use testing program for heavy-duty trucks.

Warranties

Section 207 of the CAA provides for two types of warranties. Under Section 207(a), the manufacturer must warrant to the consumer that the vehicle is "designed, built, and equipped" to conform with applicable emission standards at the time of sale and is free from defects that would cause the vehicle to fail to conform to standards during the useful life of the vehicle. Congress also provided a second warranty under Section 207(b) that is based on the performance of the vehicle. In the performance warranty, the manufacturer warrants that the emissions system will perform properly throughout its useful life as long as the vehicle is maintained in accordance with the manufacturer's instructions and the consumer is required to bear a penalty or sanction as a result of the failure. The warranty period is two years or 24,000 miles generally and eight years and 80,000 miles for "specified major emission control components." The specified major components include only a vehicle's catalytic converter, electronic emissions control unit, and onboard diagnostics device, unless other components are designated by the EPA.

Tampering and Defeat Devices

Once a manufacturer has built a vehicle or engine to meet emission standards, it is important to ensure that users do not tamper with the vehicle or engines to remove, alter, or otherwise circumvent the emission control system. Congress therefore included Section 203(a)(3)(A) in the CAA, which makes it illegal for any person "to remove or render inoperative any device or element of design installed on or in a motor vehicle or . . . engine" to meet emission standards. Similarly, Section 203(a)(3)(B) make it illegal "for any person to manufacture or sell . . . or install, any part or component intended for use with . . . any motor vehicle or . . . engine where a principal effect of the part or component is to bypass, defeat, or render inoperative any device or element of design installed" to meet emission standards. This second prohibition, in addition to forbidding aftermarket manufacturers from building devices to, for example, bypass a catalytic converter, also forbids vehicle and engine manufacturers from building their vehicles and engines to apply emission control devices during emission tests but not apply them during non-test conditions. As noted above, the EPA recently alleged that several heavy-duty engine manufacturers had employed such defeat devices in their engines for heavy-duty trucks, leading to a series of enforcement actions taken against those manufacturers.

Aircraft

The EPA also has authority to promulgate standards for emissions from aircraft engines.[97] Compliance with such standards is assessed by the Secretary of Transportation, in connection with the "issuance, amendment, modification, suspension, or revocation of any certificate authorized by the Federal Aviation Act or the Department of Transportation Act."[98] Aircraft emission standards were promulgated in 1982 and amended in 1984[99] and 1997.[100] The EPA generally follows international standards for aircraft emissions.

Preemption

In 1967, Congress preempted states from adopting their own emission standards for new motor vehicles, except that the EPA was required to waive this preemption for California standards, unless the EPA found any of the following: (1) that the California standards are not as stringent as comparable federal standards; (2) that the California standards are required to meet compelling and extraordinary conditions; or (3) that the California standards are inconsistent with Section 202(a) of the CAA. Congress specifically noted that states could continue to regulate the use, operation, and movement of motor vehicles. In 1977, Congress granted increased flexibility to California, allowing the EPA to waive preemption for California standards that are as stringent "in the aggregate" as federal standards.[101] Congress also allowed other states with nonattainment areas to adopt California standards, as long as the state and California provided two years of lead time.[102]

The 1990 CAA Amendments provided two significant revisions to the preemption provisions for mobile sources. First, the amendments added two clauses to Section 177. Under the new provisions, states that adopt California standards for new motor vehicles may not directly or indirectly limit the sale of California-certified vehicles and may not take any action that would have the effect of creating a "third vehicle." Second, Congress added Section 209(e) to the CAA, which created a regime for preemption of state standards for nonroad engines that was similar to the existing regime for motor vehicles. However, Section 209(e) had some significant differences from the existing motor vehicle provisions, which are discussed in the following sections.

California Motor Vehicle Standards

The EPA has traditionally given California considerable discretion to create its own distinct regulatory program for motor vehicles. The EPA's Administrator has stated:

> [the] structure and history of the California waiver provision clearly indicate a Congressional intent and an EPA practice of leaving the decision on ambiguous and controversial public policy to California's judgment. . . . I would feel constrained to approve a California approach to the problem

which I might also feel unable to adopt at the federal level in my own capacity as regulator.[103]

The EPA's approach was affirmed by the D.C. Circuit in *Motor and Equipment Manufacturers Association v. EPA*.[104] In that decision, the court quoted the legislative history of Section 209(b), indicating that the waiver provision is intended "to afford California the broadest possible discretion in selecting the best means to protect the health of its citizens and the public welfare."[105] A more recent case, *Motor and Equipment Manufacturers Association v. Nichols*, reaffirmed this approach.[106] In that case, manufacturers of aftermarket parts claimed that California's regulations violated Section 202(m) of the statute because the California regulations did not provide access to onboard diagnostics information for the aftermarket. The court rejected this claim based on the statutory language of Section 202(m). However, the court also agreed with the EPA's contention that it was not required to weigh California's compliance with the provisions of Section 202(m) in the EPA's waiver determination because compliance with Section 202(m) was not one of the three enumerated factors that the EPA must weigh in determining whether to grant California a waiver. The court noted that requiring California to meet requirements in Section 202 other than those enumerated in Section 209(b) would make it virtually impossible for California to exercise the broad discretion that Congress provided in Section 209.[107]

Motor Vehicle Programs in Other States

Until the past decade, California was the only state that took advantage of the opportunity to promulgate state motor vehicle emission standards. Though Congress added Section 177 to the CAA in 1977, other states did not begin to make use of this provision until the 1990s. The impetus for the recent interest in Section 177 was California's 1990 promulgation of its LEV program. Under the program, manufacturers could build light-duty vehicles and trucks to meet any of five levels of emission standards. The five levels were, in order of stringency, Tier 1 standards, transitional low emission vehicle (TLEV) standards, LEV standards, ultra LEV (ULEV) standards, and zero emission vehicle (ZEV) standards. However, to ensure that manufacturers do not merely build vehicles that meet only the least stringent standards, California required manufacturers to meet a fleet average standard that in effect requires the manufacture of a significant number of lower-emitting vehicles. This fleet average increased in stringency from the beginning of the program until 2003, when it leveled out. California also required that a portion of each manufacturer's fleet be ZEVs, beginning in 1998 at two percent and growing to ten percent by 2003.

Initially, two states, Massachusetts and New York, promulgated and implemented programs under Section 177 mandating California's LEV requirements in those states. Automobile manufacturers attempted to block these state regulations by arguing that the regulations, though they are identical to California motor vehicle regulations, violate Section 177. Courts in both the First and Second Circuits upheld the New York and Massachusetts programs.[108] Maine and Vermont subsequently promulgated programs requiring the California LEV standards in those states. In addition, the Ozone Transport Commission (OTC), which covers eleven northeastern states, the District of Columbia, and northern Virginia, requested under Section 184 of the CAA that the EPA order all states in the OTC to use their authority under Section 177 to promulgate state LEV programs.[109] These state and regional actions were the principal catalysts for manufacturers' acceptance of the National Low Emission Vehicle program, discussed above, implemented by the EPA in 1998. The EPA granted the request of the OTC to require state programs under Section 184. However, the Court of Appeals for the D.C. Circuit reversed that order, stating that the EPA's order requiring states to implement California standards was essentially a federal requirement mandating standards more stringent than the federal Tier 1 standards, which the EPA is forbidden, under Section 202(b)(1)(C), to require before model year 2004.[110]

Subsequent to the initial round of litigation, California decided to amend its LEV program to delay the ZEV production mandate until 2003.[111] However, neither New York nor Massachusetts amended their regulations to correspond to the new California regulations. New York failed to revise its regulations at all, and was challenged by manufacturers. In *American Automobile Manufacturers Ass'n v. Cahill*, the Court of Appeals for the Second Circuit agreed with manufacturers that New York's ZEV mandate was a standard under Sections 209 and 177 and thus needed to be identical to California's ZEV mandate. The fact that New York's ZEV mandate was identical to an earlier version of California's mandate did not save it from preemption.[112]

Massachusetts did revise its ZEV mandate, but it revised the mandate to be identical not with California's regulations, but with separate voluntary memoranda of understanding that California had signed with various individual manufacturers. The First Circuit, using rationale similar to that in *Cahill*, found that Massachusetts's ZEV regulations were preempted under Sections 209 and 177 because the memoranda of understanding were not "standards" under those sections because they were "voluntary contractual agreements rather than legislation or formal administrative regulations."[113]

State Nonroad Engine Programs

When Congress passed the 1990 CAA Amendments, it included a regime for preemption of state standards regulating emissions from nonroad engines that is very similar to that already created for motor vehicles. Under Section 209(e), states and localities are forbidden from promulgating emission standards for new locomotives and new farm and construction equipment with horsepower below 175. With regard to other nonroad engines, California may enact and enforce emission standards if it receives authorization from the EPA. The criteria for California to receive authorization under Section 209(e) are virtually identical to the criteria for California to receive a waiver of preemption under Section 209(b) for motor vehicles. Moreover, once California receives authorization, other states with nonattainment areas may promulgate standards identical to California's, under Section 209(e)(2)(B), which is similar to Section 177.

However, there are two significant differences between preemption of state standards for nonroad engines and state standards for motor vehicles. First, there are two specific categories of new nonroad engines for which no state, even California, may promulgate standards: (1) new nonroad engines below 175 horsepower used in farm and construction equipment and (2) new nonroad engines used in locomotives. Second, the preemption of state standards was not specifically limited to standards for new nonroad engines. The EPA's initial regulations, which delineated the scope of preemption of state standards, interpreted this omission to imply that the preemption was limited to state standards for new nonroad engines, as the preemption for motor vehicles is limited.[114] Several parties challenged this interpretation, and the D.C. Court of Appeals, in *Engine Manufacturers Association v. EPA*,[115] agreed with the challengers that the omission of the word "new" meant that standards for both new and used nonroad engines were preempted. The court, however, upheld all other aspects of the EPA's rule, including the EPA's determination that states are not preempted from controlling, regulating, or restricting the use, operation, or movement of nonroad engines.

Preemption of State Aircraft Regulations

Like standards for other mobile sources, state standards for aircraft engines are preempted by the CAA. Unlike emission standards for other mobile sources, however, Congress did not allow any waiver of preemption for California or other states. Section 233 of the CAA tersely states that no state standard for any air pollutant from any aircraft or aircraft engine is permitted unless such standard is identical to federal standards. Given the international nature of air travel, it is not surprising that Congress believed that any state standard regulating aircraft engines would be an undue interference with air travel.

Notes

The views expressed in this chapter are those of the author and do not necessarily reflect any position of the U.S. Environmental Protection Agency. This chapter includes material originally written for the corresponding chapter on regulation of mobile sources in the previous edition of the *Clean Air Act Handbook*, which chapter was co-written by Michael J. Horowitz and Patrick Schlesinger.

1. U.S. EPA, Health Assessment Document for Diesel Exhaust: SAB Review Draft, EPA/600/8-90/057E (2000).

2. Pub. L. No. 89-272.

3. 31 Fed. Reg. 5170 (1966).

4. Pub. L. No. 90-148.

5. *Id*. § 208(a).

6. *See* CONGRESSIONAL RESEARCH SERVICE, HISTORY AND FUTURE OF SPARK IGNITION ENGINES, REPORT FOR THE SENATE COMM. ON PUBLIC WORKS; *Hearings on Automobile Steam*

Engine and Other External Combustion Engines Before the Senate Comm. on Commerce and the Subcomm. on Air & Water Pollution of the Senate Comm. on Public Works, 90th Cong. (1969).

7. Pub. L. No. 91-604.

8. *Id.* § 202(a)(1) and (2).

9. The section numbers provided in the 1970 CAA have, for the most part, been retained in later amendments.

10. 478 F.2d 615 (D.C. Cir. 1973).

11. *Id.* at 648.

12. *Id.* at 640.

13. Natural Resources Defense Council v. EPA, 655 F.2d 318, 328, 333 (D.C. Cir. 1981). *See also* Husqvarna v. EPA, 254 F.3d 195, 201.

14. Pub. L. No. 95-95.

15. Public Law No. 101-549 (November 15, 1990).

16. 40 C.F.R. § 86.1803-01.

17. The Office of Technology Assessment has since been eliminated by Congress.

18. EPA420-R-98-008.

19. 65 Fed. Reg. 6698 (2000).

20. *Id.* at 6701.

21. *Id.* at 6698.

22. 40 C.F.R. § 86.1811-04(c)(6).

23. *Id.* at § 86.1811-04(d).

24. 40 C.F.R. pt. 86 subpt. R.

25. 62 Fed. Reg. 31,192 (1997) and 63 Fed. Reg. 925 (1998).

26. 63 Fed. Reg. 11,374 (1998).

27. CAA § 206(h).

28. 61 Fed. Reg. 54,851 (1996).

29. 40 C.F.R. § 64.1708-99(e).

30. 65 Fed. Reg. 6790–91 (2000).

31. 57 Fed. Reg. 13,220 (1992).

32. 983 F.2d 259 (D.C. Cir. 1993).

33. 467 U.S. 837 (1984).

34. 59 Fed. Reg. 16,262 (1994).

35. 58 Fed. Reg. 16,002 (1993).

36. 65 Fed. Reg. 6748–49 (2000).

37. 58 Fed. Reg. 9648 (1993).

38. 40 C.F.R. § 86.094-17.

39. 63 Fed. Reg. 70,681 (1998).

40. 66 Fed. Reg. 18,155 (2001).

41. 60 Fed. Reg. 40,474 (1995).

42. 40 C.F.R. § 86.094-38(g).

43. Motor and Equipment Manufacturers Ass'n v. EPA, 142 F.3d 449 (D.C. Cir. 1998).

44. *Id.*

45. 57 Fed. Reg. 31,888 (1992).

46. CAA § 202(j)(4).

47. 55 Fed. Reg. 30,622 (1990) (codified at 40 C.F.R. § 86.091-15).

48. CAA § 202(a)(3)(B).

49. 58 Fed. Reg. 15,781 (1993).

50. 62 Fed. Reg. 54,694 (1997).

51. 65 Fed. Reg. 59,926 (2000).

52. 62 Fed. Reg. 54,694 (1997).

53. 66 Fed. Reg. 5002 (2001).

54. 40 C.F.R. §§ 86.007-11 and 86.008-10.

55. National Petrochemical & Refiners Ass'n, et al. v. EPA, 287 F.3d 1130 (D.C. Cir. 2002).

56. 65 Fed. Reg. 59,899 (2000).

57. 63 Fed. Reg. 59,330–34 (1998).

58. *See* CAA § 203(a)(3) and 40 C.F.R. § 86.004-2.

59. 63 Fed. Reg. 59,330–34 (1998).

60. 65 Fed. Reg. 59,896 (2000).

61. 64 Fed. Reg. 58,490 (1999).

62. 66 Fed. Reg. 64,679 (2001).

63. International Truck, et al. v. EPA, No. 00-1510 (D.C. Cir.).

64. 65 Fed. Reg. 59,916–18, 59,924–26, 59,929 (2000).

65. 66 Fed. Reg. 5044 (2001).

66. 58 Fed. Reg. 15,781 (1993).

67. 58 Fed. Reg. 21,359 (1993).

68. CAA § 241.

69. CAA § 243.

70. CAA § 241.

71. 58 Fed. Reg. 64,679 (1993).

72. 59 Fed. Reg. 50,042 (1994).

73. CAA § 249.

74. 59 Fed. Reg. at 50,042.

75. 58 Fed. Reg. 11,888 (1993); 57 Fed. Reg. 60,038 (1992).

76. U.S. EPA, Nonroad Engine and Vehicle Emission Study, EPA-21A-2001 (1991).

77. 59 Fed. Reg. 31,306 (1994).

78. Engine Manufacturers Ass'n v. EPA, 88 F.3d 1075 (D.C. Cir. 1996).

79. 60 Fed. Reg. 34,582 (1995).

80. 61 Fed. Reg. 52,088 (1996).

81. 63 Fed. Reg. 18,978 (1998).

82. 63 Fed. Reg. 56,967 (1998).

83. 64 Fed. Reg. 73,300 (1999).

84. 67 Fed. Reg. 68,242 (2002).

85. *Id.*

86. 68 Fed. Reg. 9745 (2003).

87. 63 Fed. Reg. 56,967 (1998).

88. 64 Fed. Reg. 15,208 (1999) and 65 Fed. Reg. 24,268 (2000).

89. Husqvarna v. EPA, 254 F.3d 195 (D.C. Cir. 2001).

90. 64 Fed. Reg. 23,906 (1999).

91. 65 Fed. Reg. 24,286 (2000).

92. 41 Fed. Reg. 31,471 (1976).

93. 40 C.F.R. § 86.610.

94. Chrysler Corp. v. EPA, 631 F.2d 865, 891 n.133 (D.C. Cir. 1980) (quoting EPA decision document).

95. *Id.* at 888.

96. *Id.* at 889.

97. CAA § 231.

98. CAA § 232.

99. 49 Fed. Reg. 41,002 (1984); 49 Fed. Reg. 31,875 (1984); 47 Fed. Reg. 58,470 (1982).

100. 62 Fed. Reg. 25,356 (1997).

101. CAA § 209(b).

102. CAA § 177.

103. 40 Fed. Reg. 23,101, 23,104 (1975).

104. 627 F.2d 1095 (D.C. Cir. 1979). See also Ford Motor Co. v. EPA, 606 F.2d 1293 (D.C. Cir. 1979).

105. *Id.* at 1110 (citing H.R. REP. No. 95-294, at 301–02 (1977)).

106. 142 F.3d 449 (D.C. Cir. 1998).

107. *Id.* at 462–64.

108. Motor Vehicle Mfrs. Ass'n v. New York DEC, 79 F.3d 1298 (2d Cir. 1996); Motor Vehicle Mfrs. Ass'n v. New York DEC, 17 F.3d 521 (2d Cir. 1994); American Auto. Mfrs. Ass'n v. Greenbaum, No. 93-10799-MA, 1993 U.S. Dist. LEXIS 15337 (D. Mass. Oct. 27, 1993), *aff'd*, 31 F.3d 13 (1st Cir, 1994).

109. 60 Fed. Reg. 4712 (1995).

110. Virginia v. U.S. EPA, 108 F.3d 1397 (D.C. Cir. 1997).

111. California Executive Order G-96-048, July 24, 1996.

112. American Automobile Manufacturers Ass'n v. Cahill, 152 F.3d 196 (2nd Cir. 1998).

113. Association of International Automobile Manufacturers v. Massachusetts Dep't of Environmental Protection, 208 F.3d 1 (1st Cir. 2000).

114. 59 Fed. Reg. 36,969 (1994).

115. 88 F.3d 1075 (D.C. Cir. 1996).

CHAPTER 11

Regulation of Fuels and Fuel Additives

JONATHAN S. MARTEL

Introduction

This chapter focuses on vehicle fuels as the counterpart to the vehicle in determining air pollutant emissions. Common conventional fuels such as gasoline and diesel fuel contain hundreds of separate organic chemical compounds. These compounds may evaporate into the air, react in the atmosphere to create other pollutants (e.g., ozone and particulate matter), and interact to affect the fuel's combustion properties and tailpipe emissions. In addition, gasoline and diesel fuel contain additives designed to enhance performance and to improve vehicle maintenance. These additives introduce many more chemical compounds that also are combusted and emitted. Unlike gasoline and diesel fuel, alternative fuels such as compressed natural gas (CNG), liquefied petroleum gas (LPG), methanol, and ethanol generally consist of a single compound and if liquid may be blended with gasoline. Even the simpler alternative fuels, however, react with constituents of the air during combustion to generate pollutants.

Measuring the emissions impacts of fuels presents special challenges. The motor vehicle emission standards discussed in Chapter 10 are based on emissions testing using standardized test fuels. Vehicles in use actually encounter fuels with varying compositions. The fuel composition can affect the same pollutants that are addressed in the vehicle regulations: hydrocarbons and nitrogen oxides (NO_x) that are the precursors to ozone and urban smog, toxic air pollutants, carbon monoxide (CO), and particulate matter. Further, changes in fuel composition can have different effects depending on the characteristics of the vehicle in which the fuel is burned. Therefore, understanding the effects of fuel changes on real-world emissions can be complicated and depends on extensive testing of many different vehicles while varying isolated fuel properties.

Despite the large potential health impact of fuel formulation, Environmental Protection Agency (EPA) attention to controlling pollutants by regulating the ingredients of fuels was limited prior to the Clean Air Act Amendments of 1990. Since the advent of Clean Air Act (CAA) regulation of motor vehicle emissions, the focus has primarily been on limiting emissions through vehicle technology. Indeed, the EPA based the elimination of lead additives, the first and most important regulation of gasoline, on the grounds that the lead would interfere with the effectiveness of catalytic converter technology. However, as vehicle technology has progressed and further improvement becomes more difficult in the face of persisting air quality problems, regulators have focused on the fuels that vehicles use. In particular, the dramatic expansion of fuels regulation programs in the 1990 CAA Amendments reflects this increased focus as part of the effort to meet the National Ambient Air Quality Standards (NAAQS) for ozone and CO and to make concrete progress in controlling toxic air pollutants. Most recently, the EPA has moved toward a "systems" approach, revising fuel and vehicle regulations simultaneously to address interactions between the two.

The fungibility of fuels and fuel additives and the existing distribution system for gasoline and diesel fuel in particular present unique challenges for EPA regulation and enforcement. In contrast to stationary sources and vehicles, it may not be possible for regulators to identify the manufacturer of fuels or additives in the distribution system. As fuels such as gasoline and diesel fuel make their way through the distribution system, transported from a refinery, by pipeline, barge, and truck through storage and terminal facilities and ultimately to retail stations, fuel components and additives may be blended into the fuel and products from various refineries may be blended together. Moreover, the regulated product ultimately disappears entirely, when it is combusted in consumers' vehicles. Therefore, regulators may have extreme difficulty connecting the product with its manufacturer.

As the fuels and fuel additive programs have developed, the EPA has addressed these complexities in a variety of ways. For enforcement, the EPA has developed an approach that relies on a system of record-keeping requirements together with presumptive and vicarious liability. In general, when the EPA finds fuel that is not in compliance with regulatory requirements, it presumes that each party that handled the product upstream is responsible for the violations, unless a party can show that it did not cause the problem. In addition, the EPA holds refiners vicariously liable for violations discovered at their branded distribution outlets, thus relying on branded refiners' control over downstream parties that operate under their brand name.

Conceptual Overview of Programs

The fuels provisions of the CAA are codified together at Section 211.[1] Section 211 establishes a few different approaches to regulation. First, the EPA has general authority to obtain information from manufacturers about all fuels and fuel additives and to take regulatory action when information warrants it. Subsections (a), (b), and (e) authorize the EPA to require registration, submission of basic information, and testing by manufacturers regarding health effects of fuels and additives. Subsection (c) gives the EPA general authority to regulate fuels and fuel additives if the EPA administrator believes that any emission product of the fuel or additive causes or contributes to air pollution or if any such product will impair the performance of a vehicle's emissions control equipment. Under these provisions, the EPA is equipped to gather information and has discretionary and general authority to take affirmative action to address identified problems.

The second regulatory approach essentially shifts the burden of persuasion to the manufacturers, requiring them to show that their new fuels and additives will not harm emissions control equipment and will thus not increase emissions. Section 211(f) prohibits manufacturers from introducing new fuels or additives into commerce or increasing their concentration unless the fuel or additive is "substantially similar" to any fuel or additive used in certification testing of vehicles. Presumptively, vehicles operating on fuels similar to those used in certification testing will meet the certification emissions standards when using those similar fuels. The EPA administrator is also authorized to waive the "substantially similar" prohibitions upon application of a manufacturer of a new fuel or additive. To do so, the applicant must establish that the new fuel or additive, or an increased concentration of an additive, as well as the emission products of the fuel or additive will *not* cause or contribute to a vehicle's failure to comply over its useful life with the emissions standards to which the vehicle is certified.

The third regulatory approach entails the implementation of very specific programs that Congress set out in detail in the statute to address problems in a particular manner. In Section 211(h), Congress built on EPA regulations promulgated under Section 211(c) to control the volatility of gasoline; in Section 211(k), Congress established by far the most specific fuels program for the reformulation of gasoline; and in Section 211(l), Congress required that gasoline contain detergent additives, pursuant to EPA specifications, to prevent the accumulation of engine and fuel supply deposits. In addition, in Section 211(i), Congress built on EPA regulations promulgated under Section 211(c) to control sulfur and aromatic hydrocarbon levels in diesel fuel to reduce emissions of particulate matter from diesel engines and to prevent sulfur in the fuel from plugging "trap oxidizer" technology needed to meet the EPA's new diesel engine particulate emission standards. Section 211(m) contains the one fuels program that the EPA directed states to adopt. Congress specified that states require the addition of oxygenates to gasoline to lower CO emissions in the winter months when CO pollution is a problem. Finally, Congress enacted Section 211(g) and (n) to support the EPA program previously adopted under Section 211(c) to phase down leaded gasoline. Section 211(g) prohibits misfueling unleaded gasoline engines with leaded gasoline, and Section 211(n) flatly prohibits any person from selling leaded gasoline for use in motor vehicles.

In addition to these substantive regulatory programs, Section 211(d) gives the EPA special authority to obtain civil penalties and seek injunctions to enforce the fuels provisions. Administrative penalties can be assessed in accordance with the general provisions in Section 205 of Title II.

Historical Development

Fuels regulation began with the basic registration requirements in Section 211(a) and (b).[2] Under the 1967 Air Quality Control Act, the Secretary of Health, Education, and Welfare (HEW) could designate fuels for registration, and the manufacturers would then have to provide their name and the fuel's name as well as basic information about additives in the fuel, including the name, manufacturer, recommended range of concentration, purpose in use, and chemical structure, when available. In 1969, the secretary of HEW proposed regulations for registration of gasoline additives that would have required manufacturers to furnish available information on emissions and health effects resulting from use of the additives and have also required that they conduct research to provide information on the emissions impact of the additives if it was not available at the time of registration. Controversy about these emissions and research requirements held up final action on those regulations.

The 1970 CAA expanded on the basic statutory registration requirements to give the EPA explicit authority in Section 211(b)(2) to require health-effects testing as a condition of registering a designated fuel. (The EPA succeeded HEW as the agency implementing the CAA soon after the 1970 Act.) To respond to identified health concerns, Congress added Section 211(c) authorizing the EPA administrator to regulate commerce in fuels and additives. While Congress recognized the potential for direct endangerment to public health from evaporation of fuel, the dominant concerns leading to this expansion were concerns about the effects of leaded gasoline both on catalytic converter technology being developed to control hydrocarbon emissions and the health effects of tailpipe emissions of the actual lead. The legislative history in the House reflects particular concern that the implementing agency's burden to prove health concerns was too great and that the agency should have the authority to require industry to provide the research necessary to determine health dangers. This authority for the EPA to require industry testing was ultimately codified in Section 211(b)(2).[3] The 1970 act also added authority for the EPA administrator to recover civil penalties in U.S. district court of $10,000 per day for regulatory violations.

Following enactment of the 1970 act, the EPA finally took action to promulgate basic registration regulations for fuels and fuel additives under Sections 211(a) and (b).[4] However, the agency had not yet exercised its authority under Section 211(b)(2) to require health-effects testing and submission of information about the impact on emissions and emissions control equipment when Congress amended the CAA in 1977. The House committee expressed frustration about the "unwarranted delay and gross inadequacy" of the EPA's efforts and failure to require testing and the agency's intent (reflected in its proposed regulations) to require only that manufacturers test selected additives. The House committee was concerned that the EPA would first have to prove probable harm before industry testing would be required, and that such shifting of the burden of developing proof would be unacceptable where the number of registered fuels and additives for screening was already high.[5] In response to the EPA's failure to exercise its authority and the inadequacy of the EPA's proposed approach, Congress in the 1977 amendments enacted a new Section 211(e) requiring the EPA to promulgate regulations within one year implementing its health-effects testing authority.

The EPA did, however, take major regulatory action following the 1970 act to establish a program to phase down the lead content in gasoline, pursuant to Section 211(c). (Lead, in the form of the organo-metallic compound tetraethyl lead, is added to gasoline as an octane enhancer.)[6] The EPA first acted to prohibit leaded gasoline for use in cars equipped with catalysts, requiring retailers to provide unleaded gasoline.[7] Thereafter, the EPA acted to reduce lead content of all gasoline to reduce the danger to health from lead emissions. The initial panel of the Court of Appeals for the District of Columbia Circuit invalidated the EPA's action on the grounds that the EPA had not shown, under the 1970 version of Section 211(c), that lead emissions "will endanger the public health or welfare."[8] In particular, the initial panel noted the broader language governing EPA standards applicable to new motor vehicles under Section 202(a) of the CAA for emissions "which, in [the administrator's judgment,] cause, or contribute to, air pollution which may reasonably be anticipated to endanger public health or welfare." The court, *en banc*, reversed the original panel, holding that the "will endanger" language authorized the EPA to take precautionary or preventive action.[9] Congress, in the 1977 amendments, codified the full D.C. Circuit's interpretation, using language parallel to that in Section 202(a).[10]

Controversy regarding another octane-enhancing organo-metallic compound, called MMT,[11] prompted additional congressional action on fuels in the 1977 amendments. The automobile companies raised concerns that MMT, which was being used in place of lead, also damages catalytic converters, increasing hydrocarbon emissions.[12] The House committee noted the MMT controversy as illustrating the need for a preventive approach to testing new additives before their use becomes widespread.[13] In addition, the Senate committee recognized that EPA regulation under Section 211(c) could not adequately protect emissions control equipment currently in use, owing to the time needed for the EPA to satisfy the affirmative demonstrations and procedural safeguards of that subsection.[14] The MMT controversy and the potential for new fuels and additives to harm existing cars motivated Congress to adopt Section 211(f)'s "substantially similar" provision. This provision shifts the burden to manufacturers to show that a fuel or additive will *not* have a harmful impact on emissions control equipment.[15] This provision prohibited manufacturers, beginning March 31, 1977, from introducing new fuels or additives into commerce or increasing additive concentrations that are not "substantially similar" to certification fuel. The "substantially similar" provision also allows the EPA to waive the prohibition when an applicant shows that the fuel or additive will not cause or contribute to a failure of an emissions control device to comply with certification emissions standards. Specifically addressing MMT, paragraph (2) prohibited manufacturers, beginning November 30, 1977, from selling gasoline containing a concentration of manganese above 0.625 grams per gallon, unless the EPA granted a waiver.

In the 1977 amendments Congress also added Section 211(g) to ease the burden on small refiners resulting from restrictions on octane-enhancers from the EPA's lead phasedown regulations and the limit on new octane-enhancing additives such as MMT under Section 211(f).[16] This provision, which was repealed in the 1990 amendments, limited the EPA's authority to regulate small refiners in the lead phasedown program. In the absence of octane-enhancing organo-metallic additives such as tetraethyl lead and MMT, refiners raise the octane of gasoline by adding aromatic hydrocarbons, which are produced through "catalytic cracking" of larger hydrocarbons. This capital expense for "cat cracking" refinery units would constitute a proportionally greater burden for small refiners.

Following the 1977 amendments, the EPA rejected the first waiver applications for MMT[17] and acted on a variety of other waiver applications. Despite its new mandatory duty under Section 211(e) to promulgate fuel testing requirements for purposes of registration, the EPA still failed to promulgate these regulations. Under Section 211(c), the EPA did act shortly before the 1990 amendments to address two distinct problems. First, the agency adopted controls on gasoline volatility during the summer to limit the evaporative emissions of hydrocarbons that contribute to summer ozone formation. This was, in part, a response to unintended consequences of the lead phasedown program. As described earlier, to replace the octane that lead additives provided and that MMT was not allowed to provide, refiners used more volatile aromatic hydrocarbons and added to gasoline increased amounts of butane. (As discussed in detail later, gasoline volatility also increased in response to vehicle technology changes that made engines more tolerant of gasoline that is high in butane and is therefore cheaper and more volatile.) The EPA also acted to limit the sulfur content of diesel fuel because high sulfur levels would interfere with new technology designed to trap particulate emissions from diesel engines.[18]

The 1990 amendments broadly expanded the CAA fuels programs. Unlike the lead problem in 1970 and the MMT problem in 1977, Congress went beyond general statutory solutions applicable to those and other problems that might arise. This time Congress, less trusting of the EPA's willingness to exercise more general authority, specified very particular solutions to particular environmental problems. To accomplish this level of detail and mandate a variety of specific programs, a dramatic expansion of Section 211 was required.

The most far-reaching and detailed of these provisions was the new Section 211(k), which mandated a new program for the reformulation of gasoline to reduce emissions of volatile organic compounds (VOCs) and toxic air pollutants. Section 211(k) alone comprises substantially more statutory text than the entire fuels program previously filled. The legislative history of the 1990 amendments indicates that Congress focused much more attention on this than on any other fuels provision. Rather than simply preventing fuels from causing new emissions problems or interfering with vehicles' emissions control equipment, Congress designed the reformulated gasoline program, applicable in the most polluted ozone nonattainment areas, to reduce emissions from the gasoline currently on the market. As with the volatility controls, one common perception in Congress was that refiners had replaced lead additives and the octane provided by lead with toxic and volatile aromatics and that this had increased emissions of these other pollutants. Congress believed that substituting organic compounds containing oxygen—called oxygenates—to provide "clean octane" could reduce emissions.[19] The dominant oxygenates in use were ethanol and MTBE.[20] Ethanol is an alcohol derived from grain and primarily corn. MTBE is an ether made by combining isobutylene, a refinery component that can be made from natural gas or other hydrocarbons, and methanol derived from natural gas. ETBE,[21] an ether made by combining isobutylene with ethanol, as well as other ethers, is also available but has not generally been cost-competitive with ethanol and MTBE. The requirement that reformulated gasoline contain oxygenates gained the particular support of the farm lobby, which saw the opportunity for increasing the market for ethanol.[22] As detailed in the discussion of the reformulated gasoline program, the ultimate fate of ethanol in the EPA's implementation of the program was to become one of the most politically controversial aspects of the entire CAA (and recently MTBE has created similar controversy). The oil industry also accepted the program for gasoline as an alternative to proposals to emphasize alternative fuels programs.[23]

In addition to reformulated gasoline, Congress (again with farm lobby support) established the oxygenated gasoline program in Section 211(m). Another benefit of oxygenates in gasoline is a reduction in CO emissions that result from incomplete combustion in cold weather. Adding oxygen to the fuel increases combustion efficiency and thus lowers CO emissions. Section 211(m) requires that states include in their state implementation plans (SIPs) programs to require that gasoline sold for use in their CO nonattainment areas during the wintertime when CO exceedances occur contain 2.7 percent oxygen by weight. Again, this program is very specific and the statute itself addresses many implementation issues, such as the amount of oxygen required, the time period that the program should apply, pump labeling, and circumstances that warrant a waiver from the program's requirements. The last new provision to address a specifically identified program is the new requirement in Section 211(l) that gasoline contain detergent additives to prevent deposits in engines and fuel supply systems. This provision is much less detailed, however, providing simply that the EPA establish specifications for such additives.

The remainder of the changes in the 1990 amendments to Section 211 comprised codification of and follow-up to the EPA's prior regulations, particularly under Section 211(c). The most substantial of these was Section 211(h), which codified and made somewhat more stringent the EPA's regulation of gasoline volatility under Section 211(c) that was promulgated shortly before enactment of the 1990 amendments. Similarly, Section 211(i) codified the EPA's regulation of the sulfur content of diesel fuel, promulgated just over two months before enactment of the 1990 amendments.[24] In addition, Congress clarified that the registration and information provisions of Section 211(a) and (b) and the EPA's regulatory authority under Section 211(c) apply to fuels and fuel additives used in nonroad engines and vehicles, paralleling the extension of the EPA's authority to regulate emissions from these engines and vehicles in revised Section 213.[25]

Congress made other minor changes to Section 211(c) to clarify certain elements of the state preemption aspects of that provision. Congress also extended the "substantially similar" program in Section 211(f) that previously applied to fuels and additives used in light-duty motor vehicles to apply to any fuel or additives used in any motor vehicle or engine, including heavy-duty diesel engines. Regarding the EPA's continuing lead phasedown program, Congress repealed the small refinery provisions in Section 211(g). In their place, Congress enacted a new Subsection (g) to codify the EPA's regulatory prohibition on fueling with leaded gasoline a vehicle requiring unleaded gasoline. It also extended this prohibition to apply to "any person." Further, in Section 211(j), Congress established a program for evaluating the effectiveness of substitutes for lead additives that are still used as lubricants to prevent valve seat wear, particularly in farm equipment,[26] and in Section 211(n) prohibited the sale of leaded gasoline for use in highway vehicles. In Section 211(o), Congress clarified that the term "manufacturer" includes importers. Finally, Congress revised the penalty provisions in Section 211(d), principally to provide for administrative penalties and to provide courts with jurisdiction to mitigate civil penalties and to enjoin violations.

Explanation of Regulatory Programs

Information Programs

Section 211(a) authorizes the EPA to designate any fuel or fuel additive for registration as a condition of selling the fuel or additive, and Section 211(b) specifies requirements for registration for designated fuels and additives. The EPA's implementing regulations are codified at 40 C.F.R. Part 79. The basic designation and registration requirements in Subparts A through D of the regulations remain unchanged from the EPA's regulations implementing the 1970 CAA. Despite the authority in Section 211(b) to require health-effects testing of fuels and additives, and the requirement in Section 211(e) that the EPA exercise that authority within one year of the 1977 amendments, the EPA did not take final action to establish the testing program in a new Subpart F until June 1994.[27]

Section 211(a) applies not only to fuels and additives used in mobile sources, but also, after provisions added by the 1990 amendments, to fuels and additives used exclusively in nonroad engines or nonroad vehicles. The placement of this provision in Title II of the CAA and the limitation of regulatory authority in Section 211(c) to mobile source fuels and additives, arguably indicates that it does not apply to stationary source fuels such as coal burned in electric utility boilers. The EPA has not attempted to apply this authority to such stationary source fuels. Currently, the EPA has only designated gasoline and diesel fuels.

The EPA's original regulations did, however, interpret the term "fuel" to include "motor vehicle engine oil" and designated additives to such oil on the grounds that motor oil reaches an engine's combustion chamber and thus can affect emissions.[28] In *Lubrizol Corporation v. EPA*,[29] the court of appeals rejected the EPA's approach to regulating any potential contributor to emissions as too broad, concluding that Congress intended by the term "fuel" to refer to the substance used to propel motor vehicles. Just before the decision, the 1977 amendments were enacted; the House committee, presumably aware of the *Lubrizol* dispute, supported the EPA's position:

> [T]he Committee, in repeating the terms "fuel" and "fuel additives," intended that these terms be construed broadly, as with existing Section 211, to include any substance that is intentionally put into a vehicle's motor, either directly or indirectly, and which is combusted in the engine. In terms of the potential effect on pollution control devices or on public health, it matters not whether any such substance makes its way from the engine to the gas tank or is put directly into the engine.[30]

The EPA retracted the designation of motor oil additives in response to the court's decision, but at the same time it gave notice of its intent to reinstate it in reliance on the committee's opinion.[31] One commentator has noted that the 1977 committee's view should not be accorded the weight that might ordinarily apply to legislative history, since Congress did not change the 1970 statutory language, and the committee was therefore simply interpreting prior language.[32] Nevertheless, while Congress could have clarified the matter in the statutory language, the EPA regarded its decision not to do so while noting the EPA's interpretation arguably to reflect Congress's intent to ratify the EPA's approach.

The basic registration requirements establish general definitions and requirements for registration with which designated fuels and fuel additives must comply before sale.[33] Certain exemptions are provided, for example, for research and development. The regulations also establish periodic reporting requirements for fuel and additive manufacturers to provide basic information about concentrations and production volumes. The general authority to require testing has been replaced with the extensive new testing requirements.[34] The regulations establish separate registration procedures for fuels and fuel additives.[35] These regulations specify all of the basic information that a manufacturer must submit to register a designated fuel or additive, including commercial identifying information, range of concentration, purpose, annual production volume, marketing distribution data, chemical composition, and information about the manufacturer's approach to testing compliance. Fuel additives must be registered only for those specific types of fuel for which they will be sold and used. The registration regulations also contain the EPA's actual designations of fuels and additives, including motor vehicle gasolincs, motor vehicle diesel fuels, and all additives used in those fuels.[36] The designations also specify certain additional information that must be submitted to register, including emissions and health effects information "to the extent known to the [additive or fuel] manufacturer." On March 17, 1997, the EPA issued a final rule modifying the fuel and fuel additive registration and testing requirements. The rule revised the definitions of "additive," "fuel manufacturer," and "small business" to limit their applicability and relieve hundreds of businesses from existing regulatory responsibilities of registration.[37] For instance, the rule revised the definition of "fuel manufacturer" to exclude oxygenate blenders if they were not also fuel refiners or importers.

The fuels and additives testing rule followed two decades of frustration in implementing the EPA's Section 211(b) authority to require health-effects testing in conformity with EPA procedures and protocols. The requirement in Section 211(e), added by the 1977 amendments, that the EPA implement this authority by August 7, 1978, for all fuels and additives registered on or after the date of promulgation stalled after a 1978 advance notice of proposed rule making.[38] In fact, rule making leading to final action only followed a 1989 lawsuit challenging the EPA's failure to act.[39] Under Section 211(e), the testing information was to be submitted for purposes of newly registered fuels and additives after promulgation of the rule, but fuels and additives already registered by that time were given three years to submit the information. As of March 1994, more than 2,300 fuels and 4,800 additives were registered by the EPA.[40] This is nearly triple the 2,600 fuels and additives that were registered at the time Congress mandated EPA action by enacting Section 211(e) in 1977.[41] In addition, Section 211(e) allows the EPA to provide for small-business exemptions, cost-sharing among manufacturers for testing, and exemptions when more testing would only duplicate existing information. By statute, health and welfare information provided to the EPA in compliance with the testing requirements must be available to the public.[42]

In the fuels testing rule, the EPA adopted a grouping system to allow manufacturers of similar products to share costs by permitting the testing of one product to serve as representative of relatively similar products. Products are grouped as additive-fuel mixtures. The criteria for sorting fuels and additives into groups is based on similarities in the chemical and physical properties of the "raw" fuel or additive-base fuel mixture. Manufacturers are individually responsible for compliance with the testing requirements and may fulfill them on an individual basis. The grouping system simply provides a voluntary opportunity to share costs to meet the requirements in a more cost-effective manner. The system is set up to ensure that fuels and additives with unique compositional characteristics are separated into groups for testing.

The framework for grouping involves sorting each fuel or additive into one of six broad "fuel families": gasoline, diesel, methanol, ethanol, methane (a compressed or liquefied natural gas), and propane (an LPG). The fuel families are defined as those containing 50 percent or more of the particular kind of fuel. This is by volume for the liquid fuels and as mole percent for the gaseous fuels. Each fuel family also includes the bulk (or general use) and aftermarket additives intended for use in such fuels. Additives registered for use in more than one fuel are included in more than one family. Base fuels for each family reflect generic or average characteristics for each family.

Each fuel family is then subdivided into three fuel/fuel additive categories: baseline, nonbaseline, and atypical. The baseline category consists of fuels and additives that resemble the base fuel of a particular family in elemental composition and that meet certain quantitative limits for particular constituents. The nonbaseline category contains only chemical elements in the baseline category that exceed the quantitative limits for particular constituents. The atypical category generally consists of fuels and additives that contain chemical elements in addition to those allowed in the baseline category. The category for additives is based on the properties of the additive mixture in the base fuel at the maximum additive manufacturer-recommended concentration.

The fuel/fuel additive categories are further subdivided into fuel/fuel additive groups. Once a group is determined, arrangements can be made for cooperative testing, and criteria are applied to select a representative of the group for the group-sponsored testing. Each group should contain fuels and additives that are sufficiently similar so that one formulation may represent all of the member products in testing. The number of groups within the various categories for the various fuel families differs depending on the variability among the products in the category. The regulations address the categories and groups within each fuel family. Treatment of a particular fuel can thus be tracked in the regulations from the general family through the more specific characteristics, placing it into a category and into a group. The grouping system is summarized in Table F94-7 in the regulations.[43] To the extent that fuels are registered for a number of potential additives that place the potential fuels into different testing groups, the manufacturer is responsible for individually testing each fuel/fuel additive combination or participating in each group.

Manufacturers' organization of testing and cost sharing for representative fuels and additives in each group is left largely to them. The EPA patterned this scheme, and procedures for dispute resolution, after the testing program under the Toxic Substances Control Act (TSCA).[44] For fuels and additives registered before May 27, 1994, manufacturers must have notified the EPA by November 27, 1994, whether they would comply with the testing requirements as part of a group. For fuels and additives not registered by May 27, 1994, manufacturers must conduct testing individually unless they certify that they intend to rely on data submitted by another group or individual manufacturer. Submitters of the test data have fifteen years to obtain reimbursement from those that rely on it.

The EPA's testing regulations focus primarily on impacts of air emissions from the fuels and additives, rather than on the effects of the raw, uncombusted materials. Evaporative emissions testing requirements apply in cases in which the fuel or fuel/fuel additive mixture meets specific volatility criteria. The EPA adopted a "tiering" system for testing so that more rigorous, resource-intensive requirements would apply in successive tiers of testing requirements, based on the results of preceding, less rigorous screening. Under Tier 1, mandatory in all cases, manufacturers must perform a literature search on health and welfare effects (including both public and in-house sources), characterize emissions, and provide qualitative exposure analysis based on production volumes and market distribution data. Under Tier 2, also mandatory, manufacturers must include biological testing for specific health endpoints, including basic inhalation studies, and additional testing involving exposure of laboratory animals to emissions for assessing carcinogenic, mutagenic, teratogenic, and acute toxicity effects. Previous studies comparable to the testing established by EPA guidelines can be submitted in lieu of new duplicative tests. Based on the EPA's evaluation of information from Tiers 1 and 2, the EPA has the discretion to determine, on a case-by-case basis, whether additional Tier 3 testing is warranted, and the objectives and scope of such tests would depend on the concerns the EPA identified from the earlier tiers or other information available to the agency. The EPA has stated that it must be able to decide whether a particular fuel or additive is likely to create unacceptable health or welfare risks, and that if such a risk decision is not possible based on Tier 1 and 2 data, the EPA would mandate Tier 3 testing.[45]

For registered fuels and additives, manufacturers were to submit certain Tier 1 information by May 27, 1997. If by that date they had submitted a contract with a qualified laboratory to conduct the Tier 2 tests, manufacturers had until May 27, 2000, to submit a final Tier 2 report. The EPA chose this longer time frame owing to the number of groups to be tested and to limited laboratory availability.[46] The EPA will specify the time frame for completion of Tier 3 testing when the EPA prescribes any particular Tier 3 requirements for particular registered fuels and additives. For "new" fuels and additives that were not yet registered on May 27, 1994, all testing requirements must be satisfied before registration, including any Tier 3 requirements that the EPA judges to be necessary. Under the EPA's regulations, new fuels and additives are those not registered by May 27, 1994, *and* not fitting "registrable criteria." Fuels and additives fit registrable criteria, and hence are treated like previously registered fuels and additives, if they meet the program's criteria for "grouping" with a previously registered fuel or general use additive in the same fuel family (such as gasoline or diesel fuel). This is because fuels and additives grouped together should be similar enough to present no increase in health and welfare risks, and interference to prevent entry into the market pending testing would have no benefit.[47] The fuel family limitation prevents market expansion into new uses for the fuel or fuel additive, and hence it prevents an increase in exposure without testing.[48] (Registered additives meeting the criteria for grouping *only* with a previously registered aftermarket additive would not be registrable because aftermarket additives have limited distribution, and considering general use additives to be registrable because they can group with aftermarket additives could significantly increase public exposure to that additive.)[49]

On July 19, 2000, the EPA issued a notice announcing that it had notified Ethyl Corporation, the manufacturer of MMT, and other affected registrants of fuels and additives containing MMT, of Alternative Tier 2 health and exposure testing requirements.[50] The stated purpose of the requirements is to assist in characterizing potential health risks associated with use of the additive in unleaded gasoline.

Lastly, the testing rule contains special provisions for small businesses, manufacturers of experimental fuels and additives, relabeled products, and aerosols. For experimental products, the EPA's long-standing registration exemptions apply so that testing requirements do not apply.[51] Relabeled products are simply repackaged and thus need only comply with basic registration information requirements. Approximately half of the 4,800 registered additives as of March 1994 were relabeled products.[52] For aerosol products that are sprayed, such as carburetor cleaners and engine starters, the EPA concluded that different testing for direct exposure would be more appropriate than emissions-type testing. For these products, manufacturers must submit basic registration information as well as a literature survey and a discussion of potential exposures. Tier 2 emissions testing would not apply. The EPA would then decide whether Tier 3 testing should be required.

Finally, small businesses (i.e., those with annual sales below $50 million) must submit only basic registration information for baseline and nonbaseline products, relying on larger companies to supply Tier 2 information for such products. For atypical products this general exemption does not apply, since larger companies may not supply the relevant information. Instead, for the atypical category, small businesses with less than $10 million in annual sales are excused from Tier 2 requirements.

New Fuels and Additives: "Substantially Similar" and Waivers

The programs already discussed are designed to provide the EPA with information on which to base affirmative action to promulgate regulations under Section 211(c) of the CAA. Before discussing the EPA's actions under Section 211(c), it is first useful to understand the second statutory approach to fuels regulation, whereby manufacturers of new fuels and additives have the burden of showing that their products will not harm emissions control equipment and performance before they can be introduced into commerce. As discussed, it was a particular controversy regarding the organo-manganese additive MMT that led Congress in the 1977 amendments to adopt this second approach in Section 211(f). Concerned that the EPA had not taken action to require testing under Section 211(a), (b), and (e) and that the hurdles to regulation under Section 211(c) were too high, Congress enacted Section 211(f). That section banned gasoline containing manganese above 0.625 grams per gallon and banned other new fuels and additives not "substantially similar" to certification fuel, subject to waiver provisions applicable to both the manganese limit and the general prohibition.

Section 211(f)(1)(A) prohibits manufacturers from first introducing into commerce or increasing the concentration in use (after March 31, 1977) of any fuel or additive for general use in light-duty motor vehicles that is not "substantially similar" to any fuel or fuel additive used in the certification of a 1975 or later model-year vehicle or engine. Fuel used in certification of gasoline-powered light-duty motor vehicles is a standardized fuel called Indolene (for exhaust emissions testing) and a mileage-accumulation fuel that must be representative of commercially available fuels (for durability testing).[53] Section 211(f)(1)(B), added in the 1990 amendments, extended this prohibition against first introducing fuels or additives (after November 15, 1990) to other motor vehicles, including heavy-duty ones. It thus reached diesel fuel, leaded gasoline, and consumer additives.[54] Diesel fuel used for certification is subject to specifications that are different for exhaust emissions testing than for service accumulation, as specified in the EPA's regulations.[55] (Section 211(f)(1)(B) applies only to fuels and additives used in vehicles for which there are certification standards. It thus does not reach alternative fuels such as ethanol for which certification standards do not yet exist, but it does apply to methanol and CNG vehicles.)[56] Section 211(f)(2) specifies the manganese prohibition. Section 211(f)(3), as discussed earlier in the legislative development section, is a retroactive prohibition on the sale of not substantially similar fuels introduced into commerce between 1974 and 1977. Section 211(f)(4) authorizes the EPA to waive these statutory prohibitions upon application of any manufacturer of any fuel or fuel additive. To qualify for a waiver, the EPA administrator must determine that the applicant has established that the fuel or additive (or the additive concentration) will not cause or contribute to any emission control equipment's failure to achieve compliance with the emissions standards to which the vehicle has been certified over the vehicle's useful life. If the administrator does not grant or deny an application within 180 days of receipt, the waiver is to be treated as granted.

This statutory scheme essentially shifts the burden of proof to the manufacturers of fuels and fuel additives to show that their products will not interfere with the effectiveness of a vehicle's emissions control equipment. As such, the waiver system establishes a permit or licensing system for the EPA to allow new fuels and additives on the market after the manufacturer bears the burden of showing that harm will not result. The EPA can, however, allow waivers to be granted by operation of law without making a factual determination by allowing the 180-day period to lapse without agency action.

In *Ethyl Corporation v. EPA*,[57] the court of appeals made clear that there is no requirement under Section 211(f) that the new fuels or additives will not endanger public health and welfare through emissions that are not the subject of vehicle or engine certification standards. At issue in *Ethyl* was the EPA's denial of Ethyl Corporation's waiver application under Section 211(f) on the grounds of "unresolved concerns regarding the potential impact of manganese emissions resulting from MMT use on public health."[58] The EPA claimed that it could choose to deny a waiver based on considerations not explicitly identified in Section 211(f), such as health effects. The EPA reasoned that Section 211(f) authorizes the EPA to grant waivers using the permissive "may" rather than the mandatory "shall," and therefore gives the EPA wide discretion to opt to deny waivers, as long as the EPA has a nonarbitrary reason for denying the waiver.

The court of appeals in *Ethyl* rejected the EPA's reasoning, holding that the EPA could not consider health effects under the waiver provision, though the agency could regulate MMT under Section 211(c)—if it had adequate evidence of adverse health effects. The court reasoned that the plain language of Section 211(f) focuses on impacts on the vehicle's ability to comply with emission standards, without reference to public health effects. First, the court determined that the word "may" simply refers to the EPA's choice to do nothing about complying with emissions standards, with the waiver treated as granted at the expiration of the 180-day period. Second, the court focused on the statutory structure, contrasting Section 211(f) with Section 211(c), which clearly authorizes the EPA to "control or prohibit" fuels and additives based on health effects. Third, the court pointed to the legislative history indicating that the EPA could allow the 180-day period to expire without action and that Congress was concerned about impacts on emission control equipment.

By eliminating the EPA's option of refusing to waive the preexisting ban in light of health concerns, the *Ethyl* case limits the EPA to affirmatively regulating new fuels and additives when the EPA has specific evidence of health effects. Of course, the case thereby also highlights the importance of information acquired through the health-effects testing rule. The case demonstrates a possible consequence of the EPA's failure to require such testing earlier: The EPA may lack information about health effects sufficient for affirmative regulation of the large number of fuels and additives now on the market.

Since Congress intended that the Section 211(f) prohibitions not depend on proactive EPA regulatory action, the EPA has not issued implementing regulations. The EPA has, however, issued an interpretive rule regarding the term "substantially similar" for gasoline and gasoline additives, which is not otherwise defined in the CAA. The EPA first interpreted the term in its 1978 guidelines for the waiver process.[59] There, the EPA defined substantially similar for additives to mean that the additive does not contain elements (other than impurities) different from certification fuel, or that the chemical structure of the additive is not identical to the chemical structure of additives specified for use in certification fuel. Thereafter, the EPA established a more extensive interpretive rule through a March 1979 proposal,[60] an October 1980 final rule,[61] and July 1981 revisions.[62] The EPA interpreted Section 211(f) as inapplicable to leaded gasoline; it did not address diesel fuels in the interpretive rule. The EPA established four criteria for a fuel to be substantially similar:

1. The fuel must contain the elements carbon, hydrogen, oxygen, nitrogen, and/or sulfur exclusively, in the molecular form of hydrocarbons, aliphatic ethers, aliphatic alcohols other than methanol, up to 0.3 volume percent methanol, up to 2.75 volume percent methanol with an equal volume of butanol or higher molecular weight alcohol, or in the form of an additive at no more than 0.25 weight percent contributing no more than 15 parts per million (ppm) sulfur to the fuel.
2. The fuel must contain no more than 2.0 weight percent oxygen.
3. The fuel must meet the physical and chemical properties of the American Society of Testing and Materials (ASTM) for unleaded gasoline (Standard D 439).
4. The fuel additive must contain only carbon, hydrogen, and any or all of the elements oxygen, nitrogen, and sulfur.

Trace impurities in fuels and additives may be present. In February 1991, the EPA made further minor revisions to the interpretive rule to increase the allowable oxygen content from 2.0 weight percent to 2.7 weight percent (for blends of aliphatic alcohols or ethers, excluding methanol) and to update the ASTM specifications reference to Standard D 4814–88.[63] The separate restriction for methanol at 0.3 volume percent remains unchanged.

Since the extension of the substantially similar prohibition in the 1990 amendments to fuels and fuel additives used in vehicles other than light-duty ones, the EPA issued an advance notice of proposed rule making to interpret what constitutes substantially similar to diesel fuel used in heavy-duty engines.[64] There, the EPA suggested a definition similar to the definition for unleaded gasoline, limiting the composition of diesel fuel to the elements carbon, hydrogen, oxygen, nitrogen, and sulfur; placing an upper limit on additive concentration; limiting impurities; and requiring that diesel fuel meet ASTM properties. Commentators have focused on the more heterogeneous nature of diesel fuel (in comparison to gasoline) that requires more varied additives with more elements, and at higher concentrations (for cetane improvers in particular). These commentators suggest that the limits on the composition of diesel fuel be more relaxed to encompass these variations.

Other than the interpretation of "substantially similar," the EPA's regulatory activity has been to resolve applications for waivers, and it has refined the criteria for a waiver through these decisions.[65] Despite concerns that alcohols (including ethanol and methanol) increase the volatility of gasoline into which they are blended, and thus increase evaporative emissions, the EPA allowed a waiver application to lapse, and thus be granted by operation of law, for ethanol at the 10 volume percent concentration.[66] Thereafter, the EPA granted waivers for various ethanol and methanol blends, conditioned on the blend meeting volatility standards set by ASTM.[67] (These ASTM volatility standards are discussed later, in connection with the EPA's volatility regulations.)

The EPA's waiver analysis has focused on exhaust emissions, evaporative emissions, materials compatibility, and driveability. If the EPA expects the fuel to have only an instantaneous effect on emissions, then a comparison of the waiver fuel and other representative fuel is sufficient. If there is concern about long-term effects of the fuel on the vehicle's equipment, then durability testing over the vehicle's useful life also is required.

As discussed earlier, since the enactment of Section 211(f) in 1977, a central focus of the EPA under that section has been the octane enhancer MMT, manufactured by Ethyl Corporation. The EPA first denied a waiver application for MMT in 1978,[68] and then again in 1981,[69] owing to concerns that MMT use would affect catalytic converters over time, ultimately increasing hydrocarbon emissions. Ethyl Corporation submitted a third application in November 1990, but withdrew it before the deadline for EPA action, and submitted a fourth application in July 1991, which the EPA denied in January 1992,[70] again on grounds of increased hydrocarbon emissions. On judicial review, the EPA sought a voluntary remand of the 1992 decision to consider new data from Ethyl Corporation. The EPA ultimately determined that Ethyl Corporation had demonstrated that MMT would not cause or contribute to vehicle or engine failure to comply with certification emissions standards (including hydrocarbon standards).[71] Nevertheless, as previously noted, the EPA denied Ethyl Corporation's waiver application on July 13, 1994,[72] based on unresolved concerns about the potential health impact of manganese emissions resulting from MMT use. Following the decision in *Ethyl Corporation v. EPA* that the EPA cannot deny a waiver based on health effects, in July 1995 the EPA granted Ethyl Corporation's November 30, 1993, waiver application.[73]

The waiver was not, however, the end of the MMT story. The EPA claimed, in correspondence with Ethyl Corporation, that Ethyl's registration for MMT under Section 211(b) was restricted to use in leaded (but not unleaded) gasoline because Section 211(f) banned use of MMT in unleaded gasoline as of 1978. The EPA explained that an additive could not be registered for use in a fuel when use in that fuel was prohibited. MMT could not be used in unleaded gasoline because MMT was not substantially similar to test fuel and the EPA had not granted a waiver. In addition, the EPA claimed that under the EPA's testing rule MMT would not be considered registrable for use in unleaded gasoline because its manganese content makes it not sufficiently similar to currently registered fuels or refinery additives. Thus, the EPA's position was that Ethyl Corporation, even if it could obtain a waiver for MMT, was not registered and hence not grandfathered under the testing rule and it must complete all testing before registration for use in unleaded gasoline.

In October 1995, in *Ethyl Corporation v. Browner*,[74] the court of appeals again decided against the EPA. The court explained that the EPA should have granted the waiver for MMT on November 30, 1993, when the agency published its finding that Ethyl Corporation had met the only requirement for obtaining the waiver. The court reasoned that MMT, if it ever lost its registration for use in unleaded gasoline, would have regained its registration on November 30, 1993, well before promulgation of the 1994 testing regulations. The court thus ordered the EPA to register MMT as an additive as of November 30, 1993, in time to be grandfathered under the testing rule.

A few other fundamental issues under Section 211(f) have also been resolved in litigation challenging the EPA's waiver decisions. In *American Methyl Corporation v. EPA*,[75] the court of appeals held that the EPA may not revoke a waiver granted under Section 211(f), but that the agency may control or prohibit the fuel or additive only through a proceeding under Section 211(c). At issue was the EPA's waiver for a methanol-gasoline blend called Petrocoal. While the EPA conceded that it did not have authority to revoke a waiver that was properly granted based on the record at the time of the original decision, it argued that it could revoke the waiver based on a conclusion— upon reexamination—that the record actually did not support the original waiver.[76] The court of appeals disagreed, concluding that the EPA's authority to correct a mistake under Section 211(f) is limited only to the period available for taking an appeal.[77] The court reasoned that Congress provided authority to correct such mistakes through action under Section 211(c) and that the legislative history of Section 211(f) reflected this understanding. The court also reasoned that EPA authority to revoke a waiver, including one granted by expiration of the 180-day period, would effectively write that time limit out of the statute.[78] In addition, allowing the EPA to revoke only waivers granted through factual mistakes but not those granted by expiration of the 180-day period would have the perverse effect of giving the greatest deference to the least-thought-out waivers.[79] At bottom, the court was bothered by the uncertainty and commercial risk that the continuing threat of revocation would create, and by the lack of discipline in the EPA's decision making that such revocation authority would foster.[80]

The following year, in *Motor Vehicle Manufacturers Association v. EPA*,[81] the court of appeals revisited the Petrocoal waiver, considering the automobile manufacturers' challenge to the EPA's waiver decision on the merits. First, the court held that the EPA could grant a waiver as long as the fuel does not cause or contribute to a failure to achieve compliance with certified vehicle emission standards, but that the EPA does not have to insist that the fuel not cause "any increase" in emissions.[82] Second, the court held that, for a fuel to qualify for a waiver, the EPA must determine that the fuel will not cause or contribute to a vehicle's failure to meet emissions standards at any time during its useful life. The court also agreed with the EPA that the agency may rule out long-term, deteriorative effects based on evidence before the agency, and thereby obviate the need for the applicant to conduct costly 50,000-mile durability testing.[83] In the case of Petrocoal, however, the court found that the EPA did not have a basis to conclude that the high levels of methanol in the fuel would not cause a deterioration problem, and it also found other deficiencies in the EPA's technical basis for granting the waiver. As a result, the court vacated the EPA administrator's waiver and remanded for the EPA to make a reasoned decision. In the end, therefore, the court, rather than the EPA, invalidated the original waiver. Thus, under this decision, together with the preceding *American Methyl* case, the EPA cannot withdraw a waiver granted under Section 211(f) based on a conceded mistake, but a court may reach the same result by invalidating the waiver as arbitrary and capricious. Since the waiver recipient presumably would not seek revocation, and since the EPA cannot revoke a waiver, invalidation of a waiver under Section 211(f) based on an EPA mistake would occur only through the challenge of a third party injured by an improper waiver.

This result does not seem to satisfy entirely the *American Methyl* court's concern that the threat of revocation would cause undue uncertainty and commercial risk for the waiver recipient. Pending litigation could create the same cloud of uncertainty regarding the validity of a waiver as has the EPA's reconsideration—at least during the pendency of the litigation. Still, the EPA's dependence on a third party to correct a mistake under Section 211(f) may enhance the EPA's decision-making discipline. While the EPA retains authority to regulate under Section 211(c), a factual record insufficient to support a waiver under Section 211(f) may nevertheless also be insufficient to support EPA regulation under Section 211(c).

The court reached a different conclusion about reconsideration of a waiver *denial*. In *Ethyl Corporation v. EPA*,[84] Ethyl Corporation argued that the EPA's erroneous denial of a waiver application is equivalent to EPA inaction for 180 days, whereby the waiver would be deemed granted. In the MMT waiver controversy, the EPA acknowledged that evidence that had developed since denial of Ethyl Corporation's fourth MMT waiver application undermined the stated basis for the denial. Nonetheless, the EPA asked the court of appeals to remand the issue to the agency to consider other possible bases for denial that were not resolved in the decision. Ethyl Corporation argued that the court should address whether the waiver was improperly denied and, if so, hold that it would then be entitled to the waiver. In a brief opinion, the court concluded that the EPA could reconsider a denial of a waiver based on events pending appeal. The court reasoned that the 180-day automatic waiver provision is a dramatic penalty for agency delay but that there is "no basis to extend Congress's remedy for delay into a similarly radical remedy for error."[85]

General Authority to Regulate Fuels and Fuel Additives

Review of Statutory Provisions

Section 211(c) provides the EPA's general authority to regulate fuels and fuel additives and is thus arguably the most important provision in Section 211. The major concern motivating enactment of this provision in the 1970 act and major regulatory action thereafter involved the phasedown of leaded gasoline. However, it is also the authority the EPA used to regulate gasoline volatility and sulfur in diesel fuel, both of which were codified into separate provisions of the 1990 amendments. The EPA has also relied on this provision, in conjunction with the more specific authorities, for the reformulated gasoline and detergent additives program.

Before considering the EPA's regulatory programs under Section 211(c), it is useful to review the statutory scheme. The EPA's authority to regulate applies to any fuel or additive for use in a motor vehicle, motor vehicle engine, nonroad engine, or nonroad vehicle if either of two concerns are present. Under Section 211(c)(1)(A), the EPA may regulate if an emission product of the fuel or additive causes (or contributes to) air pollution that may reasonably be anticipated to endanger public health or welfare. Under Section 211(c)(1)(B), the agency may regulate if emission products of the fuel or additive will significantly impair the performance of emissions control equipment that is in general use, or that has been developed and would be in general use if the fuel or additive were regulated. This dual focus on direct health effects from emissions and emissions products harming control equipment, including equipment under development, parallels the controversy about the health impact of lead emissions and the impact on then-developing catalytic converter technology that motivated Congress's action in 1970. As discussed below concerning limits on sulfur content of gasoline and diesel fuel, the EPA's most recent action to reduce diesel sulfur was also based on the impairment of emissions control equipment under this provision.

Further, the statute specifies elements of regulatory analysis that must precede regulation. There are three such additional criteria:

- First, before regulating based on health effects under (A), the EPA must consider all relevant medical and scientific evidence available, including other means of achieving emission standards under Section 202.
- Second, before regulating based on interference with emission control equipment under (B), the EPA must consider scientific and economic data, including a cost-benefit analysis comparing emission control devices that would depend on the fuel regulation to those control devices that would not. The EPA is given special authority to require vehicle manufacturers to furnish their existing information about emissions resulting from particular fuels or additives, or the impact on emissions control devices of such products.
- Third, the EPA must also find as a condition before prohibiting a fuel or additive that the prohibition will not cause the use of any other fuel or additive that will produce emissions that will endanger health or welfare to the same or greater degree.

All of these additional criteria again reflect the controversy about the health effects of lead additives and concern that leaded gasoline would interfere with the catalytic technology needed to meet the then–very stringent 1970 vehicle emission standards.

Section 211(c)(4) addresses preemption of state fuel and fuel additive regulations, which has become increasingly important as states seek to find additional sources of emission reductions to achieve the ozone NAAQS under Title I of the CAA. Subparagraph (A) establishes the general preemption rule that states may not prescribe or attempt to enforce, for purposes of motor vehicle emission control, any control or prohibition respecting any characteristic or component of a fuel or fuel additive if either the EPA has found that no such federal control is necessary under Section 211(c)(1) or the EPA has already prescribed a control or prohibition on that characteristic or component of a fuel or additive. One exception to preemption in the general rule is that states may adopt any control or prohibition that is identical to that of the EPA.

Subparagraphs (B) and (C) provide a second and third exception to preemption. Under Subparagraph (B), preemption does not apply to California, which gets an "automatic" waiver of fuel preemption because it is the only state that can develop its own motor vehicle standards. Congress presumably believed California should be able to develop corresponding fuel regulations as well. Under Subparagraph (C), other states may adopt fuel and additive regulations in their SIPs subject to EPA approval only if the EPA finds that the state regulation is necessary to achieve the NAAQS that the SIP implements. Even if these other states adopt California vehicle standards under CAA Section 177, they must still show that any corresponding fuel controls not identical to federal fuel controls are "necessary" for attainment.[86]

Lead Phasedown

The EPA's first regulatory program under Section 211(c) was, as Congress contemplated, to phase down leaded gasoline. Congress, adding new Section 211(n) in the 1990 amendments, completed the phasedown of leaded gasoline by banning its use in motor vehicles after December 31, 1995. Still, this program and its regulatory history are important as the template for resolving many issues that the EPA has applied in later fuels programs, including the extent of the EPA's authority under Section 211(c); averaging, trading, and banking programs; liability issues; and penalty issues. It was also the context in which many of these threshold issues were litigated. The lead phasedown regulations are codified, along with the EPA's other affirmative controls on fuels and fuel additives, at 40 C.F.R. Part 80.

The EPA first acted under Section 211(c)(1)(B) in January 1973[87] to ban lead in gasoline[88] for use in cars with catalytic converters and marked as requiring unleaded gasoline only. The EPA also required that auto manufacturers label the cars requiring unleaded gasoline on the instrument panel and near the fuel tank inlet[89] and that they manufacture such vehicles with gas tank inlet restrictors.[90] (It is unclear how these requirements applicable to *vehicle* manufacturers constitute *fuel* controls under Section 211(c).) Gasoline retailers must also display a notice that leaded gasoline may not be used in cars labeled "unleaded gasoline only";[91] and they must dispense leaded gasoline from a nozzle too big to fit the inlets of cars with the restrictors to prevent refueling with leaded gasoline.[92] The EPA's initial regulations required retailers to provide at least one grade of unleaded gasoline. In the challenge to these first regulations under Section 211(c), the court of appeals in *Amoco Oil Co. v. EPA (Amoco I)* upheld the EPA's findings under Section 211(c) and upheld the affirmative marketing requirement as a control on the sale of leaded gasoline.[93]

Almost one year later, in December 1973, the EPA acted to phase down the average lead content in all gasoline under Section 211(c)(1)(A) in order to address the danger to health from lead in tailpipe emissions.[94] As discussed earlier regarding the historical development of the fuels program, the initial panel of the Court of Appeals for the District of Columbia, acting pre-*Chevron* in *Ethyl Corporation v. EPA*,[95] invalidated the EPA's health-based regulations under a demanding interpretation of the "will endanger the public health or welfare" language of Section 211(c) before the 1977 amendments. The initial panel also held that the EPA had acted arbitrarily in finding that lead from auto emissions significantly contributed to elevated blood levels of lead. The court of appeals, however, reversed the initial panel's decision on rehearing *en banc*, deferring to the EPA's broader interpretation of the "will endanger" language. The court held that the EPA could act in a precautionary manner and that the agency could base its decision on inconclusive but suggested results of the studies together with policy judgments about the risk of lead impacts from all sources.[96] Congress codified this broader view of Section 211(c) in the 1977 amendments.

The EPA's original health-based regulations required refiners to limit lead content to 1.7 grams per gallon beginning in 1975, steadily decreasing it to 0.5 grams per gallon in 1979, on average for a refiner's leaded and unleaded gasoline pooled together.[97] Thus, refiners that sold more unleaded gasoline could use more lead per gallon of leaded gasoline. Small refiners were exempted until 1977 because of the high capital and operating costs needed to produce unleaded gasoline with sufficient octane supplied through other refinery components, primarily aromatic hydrocarbons. The lead-time needs for small refiners became the subject of congressional concern in the 1977 amendments, which led to a special provision then codified at Section 211(g) to give small refiners until October 1982 to meet specified lead standards, but also to allow the EPA to further regulate such refiners thereafter.[98]

The EPA changed course in 1982 after once postponing the ultimate 0.5 grams per gallon standard,[99] adopting regulations to require small refiners to meet that standard as of October 1982,[100] and considering a relaxation of that standard for small or all refiners.[101] The EPA then adopted "grams per leaded gallon" limits on lead in leaded gasoline only, replacing limits averaged over leaded and unleaded gasoline together.[102] This would avoid refiners' ability to concentrate higher levels of lead in a declining market for leaded gasoline, as the fleet turned over to cars with catalytic converters requiring unleaded gasoline. The 1982 regulations set a limit of 1.10 grams per leaded gallon for large refiners. In developing the new grams-per-leaded-gallon scheme, the EPA considered a less stringent permanent standard for small refiners, but it ultimately decided to give small refiners until July 1983 to meet the same standard as applied to large refiners, with a less stringent interim standard applicable to small refiners until that time. This scheme for small refiners was challenged in *Small Refiners Lead Phasedown Task Force v. EPA*[103] and invalidated on notice-and-comment grounds in a seminal decision regarding notice-and-comment procedures applicable to all agency rule-making.

In 1985, the EPA acted again to phase down the level of lead in leaded gasoline to current requirements.[104] The regulations specified limits on average lead content for leaded gasoline in any calendar quarter of 1.10 grams per leaded gallon before July 1, 1985; 0.50 gram per leaded gallon during 1985; and 0.10 gram per leaded gallon beginning in 1986.[105] To ease the burden of the new phased-in limits, the EPA shortly thereafter promulgated a "banking rule"[106] to allow those who could use less lead during 1985 to create lead usage rights or credits that could be banked during 1985 and then withdrawn and used to meet the more stringent standards when they became effective, but before 1988. These credits could also be transferred during that time.[107] The EPA also provided in the banking rule that those refiners meeting lower lead limits under more stringent California standards could not use them to generate credits, which otherwise could be used to raise lead levels in gasoline sold elsewhere. Such action to treat more stringent state standards as part of the regulatory "background" that should not result in higher emissions elsewhere was upheld as not discriminating against California refiners and not arbitrary in *Union Oil Co. v. EPA*.[108]

Compliance with the lead phasedown limits is calculated on average for a refinery by dividing the total grams of lead used in production by the total gallons of leaded gasoline produced.[109] The regulations require that refiners submit records to the EPA regarding lead inventories and gasoline production and calculations from these inventories of average lead content.[110] The same average standards apply to importers of gasoline, who must also submit information regarding the lead content of imported products.[111] The lead phasedown regulations also provide for "inter-refinery averaging," which essentially amounts to trading credits, or pooling production, for purposes of average compliance.[112]

To generate usage rights or credits during lead phasedown, the product produced or imported had to be "gasoline." The fundamental definition of gasoline in the EPA's regulations was a central issue in *United States v. Coastal Refining and Marketing, Inc.*[113] There, the government sought penalties from Coastal for generating lead usage rights based on shipments that the government contended were not gasoline. The regulations define gasoline in the general provisions applicable to all its regulatory programs as "any fuel sold in any State for use in motor vehicles and motor vehicle engines, and commonly or commercially known or sold as gasoline."[114] Coastal's product had octane levels at the low end of what is ordinarily sold as gasoline. The court of appeals focused on ASTM specifications as a benchmark for what is commonly known as gasoline. Finding that Coastal's product met the ASTM specifications, the court concluded that it was "commonly or commercially known" as "gasoline." In addition, the court found that Coastal's presentation of evidence of at least a single sale in one state of the same type of product as gasoline was sufficient under the definition. Since Coastal presented evidence that four service stations sold gasoline with the low octane of Coastal's product, it satisfied the definition.

The liability scheme in the EPA's lead phasedown program has been an important template for its other fuels programs. The EPA extended liability for misfueling leaded gasoline into cars labeled as requiring unleaded through the distribution network. In its initial regulations, the EPA imposed liability on distributors and refiners for retail sale of lead-contaminated gasoline as unleaded.[115] The *Amoco I* court recognized the validity of the EPA's basic argument for its presumptive liability scheme that the contamination could be caused upstream of the retail station and that it would be extremely difficult for the EPA to determine the cause of the problem in each case.[116] However, the court rejected the EPA's vicarious liability requirements, irrespective of fault, for distributors and refiners. The court held that a distributor could not be held liable if it could show that its employees and agents did not cause the violation and that a refiner could not be held liable if it could show that its employees, agents, and lessees did not cause the violation and that a reasonable program of contractual oversight could not have prevented the violation.[117]

In response to the *Amoco I* decision, the EPA revised the liability provisions, allowing distributors and refiners to avoid liability by showing that they did not cause the violation, but retaining refiners' strict vicarious liability for retailers whose assets or facilities are substantially owned, leased, or controlled by the refiner. In *Amoco Oil Co. v. EPA (Amoco II)*,[118] the court of appeals again invalidated the EPA's approach, concluding that extending vicarious liability to make refiners liable for the negligent acts of their lessees would be arbitrary.[119] In response to *Amoco II*, the EPA's current regulations provide that refiners can avoid liability at their branded facilities if they can show that they did not cause the violation and that the violation was caused either by sabotage or vandalism or by another in violation of a contractual undertaking imposed by the refiner and despite reasonable contractual oversight by the refiner.[120] The regulations define "was caused" to mean that "the refiner must demonstrate by reasonably specific showing by direct or circumstantial evidence that the violation was caused or must have been caused by another."[121]

The courts have also addressed the liability scheme in the lead phasedown program in the context of enforcement actions. In *United States v. Pilot Petroleum Associates, Inc.*,[122] the court rejected Pilot's argument that, as a "middleman," it did not "cause" violations. Rather, the court concluded that, since Pilot was the middleman that "caused" the transportation of gasoline, it was a "distributor" and failed to meet its burden to show that it did not cause the violations. In *United States v. Sharp*,[123] the court rejected a refiner's attempt to satisfy the affirmative defense elements for violations discovered at its branded retail outlet. While the refinery was able to establish that it did not cause the violation and that the violation was contrary to contractual obligations of the retailer to the refiner, the refiner failed to show that it took reasonable steps to ensure compliance with the contractual obligations. The court held that merely mailing literature about unleaded gasoline did not constitute reasonable efforts to ensure compliance. In particular, the court noted that periodic sampling of the delivery vehicles and the retail facilities was not undertaken.[124]

Since the popularization of self-service refueling stations, the courts and Congress have addressed liability for customer misfueling. In *United States v. Schilling*,[125] a district court addressed the meaning of "causing" a violation in the context of retail self-service refueling. In an enforcement action against a retailer for "allow[ing] the introduction of leaded gasoline"[126] into a car requiring unleaded, contrary to the regulatory prohibition, the retailer claimed that he could demonstrate, pursuant to the affirmative defense provisions, that he did not cause the misfueling because the customer refueled the vehicle. The court rejected this argument, holding that the affirmative defense would require a showing that an external factor caused the attendant to "allow" the customer to misfuel the vehicle.[127] In the 1990 amendments, Congress extended liability for misfueling to consumers in a new Section 211(g), providing that "no person shall introduce, or cause or allow the introduction of, leaded gasoline" into a vehicle labeled unleaded only, or which the person knows or should know is designed for unleaded gasoline.

The boundaries of the preemption provisions of Section 211(c)(4) were also first tested in the lead phasedown context. First, in 1972, in *Allway Taxi, Inc. v. City of New York*,[128] the court upheld New York's regulation requiring that taxi fleets use low-lead gasoline before the EPA's lead regulations. At that time, the EPA had not satisfied either condition for preemption under Section 211(c)(4)(A): it had not regulated under Section 211(c)(1) and had not found that no control was necessary. Once the EPA's initial lead regulations were promulgated in 1973, requiring marketing of unleaded gasoline and then a phasedown in lead content, the court of appeals in *Exxon Corporation v. City of New York*[129] concluded that nonidentical (and more stringent) New York City regulations were preempted. Even in the interim period after promulgation, but before the EPA lead-content controls were to become effective, the court concluded that the monitoring and reporting provisions designed to ensure that the industry would be prepared to manufacture the low-lead gasoline were sufficient to preempt the local lead-content regulations. The court also noted that New York had not invoked the SIP mechanism to overcome preemption where necessary to achieve the NAAQS. (This point, however, seems misplaced because the EPA did not establish the NAAQS for lead until the year after the *Exxon* court's decision.) Further, the court of appeals concluded that the EPA's lead regulations also preempted New York City's controls on gasoline volatility to address the problem of evaporated hydrocarbons, since the EPA had already prescribed nonidentical regulations "applicable to such fuel or additive."[130] In the 1990 amendments, Congress modified Section 211(c)(4) presumably to reverse this decision.

This section limits preemption to control or prohibition of "any characteristic or component of a fuel" if the EPA has found that no control or prohibition "of the characteristic or component" is necessary, or if the EPA has prescribed a control or prohibition applicable to such "characteristic or component of a fuel or fuel additive."

Finally, Congress acted by adding Section 211(n) in the 1990 amendments to ban the sale of leaded gasoline for use in any motor vehicle after December 31, 1995. The EPA had proposed in 1985 to ban the sale of leaded gasoline beginning in 1988, but it had never taken final action to do so.[131] On February 2, 1995, the EPA published a final rule, pursuant to Section 211(n), prohibiting the introduction of gasoline that is produced with the use of any lead additive, or that contains more than 0.05 grams of lead per gallon, into commerce for use as motor vehicle fuel after December 31, 1995.[132] Throughout the lead phasedown program, concerns were raised that low-lead or unleaded gasoline would cause excessive valve seat wear in engines designed to operate on leaded gasoline, particularly for older engines concentrated in the farm community. After an EPA and Department of Agriculture study of this issue, Congress added Section 211(j) to the 1990 amendments to provide for special registration under Section 211(a) of substitutes for lead additives that would reduce valve seat wear. However, the agency has not taken any further action on registration and testing lead substitute gasoline additives.[133]

Volatility Regulation under Sections 211(c) and 211(h)

After lead phasedown, the EPA's next major step under Section 211(c) to lower emissions resulting from fuel formulation was volatility controls. These were first promulgated in March 1989.[134] Evaporative hydrocarbon emissions from gasoline constitute ozone precursors. As discussed earlier, gasoline volatility had increased in the 1970s as a result of refiners' need to replace the octane formerly supplied by lead additives with aromatic hydrocarbons and refiners' incentive to use the light and volatile hydrocarbons (especially butane) generated by the production of aromatics through catalytic cracking of larger hydrocarbons. Also, newer technology cars can tolerate more volatile gasoline, and refiners have an incentive to increase volatility as much as vehicles will tolerate because volatility is increased by adding butane, a relatively inexpensive refinery component. The tolerance of cars for higher-volatility gasoline (and more butane) increased with the advent of fuel-injector technology to replace carburetors in the 1980s. Fuel injectors, unlike carburetors, keep the gasoline in the fuel supply system under pressure, thus keeping it in its liquid state. This prevents the "vapor lock" that would otherwise occur when high-volatility gasoline turns to its gaseous state in the fuel system.

Options to address the evaporative emissions from gasoline vehicles included requiring that pumps be equipped to capture refueling emissions, that vehicles carry "onboard" canisters to capture evaporative and refueling emissions, and that gasoline be formulated to limit the most volatile hydrocarbon fraction. In the course of establishing evaporative emissions standards for vehicles, the EPA recognized that more volatile fuels used in the field led to much higher evaporative emissions than the test fuels used for certification. This led the EPA to study evaporative emissions and to conclude that in-use fuel volatility reduction would be feasible and cost-effective and would result in immediate benefits, which in turn resulted in the EPA's proposal of such controls in 1987.[135] (The same day, the EPA proposed onboard refueling vapor recovery requirements, which depend on time for fleet turnover to achieve substantial reductions.) Since VOC emissions resulting from gasoline evaporation are an ozone precursor problem only in the summer months, the EPA's program is limited to the summer ozone season. In 1989, the EPA took final action to promulgate the basic framework for the volatility program and initial standards applicable beginning in the summer of 1989.[136] In 1990, the EPA promulgated more stringent but simplified Phase II standards to begin in May 1992.[137] Shortly thereafter, Congress codified the volatility program with certain changes by enacting new Section 211(h) as part of the 1990 amendments. The EPA promulgated regulations implementing the changes required by Section 211(h) at the end of 1991.[138]

The standard industry approach to measuring gasoline's volatility is in terms of pounds per square inch (psi) of Reid vapor pressure (RVP).[139] The higher the RVP, the higher the gasoline's volatility, or tendency to evaporate. Gasoline with the same RVP will evaporate more readily in warmer temperatures than in cooler temperatures. It will also evaporate more readily at higher elevations. Refiners adjust gasoline volatility throughout the year according to the prevailing temperature and the region where the gasoline is used. This adjustment is important to ensure that sufficient vapor reaches the cylinder in cold weather and to prevent vapor lock in hot weather and at high elevations.[140] Thus, refiners provide gasoline with a higher RVP to cooler (and less elevated) areas and during cooler months of the year. To assist industry with adjusting gasoline RVP to avoid drivability problems, the ASTM developed a system assigning a "class" to each state for each month of the year and specifying an upper RVP limit for gasoline for each class. (Gasoline with too low of a volatility is rare because refiners have an economic incentive to add as much high-volatility butane as possible.) The EPA's program follows the basic ASTM structure, reducing RVP in the summer months by the same increment nationwide to achieve similar reductions in evaporative emissions, but adopting higher RVP standards for cooler areas than for warmer areas.

The EPA's approach was to establish a two-phase program to reduce gasoline volatility nationwide (except for Alaska and Hawaii, where ozone pollution is not a problem and supply costs would be great). The 1989 Phase I regulations, which began in May 1989, set RVP standards of 10.5 psi, 9.5 psi, and 9.0 psi. The regulations specified standards applicable to each state (or, in some cases, portions of a state), on a month-by-month basis. The EPA established a summer ozone season of June 1 to September 16 for the standards to apply at retail stations. To ensure the proper changeover to the summer RVP gasoline, enforcement begins on May 1 for all other points upstream in the distribution system. The standards for the various areas in Phase I largely tracked the voluntary ASTM classification system.[141] This approach was designed to achieve equivalent per-vehicle emissions in all areas of the country during the summer months. In 1990, the EPA promulgated Phase II volatility regulations to take effect beginning in May 1992.[142] (The EPA also included a provision for the EPA administrator to grant testing exemptions from the volatility limits for gasoline used in research or emissions certification testing, as long as the test program is reasonable and certain information is provided to the EPA.)[143] Under Phase II, gasoline RVP standards were set at 7.8 psi for northern areas and 9.0 psi for southern areas. The EPA's Phase II rule involved analysis of climatic conditions in each state to better ensure equivalent per-vehicle emissions across the country. It was also designed to reduce month-to-month and state-to-state variability for ease of distribution and enforcement.[144] This was also simplified so that all areas receive 9.0 psi gasoline in May and have a single standard from June to September. In addition, under Phase II any state would receive gasoline meeting only one standard.

New Section 211(h), added as part of the 1990 amendments, mandates that EPA regulations prohibit the sale of gasoline with an RVP above 9.0 psi during the high-ozone season (as defined by the EPA administrator) for only the forty-eight contiguous states and the District of Columbia. The statute also mandates the approach under the EPA's prior Section 211(c) regulations to establish more stringent RVP standards to achieve comparable evaporative emissions on a per-vehicle basis across the country, taking into consideration enforceability and economic factors that the agency considered in Phase II to simplify the program. However, Section 211(h) departed from the prior regulations by allowing more stringent standards in ozone nonattainment areas, while specifying in Section 211(h)(2) that the regulations under that subsection shall not prohibit gasoline with an RVP of 9.0 psi in any area designated in attainment. The provision does specify an exception for the EPA to impose more stringent RVP requirements in attainment areas. This is presumably to address maintenance concerns for an area that was formerly in nonattainment and that has been redesignated as in attainment. In 1991, the EPA revised the Phase II standards to go into effect for nonattainment areas only and to specify a 9.0 psi standard for the attainment (and unclassifiable) areas.[145] The EPA explained that, for areas that receive 7.8 psi gasoline and are redesignated, the standard would remain 7.8 psi until the area has completed, and the EPA has approved, a maintenance plan providing for 9.0 psi gasoline. Upon redesignation to nonattainment, the standard would remain 9.0 psi until the EPA promulgates a change.[146]

In addition to the general standards, in its Phase I rule the EPA provided a special "interim" allowance of 1.0 psi for blends of 10 percent ethanol in gasoline, and it adopted this allowance on a permanent basis in the Phase II rule.[147] Ethanol is generally blended into gasoline at the distribution terminal, downstream of the refinery,[148] and raises the volatility of the gasoline into which it is blended by approximately 1.0 psi. Since ethanol has not generally been blended into specially formulated base gasoline, ethanol blends have had an RVP of 1.0 psi higher than other gasoline sold in any particular area. By providing a 1.0 psi allowance for ethanol blends, the EPA retained the status quo, whereby ethanol blends would continue to raise the RVP of the base gasoline by 1.0 psi. Since the EPA limited the RVP of the base gasoline, the RVP of ethanol blends would also be reduced, compared with previously unregulated gasoline, by the same increment as other gasoline. New Section 211(h)(4) codified the ethanol 1.0 psi allowance. This provision specifies that a distributor, blender, marketer, reseller, carrier, retailer, or wholesale purchaser-consumer (WPC) shall be deemed in compliance if it can show that the gasoline portion of the blend is in compliance, the ethanol portion does not exceed its waiver condition under Section 211(f)(4) (10 volume percent), and no other additive has been added to increase the RVP of the ethanol portion of the blend. To qualify for the 1.0 psi allowance, ethanol must be denatured and blended into gasoline at 9 to 10 volume percent, and the shipping documents must indicate the concentration of ethanol.[149]

While the EPA conformed its regulations to the program limitations in Section 211(h), it is noteworthy that those limitations are applicable on their face to regulations "under this subsection." Nothing in Section 211(h) or the EPA's implementing regulations removed the EPA's exercise of authority for its volatility program under Section 211(c). It is therefore at least arguable that the EPA could override the limitations in Section 211(h) by invoking its Section 211(c) authority. Since nowhere does Section 211(h) specify any preemptive limitation on states' authority to regulate gasoline volatility, the agency's continued insistence that states show that their more stringent volatility controls are "necessary" indicates that the agency continues to believe that the regulations are promulgated pursuant to Section 211(c)(1) as well as Section 211(h). Under the supremacy clause of the U.S. Constitution, Section 211(h) would nevertheless preempt state regulations that conflict with the federal scheme, even though Section 211(h) does not explicitly address federal preemption. Such federal regulations also might arguably be held to preempt state regulations that can be shown to frustrate the purposes of the federal scheme, for example by causing supply or distribution problems in meeting federal requirements or unduly disrupting a federal interest in national uniformity. The applicability of the Section 211(c) preemption scheme and the supremacy clause is an issue for all fuels programs that do not explicitly address preemption, including the diesel sulfur, reformulated gasoline, detergent additives, and oxygenated gasoline programs. It is unlikely that Congress intended all of these programs to preempt all state action regarding these aspects of fuels, given the special provisions to balance these concerns in Section 211(c). Further, such broad preemption might also arguably preclude California's special authority regarding these types of programs that is generally preserved in Section 211(c). There is no indication in the legislative history that Congress intended such a result.

The EPA has approved requests by several states to adopt more stringent volatility controls in their state implementation plans as necessary to achieve the ozone NAAQS under Section 211(c)(4)(C).[150] The EPA's approach to determining what is "necessary" was to find that a state control is necessary if no other measures exist that would bring about timely attainment, or if other measures exist and are technically possible to implement but are unreasonable or impracticable.[151] The EPA has explained in these cases that its assessment of what constitutes a reasonable option is a "complicated policy determination" and that cost and public acceptance of alternatives are relevant factors. Once options that the EPA considers reasonable are addressed, the state is free to determine what control measure, such as volatility control, should next be employed.[152] Congress codified this approach in Section 211(c)(4)(C) in the 1990 amendments. A remaining question is whether the EPA may consider if state volatility controls are necessary to maintain NAAQS after they have been achieved. While the statutory language explicitly refers to attainment and excludes any reference to maintenance, it seems odd that Congress would have intended that states could adopt more stringent fuel controls to achieve the NAAQS but could not do so to avoid relapsing into nonattainment. It is also important to note that Section 211(c)(4)(C) authorizes the EPA to approve more stringent state fuel controls as "necessary," but it does not obligate the agency to do so. Other considerations may constitute a basis to disapprove state measures even when they are necessary, such as a case in which national supply would not be sufficient.

The EPA also did not include an "enforcement tolerance" in the Phase I regulations but expected that gasoline would meet the standards in use. The agency explained that refiners would include a "compliance margin," producing gasoline with RVP slightly below the standard to ensure that EPA enforcement testing would find the gasoline to meet the standards.[153] In Phase II, the EPA adopted a 0.3 psi enforcement tolerance as a matter of enforcement policy, so that the agency would take enforcement action only if the RVP measures 0.3 psi above the standard.[154] The regulations specify particular sampling methodologies for determining compliance.[155]

The EPA based its enforcement and liability schemes, established in Phase I, on its experience in the lead phasedown program. Upstream, the standard is the standard applicable in the geographic area and time period in which the gasoline is intended to be sold, or the most stringent standard if the intended area cannot be determined. The EPA recognized that certain products intended for further blending before retail sale might not meet RVP standards, and it provided that it would not take enforcement action against such a product if the product is clearly labeled as unfinished and not meeting standards and if the buyer or recipient has certified that it understands the circumstances.[156] In addition, gasoline intended for export is not covered because gasoline is defined as fuel "sold in any State."[157] Enforcement is through in-field sampling and testing at refinery shipping tanks, importer shipping tanks, pipelines and other common carrier facilities, bulk terminals and plants, and service stations.

Thus, rather than tracing violating gasoline through documentation to determine liability, the EPA decided to rely on testing and presumptive liability. The program does not include new record-keeping and reporting requirements beyond those previously required for the lead phasedown program. Recall, however, that the prior regulations do provide authority to collect information about potential violations of any regulations under Section 211(c).[158]

The RVP liability scheme[159] is closely patterned after the lead phasedown program.[160] The scheme includes generally the same approach to presumptive liability for upstream parties for violations discovered downstream and to vicarious liability for refiners when violations are discovered at their branded downstream facilities. Refiners and importers (at the top of the distribution stream) are solely liable for violations found at their facilities. For violations found at a carrier's facility (i.e., in a truck), the carrier is presumptively liable, as are the refiner, any ethanol blender that produced the gasoline, and the distributor or reseller. For violations found outside the carrier's facility, the carrier is liable only if the EPA can show that the carrier caused the violation. In *In Re Commercial Cartage Co., Inc.*,[161] the Environmental Appeals Board recently clarified that transportation alone is insufficient for a carrier to "cause" a violation. Rather, to cause a violation, the carrier must either intentionally or negligently have brought gasoline above the RVP standard to an area subject to the standard.

For RVP violations found at unbranded distributor facilities or ethanol blending plants, the distributor or blender would be presumed liable, as would the refiner. If the distributor, reseller, or ethanol blending facility at which the violation is found is branded, the distributor, reseller, or blender is presumptively liable, plus the refiner is vicariously liable. For violations found at unbranded retail outlets or WPC facilities, the retailer or WPC would be presumed liable, as would distributors, any ethanol blender that produced the gasoline, and the refiner. If the violation is found at any downstream facility that operates under the refiner's brand name, then the refiner is vicariously liable.

For each of the parties in the distribution network, the regulations establish affirmative defenses[162] that define the scope of presumptive liability and, in the case of refiners with branded distribution networks, vicarious liability. In general, presumptively liable parties have an affirmative defense if they can show that they (and their employees and agents) did not cause the violation and that they have a quality assurance oversight program (e.g., periodic sampling and testing to monitor the volatility of the gasoline they handle). Refiners must, in addition, show test results demonstrating that the gasoline was in compliance when it was delivered to the next party in the distribution system. Retailers and WPCs must simply show they did not cause the violation, and they need not demonstrate an oversight program. Ethanol blenders must show that they did not cause the violation, that they had an oversight program, and that the gasoline contained no more than 10 volume percent ethanol when delivered to the next party in the distribution system.

In addition, the new Section 211(h)(4) added a specific affirmative defense for ethanol blenders who can show that the gasoline portion of the blend complied with the RVP limits, that the ethanol portion did not exceed 10 volume percent, and that no additional alcohol or other additive had been added to increase the RVP of the ethanol portion. Finally, when violations are discovered at refiners' branded downstream facilities, the refiner must show that (1) the violation was not caused by the refiner's employees or agents; (2) test results demonstrate compliance when it was transported from the refinery; and (3) the violation was caused either in violation of law (or by sabotage or vandalism) or that it was caused by another in the distribution network in violation of a contractual obligation with the refiner and despite the refiner's reasonable efforts to ensure compliance with the contractual obligation.

The EPA's imposition of liability on common carriers in the volatility rules was challenged in *National Tank Truck Carriers, Inc. v. EPA*.[163] The regulations define a "carrier" as a distributor that transports or causes the transportation or storage of gasoline without taking title to or otherwise owning the gasoline, and without altering the quality or quantity of the gasoline.[164] Common carriers generally do not take title. However, those that "splash blend" ethanol by adding the ethanol to the gasoline in the truck are defined in the EPA regulations not as carriers but as ethanol blenders and refiners.[165]

The carriers first urged that the EPA should rely on record-keeping and reporting requirements to hold liable only the party whom the documents establish caused a violation but should not hold a carrier presumptively liable for violations found in their trucks. The EPA responded that carriers could misroute gasoline to the wrong destination and that presumptive liability throughout the distribution system is preferable to tracing documentation for enforcement. The EPA also explained that the absence of such presumptive liability for carriers in the lead phasedown program had made enforcement against carriers and obtaining information from them in investigations more difficult.[166] The court of appeals upheld the EPA's policy choice of a presumptive liability scheme as not arbitrary or capricious.[167]

Second, the carriers argued that when blending ethanol they have no control over the mix and should not be considered refineries, with the additional presumptive liability for violations found downstream and the more stringent elements of the affirmative defense. The court, however, concluded that the EPA's different approach for such blenders was warranted.[168] Finally, however, the carriers successfully attacked the EPA's original requirement that carriers produce documentation indicating the compliance of their load as an element of an affirmative defense to liability for a violation found in the truck. The EPA had not imposed a requirement that shippers provide such documentation to the carriers. The court concluded that the EPA did not have an adequate rationale for requiring carriers to produce documents that only others could create without requiring that the others furnish the documents.[169] The court's remedy was to strike the documentation element from the carrier affirmative defense, allowing the EPA to reinstate it if the agency were to supply a reasoned explanation.[170] The EPA has not done so, and there is thus no such documentation requirement in the current regulations.

Diesel Sulfur Regulation under Sections 211(c) and 211(i)

As with volatility controls, the EPA first acted to limit the sulfur and aromatic content of diesel fuel just before enactment of the 1990 CAA Amendments,[171] under Section 211(c), and Congress thereafter codified the sulfur requirements (with limited changes) in the 1990 amendments by adding new Section 211(i). EPA's recent action to tighten diesel sulfur restrictions dramatically together with new diesel engine standards highlights the Agency's trend toward "systems" regulation of vehicles and fuels together.

Highlighting the close connection between fuel and vehicle regulations, the EPA began exploring the effects of diesel fuel sulfur levels in the course of its rule making to tighten the particulate emission standards for heavy-duty diesel trucks and urban buses. At the time the EPA promulgated these more stringent standards in 1985,[172] industry raised concerns that sulfur in the fuel generates particulate sulfate emissions and would plug "exhaust aftertreatment" technology (such as catalyzed particulate traps) that would be needed to meet the standards. Since the new standards would not apply until model year 1991, the EPA responded that it did not have sufficient information to take action at that time but that it would continue to study the issue.

Subsequent studies indicated that reductions in diesel sulfur would reduce sulfur dioxide and sulfate particulate emissions as well as reduce engine wear and also that reductions in aromatic content in diesel fuel would reduce carbonaceous and sulfate particulate emissions. In addition, sulfur reductions would allow engine manufacturers to use more cost-effective exhaust aftertreatment technologies to meet the particulate standards, which would also result in indirect collateral reductions in hydrocarbon and CO emissions.[173] After completion of these studies, the diesel engine manufacturing and petroleum refining industries submitted a joint proposal for regulations to address the sulfur and aromatics content of diesel fuel and to allow engine certification to reflect changes in the in-use fuel. This was a forerunner to the regulatory negotiation approach used to develop other EPA rules, including the reformulated gasoline program, discussed later. The EPA proposed and then took final action to adopt these standards.

The regulations limited the sulfur content of diesel fuel for use in motor vehicles to 0.05 weight percent,[174] reduced from preregulation average levels of 0.25 weight percent.[175] In addition, to cap aromatics content at then-current levels,[176] the EPA set the equivalent standards of a cap on aromatics at 35 volume percent or a minimum cetane index of 40.[177] The EPA also adopted specifications for certification diesel fuel to reflect these changes. Because diesel oil is also used for purposes other than fueling motor vehicles (such as for home heating oil), the EPA needed to develop a system to separate the diesel fuel for which the sulfur limit applies from other diesel oil. To accomplish this, diesel fuel not intended for use in motor vehicles must be dyed with a chemical.[178] The EPA's original regulations specified a blue-green dye. However, because of the use of blue dye in certain aviation fuel, the EPA changed the dye to red dye solvent red 164 beginning October 1, 1994.[179]

New Section 211(i)(1) codified the 0.05 weight percent limit on the sulfur content of motor vehicle diesel fuel, as well as a minimum cetane index of 40, beginning October 1, 1993. Paragraph (2) specifically requires the EPA to adopt implementing regulations, authorizes the EPA to require manufacturers and importers to dye diesel fuel not intended for use in motor vehicles to segregate it, and authorizes the EPA to establish an equivalent aromatic level to the cetane index specification. Paragraph (3) codified the EPA's approach to the certification fuels, set the sulfur content for certification of heavy-duty engines in the 1991 to 1993 model years at 0.10 weight percent, and provided that diesel certification fuel must comply with the EPA's diesel sulfur regulations thereafter. Finally, paragraph (4) provides that the EPA may exempt Alaska and Hawaii from the diesel sulfur requirements in the same manner as territories may be generally exempted from CAA requirements under Section 325 of the CAA (based on unique geographical, meteorological, economic, or other significant local factors). The EPA has granted exemptions from the diesel sulfur requirements to Alaska[180] and the Northern Marianas Islands[181] on this basis. Section 211(i) also departed from the EPA's prior regulations in that it eliminated a two-year extension for small refiners and expanded the prohibitions beyond specific parties in the fuel distribution system to apply to "all persons." The EPA implemented these changes in 1992.[182]

Most recently, on January 18, 2001, the EPA published its final rule regulating heavy-duty engines and fuels as a single system, and regulating the sulfur content of diesel fuel.[183] New emission standards will take effect for model year 2007, intended to reduce particulate matter and nitrogen oxides by 90 and 95 percent, respectively, from heavy-duty trucks and buses, which the EPA believes account for one-quarter of particulates and one-third of nitrogen oxides from mobile sources. Because the high-efficiency catalytic exhaust emission control devices and comparable technologies employed are damaged by sulfur, under authority of Section 211(c)(1)(B) to regulate fuel components that impair the performance of an emissions control device, the EPA is reducing the level of sulfur in highway diesel fuel by 2006, seeking a 97 percent reduction to 15 ppm, from the current 500 ppm.[184] Under a "Temporary Compliance Option," 80 percent of diesel fuel from any given refinery must meet the 15 ppm cap in 2006–2008, with credits allowed for overachieving refiners that can be used for averaging among the refiner's own refineries, banked for future years, or sold to another refiner.

A coalition of petroleum industry trade associations representing refiners and marketers, along with diesel engine manufacturers, challenged the diesel sulfur limits as arbitrary and capricious in *National Petrochemical & Refiners Ass'n v. EPA.*[185] The D.C. Circuit rejected the plaintiffs' arguments that the EPA failed to show that the emission-control technology for NO$_x$

would not be in use even with the fuel standard, and that the PM control technology does not require ultra-low sulfur fuel, finding that the EPA had ample support for its conclusions. The court of appeals specifically referenced the 1974 *Amoco I* decision in which lead reductions to protect catalytic converters as supporting the EPA's action for diesel sulfur content. The court of appeals also rejected challenges to the phase-in as arbitrary and capricious and contentions that the standards would result in fuel shortages.

As with the volatility program and the lead phasedown program, the enforcement scheme for the diesel sulfur regulations is based on presumptive liability rather than extensive documentation requirements.[186] Refiners and importers are liable for violations found at their facilities, without affirmative defenses.[187] They are also presumptively liable for violations found throughout their unbranded distribution networks and are vicariously liable for violations found at their branded distribution facilities. Carriers are presumptively liable for violations found in their trucks, but otherwise they are liable only if the EPA can show that they caused the violation by fuel switching, blending, mislabeling, or other means.[188] Distributors, resellers, retail outlets, and WPCs are presumptively liable for violations found at their facilities.

The affirmative defenses against presumptive liability for refiners and importers include as elements a demonstration that the party (including employees and agents) did not cause the violation, evidence of an oversight program, and test results showing compliance when the product was delivered.[189] For carriers, distributors, and resellers, the elements of the affirmative defense to presumptive liability include only a demonstration that the carrier, distributor, or reseller (including employees and agents) did not cause the violation and evidence of an oversight program.[190] For retailers and WPCs, the affirmative defense to presumptive liability requires only a showing that the retailer or WPC (including employees and agents) did not cause the violation.[191] The elements of refiners' affirmative defense against vicarious liability at their branded downstream facilities include the additional elements of a showing that the violation was caused by an action in violation of law (or by sabotage or vandalism); or was caused by another party in the distribution system in violation of a contractual undertaking imposed by the refiner and despite reasonable enforcement to ensure compliance with the contractual undertaking.[192] Refiners must show by reasonably specific direct or circumstantial evidence that the violation was or must have been caused by another party.[193]

Gasoline Sulfur Regulation under Section 211(c)

In conjunction with its Tier 2 vehicle standards issued in 2000 to reduce tailpipe emissions from passenger vehicles, the EPA also imposed lower sulfur standards for gasoline.[194] This rule was the EPA's first effort to regulate vehicles and fuels as a system, subsequently followed in the diesel and diesel sulfur rule discussed above. The EPA determined that gasoline sulfur would significantly impair the emission control systems that will be used in Tier 2 technology vehicles under Section 211(c)(1)(B).

The regulation requires most refiners to meet a corporate average gasoline sulfur standard of 120 ppm and a cap of 300 ppm by 2004. In 2005, the refinery average will be set at 30 ppm, with a corporate average of 90 ppm, and a cap of 300 ppm. Gasoline produced for sale in parts of the Western U.S. will be allowed to meet a 150 ppm refinery average and a 300 ppm cap through 2006, but must meet the 30 ppm average and 80 ppm cap by 2007. In 2006, refiners must meet a 30 ppm average sulfur level with a cap of 80 ppm. The regulations allow for the trading of sulfur credits and provide hardship allowances for small refineries.[195]

Small refiners (those who employ no more than 1,500 employees and have a corporate crude oil capacity of no more 155,000 barrels per day) can comply with less stringent interim standards through 2007, when they must come into compliance with the final sulfur standards. Small refiners that demonstrate a severe economic hardship can apply for an additional extension of up to two years.[196]

In April 2001, the EPA issued a direct final rule to correct and revise certain provisions of the Tier 2/gasoline sulfur rule.[197] The direct final rule (1) makes minor corrections to clarify the gasoline sulfur standards; (2) revises the boundaries of the Geographic Phase-in Area (GPA) to include counties and tribal lands in states adjacent to the eight original GPA states, in order to ensure a smooth transition to low sulfur gasoline and mitigate the potential for gasoline shortages; (3) amends certain provisions of the small refiner and Averaging, Banking, and Trading (ABT) programs to assist domestic and foreign refiners and importers in establishing gasoline sulfur baselines for credit and allotment generation purposes; and (4) revises certain sampling and testing provisions for low sulfur gasoline to enable certain refiners to generate early credits and/or allotments under the ABT program.

Reformulated Gasoline

The reformulated gasoline provisions codified in Section 211(k) constitute Congress's most ambitious effort toward highly detailed and prescriptive requirements for regulations anywhere in the fuels program and, perhaps, anywhere throughout the CAA. In response to efforts in the development of the 1990 amendments to develop purportedly "clean" alternative fuels (such as methanol, ethanol, CNG, and LPG), the automobile and oil industries joined forces to promote the possibility of reducing harmful emissions from gasoline, and began a major auto-oil research program to investigate the best way to do so. Legislation that began with general requirements to achieve the greatest possible reductions in emissions, considering certain factors, ultimately acquired additional details of how the EPA's regulations should accomplish this goal.

Overview of Statutory Requirements

Congress specified in Section 211(k)(5) that only reformulated gasoline may be supplied to certain "covered areas" beginning January 1, 1995. Section

211(k)(10) defines these covered areas to include nine large cities with the worst ozone pollution problems, and any ozone nonattainment area redesignated to the "severe" category. Under Section 211(k)(6), a governor may apply to the EPA to opt into the program for any ozone nonattainment area. The EPA has interpreted Section 211(k)(6) to allow governors who have opted into the program to opt out of the program later.[198] Section 211(k)(8) establishes "anti-dumping" rules that apply to prevent degradation elsewhere that might result if refiners were to redirect "dirty" components removed from reformulated gasoline to gasoline destined for other areas.

The EPA also promulgated the reformulated gasoline program under the dual authority of Section 211(c). The EPA chose this approach originally to preserve uniformity, preempting states from adopting nonidentical regulations. (As noted in the volatility context, it is unclear whether states that adopt more stringent reformulated gasoline regulations would be preempted as frustrating a national uniformity purpose, or whether the EPA would deny approval under Section 211(c) based on supply or uniformity concerns, even if the regulations were "necessary.") While California may develop its own fuels regulations under Section 211(c)(4), and has developed its own reformulated gasoline program, the federal program still applies. California refiners must therefore satisfy the requirements of both programs. As discussed later, the EPA ultimately relied on Section 211(c) to require that reformulated gasoline achieve reductions in NO_x emissions, a concern not addressed in Section 211(k).

Section 211(k)(1) establishes the overarching requirement that the EPA promulgate regulations to obtain the greatest reduction in emissions of ozone-forming VOCs (during the summer ozone season) and emissions of toxic air pollutants[199] (throughout the year) achievable through reformulation of gasoline, considering factors such as cost, other health and environmental impacts, and energy requirements. Section 211(k)(2) establishes four fundamental requirements for the regulations. First, reformulated gasoline is not to cause an increase in NO_x emissions, and the EPA could waive the other three requirements to ensure this end. Second, reformulated gasoline must contain oxygenates to provide at least 2.0 weight percent oxygen in the fuel. Third, benzene (a carcinogenic compound) is limited to 1.0 volume percent. Fourth, heavy metals are entirely prohibited, except that the EPA can waive this prohibition if a metal will not increase toxic emissions (on a mass or cancer-risk basis).

Section 211(k)(3) addresses the complicated issue of how the EPA is to require the greatest reduction achievable in ozone-forming and toxic emissions. That paragraph provides that the EPA's regulations are to require compliance with the more stringent of a specific formula fuel or certain performance standards. The performance standards include two "phases." The initial standard is a 15 percent reduction in VOC emissions and toxic emissions, on a mass basis. Then, beginning in 2000, the performance standard changes to 25 percent, which the EPA can adjust either downward to 20 percent or upward, based on cost and feasibility. To measure the "performance" of a reformulated gasoline, the statute specifies three important factors. First, all testing and measurements are to be conducted using 1990 model-year vehicles; the program, therefore, does not take account of changes in vehicle technology after 1990. Second, the EPA is to take account of emissions from the entire vehicle, including tailpipe emissions and all evaporation—during operation ("running losses"), immediately after operation ("hot soak"), and during refueling. Finally, Section 211(k) specifies fuel properties of a "summertime baseline" gasoline (that apparently is close to the 1990 industry summertime average properties) and provides that the EPA establish "baseline" properties for wintertime gasoline that represent 1990 industry average gasoline. In sum, performance of reformulated gasoline is thus to be measured with 1990 vehicle technology, for the entire vehicle, against these baseline gasolines.

Section 211(k)(4) provides that the EPA is to establish procedures to certify reformulated gasoline that complies with the emissions requirements within 180 days of submission. Only gasoline certified as reformulated can be sold in covered areas. Under Section 211(k)(4), the EPA's first task was to determine the level of emissions from 1990 vehicles when using the baseline gasolines and to establish a methodology for measuring emissions from these cars when using other gasoline formulations. This was a complicated issue that is addressed in more detail in the later discussion of the EPA's implementation. The EPA then had to determine whether the specified formula fuel achieved reductions beyond the specified performance standards. The EPA concluded that it did not, and the formula therefore is not important in the EPA's regulatory scheme.

In meeting the standards, Section 211(k)(7) provides that the EPA's regulations are to allow refiners, blenders, and importers to obtain credits for using more oxygen than required, less aromatic hydrocarbons than required, and less benzene than required. Under the provision, these parties may trade those credits to others within the same nonattainment area. This credit scheme follows the precedent the EPA established in the lead phasedown program.

Finally, Section 211(k)(8) requires that the EPA establish an anti-dumping program to ensure that gasoline that is not reformulated does not result in higher emissions of VOCs, NO_x, CO, and toxic air pollutants. The anti-dumping program applies to gasoline from each refiner, blender, or importer separately, so that emissions cannot increase for each such party above the emissions from that party's gasoline in 1990. Each party's 1990 "baseline" gasoline is to be established based on data regarding the composition of that party's gasoline in calendar year 1990. When such data is not available, the EPA is to determine compliance based on comparison to the "statutory" baseline gasoline used to measure performance of reformulated gasoline (that approximates industry-average gasoline properties).

Overview of Regulatory Development

While the statutory provisions for reformulated gasoline are themselves among the most complex in the CAA, the issues to be resolved in implementing the program in a manner that would minimize disruption of the gasoline distribution network were even more daunting. The most complicated technical issue was the methodology for determining the emissions levels that a particular gasoline formulation would generate across the 1990 model-year fleet of vehicles, from both the tailpipe and evaporation, under all relevant conditions and throughout those vehicles' useful lives. The approach the EPA followed was to aggregate test data from many vehicles to develop a mathematical emissions model for the impact of varying particular fuel properties on emissions. Based on testing many 1990 vehicles at various points in their useful lives, it was possible to develop a relationship between various characteristics of gasoline and emissions. Another different methodology that the EPA rejected was to require refiners to establish the performance of their gasoline through a particular vehicle testing protocol.[200] Other complicated issues involved working out an enforcement scheme and an averaging and trading regime that would be workable in an existing distribution system characterized by extensive fungible mixing of gasoline from multiple refiners, thus making segregation of gasoline destined for particular ozone nonattainment areas very difficult.

To address these and other complications, the EPA entered into regulatory negotiation (reg neg) pursuant to the Negotiated Rulemaking Act of 1990,[201] with representatives of the auto and oil industries, state officials, oxygenate suppliers (including those producing the primary oxygenates MTBE and ethanol), environmentalists, and others. The reg neg addressed the reformulated gasoline and anti-dumping requirements of the statute. Since the EPA faced a November 15, 1991, statutory deadline to promulgate the regulations, it issued its initial proposal in July 1991 during the negotiation, outlining various issues that the negotiating committee was considering.[202] After the committee reached a reg neg agreement, the EPA published a supplemental proposal in April 1992 consistent with that agreement.[203]

The reg neg agreement signed on August 16, 1991, as elaborated upon in the 1992 proposal, established the basic framework for the current regulations. This proposal also crystallized the issue regarding the treatment of the oxygenate ethanol in the program that was to lead to extreme controversy and to delay ultimate promulgation of the EPA's final rule until 1994. Under the reg neg agreement, the EPA would establish two models to determine emissions from 1990 vehicles when using a gasoline having particular properties. The reg neg agreement provided for a two-step approach. In the first step, a "simple model" would be used to determine that the fuel achieved sufficient reductions in VOCs and toxic emissions, based on the fuel's oxygen, benzene, heavy metal, and aromatics content, as well as RVP. The EPA only had data at the time to quantify the effect of these parameters on emissions. The model assumed the statutory limitations on oxygen, benzene, and heavy metals, and specified RVP levels of 8.1 psi for northern areas and 7.2 psi for southern areas, to achieve at least 15 percent reductions for northern areas and even lower RVP levels to achieve similar incremental reductions beyond the volatility rule limits for southern areas. Reductions in VOCs for southern areas would be substantially higher compared with the single statutory baseline gasoline with an 8.7 psi RVP. Refiners would hold the other fuel properties at the average value for their 1990 production. Refiners' "1990 baseline" would thus be used for simple model reformulated gasoline, and would serve as the baseline for the anti-dumping program.

The EPA would thereafter propose a "complex model" that would take account of more fuel properties (olefins, sulfur, T50, and T90)[204] in determining the emissions that would result, based on data being developed to quantify the emissions impact of these additional parameters. Also, the EPA agreed first to propose the Phase I standards that would apply from 1995 to 1999, and then to propose the more stringent Phase II standards to begin in 2000 at the same time as it would propose the complex emissions model. The reg neg agreement specifically provided for standards that would be more stringent in southern areas subject to lower RVP limits in the volatility program and less stringent standards applicable in northern areas subject to higher RVP limits in the volatility program. This was in response to the problem posed by a single summertime baseline gasoline specified in the statute with an RVP of 8.7. The volatility program independently required gasoline in southern nonattainment areas to have an RVP of 7.8. That RVP control alone would achieve a 15 percent reduction in VOC emissions. To ensure that the incremental benefits from reformulated gasoline would be equivalent in northern and southern areas, the reg neg agreement provided for more stringent RVP limits in the simple model for southern areas, and hence a substantially larger reduction in emissions compared with the summertime baseline gasoline.[205] To preserve existing distribution arrangements, the reg neg agreement provided for compliance on average at the refinery level, with a "survey" system designed to ensure that gasoline averaged separately in each nonattainment area would be in compliance.

The controversy regarding the role of ethanol in reformulated gasoline also began with the reg neg agreement.[206] Ethanol, largely derived from corn, has been used increasingly as a volume extender and octane enhancer since the 1970s when the OPEC oil embargo raised concern about oil imports and lead phasedown created a need for alternative sources of octane. It has been the subject of government support, including federal and state tax subsidies, government-sponsored research and development, and other legislative initiatives designed to stimulate development of alternative fuels and especially domestic renewable fuels.[207] As discussed with respect to the volatility program, ethanol raises the RVP of gasoline by approximately 1.0 psi. Since the summertime baseline gasoline has a single 8.7 psi RVP, ethanol would have to be blended into gasoline starting with an RVP one psi below other gasoline to achieve the same reductions compared with the baseline.[208]

The reg neg agreement did not explicitly provide that ethanol blends could comply despite a higher RVP than other fuel. The ethanol industry would argue that they understood the 1 psi "waiver" in Section 211(h) and the EPA's volatility rule to apply to reformulated gasoline as well. In this manner, they would argue they believed blenders could continue to add ethanol to any gasoline in a nonattainment area and be in compliance with the standards.

The EPA's April 1992 proposal did not incorporate a special volatility "waiver" for ethanol; this led the ethanol industry to raise the concern that ethanol would improperly be excluded from the reformulated gasoline market, since refiners would simply blend MTBE into the fuel to supply the required oxygen content without raising the volatility of the blend. They argued that refiners would not provide gasoline having extra-low volatility to allow for ethanol to be blended into the gasoline downstream and still comply with the standards. In a November 17, 1992, opinion, the EPA's general counsel rejected applicability of the 1 psi waiver provision in Section 211(h) to Section 211(k) and reformulated gasoline. Thereafter, the EPA continued to work to develop a mechanism to enhance the use of ethanol to meet the oxygen content requirement, despite the volatility increase that ethanol causes, and to respond to numerous other proposals from ethanol supporters to encourage or require the use of ethanol in reformulated gasoline. The ethanol supporters continued to urge that the benefits of ethanol as a renewable source of energy made from domestically grown grains justified encouraging its use in reformulated gasoline.

In February 1993, the EPA issued another proposal, signed on the last day of the first Bush administration, that included the complex emissions model and the Phase II standards that were to apply beginning in 2000.[209] In addition, the EPA proposed in that notice a new performance standard under Section 211(c) of the CAA for NO_x emissions reductions to apply, beginning with Phase II in 2000, noting the increasing attention to NO_x as an important ozone precursor.[210] Finally, the 1993 proposal contained special provisions to require that refiners marketing gasoline containing ethanol or other renewable oxygenates (such as ETBE) could meet less stringent standards and that those not using ethanol would have to meet more stringent standards. The result was the equivalent of a 1 psi waiver for the first 30 percent market share of ethanol blends in northern areas with the resulting increase in volatility and evaporative emissions to be offset by more stringent RVP standards applicable to the rest of the reformulated gasoline pool.[211]

The Clinton administration ultimately abandoned this ethanol plan. The EPA explained that the previous plan was unworkable, and that despite no increase in the average RVP of the in-use gasoline, 40 to 50 percent of the VOC control required under Section 211(k) would be lost as a result of the plan, for various technical reasons.[212] In particular, the EPA emphasized that ethanol blends "commingled" in consumers' fuel tanks with nonethanol blends would increase the volatility of the mixture, thus degrading the emissions benefits from the nonethanol portion and the overall emissions benefits. In its place, the EPA adopted a simpler mandate that a percent of the oxygenates needed to comply with reformulated gasoline requirements be supplied by "renewable oxygenates." After proposing this plan at the same time as it promulgated final rules for the other aspects of the reformulated gasoline program in February 1994,[213] the EPA took final action on the plan in August 1994.[214] Under this plan, 30 percent of the required 2.0 weight percent oxygen in reformulated gasoline (but only 15 percent during the first year of 1995) would have to be produced from "renewable oxygenates." This includes those oxygenates produced from non–fossil fuel feedstocks. Also, during the summer VOC-controlled months, only oxygenates that do not cause an increase in gasoline volatility would qualify. Thus, ethanol would qualify in the winter months, but only ETBE (derived from ethanol) would qualify in the summer.

The oil industry challenged the legality of the EPA's renewable oxygenate requirements in *American Petroleum Institute v. EPA*.[215] The EPA justified the inclusion of the renewable oxygenates requirement as appropriate to ensure that the emissions reduction requirements for reformulated gasoline are achieved in a manner that optimizes the energy, cost, environmental, and other impacts of the program. In particular, the agency asserted that Section 211(k)(1) provides a general grant of authority to the EPA to establish reasonable requirements that are not limited to establishing emissions reduction standards.[216] The EPA also relied on legislative history indicating that particular members of Congress expected that the reformulated gasoline program would expand the market for renewable oxygenates such as ethanol.

The court of appeals in *American Petroleum Institute v. EPA* concluded that the plain meaning of Section 211(k)(1) precluded the adoption of reformulated gasoline regulations that were not directed toward reduction of VOC and toxic emissions.[217] The court noted that the EPA conceded that the renewable oxygenate rule would not provide additional emission reductions for VOCs or toxics. Accordingly, the court held that the EPA's interpretation of Section 211(k) to adopt the renewable oxygenate rule and effectively guarantee the market for ethanol was improper.[218]

Regulations

The EPA's regulations follow the elements of the reg neg agreement very closely. Elements of the final rules that are beyond the scope of the reg neg agreement include the renewable oxygenates program, the Phase II standards for NO_x and VOC, and an additional Phase II NO_x standard.[219]

The VOC emissions requirements apply during the summer ozone season of June 1 to September 15 at retail outlets and, beginning May 1, upstream (consistent with the summer volatility control season). The toxics emissions requirements apply throughout the year. The simple model for VOC emissions,[220] which was used until the complex model became mandatory after December 31, 1997, required 2.0 weight percent oxygen and RVP limits of 7.2 psi in southern areas and 8.1 psi in northern areas (yielding about 15 percent VOC emissions reductions relative in both areas relative to current RVP limits).[221]

To justify averaging for VOC compliance, which Section 211(k) does not specifically address, the EPA reasoned that more reductions would be "achievable" under Section 211(k)(1) through such averaging. Hence, for refiners that met the RVP and oxygen standards through averaging, the standards were 7.1 and 8.0 psi, and 2.1 weight percent oxygen. Other parameters were to be held at the refiner's 1990 baseline.

To ensure that NO_x emissions did not increase due to the effects of oxygenates and adjustments to other parameters when oxygenates are added, under the simple model oxygen content could not exceed 2.7 weight percent during the summer months, but oxygen content could reach 3.5 weight percent outside the ozone season (unless a state requests that oxygen be limited to 2.7 weight percent in the nonozone season).

The simple model for toxics[222] was based on the aromatics and benzene content of the fuel. Benzene is a component of gasoline; benzene emissions result from fuel evaporation rather than combustion. The other toxic pollutants (1,3 butadiene, acetaldehyde, formaldehyde, and polycyclic organic matter, or POM) are not found in fuel and result from fuel combustion. Hence, benzene was a consideration only in the summer months for which data on fuel evaporation is available.[223] The EPA concluded that toxics emissions reductions beyond 15 percent in Phase I were not cost-effective, and thus set the standard at the 15 percent minimum. As with VOC averaging, however, for refiners who use averaging to comply with the toxics standard, the more stringent standard of 16.5 percent applied.[224]

The EPA's complex model must be used to certify fuels as of January 1, 1998. The complex model is an equation into which the levels of various fuel parameters can be input to generate a percentage emissions reduction from baseline gasoline. It reflects assumptions regarding factors, such as inspection and maintenance programs and driving conditions, represented by the EPA's MOBILE model,[225] and combines through complicated regression analyses data from various vehicle testing programs. In addition, the final rule provides for private organizations to "augment" the complex model through a testing program meeting regulatory requirements (subject to EPA preapproval), to refine the model's predictions or to extend the model to account for the effects of adjusting additional parameters.[226]

The EPA's Phase II standards are subject to compliance through the complex model only. The standards are therefore expressed as percentage emissions reductions from the baseline gasoline, and refiners have freedom to adjust any of the parameters in the complex model that the model shows will generate the required reductions. The Phase II standards that applied as of January 1, 2000, required for VOC control 25.9 percent reductions in northern areas and 27.5 percent reductions in southern areas, as measured against the baseline gasoline. This amounts to a greater incremental benefit from Phase I for northern areas, since southern areas started with more stringent volatility controls. For toxics, the EPA set the Phase II standards at the statutory minimum 20 percent reductions. The EPA explained that the incremental cost of avoiding cancer deaths by increasing the toxics reductions beyond that point would be exorbitant, at least for some refiners.[227] Finally, acting under the independent authority of Section 211(c), the EPA adopted a NO_x emissions reduction requirement of 5.5 percent for both northern and southern areas.[228] Reductions in sulfur (and olefin levels to a lesser extent) tend to reduce NO_x emissions. The EPA concluded it makes sense to address NO_x emissions at the same time through the same program designed to target ozone nonattainment areas, especially since evidence accumulated since the 1990 amendments has confirmed the importance of NO_x reductions for ozone control.[229] All of these standards are slightly more stringent for refiners that comply on average, since the cost savings of averaging makes more reductions "achievable."[230]

As summarized below in the discussion of the oxygenated gasoline program, use of MTBE has become highly controversial due to its propensity for contamination of groundwater upon release from underground storage tanks or other containment. As part of broader efforts to decrease reliance on MTBE, the EPA proposed on July 12, 2000, to adjust the VOC performance standard under Phase II of the reformulated gasoline program for ethanol blends that contain 3.5 weight percent oxygen, adjusting the standard down by one percentage point each in the north and south, to 26.4 and 28 percent, respectively.[231]

The anti-dumping requirements are designed to ensure that a refiner's or importer's conventional gasoline supplied to areas not receiving reformulated gasoline does not deteriorate in emissions performance, compared with that refiner's or importer's 1990 gasoline quality. Under Section 211(k)(8), these requirements apply independently for average per gallon emissions of VOC, CO, NO_x, and toxic air pollutants. The regulations address only exhaust benzene, total exhaust toxics, and NO_x emissions from conventional gasoline. Under the simple model, there are caps on sulfur, olefin, and T90 levels in conventional gasoline. The EPA explained that these requirements, together with other programs (such as volatility), will ensure that levels of VOC and CO emissions will not increase compared with each refiner's and importer's 1990 levels.[232] The exhaust benzene emissions from conventional gasoline were measured under the simple model before January 1, 1998, based on benzene and aromatic content. Olefin, sulfur, and T90 levels were capped at 25 percent above the refiner's or importer's baseline levels. As of January 1, 1998, compliance for toxics and NO_x is determined using the complex model. Refiners can demonstrate compliance either for each refinery separately or for a group of refineries that the refiner operates.[233]

The important issue of "baseline determination" applies both for the anti-dumping program and for purposes of holding refiners and importers to their 1990 levels of olefins, sulfur, and T90 under the reformulated gasoline simple model.[234] These baseline determinations are important because those who might obtain a "dirtier" baseline can provide "dirtier" gasoline both for simple model reformulated as well as conventional gasoline. The EPA developed extensive procedures to determine a domestic refiner's 1990 levels of the various parameters, using data from 1990 production or data from later production at the same refinery or through analysis of the refinery's 1990 configuration to determine what 1990 levels must have been.[235] Refiners are not allowed to choose whether to present data to calculate their 1990 baseline, which approach to use, or whether to default to the statutory baseline; if allowed to choose, they would simply choose the least stringent option. Rather, data will be used if it is available, and the refiners must use independent commercial auditors to certify the accuracy and availability of the data. Thus, the default to the "statutory" baseline specified in Section 211(k)[236] will not apply to domestic refiners.

For importers, the regulations provide that an individual baseline may be established either by using actual data confirming the characteristics of their 1990 imports or by default to the statutory baseline. Since most importers lack sufficient 1990 data for all of their imports, most will default to the statutory baseline. Calculations using data from subsequent years or from refinery configurations where the imported gasoline was produced are not allowed, because the EPA did not believe it could verify the refinery-of-origin for imports or the reliability and availability of data from foreign refineries.[237]

This difference in treatment created the second major political issue for reformulated gasoline implementation. The Venezuelan national oil company, Petroleos de Venezuela, S.A. (PDVSA), which supplies gasoline primarily to the northeast U.S. market, objected that this difference in treatment between foreign and domestic refiners discriminates against foreign refiners. PDVSA argued that this regulatory scheme violates national treatment guarantees of the General Agreement on Tariffs and Trade (GATT) and does not qualify for an exception applicable to measures "necessary to protect human, animal or plant life or health."[238] The statutory baseline would be more stringent in sulfur and olefin content than a baseline calculated from its own 1990 production for the U.S. market. In particular, requiring that PDVSA hold olefin and sulfur levels at the statutory baseline rather than at its own 1990 average levels would make PDVSA's participation in the reformulated gasoline market more difficult in the simple model period, and would require PDVSA to make changes to lower olefin and sulfur levels down to the statutory baseline for its conventional gasoline production. The EPA considered whether some diplomatic arrangement could be devised for the EPA to assure the availability and reliability of data for a foreign refiner's product destined for the U.S. market; it did not develop such a solution by the time of the reformulated gasoline final rule promulgation. Thereafter, the EPA continued to work with PDVSA and others to develop a solution. In May 1994, the EPA proposed procedures for foreign refiners to develop baselines based on their own 1990 production for the U.S. market by petition that importers could apply to gasoline imported from a particular foreign refinery.[239] To establish its own baseline, the foreign refiner would supply data from the refinery and a report from an independent EPA-approved auditor. The foreign refiner would further have to agree to EPA inspections and audits at the refinery. Finally, the gasoline from the foreign refinery would have to be segregated and tracked to ensure that the refinery-of-origin could be identified. Other refiners seeking their own 1990 baseline had yet to come forward at the time of this proposal. Thereafter, political concerns led Congress to enact a rider to an appropriations bill prohibiting the EPA from expending funds to take final action on the May 1994 proposal.[240] Venezuela requested that a GATT panel be established to consider the GATT consistency of the EPA's rules governing the baseline determination for reformulated gasoline under the simple model and conventional gasoline, and Brazil joined the challenge as well.

In the meantime, the World Trade Organization came into being, and this dispute resulted in the first decision handed down by a WTO dispute resolution panel. The panel rejected the U.S. discrimination between foreign and domestic producers, and the environmental rationale put forward by the United States in its defense, declaring the measure inconsistent with the GATT. [241] A WTO appellate body affirmed this decision.[242] Subsequently, on August 28, 1997, the EPA issued revisions to the baseline requirements for imported conventional gasoline, applicable to both foreign refiners and importers that produce, import, or distribute gasoline for sale in the United States.[243] Foreign refiners may now choose to petition the EPA to establish an individual baseline reflecting the quality and quantity of gasoline produced at a foreign refinery in 1990 that was shipped to the United States. The foreign refiner must meet the same requirements relating to the establishment and use of individual refinery baselines as are met by domestic refiners. The EPA indicated that it believed these provisions to be consistent with U.S. obligations under the WTO.[244]

The EPA's enforcement scheme imposes the most complicated requirements on refiners and importers at the top of the distribution network, who are responsible for certification of fuel formulations and a variety of requirements designed to ensure that the proper gasoline is made. All gasoline either must be certified as reformulated or be treated as conventional. All gasoline certified as reformulated must meet reformulated gasoline requirements, wherever it is sold, but only reformulated gasoline may be sold in the covered areas.[245]

Special enforcement requirements apply to refiners and importers that choose to meet standards on average for RVP, oxygen, and benzene under the simple model, and VOC, toxics, and NO_x under the complex model. These requirements are designed to limit geographic variation in gasoline quality to assure that each area gets gasoline that, on average, meets the emissions reduction requirements. First, gasoline subject to averaged compliance is subject to minimum and maximum levels for each averaged parameter. Then, refiners, importers, and oxygenate blenders that meet the standards on average must survey the gasoline quality in each covered area each year.[246] If that average does not meet the per-gallon standards, then the minimum or maximum standard, as well as the standard for average compliance, is tightened in the following years for all refineries that supplied gasoline to the area.[247] The averaged standards are already more stringent than the per-gallon standards. Credit trading among refiners and importers is available only for oxygen and benzene levels.

Oxygen credits and averaging is complicated in two circumstances. First, the oxygenated gasoline program under Section 211(m) (discussed in detail later) requires at least 2.7 weight percent oxygen in winter months in CO nonattainment areas. Some of these areas are also subject to a reformulated gasoline requirement for 2.0 weight percent oxygen throughout the year. Refiners may not rely on oxygen levels needed to comply with the winter requirements to generate credits that could otherwise be used to diminish oxygen content below 2.0 weight percent during the rest of the year. Second, certain oxygenates such as ethanol are typically added to gasoline downstream of the refinery and the gasoline must be specially formulated for this purpose in order for the finished product to comply with the reformulated gasoline standards (after the volatility boost that ethanol causes). This reformulated blendstock for oxygenate blending (RBOB)[248] must include in the transfer documentation the kind and amount of oxygenate that may be blended into it, and must comply with all standards except oxygen. Also, RBOB must be segregated from reformulated gasoline and from other RBOB with different oxygenate requirements. Further, RBOB refiners and importers must have contractual relationships with the oxygenate blenders to ensure proper downstream blending, and the refiner or importer must conduct quality assurance programs for the downstream blending operations. (RBOB suitable for blending with any oxygenate or with "ethers only" does not have to comply with certain constraints.)

Refiners, importers, and oxygenate blenders are subject to extensive registration,[249] record-keeping,[250] reporting,[251] and "attest engagement"[252] requirements. These parties must submit quarterly reports regarding each batch of reformulated gasoline or RBOB produced or imported. Additional reporting requirements apply to those who comply on average for any standard. Averaging reports for RVP, VOC, and NO_x are due for each summer ozone season; oxygen, benzene, and toxics averaging reports are due for each year. Refiners, importers, and oxygenate blenders also must register with the EPA to provide information about facilities and independent laboratories that will conduct testing, and a facility registration number to be used in all reports. These parties must commission an "attest engagement" on an annual basis to conduct an independent review of information contained in the reports to the EPA. Refiners and importers must create product transfer documents that include, in addition to the RBOB blending information discussed earlier, information about whether the gasoline is reformulated, whether it meets summer VOC-controlled requirements, and any applicable segregation requirements. Finally, the regulations provide a special exception for the EPA to allow refiners and importers to distribute noncompliant gasoline under extraordinary circumstances, when it is in the public interest to do so.[253]

The accuracy of refiner and importer records is especially important for enforcement in the reformulated gasoline program because of the common fungible mixing of gasoline after it leaves the refinery. The EPA cannot test gasoline downstream to verify that it complies with the certified formulations that ensure compliance with the emissions standards for each refinery or importer. Because the EPA cannot "look behind" the refiner's or importer's records in most cases, the regulations require refiners and importers to carry out a program of independent sampling and testing to assure the accuracy of the records. This is in addition to the "attest engagement" requirement to review the records themselves. Refiners and importers must retain records for a period of five years.[254]

The EPA's program is generally designed to accommodate the fungible mixing of gasolines that currently exists in the distribution network. However, there are a number of limitations. First, gasoline that is VOC-controlled for summer season use must be segregated from non-VOC-controlled gasoline in advance of the summer season. Second, northern (Control Region 1) gasoline must be segregated from southern (Control Region 2) gasoline. Third, during the summer VOC-controlled season, gasoline containing ethanol must be segregated from gasoline containing other oxygenates (to prevent the ethanol from raising the volatility of the overall mix through commingling). Fourth, gasoline designated for use in areas subject to reformulated gasoline and oxygenated gasoline requirements (oxygenated fuels program reformulated gasoline, or OPRG) must be segregated from other reformulated gasoline.

Parties downstream of refiners and importers must ensure that properly designated reformulated gasoline is sold in the correct season and in the correct areas, according to the product transfer documents. Also, downstream parties are responsible for ensuring that the reformulated gasoline complies with certain minimum and maximum limits on parameters that apply to gasoline that is to meet standards on average. For violations of these requirements, the EPA's presumptive and vicarious liability scheme utilized in the other fuels programs applies, and the EPA relied on its experience with these other programs to support its scheme for reformulated gasoline.[255] Parties are presumed liable for violations discovered at their facilities, and upstream parties are also presumptively liable. (As in the volatility program, however, carriers that do not alter the gasoline are presumptively liable only for violations found in their trucks, but would be presumptively liable if they blend oxygenates or other components.) Refiners are also vicariously liable for violations found at their downstream branded facilities. The affirmative defense to presumptive liability requires that the party show that it did not cause the violation, that the product transfer documents were proper, and that the party carried out a quality assurance program to verify compliance with minimum and maximum limits. For a defense to vicarious liability, the refiner must also show that another caused the violation; that the violation was contrary to a contractual obligation to the refiner; and that the refiner carried out a contractual oversight program to ensure compliance with it.

The reformulated gasoline program also includes a special exemption from certain enforcement requirements for gasoline subject to California's independent reformulated gasoline requirements.[256] The EPA concluded that California's own Phase II program would achieve greater emissions reductions than federal reformulated gasoline. Thus, while the federal standards still apply in California, compliance with California's requirements would also assure compliance with the federal requirements. Since compliance with both the federal and California enforcement regimes would be burdensome, the regulations allow those producing reformulated gasoline for use only in California to be exempt from a number of the enforcement-related requirements of the federal program. These exemptions would be lost for any California-approved formulations that would not achieve compliance with federal standards, or to gasoline produced in California but sold outside that state. By rule issued September 15, 1999, the EPA extended Phase I exemptions into Phase II for California refiners, importers, and blenders, protecting them from certain enforcement provisions in the Federal reformulated gasoline program.[257]

The regulations also specify test methods for all of the relevant gasoline parameters.[258] The EPA addressed enforcement tolerances for these parameters in the preamble to the final rule.[259] Without test tolerances, refiners may have to produce gasoline that surpasses applicable maximum or minimum limits, creating a "margin of safety" to account for variability that may result in violations discovered through testing. The EPA concluded that test tolerances are not required under Section 211(k). The EPA explained that test tolerances within the EPA's enforcement discretion constitute a policy that the EPA will not enforce unless testing shows failure to meet a standard by more than the test tolerance amount. In holding downstream parties responsible for the maximum and minimum limits, the EPA specified enforcement tolerances so that the downstream parties would not insist that refiners and importers build a "margin of safety," surpassing those limits in production. The EPA set these tolerances for the parameters relevant under the simple model and that are subject to maximums and minimums: oxygen (0.3 weight percent, consistent with the oxygenated gasoline program recommended tolerance), benzene (0.21 volume percent, pending further refinement), and RVP (0.30 psi, consistent with the volatility rule's current enforcement test tolerance).[260]

For anti-dumping enforcement, refiners and importers must account for and track gasoline blendstocks, blendstocks for oxygenate blending, and nongasoline products. This is designed to avoid an incentive to transfer blendstocks to those with less stringent 1990 baselines instead of producing gasoline that must meet the transferor's more stringent 1990 baseline. The accounting and tracking requirements apply where the refiner's or importer's blendstock-to-gasoline ratio exceeds by more than 10 percent that ratio averaged over the period 1990 to 1993. In other words, it applies for refiners that shift more production to blendstocks, raising concern about whether such refiners might otherwise be shifting gasoline production to those with less stringent baselines. The treatment of blendstocks is addressed extensively in the final rule preamble.[261]

The enforcement scheme for refiners and importers to comply with the anti-dumping program for conventional gasoline includes refiner and importer sampling and testing requirements, as well as record keeping and reporting, transfer documentation, and annual "attest engagements" (audits).[262] The EPA explained in its proposal that an EPA auditing program improved compliance dramatically in the lead phasedown program.[263]

Refiners and importers of conventional gasoline must also register with the EPA. They must also maintain records of the composition of the conventional gasoline and blendstocks they produce or import, and must retain documents (including transfer documents) relating to the purchase or sale of feedstocks and other products. As with the reformulated gasoline requirements, due to the same averaging and fungible mixing concerns, independent sampling and testing, as well as attest engagements, are required to ensure the accuracy of the records. Those blending oxygenates downstream must maintain records to the extent the oxygenate is used in the upstream refiner's or importer's compliance calculations. Other downstream responsibilities are limited to ensuring that conventional gasoline is not sold in areas covered by the reformulated gasoline requirements. Based on experience since the promulgation of the reformulated gasoline provisions in 1994, the EPA, on December 28, 2001, adopted certain new procedures relating to both reformulated and conventional fuels, allowing refiners to use conventional gasoline to produce reformulated gasoline, and to reclassify reformulated gasoline with regard to VOC classification, activities which were previously prohibited.[264] The changes came partly in response to recommendations of the second Bush administration's National Energy Policy Development Group in 2001, but were adopted sooner than other recommendations because these had been previously proposed by the EPA.[265] The administration's National Energy Policy, issued May 17, 2001, had directed the EPA to "study opportunities to maintain or improve the environmental benefits of state and local 'boutique' clean fuel programs while exploring ways to increase the flexibility of the fuels distribution infrastructure, improve fungibility, and provide added gasoline market liquidity."[266]

Under the new regulations, refiners may reclassify conventional gasoline as reformulated or reclassify reformulated gasoline with regard to VOC control. Previously, the EPA was concerned that this would allow a refiner to include conventional fuel in its anti-dumping calculations that would later be reclassified and used as reformulated fuel. Under the new regulations, a batch of previously certified fuel may be used as a blendstock by refineries if they determine the volume and properties of each batch, its designation as conventional, reformulated, or reformulated blendstock for oxygenate blending, and, for reformulated fuels, its VOC designation; the volume and properties of each batch are reported to the EPA as a negative batch under the same designation as it was originally received or produced by the refinery.[267] Thus, conventional fuel may be upgraded to reformulated, reformulated can be reclassified as conventional, non-VOC-controlled reformulated can be upgraded to VOC-controlled, and reformulated VOC Region 2 fuel can be reclassified for VOC Region 1.[268]

On December 3, 2001, the EPA proposed changes regarding reformulated gasoline and reformulated blendstock for oxygenate blending, proposing April 15 as a new annual compliance date, on or after which no persons except retailers and wholesale purchaser consumers would be able to accept receipt of any reformulated fuel other than summer grade.[269] The EPA intends to reduce the competitive pressure that keeps terminals from accepting summer-grade refor-mulated fuel for as long as possible.

In February 2002, the EPA issued a final rule that eliminated the blend-stock accounting requirements in its reformulated gasoline regulations.[270] This action is designed to give more flexibility to refiners and terminal oper-ators during the springtime transition to summer-grade reformulated gaso-line by eliminating significant record-keeping and reporting requirements. In tandem with this regulatory action, the EPA issued new enforcement guid-ance to allow gasoline terminal operators a broader testing tolerance than previously allowed for the initial transition from winter to summer fuel.[271] The EPA also decided not to adopt its proposal to establish a new April 15 annual compliance date for reformulated gasoline and reformulated blend-stock for oxygenate blending.

In issuing this rule, the EPA determined that the blendstock accounting requirements were no longer necessary.[272] The blendstock accounting regula-tions were originally intended to prevent excessive transfers of dirty blend-stocks from refineries with clean baselines to refineries with dirty baselines. However, the EPA has determined that refineries today have little or no incen-tive to transfer blendstocks to other refineries for the purpose of evading a more stringent baseline. When refineries produce more total gasoline than was produced in 1990, the additional gasoline over the 1990 baseline must meet the statutory baseline for all refineries regardless of the refinery's indi-vidual baseline. The EPA found that the shifting of blendstocks from one refinery to another where both refineries produce more gasoline than they did in 1990 has very little potential to cause any environmental harm. In addition, restrictions placed on refiners by the Mobile Source Air Toxics rule make refineries much less likely to accept high toxics-emissions gasoline blendstocks from other refineries.

Detergent Additives

Section 211(l) requires that all gasoline, beginning January 1, 1995, contain detergent additives to prevent deposits in engines and fuel supply systems. The EPA is to establish specifications for such additives. With engineering changes designed to enhance engine performance, sensitivity to deposits resulting from fuel combustion has increased. Of particular concern are port fuel injector deposits (PFID) and intake valve deposits (IVD). Unfortunately, higher concentrations of detergent additives intended to prevent PFID and IVD may also increase combustion chamber deposits. Performance engineering has made combustion chamber deposits more likely to cause engine knock-ing and thus require higher-octane fuel. Since base gasoline for various refin-ers is generally not distinct and is mixed fungibly in the fuel supply system, oil companies have marketed their gasoline by promoting the effectiveness of their detergent additives in preventing deposits and thereby protecting per-formance. The market therefore led to detergent additization of 90 percent of the gasoline supply to address PFID deposits, and 60 to 75 percent for purposes of IVD control.[273] Industry has developed much data based on roughly standardized test procedures in response to these performance concerns. While it is not surprising that tailpipe emissions of hydrocarbons, NO_x, and CO increase with engine performance deterioration due to deposits, the data quantifying deposit effects is limited and the variation from car to car is likely to be very great.

The EPA proposed an extensive detergent certification program in December 1993.[274] Since there is market pressure to develop better additives, the EPA decided it was not appropriate to require specific detergents, and that a performance standard accommodating innovation and improvement would be preferable. Therefore, the EPA proposed requirements based on vehicle testing. Owing to the time needed for such testing to certify detergent additives, the EPA also proposed a simplified interim program for the first year of the program, to provide lead-time for manufacturers to certify detergents according to the promulgated procedures. The EPA issued a final rule pursuant to Section 211(l) on July 5, 1996, establishing the final certification program for detergent additives and adopting the essential elements of the proposed program.[275]

The detergent program faces an additional analytical step compared with the other fuel programs. Rather than measuring emissions from a particular fuel, one must calculate the deposits and establish deposit limits that would be likely to cause adverse emissions effects. Based on limited data relating deposits quantitatively to emissions, the EPA generally presumed qualitatively in establishing deposit standards that emissions effects would occur at the same time or before the engine performance problems that have led to industry deposit standards. The EPA did not propose standards for combustion chamber deposits, because test procedures and data were not yet sufficient to establish a standard.[276]

The EPA proposed extensive requirements to ensure that representative fuels are selected for certification testing, including three general options, focusing on the fuel parameters identified as affecting PFID and IVD tendency (sulfur, olefins, aromatics, T90, and oxygenates). First, the EPA proposed that detergents could be certified for use in any gasoline, with specific requirements for formulating test fuels that are representative of all in-use fuels. Second, detergents could be certified for use in a particular geographic region of the country that tracks the gasoline distribution network, with specific requirements to ensure that the test fuels reflect pools of in-use gasoline with boundaries conforming to patterns in the gasoline distribution system.[277] Finally, detergents could be certified for use in a particular refiner's gasoline only with testing in that gasoline alone, as long as that fuel is segregated in the distribution system.

The EPA's enforcement program had to be designed to rely principally on record-keeping requirements because testing to identify and measure the concentration of detergents in gasoline is largely impracticable. Therefore, the sampling and testing approach utilized in the EPA's other enforcement programs would not work for detergents. The basic requirements are that gasoline be additized in conformity with the registration requirements, that an accounting procedure to ensure proper additization be undertaken, and that product transfer documents accompany the products through the distribution system.[278] The EPA enforcement is largely through review of records that must be retained for five years.

On November 5, 2001, the EPA revised the information that must be provided on gasoline additive composition by the manufacturer at the time of certification, and clarified requirements to limit variability in composition of additive production batches from that reported during certification.[279]

Oxygenated Gasoline

CO pollution results from inefficient combustion in cold winter weather. Ambient CO problems are usually attributable to motor vehicle emissions. Ambient exceedances of the CO NAAQS tend to concentrate close to major roadways and in downtown street "canyons," and CO nonattainment areas therefore tend to be small, compared with ozone nonattainment areas. Oxygenates improve combustion and substantially reduce CO emissions, particularly during cold operating conditions. Of course, to address a CO nonattainment problem, cars entering the CO nonattainment area must refuel with oxygenated gasoline, even if refueling occurs outside the nonattainment area. Under the oxygenated gasoline program, therefore, gasoline sold throughout metropolitan areas encompassing CO nonattainment areas must contain oxygenates. This program has proven very effective, as the resulting substantial reductions in CO emissions have helped many CO nonattainment areas to achieve attainment rapidly, without waiting for more stringent CO standards applicable to new motor vehicles to generate larger reductions through fleet turnover.

The oxygenated gasoline program in Section 211(m) is different from all other fuels programs under Section 211 because it is a SIP program that states are required to adopt and implement as state regulations.[280] The EPA's role in implementing the oxygenated gasoline program has been to provide guidance to states in developing their programs and to review and approve state oxygenated gasoline SIP revisions. Section 211(m) also assigns the EPA certain responsibilities to make decisions about the period in which the program is applicable for each area, the applicable testing tolerance, waivers from the requirements, and the structure of oxygen credit trading programs.[281]

Paragraph (1) of Section 211(m) addresses applicability. The program applies to states with CO nonattainment areas having a CO design value of 9.5 parts per million or above, based on EPA methodology. States were to submit SIP revisions adopting the program, effective November 1992, for areas meeting this threshold for 1988–1989. Areas meeting the threshold for a later two-year period must submit oxygenated gasoline program SIP revisions within eighteen months after the two-year period, and the program is to take effect by November 1, three years after the two-year period.

Paragraph (2) describes the program's requirements. The SIP is to require that the gasoline be oxygenated in the larger of the consolidated metropolitan statistical area (CMSA) or metropolitan statistical area (MSA) in which the CO nonattainment area is located. The Office of Management and Budget develops MSAs and CMSAs based on data from the Bureau of the Census to estimate generally the scope of metropolitan areas for a variety of federal purposes.[282] A few MSAs and CMSAs extend into states that do not have CO nonattainment areas. Those states have not been obligated to establish the program for their portion of the MSA or CMSA, since Section 211(m) applies only to states in which CO nonattainment areas are located. The gasoline is to contain 2.7 weight percent oxygen. This level corresponds to 15 volume percent MTBE, the maximum concentration waived for use in gasoline under Section 211(f)(4). Ethanol at 10 volume percent, providing 3.5 weight percent oxygen, would also satisfy the program's requirement. The oxygen level is subject to a test tolerance established by the EPA administrator. The EPA has established a test tolerance of 0.3 weight percent oxygen, consistent with the tolerance for oxygen levels in the reformulated gasoline program. The program applies during the portion of the year in which the area is prone to high CO concentrations, as determined by the EPA administrator. The EPA issued guidance on control periods[283] for areas subject to the program, and takes final action on these control periods in approving the states' SIP submissions. The EPA can reduce a control period if the state can demonstrate that, due to meteorological conditions, no CO exceedances will occur outside the reduced period.

Paragraph (3) establishes additional bases for waivers from program requirements (beyond control period reductions). First, the EPA can waive the requirements in whole or in part if the state can demonstrate that oxygenated gasoline will prevent or interfere with the area's attainment of a national, state, or local ambient air quality standard for another pollutant. Several states have raised concerns about oxygenated gasoline impacts on other air pollutants. California and Utah raised concerns that oxygenates cause an increase in NO_x emissions, which could interfere with ozone, particulate matter, and nitrogen dioxide attainment in California areas and particulate matter attainment in Utah. These states have submitted petitions for waivers to the EPA, which are still pending at the agency.[284] The EPA has concluded, for the reformulated gasoline program, that oxygenates should not increase NO_x emissions when other changes in the gasoline formulation to accommodate the oxygenates are taken into account; this conclusion applies only to 1990 technology vehicles considered in the reformulated gasoline program. In older technology cars (particularly those with carburetors rather than fuel injectors), oxygenates may cause a slight NO_x increase.[285]

The second and third bases for waivers under paragraph (3) have not been utilized. The second basis for a waiver is a state's demonstration that mobile sources of CO do not contribute significantly to CO levels in an area. As noted, concentrated industrial combustion is generally not the dominant cause of CO nonattainment. The third basis for a waiver is a petition from any person that there is an inadequate supply of, or distribution capacity for, oxygenated gasoline or oxygenates. The EPA issued guidance for such waivers in light of concern that the distribution system would be insufficient to comply all over the country as early as 1992. However, these problems did not materialize and the waiver provisions have not been used. The specific statutory provision for the EPA to address oxygenate supply problems does, however, highlight the preemption concerns that state oxygenate regulations could raise. This provision makes clear that state requirements could interfere with the federal scheme, even if adopted to comply with that scheme. This suggests that state requirements going beyond federal requirements could likewise interfere with the overall scheme, and might therefore be preempted. In the case of oxygen control, the EPA has promulgated the reformulated gasoline controls under Section 211(c), and the preemption provisions of that subsection may therefore apply as well. There, the EPA could approve or disapprove state controls based on the state's needs and the degree of interference with federal goals of uniformity and adequacy of supply and distribution systems.

Paragraphs (4) and (5) establish additional EPA obligations for implementation. The EPA satisfied its obligations under paragraph (4) to promulgate regulations for pump labeling to indicate that the gasoline dispensed is oxygenated and will reduce CO emissions.[286] The EPA also satisfied its obligations under paragraph (5) to promulgate guidelines for an oxygen credit-trading system so that those using more oxygen than required could offset those using less, within the same area.[287] This would allow those using ethanol to provide 3.5 weight percent oxygen to offset others using less than 2.7 weight percent. A limited number of states have adopted credit-trading programs. This is because enforcement of a trading program entails record-keeping and other requirements that are more complicated than simply requiring each gallon of gasoline in the system to meet the standard, and is therefore not worthwhile unless there is a substantial industry interest in taking advantage of credit-trading. The EPA has also issued general implementation guidelines for enforcement and other aspects of a per-gallon program.[288]

Finally, paragraphs (6) and (7) address the status of the program after CO attainment deadlines. According to paragraph (6), the program is not required in areas that are in attainment for CO, but the program is to remain in effect to the extent necessary for maintenance after redesignation. The EPA has not insisted that areas submit the program as a condition for redesignation if they do not expect that they will need the program for redesignation, for maintenance, or as a contingency measure. Under paragraph (7), if the EPA determines that a serious CO nonattainment area has failed to attain by the applicable date, then the state is to submit an additional SIP revision within nine months of the determination to raise the minimum oxygen concentration to 3.1 weight percent.

Implementation of the oxygenated gasoline program has become highly controversial due to concerns raised about the health effects of MTBE, the dominant oxygenate used for compliance, leading to debate over the reformulated gasoline oxygen requirement as well.[289] MTBE use (which causes a distinct odor in gasoline) led to reports at the outset of the program in November 1992 of acute health effects such as dizziness. This did not threaten to interfere with other ambient standards, and thus the waiver provision has not applied. Nevertheless, concerns were quickly raised, first in Alaska and New Jersey, about the health impacts of this oxygenate as an air pollutant. Highlighting the EPA's failure to implement the health-effects testing provisions of Section 211(b) and (e), the agency initially had very little information about the health effects of MTBE or other oxygenates, and needed to embark on a testing program to explore these concerns.

In response to the health concerns that have been raised, a number of health studies of oxygenates and particularly MTBE have been undertaken. In particular, concerns about cancer risk from exposure to MTBE have been raised. The EPA concluded in its initial assessment that, based on animal studies, MTBE is a low-potency possible human carcinogen.[290] Ultimately, after widespread discoveries of MTBE in groundwater, with unknown human health implications, attention has turned to MTBE's propensity for groundwater contamination and its relative mobility there once released, and its detriment to clean water relative to its benefits for clean air.

In 1998 the EPA established a Blue Ribbon Panel on Oxygenates in Gasoline, which concluded in July 1999 that MTBE poses a risk to water supplies through leaks from underground storage tanks and other sources, that use of MTBE should be substantially reduced (some members supporting a complete phase-out), and that Congress should provide authority to provide federal and state authority to accomplish this goal.[291] On March 24, 2000, the EPA issued an advance notice of proposed rule making through which it intended to issue a rule to limit or eliminate use of MTBE.[292] California acted aggressively to address MTBE after reports of extensive contamination of groundwater in the state, and the governor directed the removal of MTBE from gasoline in California by the end of 2002.[293] New York enacted legislation to ban MTBE by 2004, and several other states have either banned MTBE already or are considering such a step.[294] Various bills have been introduced into Congress either to remove the 2 percent oxygenate requirement from the CAA or to ban MTBE and, by default, to promote ethanol as the alternative.[295] The ultimate fate of MTBE in Congress remains to be decided.

In *Oxygenated Fuels Ass'n, Inc. v. Davis*,[296] a trade association including major MTBE producers challenged California's regulation banning use of MTBE in California gasoline as of December 31, 2002. In dismissing the case, the court rejected the plaintiffs' arguments that the MTBE ban violated the supremacy clause of the U.S. Constitution. The plaintiffs argued that the ban was preempted by Congress's intent to occupy the field with regard to the regulation of oxygenated gasoline content (implied preemption) and by Congress's objectives in the CAA (conflict preemption); and was expressly preempted by the reformulated gasoline rule. Although the CAA contains an express provision prohibiting a state from regulating fuels for the purposes of emissions control, the court relied primarily on another CAA provision allowing California to prescribe its own fuel regulations (because California regulated auto emissions before Congress did).[297] The court also ruled that the ban did not violate the dormant commerce clause of the U.S. Constitution.

In *Oxygenated Fuels Ass'n, Inc. v. Pataki*,[298] the plaintiffs challenged on similar grounds the constitutionality of the New York law that bans the use, sale, or importation in New York of MTBE fuels as of January 1, 2004. The district court denied the plaintiffs' motion for summary judgment, rejecting their preemption arguments that the New York law legislates in a field expressly preempted by Congress and the EPA; that Congress intended to occupy the field (implied preemption); and that the law will be an obstacle to the objectives of Congress (conflict preemption). The court relied on a narrow construction of the express preemption provision in the CAA, which preempts state regulation for the purposes of emissions control, while the New York law was enacted for purposes of groundwater protection.[299]

A third case decided in 2001, *In re MTBE Products Liability Litigation*,[300] involved multiple petroleum companies seeking dismissal of class actions arising out of alleged MTBE contamination of private water wells. The court held that federal regulation of MTBE did not preempt state law claims and that damage claims should not be dismissed in favor of state environmental agencies' "primary jurisdiction." The court dismissed some claims for lack of standing and allowed others to proceed under market-share and concert-of-action theories of liability. The ruling shows that the status of MTBE under strict products liability and other tort theories will continue to evolve.

Penalties Provisions

In the 1990 amendments Congress also revised the penalties provisions of Section 211(d), affecting all fuels programs. Under prior law, persons who violated the information requirements of Subsections (a) and (b), the substantially similar requirements of Subsection (f), or the regulations under Subsection (c) were required to pay a civil penalty of $10,000 for each and every day the violation continued. The penalty could be recovered only through a civil suit in federal district court in the district of the person's principal place of business or the district where the person does business. Only the EPA administrator could, upon application, remit or mitigate penalties after determining the facts. Several courts concluded that the statutory penalty amount was determinative and that the district courts did not have equitable jurisdiction to remit or mitigate penalties, since Congress gave the EPA administrator that exclusive authority after the penalty's imposition by the court.[301] These penalty provisions are codified in the EPA's general fuels regulations in 40 C.F.R. Part 80, Subpart A.[302]

In the 1990 amendments, Congress revised the penalty scheme in a number of respects. As revised, violators of the statutory, regulatory, or information requirements under Section 211 are liable for the increased sum of *not more* than $25,000 for every day of the violation, plus the amount of

economic benefit or savings resulting from the violation. Civil penalties are
to be assessed in accordance with the motor vehicle civil penalty provisions
in Section 205(b), which grants the court authority to take account of various
mitigating or exacerbating factors (such as history of compliance) in setting
the penalty amount. Section 211(d) further grants to the district courts jurisdiction to enjoin violations and to award "other appropriate relief." The
courts may also compel the furnishing of information and conducting of
tests required under Subsection (b). Section 211(d) further specifies that a
violation of regulations under Subsections (c), (k), (l), or (m) of the standard
based on a multiday averaging period constitutes a separate day of violation
for each day in the averaging period.

In addition, civil penalties may also be collected in accordance with the
administrative penalty scheme of Section 205(c). That subsection authorizes
the EPA administrator to assess penalties through an administrative action
pursuant to the record and hearing procedures of the Administrative Procedure Act[303] in lieu of an action in district court under Section 205(a). The
maximum amount that the EPA may seek in such an administrative action is
$200,000, unless the EPA administrator and the Attorney General jointly
determine that a larger penalty amount is appropriate for an administrative
assessment. The EPA administrator may compromise or remit such administrative penalties and may attach conditions for doing so, thereby allowing
the violator to take some other action to substitute for some or all of the
monetary penalty. Actions subject to administrative enforcement cannot also
be subject to a civil suit. Judicial review of an administrative penalty is in the
District Court for the District of Columbia, or in the district court where
the violation is alleged to have occurred, where the person resides, or where
the person's principal place of business is located, and must be filed within
thirty days of the administrative penalty order. The court may set aside the
penalty if the EPA administrator's finding of violation is not supported by
substantial evidence in the record, or if the administrator's assessment is an
abuse of discretion. The court may not assess *additional* penalties unless the
EPA's assessment was an abuse of discretion. The EPA can seek to collect
civil penalties through a civil action in district court, and persons who fail to
pay on a timely basis are liable for the United States' enforcement expenses,
including attorneys fees and costs, plus a 10 percent nonpayment penalty for
each quarter that the penalty payment is late.

The EPA's reformulated gasoline and anti-dumping and detergents programs contain their own penalty regulations based on the new statutory provisions. The reformulated gasoline and anti-dumping penalty provisions[304]
specify penalties of up to $25,000 per day of violation, plus the amount of
economic benefit or savings resulting from any violation. Violations of
each standard are separate violations, and a violation based on a multiday
averaging period, including credit creation or credit transfer violations, constitutes a violation for every day in the averaging period. Violations of per
gallon standards constitute a separate violation for every day that the product remains any place in the distribution system, beginning on the day the

product is produced or imported and distributed for sale and ending with dispensation to an ultimate consumer, unless the violation is corrected earlier. There is a regulatory presumption that the length of time in the system is twenty-five days, unless the violator demonstrates that this period was shorter. If required testing is not accomplished, the regulations also establish presumptive levels for the various fuel parameters. Finally, violations of affirmative requirements continue as long as they are not accomplished.

The detergents penalty provisions[305] are similar, providing for $25,000 in penalties for every day of violation, plus the amount of economic benefit or savings. As with the reformulated gasoline and anti-dumping program, violations continue for each and every day the gasoline or other nonconforming product remains any place in the gasoline distribution system, and document violations continue for each day the documents are not in compliance. However, the regulations do not specify a presumptive length of time that the product is deemed in the distribution system. For volume additive reconciliation (VAR) standards (which are in reality standards for average compliance over the reconciliation period), the violation is for each day of the VAR compliance period.

Outlook

Economic growth and Americans' love of the automobile will always pressure regulators and industry to find new ways to combat the resulting air pollution. Regulation of fuels and additives is now an important part of that effort. Required health testing of fuels and additives, though late in coming, will also now be an important factor in the effort. As with all environmental regulation, the easiest gains come first and additional gains are more difficult or expensive. This is likely to be the case for fuels as well. Ultimately, the more difficult or expensive infrastructure and technical hurdles associated with alternatives to gasoline and diesel fuel are likely to gain increasing attention. One conclusion is sure: The need for perpetual progress will always exist to counteract perpetual growth in Americans' use of motor vehicles.

Notes

1. CAA § 211; 42 U.S.C. § 7545.

2. *See* Air Quality Control Act of 1967, Pub. L. No. 90-148, § 2, 81 Stat. 502 (amending CAA Section 211 to authorize secretary of Health, Education, and Welfare to require registration of fuels as a condition to their introduction into commerce).

3. *See* SENATE COMM. ON PUBLIC WORKS, 93D CONG., 2D SESS., A LEGISLATIVE HISTORY OF THE CLEAN AIR AMENDMENTS OF 1970 at 836 (Comm. Print 1974) (statement of Rep. Vanik).

4. *See* 40 C.F.R. pt. 79, promulgated at 40 Fed. Reg. 52,011 (1975) and amended at 41 Fed. Reg. 21,324 (1976).

5. *See* SENATE COMM. ON ENVIRONMENT AND PUBLIC WORKS, 95TH CONG., 2D SESS., A LEGISLATIVE HISTORY OF THE CLEAN AIR ACT AMENDMENTS OF 1977 at 2775 (Comm.

Print 1978) (hereinafter 1977 LEGISLATIVE HISTORY) (H.R. REP. No. 95-294, 95th Cong., 1st Sess.).

6. "Octane" is the measure of a gasoline's resistance to ignition under pressure from the piston in the cylinder. Gasoline with too low of an octane level will ignite as a result of such pressure before the spark plug ignites the fuel at the appropriate time. This early ignition causes the sound known as "knocking" or "pinging."

7. 40 C.F.R. pt. 80, promulgated at 38 Fed. Reg. 1,255 (1973).

8. Ethyl Corp. v. EPA, 7 Env't Rep. Cas. 1353 (D.C. Cir.), rev'd on reh'g en banc, 541 F.2d 1 (1975), cert. denied, 426 U.S. 941 (1976).

9. See Ethyl, 541 F.2d at 13.

10. Thus, Section 211(c)(1) now provides that the EPA may regulate fuels and additives "if in the judgment of the Administrator any emission product of such fuel or fuel additive causes, or contributes, to air pollution which may reasonably be anticipated to endanger the public health or welfare."

11. Methylcyclopentadienyl manganese tricarbonyl. MMT is a manganese- rather than lead-based organo-metallic compound.

12. See 1977 LEGISLATIVE HISTORY at 759 (Senate debate on S. 252) (Statement of Sen. Muskie).

13. See 1977 LEGISLATIVE HISTORY at 2775 (H.R. REP. No. 95-294, 95th Cong., 1st Sess.).

14. See 1977 LEGISLATIVE HISTORY at 1464 (S. REP. No. 95-127, 95th Cong., 1st Sess.).

15. See 1977 LEGISLATIVE HISTORY at 362 (Conference Report).

16. See 1977 LEGISLATIVE HISTORY at 1465 (S. REP. No. 95-127, 95th Cong., 1st Sess).

17. See, e.g., 43 Fed. Reg. 41,424 (1978).

18. 55 Fed. Reg. 34,138 (1990).

19. The Baucus-Chaffee Statement of Senate Managers regarding the conference bill stated:

> Over the 20-year history of the Clean Air Act most of the regulatory effort has focused on the vehicle itself with requirements for new pollution control technology like the catalytic converter or the evaporative canister system. Very little attention has been paid to fuel quality during that same period. Lead has been phased down because it interferes with the operation of the catalytic converter. In other respects fuels have actually become dirtier in the last 20 years. The octane provided by the lead was replaced with octane from aromatic hydrocarbons which are toxic and have other negative air pollution effects. And the volatility of gasoline has increased dramatically causing increased evaporative emissions.

SENATE COMM. ON ENVIRONMENT AND PUBLIC WORKS, 103D CONG., 1ST SESS., A LEGISLATIVE HISTORY OF THE CLEAN AIR ACT AMENDMENTS OF 1990 at 851 (Comm. Print 1993) (hereinafter 1990 LEGISLATIVE HISTORY) (statement by Senator Durenberger). See also Waxman, Wetstone, Barnett, Cars, Fuels, and Clean Air: A Review of Title II of the Clean Air Act Amendments of 1990, 21 ENVTL. L. 1947 at 1972–73 (1991) (describing increase in emissions of toxic and smog-forming emissions due to elimination of lead from gasoline).

20. Methyl tertiary-butyl ether.

21. Ethyl tertiary-butyl ether.

22. See, e.g., 1990 LEGISLATIVE HISTORY at 1073 (Conference Report on Senate debate) (statement of Sen. Dole) ("Kansas farmers should see real opportunities contained within the reformulated fuels portion of the bill. . . . This bill puts in place a workable program to use clean-burning renewable fuels to combat urban smog in our Nation's dirtiest cities.").

23. 1990 LEGISLATIVE HISTORY at 851 (Conference Report on Senate debate) (Statement of Sen. Durenberger) ("The oil companies became seriously interested in [reformulated gasoline] only after the President proposed an alternative fuels program.").

24. 55 Fed. Reg. 34,138 (1990).

25. Most nonroad engines and vehicles use the same gasoline and diesel fuels that motor vehicles use. However, certain nonroad engines and vehicles, such as marine vessels with their very large internal combustion engines, may use fuel that the EPA did not previously have authority to regulate.

26. *See* 1990 LEGISLATIVE HISTORY at 5052 (Senate debate on S. 1630) (Statement of Sen. Symms) (farm equipment will wear out if unleaded gasoline is used due to valve seat wear; farm equipment losses could be significant); *id.* at 6683–84 (Statement of Sen. Durenberger) (describing impact on farm equipment of ban on leaded gasoline and letter from the EPA regarding impact on farm equipment).

27. 59 Fed. Reg. 33,042 (1994).

28. 40 Fed. Reg. 52,009 (1975).

29. 562 F.2d 807 (D.C. Cir. 1977).

30. 1977 LEGISLATIVE HISTORY at 2776 (H.R. REP. No. 95-294, 95th Cong., 1st Sess.).

31. 43 Fed. Reg. 28,490 (1978).

32. David P. Currie, *The Mobile Source Provisions of the Clean Air Act*, 46 U. CHI. L. REV. 811, 880 (1979).

33. *See* 40 C.F.R. pt. 79, subpts. A–C.

34. *See* 40 C.F.R. pt. 79, subpt. F.

35. *See* 40 C.F.R. pt. 79, subpts. B and C.

36. *See* 40 C.F.R. pt. 79, subpt. D. The EPA's 1994 regulatory agenda indicated that the EPA is currently developing a "proposal to cover certain new fuels and fuel additives entering the market, and plans to take final action by the end of 1995." 59 Fed. Reg. 58,200, 58,282 (1994). However, the 1995 regulatory agenda indicates that it does not now plan further action to revise the registration regulations. 60 Fed. Reg. 23,928, 24,026 (1995).

37. 62 Fed. Reg. 12,564-01 (1997).

38. 43 Fed. Reg. 38,607 (1978).

39. Thomas v. Browner, C.A. No. 89-6269 (D. Or. 1989).

40. 59 Fed. Reg. at 33,042 (1994).

41. *See* H.R. REP. No. 294, 95th Cong., 1st Sess. 308 (1977), *reprinted in* 1977 U.S.C.C.A.N. 1387.

42. *See* § 211(b)(2)(A).

43. *See* Table F94-7 at 40 C.F.R. § 79.56.

44. *See* 40 C.F.R. pt. 791 (TSCA rules) and 40 C.F.R. § 79.56(c) (fuels rule).

45. *See* 59 Fed. Reg. at 33,083 (1994).

46. *See id.* at 33,046–47.

47. *See* 59 Fed. Reg. at 33,050 (1994).

48. *Id.*

49. *Id.*

50. 65 Fed. Reg. 44,775 (2000).

51. *See* 40 C.F.R. §§ 79.4(a)(3) and 79.4(b)(2).

52. *See* 59 Fed. Reg. at 33,086 (1994).

53. Heavy-duty engines are certified through a "bench test" of the engine apart from the vehicle, whereas light-duty vehicles are certified as an entire unit. Durability testing is through "service accumulation" for the heavy-duty engines, in contrast to "mileage accumulation" for the light-duty vehicles that are actually driven for purposes of durability testing.

54. *See* H.R. Rep. No. 490, pt. 1, 101st Cong., 2d Sess. 313 (1990).

55. These specifications for certification diesel fuel are codified in the EPA's regulations at 40 C.F.R. § 80.113(b).

56. The EPA's 1994 regulatory agenda indicated that the agency was developing emissions standards for ethanol-fueled vehicles, and planned a proposal in 1996 with final action in 1997. 59 Fed. Reg. at 58,265 (1994). Once such standards are established, Section 211(f)(1)(B) would apply to ethanol fuels.

57. 51 F.3d 2053 (D.C. Cir. 1995).

58. 59 Fed. Reg. 42,227 at 42,228 (1994).

59. 43 Fed. Reg. 11,258 (1978).

60. 44 Fed. Reg. 16,033 (1979).

61. 45 Fed. Reg. 67,443 (1980).

62. 46 Fed. Reg. 38,582 (1981).

63. 56 Fed. Reg. 5352 (1991).

64. 56 Fed. Reg. 24,362 (1991).

65. The EPA has not undertaken rule making for waiver applications. The EPA clarified in its 1978 waiver guidelines that the burden of testing, data, and evidence is on the applicant for a waiver. Also, the EPA clarified that a waiver granted to one manufacturer is applicable to any similarly situated manufacturer. This raises an issue whether waivers have general applicability and future effect, and should therefore be considered "rules" under the Administrative Procedure Act (APA) that should be promulgated through notice-and-comment rule making. The EPA, however, has not proposed waiver decisions for public comment, though it has generally published a notice seeking public comment on waiver applications that are submitted. In support of the EPA's adjudicatory approach, Section 211(f)(4) clearly indicates that waivers constitute an exemption from a statutory prohibition, and a particular applicant bears the burden to present evidence meeting the statutory criteria. A waiver thus seems to meet the APA definition of a license, which the EPA may issue through an order pursuant to informal adjudication. The 180-day deadline for a decision, together with an automatic waiver if the EPA does not decide within that time frame, also may indicate that Congress did not intend the EPA to undertake rule making.

66. *See* 46 Fed. Reg. at 38,584 (1981).

67. *See* Synco 76 Fuel Corp. waiver (10 percent ethanol, with an additive), 47 Fed. Reg. 22,404 (1982); E.I. Dupont waiver (5 volume percent methanol with cosolvent alcohols), 50 Fed. Reg. 2615 (1985); ARCO waiver (4.75 volume percent methanol with GTBA), 46 Fed. Reg. 56,361 (1981); Texas Methanol waiver (5 volume percent methanol, with cosolvent alcohols), 53 Fed. Reg. 3636 (1988).

68. *See* 43 Fed. Reg. 41,424 (1978).

69. 46 Fed. Reg. 58,630 (1981).

70. 57 Fed. Reg. 2535 (1992).

71. 58 Fed. Reg. 64,761 (1993).

72. *See* MMT waiver decision, 59 Fed. Reg. 2227 (1994).

73. 60 Fed. Reg. 36,414 (1995).

74. Ethyl Corp. v. Browner, No. 94-1516, 1995 WL 612905 (D.C. Cir. Oct. 20, 1995).

75. 749 F.2d 826 (D.C. Cir. 1984).

76. 749 F.2d at 837.

77. 749 F.2d at 835.

78. 749 F.2d at 836.

79. 749 F.2d at 835.

80. 749 F.2d at 840.

81. 768 F.2d 385 (D.C. Cir. 1985).

82. 768 F.2d at 390.

83. 768 F.2d at 392.

84. 989 F.2d 522 (D.C. Cir. 1993).

85. 989 F.2d at 524.

86. *See* Motor Vehicle Mfr's Ass'n v. New York State Dept. of Envt'l Conservation, 810 F. Supp. 1331, 1343 (N.D.N.Y. 1993) (holding that states adopting California vehicle standards need not adopt California fuel standards in order to comply with Sections 177 and 209 of the act), *aff'd in pertinent part*, 17 F.3d 521, 531–33 (2d Cir. 1994), *on remand*, 869 F. Supp. 1012 (N.D.N.Y. 1994).

87. 38 Fed. Reg. 1254 (1973).

88. The regulations define "leaded gasoline" to mean gasoline that is produced with a lead additive or that contains more than 0.05 gram of lead per gallon or more than 0.005 gram of phosphorous per gallon. 40 C.F.R. § 80.1(f).

89. 40 C.F.R. § 80.24(a).

90. 40 C.F.R. § 80.24(b).

91. 40 C.F.R. § 80.22(d).

92. 40 C.F.R. § 80.22(f).

93. 501 F.2d 722 (D.C. Cir. 1974). The court explained: "The affirmative marketing requirement does in fact 'control' the sale of *leaded* gasoline, for the regulation provides in effect that the specified retailers may sell no leaded gasoline unless and until they also offer for sale one grade of unleaded gasoline." 501 F.2d at 744.

94. 38 Fed. Reg. 13,741 (1973).

95. 7 Envt'l Rep. Cas. 1353 (D.C. Cir. 1975), *rev'd on reh'g en banc*, 541 F.2d 1 (D.C. Cir.), *cert. denied*, 426 U.S. 941 (1976).

96. 541 F.2d at 31–32, 37–38.

97. 38 Fed. Reg. at 33,741 (formerly codified at 40 C.F.R. § 80.20(a)(1) (1976)).

98. Congress repealed the small refinery provisions in the 1990 amendments as no longer relevant.

99. 44 Fed. Reg. 53,144 (1979) (formerly codified at 40 C.F.R. § 80.20(a)(6) (1980)).

100. 44 Fed. Reg. 46,275 (1979).

101. 47 Fed. Reg. 7812 (1982).

102. 47 Fed. Reg. 49,322 (1982).

103. 705 F.2d 506 (D.C. Cir. 1983).

104. 50 Fed. Reg. 9397 (1985).

105. 40 C.F.R. § 80.20(a)(1).

106. 50 Fed. Reg. 13,128 (1985).

107. 40 C.F.R. § 80.20(e).

108. 821 F.2d 678, 685 (D.C. Cir. 1987).

109. 40 C.F.R. § 80.20(a)(2).

110. 40 C.F.R. § 80.20(a)(3).

111. 40 C.F.R. § 80.20(c).

112. 40 C.F.R. § 80.20(d).

113. 911 F.2d 1036, 1039–42 (5th Cir. 1990).

114. 40 C.F.R. § 80.2(c).

115. Formerly codified at 40 C.F.R. § 80.23(a) (1973).

116. 501 F.2d at 748.

117. 501 F.2d at 749.

118. 543 F.2d 270 (D.C. Cir. 1976).

119. 543 F.2d at 274.

120. 40 C.F.R. § 80.23(b)(2).

121. 40 C.F.R. § 80.23(b)(2)(viii).

122. 712 F. Supp. 1077 (E.D.N.Y. 1989).

123. 645 F. Supp. 337 (W.D. Mo. 1986).

124. 645 F. Supp. at 343.

125. 696 F. Supp. 407 (S.D. Ind. 1986).

126. 40 C.F.R. § 80.22(a).

127. 696 F. Supp. at 411.

128. 340 F. Supp. 1120 (S.D.N.Y.), *aff'd,* 468 F.2d 624 (2d Cir. 1972) (per curiam).

129. 548 F.2d 1088 (2d Cir. 1977).

130. 548 F.2d at 1095–96.

131. *See* Proposal to Ban Unleaded Gasoline, 50 Fed. Reg. 9400 (1985).

132. 61 Fed. Reg. 3,832 (1996).

133. 60 Fed. Reg. at 24,020.

134. 54 Fed. Reg. 11,868 (1989).

135. *See* 52 Fed. Reg. at 31,275 (1987).

136. 54 Fed. Reg. 11,868 (1989).

137. 55 Fed. Reg. 23,658 (1990).

138. 56 Fed. Reg. 64,704 (1991).

139. RVP is the vapor pressure of gasoline in a closed container at 100 degrees Fahrenheit.

140. 52 Fed. Reg. at 31,278 (1987).

141. The RVP standards are codified at 40 C.F.R. § 80.27. For the EPA's analysis of the ASTM class system, see 52 Fed. Reg. at 31,288 (1987).

142. 55 Fed. Reg. 23,658 (1990).

143. 40 C.F.R. § 80.27(d).

144. *See* 55 Fed. Reg. at 23,659 (1990).

145. 56 Fed. Reg. 64,704 (1991).

146. 56 Fed. Reg. at 64,706.

147. The special provisions for ethanol blends are codified at 40 C.F.R. § 80.27(d).

148. This downstream blending is due to ethanol's affinity for water and associated problems with distributing ethanol in gasoline through the ordinary distribution system, including pipelines. Ethanol blended in carriers' trucks is called "splash blending."

149. 40 C.F.R. § 80.27(d)(1) and (2).

150. *See* 54 Fed. Reg. 16,005 (1990); 54 Fed. Reg. 19,173 (1989); 54 Fed. Reg. 23,650 (1989); 52 Fed. Reg. 25,572 (1989); 54 Fed. Reg. 26,030 (1989). In *American Petroleum Institute v. Jorling,* 710 F. Supp. 421 (N.D.N.Y. 1989), the court of appeals rejected the petroleum industry's motion for a preliminary injunction against New York's volatility rules. This was after the EPA promulgated its RVP standards and proposed to approve New York's more stringent standard, but before the EPA took final action to approve the New York program. While the court concluded that the petroleum industry was likely to prevail on the merits, it also concluded that the industry had not demonstrated a threat of irreparable injury. New York's Department of Environmental Conservation Commissioner Jorling had determined not to enforce the program, pending the EPA's final action. The court also found the possibility of EPA approval to militate against the preliminary injunction.

151. The EPA first announced this interpretation of the "necessary" standard in approving a Maricopa County, Arizona, SIP. *See* 53 Fed. Reg. 17,413 (1988) (proposal); 53 Fed. Reg. 30,228 (1988) (final rule).

152. *See, e.g.,* 54 Fed. Reg. 26,033 (1989) (New York); 54 Fed. Reg. 25,574 (1989) (New Jersey).

153. 54 Fed. Reg. at 11,869 (1989). *See* 54 Fed. Reg. at 11,877.

154. 55 Fed. Reg. at 23,660 (1990).

155. 40 C.F.R. § 80.27(b).

156. *See* 54 Fed. Reg. at 11,871 (1989).

157. *See id.*

158. 40 C.F.R. § 80.7.

159. The liability scheme for the volatility program is codified at 40 C.F.R. § 80.28.

160. *See* 54 Fed. Reg. at 11,872 (1989).

161. 1994 WL 60922 (EPA Feb. 22, 1994).

162. 40 C.F.R. § 80.28(g).

163. 907 F.2d 177 (D.C. Cir. 1990).

164. 40 C.F.R. § 80.2(t).

165. *See* 40 C.F.R. § 80.2(h), (u), and (v).

166. 907 F.2d at 181.

167. 907 F.2d at 183.

168. *Id.*

169. 907 F.2d at 184.

170. 907 F.2d at 185.

171. 55 Fed. Reg. 34,138 (1990).

172. The EPA's final rule establishing the new particulate standards was published at 50 Fed. Reg. 10,606 (1985).

173. These impacts are addressed in the preamble to the EPA's final diesel sulfur rule, 55 Fed. Reg. 34,120–21 (1990).

174. 40 C.F.R. § 80.29(a).

175. *See* 55 Fed. Reg. at 34,120 (1990).

176. *See id.*

177. 40 C.F.R. § 80.29(a).

178. 1,4 dialkyamino-anthraquinone.

179. 59 Fed. Reg. 35,854 (1994) (amending 40 C.F.R. § 80.29).

180. *See* 55 Fed. Reg. 13,610 (1994).

181. *See* 59 Fed. Reg. 26,129 (1994).

182. 57 Fed. Reg. 19,535 (1992).

183. 66 Fed. Reg. 5,002 (2001).

184. *See id.*

185. 287 F.3d 1130 (D.C. Cir. 2002).

186. 40 C.F.R. § 80.30.

187. 40 C.F.R. § 80.28(a).

188. 40 C.F.R. § 80.28(c)(2) and, for example, § 80(d)(3).

189. 40 C.F.R. § 80.28(g)(2).

190. 40 C.F.R. §§ 80.28(g)(1) and (3).

191. 40 C.F.R. § 80.28(g)(5).

192. 40 C.F.R. § 80.28(g)(4).

193. 40 C.F.R. § 80.28(g)(4)(iv).

194. 65 Fed. Reg. 6698 (Feb. 10, 2000).

195. *See* 40 C.F.R. § 80.195.

196. *See* 40 C.F.R. § 80.225.

197. 66 Fed. Reg. 19295 (Apr. 13, 2001).

198. After extending the program to certain nonattainment areas in Wisconsin following the governor's opt in, the EPA subsequently withdrew the rule on the basis of the governor's request to opt out. 60 Fed. Reg. 2,693 (1995) (extending program based on opt

in); 60 Fed. Reg. 21,724 (1995) (withdrawal of extension based on opt out). The EPA also stayed the program for opt-in areas in New York, Pennsylvania, and Maine following opt-out requests. 60 Fed. Reg. 2,696 (1995) (temporary stay); 60 Fed. Reg. 35,488 (1995) (extension of stay). Finally, the EPA has proposed final approval of the opt-out requests for the New York, Pennsylvania, and Maine counties, and has proposed procedures for processing future opt-out requests to accommodate the needs of industry for lead-time and to ensure that emissions reductions are replaced. 60 Fed. Reg. 31,269 (1995).

199. Section 211(k)(10)(c) defines toxic air pollutants to mean the aggregate emissions of benzene, 1,3 butadiene, polycyclic organic matter (POM), acetaldehyde, and formaldehyde.

200. The EPA's rationale for choosing a modeling approach over a vehicle testing approach is described in the EPA's final rule, 59 Fed. Reg. at 7720 (1994).

201. Negotiated Rulemaking Act of 1990, Pub. L. No. 101-648, 104 Stat. 4969 (Nov. 29, 1990).

202. 56 Fed. Reg. 31,176 (1991).

203. 57 Fed. Reg. 12,416 (1992).

204. T50 and T90 are the temperatures at which 50 and 90 percent of the fuel evaporates, respectively.

205. *See* 58 Fed. Reg. at 11,723 (1993).

206. The history of the ethanol debate is summarized in the EPA's final reformulated gasoline rule, 59 Fed. Reg. at 7718–20 (1994).

207. For a more thorough discussion of this background, see 59 Fed. Reg. at 39,261 (1994).

208. *See* 58 Fed. Reg. at 11,723–25 (1993) (discussion of ethanol issues).

209. 58 Fed. Reg. 11,722 (1993).

210. *See id*. at 11,722, 11,741.

211. 58 Fed. Reg. at 11,724–25 (1993).

212. 59 Fed. Reg. at 7719 (1994).

213. 58 Fed. Reg. 68,343 (1993).

214. 59 Fed. Reg. 39,258 (1994).

215. 52 F.3d 1113 (D.C. Cir. 1995).

216. For the EPA's legal justification for the renewable oxygenate program, see 59 Fed. Reg. at 39,263–66 (1994).

217. 52 F.3d at 1119.

218. *Id*.

219. The reformulated gasoline standards under the simple and complex models, both on a per-gallon and averaged basis, are codified at 40 C.F.R. §§ 80.40–80.45.

220. 40 C.F.R. § 80.42(a).

221. VOC control regions 1 and 2, corresponding to southern and northern areas, respectively, are described in the regulations at 40 C.F.R. § 80.71.

222. 40 C.F.R. § 80.42(b).

223. *See* 59 Fed. Reg. at 7722 (1994).

224. *See id*. at 7724.

225. The EPA's MOBILE emissions model quantifies in-use emissions from motor vehicles and the impact of various programs on in-use emissions.

226. The complex model analysis and the mechanism to augment the model are discussed extensively in the preamble to the final rule. *See* 59 Fed. Reg. at 7725–44 (1994). The regulatory requirements for augmenting the complex model are codified at 40 C.F.R. § 80.48–80.62.

227. *See* 59 Fed. Reg. at 7755.

228. For the EPA's analysis supporting these Phase II standards, see 59 Fed. Reg. at 7746–56 (1994).

229. *See* 59 Fed. Reg. at 7751.

230. *See* 59 Fed. Reg. at 7721.

231. 65 Fed. Reg. 42,920 (2000).

232. 66 Fed. Reg. 37,156 (2001).

233. *See* 40 C.F.R. § 80.90.

234. Regulations governing baseline determination are codified at 40 C.F.R. §§ 80.90–80.93.

235. *See* 59 Fed. Reg. 7791–8000 (1994). The EPA has withdrawn and proposed changes to criteria for establishing individual baselines. These changes involve an adjustment tied to refiners' production of JP-4 jet fuel in 1990; the valid range limits for RVP under the simple model; and criteria for conventional gasoline for refiners that are no longer able to obtain extremely sweet (low sulfur) crude, which was available in 1990 and used to develop the refiner's 1990 baseline. *See* 60 Fed. Reg. 6030 (1995) (final rule withdrawing JP-4 provisions and changes to RVP valid range); 60 Fed. Reg. 40,006 (1995) (issuing three-month administrative stay of criteria for JP-4 and sweet crude adjustments); 60 Fed. Reg. 40,009 (1995) (proposing new criteria for JP-4 and sweet crude adjustments).

236. The statutory baseline is codified in the regulations at 40 C.F.R. Section 80.91(c)(5).

237. *See* 59 Fed. Reg. at 7785–87 (1994).

238. GATT art. XX(b).

239. 59 Fed. Reg. 22,800 (1994).

240. Pub. L. No. 103-327, 108 Stat. 2322 (for fiscal year 1995) (1994).

241. World Trade Organization Panel Report, United States—Standards for Reformulated and Conventional Gasoline, Jan. 29, 1996, 35 I.L.M. 274 (1996).

242. World Trade Organization Appellate Body, United States—Standards for Reformulated and Conventional Gasoline, May 20, 1996, 35 I.L.M. 603 (1996).

243. 62 Fed. Reg. 45,533 (1997).

244. *See id.* at 45,533.

245. 40 C.F.R. § 80.78(a).

246. 40 C.F.R. § 80.68.

247. *See* 40 C.F.R. §§ 80.41(k)–(o).

248. RBOB is defined at 40 C.F.R. § 80.2(kk).

249. 40 C.F.R. § 80.76.

250. 40 C.F.R. § 80.74.

251. 40 C.F.R. § 80.75.

252. The "attest engagement" requirements are codified in Subpart F of Part 80, 40 C.F.R. §§ 80.125–80.130.

253. 40 C.F.R. § 80.73.

254. 40 C.F.R. § 80.74.

255. *See* 59 Fed. Reg. at 7778 (1994). The liability scheme is codified at 40 C.F.R. § 80.79.

256. 40 C.F.R. § 80.81.

257. 64 Fed. Reg. 49,992 (1999).

258. 40 C.F.R. §§ 80.46, 80.55, 80.56.

259. *See* 59 Fed. Reg. at 7763 (1994).

260. *See* 59 Fed. Reg. at 7764–65.

261. 59 Fed. Reg. at 7801–07 (1994).

262. These requirements are codified at 40 C.F.R. §§ 80.101–80.106.

263. *See* 57 Fed. Reg. at 13,483.

264. 66 Fed. Reg. 67098 (2001).

265. *See id.*

266. *See* 66 Fed. Reg. 57099 (2001) (announcing availability of the EPA White Paper on boutique fuels).

267. *See* 66 Fed. Reg. at 67101.

268. *See id.*

269. 66 Fed. Reg. 60,163.

270. 67 Fed. Reg. 8729 (Feb. 26, 2002). In this rule making, the EPA also updated certain ASTM designated analytical test methods for reformulated and conventional gasoline to their most recent ASTM version and updated several sampling methods to their most recent ASTM version.

271. The enforcement guidance outlines the EPA's policy on allowing a two percent testing tolerance for the volatile organic compound performance standard. The two percent enforcement tolerance will apply at terminal locations at the time the terminal first classifies the tank as complying with summer standards for federal reformulated gasoline. Letter from Sylvia K. Lowrance, Acting Assistant Administrator, EPA Office of Enforcement and Compliance Assurance, to Red Cavaney, President and CEO, American Petroleum Institute (Feb. 6, 2002) (*available at* http://www.epa.gov/otaq/rfg.htm).

272. The EPA noted that it will closely monitor new terminals and refineries to determine if they are being created for the purpose of evading a more stringent baseline. If the EPA finds that facilities are being created for this purpose, it may reinstate the blendstock accounting requirements or impose other restrictions on blendstock transfers. 67 Fed. Reg. 8729 (Feb. 26, 2002).

273. *See* 58 Fed. Reg. at 64,217.

274. 58 Fed. Reg. 64,215 (1993).

275. 61 Fed. Reg. 28,763 (1996).

276. *See* 58 Fed. Reg. at 64,221 (1993).

277. The gasoline distribution network is divided into five Petroleum Administration for Defense Districts, or PADDs. The PADDs conform to patterns in the distribution system and have commonly been used to examine regional differences in the production and supply of petroleum products. The geographic areas proposed for detergent certification are PADD-based. *See* 59 Fed. Reg. at 64,231.

278. *See* 40 C.F.R. § 80.155(a), (b), and (c).

279. 66 Fed. Reg. 55,885 (2001).

280. Subpart 3 of Part D of Title I, which specifies SIP measures for CO nonattainment areas, also includes in Section 187(b)(3) oxygenated gasoline requirements that are generally subsumed within Section 211(m). (The retention of Section 187(b)(3) in the 1990 amendments as enacted was probably a drafting oversight.)

281. *See, e.g.,* 60 Fed. Reg. 47,907 and 47,911 (1995) (EPA proposal to approve Connecticut and New York SIP revisions to shorten oxygenated gasoline control period to four months).

282. *See, e.g.,* Revised Standards for Defining Metropolitan Areas in the 1990s, 55 Fed. Reg. 12,154 (1990).

283. Control Period and Credit Guidelines Notice of Availability, 57 Fed. Reg. 47,849 (1992) (guidelines not published).

284. *See* 58 Fed. Reg. 32,531 (1993) (notice of hearing on Utah application for waiver on the grounds that use of oxygenated gasoline would increase NO_x emissions and interfere with PM_{10} attainment); 58 Fed. Reg. 21,719 (1993) (notice of hearing on California application for waiver on grounds that use of oxygenated gasoline would increase NO_x emissions and thereby interfere with attainment for NO_2, PM_{10}, and ozone).

285. *See* 60 Fed. Reg. 52,129 (1995) (in context of proposing to raise oxygen content cap for reformulated gasoline, the EPA explained that its conclusions regarding NO_x emissions were based on testing of 1990 technology vehicles; the EPA recognized emissions impacts may be different for non-1990 technology vehicles and that therefore "states may have concerns about the NO_x (or other) emissions impacts" of an increase in oxygen content).

286. 57 Fed. Reg. 47,769 (1992) (codified at 40 C.F.R. § 80.35).

287. Control Period and Credit Guidelines Notice of Availability, 57 Fed. Reg. 47,849 (1992) (guidelines not published).

288. Final implementation guidelines, dated July 27, 1992, are available from the EPA. These were not published and no notice of availability was published in the *Federal Register*.

289. Though not used as widely as MTBE, ethanol may be used in the winter oxygenated gasoline program more readily than in reformulated gasoline, because the volatility increase that ethanol causes is not a problem in cold winter months when ozone is not a problem.

290. Assessment of Potential Health Risks Tertiary of Gasoline Oxygenated with Methyl Tertiary Butyl Ether, Office of Research and Development, U.S. EPA Report No. EPA/600/R-93-206 (November 1993).

291. *See* Richard O. Faulk et. al, *Salem Revisited: Updating the MTBE Controversy,* SF97 ALI-ABA 949–950, 964–968 (2001).

292. 65 Fed. Reg. 16,903 (2000); See *Faulk, supra,* at 968.

293. *See* Faulk, *supra,* at 949, 966 (2001).

294. *See id.* at 969–970.

295. *See id.*

296. 163 F. Supp. 2d 1182 (E.D. Cal. 2001).

297. 163 F. Supp. 2d at 1186.

298. 158 F. Supp. 2d 248 (N.D.N.Y. 2001).

299. 158 F. Supp. 2d at 253–55.

300. No. 00-Civ. 1898 (BS), 2001 WL 936210 (S.D.N.Y. 2001).

301. *See* United States v. Coastal Refining and Marketing, Inc., 911 F.2d 1036, 1042–44 (5th Cir. 1990) (upholding constitutionality of Section 211(d) scheme against separation of powers and due process attack); United States v. Pilot Petroleum Associates, Inc., 712 F. Supp. 1077, 1086 (E.D.N.Y. 1989) (concluding court did not have power to mitigate penalties); United States v. Sharp, 645 F. Supp. 337, 344 (W.D. Mo. 1986) (same).

302. *See* 40 C.F.R. § 80.5, referenced for diesel sulfur requirements at 40 C.F.R. § 80.29(d).

303. 5 U.S.C. §§ 554 and 556.

304. 40 C.F.R. § 80.80(a).

305. 40 C.F.R. § 80.159.

CHAPTER 12

The Acid Rain Program

DEBRA JEZOUIT[1]

Overview

Title IV of the Clean Air Act[2] (CAA) was enacted to reduce atmospheric loading of sulfur dioxide (SO_2) and nitrogen oxides (NO_x), the two principal precursors of acid rain, by restricting emissions of these pollutants from electric utilities.[3] According to the Environmental Protection Agency (EPA),

> Of the approximately 23 million tons of SO_2 and 19 million tons of NO_x emitted annually from all sources in the United States in 1985, about 16 million tons of SO_2 and 7 million tons of NO_x were emitted by electric utilities.[4]

At the same time, Title IV represents an attempt to employ market-based principles to achieve these emission reductions. The title also was intended to encourage the use of energy conservation, renewable energy, and alternative technologies for emissions reductions.[5]

The CAA provides for a 10-million-ton reduction in SO_2 emissions from electric utilities from 1980 levels.[6] Title IV implements this goal in two stages, referred to as Phase I and Phase II in the CAA.[7] Phase I, which began on January 1, 1995, required the biggest and dirtiest (primarily coal-fired) utilities to make a preliminary reduction in SO_2 emissions. In Phase II, which began on January 1, 2000, the Phase I units were required to make further reductions in SO_2 emissions, and all remaining affected units, including new units, were required to comply with the Phase II limits, which are designed to cap annual utility SO_2 emissions at approximately 8.95 million tons.[8]

Due to the use of a market-based program, it is possible for some affected units to comply with the SO_2 limits without actually reducing emissions. To achieve the SO_2 reductions, Title IV authorizes the EPA administrator to allocate "allowances," a major feature of the legislation.[9] One allowance entitles the holder to emit one ton of SO_2. The CAA specifies the number of allowances that the EPA administrator is to allocate to each utility unit on an annual basis. The number is based on the amount of emissions that would result from each unit if it operated at a certain baseline fuel consumption and a specified emission rate. In the case of Phase I allowances, the number of allowances was identified in a statutory list, and for Phase II, the number of allowances were determined by various equations. As long as a utility unit has enough allowances to cover its emissions, it is in compliance with the CAA.[10] The program allows utility units to trade allowances so that a utility unit may purchase extra allowances to cover its emissions rather than reducing its emissions to meet its statutory allowance allocation. In contrast, utility units with extra allowances may sell them or bank them for use in future years.

A utility unit is likely to purchase extra allowances if it costs less to buy the extra allowances than to install emission controls. Since the EPA administrator allocates a finite number of allowances each year, extra allowances are available only if another unit is emitting at a level below what is permissible under the CAA, or has banked allowances from previous years. Since Title IV is concerned with overall emissions of SO_2 and not with regional emissions, which are addressed by the National Ambient Air Quality Standards (NAAQS), state implementation plans (SIPs), and new source review nonattainment and prevention of significant deterioration (PSD) provisions, the emission reduction requirements of the title are achieved using the most cost-effective means.

Title IV also provides for a reduction in emissions of NO_x by approximately 2 million tons from 1980 levels by requiring the installation of "low NO_x burner technology" (LNBT) on coal-fired utility boilers.[11] Unlike the SO_2 program, the NO_x program does not allocate NO_x allowances to coal-fired boilers. Instead, under Section 407, all coal-fired utilities must comply, either during Phase I or Phase II, depending on the type of boiler at issue, with technology-based emissions limitations set by the EPA. These emissions limitations were to be based either on LNBT, for certain types of boilers, or, for other boilers, on the best system of emission reduction technology identified by the EPA as being comparable in cost to LNBT. A utility unit that is unable to meet the applicable emission limitation may apply for an alternative emission limitation or may average its emissions with commonly owned or operated utility units and meet the standard on an averaged basis. The statute also provides incentives for using clean coal technology.[12]

The SO_2 and NO_x requirements established by Title IV and by the EPA administrator through regulations are enforced through a permit program.[13] In Phase I, the permit program was run by the administrator but, beginning in Phase II, is being administered by the states. Acid rain permits are subject to the requirements of Title IV and also of Title V, the operating permits program.

Lastly, Title IV requires accurate emissions monitoring[14] and imposes penalties and offset requirements for noncompliance with the SO_2 and NO_x emission reduction requirements.[15] Title IV also provided incentives for the use of energy conservation measures and renewable energy during Phase I.[16]

The main features of the legislation—the SO_2 program, the NO_x program, and permitting, monitoring, and compliance—are discussed in detail in the following sections. Following each section discussing the statutory provisions is a discussion of the implementing regulations.

Sulfur Dioxide Program

Statutory Provisions

Sections 403, 404, and 405 of the CAA are the principal provisions establishing the SO_2 program. Other provisions are found in Sections 409 (repowering), 410 (opt ins) and 416 (auctions and sales of allowances). In addition to the creation and allocation of marketable allowances, the Title IV SO_2 provisions provided incentives for the use of alternative technologies and energy conservation during Phase I. The various statutory provisions addressing these issues are described in the following paragraphs.

Applicability

The SO_2 program applies to new and existing utility units in the forty-eight contiguous states and the District of Columbia. This can be determined, however, only upon a review of various sections of Title IV. Section 401 states that the purpose of the title is to reduce emissions of SO_2 and NO_x from "affected sources" in the contiguous United States.[17] As defined in Section 402, an "affected source" is a source comprised of one or more "affected units."[18] Affected units are defined as those units that are subject to emission reduction requirements under Title IV,[19] which are "existing utility units" and "new units."[20]

A "unit" is a fossil fuel–fired combustion device,[21] and an "existing" unit is one that commenced commercial operation before November 15, 1990, the date of enactment of the CAA amendments.[22] An existing unit does not, however, include a simple combustion turbine or a unit that serves a generator with a nameplate capacity of 25 megawatts or less.[23] A new unit is a unit that commenced commercial operation on or after November 15, 1990.[24] A utility unit is a unit that serves a generator that produces electricity for sale, or that did so in 1985, and includes certain cogeneration units.[25] The SO_2 program also applies to units that opt into the program under Section 410.

Allowances

Title IV imposes limits on SO_2 emissions through a system of marketable allowances. Section 403 contains the basic provisions regarding the allowance system. Pursuant to this section, the EPA administrator is to issue allowances to the designated representative of each existing affected unit. The designated representative is the individual who represents the owner or operator of a utility unit in the various activities undertaken under Title IV, such as allowance transactions, permit applications, and compliance plan submittals.[26] Most utilities have appointed an official of the company or a plant manager as the designated representative, but they are not required to do so. Any individual may serve as the designated representative.

The EPA administrator issues one allowance for each ton of SO_2 that the unit is allowed to emit, as specified in Sections 404, 405, 406, 409, and 410 of the CAA. New units do not receive allowances, except for those that commenced operation before December 31, 1995, as specified in Section 405(g), but are required to have allowances to cover their SO_2 emissions beginning in Phase II.[27] New units must therefore purchase allowances from existing units, which in turn requires the existing units to reduce their emissions. This preserves the SO_2 emissions cap.

The EPA administrator was required to ensure that, by Phase II, no more than 8.9 million allowances could be allocated per year, with the exception of allowances allocated pursuant to Section 405(a)(2) (bonus allowances), Section 405(a)(3) (extra allowances for certain big high-emitting units), Section 409 (allowances for repowering extensions), and Section 410 (allowances for units that opt into the SO_2 program). The administrator was required to reduce the basic Phase II allowance allocations pro rata to ensure that this limit was not exceeded.[28]

The number of allowances that each Phase I affected unit received during Phase I is listed in Section 404 of the CAA. The number of allowances that each affected unit receives in Phase II was not specified in a list; instead, Section 405 contains numerous formulas for determining the number of allowances that each unit receives. Section 403(a) required the administrator to publish a final list of Phase II allowance allocations by December 31, 1992. Units considering applying for repowering extensions and units that could elect how their allowances were to be calculated were required to notify the EPA administrator of these elections in time for inclusion in the allowance list. The list was published on March 23, 1993, and the administrator published a revised final list, pursuant to Section 403(a), on September 28, 1998.[29]

Section 403(b) provides that allowances may be freely transferred among designated representatives of affected units or any holder of allowances. (Purchases of allowances are not restricted to utilities and, in fact, there are allowance brokers). Transfers become effective upon the EPA administrator's receipt and recordation of a written certification of the transfer. Allowances may be transferred before they are issued (since utilities know in advance how many allowances they will be allocated each year), but they may not be used before the year for which they are allocated. Compliance is always determined at the end of the calendar year, under Section 403(d)(2), so that emissions may go above or below the allocation for a unit during the year as long as the unit has enough allowances at the end of the year to cover its emissions. The administrator was required to promulgate, pursuant to Section 403(d)(1), a system for issuing, recording, and tracking of allowances and allowance transactions.

Phase I Requirements

Section 404 identifies the units that became affected units beginning in Phase I and specified the number of allowances that each unit was to receive.[30] The list in Table A of Section 404 includes 110 units, all of which are 100 megawatts or greater and had SO_2 emission rates greater than 2.5 pounds per million British thermal units (lb/mmBtu). In general, the number of allowances allocated to each unit was based on an SO_2 emission rate of 2.5 lb/mmBtu applied to a baseline amount of fossil fuel consumed by the unit, determined by averaging the annual amounts of fuel consumed in 1985 to 1987.[31] Certain units that reduced their emissions before Title IV was enacted were allowed to choose between baselines, as provided in Section 404(h), to maximize their allowances. The administrator also was required to allocate 200,000 bonus allowances annually during Phase I to certain utilities in Indiana, Illinois, and Ohio, as specified in Section 404(a)(3).

Phase I Compliance Options

Although Section 404 identified the specific units that became affected in Phase I and the number of allowances they were to be allocated, the statute provided several options to allow the Phase I units to postpone or reassign their SO_2 emissions reduction requirements. First, Section 404(d) allowed a Phase I affected unit to receive a two-year "extension" of the Phase I compliance date if it used a qualifying Phase I technology or transferred its emission reduction obligations to a unit using such a technology, that is, a technology that would achieve a 90 percent reduction in SO_2 emissions.[32] A unit granted an "extension" was provided extra allowances, allowing it to emit more SO_2 for a two-year period. Units eligible for the extension were granted these extra allowances from a reserve of 3.5 million allowances, which was created pursuant to Section 404(a)(2) by withholding a certain percentage of allowances from the allocations of each of the Phase I units. These reserve allowances were allocated to the unit in addition to the allowances allocated under Section 404(a).

Second, pursuant to Section 404(b), utility units could postpone their SO_2 emission reduction requirements by reassigning their Phase I SO_2 reduction requirements to another unit under the control of the same owner or operator. The unit was required to demonstrate that reassignment to a "substitution" unit would result in at least as great a reduction in SO_2 emissions as would have been achieved without the substitution.

Third, a Phase I unit could comply with the SO_2 emission reduction requirements during Phase I by reducing utilization of or shutting down a unit, pursuant to Section 408(c)(1)(B). If the owner or operator of a unit chose to reduce utilization of or to shut down the unit, Section 408 required that party to include in the unit's compliance plan a specification of the unit or units that would provide the electricity to compensate for this reduced utilization (compensating units), or else to demonstrate that the reduced utilization would be accomplished through energy conservation or improved efficiency. Any compensating units became affected units under Section 404 and received allowances during Phase I.

Energy Conservation and Renewable Energy

Under Section 404(g), units could receive allowances for each ton of SO_2 emissions avoided through the use of qualified energy conservation measures or qualified renewable energy. A qualified energy conservation measure is defined as "a cost effective measure," as identified by the EPA administrator in consultation with the secretary of energy, "that increases the efficiency of the use of electricity provided by an electric utility to its customers."[33] Qualified renewable energy is defined as "energy derived from biomass, solar, geothermal, or wind as identified by the administrator in consultation with the Secretary of Energy."[34]

Pursuant to Section 404(g), the EPA administrator allocated allowances from a reserve of 300,000 allowances withheld from Phase II allocations if the utility met various requirements specified in Section 404(f)(2)(B), including that the utility was paying for the measures; that the utility had adopted and was implementing a least-cost energy conservation and electric power plan; and, in the case of qualified energy conservation measures, that the state regulatory authority with jurisdiction over the utility's rates had established rates and charges to ensure that the utility's net income after implementation of the measures was at least as high as if the measures had not been implemented.

The utility could receive allowances for energy conservation and renewable energy measures used after January 1, 1992, and before the earlier of December 31, 2000, or the date upon which any unit owned or operated by the utility became an affected unit. Utilities with Phase I units were eligible for energy conservation and renewable energy allowances for measures through December 31, 1994, while utilities with only Phase II units were eligible for the allowances for measures taken through December 31, 1999.

Phase II Requirements

Beginning in 2000, all existing utility units became subject to the SO_2 requirements and have been allocated allowances, pursuant to Section 405, based on an emission rate of 1.2 lb/mmBtu multiplied by the baseline fuel consumption. These basic allowances are supplemented by various bonus allowances, specified in Sections 405(b), (c), (d), and (h) and 406, and taken from a Phase II reserve. The bonus allowances have been allocated for the first ten years of Phase II. In addition, the administrator is required to allocate 50,000 bonus allowances annually above the cap to units listed in Table A and located in ten midwestern, Appalachian, and southern states. Certain units in high-growth states also receive bonus allowances, pursuant to Section 405(i).

Repowering

The Phase II provisions also contain incentives for the development of alternative technologies. Section 409 provides that units subject to the emission limitation requirements of Section 405(b) and (c) (certain Phase II units with emission rates equal to or above 1.2 lb/mmBtu) could repower with a qualifying clean coal technology to comply with the Phase II emission limitations.

Qualifying clean coal technologies are defined in Section 402(12) and include those specifically listed in that section as well as

> any (other) technology capable of controlling multiple combustion emissions simultaneously with improved boiler or generation efficiency and with significantly greater waste reduction relative to the performance of technology in widespread commercial use as of November 15, 1990 (the date of enactment of the Clean Air Act Amendments).

Units that submitted satisfactory documentation for repowering, pursuant to Section 409(a), received a four-year extension from the Phase II compliance date. In the interim they were allocated allowances based on the emission rate in the applicable SIP. These allowances may not be transferred.[35] Once the unit was removed from operation to install the repowering technology, it received transferable allowances based on an emission rate of 1.2 lb/mmBtu.[36] Repowered units that do not increase their hourly emissions of any criteria pollutant also are exempt from new source performance standards (NSPS) under CAA Section 111.[37]

Direct Sales and Auctions of Allowances

Title IV provides for the EPA administrator to hold direct sales and auctions of allowances to ensure the availability of allowances to the market. The direct sale and auction provisions are contained in Section 416. The auctions also were intended to signal price information to the market early in the acid rain program, while the direct sales were intended to ease financing for new independent power producers (IPPs) by assuring them priority in purchasing allowances.[38]

Under Section 416, beginning in 1993, the EPA administrator was required to offer for sale 25,000 allowances, for use beginning in the year 2000, at $1,500 each. IPPs, as defined in Section 416(a), that were unable to purchase allowances from utilities or at auction were entitled to a written guarantee of the availability of allowances through the direct sale and were entitled to purchase their allowances first.[39] However, because allowances began trading at a price much lower than $1,500 each and there were plenty of allowances available, IPPs did not need to take advantage of the direct sale offer. Therefore, pursuant to Section 416(c)(7), the EPA administrator terminated the program after 1995 and transferred the allowances to the auction subaccount.

The EPA administrator also was required to hold auctions of allowances beginning in 1993. Under the auction schedule, set forth in Section 416(d), the administrator was to auction 50,000 spot allowances (for use beginning in 1995) and 100,000 advance allowances from 1993 through 1995; 150,000 spot and 100,000 advance allowances from 1996 through 1999; and then 100,000 of each type thereafter. If the administrator determines that less than 20 percent of the allowances available at auction are purchased in any three consecutive years after 2002, the administrator may terminate the auctions, as provided in Section 416(f). The administrator may also reduce the number of allowances withheld and sold under the auction and direct sale provisions, pursuant to Section 416(e).

Allowances sold at auction have been obtained from a reserve of allowances created under Section 416(b) by withholding 2.8 percent of the allowances that otherwise would be allocated under Phase I and Phase II. Proceeds from the auction are returned on a pro rata basis to the units from whom the allowances were withheld, pursuant to Section 416(c)(6) and (d)(3). All allowances withheld for the direct sale were transferred to the auction account. The EPA holds the allowance auction each March and, to date, has sold all the allowances available each year. However, if any allowances were to remain after an auction, the allowances would be returned pro rata to the units from whom they were withheld.

The Opt-In Program

Lastly, it is possible for units that are not affected units under Sections 404 or 405 (combustion sources, such as industrial boilers, or units exempt from the acid rain requirements, such as those of less than 25 megawatts) and for process sources (sources that emit SO_2 in the course of a manufacturing process) to opt into the SO_2 program. These sources may designate themselves as affected units and receive allowances, pursuant to Section 410. In this way, sources for which a reduction in SO_2 emissions may be relatively inexpensive or easy to achieve are given the incentive to make those reductions, at the same time freeing up allowances for purchase and use by other units.

Under Section 410, the EPA administrator was required to establish baselines and emission limitations for opt-in units, as well as to define the process sources that may participate in the opt-in program and establish whatever requirements are necessary for such sources to participate in an opt-in program. Opt-in sources also are subject to a reduced utilization provision: Section 410(f) prohibits an opt-in unit from transferring or banking allowances generated from reduced utilization or shutdown unless the reduced utilization or shutdown resulted from the replacement of "thermal energy" from the opt-in unit with thermal energy from an affected unit. The statute did not define "thermal energy" but left it to the EPA to define the term by regulation. Section 410(f) also prohibits the administrator from allocating allowances to an opt-in unit "in an amount greater than the emissions resulting from operation of the source in full compliance with the requirements of this chapter." This prohibition affects the emission rate that the EPA uses in its allowance calculations.

Industrial sources also are the subject of an emissions inventory that was conducted by the administrator pursuant to Section 406 of the CAA Amendments.[40] Under this provision, if the inventory indicated that SO_2 emissions from industrial sources were likely to exceed 5.6 million tons per year, the administrator was required to take actions to control those emissions so that the 5.6-million-ton cap would not be exceeded.

Such actions could not include prohibiting industrial sources from opting into the SO$_2$ program,[41] but the EPA considered this cap in developing the opt-in regulations.

Section 410(h) also contains provisions for small diesel refineries engaging in desulfurization to receive allowances as calculated pursuant to that subsection.

Regulatory Provisions

On January 11, 1993, the agency published a package of "core rules" containing requirements for acid rain permits, the allowance system (including the Phase I allowance allocations), continuous emissions monitoring systems (CEMS), excess emissions penalties, and administrative appeals, codified in 40 C.F.R. Parts 72, 73, 75, 77, and 78, respectively.[42] In addition, the EPA promulgated a rule governing the auction and sale of allowances on December 17, 1991,[43] codified in Part 73, Subpart E; published the list of Phase II allowance allocations on March 23, 1993,[44] codified in Part 73, Subparts B and G; and promulgated a rule prescribing the requirements for SO$_2$ combustion sources choosing to opt into the acid rain program on April 4, 1995, codified in Part 74.[45] The agency also has issued several rule revisions to clarify and streamline the regulations.

The EPA developed the acid rain rules using an advisory committee established pursuant to the Federal Advisory Committee Acts. The Acid Rain Advisory Committee was comprised of forty-four members, and it included representatives of utilities, coal companies, emissions control equipment vendors, environmental groups, state public utility commissions, state and local air pollution control agencies, and labor organizations. Although consensus was reached on many issues, many aspects of the core rules subsequently were the subject of litigation.

The EPA also has developed various forms for permit applications, monitoring plans, and certificates of representation. The forms can be obtained directly from the EPA's Web site at http://www.epa.gov/airmarkets/.

Applicability

Section 72.6 of the permit rule spells out the different types of units that are affected units under the acid rain program, including applicability requirements for cogenerators, qualifying facilities, IPPs, and solid waste incineration units.[46] In general, the rule is consistent with the statutory provisions previously discussed. In Section 72.7, however, the EPA created an exemption for new units that serve generators with a nameplate capacity of 25 megawatts or less and that burn fuel with a sulfur content of 0.05 percent or less by weight, determined according to the provisions of Section 72.7(d)(2). Such units may submit a statement to the permitting authority identifying their eligibility for an exemption from the requirements of the acid rain program. They must, however, agree to surrender or waive the right to any allowances that have been or would be allocated to them under Part 73 for any year for which the exemption applies. A unit that is retired from service before the issuance or renewal of a Phase II acid rain permit also is eligible for exemption from the program under Section 72.8, by submitting a statement of the unit's retired status to the permitting authority. Such units retain their allowance allocations. If the unit intends to resume operations, the designated representative must submit an acid rain permit application to the permitting authority at least twenty-four months prior to the date the unit will resume operation.

Phase I Allowance Allocations

Section 73.10(a) of the core allowance rule contains the list of Phase I allowance allocations. Although this list is based on the list in Table A of Section 404 of the statute, it reflects the deductions made to create the Phase I extension reserve and the auction and direct sale reserve.

Phase II Allowance Allocations

Section 73.10(b) contains the allowance allocations for Phase II units. These allocations were promulgated in a separate rule making, published on March 23, 1993,[47] and revised in a subsequent rule making published on September 28, 1998,[48] and cover approximately 2,200 existing utility units. They are based on a corrected National Allowance Data Base and Supplemental Data File, which went through an informal rule-making process and which contained all the data necessary for making the calculations required by the CAA to determine the allowance allocations.[49] They also were based on twenty-nine different equations in the statute.[50]

Section 73.10(b) specifies two allowance allocations for each existing affected unit, one for 2000 through 2009, to account for bonus allowances, and the other beginning in 2010.

Repowering allowances for the year 2000 were withheld from Phase II basic allowances, pursuant to Section 405(a)(2) of the CAA, whereas repowering extension allowances for the years 2001 through 2003 are additional allocations above the cap.

Allowance Tracking System

Part 73 establishes the requirements for the allowance tracking system. Pursuant to Section 73.31, the EPA administrator establishes an account for each affected unit and for new units and other allowance holders that have filed certificates of representation with the administrator. The accounts reflect all allowance transactions, including allocations, transfers, and deductions for offsets (Section 73.30). Only the "authorized account representative" may undertake matters related to the account, pursuant to Section 73.33. For an affected unit, the designated representative must be appointed as the authorized account representative.

Each account is divided into subaccounts, as prescribed in Section 73.32, which reflect current-year allowances, future-year allowances, and, for unit accounts, allowances to be used for compliance for the current year. Each allowance is identified by a serial number, which identifies the date on which the allowance may be used for compliance (Section 73.34). The EPA uses this allowance tracking system to determine each unit's compliance with its emissions requirements.

All allowance transactions are recorded by the EPA pursuant to the provisions of Section 73.52. The EPA will not record a transfer of allowances until receiving notification from the authorized account representative pursuant to Section 73.50. Thus, allowance transactions may take place without public notification, but all transfers must be recorded before allowances may be used for compliance. Units have until March 1 (February 29 in leap years) to complete and submit for recordation all allowance transactions required for compliance with the preceding year, pursuant to Section 73.35(a). Any disputes as to allowance recordation are to be resolved according to the provisions of Section 73.37.

Energy Conservation and Renewable Energy

The requirements concerning the energy conservation and renewable energy program are contained in Subpart F to Part 73. A list of qualified energy conservation measures and qualified renewable generation is contained in Appendix A to the Subpart. Appendix A also specifies the supply-side measures that may be used for reduced utilization plans. In addition, measures that are not listed in Appendix A but that meet the criteria of Section 73.81(a)(2), in the case of energy conservation measures, and (c)(2), in the case of renewable energy generation, also were eligible for the program. Specific exclusions from the program are contained in Section 73.81(b) and (d).

Section 73.82 specifies the process for applying to the program, as well as the calculation for the number of allowances to be allocated. Sections 73.83 and 73.84 describe the approval process. Applications are processed on a first-come, first-served basis until the reserve is depleted. Section 73.85 ensures that both the energy conservation category and the renewable energy generation category will receive at least 60,000 of the 300,000 allowances to be awarded through the program.

Repowering

Units choosing to meet their emission reduction requirements by installing repowering technology and seeking an extension from the Phase II compliance deadline for this purpose were required to comply with the requirements of Section 72.44 of the permit rule. Under this section, the designated representative for the coal-fired unit in question had to submit to the permitting authority by January 1, 1996, a repowering extension plan and submit to the EPA administrator by June 1, 1997, a petition for approval of a repowering technology. Certain repowering technologies are listed in the definition of a qualified repowering technology under Section 72.2, but others could be certified by the vendor as meeting the necessary criteria.

Once the administrator conditionally approved a repowering technology, the permitting authority was to issue a permit containing a schedule of compliance for the technology's construction, installation, and commencement of operation. Upon final approval of the technology, the administrator was to allocate allowances to the unit pursuant to Section 72.44(f)(3).

Direct Sales and Auctions

The EPA administrator began holding auctions and direct sales of allowances in 1993, pursuant to the provisions of Subpart E of Part 73. Under Section 73.70, the administrator is required to hold the auction of allowances by March 31 of each year. Authorized account representatives also may offer allowances for sale at auction and may specify a minimum price for their sale, pursuant to Section 73.70(c). These allowances will be auctioned off only after all allowances from the auction subaccount are sold, under Section 73.70(d). Section 416(f) of the CAA allows the EPA to delegate or contract for the running of auctions and sales, as also provided in Section 73.73(a) of the regulations. After considering delegating the administration of the auctions to another agency and accepting proposals from industry, the EPA contracted with the Chicago Board of Trade to run the auctions. The Chicago Board of Trade has created a futures market for allowances.[51]

Bidding procedures are specified in Section 73.71. Bids must be submitted on official bid forms and be accompanied by a certified check or letter of credit for the total bid price. Bidders may bid for any number of allowances up to the total available and may submit more than one bid, as long as all bids are submitted by three days before the date of the auction. Upon receipt of bids at the auction, the EPA administrator is to rank all bids in descending order of bid price. The administrator is to sell allowances from the allowance subaccount first and then, if bids still remain, will sell allowances offered by authorized account representatives. The latter are sold based on a discriminating price system, under Section 73.70(d), so that the highest bids are matched with the lowest minimum prices until all allowances are sold, no bids remain, or remaining bids do not meet minimum prices. The administrator is to publish the names of winning bidders and their bids, the amounts of losing bids, and the lowest price at which allowances are sold, pursuant to Section 73.30(e), and will transfer allowances as soon as payment is collected, under Section 73.30(f).

Opt Ins

The EPA promulgated a rule on April 4, 1995, that contains provisions primarily for combustion sources seeking to opt into the acid rain program.[52] These provisions are set forth in Part 74. To date, the EPA has not issued a rule specific to process sources.

The terms "combustion source" and "process source" are not defined in Title IV, but Section 410(a) makes a distinction between a "unit that is not, nor will become, an affected unit" and a "process source." The EPA refers to the former as a "combustion source" and has defined the term in Section 72.2 of the permits rule as a fossil fuel–fired boiler, turbine, or internal combustion engine; whereas "process source" was described in the preamble to the proposed opt-in rule as a stationary source that emits SO_2 by processing or manufacturing materials.[53]

In general, the rule provides that combustion sources opting into the SO_2 program shall be subject to all the same requirements as affected units. In certain instances, however, the EPA found a need to propose unique requirements for such sources. Thus, under Section 74.14, an opt-in source may submit a draft permit application and monitoring plan to the administrator and then has the opportunity either to withdraw that application or to confirm it after receiving a draft permit specifying the number of allowances the source would receive. The opportunity to withdraw is included because the allocation might determine whether a source would participate in the program; unlike for affected sources, the allocation for an opt-in source is not already specified in the CAA.

The EPA also has clarified, in Section 74.10, that calculations and other activities involving allowances will remain the responsibility of the administrator and will not be undertaken by the permitting authority. The provisions for selecting a baseline and SO_2 emissions rate are contained in Sections 74.20 through 74.25, and the allowance allocation formula is specified in Sections 74.26 and 74.28. Combustion sources are subject to the same 1985 to 1987 baseline as affected sources, where feasible. They also are subject to the lesser of 1985 actual or allowable emission rates, except when their current allowable SO_2 emission rate is lower, owing to the language in Section 410(f) prohibiting emissions greater than those resulting from "operation of the source in full compliance with the requirements of this chapter." Allowances are then calculated as for affected units, except that opt-in sources are allowed a partial allowance allocation for their first year in the program (assuming they do not opt in at the beginning of the year).

In Sections 74.44 through 74.50 of the regulations, the EPA addressed the reduced utilization provision of Section 410 of the CAA. The EPA defined reduced utilization based on input to the boiler and uses a trailing average of three years to determine utilization. In deducting allowances resulting from reduced utilization, the EPA would use the historic emission rate used in calculating the initial opt-in allowance allocation. The agency also defined "thermal energy" as being limited to the steam output used in an industrial process, as distinguished from the electrical output, thus limiting the number of allowances that would be transferable.

The rule also allows opt-in sources to withdraw from the acid rain program, setting forth in Section 74.18 the conditions that must be satisfied to withdraw, including the surrender of future-year allowances.

Finally, the EPA considered issuing regulations that would address the uncertainty involved with opt-in allowances, since they are subject to cancellation.[54] However, the agency concluded that purchasers would take this uncertainty into account in negotiating a contract or price for the allowances and so did not attempt to regulate, other than to prohibit such allowances from being offered for sale in the EPA auction.

Nitrogen Oxides Program

Statutory Provisions

The provisions pertaining to NO_x control are contained in Section 407 of the CAA. The section establishes technology-based emission limitations and does not employ the same market-based incentives as the SO_2 provisions.

Applicability and Time for Compliance

Section 407 applies to coal-fired units only and provides that on the date that a coal-fired unit becomes an affected unit under Sections 404, 405, or 409 of the SO_2 provisions, it also becomes an affected unit under the NO_x provisions. Phase I extension units and repowered units become affected units under the NO_x provisions on the dates that their SO_2 extensions terminate (January 1, 1997, and January 1, 2004, respectively).

The dates on which coal-fired units were required to comply with NO_x emission limitations are contained in Section 407(b). Subsection (b)(1) required the EPA administrator initially to establish emission limitations for only certain types of boilers: tangentially fired boilers and dry bottom wall-fired boilers not including cell burners (known as Group 1 boilers). Section 407(b) required Phase I units with Group 1 boilers to meet the NO_x emission limitations by January 1, 1995. Phase II, Group 1 units did not become subject to the limitations until January 1, 2000. All other types of utility boilers (termed Group 2 boilers, which include wet bottom wall-fired boilers, cyclones, and cell burners) are covered by Subsection (b)(2), and compliance with the Group 2 limits was not required until Phase II.

Emission Limitations

Section 407(b)(1) specifies that the maximum rates of NO_x emitted from Group 1 units should be 0.45 lb/mmBtu for tangentially fired boilers and 0.50 lb/mmBtu for dry bottom wall-fired boilers, "[p]rovided, [t]hat the administrator may set a rate higher than that listed for any type of utility boiler if the administrator finds that the maximum listed rate for that boiler type cannot be achieved using low NO_x burner technology." The section thus implies that the administrator should promulgate the Group 1 emission limitations based on "low NO_x burner technology." The precise meaning of the term "low NO_x burner technology," however, was a subject of much dispute in the course of the NO_x rule making.

Section 407(b)(2) required the EPA administrator by January 1, 1997, to base rates for the Group 2 boilers "on the degree of reduction achievable through the retrofit application of the best system of continuous emission reduction, taking into account available technology, costs and energy and environmental impacts, and which is comparable to the costs of nitrogen oxides controls set pursuant to subsection (b)(1)." The way in which the EPA defined "low NO$_x$ burner technology" therefore affected the degree of control that would be placed on Group 2 boilers, due to the requirement that the costs be "comparable."

The statute also provided the administrator with the authority to revise the Group 1 emission limitations to be more stringent if the administrator determined that more effective LNBT was available. However, any Phase I boiler that was subject to the initial Group 1 emission limitations would not be required to meet the revised emission limitations.

Alternative Emission Limitations

Under Section 407(d), a permitting authority was allowed to authorize a less stringent emission limitation for a unit that demonstrated that it could not meet the applicable emission limitation using either LNBT, in the case of a Group 1 unit, or the technology on which the administrator based the emission limitation, in the case of a Group 2 unit. To make this demonstration, the unit had to install the appropriate control technology and operate it for fifteen months, provide data showing that the unit could not meet the emission limitation, and specify an emission rate that the unit could meet. The permitting authority had to issue an operating permit to allow the unit to emit in excess of the emission limitation during the demonstration period and, if the unit demonstrated the infeasibility of the emission limitation, revise the permit to reflect the alternative emission limitation (AEL) that was demonstrated.

Compliance Extension

If a Phase I, Group 1 unit could demonstrate that the necessary technology to meet the applicable emission limitation was not in adequate supply to enable its installation and operation at the unit by 1995, the administrator was to extend the deadline for compliance by fifteen months, also pursuant to Section 407(d).

Emissions Averaging

The owner or operator of two or more units subject to the Title IV NO$_x$ emission limitations may request permission to average the emissions of the units in question and have the average meet the applicable emission limitations. This compliance option was available in Phase I and continues to be available in Phase II. The units must comply with alternative emission limitations that ensure that the actual annual NO$_x$ emission rate averaged over the units in question is less than or equal to the average annual NO$_x$ emission rate for the units if they had been operated according to the applicable emission limitations under the statute.

Regulatory Provisions

The EPA published the final rule implementing Section 407 at 40 C.F.R. Part 76 on March 22, 1994.[55] Initially, the EPA attempted to promulgate the NO_x rule through a regulatory negotiation process, but in the end the agency went through a standard rule-making process. Although a NO_x subcommittee of the Acid Rain Advisory Committee was established, and attempts were made to reach some consensus on the various issues, the advisory committee process was not successful and the rule was challenged by industry groups, leading to a revision of the rule on April 13, 1995.[56] In addition, the EPA revised Part 76 to incorporate the Group 2 limits on December 19, 1996.[57]

Applicability and Time for Compliance

As prescribed in the statute, the rule applies to existing coal-fired utility units and the few new coal-fired utility units that were allocated allowances under Section 405.[58] The remainder of new units are not subject to Part 76 but will reduce NO_x emissions according to the NSPS, which the EPA was required to revise under Section 407(c). The EPA addressed this NSPS revision under a separate rule making published on September 16, 1998.[59]

Section 76.2 of the rule clarifies the dates on which certain units become subject to the NOx requirements. Due to litigation over the final Group 1 NO_x rule, the general compliance date for Phase I, Group 1 boilers was delayed by one year, to January 1, 1996. Phase II units with Group 1 or Group 2 boilers were required to comply with the NO_x requirements beginning January 1, 2000.

The EPA included an Appendix A with its rule clarifying when each Phase I, Group 1 unit and Phase I units with cell burners would be required to comply with the NO_x emission limitations and specifying the applicable emission limitation.

Definition of Low NO_x Burner Technology

There was much debate during the NO_x rule-making process as to whether the term "low NO_x burner technology" in the statute meant simply low NO_x burners alone, or low NO_x burners combined with "overfire air," a term referring to various methods of introducing air into the boiler's combustion chamber to prevent the formation of NO_x. Although the EPA initially promulgated a final definition of LNBT that included overfire, the agency's position was challenged in litigation over the rule and the U.S. Court of Appeals for the D.C. Circuit rejected the agency's interpretation of the definition of LNBT. In its revised rule, following the court's decision, the EPA did not include overfire air technology as any part of the definition of LNBT.

Emission Limitations

For the Phase I, Group 1 units, Section 76.5 adopted the maximum emission limitations set forth in the statute of 0.45 lb/mmBtu for tangentially fired boilers and 0.50 lb/mmBtu for dry bottom wall-fired boilers. The EPA evaluated the performance of all commercially available LNBT and determined that the statutory emission limitations were appropriate since they could be met by the majority of units using LNBT.[60] For the Phase II, Group 1 units, Section 76.7 lowered the limits to 0.40 lb/mmBtu for tangentially fired boilers and 0.46 lb/mmBtu for dry bottom wall-fired boilers. The limits for the Group 2 boilers are contained in Section 76.6. The limits are 0.68 lb/mmBtu for cell burners; 0.86 lb/mmBtu for cyclone boilers with a maximum continuous steam flow at 100 percent of load of greater than 1060, in thousands of lb/hr; 0.84 lb/mmBtu for wet bottom boilers; and 0.80 lb/mmBtu for vertically fired boilers.

Alternative Emission Limitations

Pursuant to Section 407(d), a Phase I or Phase II unit would be granted an AEL if it "cannot meet the stated limitation using low NO_x burner technology." Section 76.10 required a unit applying for an AEL to satisfy three criteria. First, the unit needed to have installed LNBT or an approved alternative technology or, in the case of Group 2 boilers, the appropriate NO_x emission control technology on which the applicable emission limitation for Group 2 was based. Second, the burner technology that was installed must have been designed to meet the applicable emission limitation. Last, the unit had to be operated throughout a fifteen-month demonstration period both to show the inability of the unit to meet the applicable emission limitation and to demonstrate the rate that the unit can achieve.[61]

Compliance Extension

Section 76.12 of the rule permitted Phase I, Group 1 units to apply for a fifteen-month extension of the compliance deadline if they demonstrated that the necessary LNBT was "not in adequate supply to enable installation and operation at the unit, consistent with system reliability, by January 1, 1995." Units participating in an approved clean coal technology demonstration project also were eligible for the extension.

Emissions Averaging

The provisions regarding emissions averaging are contained in Section 76.11 of the NO_x rule. The rule permits averaging among units in multiple jurisdictions. Section 76.11 requires all units in an averaging pool to have at least one common owner or operator. Moreover, Section 76.11 also requires all such units to share a single common designated representative, for administrative purposes, and this must be the same designated representative as is used under the SO_2 program. However, pursuant to Section 72.22, the units do not need to share a common alternate designated representative if they are in different states.

Early Election

In Section 76.8 of the rule, the EPA created an early election program for Phase II, Group 1 boilers. There is no corresponding provision in the statute. The EPA created this program to encourage early compliance with the Phase I, Group 1 standards.[62] Under this provision, a Phase II, Group 1 unit that elected by January 1, 1997, to comply with the Phase I standard and that demonstrated compliance by the end of 1997 would be grandfathered from complying with any revised standard until January 1, 2008. Such units could not participate in Phase I emissions averaging plans, so as not to undermine intended Phase I NO_x reductions,[63] but are free to participate in Phase II plans, provided that they are subject to the revised Group 1 emission standards. Such units also may withdraw from, or "opt out" of, their election, effective at the beginning of a new year, but once a unit has opted out, it may not become an early election unit again.

Permitting, Monitoring, and Enforcement Provisions

The requirements of Title IV and the regulations promulgated under that title are enforced through acid rain permits. These permits are subject to the requirements of Title V, the operating permit program, but also must comply with the specific provisions of the acid rain title. In addition, the acid rain program requires the installation of CEMS on all affected units. Finally, Title IV imposes excess emission penalties and offset requirements on any affected unit that emits more than the title allows. These provisions are discussed in the following paragraphs.

Permits

Statutory Provisions Regarding Permits

Acid rain permits are issued pursuant to Section 408 for a period of five years. They were issued by the EPA administrator during Phase I and are being issued by the states during Phase II. Under Section 408, the designated representative or owner or operator of a Phase I affected source must have submitted a permit application to the administrator by February 15, 1993. Phase II permit applications were due by January 1, 1996.

Each permit application must be accompanied by a compliance plan, which must cover all the affected units that comprise the affected source. In general, the compliance plan for most units will be very simple. For the SO_2 program, since the alternative methods of compliance are no longer available, all the permit applicant needs to do is check a box on the form to indicate that the unit will hold sufficient allowances by the allowance transfer deadline to cover the unit's SO_2 emissions for the applicable compliance year. For the NO_x program, the unit must check the box on the form agreeing to meet the applicable emission limitations, or provide more detailed information if an emissions averaging plan is chosen for compliance. More detail also is required for opt-in sources. The permit application and compliance plan are binding on the designated representative and the owner or operator and are enforceable in lieu of a permit until the permit is issued.

Pursuant to the statute, sources with new units that are affected under Phase II must submit permit applications and compliance plans to the permitting authority by the later of January 1, 1998, or two years before the unit commences operation. However, many new units have been submitting their acid rain permit applications less than two years before the unit is scheduled to commence operation. Although this is a violation of the statute, the EPA has not taken enforcement actions for such violations since it has determined that acid rain permit applications can be reviewed and approved in significantly less time. The EPA cannot force the states to follow suit; however, most states also are accepting acid rain permit applications less than two years before a new unit is scheduled to commence operation. Such states generally are requiring that acid rain permit applications be submitted at least a year in advance of scheduled operation.

Section 408(i) provides that no permits will be issued until the designated representative of the unit at issue has filed a certificate of representation with the EPA administrator. This subsection also requires multiple owners of affected units to state in the certificate that allowances and the proceeds resulting from allowance transactions will be divided in proportion to each owner's interest.

Permit Regulations

The standard permit requirements are contained in Section 72.9. They require the designated representative of each affected source to submit a permit application and compliance plan and require the source to comply with the monitoring requirements of Part 75 and the SO_2 and NO_x requirements of the acid rain program. They also contain requirements for submitting excess emissions offset plans and for record keeping and reporting, and they provide for liability under Section 113 of the CAA for any violation of the acid rain program.

The provisions regarding the designated representative are contained in Subpart B of Part 72. Section 72.20 requires each affected source, including all affected units at the source, to have only one designated representative, who legally binds the owner and operator of the affected source by his or her actions. Each source also may designate an alternative designated representative under Section 72.22. Subpart B also contains the requirements for the certificate of representation and for changing the designated representative.

The specific requirements for acid rain permit applications are contained in Subpart C. The requirements for compliance plans are contained in Subpart D and the acid rain permit contents are identified in Subpart E.

Subpart F of Part 72 contains the procedures for federal issuance of acid rain permits. Subpart G identifies the procedures for EPA approval of state acid rain permit programs and state issuance of Phase II permits. Section 72.74 provides that the EPA administrator be responsible for issuing Phase II permits for any area that does not have an approved permitting program.

Subpart H contains special procedures for revision of acid rain permits. A permit revision may be submitted for approval at any time under Section 72.80. Depending on the type of permit revision at issue, however, different procedures will be followed for approval. The section specifies four different procedures: permit modifications (Section 72.81); fast-track modifications (Section 72.82); administrative permit amendments (Section 72.83); and automatic permit amendments (Section 72.84). Finally, under Subpart I, each source is required to submit to the administrator an annual compliance certification for each affected unit within the source. This report must be submitted within sixty days after the end of the year and must include information on the unit's compliance with the acid rain requirements and the number of allowances to be deducted for the year. Subpart I also includes two appendices setting forth methods of annualizing emissions limits and converting emissions limits to lb/mmBtu.

Monitoring

Statutory Provisions Regarding Monitoring

Section 412 required the owner or operator of each Phase I unit to install and operate CEMS on that unit, ensure the quality of the data, and comply with record-keeping and reporting requirements by November 15, 1993. The deadline for Phase II units was January 1, 1995. For new units it is the date of commencement of commercial operation.

The statute required the EPA administrator to specify the requirements for CEMS, as well as to specify when an alternative monitoring system that is "demonstrated as providing information with the same precision, reliability, accessibility and timeliness as that provided by CEMS" may be used. Section 412 also directed the administrator to promulgate quality assurance requirements, which were to include a review of data for SO_2, NO_x, opacity, and volumetric flow, as well as regulations establishing record-keeping and reporting requirements. Finally, the statute required the administrator to establish a means of calculating emissions for any period in which the CEMS data or data from an alternative monitoring system is unavailable. The monitoring regulations have been the most controversial of all the acid rain regulations that the EPA has promulgated and have undergone several revisions.

Monitoring Regulations

The monitoring requirements are contained in 40 C.F.R. Part 75. The specific provisions for monitoring SO_2, NO_x, CO_2, and opacity are set forth in Subpart B, as are provisions for monitoring emissions from common and multiple stacks. Certain oil- and gas-fired units are eligible to use the optional monitoring procedures for SO_2 in Appendix D and for NO_x in Appendix E to Part 75, instead of having to install CEMS.

Subpart C contains provisions for certification. Pursuant to Section 75.20, the designated representative must apply to the EPA administrator for certification of each CEMS or continuous opacity monitoring system (COMS) to be used in the acid rain program. The application must demonstrate that the tests specified in Section 75.20(c) were performed and that the monitoring system met the specifications set forth in Appendix A to Part 75. Each unit must be operated according to the quality assurance and quality control procedures set forth in Appendix B. Both the certification and quality assurance specifications include relative accuracy test audits, to ensure that monitor error falls within a certain percentage of the average reference method measurements, and bias tests, to determine if a monitor is measuring consistently low.

The monitoring rule also contains requirements for filling in data whenever it is not recorded by the monitoring system. These "missing data" provisions require the owner or operator, pursuant to Section 75.30, to provide substitute data according to the procedures set forth in Section 75.31. In addition, units with add-on emission controls may choose to provide substitute data according to the provisions of Section 74.34.

The owner or operator of an affected unit may apply to the EPA administrator for approval of an alternative monitoring system, as provided by Section 412, pursuant to the requirements of Subpart E. The owner or operator must demonstrate that the alternative system has at least the same precision, reliability, accessibility, and timeliness as a CEMS, according to the criteria in Sections 75.41 through 75.44. The owner or operator must also demonstrate that the quality assurance tests specified in Appendix B can be performed on the alternative system and that it can account for missing data.

Finally, the owner or operator of an affected unit must comply with the record-keeping requirements of Subpart F, maintain a monitoring plan pursuant to Section 75.53, and comply with the reporting requirements of Subpart G. Emissions data must be reported electronically to the EPA on a quarterly basis, within 30 days after the end of a calendar quarter.

Excess Emissions Penalty

Statutory Provisions Regarding the Penalty
Section 411 provides that any affected unit that emits SO_2 or NO_x in excess of allowances held or the applicable emissions limitation is liable for a penalty of \$2,000 per ton of excess emissions, adjusted yearly for inflation. This penalty is in addition to any other penalty that may be assessed against the unit for the same violation under any other provision of the CAA. The owner or operator of the unit must offset the excess emissions by an equal tonnage in the following year, unless the EPA administrator prescribes a longer period for the offset, and must submit a plan to the administrator detailing how the required offsets will be achieved.

Regulations Regarding the Penalty
The excess emissions regulations are set forth in 40 C.F.R. Part 77 and provide for the offset plans and penalties required by the statute. In addition, Section 72.9(c)(2) provides that each ton of SO_2 emitted in excess of the number of allowances held shall constitute a separate violation of the CAA.

Administrative Appeals Rule

In Part 78, the EPA provides procedures for appeal of final administrative actions regarding permits, monitoring, and allowances. A petitioner may seek review from the Environmental Appeals Board, pursuant to Section 78.3. The Environmental Appeals Board will issue an order pursuant to Section 78.20(c) or, if a hearing is requested, may refer the proceeding to a presiding officer, pursuant to Section 78.6, who in turn will issue a proposed decision to the Environmental Appeals Board under Section 78.18. The board's decisions are final agency actions for purposes of the judicial review provisions of Section 307 of the CAA.

Notes

1. The first edition was written by Jill E. Grant.
2. CAA §§ 401 *et seq.*
3. CAA § 401(a).
4. 58 Fed. Reg. 3,590 (1993).
5. CAA §§ 401, 404(f), 409, 415.
6. CAA § 401(b).
7. CAA §§ 404, 405.
8. CAA §§ 403(a), 404.
9. CAA § 403.
10. CAA § 403(g).
11. CAA § 407.
12. CAA §§ 409, 415.
13. CAA § 408.
14. CAA § 412.
15. CAA § 411.
16. CAA § 404(f).
17. CAA § 401(b).
18. CAA § 402(1).
19. CAA § 402(2).
20. CAA §§ 402(2), 403(e), 404(a), 405(a).
21. CAA § 402(15).
22. CAA § 402(8).
23. *Id.*
24. CAA § 402(10).
25. CAA § 402(17).
26. The term "designated representative" is defined in CAA § 402(26).
27. CAA § 403(e).
28. CAA § 403(a).
29. 63 Fed. Reg. 51,706 (1998).
30. CAA § 404(a)(1) & tbl. A.
31. The term "baseline" is defined in CAA § 402(4).
32. CAA § 402(19).
33. CAA § 404(f)(1)(A).
34. CAA § 404(f)(1)(B).
35. CAA § 409(c).
36. *Id.*

37. CAA § 409(d).

38. 56 Fed. Reg. 65,592 (1991).

39. CAA § 416(c)(3)–(5).

40. This is a provision of the CAA Amendments of 1990 that did not amend the Clean Air Act.

41. CAA § 406(c).

42. 58 Fed. Reg. 3,590 (1993).

43. 56 Fed. Reg. 65,592 (1991).

44. 58 Fed. Reg. 15,634 (1993).

45. 58 Fed. Reg. 50,088 (1993).

46. The requirements for these units were finalized in the Phase II allocation rule. 58 Fed. Reg. 15,634 (1993).

47. *Id.*

48. 63 Fed. Reg. 51,706 (1998).

49. The allowance databases are published at 58 Fed. Reg. 15,720 (1993).

50. 58 Fed. Reg. at 15,640.

51. 56 Fed. Reg. at 65,594 (1991).

52. 60 Fed. Reg. 17,100 (1995).

53. 58 Fed. Reg. at 50,090 (1993).

54. *Id.* at 50,103.

55. 59 Fed. Reg. 13,538 (1994).

56. 60 Fed. Reg. 18,761 (1995).

57. 61 Fed. Reg. 67,112 (1996).

58. 40 C.F.R. § 76.2.

59. 63 Fed. Reg. 49,442 (1998).

60. 59 Fed. Reg. at 13,548–49.

61. 40 C.F.R. § 76.10(a)(2).

62. 59 Fed. Reg. at 13,557.

63. *Id.* at 13,560–61.

CHAPTER 13

Stratospheric Ozone Protection

DIANE E. McCONKEY
PETER WYCKOFF[1]

Introduction

This chapter describes the law applicable in the United States that aims to heal and preserve the stratospheric ozone layer from the effects of chlorofluorocarbons (CFCs) and other ozone-depleting substances (ODS). The ozone layer shields humankind and other forms of life from harmful levels of ultraviolet radiation. The chemical industry's expansion after World War II brought with it massive production of CFCs and other halogenated chemicals. This level of production initially appeared to be a blessing, especially in the case of CFCs, since CFCs were inert, virtually nontoxic, and highly useful. Scientists progressively learned during the 1980s, however, that the blessings of massive use of CFCs and other halogenated chemicals carry a high price. CFCs and other such chemicals destroy ozone molecules in the stratosphere, potentially resulting in serious, albeit indirect, harm to human health and welfare.

In response to this potential for growing harm and possible global catastrophe, the U.S. government and other governments around the world shaped a broad and unprecedented program for stemming and reversing the process of ozone destruction. This program took the form of a treaty, the Vienna Convention for the Protection of the Ozone Layer, and a protocol to that treaty, the Montreal Protocol on Substances that Deplete the Ozone Layer.[2] In addition, the European Union and individual national governments implemented the Montreal Protocol with regulatory structures at the domestic level and supplemented the protocol with various other measures, such as mandatory labeling and restrictions on the release of ODS. In the United States, such domestic programs found expression first in the Clean Air Act (CAA) Amendments of 1990 and then in regulations of the U.S. Environmental Protection Agency (EPA). There are virtually no regulatory programs at the state and local levels for protection of the ozone layer.

This body of international and domestic law is important because it regulates current industrial behavior, but also because it presents a valuable template for dealing with other global threats to the biosphere (e.g., the release of greenhouse gases and reduction of vegetation capable of absorbing such gases). The Montreal Protocol offers—in terms of both its development and substance—a remarkably successful example of effective international cooperation. It has resulted in a dramatic reduction in worldwide production of ODS. Annual production by the developed world of CFCs alone dropped from a level in 1986 of approximately 1,000,000 metric tons (adjusted to take relative ozone-depletion potential into account) to a level in 2000 of approximately 50,000 metric tons.[3] Moreover, the Multilateral Fund, established under the protocol for the purpose of supporting developing countries in their efforts to shift to ozone-safe technologies, disbursed a total of more than $1.2 billion between 1991 and late 2001 to approximately 120 such countries.[4] The Montreal Protocol's Scientific Assessment Panel in mid-2002 concluded that the protocol "is working, and the ozone-layer depletion from the Protocol's controlled substances is expected to begin to ameliorate within the next decade or so."[5]

International Agreements and Conventions

The Vienna Convention

In March 1985, twenty countries and the Commission of the European Communities signed the Vienna Convention. The Vienna Convention imposed general obligations on the signatories but did not prescribe specific control measures. Under the terms of the treaty, the parties promised to take "appropriate measures" to "protect human health and the environment against adverse effects resulting or likely to result from human activities which modify or are likely to modify the ozone layer."[6] In addition, the parties agreed to conduct research, to exchange scientific and technical data, and to work toward the adoption of control measures consistent with "relevant scientific and technical considerations."[7]

The Montreal Protocol

Overview

The principles contained in the Vienna Convention came to fruition with the adoption, in September 1987, of the Montreal Protocol.[8] The Montreal Protocol entered into force on January 1, 1989, with ratifications by twenty-nine nations, including the United States, as well as the European Commission (on behalf of the European Community).[9] The Montreal Protocol is an innovative instrument addressing environmental policy making on a global scale. Several of its most striking features are as follows:

- It is preventative, as opposed to purely reactive. It was designed with the purpose of avoiding environmental harms, rather than reacting to them after the damage was done.

- It evinces a solid commitment to the advancement of scientific knowledge. The evolving understanding of ozone depletion has been the driving force behind the amendments to the protocol.
- It imposes substantial short-term economic restrictions on individual signatories. Unlike the Vienna Convention, it specifically sets forth phaseout requirements for a variety of ODS.
- It restricts supply to achieve a gradual transformation consistent with environmental goals. This feature sets it apart from laws and regulations that restrict emissions or specific end uses.
- It embraces decision making by consensus as the preferred mode of operation. Decisions are drafted with the goal of making them acceptable to all parties.
- It pays particular heed to the needs of developing countries. These countries are assigned a less stringent phaseout schedule for ODS. In addition, they are eligible for economic assistance to help them put in place the technology needed to produce viable substitutes.

The parties to the Montreal Protocol have met on a yearly basis every year since 1989. Several of these meetings have resulted in significant amendments or adjustments. Amendments are adopted by consensus, if possible, and by a two-thirds majority vote, if consensus is not possible.[10] Once adopted, amendments enter into force if ratified by at least two-thirds of the parties.[11] After the parties have established production or consumption controls for a substance, they may "adjust" the phaseout of that substance without going through the formal amendment process. Adjustments, like amendments, are adopted by consensus, if possible, and by a two-thirds majority vote, if consensus is not possible. If a two-thirds majority vote is taken, it must reflect a majority of both the developing countries and the developed countries present and voting. Unlike amendments, however, adjustments are not subject to ratification, but rather are binding on all parties without further procedures.[12]

Control Measures

Control measures under the Montreal Protocol (in Article 2, 2A–2H) have generally taken the form of phased reductions in production and consumption of certain "controlled substances." The reduction schedule usually leads to a complete phaseout by a given date. In many cases, related compounds are grouped together for purposes of measurement and control.

The terms "production" and "consumption" carry special meanings in the Montreal Protocol context. "Production," as defined by the protocol, does not include amounts destroyed by approved technologies, amounts used as feedstock to manufacture other chemicals, or amounts recycled and reused.[13] The protocol defines consumption as "production plus imports minus exports."[14] "Consumption" thus should not be understood as synonymous with "use." The protocol does not regulate directly the *use* of controlled substances.

The Montreal Protocol currently regulates seven categories of ODS: CFCs,[15] halons,[16] carbon tetrachloride,[17] methyl chloroform,[18] methyl bromide,[19] hydrobromofluorocarbons (HBFCs),[20] hydrochlorofluorocarbons (HCFCs),[21] and bromochloromethane.[22] As originally adopted, the protocol froze production of CFCs and halons at 1986 levels and required a reduction to 50 percent of 1986 levels by June 30, 1999.[23] Subsequently, new scientific data conclusively demonstrated the link between the use of these chemicals and stratospheric ozone depletion.[24] Owing to widespread agreement that the original controls were inadequate to avert serious environmental and health risks, the parties decided to accelerate the phaseout schedule and to add additional ozone-depleting compounds to the list of controlled substances.

The London Amendments, adopted in June 1990, required a complete phaseout of CFCs and halons by the year 2000.[25] Two new compounds were also scheduled for phaseout: carbon tetrachloride by 2000 and methyl chloroform by 2005.[26] In addition, the parties adopted a nonbinding declaration of intent to phase out HCFCs, preferably by 2020, and in any case no later than 2040.[27] Finally, the parties agreed to review the revised phaseout dates in 1992 with the goal of further accelerating the schedule.

At the 1992 Copenhagen meeting, the parties adopted further accelerated the reduction and phaseout schedule. Under this schedule, January 1, 1994, was the phaseout date for halons.[28] January 1, 1994, was also the deadline for interim reduction requirements for CFCs (25 percent of 1986 production levels)[29] and methyl chloroform (50 percent of 1989 production levels).[30] Production of carbon tetrachloride was limited to 15 percent of 1989 consumption levels as of January 1, 1995.[31] Complete phaseout of CFCs, carbon tetrachloride, and methyl chloroform occurred on January 1, 1996.[32]

The Copenhagen Amendments also imposed controls on three additional substances: HCFCs, HBFCs, and methyl bromide. For HCFCs, controls were based in part on each country's history of CFC consumption, as well as consumption of HCFCs. The baseline year was 1989. The base level is currently the party's 1989 HCFC consumption plus 2.8 percent of the party's 1989 CFC consumption. A consumption freeze took effect in 1996. Parties must reduce consumption 35 percent by January 1, 2004; 65 percent by January 1, 2010; and 90 percent by January 1, 2015. As of January 1, 2020, parties must achieve 99.5 percent reduction, and must ensure that consumption is restricted to the servicing of refrigeration and air-conditioning equipment existing as of that date. The complete consumption phaseout will occur on January 1, 2030.[33]

In Copenhagen, the parties agreed to cease production and consumption of HBFCs as of January 1, 1996, with no interim phaseout steps.[34] For methyl bromide, the parties agreed to freeze production at 1991 levels as of January 1, 1995.[35]

In 1997, the parties returned to Montreal for their ninth meeting, at which they established a phaseout schedule for methyl bromide. That schedule requires parties to reduce production and consumption 25 percent by January 1, 1999; 50 percent starting January 1, 2001; and 70 percent starting January 1, 2003. The complete methyl bromide phaseout will occur on January 1, 2005.[36] At their eleventh meeting, which occurred in Beijing in 1999, the parties agreed to cap HCFC production beginning in 2004. This requirement is in addition to the HCFC consumption controls already established. The parties also agreed to ban production and consumption of a newly controlled substance, bromochloromethane, as of January 1, 2002.[37]

Essential Use Exemptions

The essential use process provides an important exception to the control obligations imposed by the Montreal Protocol. The parties may exempt from the phaseout requirements any use deemed by them to be "essential."[38] The decisions of the parties have established a framework for essential use determinations. A specific use qualifies as being essential only if

- It is necessary for health or safety, or is critical for the functioning of society (encompassing cultural and intellectual aspects); and
- There are no available technically and economically feasible alternatives or substitutes that are acceptable from the standpoint of environment and health.[39]

Furthermore, the parties are to permit production and consumption of a directly controlled substance for an essential use only if

- All economically feasible steps have been taken to minimize the essential use and any associated emission of the controlled substance; and
- The controlled substance is not available in sufficient quantity and quality from existing stocks of banked or recycled controlled substances, also bearing in mind the developing countries' need for controlled substances.[40]

The essential use process runs on an annual basis. Only parties have the authority to nominate an essential use. Thus, a company wishing to receive an exemption must ask its government to submit a nomination on its behalf.[41] Parties must submit the nomination to the United Nations Environment Programme (UNEP) Ozone Secretariat by January 31 of the year in which they expect to receive a decision.[42] The nomination may specify any future year or years as the effective period for the exemption.[43]

For purposes of reviewing essential use applications, the parties have established an expert panel, the Technology and Economic Assessment Panel (TEAP).[44] The initial evaluation is carried out in one of the TEAP's Technical Options Committees (TOCs), each of which specializes either in specific end uses or in specific substances. The relevant TOC prepares a report for the panel's use. By April 30 of the year of nomination, the panel must issue its own report, stating whether it is able to recommend approval.[45] The panel report is then studied in working group sessions, where a final recommendation is formulated. At their annual meeting, the parties consider the recommendation and decide whether to grant an essential use exemption.[46]

Exemptions authorize the applicant to obtain a specific volume of the ODS for one or more calendar years.[47]

Exemptions for Export to Developing Countries

One important exemption from the control measures in Article 2 of the Montreal Protocol is that notwithstanding the phaseout, developed countries may produce limited amounts of most substances subject to the control measures specifically for export to developing countries to meet the basic domestic needs of those countries. As discussed below, developing countries that qualify under Article 5 of the protocol are subject to less stringent phaseout schedules than other parties. Since production tends to be concentrated in the developed world, this exemption allows developing countries to continue to obtain needed supplies of ozone depleting substances during a transitional period.[48]

Exemptions Specific to Methyl Bromide

The control measures for methyl bromide specifically exclude amounts used for quarantine and pre-shipment applications.[49] The parties have defined "quarantine" applications as "treatments to prevent the introduction, establishment and/or spread of quarantine pests (including diseases), or to ensure their official control, where (i) official control is that performed by, or authorized by, a national plant, animal or environmental protection or health authority; (ii) quarantine pests are pests of potential importance to the areas endangered thereby and not yet present there, or present but not widely distributed and being officially controlled."[50] The parties' current definition of "preshipment applications" is "those non-quarantine applications within 21 days prior to export to meet the official requirements of the importing country or existing official requirements of the exporting country. Official requirements are those which are performed by, or authorized by, a national plant, animal, environmental, health or stored product authority."[51]

In addition, the parties have indicated that they may approve limited production or consumption of methyl bromide following the complete phaseout on January 1, 2005, if such production or consumption is necessary for "critical uses."[52] In Decision IX/6, the parties agreed on the following criteria for critical uses: "(i) The specific use is critical because the lack of availability of methyl bromide for that use would result in a significant market disruption; and (ii) There are no technically and economically feasible alternatives or substitutes available to the user that are acceptable from the standpoint of environment and health and are suitable to the crops and circumstances of the nomination." The parties further stipulated that "production and consumption, if any, of methyl bromide for critical uses should be permitted only if: (i) All technically and economically feasible steps have been taken to minimize the critical use and any associated emission of methyl bromide; (ii) Methyl bromide is not available in sufficient quantity and quality from existing stocks of banked or recycled methyl bromide, also bearing in mind the developing countries' need for methyl bromide; (iii) It is demonstrated that an appropriate effort is being made to evaluate, commercialize and secure national regulatory approval of alternatives and substitutes, taking into consideration the circumstances of the particular nomination. . . . Non-Article 5 Parties must demonstrate that research programmes are in place to develop and deploy alternatives and substitutes."[53]

Control of Trade with Nonparties

The Montreal Protocol (in Article 4) places severe restrictions on trade with nonparties. Imports from nonparties of most substances subject to control under the protocol are banned outright.[54] Exports to nonparties of these substances are also banned.[55] Products containing CFCs and halons are identified in an annex to the protocol, and parties that do not register an objection to the annex must ban the import of these products from nonparties.[56] The parties are moving toward similar bans for products containing other controlled substances.[57] In addition, the parties are moving toward bans on the import of products produced with, but not containing, controlled substances.[58]

In regard to technology, parties are required to discourage the export to nonparties of technology for the production and use of any of the controlled substances that are themselves banned from export. This restriction does not apply to technology that promotes containment, destruction, or recycling of controlled substances; development of alternatives; or reductions in emissions.[59]

Developing Countries

Developing countries are treated with particular deference under the Montreal Protocol. Those countries that meet the qualifying test under Article 5[60] benefit from delayed compliance schedules. With respect to CFCs, halons, carbon tetrachloride, and methyl chloroform, Article 5 countries are subject to the control measures adopted at the London meeting, with a ten-year delay. Thus, for example, the complete phaseout of CFC production and consumption will not occur in these countries until January 1, 2010.[61] Article 5 countries must achieve a complete phaseout of HCFCs in 2040 and of methyl bromide in 2015. However, the phaseout dates for HBFCs and bromochloromethane were the same for Article 5 countries as they were for other parties to the protocol.[62]

Since its beginning, the protocol has recognized the need to assist developing countries in acquiring the necessary technology to replace ODS with substitutes. The Interim Multilateral Fund established by the parties in London in 1990 was designed to assist in the transfer of technology to Article 5 countries. The fund began operations on January 1, 1991.[63] It was given permanent status in Copenhagen the following year.

The Multilateral Fund is governed by an executive committee made up of seven representatives from Article 5 countries and seven representatives from non-Article 5 countries.[64] The United States holds a permanent seat on the executive committee. When possible, decisions are made by consensus. Otherwise, they may be made by a two-thirds majority of those present and voting, as long as this number includes a majority from both groups of seven representatives.[65] The fund is financed through contributions by non-Article 5 parties.

Three "implementing agencies" help to carry out the mission of the Multilateral Fund. The World Bank aids the executive committee in the administration and management of the fund. The United Nations Development Programme (UNDP) undertakes "feasibility and preinvestment studies" and other forms of technical assistance. The Environment Programme, UNEP, assists in "political promotion of the objectives of the Protocol, as well as in research, data-gathering, and the clearinghouse functions."[66]

Each Article 5 party interested in receiving financial assistance must submit to the executive committee a plan for meeting Montreal Protocol requirements. This plan, known as a "country programme," serves as a basis for cooperation with the implementing agencies but is not an absolute prerequisite to funding specific projects. Subsequently, the implementing agencies are invited to develop a "work programme" in conjunction with each participant. Work programs should include descriptions of specific projects to be undertaken, a timeline, and an estimated budget.[67]

Assessment and Review of Control Measures

Every four years, the parties are to assess control measures imposed under the Montreal Protocol (in Article 6). For this purpose, the parties are directed to convene panels with relevant expertise at least one year before each assessment. The expert panels must report to the parties within a year of their appointment.[68]

Reporting of Data

The parties must provide to the secretariat statistical data on annual production of controlled substances, amounts used for feedstocks, amounts destroyed by approved technology, and imports and exports to both parties and nonparties (under Article 7). In addition, the parties are required to submit data on production, imports, and exports for the baseline year for each group of controlled substances.[69]

Noncompliance

Article 8 requires the parties to adopt procedures for determining and addressing noncompliance. These procedures are now contained in Annex 7 to the Montreal Protocol. The noncompliance procedures establish an implementation committee to consider any party's failure to comply with obligations under the Montreal Protocol and to report on such failure at the meeting of the parties. The parties may then take steps to bring the noncomplying party into full compliance.[70] Such steps could include appropriate assistance; issuance of cautions; or suspension of specific rights and privileges under the Montreal Protocol.[71] Instances of noncompliance may be brought to the committee's attention by another party, the secretariat, or the actual noncomplying party.[72]

Research, Development, Public Awareness, and Exchange of Information
In addition to their specific obligation to assist developing countries, the parties to the Montreal Protocol (under Article 9) are to cooperate in research, development, and information exchange. Such efforts should focus on technology for containment, recovery, recycling, destruction, or reduction of the emissions of controlled substances; possible substitutes; and "costs and benefits of relevant control strategies."[73] The parties are also under a general obligation to publicize the effects of ODS on the environment.[74] Information on Article 9 activities must be submitted to the secretariat every two years.[75]

The 1978 Ban on CFCs for Use in Aerosol Propellants Issued under U.S. Statutes

In 1978, under authority of the Toxic Substances Control Act (TSCA), the EPA banned the manufacture, import, processing (including processing for export), and distribution in commerce of CFCs for any aerosol propellant use.[76] The EPA provided for several "essential use" exemptions from this ban.[77] Simultaneously, the Food and Drug Administration (FDA) declared that any food, drug, device, or cosmetic in a self-pressurized container containing a CFC propellant is adulterated or misbranded in violation of the Federal Food, Drug, and Cosmetic Act, unless such use has been exempted or approved as "essential" by the FDA.[78]

Until its accession to the 1985 Vienna Convention and the 1997 Montreal Protocol, the United States did not take any other aggressive action to address the impacts of emissions of "greenhouse gases" on the global environment.[79] In response to the U.S. ratification of the Montreal Protocol, the EPA issued regulations in the late 1980s to govern domestic implementation of the Protocol.[80] However, those regulations were soon superseded by the 1990 CAA Amendments and subsequent rule making.

Title VI of the 1990 CAA Amendments

General Information

Title VI of the 1990 CAA Amendments[81] was intended to address "a very important environmental problem—the destruction of the stratospheric ozone layer."[82] Loss of stratospheric ozone was expected to lead to "increased rates of disease in humans, including increased incidence of skin cancer, cataracts, and, potentially, suppression of the immune system," as well as damage to crops and marine resources.[83]

The best-known use of ODS is the use of CFCs in refrigerant and cooling systems. However, ODS have been used in a wide variety of applications, including foams, solvent cleaning, fire suppression and explosion protection, sterilants, aerosols, agricultural fumigants, adhesives, coatings, and inks.[84]

Title VI represents a sharp departure from the standard "end of the pipe" command-and-control pollution abatement scheme found in much of the CAA and many other environmental laws, which typically mandate allowable levels of emissions and the application of specific technologies. In contrast, Title VI uses restrictions on the supply of ODS to drive their eventual elimination from the marketplace. Title VI is also unique in that its provisions are linked to international treaty developments. Specifically, if the Montreal Protocol is amended in ways that make its provisions more stringent than those of CAA Title VI, the protocol controls.[85]

Production and Consumption Phaseout

The main operative provisions of Title VI of the CAA, as amended in 1990, call on the EPA to provide for the eventual phaseout of domestic production and import of listed ODS. The EPA is authorized to establish baseline production and consumption allowances, to regulate the transfer of allowances, and to set phaseout schedules. The EPA may also accelerate the phaseout schedules as necessary.[86] These steps must be accomplished in a manner consistent with U.S. obligations under the Montreal Protocol.[87] The EPA implementing regulations for the production and consumption phaseout appear at 40 C.F.R. Part 82 Subpart A.

Classification and Listing of Substances

CAA Section 602 sets forth initial lists of Class I and II ODS, including isomers of listed substances.[88] The Class I ODS listed in the CAA are CFCs, halons, carbon tetrachloride, and methyl chloroform. Only HCFCs are listed as Class II ODS. Pursuant to Section 602(c), the EPA has authority to add substances to either list based on the substance's potential harmful effects on the stratospheric ozone layer.[89] Such action may be taken *sua sponte* or in response to a listing petition.[90] The EPA may move a Class II substance onto the Class I list, but it may not otherwise remove any substance from the Class I or II lists.[91] In 1993, the EPA added methyl bromide and HBFCs to the list of Class I ODS.[92]

Phaseout Schedules

Sections 604 and 605 of the CAA established both interim reduction requirements and deadlines for the total phaseout of production and consumption of Class I and II ODS. Recognizing that there might be a need to speed up the pace of the ODS phaseout, Congress authorized the EPA, pursuant to

CAA Section 606, to accelerate the statutory phaseout schedules if (1) scientific evidence indicates the need for faster action, (2) technological advances make such action feasible, or (3) the Montreal Protocol is modified to require faster phaseout schedules. Since enactment of the 1990 CAA Amendments, all three of these eventualities have come to pass, and the EPA has exercised its Section 606 authority to accelerate the phaseout schedules contained in the Act.

Section 604(a) of the CAA calls for a complete ban on the production of Class I substances by January 1, 2000 (January 1, 2002, for methyl chloroform),[93] with annual reduction requirements expressed as a percentage of "baseline year" production.

Section 605(a) of the CAA prohibits the use or introduction into commerce of any Class II substance as of January 1, 2015, unless such substance (1) has been used, recovered, and recycled, (2) is used and entirely consumed (except for trace quantities) in the production of other chemicals, or (3) is used as a refrigerant in appliances manufactured before January 1, 2020. Production above the Class II baseline year production level is banned as of January 1, 2015, and a complete ban on production of all Class II substances is effective on January 1, 2030.

In late 1993, in response to changes to the Montreal Protocol,[94] new scientific information, and petitions and comments received from environmental and industry groups, the EPA accelerated the phaseout deadline for most Class I substances to January 1, 1996.[95] At the same time, the EPA took steps to implement the 1992 Copenhagen Amendments to the Montreal Protocol[96] by accelerating the phaseout of HCFC-141b, HCFC-142b, and HCFC-22.[97] Production and import of HCFC-141b are banned effective January 1, 2003.[98] As of January 1, 2010, no person may produce or consume HCFC-142b or HCFC-22 except for use in equipment manufactured prior to January 1, 2010.[99] The complete phaseout of HCFC-142b and HCFC-22 production and consumption will occur on January 1, 2020.[100] With regard to other HCFCs, as of January 1, 2015, production and consumption are banned except for use as a refrigerant in equipment manufactured prior to January 1, 2020.[101] The complete phaseout of all HCFC production and consumption will occur on January 1, 2030.[102]

The EPA initially listed the phaseout date for methyl bromide as 2001, in accordance with Section 602(d). In 1998, Congress amended the CAA to require the EPA to harmonize the domestic methyl bromide phaseout schedule with the schedule established under the Montreal Protocol.[103] The EPA subsequently issued regulations establishing the phaseout date for methyl bromide as January 1, 2005, with interim reductions of 25 percent in 1999, 50 percent in 2001, and 70 percent in 2003.[104]

Allowance System for Class I Substances

To bring CAA and Montreal Protocol reduction requirements down to the level of individual companies, the EPA has had to address the issue of apportionment. The EPA's first initiative in this area was the establishment of the "allowance program" for Class I substances.[105] Under this program, each "person"[106] who was producing[107] or consuming[108] a listed Class I substance in the applicable baseline year was apportioned a chemical-specific "production" or "consumption" baseline.[109] The regulations specified what percentage of its baseline the company was to receive in the form of allowances for a given calendar year. To produce one kilogram of a Class I substance, a company was required to expend one production allowance and one consumption allowance. To import the same amount, the company was required to expend one consumption allowance. Allowances shrank each year in accordance with the phaseout schedule for the listed substance. They were valid only in the specific calendar year[110] for which they were apportioned, and any unexpended allowances were forfeited. The allowance program was in full effect for all Class I substances until January 1, 1996, the phaseout date for most Class I substances.[111] Between January 1, 1996, and January 1, 2005, the only Class I substance for which production and consumption allowances are available is methyl bromide. As of January 1, 2005, no production or consumption allowances will be granted for any Class I substance.[112]

Allowance System for Class II Substances

The allowance system for Class II substances is substantially similar to the system developed for Class I substances.[113] Companies that produced or imported HCFC-141b, HCFC-22, or HCFC-142b during any of the years 1994, 1995, 1996, or 1997 are assigned chemical-specific "production" or "consumption" baselines.[114] Companies with HCFC-22 or HCFC-142b production or consumption baselines receive allowances equal to 100 percent of their baseline through the year 2009; the EPA has stated that it will address the percentage to be allocated in 2010 and beyond in a subsequent rule making.[115] Because the publication of the Class II allocation rule coincided with the U.S. HCFC-141b phaseout, companies with historic levels of HCFC-141b production or consumption do not receive production or consumption allowances for this substance. However, companies with baseline HCFC-141b production do receive 100 percent of their baseline in the form of "export production allowances," which allow production of HCFC 141b for export to other developed countries that have agreed to be bound by the applicable HCFC control measures under the protocol.[116]

Exports to Article V Countries

Both the Class I and Class II allowance programs give participating producers the opportunity to secure additional allowances, known as "Article 5 allowances," for export to developing countries operating under Article 5 of the Montreal Protocol.[117] Each person who was apportioned baseline production allowances for Class I or Class II substances is also apportioned Article 5 allowances, which are available beyond the U.S. phaseout date for the substance in question, due to the delayed phaseout schedules in Article 5 countries. Article 5 allowances are generally equal to 15 percent of baseline production.[118] The EPA requires each person granted Article 5 allowances to report each quarter on exports to Article 5 countries.[119] Interpollutant and intercompany transfers of Article 5 allowances are permitted, subject to an offset requirement of one percent in the case of Class I substances and one-tenth of a percent in the case of Class II substances.[120]

Transformation and Destruction

For all Class I and Class II substances, the regulations provide that persons may produce or import controlled substances despite the phaseout, if they produce or import the substances explicitly for uses resulting in transformation or destruction.[121] The rationale is that the definition of production[122] does not include the manufacture of controlled substances that are either transformed or destroyed by an approved technology. The EPA defines "transform" as "to use and entirely consume (except for trace quantities) a controlled substance in the manufacture of other chemicals for commercial purposes."[123] EPA regulations list the destruction technologies approved by the parties to the Montreal Protocol.[124]

Transformation or destruction may occur either in the U.S. or abroad. All second- or third-party transformers or destroyers, regardless of location, must provide the producer or importer with an IRS certificate of intent to transform or a verification of destruction. The producer or importer must submit these certificates or verifications to the EPA and must report each quarter on the quantities of controlled substances transformed or destroyed.[125]

If methyl bromide that was originally intended for emissive uses is subsequently transformed or destroyed, the producer or importer may petition the EPA to replace the allowances expended. This provision will continue in effect until the methyl bromide phaseout on January 1, 2005.[126]

Transfers and Trades

Sections 607 and 616 of the CAA authorize, subject to EPA review and approval, certain transfers and exchanges of both production and consumption allowances in any given calendar year. Transfers may occur between the United States and another party to the Montreal Protocol; between two U.S. companies; or within a single company. Inter-pollutant transfers are allowed in some circumstances. All transfers are subject to EPA review and approval.

For example, if a U.S. company were to sell its HCFC-22 production allowances to another U.S. company, it would be performing an "intercompany" transfer. Alternatively, the company could convert its HCFC-22 production allowances into HCFC-142b production allowances, on an ODP-weighted basis. That action would be referred to as an "inter-pollutant" transfer. The company would also have the option of combining an inter-company transfer with an inter-pollutant transfer by exchanging its HCFC-22 production allowances for an ODP-equivalent amount of HCFC-142b production allowances held by another company. Inter-company transfers of Article 5 allowances and export production allowances are permissible. Inter-pollutant transfers are not permitted for export production allowances and are permitted only for certain types of Article 5 allowances.[127]

As to inter-party transfers, Section 616 of the CAA authorizes transfers of production allowances to or from other parties to the Montreal Protocol, as long as certain conditions are met. If the U.S. transfers production allowances to another party, the EPA must revise aggregate U.S. production limits to reflect the transfer.[128] Article 5 allowances also may be transferred internationally.[129]

Upon application to the EPA, a person may obtain additional consumption allowances equivalent to the amount of a substance that person exports to another party to the protocol.[130] In limited circumstances, a person may also increase consumption allowances by obtaining consumption allowances from another party to the protocol.[131]

Under Section 607, the EPA may authorize a transfer of production or consumption allowances only if it will result in less production than would occur absent the transfer. Therefore, for each domestic transfer, the EPA deducts an amount from the transferor's allowance balance equal to one percent of the amount transferred, in the case of Class I substances, or one-tenth of a percent, in the case of Class II substances. This additional deduction is known as an "offset."[132] Transfers of Article V allowances and export production allowances are also subject to the offset requirement.

Exemptions for Essential Uses

EPA regulations contain exemptions from the production and consumption ban for persons who possess allowances to produce or import specific amounts of Class I substances for designated "essential uses."[133] These exemptions are the domestic equivalent of the essential use exemptions under the Montreal Protocol.

Section 604(d) of the CAA authorizes the EPA to create certain exemptions to the phaseout of Class I substances. The EPA has relied on this authority to implement essential use exemptions approved by the parties to the Montreal Protocol. In particular, the EPA has relied on the exemptions in 604(d)(1) and (2) in amending its accelerated phaseout regulations to authorize limited production of CFCs for metered dose inhalers (MDIs) and of methyl chloroform for use in cleaning, bonding, and surface activation applications for the space shuttle and Titan rockets.[134] The CAA criteria for each of these exemptions are in addition to the criteria considered by the parties. Thus, the EPA does not necessarily grant the full amount of production or import approved by the parties for the use in question. In addition, with regard to MDIs, the EPA consults with FDA before determining what amount of newly produced or imported CFCs is "necessary" for use in MDIs.[135]

In addition to creating an essential use allowance system, the EPA has issued regulations implementing the global exemption granted by the parties for laboratory and analytical uses of Class I substances.[136] Any person may use this exemption without need of allowances.[137]

Exemptions Specific to Methyl Bromide

In 1998, Congress amended Section 604 of the Clean Air Act to authorize the EPA to implement the two exemptions from the methyl bromide phaseout that are contemplated under the Montreal Protocol: the quarantine and preshipment exemption, and the critical use exemption.[138] Section 604(d)(5) states that "[t]o the extent consistent with the Montreal Protocol's quarantine and preshipment provisions," the EPA "shall exempt" from the production and consumption phaseout quantities of methyl bromide used "to fumigate commodities entering or leaving the United States or any State (or political subdivision thereof) for purposes of compliance with Animal and Plant Health Inspection Service requirements or with any international, Federal, State or local sanitation or food protection standard." The EPA's implementing regulation provide a general exemption from the methyl bromide production and import restrictions for quantities produced or imported solely for quarantine or preshipment applications, as defined in the regulation. No special allowances are required.[139]

With regard to critical uses, Section 604(d)(6) of the Clean Air Act states that "[t]o the extent consistent with the Montreal Protocol, the Administrator, after notice and the opportunity for public comment, and after consultation with other departments or institutions of the Federal Government having regulatory authority related to methyl bromide, including the Secretary of Agriculture, may exempt the production, importation, and consumption of methyl bromide for critical uses." Because the Montreal Protocol does not permit production or import for critical uses until after the complete phaseout on January 1, 2005, critical use exemptions will not be available at either the international or the domestic level until after that date.[140] The EPA has not yet promulgated regulations implementing the critical use exemption.

Import of Used ODS

Any person who wishes to import a used Class I or Class II controlled substance must submit a petition to the EPA at least forty working days before the shipment is to leave the foreign port of export. The petition must include such information as the name and quantity of the substance; contact information for the importer, the source facility, and the exporter; information regarding the previous use and the equipment from which the substance was recovered; the U.S. port of entry, the expected date of shipment, and the identity of the transport vessel; a description of the intended use; information regarding recovery and reclamation; the export license; and a certification of accuracy. The import may not proceed unless the importer receives a nonobjection notice from the EPA. While the regulations provide that the EPA has forty days to review the petition, there is no provision for automatic approval if the EPA fails to act within that period.[141]

Reporting and Record Keeping

The EPA has set forth reporting and record-keeping requirements for persons who produce, import, export, or transship controlled substances; persons involved with destruction or transformation of controlled substances; persons allocated essential use allowances; persons operating under the global essential use exemption for laboratory and analytical uses of controlled substances; and persons operating under the methyl bromide quarantine and preshipment exemption. Records and copies of required reports must be retained for three years.[142] Reports are generally required on a quarterly or an annual basis, and unless otherwise specified must be mailed within forty-five days of the end of the reporting period.[143]

Prohibitions

For all Class I substances except methyl bromide, no person may produce in excess of unexpended essential-use allowances or exemptions, or unexpended Article 5 allowances.[144] Furthermore, no person may import these substances in excess of unexpended essential-use allowances or exemptions.[145] Every kilogram of excess production or importation constitutes a separate violation.[146]

No person may produce methyl bromide in excess of unexpended production allowances or Article 5 allowances held by that person, unless the production is for quarantine or pre-shipment applications.[147] Similarly, no person may produce or import methyl bromide in excess of unexpended consumption allowances held by that person, unless the production or import is for quarantine or pre-shipment applications.[148] (A producer must have both production and consumption allowances to produce a chemical, as production is counted against both production and consumption limits. However, importers of methyl bromide need only consumption allowances, as imports count only against consumption.)[149] Every kilogram of excess production or importation constitutes a separate violation.[150] Production and consumption allowances for methyl bromide will cease to be available on January 1, 2005.[151] The EPA may grant critical use exemptions for certain uses of methyl bromide to allow limited production and import beyond January 1, 2005, for uses other than quarantine and pre-shipment applications.[152]

Prohibitions for Class II substances are similar to those for Class I substances. For those substances subject to the allowance system, production requires use of production allowances in conjunction with consumption allowances, or alternatively, use of either Article 5 allowances or export production allowances. Import requires use of consumption allowances.[153] After the phaseout date of each substance, production and consumption allowances will cease to be available for that substance.

Both Class I and Class II substances are subject to prohibitions on trade with nonparties.[154] In addition, if a party informs the United States that it has established a ban on the manufacture and import of products containing certain Class I controlled substances, the EPA will ban the export of such controlled products to that party.[155] These regulatory prohibitions reflect trade bans agreed to by the parties to the Montreal Protocol.

Labeling

General Requirements

CAA Section 611 requires that a warning label be placed on containers containing a Class I or Class II substance, products containing Class I substances, and products manufactured with Class I substances (unless no safe alternatives are available).[156]

CONTAINERS OF CONTROLLED SUBSTANCES AND PRODUCTS CONTAINING CONTROLLED SUBSTANCES Warning labels must be placed on products containing Class I substances and such labels must be passed through the stream of commerce,[157] even when the ultimate seller has not itself placed the Class I substance in the product.[158] Effective January 1, 2015, all products containing Class II substances also must be labeled. Until then, a product containing a Class II substance will require a label only if the EPA determines, by rule making, that such a label is required.[159]

A container of a controlled substance must be labeled as such only if the substance must be transferred to another container, vessel, or piece of equipment to realize its intended use. Otherwise the container must be labeled as a "product containing a controlled substance."[160] In other words, if the controlled substance is used in the container without being transferred, the container would be considered a "product containing" and must be labeled accordingly. For example, a bulk container of halon attached to a total flooding fire protection system would be a "product containing" a Class I substance because the halons are used directly from the tank itself. In contrast, CFCs sold in small cans for recharging air conditioners would be used only after being transferred to an air conditioner, and would be labeled as "containers containing."[161]

PRODUCTS MANUFACTURED WITH CONTROLLED SUBSTANCES The EPA's labeling regulations provide that a manufacturer must label its product as "manufactured with a controlled substance" only if that manufacturer itself used a controlled substance in making the product.[162] This limitation is intended to simplify compliance for manufacturers who purchase components from many vendors.[163] The inclusion, therefore, of a component product which was manufactured with a controlled substance in the manufacture of a second product, the manufacture of which does not otherwise involve the use of controlled substances, does not constitute "manufacturing with a controlled substance."[164] The supplier must label the component, but the manufacturer does not have to pass the label through on the outside of the final product, unless the manufacturer itself otherwise used controlled substances in making the final product.

There are several exemptions from the definition of "product manufactured with a controlled substance." The definition expressly excludes the following:

- "Incidental uses" of controlled substances, that is, those situations where "a product has not had physical contact with the controlled substance"
- Situations where the manufacturing equipment or the product has had physical contact with a controlled substance, but only in an intermittent manner (and not as a routine part of the direct manufacturing process)
- Instances in which the controlled substance has, except for trace quantities, been transformed into a nonregulated substance
- Situations in which the controlled substance has been destroyed using one of the five destruction processes approved by the parties to the Montreal Protocol that achieves a destruction efficiency of 98 percent or greater[165]

Under a process established to assist the public in complying with Section 611, the EPA has issued a series of official applicability determinations providing guidance.[166] A number of these determinations clarify the meaning of "manufactured with." For example, one company informed the EPA that it had fixtures on its conveyer belt to hold its products in place during the manufacturing process. The fixtures were periodically cleaned by a Class I substance, and the company wondered whether such cleaning rendered the products "manufactured with" a Class I substance and therefore subject to the labeling requirement. The EPA determined that the products were not subject to the labeling requirement because the product itself had not come into contact with a controlled substance.[167]

Exemptions from the Labeling Requirements

There are several exemptions from the labeling rule, including the following:

- Products containing trace quantities of a controlled substance as a residue or impurity that serves no useful purpose need not be labeled as a "product containing" a controlled substance. If the product was *manufactured* with a controlled substance, however, it must be labeled as such.
- Containers containing trace quantities of a controlled substance as a residue or impurity need not need be labeled as a "container containing" a controlled substance.
- Waste containing controlled substance or blends of controlled substances bound for discard need not be labeled. Waste that is bound for recycling, however, must be labeled.
- Products manufactured solely for export (as long as the product is clearly designated as intended for export only).

- Products repaired using a process that involves a controlled substance. Similarly, companies that purchase spare parts that were manufactured using a controlled substance and subsequently sell the spare part for the sole purpose of repair need not pass the label through if the spare parts are removed from the manufacturer's original packaging.
- Products, processes, or substitute chemicals undergoing research and development in which a controlled substance is used.[168]

In addition, products manufactured before May 15, 1993, are not covered by the rule.[169]

The Distinction between Products with Class I and Class II Substances

Until January 1, 2015, Section 611 treats products manufactured with a Class I substance differently from those manufactured with a Class II substance. A product "manufactured with" a Class I substance *must* bear a label unless the EPA explicitly determines it to be exempt; products manufactured with a Class II substance need not bear a label absent an explicit EPA determination to the contrary.[170]

Before 2015, the EPA may exempt products manufactured with a Class I substance from the labeling requirement if it determines that there is no substitute product or manufacturing process that (1) does not rely on the use of the Class I substance, (2) reduces the overall risk to human health and the environment, and (3) is currently or potentially available.[171] The labeling requirements may be imposed on a product manufactured with a Class II substance before January 1, 2015, if the EPA determines by rule making that there *is* a substitute product that (1) does not rely on the use of the Class II substance, (2) reduces the overall risk to human health and the environment, and (3) is currently or potentially available.[172] The EPA can make this determination on its own or in response to a citizens' petition.

Effective January 1, 2015, products manufactured with Class I and Class II substances shall be treated equally. All products manufactured with Class I and II products must be labeled, including Class I products previously exempted and Class II products previously not regulated.

The Petition Process

The EPA established a petition process for those seeking (1) to exempt from the labeling requirement temporarily a product manufactured with a Class I substance or (2) to require a label for a product manufactured with a Class II substance.[173] While the petition process has been little used in recent years, the EPA earlier granted two temporary exemptions from the labeling requirements for products manufactured with Class I substances.[174]

Petitions must contain "adequate data" to support the request. A party seeking an exemption must continue to label its product or container while a determination is pending. Within 180 days of receiving a complete petition, the EPA must take action to grant or deny the petition.[175]

Imports

Importers of foreign products or containers must label the items before their entry into the United States if they were manufactured with or contain a controlled substance. The importer is responsible for determining whether the imported product or container is required to be labeled upon import.[176] The importer may rely on its supplier for information regarding the use of controlled substances in the product's manufacture.[177]

Label Placement and Content

The following warning label must be affixed to any covered product or container in a "clearly legible and conspicuous" manner before its introduction into interstate commerce:

> WARNING: Contains [or Manufactured with, if applicable] [*insert name of substance*], a substance which harms public health and environment by destroying ozone in the upper atmosphere.[178]

In general, the label must "appear with such prominence and conspicuousness as to render it likely to be read and understood by consumers under normal conditions of purchase."[179] The EPA has noted that for most products and containers, this standard will be met by placing the label on the principal display panel (PDP).[180] The EPA has based its preference for use of the PDP in part on the fact that most companies are required to have a PDP under Consumer Product Safety Commission requirements.[181] The label must also be in legible type and in sharp contrast to any background on which it appears.[182]

If a product or container has an outer wrapping or packaging that obscures the PDP, the label can be placed on that outer covering. When a PDP does not exist, the warning can be conveyed by other means, including a hang tag, tape, card, sticker, invoice, bill of lading, or similar means.[183]

In addition to bearing the required warning statement, the label must include the relevant substance's standard chemical name, with the exception of certain commonly recognized abbreviations for such chemical names.[184] When a product or container contains or was manufactured with more than one substance, such information may be indicated on a single warning statement as long as the statement makes clear which substances are contained in, and which are used in the manufacture of, the item.[185]

Safe Alternatives Policy: The EPA's SNAP Program

Section 612 of the CAA calls for the replacement of listed ODS, to the "maximum extent practicable . . . by chemicals, product substitutes, or alternative manufacturing processes that reduce overall risks to human health and the environment."[186] The EPA's Significant New Alternatives Policy (SNAP) program implements Section 612.[187] The SNAP program is intended to control the commercialization of substitutes for ODS and to ensure that such substitutes do not result in greater harm to the environment than chemicals currently on the market. After reviewing any relevant health and environmental effects data, the SNAP program identifies and classifies "acceptable" substitutes for existing applications of ODS and restricts or totally prohibits the use of "unacceptable" substitutes. The EPA is thus afforded an opportunity for "pre-market" review of and, if necessary, imposition of regulatory controls on specific chemicals and products containing those chemicals.[188]

Submission Requirements

Section 612(e) requires producers to submit a SNAP notification to the EPA, including all unpublished health and safety studies, ninety days before introducing new or existing chemicals into interstate commerce for any significant new uses as substitutes for Class I substances.[189] The EPA has, by regulation, extended these requirements to Class II substances.[190] The agency requires a fairly extensive set of information to support a SNAP submission.[191] Information can be claimed as confidential, but such claims must be substantiated.[192] To date, the EPA has reviewed hundreds of SNAP submissions.

The EPA Review Process

Preexisting substitutes can continue to be marketed until the EPA makes a final acceptability determination by rule making. Producers of new substitutes may introduce them into commerce ninety days after submitting notification to the EPA, even if the EPA extends the review period or has not rendered a final acceptability determination. If the EPA fails to take any regulatory action (e.g., classifying the substitute's use as "unacceptable" or otherwise restricted) within the ninety-day review period, the submitter is free to commercialize the substance until the EPA takes regulatory action.[193]

If a submitter intends to introduce a "new chemical" into interstate commerce as a substitute for a Class I or II ODS, the substitute must undergo joint SNAP-TSCA Section 5 premanufacture notice (PMN) review.[194] Restrictions may result from either SNAP or PMN review. Submitters should be aware that restrictions resulting from the PMN review process may effectively bar a company from marketing the product as an ODS substitute, even if the EPA has not issued a final SNAP acceptability determination.[195]

Acceptability Determinations

The EPA's acceptability determinations are based on comparative risk assessments for specific uses. Review criteria include atmospheric effects and related health and environmental impacts, ecosystem risks, occupational risks, consumer risks, general population risks from ambient exposure to substitutes with direct toxicity and to increased ground-level ozone, flammability, and the cost and availability of the substitute.[196] The substitute's technical performance is not normally evaluated, except when such factors affect the substitute's health or environmental effects (e.g., fire suppression or refrigeration systems).

The EPA gives notice of its acceptability determinations in the *Federal Register*. There are five kinds of SNAP determinations: (1) acceptable, (2) acceptable subject to use conditions, (3) acceptable subject to narrowed use limits, (4) unacceptable, and (5) pending.[197] In the first category, acceptable substitutes are listed without rule making, since such listings do not impose any sanction or remove any prior license to use a substance. For the second, third, and fourth categories, the EPA adds or removes substitutes through rule making.[198] Lastly, a pending classification is used when the EPA has received a SNAP notification but has yet to make an acceptability determination.[199]

To date, the EPA has published acceptability determinations for most Class I substances.[200] It has approved all of the currently used ODS substitutes, although it has restricted several to uses for specific applications. The EPA has also listed several potential substitutes as unacceptable owing to safety concerns or the existence of alternatives with lower ozone-depleting potential.[201]

Exemptions

The EPA has promulgated a series of regulatory exemptions from the SNAP requirements.[202] These include uses of substitutes already listed as "acceptable" by the EPA, research and development, test marketing, and "small sector" uses, auxiliary formulation changes, certain feedstock uses, and small volume (10,000 pounds or less) uses within SNAP sectors. Some of these exemptions entail prior notification to the EPA and record keeping (including annual production and sales information) by the person introducing the substitute in its final form into interstate commerce. Generally, this would be the manufacturer or formulator, but such requirements could fall on the end user.[203]

Prohibitions and Penalties

Persons are prohibited from using any substitute that they know or have reason to know is in violation of any SNAP requirement, including restrictions in acceptability determinations; from using any substitute without adhering to such restrictions; or from using any unacceptable substitutes.[204] SNAP violations can result in administrative, civil, and criminal fines and penalties pursuant to Section 113 of the act. (See Chapters 17 and 18 on enforcement.)

The EPA can prohibit use of a substitute only if it has identified an alternative that (1) reduces the overall risk to human health or the environment and (2) is currently or potentially available.[205] The EPA defines "potentially available" to include alternatives which the agency "reasonably believes" to be technically feasible, even absent completion of all testing, production, and commercialization, if the agency otherwise has sufficient information to make an acceptability determination.[206]

Existing (already purchased) supplies of unacceptable substitutes in the possession of end users as of March 18, 1994, may be used until exhausted. Use of unacceptable substitutes purchased after March 18, 1994, is prohibited.[207] When appropriate, the EPA will apply a four-part test[208] to determine whether to grandfather the production and use of particular substitutes by setting the effective date of acceptability determinations in the future.

Recycling and Emissions Reduction

Statutory Framework

Section 608(a) of the CAA requires the EPA to establish standards regarding the use and disposal of Class I and Class II substances particularly during the service, repair, or disposal of appliances and industrial process refrigeration.[209] The CAA requires that emissions from appliances be reduced to the lowest achievable level and that recapture and recycling of such substances be maximized.[210] Section 608(a) also calls for regulation of the use and disposal of Class I and Class II substances in other contexts, but without specifying which ones.[211] Section 608(b) requires the EPA to adopt standards and requirements for the safe disposal of Class I and II substances by requiring that all such ODS contained in bulk appliances, machines, or other goods be removed before disposal or delivery for recycling. Section 608(c) embodies self-effectuating prohibitions against the venting into the environment of Class I or Class II substances, and eventually their substitutes, during servicing or disposal of air-conditioning or refrigeration equipment excepting *de minimis* releases that occur while the recycling and recovery requirements are followed.[212]

Regulatory Implementation

The EPA during 1993–1995 promulgated foundational regulations implementing Section 608 with respect to CFCs and HCFCs used in air-conditioning and refrigeration.[213] Those regulations appear as Subpart F of 40 C.F.R. Part 82.[214] Prompted by a citizens' suit, the agency in March 1998 established regulations implementing Section 608 with respect to halons used in fire suppression and explosion prevention.[215] The halon regulations appear as Subpart H.[216] In June 1998, the EPA proposed (1) Section 608 regulations for certain ODS substitutes in the air-conditioning and refrigerant sectors, namely, hydrofluorocarbons (HFCs) and perfluorocarbons (PFCs) and (2) amendments to Subpart F that would strengthen current leak repair requirements.[217] An overview of only Subpart F follows; Subpart H has a highly specialized applicability, and disposition of the 1998 proposal, while still pending, is uncertain.[218]

Subpart F of 40 C.F.R. Part 82: Refrigerant Recycling

The EPA's foundational regulations governing CFC and HCFC refrigerants apply to (1) any person servicing, maintaining, or repairing appliances, except for motor vehicle air conditioners (MVACs); (2) any person disposing of appliances, including MVACs; and (3) refrigerant reclaimers, appliance owners, and manufacturers of appliances and recycling and recovery equipment.[219] Persons engaged in the servicing and disposal of covered equipment must adhere to certain standards, practices, equipment, and certification requirements. The regulations also establish requirements for leak repairs and for the removal and sale of refrigerant. Full compliance with the regulations was required by November 14, 1994, although the EPA has since amended and stayed several minor provisions.

AFFECTED EQUIPMENT   The regulations affect the servicing and disposal of most air-conditioning and refrigeration equipment,[220] including household air conditioners and refrigerators, commercial air conditioners and chillers, commercial refrigeration,[221] industrial process refrigeration,[222] refrigerated transport, and air-conditioning in vehicles not covered by CAA Section 609, which applies to the service of MVACs[223] containing Class I or II substances.[224]

SERVICE PRACTICES   Technicians must recover refrigerant rather than vent it into the atmosphere, excluding *de minimis* releases, which vary depending on the type of equipment being serviced.[225] Before equipment (other than small appliances or MVACs) can be opened for maintenance, service, or repair, any refrigerant must be evacuated to the levels set forth in the regulations[226] from the entire system or the part to be serviced (if the latter can be isolated) to a system receiver[227] or a certified recycling or recovery machine.[228] If a small appliance is opened for maintenance, service, or repair, the technician must either recover the refrigerant to specified levels that vary according to the type of recycle and recovery equipment used, or evacuate the small appliance to four inches of mercury vacuum.[229] Equipment (other than small appliances or MVACs) with leaks that make the required evacuation levels impossible to achieve, and some nonmajor repairs,[230] are exempt from these requirements.[231] To prevent contaminated refrigerant from entering the market, refrigerant must be reclaimed[232] by a certified reclaim entity before being transferred between equipment owned by different persons.[233]

CERTIFICATION OF RECYCLING AND RECOVERY EQUIPMENT   To ensure that the equipment that is recycling and recovering refrigerant is capable of limiting emissions of CFCs and HCFCs, the regulations require that any such equipment used during the maintenance, service, repair, or disposal of appliances be certified by an approved equipment-testing organization.[234] Removal of refrigerant in equipment manufactured before November 15, 1993, must meet different requirements than that manufactured after November 15, 1993.[235] In addition, equipment used with small appliances, MVACs, or MVAC-like appliances is subject to separate certification requirements.[236] For all equipment, manufacturers or importers must affix labels stating that the equipment has been certified by an approved equipment-testing organization and meets the minimum requirements for recycling or recovery equipment.[237] In addition, manufacturers must have their equipment tested or inspected at least once every three years to ensure that the equipment is still capable of meeting EPA requirements.[238] Certification may be revoked if the recycling and recovery equipment subsequently fails to meet the certification criteria.[239] Beginning November 15, 1993, all equipment is to be in compliance with the certification requirements.[240]

LEAK REPAIRS   Owners of commercial refrigeration equipment containing at least fifty pounds charge[241] and owners of industrial process refrigeration equipment must repair any leaks causing a loss of refrigerant that exceeds 35 percent of the total charge during a twelve-month period.[242] Owners of appliances other than commercial and industrial process refrigeration equipment with more than fifty pounds of charge must repair any leaks causing a loss of refrigerant that exceeds 15 percent of the total charge during a twelve-month period.[243] Owners must repair all leaks within certain timeframes, unless the owner intends to replace or retire the leaking equipment within one year of discovering the leak.[244] The owner must base its knowledge of leaks on the service records and the amounts of refrigerant added to the machines. Therefore, it is in the owner's best interest to provide sufficient information to a technician repairing the equipment so that the technician can accurately determine whether a leak exists or must be repaired. An owner may not intentionally shield itself from information that would have revealed a leak.[245]

REFRIGERANT DISPOSAL   Persons disposing of an appliance that is not a small appliance, MVAC, or MVAC-like appliance must evacuate the refrigerant to specified levels.[246] Persons disposing of a small appliance, MVAC, or MVAC-like appliance must recover any remaining refrigerant to the appropriate levels[247] or verify that it has been evacuated.[248] Anyone accepting this equipment for disposal must notify the appliance supplier that the refrigerant must be properly removed before delivery.[249]

RECLAIMER CERTIFICATION   A person who is in the business of reclaiming used refrigerant for resale must certify to the EPA that the person will (1) return the refrigerant to the standard of purity set forth in Appendix A to Subpart F (which is based on a standard set by the Air Conditioning and Refrigeration Institute, ARI 700-1993), (2) verify achievement of that goal on an ongoing basis using Appendix A, (3) release no more than 1.5 percent of the refrigerant during the reclamation process, and (4) dispose of resulting wastes lawfully.[250] There is a grandfather exemption for any person who was properly certified under the Section 608 regulations in existence before October 18, 1994.[251] The EPA may revoke a certification for cause.[252]

TECHNICIAN CERTIFICATION Only certified technicians may open appliances, except MVACs, for maintenance, service, or repair.[253] Only certified technicians may dispose of appliances, except small appliances, MVACs, and MVAC-like appliances.[254] Anyone who sells a Class I or Class II substance as a refrigerant must have assurance in general that the refrigerant will be handled by a certified technician, if the buyer is not an appliance manufacturer.[255] All technicians must pass an exam administered by an EPA-approved testing program.[256]

REPORTING AND RECORD KEEPING Reporting and record-keeping requirements, which vary depending on the activity in which the person engages, apply to persons involved in the manufacture, sale, service, maintenance, repair, or disposal of Class I or Class II substances. These requirements apply to owners and operators as well as to sellers, purchasers, testing organizations, reclaimers, disposers, and technicians.[257]

Motor Vehicle Air Conditioners

Statutory Framework

By the late 1980s, MVACs[258] accounted for a large percentage of the usage of CFC-12 in the United States. Consequently, when Congress fashioned Title VI in 1990, it included provisions addressing the servicing, maintenance, repair, and disposal of MVACs and MVAC-like appliances. Those provisions lie primarily in Section 609, but also in Section 608(c).

Section 609 directs the EPA to promptly promulgate regulations establishing standards and requirements governing the servicing of MVACs. It then contains three directives aimed mainly at the motor vehicle servicing business. First, no person in that business may perform a service on an MVAC that involves refrigerant[259] unless that person properly uses approved refrigerant recycling equipment and has been properly trained and certified. This prohibition took effect January 1, 1992, except in the case of small-volume shops, which had a one-year grace period. Second, within the same timeframes, any person in the business of servicing MVACs must certify to the EPA that the person has obtained and is properly using approved refrigerant-recycling equipment and allows only individuals who have been properly trained and certified to service the MVACs. Finally, Section 609 prohibits the sale or distribution of any Class I or II substance in containers less than twenty pounds to any person except someone who has complied with the first two requirements.

Section 608(c)(1) prohibits any person after July 1, 1992, from knowingly releasing any Class I or Class II refrigerant (e.g., CFC-12) while servicing or disposing of an "appliance," which is defined in Section 601 to include any "air conditioner." Similarly, Section 608(c)(2) prohibits any person after November 15, 1995, from knowingly releasing any substitute for a Class I or II refrigerant (e.g., HFC-134a) in the same circumstances. These prohibitions do not apply, however, to "de minimis releases associated with good faith attempts to recapture and recycle or safely dispose of" any such substance.

Implementing Regulations

The EPA has promulgated regulations implementing those provisions of Sections 609 and 608 in two sets. The first set consisted of a foundational rulemaking in 1992 and a supplemental rulemaking in 1995. This set established, in the form of Subpart B of 40 C.F.R. Part 82, not only the three directives specified in Section 609, but also (1) detailed technical standards governing recycling and recovery equipment and proper use of that equipment and (2) detailed record keeping and reporting requirements.[260] In effect, the primary focus of the 1992 and 1995 rules was management of the continued use of CFC-12 in MVACs.[261] In contrast, the second set of regulations, promulgated in 1997, focused primarily on disposal of MVACs and on the growing use of substitutes for CFC-12, including HFC-134a, in MVACs.[262]

The following material first describes the main provisions of Subpart B as established by the 1992 and 1995 promulgation, and then describes the additions made by the 1997 promulgation.[263]

PROVISIONS OF THE 1992 AND 1995 PROMULGATIONS   As of November 15, 1992, a Class I or II substance that could be used as a refrigerant and is in a container holding less than twenty pounds of the substance can be sold only to persons who service MVACs in accordance with the regulations or to persons who certify that the container is for resale only.[264]

As of August 13, 1992, all persons servicing MVACs must be properly trained and certified and using approved equipment.[265] Technician training and certification programs can be certified if they meet the standards located in the appendices to Subpart B for training, test subject material, test administration, and proof of certification. Once a program is approved, the program director must periodically review and update the material. The EPA may specify the need for recertification in the future and it may revoke a program's approval at any time.[266]

As of January 1, 1993, all persons servicing MVACs are also required to certify to the EPA that they have acquired approved equipment and that they (or their employees) are properly trained and certified to use the equipment.[267] Certificates of compliance are not transferable in the event of a change of ownership of the servicing establishment. Record-keeping requirements are imposed on (1) any person who owns approved recycling equipment and sends the refrigerant to another facility, (2) any person who owns approved recycling equipment and authorizes people to use it, and (3) any person who sells any Class I or II refrigerant substance in a container of less than twenty pounds.[268] Finally, any person selling a Class I or II refrigerant substance is required to display prominently in the sales area a sign announcing that

It is a violation of federal law to sell containers of class I and class II refrigerant of less than 20 pounds of such refrigerant to anyone who is not properly trained and certified to operate approved refrigerant recycling equipment.[269]

The EPA imposes uniform standards for both recover and recycle and recover-only equipment and for their use.[270] Equipment meeting these standards must be certified by the EPA or by an independent standards testing organization approved by the EPA. Any testing organization may apply to the EPA for approval to certify equipment in accordance with the regulatory standards.[271] The EPA may revoke an organization's approval at any time if it conducts certification tests in a manner not consistent with that set forth in its application.[272] Equipment purchased before certain dates will be considered approved if it is deemed "substantially identical" to equipment approved according to the EPA's standards.[273] The EPA will have available a list of approved equipment.[274]

The equipment must be "properly used" in accordance with the standard referenced in the regulation and with the manufacturer's guide.[275] For recover and recycle equipment, proper use means recycling the refrigerant before returning it to the MVAC. For recover-only equipment, proper use means recycling the refrigerant on site or sending it off site for reclamation.[276]

Potential violations of Section 609 and the implementing regulations include failure to use approved equipment, use of technicians who are not certified, failure to keep proper records, and small can sales violations. Other violations include operating an unapproved course issuing technician certifications or an unaccredited laboratory approving equipment.[277]

PROVISIONS OF THE 1997 PROMULGATION   In EPA's view, the release of HFC-134a into the atmosphere from MVACs has been prohibited—and hence recovery in effect required—since November 15, 1995, because of the self-executing phrasing of Section 608(c)(2). However, beginning with that date there were significant gaps in the regulatory structure, namely, lack of a requirement for recycling HFC-134a that is recovered from MVACs, and lack of performance standards for recover/recycle and recover-only equipment for HFC-134a and refrigerant blends containing that substance. Thus, a major purpose of the 1997 rulemaking was to fill those gaps and integrate regulation of HFC-134a into the Subpart B regulatory structure.[278] More specifically, the 1997 promulgation sets (1) equipment standards for recovery and/or recycling of HFC-134a and substances other than CFC-12 and HFC-134a, (2) criteria for technician training and certification with respect to refrigerants other than CFC-12, such as HFC-134a, and (3) criteria for certification of organizations for testing equipment for recovery and/or recycling of such refrigerants.

The 1997 rule making filled another gap, this one relating to the handling of refrigerants recovered during the disposal of motor vehicles. The EPA clarified that certified technicians and disposal facility personnel may recycle and resell such refrigerants under specified conditions; such persons are not limited to sending the refrigerants to a reclaimer.[279]

Finally, the 1997 rule making explicitly allowed for the first time, and set conditions for, the practice of operating a mobile recovery/recycling business, in which mobile units visit motor vehicle servicing and disposal facilities for the purpose of conducting recovery and recycling operations. The EPA hopes that such a practice will improve the rate of refrigerant recovery and re-use.[280]

Ban on Nonessential Products with Ozone-Depleting Substances

Class I Nonessential Products Ban

Section 610(b) of the CAA requires the EPA to promulgate regulations that "identify nonessential products that release Class I substances into the environment (including any release occurring during manufacture, use, storage or disposal) and prohibit any person from selling or distributing any such product . . . in interstate commerce"[281] and sets forth factors that the EPA must consider in making such determinations.[282] Section 610(b)(1) through (2) specifies particular CFC-containing products that must be banned, while Section 610(b)(3) grants the EPA discretion to prohibit the sale or distribution of other nonessential consumer products that release Class I substances. The EPA's implementing regulations[283] set forth three basic prohibitions.

First, as of February 16, 1993, the EPA banned the sale or distribution in interstate commerce of CFC-propelled plastic party streamers and noise horns, nonessential products identified by Congress in Section 610(b)(1).[284] Any sale, offer for sale, distribution, or offer for distribution of any of the banned products constitutes a violation of the regulations. To prove a violation, the EPA uses sales invoices or receipts, advertising or promotional material, bills of lading, shipping invoices, product labels, manufacturing or production data, or manufacturer statements indicating that a product contains Class I or II substances.[285]

Second, as of February 16, 1993, the EPA restricted the sale of certain CFC-containing electronic and photographic cleaning fluids.[286] This restriction covers "any cleaning fluid for electronic and photographic equipment that contains a chlorofluorocarbon (1) Including but not limited to liquid packaging, solvent wipes, and gas sprays; and (2) Except for those sold or distributed to a commercial purchaser."[287]

These products may be sold to commercial purchasers[288] as long as the purchasers present identification at the point of sale indicating that they are commercial entities.[289] The EPA considers it a violation of the regulation if the purchaser does not have and cannot produce the requisite documentation or if the seller fails to request proper identification.[290] The sellers or distributors must prominently display a sign warning purchasers that it is a violation of federal law to sell such products to anyone who is not a commercial user of the product.[291]

Third, effective January 17, 1994,[292] the EPA banned as nonessential uses plastic flexible or packaging foams manufactured with or containing CFCs[293] and aerosol products or other pressurized dispensers containing CFCs.[294] The EPA concluded that flexible and packaging foams using CFCs and aerosols and other pressurized dispensers[295] using CFCs were nonessential products based on information indicating that adequate substitutes for CFCs are widely available and currently in use in these products.[296] The EPA allowed for essential use exemptions for specific cases within product categories when alternatives were not available.[297] The specific nature of these product bans and exemptions has resulted in the issuance of several EPA applicability determinations. For example, for several products used in the automotive industry, the EPA has issued clarifications as to whether they are considered bulk containers or products.[298]

On November 15, 2001, the EPA issued a final rule that amended the list of banned products to include for the first time air-conditioning and refrigeration products that contain Class I substances. In the same rule making, the EPA also broadened the prohibition on plastic foam products and eliminated some of the exemptions that had formerly applied to aerosol products and pressurized dispensers.[299]

Class II Nonessential Products Ban

CAA Section 610(d)(1) prohibits the sale or distribution after January 1, 1994, of "(A) any aerosol product or other pressurized dispenser which contains a class II substance;[300] or (B) any plastic foam product[301] which contains, or is manufactured with, a class II substance."[302] Unlike the Class I ban, which required EPA regulatory action to go into effect, the Class II ban is self-executing. Nevertheless, the EPA issued regulations to implement the Class II ban "to better define the products banned under Section 610(d) and to grant authorized exceptions under 610(d)(2)."[303]

Under Section 610(d)(2), the EPA may grant exceptions from the Class II ban when the use of an aerosol product or pressurized dispenser is deemed essential owing to flammability or worker safety concerns and when the only available alternative is use of a Class I substance.[304] The EPA has interpreted these requirements to limit the universe of products eligible for exceptions to the Class II ban to those aerosol products and pressurized dispensers exempt from the Class I ban, and it therefore considered granting exceptions to only eleven products also exempt from the Class I ban.[305] The EPA ultimately exempted the following products from the Class II ban: medical devices identified as essential by the FDA in 21 C.F.R. Section 2.125; lubricants, coatings, or cleaning fluids for electrical or electronic equipment; lubricants, coatings, or cleaning fluids used for aircraft maintenance; specified mold release agents; spinnerette lubricant or cleaning sprays; document preservation sprays containing HCFC-141b; portable fire extinguishing equipment sold to commercial users, owners of boats or marine vessels, and owners of noncommercial aircraft; and wasp and hornet sprays used near high-tension power lines.[306]

Finally, CAA Section 610(d)(3)(B) also excludes from the Class II ban on plastic foam products both foam insulation products and those integral skin, rigid, or semirigid foams necessary to meet Federal Motor Vehicle Safety Standards, when no adequate substitute substance (other than a Class I or Class II substance) is practicable for effectively meeting such standards.[307]

The regulations define foam insulation products narrowly as (1) closed cell rigid polyurethane foam, (2) closed cell rigid polystyrene boardstock foam, (3) closed cell rigid phenolic foam, and (4) closed cell rigid polyethylene foam when such foam is suitable in shape, thickness, and design to be used as a product that provides thermal insulation around pipes used in heating, plumbing, refrigeration, or industrial process systems.[308] Foams that do not meet the definition of "foam insulation" are subject to the Class II ban unless they are exempt foams used to meet automotive safety standards.

The EPA concluded that all foams used in automotive applications except integral skin foams were produced without CFCs or HCFCs. Consequently, the regulations exempted only the use of integral skin foams from the Class II ban.[309] Moreover, because the EPA anticipated that an adequate substitute substance, water-blown integral skin foam, would be available by January 1, 1996, it provided that the exemption for integral skin foam made with HCFCs would cease to be effective on that date.[310]

Federal Procurement

Statutory Framework

Under CAA Section 613, the EPA must promulgate regulations requiring federal agencies to modify their procurement regulations to maximize the use of safe alternatives to ODS and to conform their procurement regulations to the policies and requirements regarding ozone protection under the CAA. Before the enactment of the regulations implementing Section 613, the process of federal procurement was generally governed by the Federal Acquisition Regulation (FAR).[311] Nearly all federal agencies have promulgated regulations to supplement the FAR.[312]

Implementing Regulations

The EPA's implementing regulations, 40 C.F.R. Part 82, Subpart D,[313] promulgated on October 22, 1993, provide that the executive branch must conform its procurement regulations to the requirements and policies of Title VI by October 24, 1994; substitute ODS with non-ODS to the maximum extent practicable;[314] prohibit the purchase of Class II substances or products containing such substances, consistent with the applicable phaseout schedules; require all contractors and subcontractors to comply with these provisions; and implement prohibitions on and proper labeling of substances used in MVACs. For agencies subject to the FAR, amendment of that regulation satisfies the EPA requirements.

The regulations set forth in Subpart D do not specify in any detail the manner in which federal agencies are to reduce their use of ODS or related products. Each agency will be required to translate the general requirements of the regulations into its actual purchasing decisions by identifying alternatives to currently used products and to possibly find different approaches which could avoid the need to purchase ODS entirely. The regulations are intended to give agencies flexibility to maximize the substitution of safe alternatives "to the extent practicable," to use the wording of Section 612.[315]

The federal government eventually amended the FAR to comply with Subpart D. Interim amendments were promulgated in 1995 and made final in 1996.[316]

Enforcement

The enforcement powers that the Clean Air Act provides the EPA and citizens for general purposes, especially those in Sections 113, 114 and 304, are also available to them for enforcement of Title VI and the regulations that implement Title VI.[317] (For a detailed description of those enforcement powers, see Chapters 17 and 18.) In addition, the states retain full authority to adopt and enforce measures for protecting the stratospheric ozone layer that are at least as protective as Title VI and its implementing regulations.[318]

Beginning in the mid-1990s, the EPA devoted substantial attention to enforcement of Title VI and those regulations, aiming in particular to prevent and deter illegal imports of CFCs.[319] The EPA has enlisted the resources and authorities of the U.S. Customs Service and the U.S. Internal Revenue Service,[320] so that CFC smugglers have found themselves subject to a wide array of non-CAA charges, such as the making of false statements to the Customs Service; failure to pay CFC excise taxes;[321] failure to pay income taxes; conspiracy to defraud the EPA, IRS, and Customs Service; and money laundering.[322] Moreover, according to the EPA, purchasers of black market CFCs can be subject to the criminal charge of knowingly buying or possessing contraband, or can have their supply of allegedly contraband CFCs confiscated.[323]

The EPA also has addressed actively the improper disposal of ODS-containing appliances—for example, household refrigerators—by metal recyclers and scrap processors, including municipal garbage disposal operations.[324] Similarly, it has focused its civil enforcement powers on the servicing of air-conditioning and refrigeration equipment, including motor vehicle air conditioners.[325]

In 2001, the EPA attempted for the first time in the context of Title VI to address compliance issues on an industrywide basis. Apparently concerned with leaks of CFCs from industrial refrigeration equipment, the EPA collaborated with the leading bakery trade association to formulate a partial-amnesty program aimed at encouraging bakeries to replace their existing equipment with ODS-free equipment.[326]

The EPA over the past decade has issued three civil penalty policies specifically tailored to alleged violations of Title VI requirements. One of the policies deals with the restrictions on production and importation of ODS, another with restrictions on the servicing of motor vehicle air conditioners, and the last with restrictions on maintenance, servicing, repair, and disposal of appliances.[327]

Notes

1. This chapter was originally written as a cooperative effort by the Clean Air Practice Group of the law firm of Gardner, Carton & Douglas. Eran Gasko and Diane E.

McConkey served as the principal co-editors. Significant contributions were made by Mary Beth Cyze, Tracey L. Mihelic, Robert J. Mueller, Patrick C. Rock, and Peter H. Wyckoff. The chapter was updated in 2002 by Ms. McConkey and Mr. Wyckoff. Diane McConkey is now an attorney with the EPA Office of General Counsel. The views expressed are those of the authors and do not reflect the views of the U.S. Environmental Protection Agency.

2. RICHARD E. BENEDICK, OZONE DIPLOMACY: NEW DIRECTIONS IN SAFEGUARDING THE PLANET 44–45 (1991).

3. Ozone Secretariat, UNEP, *Production and Consumption of Ozone Depleting Substances under the Montreal Protocol, 1986–2000,* Table 1 (April 2002), *available at* http://www .unep.org/ozone/15-year-data-report.pdf.

4. UNEP, *Conference Sets Global Agenda for Protecting Ozone Layer* (press release) (Colombo, October 19, 2001), *available at* http://www.unep.org/ozone/pdf/pressrel-191001.pdf.

5. UNEP/WMO, Executive Summary, Final, "Scientific Assessment of Ozone Depletion: 2002," at 18 (released 23 August 2002), *available at* http://www.epa.gov/ozone/science/execsumm-saod2002.pdf.

6. The Vienna Convention for the Protection of the Ozone Layer [hereinafter Vienna Convention], art. 2 ¶ 1.

7. *Id.* art. 2–4.

8. A good starting point for research on the Montreal Protocol on Substances that Deplete the Ozone Layer [hereinafter Montreal Protocol] is the UNEP Ozone Secretariat Web site: http://www.unep.ch/ozone/index.shtml.

9. Benedick, *supra* note 1, at 115, 117. The ratifying nations collectively represented approximately 83 percent of global CFC and halon usage. *Id.* at 117. The number of ratifications has since increased dramatically. Current ratification data for the Montreal Protocol and its amendments are available at http://www.unep.ch/ozone/ratif.shtml.

10. Vienna Convention art. 9(3)–(4).

11. Vienna Convention art. 9(5).

12. Montreal Protocol art. 2(9).

13. Montreal Protocol art. 1 ¶ 5.

14. *Id.* art. 1 ¶ 6.

15. CFCs are best known for their use in refrigeration and air-conditioning systems. They have also been used as propellants in aerosol devices, foam blowing agents, solvents, and sterilants. *See* Ozone Secretariat: United Nations Environment Programme, Action on Ozone (2000 ed.) at 4.

16. Halons are typically used for fire suppression and explosion protection. *See* 58 Fed. Reg. 65,018, 60,523 (Dec. 10, 1993).

17. Carbon tetrachloride functions as a solvent in the production of materials undergoing chlorination (e.g., chlorinated rubber for use in weatherproof paints). In addition, it is used as a process solvent in pharmaceutical manufacturing. *See* 1994 Report of the UNEP Technology and Economic Assessment Panel at 31–32.

18. Methyl chloroform (1,1,1,-trichloroethane) is a solvent. It acts as a bonding agent for rocket motors used in the U.S. space shuttle and the Titan rocket. *See* 58 Fed. Reg. 65,018, 60,523 (Dec. 10, 1993); 66 Fed. Reg. 1462, 1465 (Jan. 8, 2001).

19. Methyl bromide is used principally as a soil fumigant in agriculture. *See* 65 Fed. Reg. 70,795, 70,797 (Nov. 28, 2000).

20. There are few commercial uses of HBFCs. According to the 1995 Report of the UNEP Technology and Economic Assessment Panel [hereinafter 1995 TEAP Report], the only significant use of HBFCs is the use of HBFC-22B1 as a halon substitute (e.g., for fire

protection in race cars). HBFCs are normally available as side-streams or residues of halon or methyl bromide manufacturing; specialty manufacturing would be extremely expensive. Thus, phaseout of halons and methyl bromide will effectively cut off the supply of HBFCs. 1995 TEAP Report at 75.

21. HCFCs function as drop-in substitutes for CFCs. They are preferred to CFCs because they have lower ozone-depleting potential (ODP). Nevertheless, they are viewed as temporary substitutes that will be phased out in turn. *See* 58 Fed. Reg. 65,018, 60,526 (Dec. 10, 1993).

22. Bromochloromethane, also known as chlorobromomethane or CBM, is being marketed as a substitute for methyl chloroform and CFC-113 in solvent cleaning. 1998 Report of the UNEP Technology and Economic Assessment Panel at 4.

23. Only the following CFCs and halons were covered under the original agreement: CFCs 11, 12, 113, 114, and 115; halons 1211, 1301, and 2402.

24. *See* Benedick, *supra* note 1, at 108–11 (describing 1987 Antarctic expedition and 1988 report of Ozone Trends Panel).

25. This and future controls include the CFCs and halons originally regulated, as well as "other fully halogenated CFCs." *See* Montreal Protocol art. 2C; annex B.

26. Dale S. Byrk, *The Montreal Protocol and Recent Developments to Protect the Ozone Layer*, 15 HARV. ENVTL. L. REV. 275, 285–86 (1991).

27. *See* Benedick, *supra* note 1, at 175.

28. Montreal Protocol art. 2B ¶ 2.

29. *Id.* art. 2A ¶ 3; art. 2C ¶ 2.

30. *Id.* art. 2E ¶ 2.

31. *Id.* art. 2D ¶ 1.

32. *Id.* art. 2A ¶ 4; art. 2C ¶ 4; art. 2D ¶ 2; art. 2E ¶ 3.

33. *Id.* art. 2F.

34. *Id.* art. 2G.

35. *Id.* art. 2H.

36. Report of the Ninth Meeting of the Parties to the Montreal Protocol on Substances That Deplete the Ozone Layer, UNEP/OzL.Pro.9/12.

37. Report of the Eleventh Meeting of the Parties to the Montreal Protocol on Substances That Deplete the Ozone Layer, UNEP/OzL.Pro.11/10.

38. *See, e.g.,* Montreal Protocol art. 2A ¶ 4 ("This paragraph will apply save to the extent that the parties decide to permit the level of production or consumption that is necessary to satisfy uses agreed by them to be essential").

39. Decision IV/25.

40. *Id.*

41. In the United States, the EPA acts as the reviewing agency for essential use applications, but it is the Department of State that forwards nominations to UNEP.

42. Decision VIII/9 ¶ 8.

43. *See* TEAP Handbook on Essential Use Nominations (June 2001) at 6.

44. Creation of expert panels to assess control measures is authorized by Article VI of the Montreal Protocol.

45. Decision VIII/9 ¶ 8.

46. At their Thirteenth Meeting in 2001, the parties authorized limited amounts of production and consumption of CFCs for use in metered-dose inhalers for asthma and chronic obstructive pulmonary disease and CFC 113 for torpedo maintenance.

47. *See* Decision V/18; TEAP Handbook on Essential Use Nominations (June 2001) at 6.

48. *See, e.g.,* Montreal Protocol art. 2A ¶ 3–9.

49. *Id.* art. 2H.

50. Decision VII/5.

51. Decision XI/12.

52. Montreal Protocol, art. 2H ¶ 5.

53. Decision IX/6.

54. Montreal Protocol art. 4(1).

55. *Id.* art. 4 ¶ 2.

56. *Id.* art. 4 ¶ 3; Annex D.

57. *Id.* art. 4 ¶ 3.

58. *Id.* art. 4 ¶ 4.

59. *Id.* art. 4 ¶ 5–7.

60. To qualify for relaxation of the protocol's requirements, a developing country must be one "whose annual calculated level of consumption of the controlled substances in Annex A [the originally identified CFCs and halons] is less than 0.3 kilograms per capita on the date of the entry into force of the protocol for it, or any time thereafter until January 1999." *Id.* art. 5 ¶ 1.

61. *Id.* art. 5 ¶ 1.

62. *Id.* art. 5 ¶ 8.

63. Alexander Wood, *The Multilateral Fund for the Implementation of the Montreal Protocol*, 5 Int'l Envtl. Aff. 335, 338–40 (1993).

64. Montreal Protocol annex XI ¶ 1–2.

65. *Id.* art. 10 ¶ 9.

66. *Id.* annex X (A)(4).

67. *Id.* annex XIII (I).

68. *Id.* art. 6.

69. *Id.* art. 7.

70. *Id.* annex VII.

71. *Id.* annex VIII.

72. *Id.* annex VII ¶ 1–4.

73. *Id.* art. 9 ¶ 1.

74. *Id.* art. 9 ¶ 2.

75. *Id.* art. 9 ¶ 3.

76. *See* 40 C.F.R. pt. 762 (1994), deleted at 60 Fed. Reg. 31,917, 31,919, and 31,922 (1995).

77. 40 C.F.R. § 762.58 (1994).

78. 40 C.F.R. § 762.58 (1994).

79. The TSCA CFC ban was superseded by the subsequent ban on CFC propellants under Section 610 of the 1990 CAA Amendments and the EPA's issuance of implementing regulations at 40 C.F.R. 82.64(c) and 82.66(d), rendering obsolete the TSCA regulations at 40 C.F.R. pt. 762, which have been deleted. *See* 60 Fed. Reg. 31,917, at 31,919, and 31,922 (1995).

80. 53 Fed. Reg. 30,566 (August 12, 1988).

81. CAA §§ 601–18; Pub. L. No. 101-549, 104 Stat. 2399 (1990). Information on the EPA implementation of Title VI of the CAA is available on the EPA Web site at http://www.epa.gov/ozone/.

82. Cong. Rec. S 17232 (October 26, 1990) (statement of Sen. Baucus: Conference Report on S. 1630, the Clean Air Act Amendments of 1990).

83. Sen. Rep. No. 101-228, 101st Cong., 1st Sess.

84. *See, e.g.,* Ozone Secretariat: United Nations Environment Program, Action on Ozone, at 4 (2000 ed.) (uses of CFCs); 58 Fed. Reg. 65,018, 60,521–23 (Dec. 10, 1993) (uses of CFCs, HCFCs, methyl chloroform, halons).

85. CAA § 614.

86. *See* CAA §§ 602, 604–07, and 616.

87. CAA § 614.

88. *See* 40 C.F.R. pt. 82, subpt. A, apps. A and B, for a current listing of all Class I and Class II ODS regulated under Title VI. Class I substances have comparatively high ozone-depleting potentials (ODP) and hence are subject to relatively short phaseout timelines under the CAA and the Montreal Protocol. The original Class I list included several CFCs (groups I and III), halons (group II), carbon tetrachloride (group IV), and methyl chloroform (group V). These are the same substances as those listed in Annexes A and B of the London Amendments to the protocol. The current listing of Class II substances consists of certain HCFC's—partially halogenated compounds which generally have lower ODP than substances on the Class I list. These substances are listed in Annex C of the London Amendments. Most of these substances have never been commercially available. Class II substances are also subject to phaseout deadlines as well as other interim controls (e.g., recycling requirements). The EPA has not established any groups for Class II substances. *See* 40 C.F.R. pt. 82, subpt. A, app. B.

89. Section 602(a) requires the EPA to add a substance to the Class I list if it "causes or contributes significantly to harmful effects on the stratospheric ozone layer." Under section 602(b), the EPA must add a substance to the Class II list if it "is known or may reasonably be anticipated to cause or contribute to harmful effects on the stratospheric ozone layer." To date, the EPA has added methyl bromide (group VI), an agricultural fumigant, and hydrobromofluorocarbons (HBFCs) (group VII), fire suppression agents, to the original Class I substances list. These listings were in response to the listing of these substances under the Montreal Protocol. *See* 58 Fed. Reg. 65,018 (1993). In 2002, again following a change to the Montreal Protocol, the EPA proposed to add chlorobromomethane (CBM) to the list of Class I ODS. 67 Fed. Reg. 65,916.

90. CAA § 602(c)(3).

91. CAA § 602(c)(4).

92. 58 Fed. Reg. 65,018 (1993).

93. The phaseout deadlines and reduction targets are linked to "baseline year" production levels. The EPA must determine a representative calendar year as the baseline year for any Class I substances listed by the EPA after publication of the initial Class I list, and for all Class II substances. The baseline year for Class I substances in groups I (certain CFCs) or II (halons) is 1986. The baseline year for groups III (certain CFCs), IV (carbon tetrachloride), and V (methyl chloroform) is 1989. The baseline year for groups VI (methyl bromide) and VII (HBFCs) is 1991. *See* 40 C.F.R. §§ 82.5–82.6; 58 Fed. Reg. at 65,042–44 and 65,065–66 (1993).

94. The 1992 Copenhagen Amendments to the protocol called for the complete phaseout of CFCs, carbon tetrachloride, and methyl chloroform by January 1, 1996, and of halons by January 1, 1994.

95. 58 Fed. Reg. 65,018 (December 10, 1993).

96. These amendments called for each party to cap production of all Class II substances at a sum equal to 3.1 percent of the party's 1989 ODP weighted consumption of the CFCs listed in group I of the Class I substances list plus the ODP weighted level of HCFCs consumed in that year. The Copenhagen Amendments also called for a more stringent set of reductions until the final 2030 phaseout deadline. *See* Article 2F of the Protocol.

97. *See* 40 C.F.R. § 82.4; 58 Fed. Reg. at 65,025–26 (1993).

98. 40 C.F.R. § 82.16(b). The EPA's Allowance System for Controlling HCFC Production, Import and Export includes a petition process under which HCFC formulators

may petition for a limited number of HCFC-141b production or import allowances beyond January 1, 2003. 68 Fed. Reg. 2820, 2825–2831.

99. 40 C.F.R. § 82.16(c).

100. 40 C.F.R. § 82.16(e).

101. 40 C.F.R. § 82.16(d).

102. 40 C.F.R. § 82.16(f). Notwithstanding the chemical-by-chemical phaseouts and the general HCFC phaseout on January 1, 2030, an exception exists for amounts produced for transformation or destruction.

103. 1999 Omnibus Consolidated Emergency Supplemental Appropriations Act (Public Law No. 105-277, October 21, 1998), Section 764.

104. 64 Fed. Reg. 29,240 (June 1, 1999); 65 Fed. Reg. 70,795 (November 28, 2000).

105. 57 Fed. Reg. 33,754 (1992); 56 Fed. Reg. 9,518 (1991).

106. "Person" means "any individual or legal entity, including an individual, corporation, partnership, association, state, municipality, political subdivision of a state, Indian tribe; any agency, department, or instrumentality of the United States; and any officer, agency, or employee thereof." 40 C.F.R. § 82.3(t).

107. Production is defined as the manufacture of a substance from any raw material or feedstock chemical, but excludes (1) the manufacture of a controlled substance that is then transformed; (2) the reuse or recycling of a controlled substance; (3) amounts that are destroyed by the approved technologies; or (4) amounts that are spilled or vented unintentionally. *See* CAA § 601(11); 40 C.F.R. 82.3(ee); 58 Fed. Reg. at 65,045–46, 65,064 (1993).

108. Consumption is defined as domestic U.S. production plus imports, minus exports to parties to the Montreal Protocol. CAA § 601(6). Consumption does *not* include the import or export of recycled or used controlled substances, or the bulk transshipment of controlled chemicals between two foreign countries through the United States. *See* 40 C.F.R. § 82.3(i); 58 Fed. Reg. at 65,063 (1993).

109. *See* 40 C.F.R. § 82.5 (production allowances) and 40 C.F.R. § 82.6 (consumption allowances).

110. Each calendar year is known as a "control period." 40 C.F.R. § 82.3(k).

111. *See* 40 C.F.R. § 82.4(a), (c).

112. *See* 40 C.F.R. § 82.4(b), (d).

113. 68 Fed. Reg. 2820 (January 21, 2003).

114. The EPA opted not to establish baseline allowances for other HCFCs in its January 21, 2003, final rule because "the HCFC market may continue to evolve and . . . some sectors may switch from the higher ozone-depleting HCFCs, such as HCFC-141b, HCFC-22, and HCFC-142b to the lower ozone-depleting HCFCs, such as HCFC-123, HCFC-124, and HCFC-225ca and HCFC-225cb." 68 Fed. Reg. at 2823.

115. 68 Fed. Reg. at 2823.

116. Countries with a history of HCFC production must have ratified the Beijing Amendments, which place a cap on total HCFC production. Other parties to the protocol need only have ratified the Copenhagen Amendments, which contain the original control measures for HCFCs. 68 Fed. Reg. 2836.

117. *See* 60 Fed. Reg. 24,970, 24,980 (1995); 68 Fed. Reg. at 2837.

118. 40 C.F.R. § 82.9(a); 60 Fed. Reg. at 24,994. Due to a restriction in Section 605 of the CAA, Article 5 allowances for HCFCs will be limited to 10 percent of baseline between 2015 and 2029. 68 Fed. Reg. at 2837.

119. 40 C.F.R. §§ 82.11(a)(1), 82.24(b); 60 Fed. Reg. at 24,997, 68 Fed. Reg. at 2842.

120. 40 C.F.R. § 82.12(b), (c), 82.23; 60 Fed. Reg. at 24,998–99; 68 Fed. Reg. at 2836.

121. 58 Fed. Reg. at 65,045–46; 68 Fed. Reg. at 2843.

122. *See* 40 C.F.R. § 82.3; 58 Fed. Reg. at 65,045.

123. 40 C.F.R. § 82.3.

124. The regulations list the following technologies as approved destruction processes: liquid injection incineration, reactor cracking, gaseous/fume oxidation, rotary kiln incineration, cement kilns, radio frequency plasma, and municipal waste incinerators only for the destruction of foams. 40 C.F.R. § 82.3.

125. 40 C.F.R. § 82.13(f), (g), (k), (l).

126. 40 C.F.R. § 82.9(e).

127. *See* 40 C.F.R. § 82.23. The Class II allocation system does not provide for interpollutant transfers for export production allowances or Article V allowances. However, any person may convert Article V allowances for one Class I controlled substance to Article V allowances for a different Class I controlled substance within the same "group." 40 C.F.R. § 82.12(b)(2). The breakdown of Class I groups appears at 40 C.F.R. pt. 82 app. A.

128. 60 Fed. Reg. 24,971–72.

129. 40 C.F.R. §§ 82.9(c), 82.18(c).

130. 40 C.F.R. §§ 82.10(a), 82.20(a).

131. 40 C.F.R. §§ 82.10(a)–(c), 82.20(b).

132. 40 C.F.R. §§ 82.12(a), 82.23.

133. 40 C.F.R. § 82.4(n).

134. *See, e.g.,* 66 Fed. Reg. 1462 (January 8, 2001).

135. *See* § CAA 604(d)(2).

136. 66 Fed. Reg. 14,760 (March 13, 2001).

137. 40 C.F.R. § 82.4(n); App. G.

138. 1999 Omnibus Consolidated and Emergency Supplemental Appropriations Act (Pub. L. 105-277, October 21, 1998), Section 764.

139. 68 Fed. Reg. 238 (January 2, 2003); 40 C.F.R. § 82.4(a)(2), (c)(2), (k)(2).

140. *See* 68 Fed. Reg. at 248.

141. For Class I substances, *see* 40 C.F.R. §§ 82.4(j), 82.13(g); 67 Fed. Reg. 79,861 (Dec. 31, 2002). For Class II substances, *see* 40 C.F.R. §§ 82.15(b)(2), 82.24(c)(3); 68 Fed. Reg. at 2857.

142. 40 C.F.R. § 82.13(d).

143. 40 C.F.R. § 82.13(c).

144. 40 C.F.R. § 82.4(b). The various prohibitions are generally subject to an exception for controlled substances produced for transformation or destruction.

145. 40 C.F.R. § 82.4(d). This prohibition does not apply to transshipments or heels, or to used controlled substances brought in under the petition process.

146. 40 C.F.R. § 82.4(b), (d).

147. 40 C.F.R. § 82.4(a).

148. 40 C.F.R. § 82.4(c). This prohibition does not apply to transshipments or heels, or to used controlled substances brought in under the petition process.

149. 40 C.F.R. § 82.4(k).

150. 40 C.F.R. § 82.4(a),(c).

151. 40 C.F.R. §§ 82.6, 82.7.

152. *See* 65 Fed. Reg. 70,795, 70,799 (November 28, 2000).

153. 40 C.F.R. § 82.15.

154. 40 C.F.R. §§ 82.4(l), 82.15(e). In general, a U.S. company may not export a substance to or import a substance from a country that has not ratified the amendments containing relevant control measures for the substance in question. The Class II trade prohibitions take effect January 1, 2004.

155. 40 C.F.R. § 82.4(m).

156. CAA § 611(b), (d)(2). The CAA Section 611 implementing regulations are at 40 C.F.R. pt. 82, subpt. E, §§ 82.100–82.124. *See* 58 Fed. Reg. 8136 (1993) (final rule) (hereinafter final rule); 57 Fed. Reg. 19,166 (1992) (proposed rule); 60 Fed. Reg. 4010 (1995) (amendments) (proposed at 58 Fed. Reg. 69,568 (1993)).

157. Section 611 applies only to products entering interstate commerce. A product or container may enter interstate commerce at one of three points: (1) when it is released from the facility in which it was manufactured, (2) when it enters the warehouse from which the domestic manufacturer releases the product for sale or distribution, or (3) at the site of U.S. Customs Service clearance for import. *See* 40 C.F.R. § 82.104(n); 58 Fed. Reg. at 8142 (1993).

158. 40 C.F.R. § 82.112.

159. CAA § 611(c).

160. 40 C.F.R. § 82.104(s).

161. 40 C.F.R. § 82.104(f); 58 Fed. Reg. at 8150 (1993).

162. 40 C.F.R. § 82.104(o). The *proposed* labeling rule would have required all products containing component parts manufactured with a controlled substance to bear a warning label. 57 Fed. Reg. at 19,197 (proposed 40 C.F.R. § 82.104(f)) (1992). This requirement was deleted from the final rule due to the negative reactions of many commenters. 58 Fed. Reg. at 8143–46 (1993).

163. *See generally* 58 Fed. Reg. at 8143–46 (1993).

164. This assumes the component is manufactured by a third party, e.g., a vendor. The EPA treats divisions of a company, wholly owned subsidiaries, and parent corporations as a single manufacturer. Therefore, if a component is manufactured with a Class I substance by a subsidiary, sold to the parent, and incorporated into the parent's final product without further processing, the parent's product must be labeled. Components transferred within the corporate family for incorporation into a final product, however, need not necessarily have a label affixed before the transfer; rather, they must only be accompanied by the labeling information. *See* 58 Fed. Reg. at 8145; 40 C.F.R. § 82.108(c).

165. *See* 40 C.F.R. § 82.104(o); 58 Fed. Reg. 8146–47 (1993). For the destruction exemption, if the controlled substance at issue is covered by another regulatory program (e.g., RCRA or the HON Rule) that contains a destruction efficiency requirement greater than 98 percent, then the destruction technique must meet the higher destruction efficiency standard. 40 C.F.R. § 82.104(c).

166. Copies of these determinations are available through the EPA's Office of Air and Radiation, Global Programs Division.

167. Section 611—Product Labeling, Applicability Determination, Record Number 28 (September 1993).

168. 40 C.F.R. § 82.106(b), 82.112(d).

169. 40 C.F.R. § 82.102(a).

170. CAA § 611(d).

171. CAA § 611(d); 40 C.F.R. § 82.102(a)(3).

172. CAA § 611(c); 40 C.F.R. § 82.102(b). The EPA recognizes that the third decision criterion is the same as that in Section 612 of the act, which governs the Significant New Alternatives Program (SNAP). See this chapter's discussion of the Section 612 SNAP program. In making determinations for products containing both Class I and Class II substances, the EPA has stated it will ensure consistency with findings "currently or potentially available" under its SNAP program. *See* 57 Fed. Reg. at 19,178–81 (1992).

173. 40 C.F.R. § 82.120.

174. *See* 59 Fed. Reg. 47,048 (1994); 59 Fed. Reg. 54,500 (1994). In addition, the agency received a petition from several environmental groups requesting that products

manufactured with Class II substances be subject to the labeling requirements. Petition Seeking Application of Ozone Depleting Labeling Requirements to Class II Substances, filed November 7, 1994; *see* 59 Fed. Reg. 65,006 (1994). That petition was subsequently withdrawn.

175. 40 C.F.R. § 82.120(a), (c), (e).

176. *See* 40 C.F.R. § 82.114(a) and 116(a); 58 Fed. Reg. at 8154–55 (1993).

177. *See* 40 C.F.R. § 82.114(c) and 116(c).

178. *See* CAA § 611(b) and 40 C.F.R. § 82.106(a). In addition to the EPA action, the FDA has published labeling language to complement the Section 611 warning label for those human drug, biological, and device products implicated by the Section 611 requirement. *See* 58 Fed. Reg. 34,812 (1993); 58 Fed. Reg. 40,656 (1993); *see also* 58 Fed. Reg. 8155–56 (1993) (discussion of concurrent EPA and FDA labeling authority).

179. 40 C.F.R. § 82.108; 58 Fed. Reg. at 8152 (1993).

180. 40 C.F.R. § 82.104(q).

181. *See* 57 Fed. Reg. at 19,170–72 (1992).

182. 40 C.F.R. § 82.110(a).

183. 40 C.F.R. § 82.108(c). For prescription drug products for which the EPA and the FDA have negotiated alternative labeling language, the warning may be placed in the package insert along with other information intended to be read by the prescribing physician. Additional language, however, must accompany any material intended to be read by the patient. *Id.*

184. 40 C.F.R. § 82.110(b).

185. 40 C.F.R. § 82.110(c).

186. A "substitute" or "alternative" for an ozone-depleting substance may include chemical substitutes, alternative manufacturing processes (e.g., process changes), and alternative technologies. 40 C.F.R. § 82.172; *see also* S. Rep. No. 228, 101st Cong., 2d Sess. 387 (1989).

187. *See* 40 C.F.R. pt. 82, subpt. G, §§ 82.170–82.184 and related appendices. 59 Fed. Reg. 13,044 (1994) (final rule); 58 Fed. Reg. 28,094 (1993) (proposed rule); 57 Fed. Reg. 1984 (1992) (ANPR). A flowchart and description of the SNAP review process can be found in the final rule, 59 Fed. Reg. at 13,059–62 (1994). The EPA has established a Web site containing a wealth of information about the SNAP program, including a complete collection of SNAP-related *Federal Register* notices, at http://www.epa.gov/ozone/snap/index.html.

188. The SNAP program is analogous to the EPA's new chemicals review process established under the Premanufacture Notice (PMN) provisions of Section 5 of TSCA, 15 U.S.C. § 2604. The SNAP program also bears some resemblance to the pesticide registration process under Section 3 of the Federal Insecticide, Rodenticide, and Fungicide Act (FIFRA), 7 U.S.C. § 136a. TSCA Section 5 requires persons who intend to engage in activities involving new chemical substances (i.e., those not listed on the "TSCA Inventory"), including any "significant new uses" of such substances, to inform the EPA at least ninety days before commencement of such activities. After a review of any relevant health or environmental effects data, the EPA may regulate such activities. If the EPA takes no action within the ninety-day review period, the PMN submitter may commercialize the substance without restriction. *See generally* 40 C.F.R. pts. 720–21.

Similarly, FIFRA Section 3 requires any person who wishes to distribute or sell a pesticide in the United States to obtain a pesticide "registration" from the EPA. The registration process entails the generation of a body of health and environmental effects data, which is submitted to the EPA for review. The EPA may impose restrictions on the manufacture, sale, or use of the pesticide product as a condition of the registration. *See generally* 40 C.F.R. pts. 152–86.

189. The SNAP program requirements apply only to substitutes actually replacing Class I or Class II substances within nine specified SNAP industrial sectors: refrigeration and air-conditioning, foam blowing, solvents cleaning, fire suppression and explosion protection, sterilants, aerosols, tobacco expansion, pesticides, and adhesives, coatings, and inks. *See* 40 C.F.R. §§ 82.172 and 82.176. Uses of ODS in other industrial sectors are *de minimis*, and are excluded from the SNAP program. *See* 40 C.F.R. § 82.176(b)(2).

190. 40 C.F.R. §§ 82.172 (definition of "substitute") and 82.176(a). Although Section 612(e) does not mention Class II substances, the EPA asserts that it has authority to require notification and to review significant new uses of substitutes for Class II substances pursuant to Sections 114 and 301(a) of the Act. "Significant new use" is defined as any use of a new or existing substitute in a major industrial use sector as a result of the phaseout of ozone-depleting compounds. 40 C.F.R. § 82.172. Although its authority seems to be limited to the review of *new* uses, the EPA has extended its review to *existing* uses by asserting that continued use is a "new use" subject to review. *See generally* 59 Fed. Reg. at 13,047–48, 13,051 (1994). The EPA's stated concern is that as the phaseout deadlines approach, use and consumption of alternatives will increase, resulting in greater releases of and potential risks posed by those chemicals. Possibly to allay concerns over this broad assertion of authority, the EPA noted that, with few exceptions, all then-existing uses were meeting SNAP acceptability conditions. *See* 59 Fed. Reg. at 13,051 (1994).

191. 40 C.F.R. § 82.178; *see* 59 Fed. Reg. at 13,054–56 (1994). The EPA encourages potential submitters to communicate with the SNAP coordinator before making a SNAP submission. *See* 59 Fed. Reg. at 13,061 (1994). The EPA has provided a standard form and an instruction manual for SNAP submissions; they appear at http://www.epa.gov/ozone/snap/submit/index.html.

192. 40 C.F.R. § 82.182. The EPA has cautioned submitters that certain health and safety data, as well as certain data submitted pursuant to other statutes, may not be claimed as confidential. In addition, publicly available information may not be claimed as confidential. Disputed claims may delay the EPA's acceptability determinations. *See* 59 Fed. Reg. at 13,056–57 (1994).

193. 40 C.F.R. § 82.174(a); *see* 59 Fed. Reg. at 13,061–62 (1994).

194. 166.40 C.F.R. § 82.178(b)(2); 59 Fed. Reg. at 13,064–65 (1994).

195. Similarly, pesticide products formulated with Class I and Class II compounds, e.g., as active or inert ingredients, that are reformulated as the phaseout goes into effect will require joint SNAP/FIFRA review. In this case, submitters must provide separate pesticide and SNAP submissions. 40 C.F.R. § 82.182(b)(3). No reformulations may be sold until FIFRA approval is received. *See* 59 Fed. Reg. at 13,065–66 (1994).

196. 40 C.F.R. § 82.180(a)(7).

197. *See* 59 Fed. Reg. at 13,062–64 (1994) for an explanation of the differing listing classifications. Appendix A to 40 C.F.R. Part 82, Subpart G, lists substitutes subject to use restrictions and unacceptable substitutes.

198. The "acceptable subject to narrowed use limits" (List #3) classification is intended for specialized "niche" uses within a particular end-use sector where no other non-ODS alternative is technically feasible or available. Certain PFC substitutes used in solvent cleaning and CFC and HBFC substitutes used in fire suppression are subject to such narrow use limitations; similar limitations for refrigerant and aerosol uses are likely to be proposed in the future. *See* 59 Fed. Reg. at 13,063 (1994). In July 2002, the EPA promulgated "narrow use limits" for HCFC-22 and HCFC-142 in foam manufacturing. *See* 67 Fed. Reg. 47,703 (2002).

199. CAA § 612(d) also provides mechanisms for persons to petition the EPA to add substances to or remove substances from the lists of prohibited substitutes and EPA-identified safe alternatives. *See* 40 C.F.R. § 82.184; 59 Fed.

200. The initial lists were published with the final rule, 59 Fed. Reg. 13,044 (March 18, 1994). The EPA issued additional acceptability determinations on August 26, 1994 (59 Fed. Reg. 44,240), January 13, 1995 (60 Fed. Reg. 3318), June 13, 1995 (60 Fed. Reg. 31,092), and July 28, 1995 (60 Fed. Reg. 38,729). Citations to and copies of subsequent determinations appear at http://www.epa.gov/ozone/snap/chron.html. These lists will *not* appear in the Code of Federal Regulations. Substitutes for Class I substances were afforded priority review due to the accelerated phaseout schedule for these ODS. *See* CAA §§ 604, 606; 40 C.F.R. pt. 82, subpt. A.

201. *See* 40 C.F.R. pt. 82, subpt. G, app. A. The EPA has listed several refrigerants and cleaning solvents as unacceptable, largely due to the fact that most contain PFCs or are highly flammable. The EPA also has listed dibromoethane as unacceptable because of its high ODP and the existence of alternatives. *See* 60 Fed. Reg. 31,092 (1995) and 59 Fed. Reg. 49,108 (September 26, 1994; proposed rule). The EPA will not approve use of any blend of Class I and Class II substances as a substitute for a Class II substance because of the higher ODP of such a mixture. However, such mixtures may be acceptable substitutes for Class I substances, which would generally have a higher ODP than the mixture. *See* 59 Fed. Reg. at 13,070 (1994). For example, the EPA has listed several HCFC/CFC and other hydrocarbon blends as unacceptable substitutes for CFC-12 refrigerants due to flammability concerns or the existence of one or more Class II substitutes for the relevant end-use that have a lower ODP than the blend. Certain uses of HCFC-141b and its blends for foam and solvent cleaning applications have also been declared unacceptable due to the existence of other non-ODS alternatives. For listings of subsequent determinations, see http://www.epa.gov/ozone/snap/chron.html.

202. 40 C.F.R. § 82.176(b).

203. Two other "exemptions" from the SNAP requirements are discussed in the preamble to the final rule. However, they are not clearly set forth in the regulatory text. All "second generation" non-ODS substitutes that replace "first generation" non-ODS alternatives are exempt from SNAP notification and review requirements. *See* 59 Fed. Reg. at 13,052 (1994). However, a second generation substitute for a first generation alternative that *is* an ODS (e.g., a Class I or Class II substance used as a substitute for another Class I or Class II substance) is subject to the SNAP requirements. To determine SNAP applicability, a potential submitter must look to the scope of intended uses and ask itself what the alternative is designed to replace. If it is replacing a non-ODS alternative, no SNAP notification is required.

The final rule preamble also indicates that substitutes for ODS contained in medical devices and food packaging are exempt from SNAP review for adverse human health effects because of the stringent regulatory standards imposed on such products under the Federal Food, Drug, and Cosmetic Act. The EPA has stated that it will rely on the Food and Drug Administration's conclusions in its SNAP applicability determinations for these products. *See* 59 Fed. Reg. at 13,066 (1994).

204. 40 C.F.R. § 82.174. The EPA's regulations prohibit only the "use" of unacceptable substitutes; "sale" of such products is still permitted. As a practical matter, producers of unacceptable substitutes are likely to have a difficult time marketing such products. The EPA's willingness to consider "grandfathering" certain uses of existing substitutes may address such situations.

The EPA has also asserted that any domestic manufacture of substitutes intended solely for export *is* subject to SNAP requirements, because the definition of "use" includes use in the manufacturing process, which occurs in the United States. *See* 59 Fed. Reg. at 13,052 (1994). This interpretation was the subject of a judicial challenge. Alliance for

Responsible CFC Policy, Inc. v. U.S. EPA, Docket No. 94-1396 (D.C. Cir., filed May 17, 1994). However, the D.C. Circuit in early 2002 put the lawsuit on inactive status ("administrative termination"), subject to reactivation by motion. Meanwhile, EPA's interpretation remains in effect. It has been in effect for all but three months since 1994. The EPA issued a three-month administrative stay of the export provisions of the final SNAP rule in 1994 in response to the Alliance lawsuit. *See* 59 Fed. Reg. 63,255 (1994).

205. CAA § 612(c); 40 C.F.R. § 82.170(b).

206. *See* 40 C.F.R. § 82.172 (definition of "potentially available").

207. 40 C.F.R. § 82.176(c).

208. This test was established in Sierra Club v. EPA, 719 F.2d 436 (D.C. Cir. 1983), which considered the retroactive application of a rule issued by the EPA regarding calculating limitations on pollutant emissions from smoke stacks. The test involves balancing the equities of "whether the new rule represents an abrupt departure from previously established practice . . . the extent to which a party relied on the [previous] rule, the degree of burden which application of a retroactive order imposes on a party, and the statutory interest in applying the new rule despite reliance of a party on the old standard." *Id.* at 467 (citations omitted). To date, only uses of HCFC-141b in existing equipment for certain solvent cleaning applications have been "grandfathered." *See* 59 Fed. Reg. at 13,057–58, 13,136 (1994).

209. CAA § 608(a)(1), (2). "Appliance" is defined as any device that contains and uses a Class I or Class II substance as a refrigerant and that is used for household or commercial purposes, including any air conditioner, refrigerator, chiller, or freezer. 40 C.F.R. § 82.152.

210. CAA § 608(a)(3).

211. CAA § 608(a)(2). Regulations covering refrigerants were to appear by mid-1992, and regulations covering other contexts by late 1994. *See* CAA §§ 608(a)(1)–(2).

212. Subsection (c) extends, effective after November 15, 1995, the prohibition against venting substances that are substitutes for Class I and II refrigerants. CAA § 608 (c)(2).

213. *See* 58 Fed. Reg. 28,660 (1993), as amended by 59 Fed. Reg. 42,950 (1994), 59 Fed. Reg. 55,912 (1994), and 60 Fed. Reg. 40,420 (1995). In February 1996, the EPA issued a still-pending proposal of wide-ranging amendments to these foundational regulations. 61 Fed. Reg. 7858. The proposed amendments included, among other things, a third-party certification program for reclaimers and laboratories, adjustments to the system for testing of recovery/recycling equipment, incorporation of changes to ARI 740, and various measures aimed at providing greater flexibility for technicians.

214. 40 C.F.R. §§ 82.150–82.166.

215. 63 Fed. Reg. 11,084 (1998). In August 1998, the EPA determined that it is not necessary, nor appropriate, to require certification of recycling and recovery equipment for halons, nor to require that halons be removed only through the use of certified equipment. 63 Fed. Reg. 42,728 (1998).

216. 40 C.F.R. §§ 82.250–82.270.

217. 63 Fed. Reg. 32,044 (1998).

218. The EPA maintains an inventory of final actions it has taken under Section 608 at http://www.epa.gov/ozone/title6/608/index.html. Besides the actions described in the text of this summary, the agency has determined, as prompted by a citizens' suit, that it is not necessary, nor appropriate, to require pursuant to Section 608 the use of gas-impermeable tarps to control emissions of the ODS pesticide methyl bromide. *See* 63 Fed. Reg. 5906 and 6007 (1998).

219. 40 C.F.R. § 82.150(b).

220. *See generally* 58 Fed. Reg. at 28,665–66 (1993).

221. For the definition of "commercial refrigeration," see 40 C.F.R. § 82.152.

222. For the definition of "industrial process refrigeration," see 40 C.F.R. § 82.152.

223. CAA § 609 specifically regulates servicing of MVACs in automobiles and trucks. However, Section 609 does not regulate servicing of air conditioners in other vehicles, such as trains, airplanes, ships, buses, construction equipment, and farm vehicles, or the disposal of MVACs. Accordingly, servicing of all equipment not explicitly covered under Section 609, and the disposal of all air-conditioning and refrigeration equipment including MVACs, is subject to the Section 608 requirements.

224. 58 Fed. Reg. at 28,665 (1993). This preamble indicates that air-conditioning and refrigeration equipment that is designed and used exclusively for military applications is exempt from the regulatory requirements. *Id.* at 28,669–70. This exemption does not apply to military equipment identical to subject equipment. The EPA considers "identical equipment" to include air-conditioning and refrigeration equipment whose system of working parts is identical to that in equipment used for a household or commercial purpose but has been modified only externally for a military application. *Id.* This preamble discussion is not reflected in any explicit regulatory provision.

225. 40 C.F.R. § 82.154(a).

226. 40 C.F.R. § 82.154(b). *See* Table 1 of 40 C.F.R. § 82.156. The evacuation requirements are determined mainly by the amount of refrigerant in the appliance.

227. A system receiver is a component of the system that is designed to hold excess refrigerant charged and can be used to hold the charge during servicing or repair. 40 C.F.R. § 82.156(a).

228. 40 C.F.R. § 82.156(a).

229. 40 C.F.R. § 82.156(a)(4).

230. A major repair is any maintenance, service, or repair involving the removal of any or all of the compressor, condenser, evaporator, or auxiliary heat exchanger coil. 40 C.F.R. § 82.152.

231. 40 C.F.R. § 82.156(a)(1). If the repair is not major and evacuation is not performed after completion of the repair, the appliance must be evacuated to a pressure no higher than 0 pounds per square inch gauge (psig) before it is opened if it is a high- or very-high-pressure appliance or repressurized to 0 psig before it is opened if it is a low-pressure appliance, without using methods that require subsequent purging. 40 C.F.R. § 82.156(a)(2)(i). If leaks cause the person to be unable to evacuate to the required levels, the person opening the appliance must isolate the leak, evacuate the non-leaking components, and evacuate the leaking components to the lowest level that can be obtained without substantially contaminating the refrigerant. 40 C.F.R. § 82.156(a)(2)(ii).

232. "Reclaimed" means that the refrigerant is clean to the standard of purity satisfying ARI 700-1993 requirements. *See* 40 C.F.R. § 82.152; 59 Fed. Reg. at 42,951, 42,956 (1994).

233. 40 C.F.R. § 82.164. Various requirements apply to persons reclaiming refrigerant for sale, including purity standards, release limitations, and certification requirements. *See also* 40 C.F.R. § 82.154(g)–(i). The EPA extended the prohibitions on the sale of reclaimed or used refrigerants that do not meet the applicable standard of purity to March 18, 1996. *See* 60 Fed. Reg. 14,608, 14,610 (1995) and the companion notice at 60 Fed. Reg. 14,611 (1995). This action was taken to give the EPA time to amend the applicable regulations at 40 C.F.R. §§ 82.152(r) and 82.164. *Id.* at 14,608–09. In February 1996, the EPA extended those refrigerant purity requirements to the end of 1996. 61 Fed. Reg. 7724 (1996). Then, in December 1996, the EPA extended the requirements indefinitely. 61 Fed. Reg. 68,506 (1996). The regulations do not prohibit the sale of unreclaimed refrigerant that was and is

to be used in MVACs and MVAC-like appliances or contained in an appliance being sold with the refrigerant in place. *See* 40 C.F.R. §§ 82.154(g)(2)–(3) and (h)(2)–(3); 59 Fed. Reg. at 42,952, 42,957 (1994).

234. 40 C.F.R. § 82.158(a). The regulations also require that all appliances offered for sale or distribution be equipped with either a service aperture or, for small appliances, a process stub to facilitate the removal of the refrigerant. *Id.* at 82.154(j), (k). This requirement does not apply to used goods. 59 Fed. Reg. at 42,951 (1994).

235. 40 C.F.R. § 82.158(a)–(d). The EPA provided this difference in treatment to avoid penalizing people who purchased the equipment before the effective date of regulation and to encourage the purchase of equipment as soon as possible rather than waiting for certified equipment to become available.

236. 40 C.F.R. § 82.158(e)–(g). The EPA allows the use of either self-dependent or self-contained recovery equipment for servicing small appliances. The efficiency levels required by these devices depend on the operability of the compressor.

237. 40 C.F.R. § 82.158(h). Additional requirements may apply to the various types of recycling and recovery equipment such as installing low loss fittings on high- and low-pressure equipment and obtaining a 5 percent purge loss. This limit was to decrease to 3 percent in May 1995. 40 C.F.R. § 82.158(b).

238. 40 C.F.R. § 82.158(j).

239. 40 C.F.R. § 82.158(k).

240. 40 C.F.R. § 82.158(a). The EPA does not require certification of equipment manufactured before November 15, 1993. Technicians are responsible for testing their own "grandfathered" equipment to ensure it meets the requirements. 58 Fed. Reg. at 28,691 (1993).

241. The EPA amended this rule to include a size limitation. 59 Fed. Reg. 42,950, 42,953–54 (1994).

242. 40 C.F.R. § 82.156(i). On July 13, 1993, the Chemical Manufacturers Association (CMA) filed a petition for review of these requirements with respect to industrial process refrigeration. CMA v. Browner, No. 93-1444 (D.C. Cir.). As part of a settlement agreement in the case, *see* 59 Fed. Reg. 30,584 (1994), the EPA stayed the leak repair requirements for industrial process equipment to allow the EPA time to reconsider these rules. *See* 59 Fed. Reg. 42,198 (1994); 59 Fed. Reg. 59,369 (1994) (inserting a stay of the effective dates of 40 C.F.R. §§ 82.156(i)(1), (i)(3), and (i)(4) into 40 C.F.R. § 82.156(i)(5)). Then, the EPA promulgated amendments making the requirements for industrial process refrigeration more flexible, thereby fully disposing of the court challenge. 60 Fed. Reg. 40,420 (1995).

243. 40 C.F.R. § 82.156(i)(5).

244. The owner must develop a plan, which must be kept on site and available for EPA inspection, to retrofit or retire the leaking equipment. 40 C.F.R. § 82.156(i)(6).

245. 40 C.F.R. § 82.156(i)(9); 58 Fed. Reg. at 28,681 (1993).

246. *See* 40 C.F.R. § 82.156(a)(3), Table 1. If the equipment is leaking so that these standards cannot be achieved, evacuation must satisfy the leaking equipment standards set forth at 40 C.F.R. § 82.156(i).

247. 40 C.F.R. § 82.156(f)(1).

248. The verification must include a signed statement from the owner of the appliance, the name and address of the person who recovered the refrigerant, and the date it was recovered. 40 C.F.R. § 82.156(f)(2).

249. 40 C.F.R. § 82.156(f)(3).

250. 40 C.F.R. § 82.164(a)–(d).

251. 40 C.F.R. § 82.164 (first sentence).

252. 40 C.F.R. § 82.164(g). The EPA has revoked certifications on two occasions. 62 Fed. Reg. 28,466 (1997); 63 Fed. Reg. 1927 (1998).

253. 40 C.F.R. §§ 82.154(e), 82.161(a), and 82.152. The EPA created four separate certification categories to cover the various types of equipment subject to Subpart F: (1) small appliances; (2) high-pressure equipment with a charge of less than fifty pounds; (3) high-pressure equipment with a charge of more than fifty pounds; and (4) low-pressure equipment. 40 C.F.R. § 82.161(a); 58 Fed. Reg. at 28,694 (1993). The original rule grandfathered technicians who received training and testing in a program established before promulgation of the regulations, provided that the program met the mandatory program requirements. The EPA has amended its regulations to require only that grandfathered programs substantially meet the mandatory program requirements. The EPA has also excluded apprentices from the certification requirements. 40 C.F.R. § 82.161(a)(6), 59 Fed. Reg. 55,912 (1994) (final rule) and 59 Fed. Reg. 41,968 (1994) (proposal).

254. 40 C.F.R. §§ 82.161(a) and 82.152.

255. See 40 C.F.R. § 82.154(m). The EPA indefinitely stayed this general rule in the case of certain appliance components that the manufacturer has precharged with refrigerant, thereby allowing sales of such components directly to consumers. 40 C.F.R. § 82.154(m)(9); 60 Fed. Reg. 24,675 (1995).

256. See 40 C.F.R. § 82.161, and Appendix D to Subpart F. See 59 Fed. Reg. 55,912 (1994) for amendments to the technician certification and training program requirements, and for a limited exemption to the certification requirements for apprentices. The EPA has revoked certifications for technician certification programs on two occasions. 61 Fed. Reg. 37,741 (1996); 62 Fed. Reg. 8011 (1997).

257. 40 C.F.R. § 82.166.

258. A "motor vehicle air conditioner" is any "mechanical vapor compression refrigeration equipment" that cools the driver's or passenger's compartment of a motor vehicle. It excludes hermetically sealed refrigeration systems used for refrigerated cargo and HCFC-22 refrigerant systems found on passenger buses. 40 C.F.R. § 82.32(d).

259. "Refrigerant" refers to any Class I or II substance used in an MVAC, or, as of November 15, 1995, any substitute for such a substance, such as HFA-134a. 40 C.F.R. § 82.32(f).

260. See 40 C.F.R. pt. 82, subpt. B, §§ 82.30–82.42 and related appendices; 60 Fed. Reg. 21,682 (1995) (supplemental final rule); 57 Fed. Reg. 31,242 (1992) (final rule); 57 Fed. Reg. 14,763 (1992) (supplemental proposal); 56 Fed. Reg. 43,842 (1991) (proposed rule); 56 Fed. Reg. 46,041 (1991) (correction to proposal). The regulations are inapplicable to assembly operations, but do apply if manufacturers' garages perform air conditioner service on company-owned fleet vehicles. See 57 Fed. Reg. at 31,244–46 (1992).

261. In 1993, the EPA under authority of Section 608 expanded the Section 609 prohibition on the sale of sub-20-lb. containers to cover any size container of a Class I or II substance, including blends that include any such substance. 58 Fed. Reg. 28,712 (now codified at 40 C.F.R. § 82.154(m)).

262. 62 Fed. Reg. 68,026.

263. EPA has established a Web site providing copies of the relevant Federal notices and a wealth of guidance. See http://www.epa.gov/ozone/title6/609/index.html. Also EPA maintains a hotline (800-296-1996) for providing information and advice.

264. See 40 C.F.R. § 82.34(b); 57 Fed. Reg. at 31,254 (1992).

265. See 40 C.F.R. §§ 82.34(a), 82.42(a).

266. 40 C.F.R. § 82.40. Two currently approved programs are sponsored by the Mobile Air Conditioning Society (MACS) and the National Institute of Automotive Service Excellence (ASE).

267. 40 C.F.R. § 82.42(a). For a sample certification form, see 40 C.F.R. pt. 82, subpt. B, app. B.

268. 40 C.F.R. § 82.42(b).

269. 40 C.F.R. § 82.42(c).

270. 40 C.F.R. § 82.36. The standards are "Recommended Service Procedure for the Containment of R-12" (SAE J1989); "Extraction and Recycle Equipment for Mobile Automotive Air-Conditioning Systems" (SAE J1990); and ARI 700-1988. *See* 40 C.F.R. pt. 82, subpt. B, app. A.

271. As of August 13, 1992, both UL and ETL Testing Laboratories, Inc. are officially approved testing organizations. 40 C.F.R. § 82.38; 57 Fed. Reg. at 31,250 (1992).

272. 40 C.F.R. § 82.38(d).

273. 40 C.F.R. § 82.36(b)(1). For criteria for determining "substantially identical" status, see 40 C.F.R. § 82.36(b)(2); 57 Fed. Reg. at 31,249–50 (1992).

274. 57 Fed. Reg. at 31,247–49 (1992) (discussing the EPA's authority to regulate both recover/recycle and recover-only equipment).

275. *See* 40 C.F.R. §§ 82.34(a) and 82.32(e).

276. 40 C.F.R. § 82.32(e). The standard of purity for reclamation is that established by the Air Conditioning and Refrigeration Institute (ARI 700-1993). 40 C.F.R. § 82.32(e).

277. Specific monetary penalties are enumerated in "Appendix IX—Clean Air Act Civil Penalty Policy Applicable to Persons Who Perform Service for Consideration on a Motor Vehicle Air Conditioner Involving the Refrigerant or Who Sell Small Containers of Refrigerant in Violation of 40 C.F.R. Pt. 82, Protection of the Stratospheric Ozone, Subpart V: Servicing of Motor Vehicle Air Conditioners, July 19, 1993," *available at* http://www.epa .gov/ttncaaa1/t6/memoranda/609_pp.pdf.

278. *See* 62 Fed. Reg. at 68,027, and guidance material at http://www.epa.gov/ ozone/title6/609/subsumm.html.

279. *See* 62 Fed. Reg. at 68,028 col. 3.

280. *See* 62 Fed. Reg. at 68,029 col. 1, and guidance material at http://www.epa.gov/ ozone/title6/609/subsumm.html.

281. CAA § 610(b). The EPA interprets "interstate commerce" to include a product's entire distribution chain up to and including the point of sale to the ultimate consumer. As such, all sales and distribution, including retail sales, are prohibited as of the effective date of the ban. *See* 57 Fed. Reg. at 1994 (1992).

282. The EPA must consider the purpose or intended use of the product, the technological availability of substitutes for the product and for the Class I substance, safety, health, and other relevant factors. For a discussion of the EPA's application of these factors to the banned products, *see* 58 Fed. Reg. at 4773–80 (1993). The EPA also considered the criteria it used in developing the 1978 ban on aerosol propellant uses of CFCs under TSCA, which overlap significantly with the factors enumerated in Section 610(b)(3). The one criterion not specifically addressed in Section 610(b)(3) and considered by the EPA is the "economic significance of the product." 57 Fed. Reg. at 1997–98 (1992).

283. *See* 40 C.F.R. pt. 82, subpt. C, §§ 82.60–82.70 and related appendices. 58 Fed. Reg. 4768 (1993) (final rule); 57 Fed. Reg. 1992 (1992) (proposed rule).

284. 40 C.F.R. § 82.64(a). The ban covers any plastic party streamer or noise horn which is propelled by a CFC, including but not limited to: (1) string confetti; (2) marine safety horns; (3) sporting event horns; (4) personal safety horns; (5) wall-mounted alarms used in factories or other work areas; and (6) intruder alarms used in homes or cars. 40 C.F.R. § 82.66(a). The EPA identified string confetti, commonly known as "silly string," as the only product fitting the description of a CFC-propelled plastic party streamer. While the EPA was unaware of any company that used CFCs in this type of product at the time of the ban, the ban nonetheless extends to such products. *See* 58 Fed. Reg. at 4772 (1993). Similarly, manufacturers reported that all horn products except for the smallest

canister of 2.1 ounces were either reformulated using HCFCs or dropped from product lines. Due to the availability of substitutes for noise horn products, the EPA banned all CFC-propelled noise horns. *Id.* at 4773.

285. *See* Compliance Guidance for Section 610 of the Clean Air Act: Nonessential Products Containing Chlorofluorocarbons, at 3.

286. 40 C.F.R. § 82.64(b).

287. 40 C.F.R. § 82.66(b). The EPA clarified that, generally, waste products (such as CFC-containing spray dusters used for cleaning electronic equipment that have been designated as waste) are not subject to the Section 610 ban because they no longer meet the definition of "product" in the regulation. *See* Stratospheric Ozone Protection Applicability Determination, Record 1 (June 1993).

288. Commercial purchaser means a person with (1) a federal employer identification number, (2) a state sales tax exemption number, (3) a local business license number, or (4) a government contract number, who uses the product in the purchaser's business or sells it to another person. 40 C.F.R. § 82.62(b).

289. 40 C.F.R. § 82.68(a). Moreover, the seller or distributor "must have a reasonable basis for believing that the information presented by the purchaser is accurate."

290. *See* Compliance Guidance for Section 610 of the Clean Air Act: Nonessential Products Containing Chlorofluorocarbons at 3–4.

291. 40 C.F.R. § 82.68(b). A mail-order company that sells electronic and photographic cleaning fluids may satisfy the regulatory requirements by displaying the required language in sales catalogs and product literature. The language must also appear on the mail-order form. To verify the commercial status of the purchaser, the order form must contain a space for the purchaser to enter the requisite identification number. If the order is placed over the phone, the sales representative must record the purchaser's commercial identification number with the order information. *See* Stratospheric Ozone Protection Applicability Determination, Record 2 (June 1993).

292. Subsequent to announcing the proposed ban on nonessential products, the EPA became aware of certain replacement parts that were placed into initial inventory before April 16, 1992 (ninety days after publication of the proposed Class I ban) and that were manufactured with, contained, or are stored in packaging material that was manufactured with or contained CFCs. These products tend to be made with open cell foam products, meaning the environmental damage resulting from use of Class I substances would have occurred during the original production of the foam. Therefore, the EPA granted limited exemptions from the Class I ban to existing inventories where the original product and replacement parts are no longer manufactured, and where the replacement parts were expressly manufactured for that specific product make or model. See 40 C.F.R. § 82.65; 58 Fed. Reg. at 69,672 (1993).

293. 40 C.F.R. § 82.66(c). The ban covers open cell polyurethane flexible slabstock foam, open cell polyurethane flexible molded foam, open cell rigid polyurethane poured foam, closed cell extruded polystyrene sheet foam, closed cell polyethylene foam, and closed cell polypropylene foam. Flexible plastic or packing foam used in coaxial cable is exempt from the ban.

294. 40 C.F.R. § 82.66(d)(1). Specific aerosol products and other CFC-containing dispensers subject to the ban include, but are not limited to, household, industrial, automotive, and pesticide uses.

295. 40 C.F.R. § 82.66(d)(1). Specific aerosol products and other CFC-containing dispensers subject to the ban include, but are not limited to, household, industrial, automotive, and pesticide uses.

296. *See* 58 Fed. Reg. at 4778 (1993) ("EPA determined . . . that adequate substitutes for CFCs in the production of flexible and packaging foams were indeed available."); *id.* at 4779 ("EPA proposed banning CFCs in aerosols and other pressurized dispensers primarily because a variety of substitutes for CFCs are now widely available and currently in use.").

297. *See* 57 Fed. Reg. at 1998 (1992). The following products are exempt from the ban: all medical devices listed in 21 C.F.R. § 2.125(e); certain types of lubricants, coating or cleaning fluids for electrical or electronic equipment; certain types of lubricants and coatings used for aircraft maintenance; some mold release agents; some spinnerette lubricants/cleaning sprays used in the production of synthetic fibers; and document preservation sprays containing CFC-113 but no other CFCs. 40 C.F.R. § 82.66(d)(2).

298. Oil Charge has been found to be a bulk container and therefore not subject to the nonessential product ban, whereas Leak Stop and Leak Finder are considered to be products and thus subject to the ban. *See* Stratospheric Ozone Protection Applicability Determination, Records 4–6 (March 1994).

299. 66 Fed. Reg. 57,512.

300. 40 C.F.R. § 82.70(b). Like the Class I ban, the Class II ban covers the sale of aerosol cleaning fluids for electronic and photographic equipment containing Class II substances to noncommercial users. The EPA clarified, however, that under Section 610(d), it can restrict the sale of only aerosol cleaning fluids as opposed to any cleaning fluids for electronic and photographic equipment. *See* 58 Fed. Reg. at 50,479 (1993).

301. The EPA interprets the term "plastic foam product" to include products composed in whole or in part of material that can be described as "foam plastic." *See* 58 Fed. Reg. at 50,479 (1993).

302. CAA § 610(d)(1).

303. 58 Fed. Reg. 69,638 (1993) (final rule); 58 Fed. Reg. 50,464, at 50,469 (1993) (proposed rule).

304. CAA § 610(d)(2).

305. *See* 58 Fed. Reg. at 50,474 (1993).

306. 40 C.F.R. § 82.70(a)(2).

307. CAA § 610(d)(3)(B). The EPA determined that the exemption from the nonessential product ban found in 40 C.F.R. § 82.70(c)(2) applies to products used for passenger motor vehicles other than multipurpose passenger vehicles. *See* Stratospheric Ozone Protection Applicability Determination, Record 7 (March 22, 1994).

308. 40 C.F.R. § 82.62(h). A discussion of how various foam products are treated under the regulations is contained in the preamble to the final rule. *See* 58 Fed. Reg. at 69,655–59 (1993).

309. 40 C.F.R. § 82.70(c)(2)(ii).

310. *Id; see also* 58 Fed. Reg. at 50,484 (1993) (discussion of the EPA's rationale for the imposition of a sunset provision on the integral skin foam exemption from the Class II ban). The EPA noted that it would revisit the sunset provision for the exemption at a future date if it received a request from the public for extending the exemption.

311. The FAR is prepared, issued, and maintained by the secretary of defense, the administrator of General Services, and the administrator of the National Aeronautics and Space Administration. The Defense Acquisition Regulatory Council and the Civilian Agency Acquisition Council are responsible for revisions to the FAR. *See generally* 40 C.F.R. subpts. 1.1 and 1.2.

312. *See generally* 48 C.F.R. pts. 2–63.

313. *See* 40 C.F.R. pt. 82, subpt. D, §§ 82.80–82.86; 58 Fed. Reg. 54,892 (1993) (final rule); 58 Fed. Reg. 19,080 (1993) (proposal). The EPA was sued for its failure to meet the

statutory deadline for promulgation of these regulations. The litigation resulted in a proposed Consent Decree requiring the EPA to propose regulations by March 1, 1993, and to promulgate a final rule by October 13, 1993. *See* 57 Fed. Reg. 56,339 (1992).

314. The regulations do not preclude the use of Class II substances in place of Class I substances before the phaseout of Class II substances. *See* 58 Fed. Reg. 54,893 (1993).

315. *See* 58 Fed. Reg. at 54,897 (§ V). EPA's Subpart D regulations are

closely related to section 612, as the purchase of safe alternatives is expected to be the principle means through which agencies will minimize their purchase of ozone-depleting substances. To ensure conformity with Section 612, the regulations adopted by agencies pursuant to today's proposed rule must require agency officials both to comply with the policy in section 612(a) of maximizing the use of alternatives to class I and class II substances in making agency purchasing decisions, and to comply with the regulations to be issued by EPA identifying unacceptable substitutes.

58 Fed. Reg. at 54,897 § IV(6) (last paragraph). The EPA expects, however, that substantial changes from current practices will in fact be practicable. See 58 Fed. Reg. at 19,085 (1993).

316. The interim amendments appear at 60 Fed. Reg. 28,500 (1995), and the final ones at 61 Fed. Reg. 31,645 (1996).

317. *See*, e.g., CAA §§ 113(a)(3) (EPA's civil enforcement authority), 113(c) (EPA's criminal enforcement authority), and 304(f)(3) (citizens' suit authority).

318. *See* CAA §§ 618 and 116.

319. *See* abstracts of successful prosecutions at http://www.epa.gov/ozone/ enforce/ index.html.

320. The EPA also has built relationships at the international level to promote effective enforcement. It was one of the founders of the International Network for Environmental Compliance and Enforcement (INECE). A description of the history, purposes, and activities of INECE appears at http://www.inece.org. *See also Law of Environmental Protection*, § 9:138 (Novick et al., eds., West Group, March 2002).

321. These taxes appear at 26 C.F.R. pt. 52 (2001).

322. *See* http://www.epa.gov/ozone/enforce/index.html.

323. *See* http://www.epa.gov/ozone/enforce/blackmkt.html.

324. *See* http://www.epa.gov/ozone/enforce/index.html.

325. *Id.*

326. 66 Fed. Reg. 63,696 (December 10, 2001). Also, the EPA has issued a more general guidance document, "Compliance Guidance for Industrial Process Refrigeration Leak Repair Regulations under Section 608 of the Clean Air Act." This guidance appears at http://www.epa.gov/ozone/title6/608/compguid/compguid.html.

327. These policies appear as appendices to EPA's Clean Air Act Civil Penalty Policy at http://www.epa.gov/compliance/resources/policies/civil/caa/stationary/penpol.pdf.

CHAPTER 14

Global Climate Change

KYLE DANISH

Introduction

Why include a chapter on global climate change in this edition of the *Clean Air Act Handbook*? There is no existing greenhouse gas (GHG) regulatory program under the Clean Air Act (CAA). Indeed, whether the CAA in its current form even authorizes the U.S. Environmental Protection Agency (EPA) to regulate carbon dioxide or other GHGs has been the subject of vigorous debate. That debate, moreover, may be mostly academic for at least the near-term because President George W. Bush has unambiguously declared his opposition to any regulation of carbon dioxide.

Those factors notwithstanding, the reasons for a global climate change chapter in this edition are many. Even in the absence of a major national regulatory program under the CAA, significant climate-related policies are under development in multiple arenas. In 2002, President Bush proposed a voluntary U.S. climate change program. Congress is considering mandatory carbon dioxide controls for U.S. electric utilities in the context of "multipollutant" legislation. Both the executive and legislative branches are working on GHG reporting programs that would provide "transferable credits" to firms that register voluntary emissions reductions. A number of states are moving forward with their own climate programs. Major U.S. firms have adopted voluntary corporate GHG emission reduction commitments. In addition, even if the United States opts to continue to stay outside the Kyoto Protocol climate change treaty, U.S. firms with operations overseas will feel its effects if the treaty enters into force. This chapter reviews the status of these various developments as of early 2003.

Nevertheless, it could be argued that none of the above activities, individually or collectively, amounts to anything like the major CAA regulatory programs discussed in other chapters of this book. Yet, many observers believe that establishment of a comprehensive, mandatory GHG reduction program in the United States is only a matter of time. Even the potential of such a program has cast a long shadow over not only other air quality initiatives but also the long-term financial planning of a range of businesses.

497

The economic and social impacts of even a moderately ambitious U.S. climate program could exceed the impacts of practically all of the environmental policies developed to date. Importantly, the magnitude and the distribution of these impacts depend in great measure on the form of GHG program developed. For these reasons, this chapter also includes a discussion of different options under consideration for a mandatory GHG reduction program in the United States.

Greenhouse Gases and Their Sources

This chapter will forgo a discussion of the science of climate change, except for a brief review of (1) the types of GHGs, (2) some of the characteristics of GHGs that are relevant for the development of climate change policies, and (3) sources of GHGs in the United States.

For the most part, climate change policies focus on six GHGs: carbon dioxide (CO_2), methane (CH_4), nitrous oxide (N_2O), and what have been called the "synthetic gases"—hydrofluorocarbons (HFCs), perfluorocarbons (PFCs), and sulfur hexafluoride (SF_6).[1] GHGs have qualities that are worth noting in developing climate policy. First, a ton of a particular GHG emitted has the same effect on the atmosphere regardless of where the source of the emission is located. In other words, the climate impact of a ton of CO_2 emitted in the United States is equal to that of a ton of CO_2 emitted in Mexico. The cost of abating a ton of emissions, on the other hand, can vary considerably among sources and among regions. For this reason, climate change policy lends itself particularly well to emissions trading.

While a ton of a particular GHG emitted has equal impact regardless of location of the source, different types of GHGs have different impacts. It is possible to construct a kind of exchange rate that measures reductions of each of the GHGs in terms of "carbon dioxide equivalent." The currently accepted formulation is called Global Warming Potential (GWP). With such a GHG exchange rate, a climate policy can give firms the flexibility of meeting an emission limitation commitment through the least-cost mix of reductions in the different gases, i.e., through "inter-gas" trading.[2]

Sources (and "sinks") of the different GHGs are widely dispersed throughout the U.S. economy. The U.S. energy sector accounts for approximately 80 percent of the nation's total GWP-weighted emissions, primarily as a result of carbon dioxide emissions from combustion of fossil fuels.[3] Biomass (soils, plants, and trees) removes and stores atmospheric CO_2 through the process of photosynthesis, and thus is referred to as a "sink." Accordingly, various agricultural and forestry activities can have a positive or a negative impact on the amount of CO_2 in the atmosphere. Emissions of methane come from landfills, natural gas production and transportation, and agricultural activities. Emissions of nitrous oxide result primarily from agricultural activities, fuel combustion in motor vehicles, and production of adipic and nitric acid. Certain production processes related to the manufacturing of aluminum, semiconductor equipment, and electrical transmission equipment result in emissions of HFCs, PFCs, and SF_6. Emissions of HFCs and PFCs also result from their use as substitutes for ozone-depleting substances.

Climate Change under the Clean Air Act

The Clean Air Act does not provide the EPA with the express authority to regulate CO_2 or any other substances on the basis of their climate impacts.[4] Whether the EPA may regulate GHGs using its implied regulatory authorities under the CAA is a question that has been the subject of vigorous debate. The discussion that follows summarizes the key legal arguments that commentators have raised for and against the EPA's authority to regulate GHGs under the CAA.[5]

In 1998, at the request of the EPA administrator, the EPA general counsel drafted a memorandum analyzing the EPA's authority under Title I to regulate GHGs emitted by power plants.[6] While emphasizing that the EPA had no immediate plans to promulgate climate change regulations, the general counsel concluded that a number of Title I provisions were "potentially applicable."[7] Then, toward the end of the Clinton administration, the EPA published in the *Federal Register* a request for comment on a petition submitted by number of environmental organizations requesting that the EPA regulate GHGs from new motor vehicles or new motor vehicle engines under Section 202(a)(1) of the CAA.[8]

In December 2002, a group of environmental organizations filed a suit in the District Court for the District of Columbia, asserting that the EPA's failure to act on the petition represents a violation of the Administrative Procedure Act.[9] In January 2003, three northeastern states filed notices of intent to sue the EPA to compel the agency to regulate carbon dioxide as a criteria pollutant under CAA Section 108.[10] In the next month, a group of seven states filed a notice of their intent to sue the EPA for failing to comply with a mandatory duty to revise the Clean Air Act New Source Performance Standards (NSPS) in order to establish a technology standard to address CO_2 emissions from power plants.[11]

In the course of the debate on these various initiatives, a number of commentators have asserted that the EPA lacks legal authority under the CAA to promulgate GHG regulations. Notably, in the process of amending the CAA in 1990, Congress considered and then rejected provisions that would have regulated emissions of GHGs.[12] The EPA officials in the Clinton administration asserted, however, that Congress's rejection of explicit GHG limits did not alter the EPA's *implied* regulatory authorities. In 1999, the EPA General Counsel Gary Guzy testified before Congress that "[the] decision in the 1990 Amendments not to adopt *additional* provisions directing the EPA to regulate greenhouse gases by no means suggests that Congress intended to limit *preexisting* authority to address any air pollutant that the Administrator determines meets the statutory criteria for regulation under a specific provision of the Act."[13] It could also be argued that Congress concluded in 1990 that the scientific evidence available at that time did not support legislating limits on

GHGs but that the EPA could use its latent authority to regulate GHGs if and when the science supported such limits.

In determining whether the EPA has implied authority to regulate GHGs under either Title I or Title II, the threshold questions are whether GHGs may be considered (1) "air pollutants" that (2) "cause, or contribute to, air pollution which may reasonably be anticipated to endanger public health or welfare."

Section 302(g) defines "air pollutant" broadly as any "air pollution agent . . . which is emitted into or otherwise enters the ambient air." Industry opponents of GHG regulation argued that CO_2 cannot be considered an "air pollution agent" because it is a natural part of the atmosphere, is emitted by a range of natural processes, and can have salutary effects on human health and the environment.[14] The EPA officials countered that these characteristics of CO_2 do not prevent it from being an air pollution agent, noting that other substances that Congress expressly deemed "air pollutants" also occur naturally and, under some circumstances, have positive effects on human health. For example, volatile organic compounds are emitted by vegetation, sulfur dioxide is emitted through geothermal processes, and even some substances deemed hazardous air pollutants, such as manganese and selenium, are good for one's health in small amounts.[15] They further observe that in Section 103(g), Congress explicitly referred to CO_2 as an "air pollutant."[16] Finally, with respect to the second prong of the threshold test, Section 302(h) of the CAA provides that "all language [in the CAA] referring to effects on 'welfare' includes effects on . . . climate."[17]

Assuming the EPA could make the threshold "air pollutant" and "health or welfare" determinations regarding CO_2 or other GHGs, the EPA still would have to make further findings to support regulation of stationary sources under Title I or regulation of mobile sources under Title II.

Under Title I, the traditional avenue for regulation would be for the EPA to determine, pursuant to Sections 108 and 109, that CO_2 is a "criteria pollutant" and for the EPA to establish primary and secondary CO_2 National Ambient Air Quality Standards (NAAQS), reflecting a level of CO_2 that protects public health with a margin of safety.[18] (See Chapter 2 for a discussion of this process.) The instrument for achieving the NAAQS is the state implementation plan (SIP) process. The SIP process is predicated on the ability of states to achieve the NAAQS in particular air quality control regions. Opponents of the EPA regulation argued that this framework has "no rational application" to emissions of CO_2 and other GHGs because the ambient levels of such substances are evenly mixed throughout the world.[19] The United States, while the largest single contributor of emissions, still accounts for less than a fifth of the world total. Accordingly, if the level of NAAQS was set below the current concentration, the country as a whole would have a "nonattainment" status, yet no SIP measures could be expected to achieve attainment.[20] Even though the NAAQS regime has a number of provisions intended to address pollutant "transport," including international transport, all of these provisions invoke the SIP process as the remedy for such transport.[21]

Regulating CO_2 or other GHGs as "hazardous air pollutants" (HAPs) pursuant to Section 112 also would be problematic. The CAA defines HAPs as pollutants that have adverse effects on human health through "inhalation or other routes of exposure."[22]

There might be a better case for the EPA's authority to set GHG-related NSPS pursuant to Section 111. Section 111(a)(1) defines an NSPS as a "standard for emissions of air pollutants which reflects the degree of emission limitation achievable through the application of the best system of emission reduction which (taking into account the cost of achieving such reduction and any nonair quality health and environmental impact and energy requirements) the Administrator determines has been adequately demonstrated." Traditionally, NSPS have prescribed particular technologies. Some commentators have argued that this eliminates the possibility of a climate change-based NSPS for power plants and other stationary sources because of the absence of any cost-effective technology to reduce CO_2 emissions at the stack.[23] However, it is arguably the case that the EPA could use its Section 111 authority either to require new or modified power plants to use gas instead of coal as a fuel or to prescribe energy efficiency standards for major energy-using sources. In addition, the EPA would not need to determine first that carbon dioxide or another GHG is a "criteria air pollutant" in order to act under Section 111.

The EPA would appear to have fewer constraints under Title II than under Title I. Under Section 202(a), the EPA may promulgate mobile source regulations if it determines a substance is an "air pollutant" that "cause[s] or contribute[s] to air pollution which may reasonably be anticipated to endanger public health or welfare." Section 202(b) provides that any regulations may not take effect until "after such period as the Administrator finds necessary to permit the development and application of the requisite technology, giving appropriate consideration to the cost of compliance within such period."[24] This language appears broad enough to authorize regulation of GHG emissions by mobile sources if the EPA makes the necessary findings. However, one scholar has argued that the legislative history suggests that Congress intended a narrower application of Sections 202(a) and 202(b).[25] According to this interpretation, Congress fashioned Section 202(a) with the sole purpose of establishing a schedule for the EPA regulation of vehicle emissions of hydrocarbons, carbon monoxide, NO_x, and particulate matter.

As discussed in the next section, the debate as to whether the EPA has authority under the CAA to regulate GHG emissions might be rejoined in the near future as the State of California takes steps to implement its 2002 law calling for regulation of GHG emissions from motor vehicles.

Key Climate Change Policy Initiatives in the United States

President Bush's Voluntary Program

On February 14, 2002, President Bush announced his U.S. Global Climate Change Policy.[26] The aim of the policy is to reduce the GHG intensity of the U.S. economy by 18 percent by 2012. GHG intensity is a measure of the ratio of GHG emissions to economic output. The Bush plan calls for expanded programs for voluntary reductions and would establish new funding for clean technologies and scientific research. The plan also provides for a review in 2012. If progress toward the 18 percent goal is deemed unsatisfactory and "sound science" justifies further action, additional measures will be considered.

Commentators have criticized the adequacy of the approach adopted by the Bush administration. First, they argue that the 18 percent intensity target does not promise much of a departure from what would occur under a business-as-usual scenario; the emissions intensity of the U.S. economy is projected to decline by 14 percent even without a program. Also, they observe that a decline in emissions intensity does not amount to a limit on emissions. Because U.S. economic output is projected to grow over the next ten years, U.S. GHG emissions will grow by 12 percent even if President Bush's emissions intensity target is achieved.[27]

A notable feature of the Bush plan is its call for improvements to the existing voluntary GHG reporting program established under Section 1605(b) of the 1992 Energy Policy Act. In July 2002, the secretaries of energy, commerce, and agriculture and the EPA administrator sent a letter to the president setting forth some preliminary recommendations on program enhancements and a timetable and process for implementation.[28] Their goal is to finalize new guidelines by January 2004, for reporting 2003 data. In developing an enhanced reporting program, the Bush administration is having to confront a complicated set of issues, including determining the required scope of reporting for participating companies; defining baselines against which to measure changes in emission levels; determining whether and how companies can report on an emissions intensity basis; establishing rules for measurement, monitoring, and verification of emissions; deciding whether and how to record emission reductions achieved through projects in other countries; determining how to credit sequestration projects; and determining what provisions are necessary to give companies transferable credits for their reported reductions.

A particularly thorny issue is how to treat "indirect" emissions, i.e., emissions (or reductions) that are a consequence of the reporting company's activities, but occur from sources owned or controlled by another company. Where a reporting program aims to provide transferable credits, reporting of reductions in indirect emissions leads to a potential double-counting or ownership problem. For example, where a factory implements an energy efficient project that lowers electricity output and therefore emissions from a power plant, the program needs to make clear whether the company owning the factory or the company owning the power plant earns transferable credits.

President Bush also has directed the secretary of energy to recommend reforms "to ensure that businesses and individuals that register reductions are not penalized under a future climate policy."[29] This concept is sometimes referred to as "baseline protection." It addresses the concern that a company that makes voluntary reductions in its emissions levels now—but whose competitors do not—may be disadvantaged under a future emissions trading program.[30]

Finally, the EPA has established the Climate Leaders program, under which participating companies set a voluntary corporatewide GHG emissions reduction target and inventory their emissions annually.[31]

Legislation in Congress

Congress has been considering various alternative approaches to domestic climate change policy, including an economy-wide regulatory program, regulatory programs focused on the power sector, and GHG reporting and registry programs.

In 2003, Senators McCain and Lieberman introduced a bill that would establish a comprehensive GHG regulatory program.[32] As proposed, the McCain/Lieberman bill would reduce annual GHG emissions from sources in the electricity generation, industrial, commercial, and transportation sectors to year-2000 levels by 2010, and to year-1990 levels by 2016.[33] The bill would allow regulated firms to meet their obligations through flexibility mechanisms, including a "cap and trade" program. The bill covers all six of the major GHGs: carbon dioxide, methane, nitrous oxide, hydrofluorocarbons, perfluorocarbons, and sulfur hexafluoride.

The basic approach of the bill for these sectors is a cap-and-trade program. For 2010–2015, the government would allot to each sector, without cost, allowances equal to some portion of its year-2000 emissions. For 2016 and thereafter, each sector would receive some portion of its year-1990 emissions.[34] The government also would distribute allowances to a fiduciary, the Climate Change Credit Corporation, which would be required to sell its allowances and use the proceeds to reduce regulatory costs borne by consumers and workers.[35] The bill does not set forth the precise percentages to be allotted to the regulated sectors, on the one hand, and to the Climate Change Credit Corporation, on the other. Nor does the bill set forth a formula for distributing allowances to regulated firms within sectors. Instead, it vests the secretary of commerce with the authority to determine these allocations, subject to a set of criteria.

The bill reflects a hybrid approach to regulation. For the electricity generation, industrial, and commercial sectors, the program would cap emissions from sources. As explained below, this approach is sometimes referred to as a "downstream" cap. For the transportation sector, however, the program would adopt an "upstream" approach; it would cap the carbon content in fuel sold for transportation uses. This upstream approach amounts to an effective cap on transportation emissions and would be easier to administer than downstream regulation of the millions of individual sources (cars, trucks, aircraft, etc.) in the transportation sector.

Firms subject to regulation would be required to hold allowances equal to their emissions. Firms would have the ability to buy allowances from other firms. In addition, the bill provides that during 2010–2015, regulated firms could meet 15 percent of their obligations through any of a set of "alternative compliance measures" including (1) allowances from other countries that have enforceable GHG emissions limitations, providing that those allowances have been "retired" in the other country; (2) net increases in sequestration that have been registered in a national GHG database; (3) registered GHG reductions implemented at sources or sinks not otherwise regulated under the program; or (4) very limited "borrowing" of credits, based on a credible demonstration that the regulated firm will achieve GHG reductions in future years.[36] Starting in 2016, regulated firms only could meet 10 percent of their requirements through these alternative compliance measures.

As discussed above, the bill would establish a national GHG database and registry, to be developed through an EPA-led regulatory process. Regulated firms would be required to report their annual emissions in the database and could use the registry to report reductions or sequestration. In addition, unregulated firms could register reductions or sequestration in the database, which they then could sell as credits to regulated firms.

In addition to the McCain/Lieberman bill, Congress has been considering various bills that would amend the CAA to establish a "multipollutant" program for electric utilities. A number of the bills in play would impose limitations on power plant emissions of CO_2, in addition to limitations on nitrogen oxides (NO_x), sulfur dioxide (SO_2), and mercury.[37] President Bush has submitted legislation that would establish an alternative multipollutant framework, the Clear Skies Act.[38] Consistent with the president's pledge not to regulate CO_2, the Clear Skies Act imposes limits on NO_x, SO_2, and mercury only.

While almost all utilities oppose the establishment of stringent CO_2 limits, different utilities hold different opinions on the benefits of establishing a CO_2 limit within a multipollutant framework generally. A utility's view depends largely on its view as to the likelihood that it ultimately will be subject to stringent CO_2 limits. Some would prefer certainty as to their CO_2 obligations in order to avoid "stranded" investments in pollution controls. Studies suggest that most utilities facing a three-pollutant framework would retrofit their coal-fired power plants with emission control technologies rather than retire them or switch them to natural gas.[39] These technologies do nothing to reduce CO_2 emissions and, indeed, could result in increased emissions because the controls themselves draw energy. Accordingly, if Congress later followed on with CO_2 limits, all of these investments would be for naught because most utilities would be forced to retire or repower their older coal-fired plants. For this reason, a four-pollutant approach might impose higher costs in the near-term (because it would require more aggressive action on coal-fired power plants) but lower overall costs than following a three-pollutant program with stringent CO_2 limits.[40]

In addition to considering various regulatory approaches to addressing climate change, Congress also has been assessing alternatives to the existing Section 1605(b) voluntary emissions reporting and registry program. A number of bills would replace the Section 1605(b) program with a more rigorous, and possibly mandatory, program. Under these bills, the reporting program initially would be voluntary, but in the event that the program failed to cover a certain percentage of the nation's GHG emissions within a certain amount of time, reporting would become mandatory for sources of a particular size.[41]

State Initiatives

States have been moving forward with their own climate change programs, which in some cases are substantially more aggressive than those proposed by the federal government. Some states, including California, Massachusetts, New Hampshire, and Oregon, have adopted regulatory programs. Others are in the process of establishing voluntary emissions reporting programs.

On July 22, 2002, California enacted the first-ever U.S. law requiring the development of emissions standards limiting GHG emissions from vehicles.[42] The law requires the California Air Resources Board (CARB) to "develop and adopt regulations that achieve the maximum feasible and cost-effective reduction of greenhouse gases from motor vehicles."[43] With the fifth-largest economy in the world and 10 percent of the U.S. car market, California's regulations could have far-reaching implications.

CARB must adopt the standards no later than January 1, 2005, after which the legislature will evaluate the appropriateness of the standards. The standards then will apply to vehicles manufactured in the 2009 model year and every model year thereafter.[44] The standards will apply to manufacturers' fleet averages, rather than on a vehicle-by-vehicle basis. The law further requires that manufacturers be provided the ability to comply through alternative mitigation measures.[45] In response to a range of political challenges, the law imposes a number of constraints on the kinds of regulation CARB can develop under the law. For example, CARB cannot establish additional fees or taxes, ban the sale of categories of vehicles (such as sport-utility vehicles), require a reduction in vehicle weight, reduce speed limits, or limit vehicle miles traveled.[46]

Most observers expect a vigorous legal challenge to the legislation, although when such a challenge will be ripe is an unresolved question. A threshold substantive issue is whether the law amounts to regulation of "fuel economy," an area of regulation the federal government reserved for itself in 1975 through the Corporate Average Fuel Economy (CAFE) law.[47] The fuel economy preemption issue has arisen in ongoing litigation regarding California's zero emission vehicle (ZEV) laws.[48] Notably, the EPA calculates fuel economy for CAFE purposes by measuring a vehicle's CO_2 emissions; this might bolster a claim that regulation of CO_2 treads on the federal government's exclusive authority to regulate fuel economy. Automakers generally have argued that the only way to reduce CO_2 emissions from motor vehicles is through fuel economy measures. California officials assert that other means are available.

If the California GHG law is not precluded by the fuel economy preemption, it still could be subject to another preemption. As discussed in Chapter 10, the CAA generally prohibits states from establishing emissions standards for new motor vehicles and vehicle engines. However, Section 209 of the CAA sets forth a process under which California may apply to the EPA for a waiver from the preemption. If the EPA grants a waiver for a California emissions standard, other states may adopt the California standard. The EPA must grant the waiver if it determines that the California standard or standards "will be, in the aggregate, at least as protective of public health and welfare as applicable Federal standards."[49] The EPA must deny the waiver if it determines that "(A) the determination of the State is arbitrary and capricious; (B) such State does not need such State standards to meet compelling and extraordinary conditions; or (C) such State standards and accompanying enforcement procedures are not consistent with [Section 209(a)] of this title."[50] The last criterion is noteworthy because a requirement that the state standard(s) be "consistent with section 202(a)" could be read to imply that if the EPA lacks authority under Section 202(a) to set emissions standards for GHG emissions from motor vehicles—a question discussed in a previous section of this chapter—than the state of California also would lack such authority.

The states of Massachusetts and New Hampshire both have passed laws imposing limits on CO_2 emissions from power plants through their own "multipollutant" cap-and-trade programs.[51] The Massachusetts law requires the state's six highest-emitting power plants to reduce their emissions of CO_2 to 1,800 pounds per megawatt hour by 2006 or, for plants intending to comply through repowering, by 2008. The New Hampshire law requires power plants in the state to reduce their CO_2 emissions to 1990 levels by 2010.

Oregon passed legislation in 1997 requiring all new power plants built in the state to have a CO_2 emissions rate 17 percent lower than the most CO_2-efficient power plant in operation in the United States.[52] To comply, plants may comply either "on-system" or through the purchase of CO_2 emission credits. The state has designated a nonprofit organization, the Climate Trust, to serve as a kind of buying agent for plants. The state sets a price for a ton of carbon and directs the Climate Trust to purchase emission reductions in sufficient quantity to offset the emissions over the lifetime of the plant.

In 2001, the New England governors and eastern Canadian premiers came to an agreement on a climate change action plan that sets forth a non-binding commitment to reduce CO_2 emissions to 1990 levels by 2010 and at least 10 percent below 1990 levels by 2020.[53] In 1999, the state government of New Jersey passed an administrative order establishing a goal to reduce the state's CO_2-equivalent emissions 3.5 percent below 1990 levels by 2005.[54]

Finally, a little over a dozen states are in various stages of developing their own voluntary GHG emissions reporting programs. States creating reporting programs include California, Colorado, Illinois, Maine, Massachusetts, Michigan, New Hampshire, New Jersey, New York, Oregon, Washington, and Wisconsin.[55] Without express action by Congress, the establishment of a federal voluntary reporting program would not pre-empt any state programs. Accordingly, U.S. companies may find themselves participating in federal and state reporting programs that subject them to different sets of rules.[56]

Voluntary Company Initiatives

A range of companies based or operating in the United States have announced voluntary corporate commitments to achieve particular GHG emission reduction targets. These include such major companies as Alcan, Alcoa, BP, DuPont,

Entergy, Ford Motor Company, General Motors, IBM, Johnson & Johnson, Nike, Royal Dutch/Shell, and Toyota.[57] The companies are taking various actions to achieve their commitments, including fuel-switching, technology changes, energy efficiency improvements, and emission trades.

One of the more notable private sector initiatives is the Chicago Climate Exchange, a voluntary climate change trading program.[58] The aim of the exchange and its participants is to develop a private trading platform, complete with verification and monitoring standards and mechanisms, that could serve as a model for a future government program. In September 2002, the exchange announced that it would begin executing domestic trades of GHG credits in early 2003.[59] The design phase of the exchange attracted the participation of a range of companies, including American Electric Power, BP, DuPont, and Ford Motor Company. The exchange has designated Brazil as a country that can provide offset projects to participating companies.

Key International Climate Change Policy Initiatives

The Kyoto Protocol

International climate change initiatives directly and indirectly affect climate change policies in the United States. Since 1994, the United States has been a party to the United Nations Framework Convention on Climate Change (UNFCCC).[60] The treaty's "ultimate objective" is "stabilization of greenhouse gas concentrations in the atmosphere at a level that would prevent dangerous anthropogenic interference with the climate system."[61]

The most significant international climate change policy development to date has been the establishment of the Kyoto Protocol to the UNFCCC and its companion rulebook, the Marrakesh Accords.[62] If the protocol enters into force, it will be the first international treaty to impose binding GHG emission limitation obligations. For now, however, such obligations would not apply to the United States. The Bush administration has declared that the United States will not ratify. Nonparties are not bound by the requirements of the protocol. The overseas facilities of U.S. companies, however, will be subject to whatever laws those countries establish to meet their Kyoto obligations.

Under the Kyoto Protocol, "Annex B" parties, consisting primarily of developed countries, are subject to quantified GHG emission limitation and reduction commitments that apply in the first "commitment period."[63] At least for now, developing countries (i.e., "non-Annex B" parties) are not subject to such commitments. With some variations, each Annex B country's emissions limit is expressed with reference to the country's 1990 emissions level and must be met as an annual average during 2008–2012.[64] For example, Japan has committed to limiting its annual average emissions during 2008–2012 to a level that is 6 percent below its 1990 emissions.

The protocol incorporates a number of "flexibility mechanisms" designed to allow Annex B countries to meet their commitments cost-effectively. The most prominent flexibility mechanisms are the Article 17 emissions trading mechanism, the Article 6 joint implementation mechanism, and the Article 12 clean development mechanism. Under the Article 17 emissions trading mechanism, an Annex B government can sell its rights to emit to another Annex B government. How does this work? To each Annex B country, the protocol grants assigned amount units (AAUs) equal to its emission limitation commitment. AAUs, therefore, correspond to a quantity of rights to emit. A country can sell some of its AAUs if it projects that it will not need its full allocation to cover its emissions during the commitment period. Article 17 also provides that Annex B governments can authorize private entities to participate in trading. To prevent overselling of AAUs, the protocol requires each Annex B country to keep a certain percentage of its AAUs in a "commitment period reserve."[65]

Under Article 6, an Annex B government or authorized private entity may acquire emission reduction units (ERUs) from another Annex B government by financing a joint implementation (JI) emission reduction or removal project in the latter's country. The project must achieve emission reductions or removals that are additional to those that would occur in the absence of the project. This requirement that the project generate "additional" rather than "anyway" reductions has proved both complicated and controversial. Another requirement is that the project must be approved by both governments involved. Under the protocol, an Annex B country that sells ERUs on the basis of a project must draw the ERUs from its holding of AAUs, which makes joint implementation essentially a project-based form of AAU emissions trading.[66]

Article 12 establishes the clean development mechanism (CDM), under which an Annex B government or authorized private entity can acquire certified emission reductions (CERs) by financing an emission reduction project in a non-Annex B country. As with joint implementation projects, CDM projects must achieve emission reductions or removals that are additional to those that would occur in the absence of the project and must be approved by both the buyer and seller governments. The CDM, however, is subject to a number of other rules that are distinct from the JI context. CDM projects must contribute to sustainable development in the host country. The types of forestry projects eligible for CERs are limited.[67] Most importantly, however, CDM projects are subject to an elaborate process of third-party review and certification to which JI projects are not subject.[68]

The protocol also allows Annex B countries to meet part of their commitment through four categories of domestic land use, land use change, and forestry (LULUCF) activities: re-vegetation, grazing land management, crop land management, and forest management.[69] The Marrakesh Accords allocated to each Annex B country a certain number of tons of carbon intake that it could count toward its quantified emission limitation or reduction commitment from forest management activities.[70] Credits from LULUCF activities are referred to as removal units (RMUs).

Accordingly, another way to express the commitments adopted by Annex B countries is that they are required to ensure that, by the end of the first commitment period, they hold in a national account some combination of AAUs, ERUs, CERs, and RMUs that equals or exceeds their 2008–2012 emissions.

Under its own rules, the protocol will not enter into force under international law unless and until it has been ratified by at least fifty-five countries, including a sufficient number of "Annex I" countries (which comprise all of the Annex B countries but for a few minor exceptions)[71] to account for 55 percent of Annex I emissions in 1990. The protocol has cleared the first hurdle and will clear the second if Russia ratifies.

A number of European countries have started establishing domestic greenhouse gas regulatory programs in anticipation of the protocol's entry into force. The United Kingdom and Denmark, for example, have developed national cap-and-trade programs for carbon dioxide emissions.[72] In addition, the European Union is evaluating the establishment of an EU-wide cap-and-trade program for large emissions sources, which would be launched in phases. In 2002, the EU environmental ministers approved a directive for the proposed program; as of early 2003, it awaits approval by the European Parliament.[73]

As noted above, the Bush administration has declared that the United States will not become a party to the Kyoto Protocol. The administration has argued that the protocol is "fundamentally flawed" because it "fails to establish a long-term goal based on science, poses serious and unnecessary risks to the U.S. and world economies, and is ineffective in addressing climate change because it excludes major parts of the world."[74]

As a nonparty, the United States will not be bound by the protocol if it enters into force. That is not to say, however, that U.S. companies will not feel its effects. If and when Kyoto countries establish domestic GHG reduction programs to meet their commitments under the treaty, U.S.-owned facilities in those countries will be subject to those domestic programs.

Another issue that arises for U.S. companies with regard to the Kyoto Protocol is whether the nonparty status of the United States bars U.S. companies from participating in emissions trading through the Kyoto flexibility mechanisms. The answer appears to be mixed. Under the protocol, emission reductions generated from within a nonparty country cannot become AAUs, ERUs, CERs, or RMUs. Accordingly, there likely will not be much demand for U.S. emission reductions in countries that are parties to the Kyoto Protocol. On the other hand, nothing in the protocol precludes a nonparty government or a company based in a nonparty country from acquiring AAUs, ERUs, CERs, or RMUs. Thus, a U.S. domestic program could recognize Kyoto units purchased by U.S. companies. However, it would be important for the U.S. program to require assurances that a Kyoto unit tendered for compliance in the United States could no longer be used within the Kyoto system. One way to prevent such double-counting would be for the purchased Kyoto unit to be placed in a Kyoto country's "cancellation" account. Under the protocol, units in a cancellation account cannot be used for Kyoto compliance.[75]

Emergence of an International GHG Emissions Trading Market

Over the past five years, an international GHG trading market has emerged, driven by negotiations of the Kyoto Protocol and the growing belief that, even in the United States, the eventual establishment of a mandatory GHG reduction program is highly probable. The Pew Center on Global Climate Change estimates that approximately 65 GHG trades for quantities above 1,000 metric tons of CO_2-equivalent occurred worldwide between 1996 and 2002.[76] The Pew Center notes that this figure likely understates total market activity because not all trades are announced publicly and the figure excludes internal corporate trades. U.S. companies participating in the nascent emissions trading market have several motivations, including to hedge risk of future regulatory exposure, to demonstrate corporate environmental leadership, and to gain experience with what could become a significant compliance tool of the future.

To date, most trades have involved independently verified emission reduction or sequestration projects. Buyers have acquired from sellers the rights to any credits (such as ERUs or CERs) that may be awarded on the basis of the verified emission reductions. While project-based transactions so far have dominated, interest is growing in government-backed emission permits from national climate change programs, such as the domestic emissions trading programs in the United Kingdom and Denmark.[77]

A project-based transaction poses a number of challenges to the advising lawyer.[78] As discussed above, rules for an upgraded U.S. voluntary reporting program and for the Kyoto Protocol's CDM are still under development. Lawyers are scrutinizing the evolution of these rules closely in order to advise clients on the kinds of projects that are likely to be credited. Even at this point, some minimum crediting criteria are clear. For example, project proponents almost certainly will have to demonstrate that the reductions achieved by the project are additional to those otherwise required by law. They also will have to account for any emissions "leakage," i.e., the risk that the project will have the effect of pushing emitting activities to another site. Another significant issue for some types of projects is establishing ownership of the reductions. As discussed above, the issue of ownership arises frequently in the case of projects involving reductions in indirect emissions, e.g., a project where a facility invests in reducing energy use, leading to a reduction in emissions from the power plants that supply the facility with energy. In such a case, both the downstream facility and the upstream power plant(s) may have claims to the emission reductions, but such double-counting would be inappropriate.

Possible Future Directions for a U.S. Mandatory Reduction Program

Experience with voluntary climate change programs in the United States suggests that such programs can slow the rate of growth of GHG emissions but cannot be relied on to achieve reductions in overall levels. Bending the trajectory of U.S. emissions levels downward likely will not be possible without the establishment a domestic GHG regulatory program. A growing literature has identified a set of options for such a program.[79]

Most options for a regulatory program focus on emissions trading approaches, using the CAA acid rain program as a model. See Chapter 12 on the acid rain program, which is found in Title IV of the CAA. The acid rain program caps total annual emissions of sulfur dioxide from electric utilities. The program distributes allowances equal to the cap to the regulated utilities. By an annual compliance deadline, utilities must surrender allowances equal to the annual emissions of their facilities. The approach allows for the development of a market in allowances. Utilities that can limit their emissions at low cost can sell allowances to utilities for which abatement costs are high. If the market is functioning well, sulfur dioxide allowances should end up distributed among regulated utilities in a way that minimizes the cost of reducing emissions. A well-designed emissions trading program can give firms and individuals the incentives and the opportunities to adopt the least-cost means of abating emissions, including switching to less carbon-intensive fuels, increasing their energy efficiency, investing in carbon sequestration, or reducing their consumption.

Developing a U.S. GHG regulatory program that relies on emissions trading involves a number of design determinations. First, it is necessary to determine whether the point of regulation will be emissions sources ("downstream") or fuel producers ("upstream"), or whether it will involve a hybrid approach. Irrespective of the determination as to what firms will be required to surrender allowances, policy makers will need to decide how allowances initially should be allocated. Finally, policy makers will need to determine whether to limit the costs of the program through a "safety valve" mechanism. These issues are discussed below.

What Firms Should Be Regulated and How?

The first decision involved in designing a trading-based GHG regulatory program is determining what firms should be required to surrender allowances. Under a downstream approach, sources would be required to surrender allowances for their emissions.[80] This is the approach reflected in the acid rain program and thus has the advantages of familiarity. As applied in the context of carbon dioxide emissions, however, a downstream system has a significant drawback. While it would be feasible to incorporate electric-generating facilities and other large industrial sources of GHGs in a downstream program, it would not be feasible to regulate the hundreds of thousands of smaller sources of GHGs, such as individual motorists or households. For these reasons, a downstream trading program likely could reach no more than 50 percent of U.S. GHG emissions.

A number of commentators are advocating an upstream approach as an alternative.[81] An upstream emissions trading program would regulate carbon as it enters the economy. It would require firms to surrender allowances for the carbon content of the fuel they sell to downstream users. The Center for Clean Air Policy has determined that an upstream program involving fewer than 2,000 regulated facilities—approximately the same number of facilities subject to the CAA acid rain program—could reach virtually all of the CO_2 emissions in the U.S. economy.[82] These facilities would include a combination of refineries, oil importers, natural gas pipelines and processing plants, and certain coal mines.

As with a downstream system, an upstream trading program would give downstream energy users the incentives and the opportunities to implement the most cost-effective means of achieving emission reductions. The incentive, however, would take a different form. Instead of being subject to an allowance holding requirement, downstream sources would face higher prices for carbon-intensive fuels. Theoretically, downstream energy users should respond to this price signal in the same way as they would to a requirement to hold allowances directly—that is, under an upstream emissions trading program, the cap on fuel carbon would induce downstream sources to adopt the least-cost mix of emission reduction measures.

Undoubtedly, a completely upstream emissions trading approach would mean that motorists and households would see price increases for gasoline and home heating fuels. If policy makers are particularly concerned about shielding consumers from such overt price increases, they might prefer alternative designs. As discussed above, the proposed McCain/Lieberman bill reflects a upstream/downstream hybrid; it would regulate the transportation sector on an upstream basis and the electricity-generation, industrial, and commercial sectors on a downstream basis.

Another hybrid approach would rely on a downstream cap-and-trade program to regulate large sources in the utility and industrial sectors and on product standards to reach emissions in the transportation, residential, and buildings sectors.[83] Such a hybrid program could build on the range of existing energy efficiency and fuel economy standards already established for appliances, equipment, and automobiles. In addition, it would be possible to design the standards as "tradable standards," which would give firms that exceed the standards allowances they could sell to others.[84]

This hybrid approach would have the political advantages of building upon familiar programs and avoiding overt fuel price increases for consumers. However, even the most cost-effective hybrid program likely would be less cost-effective than an economy-wide upstream approach. Standards provide no incentive to adopt what, in many cases, may be the lowest-cost option for lowering emissions: reduced consumption. In the transportation sector, for example, standards could force lower-emitting vehicles into the marketplace, but they would not provide any incentive for motorists to reduce their miles traveled. The absence of any incentive to reduce consumption means that a standards approach—even if the standards are tradable—likely would be a less cost-effective means of meeting any emissions limit than a cap-and-trade program that regulates fuel producers or end-users directly.

How Should Allowances Be Allocated?

The second major decision involved in the design of any program involving emissions trading is how the government initially should allocate allowances. The method by which allowances are allocated can have significant consequences both for the total cost of the program and for the distribution of costs among firms and individuals.

The conventional approach is to distribute allowances on a gratis basis to the firms that will be required to surrender them for compliance. The rationale is that the regulated companies will bear the greatest proportion of the financial impact of the regulatory program. Under the acid rain program, the government has made distributions of allowances to utilities in proportion to each utility's emissions in a historical period. This is sometimes referred to as the grandfather method. Another method of free distribution is to allocate allowances to regulated firms on the basis of their recent or projected output. As applied to utilities, this is sometimes referred to as a generation performance standard (GPS) approach. The GPS approach has a growing number of advocates; they emphasize the potential effectiveness of the GPS approach in rewarding more efficient and lower-emitting forms of generation.

A number of recent studies have suggested that the grandfathering and GPS approaches to allowance allocation might not be optimal in the context of a GHG trading program.[85] Among other things, the studies suggest that the value of the allowances in a GHG trading program likely would exceed the costs directly borne by the regulated firms because those firms will be able to pass some of their costs on to consumers.[86]

In any event, it is clear that distributing all of the allowances to regulated firms would not address the financial impacts sustained by those firms and consumers not subject to regulation. Under any GHG regulation program, these indirect impacts could be significant for coal producers, coal miners and their communities, energy-intensive firms, and consumers of electricity. Distribution of allowances only to regulated firms also would not address the likely reduction in federal tax revenues resulting from the regulatory program's impact on the economy.[87]

For these reasons, recent allowance allocation studies recommend unlinking the allocation of GHG allowances from the incidence of regulation and linking it instead to financial impacts attributable to the regulatory program. In this regard, an important finding of the studies is that the government might need to distribute only a fraction of the total allowance value to major firms, regulated and unregulated, to eliminate their equity losses from GHG regulation.[88] If correct, this means the government could distribute much of the value of the allowances to achieve other purposes, e.g., to help households offset higher electricity prices, to assist hard-hit workers or their communities, or to prevent a drop in government revenues.[89]

A number of economists and policy analysts recommend distributing allowances through an auction.[90] Similar results could be achieved by distributing allowances to a fiduciary, such as the Climate Change Credit Corporation proposed in the McCain/Lieberman bill. Analysts cite two advantages of an auction/fiduciary approach. First, it could provide a potentially more manageable mechanism for distributing the value of the allowances. Rather than distribute allowances to firms and consumers to sell, the government or the fiduciary could sell the allowances and "recycle" the revenue to those groups through payments and/or retain some of the revenues to prevent erosion of the federal tax base.

Recycled revenues also could be used to reduce "distortionary" taxes that encumber economic activity. Public-finance economists argue that existing wage-related taxes create a disincentive to work and that taxes on interest, dividends, capital gains, and corporate income discourage productive investments. According to this argument, using some of the proceeds of an allowance auction to reduce such taxes would result in economic gains that could significantly reduce the cost of GHG regulation to society as a whole.[91]

One option may be to allocate some percentage of allowance value to hard-hit industries and auction the remainder. The allowance allocation studies have found that with an upstream cap-and-trade program, the equity losses of major industries could be addressed through free distribution of less than a quarter of the allowance value. This means that a substantial proportion of allowances could be auctioned and the revenue devoted to efficiency enhancement through cuts in marginal tax rates.

Any allocation approach involving an auction would confront political challenges. First, requiring regulated firms to buy their allowances through a government-run auction could be characterized by its opponents as a new tax. Second, using revenue recycling to reduce taxes implies not only the development of a GHG trading program but also reform of the tax code. For these reasons, policy makers might opt for a phased approach, involving free distribution of a significant proportion of the allowances to major firms in the early years of a GHG program with a gradual shift to greater reliance on auctioning over time.

Should the Program Cap Costs through a "Safety Valve"?

The third critical design issue that arises in designing an emissions trading program is whether the program should provide for a "safety valve" feature. A safety-valve feature would authorize the government to sell additional allowances at a preset price. With such a mechanism in place, the market price of allowances—and therefore the marginal cost of compliance—would rise no higher than the safety-valve price. The effect would be to cap compliance costs.[92]

Establishing a safety valve, however, would mean that emissions would *not* be capped. If compliance costs turned out to be higher than expected, regulated firms could purchase more allowances at the safety-valve price and total emissions would exceed the cap. This is not to say that emissions would be entirely unlimited. Firms would have to pay the safety-valve price to obtain the rights to additional emissions. However, use of a safety-valve mechanism would mean that there was not an absolute cap.

Accordingly, the safety-valve option presents policy makers with a possible choice between emissions certainty and compliance cost certainty. Because the atmosphere is not particularly sensitive to small variations in emissions levels, absolute certainty about meeting a near-term emissions reduction target might not be a high priority. Assurances that compliance costs will not rise above a particular level, on the other hand, could be an important factor in building political support for a regulatory program.[93] A safety-valve mechanism could help remove such concerns as a barrier to action. One approach would be to set the safety-valve price at a level high enough to ensure that it is truly a last resort.

Notes

1. Chlorofluorocarbons (CFCs) also are GHGs but have been less of a focus of climate change policies because they are being eliminated subject to the Montreal Protocol on Substances that Deplete the Ozone Layer. 26 I.L.J. 1550 (1987).

2. For more information on the differences between different types of GHGs and the implications for climate change policies, *see* JOHN M. REILLY, ET AL., PEW CENTER ON GLOBAL CLIMATE CHANGE, MULTI-GAS APPROACHES TO GLOBAL CLIMATE CHANGE (2003).

3. *See* U.S. GREENHOUSE GAS INVENTORY PROGRAM, U.S. ENVIRONMENTAL PROTECTION AGENCY, INVENTORY OF U.S. GREENHOUSE EMISSIONS AND SINKS: 1990–2000 (April 2002).

4. The CAA expressly directs the EPA to regulate two types of GHGs: HFCs and CFCs. *See* Clean Air Act, Title VI, 42 U.S.C. § 7671. However, it calls for such regulation on account of the effects of those substances on the stratospheric ozone layer, not on account of their effects on the climate.

5. For a more extensive analysis of the arguments for and against the EPA's legal authority under the CAA to regulate GHGs, *see* ARNOLD W. REITZE, JR., AIR POLLUTION CONTROL LAW: COMPLIANCE & ENFORCEMENT 414–21 (2001).

6. Memorandum, EPA's Authority to Regulate Pollutants Emitted by Electric Power Generation Sources, from Jonathan Z. Cannon, EPA General Counsel, to Carol M. Browner, EPA Administrator (April 10, 1998).

7. *Id.*

8. *See* 66 Fed. Reg. 7486 (Jan. 23, 2001).

9. In 2003, a group of environmental organizations filed a suit in the District Court for the District of Columbia asserting that the EPA's failure to act on the petition represents a violation of the Administrative Procedure Act. International Center for Technology Assessment v. Whitman, No. DC-1:02 CV 2376 (D.C. Cir. filed Dec. 5, 2002).

10. *See* Letter from Thomas F. Reilly, Massachusetts Attorney General; Richard Blumenthal, Connecticut Attorney General; and G. Steven Rowe, Maine Attorney General; to Christine Todd Whitman, Administrator, U.S. Environmental Protection Agency (January 30, 2003).

11. *See* Letter from Peter Lehner and Jared Snyder, Assistant Attorneys General, State of New York, to Christine Todd Whitman, Administrator, U.S. Environmental Protection Agency (February 20, 2003) (filing notice on behalf of the Attorneys General of New York, Connecticut, Maine, Massachusetts, Rhode Island, New Jersey, and Washington).

12. When the Senate version of the 1990 amendments emerged from the Environment and Public Works Committee it included a Title VII, entitled Stratospheric Ozone and Climate Protection Act of 1989, which called for a reduction, to the maximum extent possible, of anthropogenic emissions of GHGs that were likely to adversely affect the climate. Title VII

also incorporated a tailpipe GHG emissions standard for motor vehicles. *See* The CAA Amendments of 1990, S. 1630 (1990). The final bill that came out of the Senate incorporated Title VII largely as introduced, but the tailpipe emissions standard had been dropped. *See* 136 Cong. Rec. 6579 (1989). In the process of finally enacting the amendments, references to GHGs were removed from the stratospheric ozone depletion title and from all other sections of the amendments with the exception of § 602(e), which provides: "[T]he Administrator shall publish the global warming potential of each listed [ozone-depleting] substance. The preceding sentence shall not be construed to be the basis of any additional regulation under this chapter." Congress also passed an amendment requiring power plants to report their CO_2 emissions annually; the amendment is part of the public law but was not incorporated directly into the text of the CAA. *See* P. L. 101-549, § 821 (Nov. 15, 1990).

13. Joint Hearing of the Subcommittee on National Economic Growth, Natural Resources and Regulatory Affairs of the Committee on Government Reform and the Subcommittee on Energy and Environment of the Committee on Science, U.S. House of Representatives (October 6, 1999) (Statement of Gary S. Guzy, General Counsel, U.S. Environmental Protection Agency). *Available at* http://www.house.gov/science/guzy_100699.htm (emphasis in the original).

14. *See* Peter Glaser, et al., *CO$_2$: A Pollutant? The Legal Affairs Committee Report to the National Mining Association Board of Directors on the Authority of EPA to Regulate Carbon Dioxide under the Clean Air Act* 22–23 (2001), *available at* http://www.nma.org.

15. Testimony of Gary S. Guzy, *supra* note 13.

16. *See* CAA § 103(g), 42 U.S.C. § 7403(g) (directing the EPA to develop a program to develop nonregulatory strategies to address "air pollutants, including . . . carbon dioxide . . . from stationary sources, including fossil fuel power plants.").

17. CAA § 302(h), 42 U.S.C. § 7602. *But see* Reitze, *supra* note 5, at 419. Professor Reitze asserts that a review of the legislative history of the 1970 CAA Amendments, when the relevant language was introduced, reveals no concern about global warming; only the possibility of global warming is raised. Indeed, at that time, there seems to have been a greater concern about a radical *drop* in global temperatures, leading to a new ice age. *Id.*

18. *See* CAA §§ 108–09; 42 U.S.C. §§ 7408–09.

19. Glaser, *supra* note 14.

20. *See* Reitze, *supra* note 5, at 417 (stating that "it is extremely unlikely that Congress gave the Agency the power to enact a potentially costly but futile control mechanism"); Glaser, *supra* note 14; Veronique Bugnion and David M. Reiner, *A Game of Climate Chicken: Can EPA Regulate Greenhouse Gases Before the U.S. Senate Ratifies the Kyoto Protocol?* 30 Envtl. L. 491, 515 (2000) ("The local and regional focus of the criteria air pollutant and hazardous air pollutant provisions seems to create an almost insuperable obstacle to the implementation of restrictions on the emissions of greenhouse gases through Titles I and II of the CAA.")

21. *See* CAA §§ 110(a)(2)(D), 115, 126; 42 U.S.C. §§ 7410(a)(2)(D), 7415, 7426.

22. CAA § 112(b); 42 U.S.C. § 7412(b).

23. *See* Reitze, *supra* note 5, at 417; Glaser, *supra* note 14.

24. CAA § 202(a)(2); 42 U.S.C. § 7521.

25. *See* Reitze, *supra* note 5, at 421.

26. *See generally* U.S. Global Climate Change Policy Book (February 2002).

27. *See* John Podesta, *Do the Math: Under the White House Global Warming Plan, Carbon Dioxide (CO$_2$) Pollution Would Continue Increasing at the Same Rate as the Past Decade,* A.B.A. Comm. on Climate Change and Sustainable Dev. Newsl., Vol. 5, No. 3 (March 2002); Stuart E. Eizenstat, Frank E. Loy, and David B. Sandalow, *President Bush's Disappointing Climate Proposal,* A.B.A. Comm. on Climate Change and Sustainable Dev. Newsl., Vol. 5, No. 3 (March 2002).

28. Letter from Spencer Abraham, Secretary of Energy; Donald L. Evans, Secretary of Commerce, Ann M. Veneman, Secretary of the Interior; and Christine Todd Whitman, Administrator, Environmental Protection Agency, to President George W. Bush (July 8, 2002).

29. U.S. Global Climate Change Policy Book.

30. For more information on the concepts of baseline protection and credit for early action, *see* Robert R. Nordhaus and Stephen C. Fotis, *Early Action and Global Climate Change,* Pew Center on Global Climate Change (October 1998).

31. *See* U.S. Environmental Protection Agency, Climate Leaders Program, *available at* http://www.epa.gov/climateleaders/index.html.

32. *See* S. 139, 108th Cong. (2003).

33. Under the bill, any firm in the electricity-generating, industrial, or commercial sectors would be subject to regulation if it emits (in the aggregate) over 10,000 metric tons of carbon-dioxide equivalent GHG emissions annually. *Id.* at § 3(4).

34. *Id.* at Title III, Subtitle B.

35. *Id.* at Title III, Subtitle C.

36. *Id.* at Title II, Subtitle A.

37. These "four-pollutant" bills include S. 556, 107th Cong. (Jeffords, I-VT), and S. 3135, 107th Cong. (Carper, D-DE).

38. H.R. 999, 108th Cong. (Barton, R-TX), and S. 485, 108th Cong. (Inhofe, R-OK).

39. *See* U.S. Environmental Protection Agency, U.S. Department of Energy, Analysis of Strategies for Reducing Multiple Emissions from Electric Power Plants: Sulfur Dioxide, Nitrogen Oxides, Carbon Dioxide, and Mercury and a Renewable Portfolio Standard, Report #SR/OIAF/2001-003 (2001); U.S. Department of Energy, Analysis of Strategies for Reducing Multiple Emissions from Power Plants: Sulfur Dioxide, Nitrogen Oxides, and Carbon Dioxide, Report #SR/OIAF/2000-005 (December 2000); U.S. Environmental Protection Agency, Office of Air and Radiation, Analysis of Emission Reduction Options for the Electric Power Industry (March 1999).

40. *See* D. Smith, et al., *Designing a Climate-Friendly Energy Policy: Options for the Near-Term,* Pew Center on Global Climate Change 24 (July 2002).

41. *See, e.g.,* S. 17, 108th Cong. (2003); Energy Policy Act of 2002, H.R. 4, Title XI, as passed by the U.S. Senate (April 25, 2002).

42. *See* A.B. 1493, signed on July 22, 2002, amending § 43018.5 of the CA Health and Safety Code.

43. The law explains that "maximum feasible and cost-effective reduction of greenhouse gas emissions" means the level of reductions that CARB determines meet two criteria: (1) "[c]apable of being successfully accomplished within the time provided by this section, taking into account environmental, economic, social, and technological factors"; and (2) "economical to an owner or operator of a vehicle, taking into account the full life-cycle of a vehicle." CA Health and Safety Code at § 43018.5(i)(1)(A), (B).

44. *Id.* at § 43018.5(a), (b).

45. *Id.* at § 43018.5(c)(3).

46. *Id.* at § 43018.5(d).

47. *See* 49 U.S.C. § 32919 (preempting any state law or regulation "related to fuel economy standards or average fuel economy standards for automobiles covered by an average fuel economy standard").

48. *See* Order Granting Plaintiff's Motion for Preliminary Injunction and Issuing Preliminary Injunction, Central Valley Chrysler-Plymouth v. California Air Resources Board, No. CV-F-02-5017 (E.D. Cal.) (June 11, 2002).

49. CAA § 209(b)(1).

50. *Id.* § 209(b)(1)(A)–(C).

51. *See* Emissions Standards for Power Plants, Mass. Regs. Code tit. 310 § 7.29 (2001) (setting forth Massachusetts multipollutant emission limitations for utilities) and H.B. 284-FN (effective July 1, 2002) (setting forth New Hampshire multipollutant emission limitations for utilities).

52. *See* Oregon Administrative Rules, Chapter 345, Division 24.

53. *See generally* Conference of New England Governors and Eastern Canadian Premiers, Resolution No. 26-4: Resolution Concerning Energy and the Environment (Aug. 2001), *available at* http://www.scics.gc.ca/cinfo01/850084007_e.html. The group includes the Governors and Premiers of Connecticut, Maine, New Hampshire, Rhode Island, Vermont, Quebec, Newfoundland, New Brunswick, Nova Scotia, and Prince Edward Island. The plan calls for the establishment of an implementation task force and proposes to standardize emission inventories for each jurisdiction; establish a reduction GHG reduction plan; promote alternative fuels; establish adaptation and mitigation measures; and create an emission registry for the region.

54. U.S. *on Sidelines, but States Active Amid Kyoto Debate,* Greenwire, June 3, 2002.

55. *See States Lay Groundwork for Possible U.S. Greenhouse Gas Registry,* Inside EPA, Jan. 31, 2002.

56. For more information on state climate change initiatives, *see generally* John Dernbach, *Moving the Climate Change Debate from Models to Proposed Legislation: Lessons from State Experience,* 30 Envtl. L. Rep. 10,993 (Nov. 2000) and *Climate Change Activities in the United States,* Pew Center on Global Climate Change 18–19 (June 2002).

57. *See Climate Change Activities in the United States,* Pew Center on Global Climate Change, *supra* note 56, at 18–19 (providing a list of thirty-eight businesses based or operating in the United States that have set voluntary corporate emission reduction targets).

58. For more information on the Chicago Climate Exchange, *see* http://www .chicagoclimatex.com/.

59. *See Trading Poised to Begin in First-Ever U.S. Voluntary Climate Program,* Clean Air Rep. (September 26, 2002).

60. 31 I.L.M. 849 (1992) [hereinafter UNFCCC].

61. *Id.* at art. 2.

62. Kyoto Protocol to the United Nations Framework Convention on Climate Change, 37 I.L.M. 22 (1998) [hereinafter Kyoto Protocol]; Report of the Conference of the Parties on its Seventh Session, held at Marrakesh from 29 October to 10 November (2001), FCCC/CP/2001/13 [hereinafter Marrakesh Accords].

63. The Annex B countries consist of Australia, Austria, Belgium, Bulgaria, Canada, Croatia, the Czech Republic, Denmark, Estonia, the European Community, Finland, France, Germany, Greece, Hungary, Iceland, Ireland, Italy, Japan, Latvia, Liechtenstein, Lithuania, Luxembourg, Monaco, the Netherlands, New Zealand, Norway, Poland, Portugal, Romania, the Russian Federation, Slovakia, Slovenia, Spain, Sweden, Switzerland, Ukraine, the United Kingdom, and the United States.

64. Articles 3.5 and 3.8 of the Kyoto Protocol provide limited exceptions to this approach: Article 3.5 provides that Annex I countries "undergoing the process of transition to a market economy" may use a base year other than 1990. In addition, Article 3.8 provides that Annex I parties may use 1995 as a base year for emissions of HFCs, PFCs, and SF_6.

65. *See* Marrakesh Accords, FCCC/CP/2001/13/Add.2, Decision 18/CP.7, Annex, at 54.

66. *See* Kyoto Protocol, art. 3.11.

67. Only afforestation and reforestation projects are eligible under the CDM. *See* Marrakesh Accords, FCCC/CP/2001/13/Add.2, Decision 17/CP.7, ¶ 7(a), at 22. In addi-

tion, the amount of afforestation and reforestation CERs an Annex B country may use for compliance may not be greater than the equivalent of one percent of its base year (usually 1990) emissions times five. *Id*. at ¶ 7(b).

68. Note, however, that third-party review and certification procedures apply to JI projects in which the Annex B country in which the project is sited (sometimes called the "host Party") is not in compliance with certain reporting requirements under the Kyoto Protocol. *See* Marrakesh Accords, FCCC/CP/2001/13/Add.2, Decision 16/CP.7, Annex, ¶ 24, at 13.

69. *See* Marrakesh Accords, FCCC/CP/2001/13/Add.2, Decision 12/CP.7.

70. For all Annex I countries other than Russia, the forest management allocations appear at Marrakesh Accords, FCCC/CP/2001/13/Add.1, Decision 12/CP.7, Appendix, at 63. Russia's limit appears at Marrakesh Accords, FCCC/CP/2001/13/Add.1, Decision 13/CP.7, at 64.

71. The Annex I list stems from the UNFCCC. The differences between the Annex I list and the Annex B list mostly reflect the breakup of Czechoslovakia and Yugoslavia.

72. Information on the UK emissions trading program can be found at the Web site for the UK Department of Environment, Food, and Rural Affairs, http://www.defra.gov.uk/environment/climatechange/index.htm.

73. *See* Proposal for a Directive of the European Parliament and of the Council Establishing a Scheme for Greenhouse Gas Emissions Allowance Trading within the Community and Amending Council Directive 96/61/EC, Interinstitutional File: 2001/0245 (COD) (Dec. 11, 2002), *available at* http://europa.eu.int/eur-lex/pri/en/oj/dat/2002/ce075/ce07520020326en00330044.pdf (last visited Jan. 16, 2003). Under the approved directive, the EU will implement the cap-and-trade program in two phases, a 2005–2007 phase and a 2008–2012 phase. All firms engaged in heat and power production, steel, cement, glass, tile, paper, and cardboard production will be subject to CO_2 emissions caps, which member states will establish with approval by the EU commission. In the first phase, however, sectors may opt out of the scheme, subject to certain requirements. This provision is intended to accommodate the concerns of Germany, United Kingdom, and a handful of other states, which had pushed for an entirely voluntary scheme in light of the domestic programs they already had established. Under the compromise approach, participation will be mandatory during 2008–2012. In addition, the program eventually will bring in additional sectors, including the chemical and aluminum industries, and will cover other greenhouse gases.

74. *Analysis of the Kyoto Protocol*, U.S. Global Climate Change Policy Book.

75. *See* Marrakesh Accords, FCCC/CP/2001/13/Add.2, Decision 19/CP.7, Annex, at 65.

76. *See* Richard Rosenzweig, Matthew Varilek, and Josef Janssen, *The Emerging International Greenhouse Gas Market*, Pew Center on Global Climate Change iv (March 2002).

77. For example, one of the first trades under Denmark's emissions trading program involved the purchase of allowances, not by a Danish company, but by an electric utility in the United States. Entergy, based in Arkansas, has adopted a voluntary goal of stabilizing its GHG emissions at 2000 levels by 2005. In 2001, the company purchased and "retired" 10,000 metric tons of Danish allowances, thereby preventing any company from using those allowances to authorize an equivalent amount of emissions. *See* Chris Holly, *Entergy, Danish Utility Make International Greenhouse Swap*, Energy Daily, v. 20, no. 234 (Dec. 7, 2001).

78. *See* Kyle W. Danish and Jonathan C. Rotter, *Drafting Contracts for Greenhouse Gas Offset Projects in Developing Countries*, 15 Nat. Resources & Env't 168 (2001).

79. For comparative reviews and assessments of different options proposed in the literature and in policy-making arenas, *see* ROBERT R. NORDHAUS AND KYLE W. DANISH, PEW CENTER ON GLOBAL CLIMATE CHANGE, DESIGNING A MANDATORY DOMESTIC GREEN-HOUSE GAS REDUCTION PROGRAM (forthcoming 2003); U.S. CONGRESSIONAL BUDGET OFFICE, AN EVALUATION OF CAP-AND-TRADE PROGRAMS FOR REDUCING U.S. CARBON EMIS-SIONS (2001); H. JOHN HEINZ CENTER FOR SCIENCE, ECONOMICS, AND THE ENVIRONMENT, DESIGNS FOR DOMESTIC CARBON EMISSIONS TRADING (1998); and ENVIRONMENTAL LAW INSTITUTE, IMPLEMENTING AN EMISSIONS CAP AND ALLOWANCE TRADING SYSTEM FOR GREENHOUSE GASES: LESSONS LEARNED FROM THE ACID RAIN PROGRAM (1997).

80. A number of extant proposals would establish a downstream cap-and-trade program for CO_2 emissions by electric utilities. These proposals include three bills intro-duced in the 107th Congress. *See* H.R. 1256, H.R. 1335, and S. 556. The laws established in Massachusetts and New Hampshire, discussed *supra*, reflect a downstream approach. Papers by the Progressive Policy Institute outline proposals for a downstream cap-and-trade program including not only electric power generators but also other large industrial sources. *See* J. Naimon and D. Knopman, *Reframing the Climate Change Debate: The United States Should Build a Domestic Market Now for Greenhouse Gas Emissions Reductions*, PRO-GRESSIVE POL'Y INST. (Nov. 1, 1999), *available at* http://www.ppionline.org; D. Knopman and J. Naimon, *How a Domestic Greenhouse Gas Emissions Trading Market Could Work in Practice: A Supplement to the November 1999 Policy Report "Reframing the Climate Change Debate,"* PROGRESSIVE POL'Y INST. (Mar. 1, 2000), *available at* http://www.ppionline.org. In a study for the World Wildlife Fund, the Tellus Institute analyzed and recommended a downstream cap-and-trade program for the electricity-generating sector with a range of standards and incentive programs. Alison Bailie, et al., *The American Way to the Kyoto Pro-tocol: An Economic Analysis to Reduce Carbon Pollution*, WORLD WILDLIFE FUND, TELLUS INST., AND STOCKHOLM ENV'T INST.—BOSTON CENTER (July 2001), *available at* http://www.worldwildlife.org/. Finally, three different coalitions of electric power generators have proposed various versions of a multi-emissions program with CO_2 trading for gen-erators. *See New Utility Proposal Advocates Voluntary Carbon Cuts*, INSIDE EPA (Sept. 7, 2001) (describing proposal of the coalition Energy for a Clean Air Future, which consists of PPL, Reliant, TECO Energy, Transalta, and Wisconsin Energy); *Competing Utility Emis-sions Plans May Create Congressional Hurdle*, INSIDE EPA (Aug. 17, 2001) (describing pro-posals of the coalition Clean Power Group [consisting of NiSource, Enron, Calpine, El Paso, and Trigen] and the coalition Clean Energy Group [consisting of Conectiv, Consoli-dated Edison, Northeast Utilities, PG&E National Energy Group, and Sempra Energy]).

81. Americans for Equitable Climate Solutions, with support from Resources for the Future, has proposed an upstream cap-and-trade program, called the Sky Trust. *See* Americans for Equitable Climate Solutions, *Sky Trust Initiative: Economy-Wide Proposal to Reduce U.S. Carbon Emissions* (Dec. 2000); Richard D. Morgenstern, *Reducing Carbon Emis-sions and Limiting Costs*, RESOURCES FOR THE FUTURE (February 2002), *available at* http://www.rff.org. In its evaluation of four options for a U.S. GHG cap-and-trade pro-gram, the Congressional Budget Office gave an option modeled on the Sky Trust the highest ratings. *See* U.S. Congressional Budget Office, *supra* note 79. The proposal also has received favorable notices in *The Economist* and *The New Republic*. *See A Novel Approach to Tackling Climate Change Could Satisfy Economists and Environmentalists Alike*, THE ECONO-MIST, February 14, 2002; Gregg Easterbrook, *How W. Can Save Himself on Global Warming*, THE NEW REPUBLIC, July 23, 2001.

82. T. Hargrave, *U.S. Carbon Emissions Trading: Description of an Upstream Approach*, CENTER FOR CLEAN AIR POLICY (1998), *available at* http://www.ccap.org.

83. *See* Nordhaus and Danish, *supra* note 79.

84. For a description of tradable standards, *see id.* and Heinz Center, *supra* note 79, at Appendix 5.

85. *See e.g.*, Anne E. Smith and Martin T. Ross, *Allowance Allocation: Who Wins and Loses under a Carbon Dioxide Control Program?* Center for Clean Air Pol'y (February 2002), *available at* http://www.ccap.org; Dallas Burtraw, Karen Palmer, Ranji Bharvikar, *The Effect on Asset Values of the Allocation of Carbon Dioxide Emission Allowances*, Discussion Paper 02-14, Resources for the Future (2002), *available at* http://www.rff.org; Lee Lane, *Allocation of Allowances and Consumer Impacts*, Americans for Equitable Climate Solutions (May 2002); Dallas Burtraw, et al., *The Effect of Allowance Allocation on the Cost of Carbon Emission Trading*, Discussion Paper 01-30, Resources for the Future (2001), *available at* http://www.rff.org; A. Lans Bovenburg and Lawrence Goulder, *Neutralizing the Adverse Industry Impacts of CO_2 Abatement Policies: What Does It Cost?* Working Paper 7654, Nat'l Bureau Econ. Res., Inc. (2000), *available at* http://www.nber.org/papers/w7654.

86. Indeed, one study found that, in an economy-wide upstream cap-and-trade program, free distribution of all allowances to the electricity sector actually would increase the sector's net worth by 50 percent. *See* Smith and Ross, *supra* note 85, at 5. *See also* Lawrence H. Goulder, *Mitigating the Adverse Impacts of CO_2 Abatement Policies on Energy-Intensive Industries*, 17–18 (September 2001) (finding that, in a scenario in which all allowances are distributed gratis to fuel producers, coal industry profits rise by 155 percent in 2002 and by 218 percent in 2025; coal industry equity values increase by a factor of seven over the same time period). Of course, the impacts would vary on a company-by-company basis. For example, overcompensation might not result for utilities subject to cost-of-service regulation if regulators were to require the allowances they used to be valued at zero cost for rate-making purposes.

87. A critical finding of the Smith/Ross study was that the GHG program it modeled would reduce U.S. tax revenues by $50 billion in 2010. This would correspond to 56 percent of the total value of the allowances created under the program. *See* Smith and Ross, *supra* note 85, at 21.

88. *See, e.g.*, Smith and Ross, *supra* note 85; Burtraw, Palmer, and Bharvikar, *supra* note 85; Bovenburg and Goulder, *supra* note 85; Goulder, *supra* note 86. Note, however, that these studies examined economy-wide upstream trading programs. Different results would occur under a domestic program in which a smaller proportion of emissions were regulated through market-based approaches, *e.g.*, a program that combined a downstream cap-and-trade program for large industrial sources and non-tradable standards for non-industrial emissions. *See* Smith and Ross, *supra* note 85, at 31. The lower cost-effectiveness of such a program would mean that equity losses of major industries could be greater. At the same time, the pool of allowances available to mitigate those losses would be smaller.

89. *See, e.g.*, S. 556 (Jeffords, I-VT), as passed by the Senate Environment and Public Works Committee on June 27, 2002. S. 556 would establish a utility cap-and-trade program covering emissions of CO_2, NO_x, and SO_2. Under the S. 556 scheme, the government would allocate allowances annually to five groups: consumers and households (approximately 64 percent); transition assistance for displaced workers and communities (approximately 4.8 percent); companies with electricity-intensive products, such as coal and aluminum (approximately 1.2 percent); renewable energy-efficiency/cleaner energy (20 percent); carbon sequestration (approximately .075 percent); and existing units (approximately 10 percent declining to 1 percent in 2017). For a number of the categories, allowances would go to a

trustee, who then would be responsible for selling the allowances and redistributing the revenues according to various formulae.

90. *See, e.g.*, Smith and Ross, *supra* note 85; Burtraw, *supra* note 85; Goulder, *supra* note 86; U.S. CONGRESSIONAL BUDGET OFFICE, *supra* note 79; Peter Cramton and Suzi Kerr, *Tradable Carbon Permit Auctions: How and Why to Auction Not Grandfather*, Discussion Paper 98-34, RESOURCES FOR THE FUTURE (May 1998), *available at* www.rff.org.

91. Economists are careful to note that such efficiency improvements would result only from reductions in marginal taxes. Increases in standard deductions or other per person or per household rebates, on the other hand, do not produce such economic gains. Such approaches just redistribute the costs of the GHG regulatory program.

92. *See* Henry D. Jacoby and A. Denny Ellerman, *The Safety Valve and Climate Policy*, Report No. 83, MIT JOINT PROGRAM ON SCI. & POL'Y GLOBAL CLIMATE CHANGE (February 2002), *available at* http://web.mit.edu/globalchange/www/reports.html.

93. *See* William Pizer, *Choosing Price or Quantity Controls for Greenhouse Gases*, Climate Brief #17, RESOURCES FOR THE FUTURE (July 1999), *available at* http://www.rff.org.

CHAPTER 15

Overview of the Title V Operating Permit Program

DAVID P. NOVELLO

Introduction

Title V of the Clean Air Act (CAA), added by Title V of the 1990 CAA Amendments, creates a federally mandated operating permit program to be implemented by the states.[1] The issuance of Title V permits in recent years has made major changes to the CAA implementation scheme that evolved between passage of the original act in 1970 and passage of the 1990 CAA Amendments. This chapter provides an overview of Title V's principal permitting requirements as well as the EPA's implementing regulations. (Chapter 16 describes what a facility should do after its Title V permit is issued.)

Title V calls on states to establish their own operating permit programs and to issue permits themselves. Following significant delays, by early 2003 the vast majority of states (and localities that will carry out Title V permitting) had received final EPA approval of their programs and had issued a number of permits. Environmentalists have criticized the pace of permit issuance, however, and have even successfully sued a state agency to speed up the process.[2] In 2002, the EPA inspector general also issued a report critical of the states' progress in issuing Title V permits, pointing out that states had not yet issued permits for approximately 30 percent of sources required to have a permit.[3]

Before 1990, the CAA contained permit requirements only for certain new or modified major stationary sources of air pollution. These provisions (described in Chapter 5) require such sources to obtain a permit from the state or the EPA before building. Many states are therefore authorized to issue these new source review (NSR) permits.

In addition, many states over the years had developed and implemented their own *operating* permit programs for *existing* sources of air pollution, even though such programs were not mandated by federal law.[4] These programs varied widely in their scope and requirements. With enactment of the 1990 CAA Amendments, however, all states are now required to carry out state operating permit programs that meet the minimum requirements of Title V and the EPA's implementing regulations. For facilities subject to Title V, the operating permit has become the implementation vehicle for nearly all stationary source requirements found in the CAA.

Title V required the EPA to issue regulations describing the minimum elements of state permit programs. The EPA proposed these rules for public comment on May 10, 1991,[5] and issued the final rules on July 21, 1992.[6] These regulations are the heart of CAA permitting, establishing the floor for approvable state programs. Numerous industry groups, environmentalists, and states challenged many aspects of the EPA's rules in court.[7] As of early 2003, few of the litigated issues have been resolved, and there appears to be no real movement to resolve permit revision and other issues that the parties had spent much time negotiating in the early to mid-1990s.

The EPA's permit program regulations, together with the preamble, occupy sixty-three pages in the *Federal Register*. The rules are codified in Part 70 of 40 C.F.R. and, thus, are often referred to as the "Part 70 rules." States were required to comply with these rules when they adopted their own permit legislation and regulations. It is important to remember that companies are not directly regulated under the Part 70 rules; rather, these rules represent the minimum required for state-adopted permit programs. Companies need to apply for and receive permits under each state's rules.

The EPA's rules often leave states discretion to meet the minimum elements, and many states with existing operating permit systems have kept aspects of their programs. Thus, Title V permit programs vary among the states.

In states that fail to adopt approvable programs, the EPA is required to step in and issue operating permits. To this end, in 1996 the agency issued *federal* permit regulations—found in 40 C.F.R. Part 71—to use if it needs to act as the permitting agency in any state, and also for EPA permitting of facilities on Indian tribal lands.[8] However, because state agencies that run their own programs are able to collect permit fees, states are unlikely to relinquish this role. In February 1999, the agency issued its final rules to implement Part 71 permits on such tribal lands,[9] and it revised those regulations three years later.[10]

Goals of the Title V Permit Program

The EPA included an operating permits title in the CAA amendments bill that the administration of George H. W. Bush sent to Congress in 1989.[11] The EPA advocated the operating permits concept so that all applicable CAA requirements for a source could be consolidated in one document.[12] (Permits issued under the Clean Water Act's national pollutant discharge elimination system, or NPDES, program—the model for the CAA permits legislation—serve this purpose for water pollution requirements.) The operating permit for a chemical plant, for example, would contain all relevant air emissions limitations, monitoring, and reporting requirements found in the state implementation plan (SIP). The permit would also contain hazardous air pollutant regulations under CAA Section 112, new source performance standards (NSPS) under CAA Section 111, prevention of signification deterioration (PSD) or nonattainment NSR permits, and any other applicable CAA rules.

Bringing these requirements together would allow the EPA, states, and citizens[13] to bring enforcement actions more easily against sources exceeding their emissions limitations. In the past, it has often been unclear whether specific CAA rules (especially SIP rules) apply to a particular source. Moreover, many CAA rules contain only sketchy monitoring and reporting requirements. Including all applicable provisions in the permit would make it easier to decide which rules apply and whether they are being satisfied.

The EPA had also hoped that the new permit program would lead to a streamlining of SIPs, thereby allowing quicker changes in requirements for individual sources. Lastly, the EPA needed an implementation vehicle for the new Title IV acid rain program and favored an operating permit system as this vehicle.

Opponents of the Title V operating permit program have vigorously contested these purported benefits. They have particularly protested the analogy to the NPDES permit system, arguing that NPDES grew up with the water program, while the EPA attempted to graft the Title V permit program onto a mature and elaborate system of CAA regulations.[14] The critics' major complaint, however, has been the program's price. They argue that the benefits are not worth the paperwork and compliance costs.

Applicability

The applicability provisions (found in CAA Sections 502(a) and 504(a) and Section 70.3 of the EPA's Part 70 regulations) answer two basic questions: who must obtain a Title V permit and what CAA requirements the permit must include. The first question is answered by Sections 70.3(a) and 70.3(b), which are based on CAA Section 502(a). A permit program is required to provide for the permitting of at least sources defined as "major" under the Part 70 rules; sources subject to a standard or regulation promulgated under CAA Section 111 (the NSPS or NSPS provision) or Section 112 (the hazardous air pollutant provision);[15] "affected" sources under the acid rain provisions of the act; sources required to have a PSD permit under Title I, Part C, or an NSR permit under Title I, Part D; and any other sources in a category designated by the EPA. States may also include additional sources in their permit programs.

Note that states may issue one permit for the entire source or different permits for the various units,[16] as long as the entire source is permitted one way or the other. The applicability rules determine whether a source needs to have a permit; they do not dictate that the state must issue only one permit, rather than multiple ones. Under current state operating permit programs, many large facilities receive numerous permits. Among other advantages, this allows companies to stagger information gathering, paperwork, and other burdens over several years.[17]

Definition of Major Source

The EPA's complicated definition of major source[18] cannot be briefly summarized. Suffice it to say that, as required by CAA Section 501(2), it sweeps in the 1990 amendments' many new major source thresholds for sources emitting various types of pollutants. For example, a source with the potential to emit 10 tons per year (tpy) of any one hazardous air pollutant listed under CAA Section 112(b), or 25 tpy of any combination of such pollutants, is a major source. The major source definition is based on the amount of potential emissions from the source, regardless of whether it is subject to existing requirements. Thus, a source that has the potential to emit over 10 tpy of a hazardous air pollutant must obtain a permit even if the EPA is not scheduled to promulgate a CAA Section 112 standard for that source category for several years.[19]

Part of the EPA's complicated major source definition focuses on whether various emission units will be grouped together to aggregate their emissions to determine whether these emissions thresholds are met. The definition states that a major source is "any stationary source (or any group of stationary sources that are located on one or more contiguous or adjacent properties, and are under common control of the same person [or persons under common control]) belonging to a single major industrial grouping" that emits quantities of pollutants at or above the threshold level.[20]

Different units are part of the same industrial grouping if the pollutant-emitting activities at the source have the same two-digit Standard Industrial Classification (SIC) code.[21] The EPA also aggregates units by SIC code in its PSD and NSR programs, and Congress seems to have intended for the agency to do the same for operating permits.[22] Under this approach, two dissimilar operations (e.g., a power plant and an adjacent coal mine) would be treated as different sources unless, under a test derived from the NSR program, equipment at one operation is considered to be a "support facility" of the other operation.[23]

Potential to Emit and Synthetic Minors

Moreover, whether a source is "major" depends on its potential to emit (PTE), not on actual emissions. The EPA defines "potential to emit" in a manner similar to its definition under the PSD and nonattainment NSR permit programs. Potential to emit is

> the maximum capacity of a stationary source to emit any air pollutant under its physical and operational design. Any physical or operational limitation on the capacity of a source to emit an air pollutant, including air pollution control equipment and restrictions on hours of operation or on the type or amount of material combusted, stored or processed, shall be treated as part of its design if the limitation is enforceable by the Administrator.[24]

Thus, even if the source might have an operational capacity giving it the capability to emit more than the tpy thresholds found in the definition of major source, it need not obtain an operating permit if it restricts that capability in a way that the EPA can enforce. This, however, creates a chicken-and-egg problem. An operating permit can be used to restrict the capability to pollute in an enforceable manner, but the source's aim in restricting the capability is to avoid the need to obtain a permit. In the preamble to its final rules, the EPA suggested possible ways around this problem (but it did not provide much guidance).

Since issuance of the Part 70 rules, industry and many states have clamored for easier ways to limit a source's PTE. They have also called for EPA guidance on this very important subject. In their view, far too many sources are included in the Title V system, and the EPA has not done enough to make it easier for these sources to limit their PTE and be excluded. In particular, industry and states have criticized the EPA's requirement that limitations or controls be "federally enforceable" to count as restrictions on a source's PTE. Industry groups challenged this requirement in petitions for review of the Part 70 rules as well as in other contexts. In two cases decided in 1995, the D.C. Circuit Court of Appeals seriously questioned the validity of this "federally enforceable" requirement, although not in the context of the Title V rules.[25] Then in 1996 the D.C. Circuit vacated the PTE definition in the EPA's Part 70 rules.[26]

EPA Guidance on Potential to Emit

In 1996, shortly after the D.C. Circuit's vacatur of the PTE definition in the Part 70 rules, the EPA issued a guidance memorandum that essentially said the vacatur would have no effect in the short term because state Title V rules already required that limits on a facility's PTE be federally enforceable. The EPA stated that it "interprets the court order vacating the part 70 definition as not affecting any requirement for Federal enforceability in existing State rules and programs, that is, whether Federal enforceability is required as a matter of State law."[27] This same August 17, 1996, EPA guidance memorandum extended yet a third EPA memorandum (dated January 25, 1995) on "transition policy" regarding PTE issues. In that January 25, 1995, memorandum, the EPA identified five ways in which sources may limit their PTE.

1. Federally enforceable state operating permit programs (FESOPs), that is, non-Title V permits that have been adopted into a SIP and which the EPA therefore may enforce
2. Limits established by state rules that the EPA approves into the SIP
3. General permits (discussed later)
4. Federally enforceable state construction permits
5. Title V permits (for those who wish to limit their potential to emit to avoid substantive standards, such as an air toxics standard)[28]

The EPA maintains that restrictions on a source's PTE also must meet requirements concerning what the agency calls "practicable enforceability";

the EPA's intent is that the "limitations and restrictions must be of sufficient quality and quantity to ensure accountability."[29]

In addition, the January 25, 1995, memorandum adopted a policy that would allow relaxed PTE requirements for a two-year transition period. (The EPA subsequently extended the transition period through June 30, 2001.[30]) During the transition period, state or local agencies may allow sources whose actual emissions are below 50 percent of all major source thresholds to be considered nonmajor sources. A source's emissions had to be below this level for every consecutive twelve-month period beginning on January 25, 1994. Under this "prohibitory rule" approach, sources would have to maintain adequate records on site to show that their actual emissions did not exceed the 50 percent level. According to the EPA, "A source that exceeds the 50 percent threshold, without complying with major source requirements of the Act (or without otherwise limiting its potential to emit), could be subject to enforcement."[31]

For the same transition period, states could allow sources whose operations are restricted only by a state permit that is not federally enforceable to use these state restrictions to avoid major source status. The EPA, however, imposed three qualifications to this general rule:

1. The state permit must be enforceable as a practical matter.
2. The source owner must submit a written certification to the EPA stating that it will comply with the limits as a restriction on its potential to emit.
3. The source owner must state in this certification that the EPA and citizens may enforce the emission limits.[32]

In 1998, the EPA also issued guidance to allow states to more easily create PTE limits for certain types of small sources. In this document, the EPA identified eight source categories for which a single type of activity tends to dominate emissions, and for which most sources in the category emit at levels well below their potential and also well below the major source thresholds. The guidance then described ways that companies and the states could clarify that these facilities are minor sources.[33]

Permanent Exemptions and Deferral for Nonmajor Sources

CAA Section 502(a) allows the EPA to exempt source categories from permitting requirements "if the Administrator finds that compliance with such requirements is impracticable, infeasible, or unnecessarily burdensome on such categories, except that the Administrator may not exempt any major source from such requirements." In its final rules, the EPA exempted asbestos demolition and renovation projects and wood stoves (which otherwise would need permits because they are subject to Section 112 and Section 111 standards, respectively).[34] It subsequently exempted other source categories, and in December 1999 issued a final rule allowing states to continue to defer Title V permitting for these categories until December 2003.[35]

In its 1992 rules, the EPA also decided to *temporarily* exempt (i.e., defer permitting obligations for) nearly all nonmajor sources. States need not permit them until the EPA has completed a future rule making on "how the program should be structured for nonmajor sources and the appropriateness of any [additional] permanent exemptions."[36] In 1992, the EPA predicted that it would complete this rule making within five years after it approved the first state program that deferred permitting requirements for nonmajor sources.[37] It has not taken any action since that time, however. States remain free not to defer permitting obligations for some or all nonmajor sources.[38]

The EPA granted this blanket deferral because it believed that the administrative burdens on state agencies would make permitting impracticable and infeasible in the early years, when the agencies had to struggle to get their programs under way. In short, states would be swamped by many thousands of applications. The EPA estimated that there are tens of thousands of major sources in the United States;[39] although estimates for nonmajor sources are much sketchier, hundreds of thousands may exist.

A second rationale the EPA offered for the deferral is that permitting in the early years of the program would be a nightmare for nonmajor sources, a great majority of which are owned by small businesses. These sources will need the most assistance from state agencies and the EPA, and assistance likely will not be available if the agencies are overburdened with thousands of permit applications.[40]

There are several exceptions to the EPA's general deferral for nonmajor sources. First, all nonmajor solid waste incineration units required to obtain a permit under CAA Section 129(e) and all nonmajor acid rain–affected sources (if any exist) must apply for a permit at the start of the program.[41] Second, when the EPA promulgates Section 111 or 112 standards, it will decide in those rule makings whether sources regulated by the standards will need to obtain a Title V permit.[42] In 1995 the agency indicated that nonmajor sources in several categories subject to Section 112 standards probably would not need to obtain permits for a five-year period, and it has taken no further action since that time.[43]

Applicable Requirements

Section 70.3(c)(1) answers the second applicability question: what CAA requirements the permit must include. It states that a permit for a major source must contain all applicable requirements for each of the source's regulated emission units. In other words, though a source may be classified as major owing to its sulfur dioxide emissions, all relevant CAA requirements for all pollutants—such as Section 112 standards and ozone SIP requirements—must be in the permit.[44]

For a nonmajor source required to have a permit, the EPA's rules require only that the permit include "all applicable requirements applicable to emission units that cause the source to be subject to the Part 70 program."[45] Thus, if a nonmajor source must obtain a permit only because it contains an oil-fired burner subject to a CAA Section 111 NSPS, the permit would have to address only the burner.[46]

Section 504(a) states that the permit must assure compliance with applicable CAA requirements, including those in the "applicable implementation plan."[47] The EPA has decided that the National Ambient Air Quality Standards (NAAQS) promulgated under CAA Section 109 are not an applicable requirement because they do not apply directly to sources. Rather, a NAAQS is a general ambient standard implemented through the SIP. A source therefore must comply with all applicable SIP requirements, but need not show that its emissions have not caused a violation of the NAAQS. There is one exception: The statute requires that "temporary sources" assure compliance with "ambient standards and . . . any applicable increment or visibility requirements under part C."[48] The EPA takes the position that a violation of a NAAQS caused by a particular source should be remedied through a notice of SIP deficiency under CAA Section 110(k)(5), followed by a subsequent tightening of emission limitations in the SIP. The permit would then have to incorporate the more stringent limitation.[49]

State Permit Programs and EPA Review of Programs

CAA Section 502(b) sets forth the minimum elements for state permit programs,[50] and the EPA elaborated upon these requirements in Section 70.4 of its Part 70 rules. In addition, Section 70.4 describes how the EPA is to review state programs (and program revisions). The section also includes criteria for partial and interim permit programs.

State Program Requirements

Each state (or locality) was required to submit its permit rules, a program description, and copies of enabling statutes and regulations to the EPA by November 15, 1993. The state's attorney general or the attorney for the air pollution control agency also had to sign an opinion stating that the state has legal authority to carry out the program.[51] The EPA's rules specify several requirements the state must show it can implement. Among the most significant requirements are that, with one exception, the state cannot issue permits with more than a five-year term (and permits with acid rain provisions must have exactly a five-year term); the state must make available to the public all permit applications, compliance plans, permits, and monitoring and compliance reports (although the source may be able to protect confidential business information in all documents except the permit); the state shall not issue a permit if the EPA objects; and the state must allow for judicial review of the final permit in state court.[52]

The state must demonstrate that it can decide within sixty days whether an application is complete, and issue or deny the permit within eighteen months.[53] It also must collect adequate permit fees (discussed later), make personnel and funding available to develop and administer the program, and develop a transition plan for program commencement. Under the transition plan, sources need to submit applications within one year of the EPA's program approval, and the state shall act on at least one-third of the applications in each of the three years following approval.[54] In actual fact, however, during the first ten years of the program states have not come close to meeting these deadlines for permit issuance.

Enforcement authority—both civil and criminal—is also required. States must demonstrate that they can enforce permit terms and bring legal action against sources that illegally operate without a permit. The enforcement mandates are found in Section 70.11. The enforcement provisions require, among other things, that states have the power to seek injunctive relief; recover civil penalties in a maximum amount of at least $10,000 per day per violation; and recover criminal fines of at least the same amount for knowing CAA or permit violations, or false and material representations.[55]

Another required program element addresses the problem of expiring permits. The rules require that sources submit applications in a timely manner, and that the state issue or deny permits within a specified period of time. Experience under the NPDES program, however, suggests that states often fail to issue renewal applications on time. This is not a problem for permits issued by the EPA under the Administrative Procedure Act, which provides that a permit remains in effect after its term if the permittee has submitted a timely and sufficient application for renewal.[56] States must adopt this approach or, alternatively, provide that the terms and conditions of the expiring permit remain in effect.[57]

The program requirements section contains several important provisions concerning a source's ability to make operational changes. The two provisions in Section 70.4—one implementing Title V's "operational flexibility" section, Section 502(b)(10), and the other governing what the EPA calls "off-permit" changes[58]—are described in more detail later. Considering them together with the permit revision provisions helps to clarify whether a revision is needed. Note that Section 70.4(b)(13) of the program requirements section also addresses revisions, requiring "adequate, streamlined, and reasonable procedures for expeditious review of permit revisions or modifications," but allowing states to adopt rules "substantially equivalent" to the EPA's minor permit modification procedures.

EPA Review of State Programs

As noted earlier, each state was to provide the EPA with its permit program by November 15, 1993, although few met the deadline. Within sixty days of receipt, the EPA was to determine whether the submission was complete. The EPA then was required to approve, disapprove, or partially approve the program within one year of receipt of the complete submission,[59] although the EPA often did not meet the deadlines.

The EPA publishes notice of these actions in the *Federal Register*, and accompanies a disapproval (complete or partial) with a statement of the revisions needed to gain approval. The state must make necessary revisions within 180 days of the EPA's disapproval.[60] If the state does not make the corrections—or if it never submits a program or fails to adequately implement it—the EPA must impose sanctions against the state, and ultimately step in itself to adopt and carry out a permit program in the state.[61] The sanctions, specified in the statute, include a bar on the award of highway funds, as well as imposition of a more stringent emissions offset ratio for NSR purposes.[62] As discussed immediately below, with a number of states the EPA has repeatedly avoided disapproving deficient programs, in large part because it wished to avoid imposing sanctions and becoming the permitting authority in those state.

Partial and Interim Approvals

The Part 70 rules also provide for partial and interim permit programs. The EPA may approve a partial program limited in terms of geographic scope (such as for a local air pollution agency), as long as the program ensures compliance with specified provisions of the CAA. However, the failure to submit an approvable "whole program" still could subject the state to sanctions.[63]

Under Section 502(g), the EPA may temporarily grant interim approval to a program (for no longer than two years) if the state "substantially meets" the Title V requirements. (In 1993, the EPA issued guidance on what it would require for interim approvals.)[64] A number of the EPA's early program approvals were interim in nature, either because that is what the state requested or because the EPA was unhappy with certain program elements. Following an interim approval, the state must submit a final program by the date the EPA specifies.[65]

In the ten years following the 1992 issuance of its Part 70 rules, the EPA repeatedly avoided disapproving state programs. Instead, it often issued a series of interim approvals of state programs (and interim approval extensions)—thus providing the states with more time to cure the program defects. These defects covered a range of issues, from failure to permit insignificant sources to refusal to provide full opportunity for judicial review of permits. In May 2000, the EPA issued a notice extending the interim approval of eighty-six programs until December 2001.[66] Environmentalists filed a petition for review in the U.S. Court of Appeals for the D.C. Circuit, challenging the legality of these extensions.[67] The environmentalists and the EPA settled the case in late 2000, with the EPA agreeing to publish a notice in the *Federal Register* to provide the public with the opportunity to identify and report to the EPA alleged deficiencies in Title V programs. The agency published that notice in December 2000,[68] and agreed to respond by December 2001 to public comments about alleged deficiencies in the interim programs (and by April 2002 to public comments on fully approved programs).

The EPA then issued "notices of deficiency" where it believed that the programs were truly deficient. It threatened to apply sanctions and withdraw the state program if the state did not correct the deficiencies.[69] Several states challenged these EPA notices. In other cases, and over the objection of environmentalists, the EPA decided against issuing a notice of deficiency and issued "contingent full approval" of programs where the state was cooperating in curing the deficiencies. The EPA was upheld in taking such action with New York.[70]

Permit Applications

Uncertainty over exactly what must be included in the permit application has been one of the most vexing problems for companies as states gain approval of their Title V programs. However, a white paper on applications issued by the EPA in July 1995[71] has alleviated much of this uncertainty. This guidance, which clarifies instances in which applications need not include detailed emissions information, is nearly as important as the Part 70 rules in answering important application content questions. Anyone involved in preparing a Title V application should study the white paper carefully, as well as any similar guidance issued by state agencies. (Although this July 1995 guidance is sometimes referred to as "White Paper 1" to distinguish it from a second permitting white paper issued by the EPA, it is referred to in this chapter as the "application white paper.")

Of course, an application is the company's vehicle for supplying the permit writer with information needed to craft the permit terms. Title V also mandates that the application include a compliance plan and compliance schedule. Finally, as discussed in the following paragraphs, filing a timely and complete application will protect the source if the state delays in issuing the permit.

Timely and Complete Applications

Each source in the permit program needs to submit a timely and complete application to the state agency. Otherwise, the owner or operator is in violation of the CAA, and may be assessed civil penalties.[72] A source applying for a Title V permit for the first time must file its application no later than twelve months after becoming subject to the program. (A source becomes subject when the EPA approves the program or the source fits the Section 70.3 applicability criteria, whichever is later.) The EPA's May 1991 proposal was silent on the timing for obtaining an operating permit if a source is subject to the CAA's PSD or NSR construction permitting requirements or the new CAA Section 112(g) hazardous air pollutant modification provisions. The final Part 70 rules allow such sources to submit their Title V permit applications twelve months after beginning operations, although the state may require an earlier filing.[73]

A renewal application must be filed at least six months before the end of the permit term, but in no case may the state require it to be filed more than eighteen months before expiration.[74] In the preamble, the EPA hints that it will audit state programs to see if applications for permit renewal are being acted on before the permit expires.[75]

A complete application is one that includes information "sufficient to evaluate the subject source and its application and to determine all applicable requirements."[76] Generally, the state will make a completeness determination within sixty days.[77] A completeness finding, however, does not relieve the applicant of its duty to supply additional information requested by the state in writing. Failure to do so in a timely manner causes what the EPA calls the "application shield" to evaporate.[78]

This application shield (not to be confused with the "permit shield," discussed later) is found in CAA Section 503(d); the EPA's regulatory elaboration is at Section 70.7(b). The application shield protects a source that has filed a timely and complete application by allowing it to operate without a permit if the state delays in issuing it.[79] It provides protection for both initial and renewal permits. Thus, a source that has never received a permit or whose permit has expired may continue to operate as long as a complete application for an initial permit or permit renewal has been filed on time.

Content of Applications

The EPA decided against adopting a national standard application form, although many multistate companies would have preferred one. The EPA's May 1991 proposal noted that many states already have operating permit programs. The EPA said that mandating a national form would disrupt these programs and represent an unnecessary intrusion on the states' flexibility in designing appropriate forms.[80] Instead, Section 70.5(c) lists data that the EPA requires to be included in the state's application form, including company information; a plant description; emissions-related data, including emission rates; a description of emission points and air pollution control equipment; and a description of applicable CAA requirements and test methods for determining compliance. The EPA's application white paper provides that in some instances, emission units and activities "may be treated generically in the application and permit for certain broadly applicable requirements often found in the SIP."[81]

The application white paper also provides more detail on what the application should contain, stating that detailed emissions information often need not be included in the application. According to the EPA, estimates expressed in tpy are "not required at all where they would serve no useful purpose, where a quantifiable emissions rate is not applicable (e.g., section 112(r) requirements or a work practice standard), or where emissions units are subject to a generic requirement."[82] Elsewhere, the application white paper states that "[g]enerally, the emissions factors contained in the EPA's publication AP-42 and other EPA documents may be used to make any necessary calculation of emissions."[83] It warns, however, that better emission estimates may be needed to show, for example, that a facility is not a major source, or that requirements are not applicable.[84]

Insignificant Activities and Emission Units

In a noteworthy addition from the EPA's May 1991 proposal to the final Part 70 rules, the EPA decided it "may approve as part of a State program a list of insignificant activities and emission levels which need not be included in permit applications."[85] This exemption will aid businesses because states will not have to collect absurd amounts of information on even the most trivial emissions at facilities. The rules, however, require the application to list the "insignificant activities" in certain cases. Moreover, a source may not omit information needed to calculate permit fees or to determine if a CAA requirement applies.[86]

Again, the EPA's application white paper provides more details on this important concept. It states that insignificant activities are ones that a state selects and the EPA approves, or those that "are clearly trivial (i.e., emissions units and activities with specific applicable requirements and with extremely small emissions)."[87] Appendix A to the application white paper lists a number of examples that the EPA thinks are trivial, and the white paper states that the list is intended to serve only as a starting point. It also may be possible to treat temporary activities as insignificant.[88] Thus, applicants would be well advised to speak to state regulators about excluding the activities mentioned on the list as well as other activities that do not warrant inclusion in the application.

A second EPA white paper, issued on March 5, 1996, and generally referred to as "White Paper Number 2,"[89] contains further guidance on the treatment of insignificant activities and emission units. This document, together with corresponding state guidance, should also be consulted.

Compliance Plans, Schedules, and Certifications

Many states and environmental groups criticized provisions in the EPA's May 1991 proposal that would have required only sources out of compliance with the CAA to include a compliance plan in their applications. The final rules compel all permit applicants to submit a plan, but requirements for sources in compliance are minimal: the applicant need only state that it will continue to comply with the requirements. Similarly, for standards on the books but not yet in effect at the time of permit issuance, the plan need only describe in narrative fashion how the source will comply.[90]

The plan must include a "schedule of compliance," which, for sources not in compliance, must contain "an enforceable sequence of actions with milestones, leading to compliance."[91] Again, requirements are minimal for sources already in compliance and for sources subject to regulations that will become effective during the permit term.[92]

Under CAA Section 504(a), the schedule is part of the permit. It is therefore enforceable against the source; the plan is not.

The application, as well as reports and required additional periodic compliance certifications, also must include a responsible official's certification of truth, accuracy, and completeness. A knowing violation of this requirement would subject the applicant to criminal penalties.[93] This provision leaves many in the regulated community extremely worried.

The EPA's application white paper includes an important clarification on the scope of the initial compliance certification that provides some relief: "Companies are not federally required to reconsider previous applicability determinations as part of their inquiry in preparing Part 70 permit applications."[94] For example, to certify that it is in compliance with the CAA, a permit applicant need not "look back" to determine if it really should have obtained an NSR permit several years ago. Not surprisingly, however, the EPA states that it expects companies to rectify past noncompliance and that companies remain liable for such noncompliance.[95]

Permit Content

As previously noted, the Title V permit must assure compliance with all applicable CAA requirements. The regulations on permit content (found in Section 70.6) are critical to realizing this mandate because the permit terms translate generally applicable standards and duties into source-specific emission limitations.

Permit Terms

Among other things, each permit needs to include emission limitations and standards as well as monitoring, record-keeping, reporting, and inspection and entry requirements to assure compliance with those limits.[96] The monitoring requirements deserve special attention. They state that if a CAA rule does not require periodic testing or monitoring, then the permit itself must supply "periodic monitoring sufficient to yield reliable data from the relevant time period that are representative of the source's compliance with the permit."[97] The EPA issued guidance interpreting this "periodic monitoring" language, but industry challenged the guidance and in 2000 the D.C. Circuit vacated it. The court held that the guidance constituted final agency action, and that it illegally broadened the 1992 Part 70 rules without requiring notice and comment rulemaking procedures.[98]

Following this loss, the EPA proposed to interpret the 1992 Part 70 rules as providing for "sufficiency" evaluations of already-established monitoring, and also proposed to delete language in Section 70.6(c)(1) to help ensure that such evaluations would be required in the future.[99] This "sufficiency monitoring" proposal followed several EPA adjudicatory orders in which the agency had taken a similar position on the meaning of the 1992 rules.[100] On the same day that it issued the proposal, the EPA also issued an "interim final" rule that the EPA planned to have in place until it issued a truly final rule based on the proposal.[101] Following an uproar by industry, however, the interim final rule expired in late 2002, and as of early 2003 the EPA had not acted on the sufficiency monitoring proposal. Sufficiency monitoring issues are discussed in more detail in Chapter 16.

Some units at major sources have to meet what the CAA refers to as "enhanced monitoring" requirements.[102] The EPA's rule-making on this subject, which was entangled in controversy for years, ended up calling for what the EPA termed compliance assurance monitoring (CAM). The CAM approach requires that "indicator ranges" be set for parameter monitoring, and would have sources implement "quality improvement plans" if monitoring data showed units to be operating outside the ranges for more than a specified period of time.[103] The rules, which the D.C. Circuit upheld in 1999 following a legal challenge by environmentalists,[104] play a very important role in determining what type of monitoring terms must be included in permits—and how such terms may be enforced.

The preamble to the Part 70 rules stated that federal standards promulgated pursuant to the 1990 CAA Amendments are presumed to contain sufficient monitoring provisions. Therefore, the preamble said, a permit need not add independent monitoring requirements for those standards.[105] A company needs to retain monitoring records for at least five years, submit monitoring reports to the state at least every six months, and report all deviations from permit requirements promptly.[106]

The Part 70 rules state that, while all applicable CAA requirements in the permit may be enforced by the EPA and citizens, the state "shall specifically designate as not federally enforceable any State provisions in the permit which are more stringent than the applicable requirements under the Act."[107] This language was included so that the EPA and citizens cannot enforce more stringent or extensive state air pollution controls in federal court. The purpose of this change was to prevent more stringent state requirements from essentially becoming "federalized" through the Title V permit. Thus, states will have to decide which requirements applying to the source are based on CAA requirements and which are based on state law. The latter must be so designated, perhaps by denoting them with an asterisk or placing them in a separate part of the permit. The EPA's "Response to Comments Document"[108] on the Part 70 rules states the agency's view that if, within ninety days of permit issuance, a party does not challenge in court the state's determination of whether a limitation is grounded in state law, it may not challenge that decision afterward.[109]

The permit must include provisions for a certification of compliance by the source, as required under CAA Sections 504(c) and 114(a)(3). This certification will be signed by a "responsible official," a term defined similarly under the EPA's NPDES regulations. Sources not in compliance with any CAA requirements also need to file semiannual progress reports stating whether they met compliance deadlines (and if not, why not).[110]

Section 70.6(g) allows companies an affirmative defense when they exceed permit limitations during emergencies ("upsets") that meet a number of specified criteria. To qualify for this defense, a company must notify the state agency within two working days, and describe the emergency and corrective actions taken. The rule specifies that exceedances caused by improperly designed equipment, inadequate maintenance, careless operation, and operator error will not qualify as emergencies.[111] Moreover, as in the NPDES program, the defense is available only when sources exceed limits founded on technology-based standards.[112] In its long-dormant August 1995 supplemental proposal, the EPA suggested that it might significantly limit the Section 70.6(g) emergency defense.[113]

The EPA's March 5, 1996, White Paper Number 2 includes important guidance concerning permit terms. It provides that a facility can "streamline" multiple overlapping requirements that apply to the same emissions unit by distilling them into one set of terms that will ensure compliance with all the requirements. In addition, it states that generally a Title V permit (and also the application) can cite to or cross-reference regulatory requirements—rather than repeat these requirements in the permit itself—if the information is currently and readily available to the permitting authority and the public.[114]

Equivalency Determinations and Alternative Scenarios

Under Section 70.6(a)(1)(iii), states may make "equivalency determinations" through the permit. In other words, states may adopt SIP provisions allowing sources to meet either an emission limitation in the SIP *or* an equivalent limit determined through the permit process. The section requires that a permit with an equivalency determination "shall contain provisions to ensure that any resulting emissions limit has been demonstrated to be quantifiable, accountable, enforceable, and based on replicable procedures." The preamble adds that the source's permit application must make this demonstration.[115]

This equivalency provision could greatly benefit the regulated community. If states include such provisions in their SIPs, companies will be able to make changes in source-specific emission limitations much more quickly than under the slow SIP revision process. Industry representatives and states have for years argued for (and litigated with the EPA over) allowing states to make equivalency determinations for SIP limitations based on reasonably available control technology.[116]

On a related topic, Sections 70.6(a)(8) and (10) are designed to allow for easier emissions trading, if the substantive CAA rules provide for trading. Again, the SIP is the most fertile ground in the CAA for allowing these innovative measures. The permit would serve as the vehicle for individual emissions trades.

Another important provision, Section 70.6(a)(9), requires states to include in the permit "reasonably anticipated operating scenarios" that the source identifies in its application. The source therefore can switch among several scenarios without the need for a permit revision, *if* it was able to foresee the need for the different operating modes and it asked the state to include these various permit terms. This section, along with the three provisions affecting operational flexibility discussed later, will be critical to companies wishing to minimize paperwork and delays when they change operations at their facility.

General Permits

CAA Section 504(d) allows states to issue a general permit covering numerous similar sources, as long as the permit complies with all Title V requirements and the sources apply for it. A general permit contains terms just like an individual permit. In some ways, however, it more resembles a rule because it states what a number of sources can and cannot do. The EPA and states have used general permits to great benefit in the NPDES program, especially for permitting smaller, simpler sources, and a number of states are now utilizing them under the CAA as well.

Section 70.6(d) of the EPA's rules makes clear that although public participation is required when a general permit is issued, it is not needed when a source applies to be covered by the terms of the permit. The application for coverage under a general permit need not contain all the information required for regular permit applications.

The preamble to the final Part 70 rules offers guidance on what types of sources may be covered by a general permit. States should consider whether the sources are (1) "generally homogeneous in terms of operations, processes, and emissions"; (2) "subject to case-by-case standards or requirements"; and (3) "subject to the same or substantially similar requirements governing operation, emissions, monitoring, reporting, or recordkeeping."[117] General permits may also cover discrete emission units located at many types of facilities. The preamble suggests that a general permit covering such units could be incorporated into the source's individual permit; this could lessen paperwork burdens for the state and the source.[118] In practice, states have often used general permits for smaller facilities that meet the criteria in (1) and (3) above, such as dry cleaners and gas pipeline transmission stations. In addition, some states allow a larger facility with a typical Title V permit to cross-reference a general permit applicable to production or emission units at the facility (such as degreasers).

The EPA suggested another important use of general permits: to avoid classification as a major source. If a source's PTE exceeds the major source threshold, it must obtain a regular permit and might be subject to substantive CAA requirements as well. However, the general permit can be used as an enforceable means of restricting the source's emissions so it will *not* be classified as a major source, and thus will not have to obtain a regular permit or be subject to the substantive CAA rules. Thus, in essence the source would elect coverage under a general permit to guarantee that other rules do not apply.[119] The preamble, however, provides no clue to what the general permit would have to contain for this purpose and what information the source would need to give to the state.

The Permit Shield

Most observers considered the permit shield provision in the administration's 1990 CAA Amendments bill to be the one major benefit businesses would derive from the proposed operating permit program. Compliance with the terms of the permit would be considered compliance with the terms of the act, as is generally the case with NPDES permits.[120] The NPDES permit shield, which the administration bill's Title V shield provision was modeled upon, simply states that except for any toxic pollutant standard, "[c]ompliance with a permit issued pursuant to this section shall be deemed compliance, for purposes of [certain sections of the Clean Water Act]."[121] This provides certainty by allowing companies to know their Clean Water Act obligations for the life of the permit.

However, the CAA bill passed by Congress made the shield optional with the state and contained murky language on its scope, suggesting that the shield did not protect the source from standards promulgated after permit issuance. (As is discussed in the next section, a major source permit with three or more years remaining in its term must reopen to incorporate new standards anyway.) The act's convoluted shield provision states in relevant part:

> Except as otherwise provided by the [EPA] Administrator by rule, the permit may also provide that compliance with the permit shall be deemed compliance with other applicable provisions of this Act that relate to the permittee if—
>
>   (1) the permit includes the applicable requirements of such provisions, or
>
>   (2) the permitting authority in acting on the permit application makes a determination relating to the permittee that such other provisions (which shall be referred to in such determination) are not applicable and the permit includes the determination or a concise summary thereof.[122]

Thus, the EPA's Part 70 rules mandate compliance with future CAA standards by the standard's effective date.[123] Unfortunately, that means the CAA Title V permit shield will provide much less certainty than the NPDES permit shield.

Some certainty, however, remains. A source will be protected if the state incorrectly translates a CAA standard into erroneous, overly lenient emission limitations in the permit. In this case, neither the EPA nor the state could bring an enforcement action based on the standard; only the permit terms could be enforced. Similarly, if the state decides when the permit is issued that standard x applies to the source but standard y does not, the shield would prevent the state or the EPA from arguing in an enforcement action that rule y did in fact apply. Instead, the agencies' recourse would be to reopen the permit to incorporate standard y. Even here, however, the protection is limited. If, during the permitting process, the state did not write *in the permit* that standard y was not applicable to the source (or did not at least provide a summary of what requirements were not applicable), the shield would not apply.[124]

The rules address several other situations where the permit shield may not apply. First, they implement the sentence in CAA Section 504(f) providing that a source may not be shielded from an emergency order under CAA Section 303. Second, they state that there is no shield from acid rain requirements under Title IV of the act. Finally, they clarify that a source may not be shielded from an enforcement action based on a violation that existed when the permit was issued.[125]

Permit Issuance, Judicial Review, Renewals, and Reopenings

The EPA's Part 70 rules require public participation for issuance of the initial permit, including adequate notice of what the agency calls the "draft proposed permit." The EPA also requires the public availability of all nonconfidential information submitted by the applicant, a thirty-day comment period, and an opportunity for an informal public hearing. The state must provide notice of a hearing at least thirty days in advance.[126]

The state need not hold a hearing in all instances; the request must be germane to the requirements that apply to the source.[127] For example, a hearing may not have to be held if the requester protests only the source's location. In contrast to the NPDES program, the hearing need not be a trial-type adjudicatory hearing, with formal procedures such as the cross-examination of witnesses.[128] Because this type of hearing is time-consuming and expensive, most state Title V programs call for informal hearings instead.

The state needs to provide a statement of the legal and factual basis for the draft permit conditions, but it does not have to prepare a NPDES-type "fact sheet."[129] The basis statement plays an important role if the applicant or another party decides to challenge the final permit, since it will be a critical part of the administrative record on the permit.

The few provisions on judicial review of state-issued permits are found in various parts of the rules.[130] The most important, Section 70.4(b)(3)(x), requires states to provide an opportunity for judicial review in state court for the applicant, any person who participated during the public comment period, and any other person who could obtain judicial review under state law. Challenges to state-issued permits may not be brought in federal court.

Petitions for judicial review must be filed within ninety days of the state's final action on the permit, or a shorter period that the state may choose. The only exception is when new grounds arise, and then the petition must be filed within ninety days of that time.[131] Thus, challenges to permit terms may not be raised as a defense in an enforcement action.

Under the EPA's rules, applications for permit renewals and reopenings will be processed in the same manner as applications for initial permits.[132] A major source's permit must be reopened if the EPA or the state issues a new, applicable CAA standard and three or more years remain in the permit term; the state then incorporates the standard in the permit within eighteen months. In addition, the state (or, in some cases, the EPA) may reopen the permit for other reasons specified in the rules.[133]

Provisions Affecting a Source's Operational Flexibility

Industry's major concern with the Title V permit program has always been that it could impede making operational changes at a facility. In addition to the alternate scenarios provisions described earlier, three parts of the EPA's regulations are critical in determining whether a company must obtain a permit revision before changing operations—and if a revision is needed, what procedures must be followed. These are the provisions addressing (1) operational flexibility, (2) off-permit changes, and (3) minor permit modifications. The EPA proposed a major overhaul to the flexibility and permit revision provisions in August 1995,[134] and following additional discussions with stakeholder groups subsequently noticed for comment several sets of "draft rules" that would modify the August 1995 proposal in a variety of ways.[135] But as of early 2003 the EPA had shown no indication that it planned on issuing final rules in the near future.

The minor permit modification section generated an enormous amount of controversy during development of the Part 70 rules. The other two provisions also elicited contentious debates, although these disputes were not as widely reported by the popular press. Unless the EPA overhauls this section of the rules and the states follow suit, the three provisions (and the states' elaboration of them in individual permit programs) will play a key role in determining whether a company needs a permit revision when it makes a change at its facility.

Section 502(b)(10) Operational Flexibility Changes

Congress included CAA Section 502(b)(10), the most fought-over section of Title V during the legislative debate, to aid businesses by allowing certain facility changes without a permit revision. Like the permit shield provision discussed earlier, however, the congressional compromises needed to reach agreement on Section 502(b)(10) make its meaning difficult, if not impossible, to decipher. The provision, located in the section on required program elements, says that state programs must provide

> [p]rovisions to allow changes within a permitted facility . . . without requiring a permit revision, if the changes are not modifications under any provision of Title I and the changes do not exceed the emissions allowable under the permit (whether expressed therein as a rate of emissions or in terms of total emissions): *Provided,* That the facility provides the Administrator and the permitting authority with written notification in advance of the proposed changes which shall be a minimum of 7 days, unless the permitting authority provides in its regulations a different timeframe for emergencies.[136]

Most readers of this provision discover that it takes on different meanings depending on the angle from which it is viewed. Environmental groups and many states have argued that it allows no more than the "reasonably anticipated operating scenarios" described earlier. That is, if a state includes the various terms in the permit, the source can switch among different operating scenarios without first obtaining a permit revision. A number of industry groups, on the other hand, have said that the provision allowed sources to "pool emissions" (trade emissions among various units at the source), regardless of how the permit is written.[137]

Making the matter more complicated is the provision's location in Title V's section on required program elements, Section 502(b). The operational flexibility section is the only such element that would significantly benefit industry. How does this provision relate to CAA Section 506(a), which allows states to adopt "additional permitting requirements not inconsistent with this Act," and Section 116, which allows states to adopt "any requirement respecting control or abatement of air pollution," as long as it is not less stringent than CAA requirements? Environmental groups and some states contended that Sections 506(a) and 116 precluded requiring states to build flexibility for companies into their permit programs.[138]

The EPA disagreed, concluding that these two general statutory provisions do not override the specific requirement in Section 502(b)(10) that states provide for operational flexibility in their permit programs.[139] However, between the EPA's May 1991 proposal and the promulgation of the final rules, the agency also drastically altered its regulatory provisions implementing Section 502(b)(10). The lengthy and confusing Section 70.4(b)(12) states that states *must* provide two types of flexibility and *may* provide a third type.

The most important is one of the two mandatory types. Under this provision, companies can contravene certain permit terms, as long as the changes do not result in emissions increases that exceed limits in the permit. However, only permit terms not found in the underlying EPA rule may be contravened; a violation of a SIP's terms or other EPA rule is not allowed.[140] The EPA's sole example for this provision explains that a facility could switch from one type of coating to another, as long as it did not lead to a violation of the emission limit—even though the permit required use of the first type of coating. The EPA has also provided that this flexibility does not extend to changes that would contravene the following types of permit terms: monitoring, record-keeping, reporting, or compliance certification requirements.[141]

The other required type and the optional type of operational flexibility provide for certain types of emissions trading at the facility. Once again, however, these provisions do not allow a company to exceed specified limits stated in the SIP or other underlying EPA rules.[142] Before making changes under any of the three operational flexibility provisions, the company must provide advance written notification to the state and the EPA.[143]

Off-Permit Changes

The Part 70 rules state that the CAA does not require a permit revision for "changes that are not addressed or prohibited by the permit."[144] (As discussed later, however, the EPA's August 1995 supplemental proposal would eliminate this concept.) The EPA leaves to the states the decision on whether to allow what the agency calls off-permit changes.[145] Under this provision, a company might have to obtain a permit revision to increase emissions of a particular pollutant covered by its permit, but might not need a revision if it emits a new pollutant not addressed in its permit.

The importance of this concept can hardly be overemphasized. The EPA, however, has offered little guidance on exactly what types of off-permit changes will not necessitate a permit revision.

Three important points on off-permit changes are worth noting. First, unlike the proposal, the EPA now requires contemporaneous written notification of such changes to the state and the EPA. Second, as with the Section 502(b)(10) operational flexibility provision, any change classified as a modification under any provision of CAA Title I (such as those governing PSD, nonattainment NSR, NSPS, or the new hazardous air pollutant standards) is not eligible for off-permit treatment.[146] Third, even though states may bar off-permit changes, the EPA and private citizens generally cannot enforce the prohibition under the CAA. Thus, enforcement of such state prohibitions could be brought only under state law.[147]

Minor Permit Modifications and Other Permit Revisions

The controversy surrounding the streamlined minor permit modification procedures centered primarily on the following issues:

- Whether public participation is required (i.e., whether the state must provide an opportunity for public comment or a hearing)
- How much time the state should have to review the application for a revision
- When the company can make the change at its facility (e.g., before or after the state approves the revision)

The preamble to the final rules states that the CAA does not require public participation for minor permit modifications or preclude the source from making changes before the state has acted on its application for a modification.[148]

The minor permit modification provisions, found in Section 70.7(e), are as lengthy and complicated as they are controversial. Only the highlights are provided here.[149] States need not adopt the procedures and may add extra requirements, but they are free to allow these streamlined revision procedures for all changes except ones the EPA has specifically excluded. Some of the changes not eligible for the minor modification process are those that (1) are classified as a modification under any provision of CAA Title I; (2) involve significant changes to existing monitoring, reporting, or record-keeping requirements; and (3) require a case-by-case determination of an emission limitation or other standard. Ineligible changes and revisions that the state determines are significant will be processed under procedures similar to those used for initial permits and permit renewals.[150]

Under the minor modification procedures, the company can make the change as soon as it files its application, and need not notify the public.

While the application is pending, the company must comply with the terms of the proposed modification. The EPA has forty-five days to review the application and may object; the state should issue or deny the revision within ninety days after receiving the application, and need not request public comment or hold a public hearing. The permit shield does not apply to terms adopted using these procedures—that is, enforcement actions may be brought based on the SIP or other underlying CAA requirements, even if the proposed modification is approved. Finally, states may group together several of a source's applications for minor permit modifications and act on them together periodically. The rules governing these "group processing" procedures are particularly complicated.[151]

The EPA calls the most mundane changes (such as address changes or those incorporating provisions from a PSD or NSR permit) "administrative permit amendments." Section 70.7(d) provides that the state shall act on these revisions within sixty days and need not provide any notice.

An important point, stated in the preamble to the final Part 70 rules, is that emission limits based solely on state law (i.e., not CAA requirements) may be revised under whatever procedures the state chooses. The EPA states that procedures for such changes need not meet minimum CAA Title V requirements.[152]

The August 1995 Supplemental Proposal

As has been pointed out, the EPA's August 1995 supplemental proposal (and the modified "draft rules" that the agency subsequently noticed for comment in 1997 and 1998) would significantly alter the Part 70 provisions on operational flexibility and permit revisions. As noted above, as of early 2003 there was almost no momentum toward issuing final rules based on the proposal. The following provides a brief summary of the August 1995 supplemental proposal.

The proposal builds on the fact that most facility changes resulting in Title V permit changes already will have triggered major or minor NSR. Because the state or the EPA (and in some cases the public as well) would have reviewed the NSR changes already, simply incorporating the changes into the Title V permit without additional review makes sense. Thus, the EPA's proposed revision procedures distinguish between facility changes that have already undergone NSR (probably the vast majority), and those that have not. For changes that have not been through the NSR process, some type of Title V review process would be required.[153]

The other cornerstone of the August 1995 supplemental proposal is the belief that the level of public, EPA, and affected state review should depend on the environmental significance of the facility change. For "more environmentally significant changes"—which under the proposal means changes that would trigger major NSR or Section 112(g) review, those involving "netting out" of NSR, and similar changes—the EPA would require that the changes "meet the full public process requirements specified by the federal regulations governing the underlying State review program."[154] For instance, major NSR changes would require a thirty-day public comment period.

For "less environmentally significant changes," such as many minor NSR changes, states "would have considerable discretion to match the amount and timing of process to the environmental significance of the change."[155] For *de minimis* changes, states would be able to "forego prior public, affected State, or EPA review altogether."[156] The EPA would let states decide which types of changes are *de minimis,* although the EPA would reserve the right to disagree. The general test for a *de minimis* change is taken from the landmark *Alabama Power v. Costle* case;[157] the question is whether it would yield a gain of trivial or no value.[158]

The EPA would delete off-permit changes from the Part 70 rules because, it says, they would no longer be necessary under the new revision system.[159] For the most part this is true, but the off-permit track may still be useful for some changes.

Permit Review and EPA Oversight over State Programs

Review of Permits by the EPA and Neighboring States

The EPA's permit review provisions for all but minor permit modifications track CAA Section 505 fairly closely. States must furnish the EPA with copies of each permit application, draft proposed permit, and final permit. They must also transmit copies of a draft proposed permit to states that are within fifty miles of the source and to states whose air quality may be affected that are contiguous to the issuing state. The EPA may waive the furnishing of such documents for some categories of sources (but not major sources). If the issuing state does not accept the neighboring state's recommendations, it must explain why it is rejecting them.[160]

The procedures governing EPA review are more complex. CAA Section 505(b), which was enacted over the protests of state officials, provides that the EPA shall object to issuance of a permit containing provisions the agency determines are not in compliance with applicable CAA requirements, including the SIP.[161] The EPA must object to (i.e., veto) the permit within forty-five days after receiving it, or the permit may automatically issue. If the EPA objects, the state may not issue the permit as written; a refusal to correct the problem will lead the EPA to issue or deny the permit itself. If the EPA does not object during the review period, under certain circumstances a person may petition the EPA to object to it afterward. CAA Section 502(b)(2) provides that the EPA administrator's decision to deny such a petition is subject to judicial review in the appropriate federal court of appeals.[162] Environmental groups have taken advantage of these provisions by petitioning the EPA to object to a number of state-issued permits, and on occasion challenging the EPA's failure to object. In early 2003, environmentalists in New York prevailed in such a judicial challenge, with the D.C. Circuit rejecting the EPA's claim that it could rely on a "harmless error rule" in deciding not to object to a permit where the agency has concluded that a minor deficiency exists.[163]

In its August 1995 supplemental proposal, the EPA proposed rule changes that would limit its oversight role by excluding many permit revisions from EPA review. The agency's role would depend on the environmental significance of the change and whether a person petitioned the EPA to object to the permit revision. In the longer term, the EPA's role would also depend on the outcome of its state program audits.[164]

EPA Oversight over State Permit Programs

As discussed earlier, Section 70.10(a) requires the EPA to apply sanctions against a state (and ultimately to issue Title V permits itself) if the state fails to submit an approvable permit program. These sanctions would follow the EPA's filing of a "notice of deficiency" with the state. Section 70.10(b), which implements CAA Section 502(i), calls for similar action if the EPA finds that the state is not adequately enforcing or implementing its program. From ninety days to eighteen months after making the determination, the EPA may impose sanctions or withdraw program approval. After eighteen months, the EPA *must* impose sanctions, and six months after that it must promulgate and administer a permit program in the state. The Fourth Circuit has upheld the sanctions provisions in a case in which the state of Virginia alleged that they violated the Tenth Amendment and the Spending Clause of the U.S. Constitution.[165]

Section 70.10(c) sets forth criteria for withdrawal of state programs. The rules do not set out special program withdrawal procedures, as the NPDES regulations do.[166] As discussed above in the "Partial and Interim Approvals" section, in the ten years following issuance of its Part 70 rules in 1992, the EPA has been very reluctant to impose sanctions, take over permitting in states, or withdraw approval of state permit programs.

Permit Fees

Requirement for Fee Demonstration

The Title V fee provisions were designed to ensure that states receive adequate funding to carry out their new permitting responsibilities. CAA Section 502(b)(3)(A) requires permitted sources to pay "an annual fee, or the equivalent over some other period, sufficient to cover all reasonable (direct and indirect) costs required to develop and administer the permit program requirements of this Title, including section 507 [relating to small business assistance programs]."

States need to establish fee schedules and demonstrations showing that they will collect and retain enough money to pay permit program costs. Although the EPA retreated from its May 1991 proposal position that permit fees should cover the cost of nearly the entire state air program for stationary sources (a position that, not surprisingly, was heartily endorsed by state air officials), ambiguous language in the final rules and preamble made the scope unclear.[167] The EPA issued guidance in August 1993 that provided more detail on the agency's position.[168]

"Required" fees may be used only for the permit program's direct and indirect costs. A state could not, for example, use fees necessary to run the permit program to fund social services programs or even air quality programs unrelated to Title V permits.[169] However, the EPA document responding to comments on the Part 70 rules states that "[t]he Act does not prohibit a State from assessing greater fees than required by the Act and using those additional fees for purposes other than supporting the permit program."[170]

Two Program Support Tests

The EPA's May 1991 proposal allowed states to meet one of two program support tests. The final rules essentially combine these into one test by presuming that a fee schedule will cover program costs if it results in the collection of $25 times the total tons of actual emissions of "regulated pollutant[s] for presumptive fee purposes." (This term includes volatile organic compounds, nitrogen oxides, pollutants regulated under CAA Sections 111 and 112 standards, and, except for carbon monoxide, pollutants for which a NAAQS has been promulgated.) The $25 figure is adjusted each year to reflect increases in the Consumer Price Index.

The state does not have to collect $25 per ton for *each* such pollutant. It could charge, for example, more for hazardous air pollutant emissions and less for particulate matter. Similarly, states may charge some sources more and others less and may also use charges other than emission fees (such as application fees). Although the EPA has encouraged states to base emission fees on actual, rather than allowable, emissions, they are not required to do so.[171]

Conclusion

With nearly all state permit programs finally approved and many initial permits issued by early 2003, the Title V program now is entering a new phase. Previously the program focused in large part on getting programs up and running and issuing initial permits for facilities. As the program matures, for facilities the focus will now shift to "living with" the permit and dealing with permit reopenings and renewals. The following chapter (Chapter 16) closely examines several important issues that companies need to consider after they obtain their initial Title V permit.

Notes

1. CAA §§ 165, 173.

2. *See* New York Public Interest Research Group, Inc. v. New York State Department of Environmental Conservation, 184 Misc. 2d 564, 710 N.Y.2d 521 (2000).

3. *See* "EPA Completes Plan to Tackle Air Permit Problems," *Air Daily*, Aug. 8, 2002, p. 1.

4. Before enactment of the 1990 CAA Amendments, approximately thirty-five states had their own operating permit programs for sources of air pollution. S. REP. No. 101-228, at 346–47 (1989) [hereinafter SENATE REPORT].

5. 56 Fed. Reg. 21,712 (1991). The May 1991 proposal is described in David Novello, *EPA's Proposed Air Permit Regulations: Implementing the 1990 Clean Air Act Amendments*, 21 ELR 10,511 (1991).

6. 57 Fed. Reg. 32,250 (1992).

7. The various petitions for review filed in the U.S. Court of Appeals for the D.C. Circuit were consolidated with Clean Air Implementation Project v. EPA, No. 92-103, as lead docket.

8. 60 Fed. Reg. 34,202 (1996). *See also* the proposal at 60 Fed. Reg. 20,804 (1995).

9. 64 Fed. Reg. 8,247 (Feb. 19, 1999).

10. 67 Fed. Reg. 38,328 (June 3, 2002).

11. H.R. 3030, 101st Cong. (1989) (Title IV).

12. The goals of the permit system are summarized in Senate Report, *supra* note 4, at 347–49, and in the preamble at 57 Fed. Reg. at 32,251.

13. Citizens may bring enforcement actions under the act's citizens' suit provision, CAA Section 304.

14. *See* National Environmental Development Association/Clean Air Act Project, Federal Air Permits: Realistic Hope or Regulatory Quicksand? (1990).

15. Note, however, that "a source is not required to obtain a permit solely because it is subject to regulations or requirements under section 112(r) [pertaining to hazardous air pollutant accidental release plans]." 40 C.F.R. § 70.3(a)(3).

16. The emissions units are subsets of the entire source. For example, a single production line at a manufacturing facility might be considered to be one emissions unit, or it may be comprised of several units.

17. See the May 1991 proposal, 56 Fed. Reg. at 21,727, which says that

[a]s long as the collection of individual emissions unit permits assure that all applicable requirements would be met which would be required under a permit for the whole source, and the State permits the entire source according to the Act's schedule, the State may permit each unit individually, or in groups within a source.

Although the EPA suggests that the entire facility should be permitted at the same time if feasible, it does not require this.

18. The EPA's operating permit definitions are listed in alphabetical order in 40 C.F.R. § 70.2.

19. The May 1991 proposal had solicited comment "on whether the Agency should exempt from permitting requirements those sources that are 'major' by virtue of the quantity of their emissions of particular pollutants, but whose emissions are not in any way actually regulated by a standard or other requirement under the Act." 56 Fed. Reg. at 21,725. In many ways this approach makes sense, for a permit is of little use if there are no requirements with which to comply. In fact, the administration favored this approach and tried to persuade Congress not to require issuance of "empty" or "hollow" permits, but CAA Section 502(a) as enacted mandates permitting of *all* major sources, and the EPA's final rules echo this requirement.

20. 40 C.F.R. § 70.2 (first paragraph of "major source" definition).

21. *Id.* The codes are found in the *Standard Industrial Classification Manual, 1987*.

22. 56 Fed. Reg. at 21,724; H.R. Rep. No. 101-490, at 236–37 (1990).

23. The support facility test is set out in the May 1991 proposal at 56 Fed. Reg. at 21,724. The EPA plans to incorporate this test into the Part 70 definition of "major source." 59 Fed. Reg. at 44,515.

24. 40 C.F.R. § 70.2 (definition of "potential to emit").

25. National Mining Ass'n v. EPA, 59 F.3d 1351 (D.C. Cir. 1995) (remanding part of EPA's "general provisions" to implement CAA § 112); Chemical Mfrs. Ass'n v. EPA,

No. 89-1514 (D.C. Cir. filed Sept. 15, 1995) (judgment in this and consolidated cases, without an opinion, vacating federally enforceable requirement in NSR rules).

26. Clean Air Implementation Project v. EPA, No. 96-1224, 1996 WL 393118 (D.C. Cir. June 28, 1996).

27. *See* Memorandum, Extension of January 25, 1995 Potential to Emit Transition Policy, from John Seitz to Robert Van Heuvelen, 3 (Aug. 27, 1996). Earlier, following the two 1995 court losses, the EPA had issued another guidance document: Memorandum, Release of Interim Policy on Federal Enforceability of Limitations on Potential to Emit, from John Seitz and Robert Van Heuvelen to EPA Regional Offices (Jan. 22, 1996).

28. *See* Memorandum, Options for Limiting the Potential to Emit (PTE) of a Stationary Source Under Section 112 and Title V of the Clean Air Act (Act), from John Seitz and Robert Van Heuvelen to EPA Regional Offices, 3–5 (Jan. 25, 1995).

29. *Id.* at 5. The EPA's various requirements regarding "practicable enforceability" are listed in the memorandum, and they are described in more detail in another memo that is attached to the January 25, 1995 Seitz-Van Heuvelen memorandum.

30. *See, e.g.*, Memorandum, Third Extension of January 25, Potential to Emit Transition Policy, from John Seitz and Eric Schaeffer to Addressees (Dec. 20, 1999).

31. *Id.* at 9.

32. *Id.* at 9–10.

33. Memorandum, Potential to Emit (PTE) Guidance for Specific Source Categories, from John Seitz and Eric Schaffer to Addressees (Apr. 14, 1998).

34. 40 C.F.R. § 70.3(b)(4).

35. 64 Fed. Reg. 45,116 (Aug. 18, 1999). These categories were for hard and decorative chromium electroplating and chromium anodizing tanks, ethylene oxide commercial sterilization and fumigation operations, perchloroethylene dry cleaning facilities, secondary lead smelting facilities, and halogenated solvent cleaning machines.

36. *Id.* § 70.3(b)(1).

37. 57 Fed. Reg. at 32,263.

38. *Id.* at 32,261, 32,263.

39. 56 Fed. Reg. at 21,725.

40. 57 Fed. Reg. at 32,261–62.

41. 40 C.F.R. § 70.3(b)(1), (2).

42. *Id.* § 70.3(b)(2).

43. *See* Memorandum, Title V Permitting for Nonmajor Sources in Recent Section 112 Maximum Achievable Control Technology (MACT) Standards, from John Seitz, Director of EPA Office of Air Quality Planning and Standards (May 16, 1995).

44. 40 C.F.R. § 70.3(c)(1).

45. *Id.* § 70.3(c)(2).

46. 56 Fed. Reg. at 21,727.

47. The term "applicable implementation plan" is defined as

> the portion (or portions) of the implementation plan, or most recent revision thereof, which has been approved under section 110, or promulgated under section 110(c), or promulgated or approved pursuant to regulations promulgated under section 301(d) and which implements the relevant requirements of this Act.

CAA § 302(q). Thus, it includes (1) SIPs approved by the EPA, (2) "federal implementation plans" promulgated by the EPA for states that have failed to submit an approvable plan and for American Indian lands, and (3) "tribal implementation plans" submitted by American Indian tribes and approved by the EPA.

48. CAA § 504(e).

49. 56 Fed. Reg. at 21,738.

50. CAA Section 506(a) provides that a state may adopt additional elements. It states, "Nothing in this Title shall prevent a State, or interstate permitting authority, from establishing additional permitting requirements not inconsistent with this Act."

51. 40 C.F.R. § 70.4(b)(1)–(3).

52. *Id.* § 70.4(b)(3); 56 Fed. Reg. at 21,727–28 (May 1991 proposal preamble discussion).

53. 40 C.F.R. § 70.4(b)(6).

54. *Id.* § 70.4(b)(7), (8), (11); 56 Fed. Reg. at 21,728–29 (May 1991 proposal preamble discussion).

55. 40 C.F.R. §§ 70.4(b)(3)(vii), 70.11. Note that in the preamble the EPA also encourages state and local permitting authorities to have administrative enforcement authority, as well as authority for incarceration in criminal cases. 57 Fed. Reg. at 32,293. However, these are recommendations only.

56. 5 U.S.C. § 558(c); *see also* 40 C.F.R. § 122.6 (continuation of expiring permits under the federal NPDES regulations).

57. 40 C.F.R. § 70.4(b)(10); 56 Fed. Reg. at 21,728–29 (May 1991 proposal preamble discussion).

58. 40 C.F.R. § 70.4(b)(12), (b)(14)–(15) (respectively).

59. *Id.* § 70.4(e).

60. *Id.* § 70.4(e), (f)(1).

61. CAA § 502(d), (i); 40 C.F.R. § 70.10.

62. CAA §§ 179(b), 502(d); 40 C.F.R. § 70.10(a).

63. 40 C.F.R. § 70.4(c); 57 Fed. Reg. at 32,270 (preamble discussion).

64. Memorandum, Interim Title V Program Approvals, from John Seitz, OAQPS Director (Aug. 2, 1993).

65. CAA § 502(g); 40 C.F.R. § 70.4(d).

66. 65 Fed. Reg. 32,035 (May 22, 2000).

67. Sierra Club v. EPA, No. 00-1262 (D.C. Cir.).

68. 65 Fed. Reg. 77,376 (Dec. 11, 2000).

69. *See, e.g.,* 66 Fed. Reg. 65,947 (Dec. 21, 2001) (notice of deficiency for the District of Columbia's Title V program).

70. New York Public Interest Research Group v. Whitman, 2003 U.S. App. LEXIS 3645 (2d Cir. 2003).

71. EPA OFFICE OF AIR QUALITY PLANNING AND STANDARDS, WHITE PAPER FOR STREAMLINED DEVELOPMENT OF PART 70 PERMIT APPLICATIONS (July 10, 1995) [hereinafter JULY 10, 1995, WHITE PAPER].

72. CAA §§ 503(c), 113(b)(2), 113(d)(1)(B); 40 C.F.R. § 70.5(a).

73. 40 C.F.R. § 70.5(a)(1); 57 Fed. Reg. at 32,271–72 (preamble discussion).

74. 40 C.F.R. § 70.5(a)(1). The EPA's May 1991 proposal stated that renewal applications had to be filed eighteen months before the expiration date, unless the EPA approved a shorter time period. *See* 56 Fed. Reg. at 21,732. In response to commenters who said that this was a recipe for stale applications, the EPA shortened the time to six months. However, the rules still contemplate a longer lead time (up to eighteen months) if needed to prevent expiration of the current permit before the new one is issued. 40 C.F.R. § 70.5(a)(1)(iii). The upper limit of eighteen months is based on CAA Section 502(b)(6), which requires states to adopt "[a]dequate, streamlined, and reasonable procedures" for processing applications. 57 Fed. Reg. at 32,272.

75. 57 Fed. Reg. at 32,272.

76. 40 C.F.R. § 70.5(a)(2). The July 10, 1995, white paper elaborates on this standard, and describes the process for providing supplemental information. *See* JULY 10, 1995, WHITE PAPER, *supra* note 71, at 18–20.

77. 40 C.F.R. §§ 70.5(a)(2), 70.7(a)(4). States are required to have adequate, stream-lined, and reasonable procedures for expeditiously determining when applications are complete. CAA § 502(b)(6). The EPA's rules require that procedures be in place to make this determination within sixty days. 40 C.F.R. § 70.4(b)(6). The May 1991 proposal would have required completeness determinations to be made within thirty days.

78. 40 C.F.R. § 70.7(b).

79. The May 1991 proposal would have extended the application shield to (1) sources that filed an application up to three months late and (2) sources the state con-cluded had made a good faith effort in submitting the application, as long as the source cured the defect. Proposed 40 C.F.R. § 70.7(b)(2), (3). Several commenters criticized these provisions as not authorized by the statute. The EPA agreed, and deleted them in the final rules. *See* 57 Fed. Reg. at 32,275.

80. 56 Fed. Reg. at 21,732.

81. July 10, 1995, White Paper, *supra* note 71, at 9.

82. *Id.* at 6.

83. *Id.* at 17.

84. *Id.* at 6–7.

85. 40 C.F.R. § 70.5(c); 57 Fed. Reg. at 32,273 (preamble discussion).

86. 40 C.F.R. § 70.5(c); 57 Fed. Reg. at 32,273 (preamble discussion).

87. July 10, 1995, White Paper, *supra* note 71, at 8.

88. *Id.* at 9–10.

89. Memorandum from Lydia Wegman of OAQPS, "White Paper Number 2 for Improved Implementation of the Part 70 Operating Permits Program" (March 5, 1996) [hereinafter March 5, 1996, White Paper Number 2].

90. 40 C.F.R. § 70.5(c)(8); 57 Fed. Reg. at 32,273–74 (preamble discussion).

91. 40 C.F.R. § 70.5(c)(8)(iii)(C).

92. *Id.* § 70.5(c)(8)(iii)(A), (B).

93. *Id.* § 70.5(c)(8)(iv), (d); *See* CAA § 113(c)(2)(A).

94. July 10, 1995, White Paper, *supra* note 71, at 24.

95. *Id.*

96. 40 C.F.R. § 70.6(a)(1) (emission limitations and standards); 70.6(a)(3) (monitor-ing, record keeping, and reporting); and 70.6(c)(2) (inspection and entry).

97. *Id.* § 70.6(a)(3)(i)(B). This same provision states: "Such monitoring requirements shall assure use of terms, test methods, units, averaging periods, and other statistical con-ventions consistent with the applicable requirement."

98. Appalachian Power Co. v. EPA, 208 F.3d 1015 (D.C. Cir. 2000).

99. 67 Fed. Reg. 58,561 (Sept. 17, 2002).

100. *See In the Matter of Pacificorp's Jim Bridger and Naughton Electric Utility Steam Generating Plants*, Petition No. VIII–00–1 (November 16, 2000) (Pacificorp), *available at* http://www.epa.gov/region07/programs/artd/air/title5/petitiondb/petitions/woc020 .pdf; *In the Matter of Fort James Camas Mill*, Petition No. X–1999–1 December 22, 2000) (Fort James), *available at* http://www.epa.gov/region07/programs/artd/air/title5/petitiondb/ petitions/fort_james_decision1999.pdf. Notice of these decisions was published in the *Federal Register. See* 66 Fed. Reg. 85, January 2, 2001 (Pacificorp); 66 Fed. Reg. 13,529, March 6, 2001 (Fort James).

101. 67 Fed. Reg. 58,529 (Sept. 17, 2002).

102. *See* CAA § 114(a)(3).

103. 62 Fed. Reg. 54,900 (Oct. 22, 1997) (codified at 40 C.F.R. pts. 64, 70, and 71).

104. Natural Resources Defense Council v. EPA, 194 F.3d 130 (D.C. Cir. 1999).

105. 57 Fed. Reg. at 32,278.

106. 40 C.F.R. § 70.6(a)(3)(ii), (iii).

107. *Id.* § 70.6(b).

108. Document V-C-1 in Docket A-90-33 [hereinafter Response to Comments Document]. Although the EPA responds to many public comments in the preamble to the final permits rule, most of the agency's responses to comments are contained in this document. The EPA generally prepares such a document and places it in the docket to meet its obligation to respond to significant comments raised during a rule making.

109. *Id.* at 6–12. This view is based on the requirement in the rules that actions for judicial review of a permit be brought no later than ninety days after issuance. This provision is discussed in the permit issuance and judicial review section later in this chapter.

110. 40 C.F.R. §§ 70.6(c)(1), (4), (5), and 70.2 (definition of "responsible official"); *see also* 40 C.F.R. § 122.22 (signatories to permit applications and reports under the NPDES regulations).

111. *Id.* § 70.6(g)(1), (3).

112. *Id.* § 70.6(g)(3). The preamble includes the EPA's rationale for limiting the defense to exceedances of technology-based standards. 57 Fed. Reg. at 32,279. The NPDES upset provision is found in 40 C.F.R. § 122.41.

113. 60 Fed. Reg. at 45,558–61.

114. March 5, 1996, White Paper Number 2, *supra* note 89.

115. 57 Fed. Reg. at 32,276.

116. *See* United States v. General Motors Corp., 702 F. Supp. 133 (N.D. Tex. 1988) (Texas could make equivalency determination under "alternative methods of control" provision in SIP).

117. 57 Fed. Reg. at 32,278.

118. *Id.* at 32,279.

119. *Id.*

120. H.R. 3030, 101st Cong. (1989) (Section 401, adding a new CAA Section 404(g)).

121. Clean Water Act § 402(k); *see also* 40 C.F.R. § 122.5(a)(1).

122. CAA § 504(f).

123. 40 C.F.R. § 70.6(f)(1); 57 Fed. Reg. at 32,277 (preamble discussion).

124. 40 C.F.R. § 70.6(f)(1).

125. *Id.* § 70.6(f)(3).

126. *Id.* § 70.7(h).

127. 57 Fed Reg. at 32,290; 56 Fed. Reg. at 21,743 (May 1991 proposal discussion). Compare the EPA's consolidated permit regulations, which state, "The Director shall hold a public hearing whenever he or she finds, on the basis of requests, a significant degree of public interest in a draft permit(s)." 40 C.F.R. § 124.12(a).

128. 56 Fed. Reg. at 21,742–43; *see* Chemical Waste Management, Inc. v. EPA, 873 F.2d 1477 (D.C. Cir. 1989) (neither the statute nor due process requires that hearings held under Section 3008(h) of the Resource Conservation and Recovery Act be formal "on the record" hearings).

129. 40 C.F.R. § 70.7(a)(5). This is similar to the statement of basis required for a draft minor NPDES permit, which does not require the preparation of a fact sheet. *Id.* § 124.7.

130. Most of the EPA's description of how judicial review will work is not in the rules at all, but rather in a preamble discussion in the May 1991 proposal. 56 Fed. Reg. at 21,759–60.

131. 40 C.F.R. § 70.4(b)(3)(xii). The preamble warns: "New grounds specifically do not include a government interpretation of a permit of which the source claims in an enforcement action to have been unaware." 57 Fed. Reg. at 32,265.

132. 40 C.F.R. § 70.7(h).

133. *Id.* § 70.7(f). The reopening provision addressing new standards promulgated for major sources implements CAA Section 502(b)(9). The EPA stated in the proposal that although the act states that this type of reopening would apply to "permits with a term of three or more years for major sources," interpreting the language to refer to all permits with *original* terms of three or more years would lead to absurd results. Thus, the EPA requires the mandatory reopening only when there are three or more years *remaining* in the life of the permit. 56 Fed. Reg. at 21,745.

134. 60 Fed. Reg. 45,530 (1995).

135. *See* 62 Fed. Reg. 30,289 (June 3, 1997); 63 Fed. Reg. 14,392 (Mar. 25, 1998).

136. CAA § 502(b)(10).

137. 57 Fed. Reg. at 32,266–67; Response to Comments Document, *supra* note 108, at 6-25, 6-27 to 6-28.

138. Response to Comments Document, *supra* note 108, at 6-16.

139. *Id.* at 6-17.

140. Note that permit terms may include requirements not included in the rule itself.

141. 40 C.F.R. § 70.4(b)(12)(i).

142. *Id.* § 70.4(b)(12)(ii), (iii).

143. *Id.* § 70.4(b)(12).

144. *Id.* § 70.4(b)(14). The May 1991 proposal provided the rationale:

Air permits summarize existing restrictions; a permit change is not affirmatively required to authorize every change in practices which are otherwise legal under the SIP or federal law merely because an existing permit does not address the practice. Thus, changes in industrial practices and procedures that do not run afoul of the terms of a permit can be made without seeking any change to the terms of the permit.

56 Fed. Reg. at 21,746.

145. 40 C.F.R. § 70.4(b)(14).

146. Although the EPA has flip-flopped on whether minor NSR changes constitute a "Title I modification," the agency's most recent position is that they do not. 60 Fed. Reg. at 45,545–46.

147. 40 C.F.R. § 70.4(b)(14), (15); 57 Fed. Reg. at 32,269–70 (preamble discussion).

148. 57 Fed. Reg. at 32,281–87.

149. Compare the revision procedures for NPDES and Resource Conservation and Recovery Act (RCRA) permits. Under the NPDES regulations, almost all changes must be made using the full process utilized for original permit issuance and permit renewals. Only minor, more technical changes to the permit may be made more quickly and with less process. 40 C.F.R. § 122.62, 122.63 (different procedures for "modifications" and "minor modifications"). Although the RCRA permitting regulations originally adopted a similar scheme, the EPA amended those regulations after conducting regulatory negotiations with industry and environmental groups. The new, more flexible (and more complex) system classifies a number of different types of permit changes into three classes, depending on their relative importance and the degree of process and public participation considered appropriate. Fairly detailed procedures are set forth for the three categories of modifications. *Id.* § 270.41, 270.42.

150. *Id.* § 70.7(e)(1), (e)(2)(i), (e)(4); 57 Fed. Reg. at 32,280, 32,287–89 (preamble discussion).

151. 40 C.F.R. § 70.7(e)(2).

152. 57 Fed. Reg. at 32,268; *see also* 40 C.F.R. § 70.6(b)(2).

153. 60 Fed. Reg. at 45,532.

154. *Id*. at 45,536.

155. *Id*. at 45,539.

156. *Id*. at 45,538.

157. 636 F.2d 323 (D.C. Cir. 1980).

158. 60 Fed. Reg. at 45,538.

159. *Id*. at 45,533.

160. See the definition of "affected states" in 40 C.F.R. §§ 70.2 and 70.8(a), (b).

161. Note that the May 1991 proposal stated the EPA's position that this duty is in fact discretionary, because the requirement to object is predicated on a discretionary determination by EPA that the permit does not comply with applicable CAA requirements. 56 Fed. Reg. at 12,749.

162. 40 C.F.R. § 70.8(c), (d). Note that the EPA says in the preamble that it also will veto a permit if the state has not provided adequate information to allow for meaningful EPA review, or if the state has not allowed adequate public participation and review by neighboring states. 57 Fed. Reg. at 32,290. The public petition process and judicial review of the EPA's decision on such a petition is discussed at 56 Fed. Reg. at 21,749–50, 21,751, and 21,760. CAA Section 505(b)(2) states that such a petition

> shall be based only on objections to the permit that were raised with reasonable specificity during the public comment period provided by the permitting agency (unless the petitioner demonstrates in the petition to the Administrator that it was impracticable to raise such objections within such period or unless the grounds for such objection arose after such period).

163. New York Public Interest Group v. Whitman, 2003 U.S. App. LEXIS 3645 (2d Cir. 2003). The court stated that while the EPA has discretion in finding that a permit is deficient, it must object to the permit if it makes the finding.

164. 60 Fed. Reg. at 45,541–43.

165. Virginia v. Browner, 80 F.3d 869 (4th Cir. 1996).

166. *See* 40 C.F.R. § 123.64 (NPDES rules).

167. 40 C.F.R. § 70.9(a)–(c); 57 Fed. Reg. at 32,291–92 (preamble discussion).

168. Memorandum, Reissuance of Guidance on Agency Review of State Fee Schedules for Operating Permit Programs Under Title V, from John Seitz, EPA Office of Air Quality Planning and Standards Director (Aug. 4, 1993). This guidance replaced a December 18, 1992, memorandum on fees from Seitz that industry groups promptly challenged.

169. 40 C.F.R. § 70.9(d); 57 Fed. Reg. at 32,291 (preamble discussion).

170. Response to Comments Document, *supra* note 108, at 9-5.

171. 40 C.F.R. § 70.9(b)(2); Fed. Reg. at 32,291–92 (preamble discussion).

CHAPTER 16

Life after Title V Permit Issuance: You've Received Your Permit, Now What Do You Do?

SHANNON S. BROOME
CHARLES H. KNAUSS

Introduction

As explained in Chapter 15, Title V requires any facility that is a "major source" (and certain minor sources) to obtain an operating permit that lists all of the requirements of the Act that apply to the facility. Virtually every state has now received approval of its Title V program and many states have issued a majority of their permits.[1]

Once the permit has been issued, facilities must meet all of the emissions limitations listed in the permit as well as any new monitoring and record-keeping requirements imposed by the permit. In addition, to the extent a facility fails to meet its obligations, each permit requires reporting of deviations from permit requirements to the state and an annual compliance certification to be submitted to both the state and the Environmental Protection Agency (EPA). Reporting of deviations or noncompliance may lead to enforcement actions. For this reason, it is important to consider an appeal of the permit if it includes inappropriate or unauthorized requirements. This chapter addresses evaluation of permit appeal options and special considerations related to Title V deviation reports, semiannual reports of required monitoring, and annual compliance certification.

Considering a Permit Appeal

Meeting Appeal Deadlines

Once the Title V permit is issued, the permit applicant (and other members of the public) have a right to appeal the terms of the permit. In most states, an applicant must appeal to an administrative hearing board prior to seeking review from a state court. Under 40 C.F.R. Part 70, appeals are required to be filed within ninety days of permit issuance,[2] but in most states the deadline for appeals is thirty days, and in some cases can be as short as fifteen days. Because the time frames are so short, it is important to assess *in advance* of receiving the final permit what permit terms should be appealed. As a general rule, states provide the applicant with a copy of the proposed permit that has been sent to the EPA for its forty-five-day review. At a minimum, the applicant will have the draft permit that was issued for public comment. The facility should determine based on these drafts which permit terms it will appeal if they are not changed in the final version of the permit.

In a state with a short deadline for appealing a permit, the applicant should prepare the appeal papers prior to issuance of the permit so that it is prepared to file immediately upon issuance. This is especially important because, frequently, the state agency issues the permit and then sends it by regular mail to the permittee. In these cases, the permittee may not actually receive the permit until well after the appeal period begins to run. Combining this with the delays that occur internally for the permit to reach the environmental staff person after it enters the plant's mail room (and is possibly routed to the responsible official first), a significant portion of the appeal period can be consumed before the plant environmental staff even receives the permit.

Permit Terms to Consider Appealing

Permit terms may be appealed if they are inconsistent with the state's Title V program regulations. In most cases, the state regulations mirror the federal regulations, which state the minimum required elements of state permit programs, codified at 40 C.F.R. Part 70 (and thus referred to as the "Part 70 rules"). Accordingly, the discussion below focuses on the requirements of the Part 70 rules. It is worth noting that many states provide separate grounds for appeal of permit actions, such as whether the permit term is "unreasonable" or "arbitrary." Therefore, even if the Part 70 regulations do not speak to the appropriateness of a specific permit term, there may be separate grounds upon which an appeal can be based for a particularly unreasonable term. Several permit appeals have been filed across the country since the inception of the Title V program. Provided below are three types of permit terms that are typical in an appeal with a brief explanation of the grounds for appeal.

Effective Date of the Permit

While some states provide a two-week or some other delay between the date of issuance and the effective date of the permit, many permits provide that they become effective on the date that they are issued, such that compliance is required immediately. In the latter situation, the facility will often not have received notice that the permit has been issued until days or weeks after permit issuance. If a facility does not know that a permit has been issued, it will not necessarily be complying with the new terms (e.g., monitoring and recordkeeping) that are imposed, and the facility would be required to report its failure to comply with the new permit terms for the period beginning at issuance and ending when the notice was received and the requirements implemented. Some companies have appealed the effective date of such permits on the grounds that notice of the facility's obligations must be communicated prior to imposing such obligations and associated penalties for noncompliance. State agencies have argued that facilities should be aware of what the permit terms will be based on receipt of draft permits. The states' argument fails to recognize, however, that a permit does not create obligations until it is actually issued and that permits often change in response to comments by the public or the EPA. Therefore, a permittee cannot be expected to be compliant in advance of receiving notice that the permit has, in fact, been issued.[3]

Visible Emissions Monitoring for Small Particulate Sources

Some states have imposed daily, weekly, or monthly requirements for facilities to conduct qualitative visible emissions observations of very small particulate sources that are highly unlikely to experience a violation of the applicable opacity standard (e.g., 20 percent as determined by the EPA Method 9). These types of permit terms can be appealed on the grounds that they go beyond what is necessary to assure compliance. Under Section 70.6(c)(1), the state's authority to impose monitoring is limited to that which is necessary to assure compliance with the permit. If a facility can demonstrate that the permit requirements go beyond what is needed to assure compliance, an appeal may be successful. This demonstration can be made, for example, by showing that other facilities in the state have not been required to meet this level of monitoring, or that prior permits issued to the facility contained less stringent monitoring.

Increasing Stringency of Existing Monitoring in Underlying Applicable Requirements

In some cases, permitting authorities are reviewing existing monitoring to determine if it is "sufficient" to assure compliance and, if it is not, are imposing new, additional monitoring or testing requirements. One example is a Title V permit where the original construction permit required stack testing every three years. The state attempted to impose a requirement that the facility conduct a stack test every two years. The facility appealed the requirement based on *Appalachian Power v. EPA,* in which the U.S. Court of Appeals for the D.C. Circuit vacated the EPA's 1998 Periodic Monitoring Guidance and instructed the EPA and the states that they could not rely on that guidance, or the underlying regulation at 40 C.F.R. § 70.6(a)(3)(i)(B), to supplement monitoring in Title V permits for standards that already contained some "periodic monitoring."[4] If a standard already contains periodic monitoring, a state permitting authority should not be supplementing that monitoring in the Title V permit. It is worth noting that since the *Appalachian Power* decision, the EPA has attempted to use an alternate provision of the regulations, Section 70.6(c)(1), to justify its imposition of new monitoring for standards that already contain monitoring. The ability of the EPA to rely on this more general provision to impose new monitoring again became the subject of litigation in *Utility Air Regulatory Group v. EPA*.[5] Industry advocates argued to the court that because Section 70.6(c)(1) contains a proviso that any action under that provision must be consistent with Section 70.6(a)(3), the *Appalachian Power* decision prohibits a state from conducting a sufficiency review of and supplementing existing monitoring in underlying standards. The EPA argued that Section 70.6(c)(1) creates a wholly separate legal authority that has not yet been addressed by a Court. While the court appeared sympathetic to the industry position during oral argument in the case, ultimately the court decided that the issues presented could not be decided due to problems with standing and ripeness.[6] As of mid-2003, the issue of the EPA's authority to impose additional monitoring under Section 70.6(c)(1) remains open. The EPA has indicated a desire to undertake a rulemaking to clarify monitoring but to date, no proposal has been forthcoming.

Special Considerations Related to Title V Deviation Reports, Semiannual Reports of Required Monitoring, and Compliance Certifications

The most significant new obligation under a new Title V permit is the preparation and submittal of deviation reports, monitoring reports, and annual compliance certifications. The lawyer plays a key role in this process. Each of these documents must be certified by a "responsible official" of the company. A responsible official is defined in Section 70.2 of the Title V regulations as:

> (1) For a corporation: a president, secretary, treasurer, or vice president of the corporation in charge of a principal business function, or any other person who performs similar policy or decision-making functions for the corporation, *or a duly authorized representative of such person* if the representative is responsible for the overall operation of one or more manufacturing, production, or operation facilities applying for or subject to the permit and either:
>> (i) The facilities employ more than 250 persons or have gross annual sales or expenditures exceeding $25 million (in second quarter 1980 dollars); or
>> (ii) The delegation of authority to such representatives is approved in advance by the permitting authority.
> (2) For a partnership or sole proprietorship: a general partner or the proprietor, respectively;
> (3) For a municipality, State, Federal, or other public agency: either a principal executive officer or ranking elected official. For the purposes of this part, a principal executive officer of a Federal agency includes the chief executive officer having responsibility for the overall operations of a principal geographic unit of the agency (e.g., a Regional Administrator of EPA); or

(4) For affected sources:

 (i) The designated representative in so far as actions, standards, requirements, or prohibitions under title IV of the Act or the regulations promulgated thereunder are concerned; and

 (ii) The designated representative for any other purposes under Part 70.

In many permits, the responsible official is identified by title (e.g., plant manager) or by name. In other permits, there is no such specification. In any case, the signatory to these documents must meet the definition of a "responsible official" to sign them. This requirement contrasts with typical reports submitted prior to Title V, in which the environmental manager for a facility would typically be the signatory. Such submittals would now be considered noncompliant with the regulations. If a person who is not a "responsible official" signs these documents, the EPA might allege that the facility filed a false certification, or filed no certification at all, and base penalty calculations on the failure to file.

Regulatory Provisions Related to Deviation Reporting

The Part 70 regulations mandate that semiannual reports of required monitoring and annual compliance certifications identify all deviations from permit requirements. Section 70.6(a)(3)(iii) requires the following with respect to deviation reporting:

> (A) Submittal of reports of any required monitoring at least every six months. All instances of deviations from permit requirements must be clearly identified in such reports.
>
> (B) Prompt reporting of deviations from permit requirements, including those attributable to upset conditions as defined in the permit, the probable cause of such deviations, and any corrective actions or preventive measures taken. The permitting authority shall define "prompt" in relation to the degree and type of deviation likely to occur and the applicable requirements.[7]

The term "deviation" is not defined in Part 70. The Part 71 regulations, which establish the federal operating permit program for states that do not adopt an approvable program by the statutory deadlines, do provide a definition, however, as follows:

> Deviation means any situation in which an emissions unit fails to meet a permit term or condition. A deviation is not always a violation. A deviation can be determined by observation or through review of data obtained from any testing, monitoring, or recordkeeping established in accordance with paragraphs (a)(3)(i) and (a)(3)(ii) of this section. For a situation lasting more than 24 hours which constitutes a deviation, each

24-hour period is considered a separate deviation. Included in the meaning of deviation are any of the following:

(1) A situation where emissions exceed an emission limitation or standard;

(2) A situation where process or emissions control device parameter values indicate that an emission limitation or standard has not been met;[8]

(3) A situation in which observations or data collected demonstrates noncompliance with an emission limitation or standard or any work practice or operating condition required by the permit;

(4) A situation in which an exceedance or an excursion, as defined in Part 64 of this chapter, occurs.[9]

Although the Part 71 regulations do not apply in states where the state is operating its Part 70 program, the deviation definition in Section 71.6 is informative as to how the EPA intends to interpret the term more generally.

Determining Whether a Reportable Deviation Has Occurred

While Part 70 does not define the term "deviation," the regulations are clear that "deviations from permit requirements" must be reported. Therefore, the starting point for assessing whether a deviation has occurred is understanding the permit requirements. For example, consider a permit term that requires that a facility (1) monitor certain conditions (e.g., scrubber pH), (2) conduct an investigation and take corrective action when operation occurs outside of those ranges, and (3) record the instances when such actions occur. A facility that experiences out-of-range operations and conducts the required investigation, corrective action, and record keeping, has complied with its permit and arguably has not experienced a deviation from a permit requirement.[10]

This result makes sense, of course, because indicator monitoring ranges are frequently set within the parameters in which compliance was achieved during recent performance tests or based on engineering judgment regarding what constitutes normal operation for the unit. Normally, neither the facility nor the regulator is certain at what point a parameter may indicate noncompliance under particular conditions of operation. On the other hand, if the permit imposes the operating range as an absolute requirement to be met, then the permittee would have deviated from a requirement if it operated outside the permitted range.[11]

Another area where deviations may occur is the obligation to collect and maintain records under the permit. Under many permits, visible emissions observations of stacks must be made every day and the data must be recorded and maintained for a period of five years. Similarly, many permits require daily or weekly usage logs of coatings to demonstrate compliance with pound-per-hour VOC limitations. Failure to record the data would normally be considered a deviation from permit requirements that must be reported. In addition, if the records are lost, the facility may have a deviation from the requirement to maintain records required by the permit for a period of five years.

Determining Whether to Certify "Continuous" or "Intermittent" Compliance

Under Section 70.6(c)(5)(iii), compliance certifications must contain the following information:

(A) The identification of each term or condition of the permit that is the basis of the certification;

(B) The identification of the method(s) or other means used by the owner or operator for determining the compliance status with each term and condition during the certification period, and whether such methods or other means provide continuous or intermittent data. Such methods and other means shall include, at a minimum, the methods and means required under paragraph (a)(3) of this section. If necessary, the owner or operator also shall identify any other material information that must be included in the certification to comply with section 113(c)(2) of the Act, which prohibits knowingly making a false certification or omitting material information;

(C) The status of compliance with the terms and conditions of the permit for the period covered by the certification, based on the method or means designated in paragraph (c)(5)(iii)(B) of this section. The certification shall identify each deviation and take it into account in the compliance certification. The certification shall also identify as possible exceptions to compliance any periods during which compliance is required and in which an excursion or exceedance as defined under part 64 of this chapter occurred; and

(D) Such other facts as the permitting authority may require to determine the compliance status of the source.

On March 1, 2001, the EPA proposed to amend this provision to require that the certification include a statement as to whether compliance was "continuous" or "intermittent."[12] In addition, the EPA made statements in the preamble indicating that unless a facility utilized a continuous monitoring method, it would not be permitted to certify to continuous compliance but instead must certify intermittent compliance. Under the EPA's approach, an intermittent compliance certification would be required even if a facility had met all of its monitoring obligations, the data collected showed no deviations, and there was no other material information showing deviations from permit requirements.

Industry filed comments objecting to the agency's proposal, arguing that nothing in Title V or Section 114(a)(3) indicates that the term "continuous" compliance requires continuous emissions monitoring for such a certification. Indeed, Section 504(b) of the CAA states that while the EPA administrator may prescribe by rule procedures and methods for determining compliance, continuous emissions monitoring need not be required if alternative methods are available that provide sufficiently reliable and timely information for determining compliance.

Industry further relied on the holding in *Natural Resources Defense Council v. EPA* (hereinafter *NRDC*), where the court determined that compliance assurance monitoring (CAM), 40 C.F.R. Part 64, meets the standards of the Clean Air Act and stated that the "EPA reasonably concluded that CAM will provide a reasonable assurance of compliance with emissions limitations."[13] Because CAM monitoring includes both intermittent and continuous monitoring, industry argued that intermittent monitoring provides enough data to reasonably assure continuous compliance and that any other reading would mean that the EPA views the CAM monitoring as providing a reasonable assurance of *intermittent* compliance, which is clearly not the purpose of the regulations. Similarly, industry argued that the EPA has interpreted CAA Section 504(b) to require periodic monitoring under 40 C.F.R. 70.6(a)(3) and has determined that "intermittent" monitoring satisfies the requirement of Section 504(a) to "assure" compliance and of Section 504(b) to be "sufficiently reliable and timely information for determining compliance." Therefore, commenters concluded that the only reasonable interpretation of the statute is that a source for which the monitoring required by the Title V permit shows compliance during the required monitoring events should be able to certify continuous compliance.[14]

As of mid-2003, the EPA had yet to finalize its action on the compliance certification rule, but many states have responded to the *NRDC* holding by changing their regulations to require a certification that compliance is continuous or intermittent. In light of the EPA's lack of guidance to date, states have adopted their own, often conflicting approaches to the issue. Many states have issued their own instructions for completing certification forms indicating how they should be completed and how compliance should be characterized. This means that two facilities with the same operating experience may report "intermittent" compliance in one state and report "continuous" compliance in another. Until the EPA issues its final determination on this issue, companies should refer to guidance issued by the state or inquire how the certification should be made.

Preparing to Sign the Certification

The EPA's Title V regulations require that a responsible official certify deviation reports, semi-annual monitoring reports, and annual certifications as follows:

> Based on information and belief, formed after reasonable inquiry, the statements and information in the document are true, accurate, and complete.

The scope of a company's "reasonable inquiry" has not been addressed by the EPA but should begin with the monitoring that is specified in the permit. Depending on the number of data points collected, a review of each data point prior to signing the certification may or may not be required. Whatever approach is taken, the company should document its process for conducting the inquiry in case the integrity of the certification is later questioned by a permitting authority or the EPA.

With respect to the responsible official, a facility should apply common-sense principles to ensure that this person has sufficient information to sign the certification. To form an objectively reasonable belief in the truth, accuracy, and completeness of a compliance certification or other submission, the responsible official needs to understand the legal significance of the document he or she is being asked to certify. To understand the legal significance, the responsible official must have a basic understanding of the Title V permitting program (e.g., what a Title V permit is and why the facility has one) and an understanding of the deviations being reported as well as any "close calls" that the facility has determined do not constitute reportable deviations. In addition, the responsible official needs to understand the basic steps taken by those responsible for preparing the submission to support a reasonable, objective belief that the information contained in the document is true, accurate, and complete. For example, the environmental staff should explain what data was reviewed and why they think this constituted a reasonable inquiry to uncover any deviations from permit requirements that may have occurred during the reporting period.

Ultimately, the responsible official must answer the question of whether he or she believes that the information submitted is true, accurate, and complete, and whether a reasonable, objective person would also hold that belief. If the answer is yes, the responsible official can sign the certification. If the answer is no, or uncertain, additional inquiry or changes to the submission should occur before it is signed.

Conclusion

The sands of the Title V permitting process continue to shift as the EPA revises its regulations and as state permitting authorities and permitted facilities gain experience with the program. The key to success is to review the permit carefully to accurately assess facility requirements, collect and organize data in such a manner that it can be easily accessed when conducting a reasonable inquiry, and manage the process so that the responsible official is well informed and communications with the permitting authority support the approach taken by the facility.

Notes

1. Throughout this chapter references to the state or state agency should be read to include local permitting authorities that are administering the Title V program.

2. 40 C.F.R. 70.4(b)(3)(xii).

3. One state, Indiana, has developed a workable solution to this problem by providing in Title V permits that new monitoring, record-keeping, and reporting obligations are not effective until ninety days after issuance.

4. 208 F.3d 1015 (D.C. Cir. 2000).

5. Utility Air Regulatory Group v. EPA, 320 F.3d 272 (D.C. Cir. 2003).

6. *Id.*

7. Most state programs address promptness of reporting by stating that deviations should be included in either quarterly or semiannual reports. Some states, however, require reporting within much shorter time frames, such as one business day or ten days. The permit generally defines the timing of reporting for deviations.

8. Note that the EPA considers it a reportable deviation whenever there is an indication that an emission limitation or standard has not been met. There is no allowance for a percentage of time operated out of the specified range.

9. 40 C.F.R. 71.6(a)(3)(iii)(C). Section 64.1 of the Compliance Assurance Monitoring (CAM) Rule defines the terms "exceedance" and "excursion" as follows:

> *Exceedance* shall mean a condition that is detected by monitoring that provides data in terms of an emission limitation or standard and that indicates that emissions (or opacity) are greater than the applicable emission limitation or standard (or less than the applicable standard in the case of a percent reduction requirement) consistent with any averaging period specified for averaging the results of the monitoring.

> *Excursion* shall mean a departure from an indicator range established for monitoring under this part, consistent with any averaging period specified for averaging the results of the monitoring.

10. Note that some states may take the view that all operations outside of the monitoring range should be reported as deviations even though they would not be considered violations. Because state regulations and interpretations vary, it is important to clarify exactly what the reporting requirements will be at the time of permit issuance or, if not then, at the time that a report is being filed.

11. The ability of a state to impose these so-called operational restrictions under Title V is currently the subject of controversy and has been raised in permit appeals in Ohio. Industry argues that under Section 70.1 of the Title V regulations, Title V does not create new substantive requirements. By imposing these new operating ranges, the state has narrowed the field of permissible operation even though the facility would be in compliance during operations outside the ranges. Therefore, industry argues, the state has created a new more stringent limit under the guise of monitoring, which is impermissible under Title V.

12. 66 Fed. Reg. 12,872, 12,916 (March 1, 2001).

13. 194 F.3d 130, 137 (D.C. Cir. 1999).

14. *See, e.g.,* Comments of the Air Permitting Forum on Notice of Proposed Rulemaking, 66 Fed. Reg. 12,872, 12,916 (2001), Air Docket No. A-91-52 (April 2, 2001).

CHAPTER 17

Civil Enforcement

JULIE R. DOMIKE
ALEC C. ZACAROLI[1]

Introduction

The 1990 Amendments to the Clean Air Act (CAA) included a number of key revisions to the statute affecting enforcement. The amendments established an operating permit program, broad administrative penalty and compliance order authority, and full investigatory and emergency remedial powers. They also included a new penalty assessment provision that imposes a presumption of noncompliance on alleged violators concerning certain continuing violations and shifts to the alleged violators the burden of proving continuing compliance to rebut the presumption. The 1990 amendments authorized a field citation program, allowing Environmental Protection Agency (EPA) inspectors to issue citations for minor CAA violations with much less procedural formality than an administrative or judicial enforcement action, although the agency has never promulgated rules implementing this program. Since adoption of the amendments, a fundamental debate has arisen over the proper role of the federal government in enforcing CAA requirements. The statutory scheme that initially envisioned state implementation and enforcement of air pollution laws has, in many respects, been altered by a scenario involving considerable federal oversight. As a result, many state enforcement decisions are subject to a second guess at the federal level, producing substantial uncertainty for many regulated entities. This is perhaps most prevalent in the enforcement of new source review (NSR) requirements, where state determinations regarding the applicability of these rules to a particular facility are increasingly being overturned by the EPA at the federal level—often many years after the fact.[2]

These developments, coupled with a much broader-based approach to enforcement, has dramatically altered the enforcement landscape under the CAA. For example, with the goal of attaining "global," multifacility settlements, the EPA has targeted entire industries that it suspects of endemic violations of the CAA. This is most prevalent in the context of alleged NSR violations at stationary sources, where the EPA has initiated broad-based enforcement actions against wood products companies, utilities, petroleum refiners, the pulp and paper industry, and recently, ethanol production facilities. The agency also has targeted mobile sources. Enforcement actions against several large diesel-engine manufacturers alleging use of illegal "defeat devices" resulted in settlements that covered more than 80 percent of the diesel-engine industry.

One clear advantage to this approach for the EPA is that it can force, through injunctive relief, application of stringent new controls that would be considerably more difficult to require through rule-making efforts. As more companies agree to stringent new control measures through settlements in order to avoid costly, lengthy, and uncertain litigation, the pressure on the rest of the industry for similar results increases. On one hand, individual companies facing potential global enforcement actions may feel compelled to reach similar settlements. On the other, the EPA faces increasing pressure to ensure that the obligations it imposes on individual companies through settlement of enforcement actions are applied on an industrywide basis, thereby avoiding the creation of competitive advantages through selective enforcement of the laws.

While the EPA has used its enforcement authority to achieve large-scale policy objectives, the agency not has backed away from traditional enforcement measures. Agency statistics reveal that from fiscal year 1996 to fiscal year 1999, CAA stationary source inspections increased from 2,064 to 2,633. As a result, the number of administrative compliance orders issued jumped from 154 in fiscal year 1996 to 298 in fiscal year 1998, while penalty order complaints increased from 88 to 193. In fiscal year 1999, meanwhile, the agency referred 109 cases to the U.S. Department of Justice (cases referred for DOJ prosecution generally involve larger-scale alleged violations), while it resolved 542 cases administratively.[3] These numbers declined in 2000 and 2001, falling to 8,163 and 1,058 respectively, with penalty orders dropping to 160 in 2000 and 170 in 2002.[4] To a large degree, these reductions are the result of a decline in CFC-related investigations. These, of course, do not include enforcement actions taken by the states—the primary enforcers of most CAA requirements under the statutory scheme.

This chapter outlines the current statutory, regulatory, and policy parameters of CAA civil enforcement. Because enforcement policy is always subject to change, practitioners confronted with a possible enforcement action are advised to supplement the information in this chapter with the most up-to-date enforcement policies as early in the enforcement process as possible.[5]

Investigatory Authorities

Inspection, Monitoring, and Information-Gathering Authority

The CAA gives the EPA broad authority to mandate monitoring and record-keeping requirements and to inspect or otherwise collect information from regulated sources under Section 114. The authority applies to any person who owns or operates an emission source, *or* who manufactures emission control or process equipment, whom the EPA "believes may have information necessary for the purposes of [Section 114(a)(1)]" or is "subject to any requirement of [the CAA]."[6] The EPA frequently relies on this authority as the basis for the monitoring, record-keeping, and reporting requirements in substantive standards as well as for developing the factual record for its rule makings concerning emissions standards. The authority may be delegated to the states.[7] Any information the EPA receives pursuant to Section 114 may be released to the public upon request, although procedures for protecting confidential business information and trade secrets are provided.[8]

The EPA can request sources subject to CAA requirements or any person who may have information necessary to carry out the act to take the following actions:

- Establish and maintain records (including records of control equipment parameters, production variables, and other indirect data when direct monitoring of emissions is impractical)
- Make reports
- Install, use, and maintain monitoring equipment and use audit procedures or methods
- Sample emissions at specific intervals, locations, and periods, using methods prescribed by the EPA
- Submit compliance certifications
- Provide any other information the EPA deems reasonably necessary[9]

The authority may be exercised on a "one-time, periodic or continuous basis." Accordingly, as part of an investigation, the EPA may require a source to audit or test emissions or operational parameters on a routine basis, keep records, and report the source's compliance status periodically.[10] In the enforcement context, the EPA's issuance of a Section 114 letter requesting certain information, records, or testing often provides the first indication that it suspects a source is in noncompliance. The letter will set a date by which the target must submit the information to the EPA. Although this time frame can often be negotiated with the agency, depending on the nature of the request, failure to comply with the request in a timely manner without sufficient cause subjects the source to daily civil penalties of up to $27,500 per day.[11] The agency routinely seeks penalties against sources that fail to comply with Section 114 requests.[12] The EPA may also use the Section 114 authority to require testing, record-keeping, monitoring, compliance certification, and auditing procedures to ensure continuing compliance in consent agreements and final orders issued to settle CAA Section 113(d) administrative penalty actions when traditional injunctive relief is not available.

The EPA has expanded use of its Section 114 authority as an investigative tool in recent years, using it to gather information from parties not subject to enforcement but who the EPA suspects have relevant information. For instance, in 1998 the agency relied on its Section 114 authority to compel boiler manufacturers to submit information regarding sales and installation of new equipment at power plants.[13] In some cases, the agency requested information from as far back as 1930,[14] raising the question of whether this provision can be applied retroactively. The EPA then used that information to track suspected modifications at several power plants, which led to large-scale enforcement actions against those companies based on alleged NSR violations.[15] This use of the EPA's Section 114 authority demonstrates its unique breadth.

Mobile Source Information-Gathering Authority

Under CAA Sections 206(c) and 208, manufacturers of new motor vehicles, engines, or engine parts and components, and any other persons subject to the requirements of CAA Title II, pts. A (engine and fuel standards) and C (clean-fuel vehicles), may be required to establish and maintain records, make reports, and provide information as necessary to demonstrate compliance with CAA requirements and regulations.[16] Similar to the parallel power under Section 114 of the CAA, the EPA can exert its information-collection powers broadly, asking for unlimited data over a period of several years. In addition, testing may be required "where such testing is not otherwise reasonably available" under the new motor vehicle and engine provisions of Title II. Extensive testing requirements for manufacturers of new motor vehicles and engines are set out in Section 206, pt. A.

Entry Inspections

Upon presentation of proper credentials, the EPA may enter at "reasonable times" the premises of any person who owns or operates an emission source, who is otherwise subject to the CAA, or who the EPA reasonably believes may have information relevant to CAA implementation or enforcement. Among other things, this authority allows the EPA to sample emissions, copy records, and inspect monitoring equipment or methods. Upon issuance, each CAA operating permit must contain a provision authorizing such entry inspections.[17] Inspections relating to state implementation plan (SIP) requirements must include prior notice to the state unless the EPA believes that the state will give the target source prior warning of the impending inspection. Failure to comply with the notice requirement, however, cannot be used as a defense to noncompliance with Section 114 in an enforcement action or as the basis for exclusion of the evidence or information obtained.[18] The inspection authority is broad in scope, is a powerful tool of government enforcers, and is widely accepted by the courts.[19]

CAA Section 114 allows the EPA or its "authorized representative" to conduct inspections. Because the term is not defined in the CAA, however, the EPA's authority to employ contractors as authorized representatives is unclear.[20] One circuit has upheld the EPA's interpretation allowing contractor use; two others have disallowed contractor inspections.[21]

Entry and inspection authority for mobile source requirements mirror the CAA Section 114 requirements for stationary sources. CAA Section 206(c) authorizes EPA employees or officers, upon presentation of proper credentials, to enter a motor vehicle or engine manufacturing facility; conduct tests; and inspect records, files, processes, and controls.[22] Similar inspection authority is provided by CAA Section 208(b) concerning regulated manufacturers and subcontractors.[23] Similar to Section 114, information collected by the EPA may be released to the public upon request, unless the information is entitled to protection as confidential business information.[24] Failure to comply with mobile source information collection and inspection requests may subject a person to civil penalties of up to $27,500 per day of violation.[25] Unlike the stationary source enforcement scheme, no explicit "sufficient cause" defense to penalties is provided for failure to comply with mobile source information or entry requests.

The EPA requests pursuant to CAA Sections 114(a)(2), 206(c), and 208(b) for entry and inspection of a facility are not self-enforcing. It is routine agency policy to obtain consent to enter and inspect whenever possible. Pursuant to EPA policy and practice, any reasonable attempts to constrain or encumber EPA entry and inspection of the facility will be deemed denial, or withdrawal, of consent to inspect. For example, the EPA views special safety training, demands for liability indemnification, procedures used to delay the inspection or limit inspector discretion, and restrictions on access or sampling as negating or revoking consent.[26] Under the statutory scheme, denial of consent to inspect that lacks "sufficient cause" arguably may subject the source to civil penalty enforcement, but since the EPA's remedy is to obtain a court-issued warrant, courts are unlikely to deem penalties appropriate.[27]

In the absence or withdrawal of consent to inspect the facility, the EPA may compel compliance with its inspection request only by securing from the appropriate federal district court a search warrant to enforce the request.[28] The decision to grant a search warrant is reviewed under the "reasonableness" standard applicable to protections afforded by the Fourth Amendment of the U.S. Constitution.[29] Warrants to enforce an inspection and entry request may be obtained *ex parte* and are routinely issued, provided that the EPA can show it has proper authority to inspect the premises, has reasonably limited the inspection's scope, and seeks the warrant for lawful purposes, not to harass or intimidate.[30] Upon issuance of the search warrant, a U.S. marshal may accompany the EPA to the facility to ensure execution of the court's writ.

From a practitioner's perspective, no amount of post-inspection lawyering can substitute for facility operators being prepared in the first place. Companies should assign one individual to monitor and coordinate inspections whenever they occur. Where consent will be granted, this person should check credentials (e.g., obtain a copy of the inspector's business card); keep a record of the date, time, duration, and purpose of the inspection; personally accompany the inspector at all times; and record any discussions and information provided to the inspector. If the inspection is to be conducted pursuant to a warrant, the company coordinator should understand that the purpose may be to investigate possible crimes. Accordingly, a criminal and environmental lawyer should be contacted immediately to ensure that the warrant's scope is adhered to, that constitutional rights against self-incrimination are protected, and that obstruction of justice does not occur. As concerns all inspections, appropriate corporate personnel need to be aware of the options available to protect privileged information from waiver through inadvertent disclosure.[31]

Administrative Subpoena Authority

The 1990 CAA Amendments expanded the scope and availability of administrative subpoena authority under the statute. Section 307(a) of the CAA confers power on the EPA to issue administrative subpoenas for purposes of compelling disclosure of information, production of documents, or testimony by witnesses (e.g., employees) in support of any investigation, monitoring, or reporting requirement, entry, or compliance inspection, including administrative enforcement proceedings. The subpoena authority applies equally to mobile and stationary source requirements.[32] Consistent with the CAA mobile and stationary source information-collection authorities discussed earlier, trade secrets or confidential business information (CBI) must be submitted or disclosed in response to a subpoena demand or questioning, but CBI can be protected from public disclosure if proper procedures are followed.[33] However, all "emission data," as defined in the Code of Federal Regulations, are exempt from CBI and trade secret claims.[34] After submission to the EPA, the emission data cannot be withheld if the public requests its release.[35]

Although not widely employed by the EPA, subpoena authority can prove valuable when a written information request pursuant to CAA Sections 114 or 208 would not be sufficient to discover adequate information to clarify the activity or incident being investigated. In connection with an enforcement action, the target of a subpoena is likely to be a plant manager or production supervisor who may have knowledge of the source's operating practices or the incident or activities in question. The subpoena target will usually be requested to bring all relevant documents, logs, operating ledgers, and information to the examination location (usually the EPA regional office) on a specific date and time. Even though the examination is not an adversarial proceeding per se, subpoena targets are allowed to be accompanied by a lawyer.[36] The EPA may seek to compel compliance with the subpoena in the U.S. district court in the area where the person resides or conducts business, and the court may impose contempt sanctions for failure to obey its order.[37] In addition, the United States may seek civil penalties against persons who refuse or fail to comply with a subpoena without sufficient cause, but such penalties may be pursued only through administrative penalty authority procedures.[38] Civil judicial actions are not authorized, and the EPA cannot issue an administrative order to compel compliance with the subpoena request.[39] Knowingly failing to comply with a subpoena is not defined as a specific criminal offense under the CAA.[40]

Monitoring, Record-Keeping, and Reporting Requirements

With the exception of the EPA's authority to gather information under CAA Sections 114 and 208, monitoring, record-keeping, and reporting requirements provide the primary information upon which most decisions concerning enforcement and investigation are made. All sources regulated under the CAA must comply with monitoring, record-keeping, and reporting requirements. Common sources of these requirements include construction and operating permits, federally enforceable state regulations, federal regulations, and judicial or administrative compliance orders. Required information may include continuous emission or parameter monitoring records, usage quantities, tank throughput records, equipment leak and maintenance records, ambient air quality monitoring data, and process or control equipment operation data.

Specific federal reporting, monitoring, and record-keeping requirements include, for example, new source performance standards (NSPS) under CAA Section 111 NSPS,[41] National Emissions Standards for Hazardous Air Pollutants (NESHAP) under CAA Section 112,[42] fuel and fuel-additive registration requirements under Title II of the CAA,[43] acid deposition requirements under Title IV of the CAA,[44] and requirements imposed by SIPs and NSR permits.[45] Occasionally the applicable requirement will allow intermittent periods of noncompliance for specified events or circumstances. For example, provided certain record keeping and reporting occurs, some NSPS and NESHAP standards and SIPs allow emission exceedances during start-up, shutdown, and malfunctions. The operating permit program allows states to adopt an affirmative defense to certain emissions exceedances of technology-based emission limits caused by an emergency.[46]

In addition, Section 114(a)(3) of the CAA, as revised by the 1990 amendments, requires major sources to submit annual compliance certifications. The certifications must include (1) identification of the applicable requirement that is the basis of the certification, (2) the method used for determining the source's compliance status, (3) the compliance status, (4) whether compliance is continuous or intermittent, and (5) other facts that the EPA may establish by rule. Additional monitoring, testing, record-keeping, and reporting obligations have been imposed by the enhanced monitoring (or compliance assurance monitoring) regulations promulgated under Section 114(a)(3).

In attempting to develop these regulations, the EPA sparked a contentious debate over what level of monitoring was called for under Section 114. The agency's initial enhanced monitoring proposals[47] were heavily criticized and opposed by many in the regulated community as overly burdensome. The agency ultimately adopted a rule that allows sources to demonstrate compliance based on monitoring parameters of their operation and maintenance.[48] In related activity, the EPA attempted through guidance to the state and local permitting authorities to require sources to undertake more onerous periodic monitoring pursuant to operating permit requirements under Title V of the Act. This guidance was ultimately overturned by the United States Court of Appeals for the D.C. Circuit, however, which ruled the agency could not enforce the guidance without undertaking notice-and-comment rulemaking.[49] Had the EPA's guidance survived judicial scrutiny, it would have imposed a significant new monitoring burden on stationary sources subject to operating permit requirements, and also would have led to the development of a larger body of evidence upon which the agency, citizens, and states could have based enforcement actions.

Another significant regulatory development, which to date has survived court review,[50] has had a more profound impact on enforcement. In 1997, the EPA adopted revisions to language in various areas of CAA regulations that clarified the agency's authority to use any credible evidence otherwise allowed under state or federal rules of evidence to prove violations of the CAA.[51] The rule, often referred to as the "any credible evidence" rule, is significant in that it replaced an existing practice restricting the agency to using reference-test methods to prove violations. As the name suggests, the new system permits the use of a substantially broader universe of evidence in establishing CAA violations. Many contend this approach renders previously promulgated EPA regulations far more stringent, as it renders sources potentially liable for any exceedance of emissions standards. Because many emission limits were established based on application of specific compliance test methods, they argue, only those methods should be used to demonstrate compliance, not a broader set of data. This argument has never been fully tested. The D.C. Circuit rejected a challenge to the rule as not ripe for review because no enforcement actions had been brought based on the use of the rule.[52] It therefore remains a potentially viable defense on a case-by-case basis, where agency reliance on credible evidence arguably affected the stringency of the underlying standard being enforced.

Operating Permits

Almost all applicable and enforceable CAA requirements must be reflected in a source's Title V operating permit, thereby rendering these permits basic road maps to both compliance and enforcement. In states with EPA-approved operating programs, the specific monitoring, record-keeping, and reporting requirements may vary somewhat. Each program, however, must contain the following minimum elements:

- Each operating permit must include monitoring, reporting, and record-keeping requirements sufficient to assure compliance with permit terms and conditions.
- Operating permits must require semiannual reporting of all required monitoring, prompt reporting of all deviations from permit requirements, and annual certifications of compliance concerning permit terms and conditions.[53]
- Any form, report, or compliance certification required by the operating permit regulations must contain a certification by a responsible official that the statement is true, accurate, and complete, based on information and belief formed after reasonable inquiry.[54]

- Each permit must contain a provision authorizing the permitting authority to enter and inspect the facility at any reasonable time.[55]

The compliance certification provisions require a responsible corporate official to certify, under the threat of criminal sanction for false statements, information describing methods used for determining compliance status and to specify whether compliance is continuous or intermittent.[56]

Administrative Enforcement Responses

Consistent with other major environmental laws, the CAA authorizes the filing of civil enforcement actions in federal or state courts before administrative or judicial tribunals. The plaintiff may be a citizen, a state (or a state environmental agency), or the United States (or the EPA). The relief sought may include injunctions, penalties, or both. The following discussion focuses on the breadth and limits of CAA enforcement authorities.

Although the statutory scheme of the CAA contemplates that most civil enforcement actions will be initiated by the states,[57] the Act reserves concurrent enforcement powers for the federal government. In many cases, this has resulted in federal EPA "overfiling" the state (i.e., filing a separate federal action) where the agency does not agree with the state's decision. The result has been considerable uncertainty regarding CAA compliance, as regulated entities may not be able to rely on compliance decisions by states. Whether the EPA in fact has authority to overfile, thereby potentially eliminating a source's reasonable reliance on the decision of a state as a defense, is an unsettled matter. In the context of the Resource Conservation and Recovery Act (RCRA), courts have rejected the notion that the EPA may overfile in cases involving alleged violations of requirements delegated to the state.[58] On the other hand, courts have recognized the CAA's dual enforcement scheme as allowing the EPA to bring enforcement actions where states may already have acted.[59] Therefore, while reliance on the decisions of state agencies may serve as a mitigating factor in many cases, it does not necessarily provide a bar to federal enforcement.

As a general matter, enforcement efforts are intended to focus on "significant violators."[60] As explained below, the EPA has developed certain mechanisms, including self-disclosure and penalty policies, that are designed to take into account factors that mitigate against harsh penalties for less significant violations. However, once the EPA has information indicating that a source has violated, or continues to violate, the CAA or poses a threat to public health or the environment, the government has a vast arsenal of authorities to compel compliance, assess penalties, and send a deterrence message to other regulated entities.

Due to the expansion and clarification of the administrative enforcement authorities in the 1990 amendments, the EPA has more leeway to avoid costly and potentially uncertain litigation in federal court. As a result, administrative approaches have assumed an important role in federal CAA enforcement. A wide variety of administrative enforcement options is available to the EPA.

Administrative Compliance Orders

Section 113(a) authorizes the EPA to issue an administrative order to comply with the CAA whenever it finds that any person has violated, or is in violation of, any requirement or prohibition of Title I (e.g., SIP, NSPS, NESHAP, NSR rules, or risk management planning requirements), Section 303 emergency orders, Title IV acid rain requirements, Title V permits, and stratospheric ozone protection requirements (Title VI).[61] Orders may address a violation of any of these provisions contained in any "rule, plan, order, waiver, or permit" or pertaining to nonpayment of any required fee (other than Title II mobile sources fees).[62] An administrative order issued under Section 113(a) must reasonably specify the nature of the violation and a reasonable time for compliance, which shall be as "expeditiously as practicable," but in no event longer than one year after the date of the order's issuance.[63] In setting the compliance date, the EPA must take into account the seriousness of the violation and any good faith efforts to comply by the source. An order issued to a corporation must be issued to appropriate corporate officers. In addition, a copy of the order must be sent to the relevant state air pollution control agency.[64]

Except in cases addressing violations under Section 112 concerning hazardous air pollutants, the order cannot become effective until after the violator has had an opportunity to confer with the EPA.[65] Accordingly, the conference affords the alleged violator an opportunity to present legal argument and evidence informally to convince the EPA to withdraw or modify the order. The EPA usually schedules the conference date between ten and fourteen days after the issuance of the order, depending on the nature of the violation and the severity of the alleged environmental impact.

Failure to comply with the terms of an administrative compliance order is a violation of the CAA and may subject a source to civil penalties. The EPA, however, must initiate a separate civil judicial or administrative action pursuant to CAA Sections 113(b) or 113(d), respectively, to collect penalties or mandate compliance with the terms of the order.[66] The statute explicitly provides that an administrative compliance order does not relieve a source from the responsibility to comply with the CAA or any permit condition, or otherwise prohibit the United States from exercising its other enforcement prerogatives, including the assessment of penalties, judicial imposition of injunctive relief, and imposition of criminal sanctions.[67] Although the EPA may use the order authority when penalties are deemed unnecessary, it often issues an administrative compliance order when time is of the essence or to enhance the enforcement exposure of an alleged violator perceived as uncooperative in coming into compliance.[68] The EPA may also issue an administrative order to establish the threat of criminal liability for knowing noncompliance with the terms of the order, when the underlying authority appears insufficient to compel immediate compliance.[69]

When an alleged violation pertains to a SIP requirement contained in a permit or otherwise, in addition to the general procedures discussed earlier, CAA Section 113(a)(1) requires the EPA to give the source and the state thirty days' notice before the order may be issued.[70] The notice of violation is designed to give states an opportunity to exercise their enforcement prerogatives before federal involvement. However, the notice requirement does not give a source a thirty-day grace period to continue to violate. Civil penalties may be assessed for the entire period of violation, regardless of whether the period of violation falls within or continues beyond the end of the thirty-day notice period.[71]

In addition to the general authority to issue orders directing compliance with CAA rules, requirements, standards, and prohibitions, the CAA also allows the issuance of administrative compliance orders to a source when the state fails to comply with NSR requirements.[72] Whenever the EPA finds that a state is not acting in compliance with NSR requirements concerning new construction or modification of existing sources, it may issue a finding of violation to the state and a prohibitory order to the source. Typically these orders arise in the context of a state prevention of signification deterioration (PSD) or NSR permitting action in which the EPA believes that the state's interpretation of the new source requirements violates the CAA as applied to the source. For example, the EPA may disagree with the state regarding what constitutes best available technology or lowest available emissions requirements, whether sufficient offsets have been obtained, or whether a permitting exemption was lawful. While the law is uncertain, courts have found that a source is entitled to rely on discretionary state actions implementing EPA-approved NSR programs. The case against the EPA generally is strongest when the source has begun construction or modification in good faith reliance on a state-issued permit and the business would be economically disadvantaged by the EPA's order.[73]

The EPA has additional authority to issue an order, or to seek injunctive relief in federal district court, as necessary to prevent the construction or modification of any major source that fails to meet the requirements of the PSD NSR program and permitting requirements.[74] Unlike CAA Section 113(a) administrative orders, Section 167 orders do not require the EPA to give the target an opportunity to meet and confer with the EPA before the order's effective date. In addition, a Section 167 authority does not require the EPA to give any prior notice or copy of the order to the relevant state authorities, and it does not limit the time period within which compliance must be achieved.

Pursuant to CAA Section 113(a)(2), based on an EPA finding that SIP or permit program violations are so widespread that state failure to enforce the program effectively may be inferred, the EPA may assume federal enforcement of the program after appropriate notice.[75] However, since the United States maintains concurrent enforcement authority of the CAA with the states and is not otherwise barred from enforcing a SIP or permit program, this provision is likely never to be invoked. In the unlikely event that a state simply ceases to enforce the CAA or one of its programs, this provision might allow the EPA to assume enforcement action more quickly than other regulatory provisions in the CAA (e.g., federal implementation plan provisions, which can take a number of months to notice, propose, and finalize).

Judicial Review of Administrative Compliance Orders

Generally, judicial review of an EPA-issued administrative compliance order has been held to be unavailable because the order does not constitute "final action" within the meaning of CAA Section 307(b).[76] Section 307(b) contains no definition of final action, and the statute elsewhere contains no explicit language addressing judicial review of administrative compliance orders. Attempts by some legislators during consideration of the 1990 CAA Amendments to clarify the judicial reviewability of administrative orders were unsuccessful.[77] Some courts, however, have found judicially reviewable administrative compliance orders concerning the construction or modification of new sources under CAA Sections 113(a)(5) and 167.[78] Despite case law holding that such orders are final action under certain limited circumstances, the EPA is not likely to relinquish the view that pre-enforcement review is precluded by the statute. Practitioners confronted with administrative orders must carefully weigh the facts in the case and the type of administrative order involved. In general, courts have been more sympathetic to finding a right to judicial review where the source would be subjected to severe sanctions, where the source would be substantially injured by the impact of the order (e.g., a stop construction order), or where EPA action is unfairly tardy.

Administrative Penalty Orders

The 1990 CAA Amendments provided the EPA with the authority to issue administrative orders assessing penalties for CAA violations of stationary source requirements. This eliminated the need for the EPA to pursue many actions in federal district court. Section 113(d) of the CAA authorizes the EPA to issue administrative penalty orders of up to $27,500 per day of violation. The orders may assess penalties for any violation of any requirement or prohibition of any rule, order, waiver, permit, or plan and payment of any required fee under any CAA title except Title II.[79]

An administrative penalty order may not assess a fine of more than $200,000, and it must be issued no later than one year after the first alleged date of violation. The penalty cap and time for filing may be waived by a joint determination of the attorney general and the EPA administrator, and such waivers are not subject to judicial review.[80] Administrative penalty orders may assess penalties for SIP violations, provided the thirty-day notice of violation requirement is met, and for failure to comply with NSR requirements when a CAA Section 113(a)(5) finding of state noncompliance has been made.[81]

Upon receipt of an administrative penalty order, an alleged violator has thirty days to file a request for a hearing before an EPA administrative law judge (ALJ) in accordance with the Administrative Procedures Act (APA).[82] Procedures before EPA ALJs are governed by 40 C.F.R. pt. 22, which is relatively flexible and informal. (For example, the Part 22 rules generally limit discovery to unusual circumstances, and then only by leave of the presiding officer.)[83] The suitability of a particular case for an administrative penalty order is determined by EPA policy guidance. In addition to the statutory limitations, the EPA has deemed the administrative forum ill-suited for cases requiring long-term, capital-intensive injunctive relief; having evidence of criminal activity; or needing post-filing discovery; or ones in which issues of first impression are likely to be addressed.[84] When settling an administrative penalty order action, the EPA will rely on the CAA Section 113(a) administrative compliance order authority as a substitute for judicially imposed injunctive authority for any nonpenalty relief necessary to assure compliance.

The EPA has also indicated that the amount of penalties pleaded in an administrative penalty order will equal the "preliminary deterrence" amount as determined by EPA civil penalty guidance. The preliminary deterrence amount equals the sum of the economic benefit of noncompliance plus an additional penalty to account for the seriousness of the violation (i.e., the "gravity" portion of the penalty).[85] This dollar amount essentially represents the EPA's determination of the settlement value of a case in the absence of special mitigating circumstances. In contrast, when the United States files an enforcement action in United States district court, the complaint seeks the maximum penalty possible, up to $27,500 per day for each violation. Thus, the administrative forum tends to limit a source's potential penalty exposure, especially since the EPA ALJs rarely award penalties in excess of the amount for which the EPA pleads in the administrative order and complaint.

CAA Section 205(c) provides authority for administrative assessment of civil penalties for violations of mobile source requirements enumerated in CAA Sections 205(a) (new motor vehicle and engine requirements), 211(d) (fuel regulations), and 213(d) (nonroad engines and vehicles). The maximum penalty amount assessed cannot exceed $200,000 in any one proceeding against any one violator, unless the EPA administrator and the attorney general jointly agree to waive the penalty cap.[86] An APA-type hearing can be requested within thirty days from the violator's receipt of the order.[87] Unless a request for a hearing is timely filed, the order becomes final thirty days after its issuance.[88]

Judicial Review of Administrative Penalty Orders

Judicial review of stationary and mobile source administrative penalty orders may be obtained by filing a petition in U.S. district court within thirty days from the date the administrative penalty order becomes final. Generally, under Part 22, an administrative penalty order is not "final" until after exhaustion of administrative remedies, including review by the EPA Environmental Appeals Board (EAB).[89] A copy of the notice of appeal must be sent to the EPA and the Attorney General. Jurisdiction lies in the U.S. District

Court for the District of Columbia or in the district in which the violation is alleged to have occurred, where the alleged violator resides, or where such person's principal place of business is located. The standard of review requires that the order be upheld unless no substantial evidence is on the record to support the finding of violation or unless the assessment constitutes an abuse of discretion.[90]

Collection procedures are virtually identical for enforcement of mobile and stationary source final penalty order assessments or judgments. After the penalty order becomes final in the administrative forum or after an appeal, the United States may file an action in district court to enforce the order and recover the penalty with interest from the date of the final order. The validity, amount, and appropriateness of this assessment is not subject to review in this type of enforcement action. In addition, a source that fails to pay a final penalty assessment in a timely way shall be required to pay United States' enforcement expenses, including attorneys' fees and costs and a quarterly nonpayment penalty of 10 percent of the aggregate amount of the outstanding balance at the beginning of each quarter.[91]

Stationary Source Noncompliance Penalty Assessment Actions

Section 120 authorizes the EPA, after issuing a notice of noncompliance, to assess noncompliance penalties against a source that "is not in compliance with" requirements of a SIP, NSPS, NESHAP, Section 167 PSD orders, Section 303 emergency orders, acid rain requirements, operating permits, or chlorofluorocarbon requirements.[92] The purpose of the noncompliance penalty assessment authority is to "recover the economic advantage which might otherwise accrue to a source by reason of its failure to comply" with the CAA.[93] Noncompliance penalties are prospective from the date the source receives the notice of noncompliance.[94]

Receipt of a notice of noncompliance requires a source to calculate the amount of the penalty owed as prescribed by regulation and to propose a quarterly payment schedule. Alternatively, the source may elect to submit a petition to the EPA to challenge the notice, whereupon the source is entitled to an APA-type hearing.[95] The source may also claim certain exemptions at this time.[96] Section 120 contains no limit on the amount of penalties that may be assessed, provided that the penalty meets the statutory definition relating to economic advantage as a result of noncompliance. Noncompliance penalty assessment authority may be delegated to the states.[97] In addition, Section 120 specifies that noncompliance penalties shall not bar or otherwise limit additional civil or criminal enforcement proceedings under the CAA or state or local law.[98] Exhaustion of administrative remedies, including appeal to the EAB, is required before judicial review is available in the appropriate local court of appeals.[99]

Before the 1990 amendments, Section 120 provided the only administrative penalty authority available under the CAA, and as a result was used more frequently at that time, despite its many cumbersome procedures.[100]

With the adoption of relatively streamlined administrative proceedings that provide for recoupment of economic benefit, Section 120 noncompliance penalty assessments have for the most part ceased to play a role in CAA enforcement.[101]

Field Citations

In addition to the more traditional administrative and judicial enforcement tools authorized by the amended CAA for stationary source requirements, CAA Section 113(d)(3) has authorized the EPA to create by rule a field citation program to address minor violations. Although it proposed a field citation program in 1994,[102] the EPA never finalized the rule, and, in fact, withdrew the proposal on March 19, 2002.[103] The agency has no current plans to develop the program. Nonetheless, the statute provides the EPA with authority to implement a program through which it could issue citations that do not exceed $5,000 per day of violation for "appropriate minor violations." A recipient of a field citation may petition the EPA for a non-APA type hearing to contest the levy. Pursuant to the statute, payment of the assessed penalty shall not be a defense against further state or federal enforcement action, or against the statutory maximum penalty under other penalty authorities, if the violation continues.[104] Nonpayment penalties and judicial review are available to the extent provided for CAA Section 113(d)(1) administrative penalty orders.

Emergency Orders

Two provisions in the CAA authorize the EPA to issue administrative orders to abate endangerment to human health or the environment caused by mobile or stationary sources of air pollution. Section 303 of the CAA allows the agency to issue an order requiring abatement of pollution that is found to be causing an imminent and substantial endangerment to human health or welfare or to the environment. Section 112(r)(9), meanwhile, also allows the agency to issue an abatement order where it finds the presence of an imminent and substantial endangerment, although this provision applies primarily to accidental releases of hazardous chemicals. The EPA may order abatement of pollution without having to show noncompliance with the CAA, and compliance with a permit or regulatory requirement is no defense (though it may be evidence of the lack of endangerment). The agency also retains the option of seeking a court-ordered injunction in addition to, or as an alternative to, issuing an administrative order. Moreover, in some cases the EPA may rely on other non-CAA statutory authorities to issue emergency orders to abate air pollution. The EPA takes the position that emergency orders do not constitute final action[105] and that consequently such orders should not be subject to judicial review beyond the context of a government-initiated enforcement action.[106]

Before issuing an order under Section 303, the EPA is required to consult with the relevant state authorities and "attempt to confirm the accuracy" of the information on which the order is based.[107] The order may require cessation of the pollution or any other action necessary to abate the endangerment it causes. The effective date of the order cannot extend beyond sixty days unless the United States files an action in district court to enforce the order. In this case the order remains in effect an additional fourteen days or until such date as the court may order. Failure to comply with an emergency order may subject the source to potential civil penalties of $27,500 per day for each violation.[108]

CAA Section 112(r)(9), meanwhile, allows the EPA to issue chemical accidental release prevention orders when the agency determines that an imminent and substantial endangerment to human health or welfare or to the environment may exist because of an "actual or threatened accidental release" of a "regulated substance." The order may require such relief as necessary to eliminate the danger and protect human health.[109] An order cannot be issued pursuant to Section 112(r)(9) unless the EPA has given notice to the relevant state authorities and Section 303 authority has been deemed inadequate to abate the danger. An accidental release is defined as "an unanticipated emission of a regulated substance or other extremely hazardous substance into the ambient air from a stationary source."[110] A regulated substance is defined as a substance listed by rule pursuant to Section 112(r)(3).[111] What constitutes an "other extremely hazardous substance" is not defined by the statute or rule.[112] Unlike CAA Section 303, Section 112(r)(9) places no mandated time limit or expiration date on an endangerment order. The EPA interprets Section 303 authority to apply to threatened as well as actual emissions. Consequently, it is more likely the EPA will rely on its authority under Section 303 to issue abatement orders than on its Section 112(r)(9) authority.[113]

The Federal Procurement Bar

Pursuant to Section 306, any person convicted of a crime under the CAA automatically becomes ineligible to perform contracts for the procurement of goods, materials, and services with *any* instrumentality of the federal government at the facility that gave rise to the conviction.[114] The purpose behind the federal procurement bar, originally enacted in 1970, is to prohibit the use of federal funds to subsidize, or to confer competitive advantage upon, persons violating the CAA.[115]

Previously, upon entry of the judgment of conviction, the name of the company and the facility associated with the crime were placed on a list of facilities ineligible to receive federal grants, contracts, or loans. To ensure that listed facilities did not receive federal funds, the list was periodically transmitted to the General Services Administration (GSA) and reviewed before commitment of any federal monies by any government entity. This program was historically referred to as the "mandatory" contractor listing program. Under the CAA as revised, the EPA has authority to extend the federal procurement bar to other facilities owned or operated by the convicted person. Once a person is placed on the list of ineligible facilities by virtue of a criminal conviction of the CAA, the prohibition against the listed facility entering into contracts with the federal government continues until the EPA certifies, based on a petition by the listed person, that the "condition giving rise to [the] conviction" has been corrected.[116] The EPA contractor listing and removal decisions under the CAA were formerly governed by regulations at 40 C.F.R. pt. 15. In June 1996, the EPA consolidated the CAA listing program with its suspension and debarment program under 40 C.F.R. pt. 32.[117]

Once a facility has been placed on the list, it must obtain an EPA determination that the condition that gave rise to the conviction has been corrected before it will again be eligible to contract with the government. This may be obtained through a petition to the agency.[118] The EPA determines the "condition" giving rise to the conviction depending on the facts of each case, but it has historically placed particular emphasis on the corporate policies, practices, and procedures that may have led to the violation.[119] In the past, the EPA has required facilities to provide comprehensive documentation that corporatewide policies, practices, and procedures have been enacted and implemented to ensure an environment conducive to compliance with the CAA before it will certify a facility for removal from the list.[120] If the debarring official denies a petition to remove a facility from the GSA list of ineligible facilities, the petitioner has thirty days to appeal the debarment decision to the EPA administrator.[121] After final EPA action, judicial review is available in the U.S. courts of appeals.[122] Facilities that receive federal funding and that face the possibility of discretionary debarment based on continuing and recurring CAA noncompliance, or a criminal plea agreement or trial for a CAA crime, would be wise to generate and implement, in consultation with the EPA, the necessary elements of a reinstatement petition as early as possible.

Assessment Factors for Administrative Penalty Assessments

Penalty assessments under Section 113(d)(1) administrative penalty orders and Section 113(d)(3) field citations are governed by the same CAA Section 113(e) penalty assessment factors that apply to civil judicial enforcement actions under CAA Section 113(b).[123] Noncompliance penalty assessments pursuant to CAA Section 120 are not subject to the Section 113(e) factors.[124] Penalty assessments in mobile source cases are governed by CAA Section 205(b) and (c)(2).[125] The CAA Sections 113(e) and 205(b) and (c)(2) penalty assessment factors are discussed later.

Judicial Enforcement Actions

Initiation of Civil Judicial Action

Under CAA Section 113(b) the United States may bring suit in U.S. district court to seek civil penalties and temporary or permanent injunctions against any person who owns or operates a stationary source. Suits are authorized whenever such a person has violated, or is in violation of, any requirement or prohibition of any SIP, permit, Title I (hazardous air pollutants, NSPS),

Section 303 (emergency orders), Title IV (acid rain), Title V (permits), or Title VI (stratospheric ozone protection).[126] The authority includes any requirement or prohibition in any rule, order, waiver, or permit promulgated, issued, or approved under the CAA, or for the payment of any non-Title II fee under the CAA. Actions to enforce SIPs must be preceded by a thirty-day notice to the state of the alleged violation pursuant to Section 113(a)(1). In addition, judicial enforcement for requirements pertaining to construction or modification of major stationary sources in violation of NSR requires the EPA to make a finding that a state has failed to enforce the new source requirements properly.

The CAA, and subsequent inflation adjustment rules, allow penalties for stationary source violations to be assessed up to $27,500 per day for each violation. Liability is strict.[127] Injunctive authority is permissive, and some courts have refused to impose an injunction unless the violations are likely to be repeated.[128] Venue is proper in the district where the violation is alleged to have occurred or is occurring or where the defendant resides or has a principal place of business. Notice of suit commencement must be given to the appropriate state air agency. The court may award attorneys' fees and costs of the litigation for actions unreasonably filed.

Judicial enforcement of the mobile source requirements in CAA Sections 205(a), 211(d), and 213(d) may be commenced in U.S. district court for civil penalties. Injunctive relief is available pursuant to CAA Sections 204(a) and 211(d)(2).[129] Penalties that may be assessed for mobile source violations vary from $2,500 per offense to $27,500 per day of each violation, depending on the provision violated. Any judicial action filed under CAA Section 205(b) may be brought in the U.S. district court for the district in which the violation is alleged to have occurred or in which the defendant resides. Suits may also be brought in a district that contains the EPA's principal place of business.

Prefiling Contacts

The EPA uses two methods of initiating civil judicial actions: direct and indirect referrals. A direct referral involves transmission of a litigation referral package to the Department of Justice (DOJ) from the EPA (usually authored by a regional EPA office) for filing with the appropriate court. An indirect referral (also called "prereferral negotiation") allows the EPA a relatively short period of time to attempt to settle the case, usually ninety days, before the case is referred to the DOJ for filing.[130] Either type of referral package includes a discussion of the facts, the applicable law, and the nature and extent of the alleged violations. The package also includes a description of the evidence supporting the violations; a discussion of potential defenses and weaknesses in the case and what facts need further investigation; the discovery strategy, if necessary; and an analysis of the appropriate settlement penalty based on application of the EPA penalty policy relevant to the facts of the case.

Executive Order 12778, concerning civil justice reform, requires the DOJ to make a "reasonable effort" before filing a complaint to contact the target of a civil judicial enforcement action, to notify the target of the nature of the dispute, and to attempt to settle the case.[131] The prefiling notice requirement may also be met by prior EPA contacts, for example, during prereferral negotiations. Prefiling notice of the impending suit, which also provides an opportunity for a prefiling settlement conference, is usually transmitted by a letter from the DOJ, but it can also occur by letter from the EPA in an attempt to settle the case through indirect referral procedures. Typically the letter briefly describes the alleged violations, proposes a settlement penalty acceptable to the United States, and suggests a time frame for a settlement conference and a response to the settlement offer. Failure to respond to the settlement offer by the date set out in the letter may cause the United States to file the complaint without further notice. The procedures required by the executive order are designed to reduce the burden and costs of litigation by encouraging early settlement.

Settlement Policy

Before the initiation of prefiling negotiations in civil judicial cases (or administrative penalty cases), the EPA or DOJ will have determined a penalty amount for each case that will be deemed acceptable to settle the case without litigation. The minimum acceptable penalty is calculated to recover the economic benefit[132] that the violator gained by noncompliance with the CAA and an additional penalty amount to account for the gravity (or seriousness) of the violation and for deterrence objectives.[133] Effective prefiling settlement negotiations require counsel to be familiar with the pertinent penalty policy and its application to the relevant facts of the case. Appropriate enhancements or reductions may be made to the government's settlement position based on information disclosed or legal arguments made by the alleged violator. Because the parameters of an acceptable penalty settlement evolve based on the facts of each case and the strength of the government's legal case, the acceptable penalty may be revisited and recalculated often, based on the facts and arguments elicited during pretrial discovery and settlement negotiations. Accordingly, practitioners must be knowledgeable of the current relevant penalty policies and be prepared to frame settlement negotiations within the context of those policies. Note that once the complaint has been filed in district court, the United States will seek the full penalties available under the CAA and will no longer be bound by the terms of the applicable penalty policy. In addition, defendants who are recalcitrant and uncooperative during pretrial settlement negotiations will usually face higher minimum acceptable settlement penalties than fully cooperative defendants.[134]

When a settlement is reached, the parties' agreement is embodied in a consent decree, which is proposed for court approval. Consent decrees usually contain, among other things, a penalty assessment, injunctive relief to ensure compliance with the CAA, and stipulated penalties for violations of the terms of the consent decree. Consent decrees uniformly include a clause noting that civil penalties are not deductible for tax purposes. Generally, force majeure provisions excusing late compliance with the terms of the consent decree due to acts of God will not be included unless a defendant raises the issue and justifies the necessity. In some cases, especially concerning very large monetary settlements, the United States will insist on deposit of the penalty amount into an interest-bearing escrow account at the time the consent decree is lodged. After signature by all parties, the DOJ (or the relevant U.S. Attorney's Office) lodges the consent decree and the complaint with the district court. After a period of time for public comment on the terms of the consent decree (a minimum of thirty days), the United States will petition the court for entry of the decree.[135]

Penalties

Penalty Assessment Criteria

Except for some minor distinctions noted later, courts and administrative law judges are required to consider virtually identical penalty assessment factors for both stationary and mobile source violations in civil administrative or judicial actions, including citizens' suits. (A notable exception is that the presumption of continuing violation for penalty assessment purposes applies only in stationary source enforcement actions.) Section 113(e) sets out mandatory criteria courts and the EPA must address to determine the appropriate penalty in enforcement actions in federal courts (including citizens' suits) and EPA administrative proceedings (including determinations by ALJs).[136] When assessing a penalty, the EPA or the court must consider the size of the violator's business, the economic impact of the penalty on the business, the violator's full compliance history and good faith efforts to comply, the duration of the violation as established by any credible evidence (including evidence other than the applicable test method), violator's payment of penalties previously assessed for the same violation, the economic benefit the violator gained from noncompliance, the seriousness of the violation, and any other factors justice may require.[137] The 1990 CAA Amendments added the criteria relating to the violator's compliance history and good faith efforts to comply, the duration of the violation established by any credible evidence,[138] previous payments for the same violation,[139] and the economic benefit of noncompliance.

While consideration of these criteria is mandatory under the CAA, the EPA's application of the criteria in individual circumstances has been muddied by the agency's recent global enforcement and settlement approach. As noted above, in bringing large-scale, companywide enforcement actions that often implicate several facilities, the EPA has established a model that has resulted in global settlements designed to resolve all violations on a companywide basis. These settlements often include substantial injunctive relief—including programs designed to enhance existing regulatory programs—and a single penalty. Although the penalties are considerable, they do not necessarily reflect application of the agency's traditional penalty policies, which would have resulted in larger penalties had the policies been applied in a straightforward manner.

In developing the penalty-assessment criteria, Congress looked to the Clean Water Act (CWA) penalty assessment provisions as a model and expressed its intention that the CAA criteria be applied in the "same manner" as under the CWA.[140] Courts have generally adhered to this view and applied CWA case law that requires a court to begin by calculating the statutory maximum civil penalty and then apply the appropriate penalty assessment criteria to determine if downward penalty mitigation is warranted. When assessing a penalty, a court is required to clearly indicate the weight given to each factor and the factual findings supporting the court's conclusions.[141]

Before the 1990 CAA Amendments, some courts held that the EPA's failure to approve a SIP revision in a timely way precluded the imposition of civil penalties for violation of the SIP.[142] Although the 1990 amendments clarified that the EPA delay in approving SIP revisions could not defeat liability, delay may still affect the size of the penalty assessed.[143]

Penalty Assessment for Excess Emissions of Sulfur Dioxide and Nitrogen Oxides

Under the Title IV acid rain program, affected stationary sources that emit sulfur dioxide and nitrogen oxides are subject to an administrative "excess emissions penalty" when they exceed the annual emission limit. The excess emissions penalty is due without demand by the EPA within sixty days from the close of the annual compliance period, and must be equal to $2,000 (adjusted for inflation) for each ton of excess emissions.[144] Procedures for automatic payment of this penalty are contained in 40 C.F.R. pt. 77. Neither Title IV nor any other provision of the CAA prohibits the EPA from seeking additional penalties pursuant to CAA Section 113(b). (The agency, however, has not issued an interpretation of the basis on which statutory maximum penalties would be determined.)[145] Failure of an owner or operator to determine excess emissions at the end of the annual period, and to submit any excess emission penalties in a timely way without demand, is a violation of the CAA, subject to enforcement and additional penalty assessment for each day the excess emissions penalty payment is late.[146]

Citizen Awards

In CAA Section 113(f), the 1990 CAA Amendments created a new section authorizing the payment of up to $10,000 to any person who provides information or services that lead to a criminal conviction or administrative or judicial civil penalty assessment for violation of stationary source requirements.[147] Once final regulations are issued to implement this provision, employees, business competitors, and any other persons may have a tangible monetary incentive to report another's alleged CAA noncompliance.[148] The funds for such rewards are subject to congressional appropriation.

Bar against Challenges to Collateral Matters
in Enforcement Actions

CAA Section 307(b)(2) precludes challenges in an enforcement proceeding of any action that could have been reviewed pursuant to Section 307(b)(1). Section 307(b)(1) allows for judicial review of final agency actions and EPA rule makings. Thus, once an agency rule making or EPA or delegated state permit decision concerning CAA requirements' applicability to a particular source or source category becomes final EPA action capable of judicial review, such determinations cannot later be challenged in a civil or criminal enforcement proceeding.[149] The bar to collateral review in an enforcement action places a premium on participation in, and where necessary the judicial review of, EPA rule making or other final actions that may establish enforceable requirements upon an industry or facility. Such judicial review must be sought within sixty days after the challenged final agency action or sixty days after new grounds arise.[150] The limit on collateral review in enforcement challenges has been extended to terms and conditions in a Title V operating permit.[151]

Defenses to Penalties for Violations of Subpoenas
and Information Requests

The 1990 CAA Amendments, in Section 113(e)(1), added a new defense for a person subject to an EPA subpoena or information request, which states that "[t]he *court* shall not assess penalties for noncompliance with administrative subpoenas under section 307(a) [subpoena], or actions under section 114 [information request] of this Act, where the violator had sufficient cause to violate or fail or refuse to comply with such subpoena or action" (emphasis added).[152] Although the legislative history does not explain the basis for this defense, the likely reason is to prevent enforcement of administrative subpoenas and information requests from being declared an unconstitutional violation of due process, pursuant to *Ex Parte Young*[153] and its progeny.[154] The good faith exception to the assessment of penalties ensures that an alleged violator's opportunity to challenge the assessment in court may be achieved without incurring chilling, coercive penalties.[155] Most courts have construed a similar "without sufficient cause" defense in the Comprehensive Environmental Response, Compensation, and Liability Act to require an objectively reasonable, good faith belief by the alleged violator that a valid defense to noncompliance existed.[156]

The statutory limitation of the sufficient cause defense to courts but not to the EPA creates a unique problem for its application to penalties for subpoena enforcement. The EPA can enforce subpoenas only in administrative penalty order proceedings, if at all. Under a literal reading of the statutory language, EPA ALJs are not required to apply the sufficient cause defense in subpoena enforcement actions. However, the CAA Section 113(e)(1) penalty assessment criteria, including the "as justice may require" factor, must be addressed by the EPA ALJs. This should allow sources to claim the defense against penalty assessment in appropriate cases. No court has yet decided whether a court that judicially reviews an ALJ penalty assessment must apply the defense.

Presumption of Continuing Violation

Section 113(e)(2), added by the 1990 amendments, establishes a novel scheme for the imposition of a presumption of continuing violations for the assessment of civil penalties under CAA Sections 113(b) (civil judicial actions), 113(d)(1) (administrative penalty orders), 304(a) (citizens' suits), and 120 (noncompliance penalties) for violations that continue for more than one day.[157] To invoke the presumption, the EPA or an authorized state must give a source notice of the violation. If the plaintiff (i.e., a citizen or the United States) makes a prima facie showing that the "conduct or events giving rise to the violation are likely to have continued or recurred past the date of notice," the act mandates that "the days of violation shall be presumed to include the date of notice and each and every day thereafter." The presumption can be rebutted if the violator proves by a preponderance of the evidence that the violation was not continuing in nature or there were intervening days without violations.[158]

The apparent need for this provision arose from the impact of several judicial decisions construing the 1977 CAA. These decisions effectively required the government to carry the burden of proving continuing violations with direct evidence from each day of alleged violation, and had the effect of prohibiting the use of circumstantial evidence based on expert testimony to prove continuing violations.[159] The presumption of continuing violation was designed to shift the burden to the source to demonstrate its continuing compliance and to overrule the contrary case law.[160] To stop the clock and limit penalty exposure, a source must be vigilant when the EPA (or a state) issues a notice of violation. Upon receipt of such notice, it is critical that the source quickly assess whether the alleged violation could be considered ongoing in nature and assemble proof demonstrating intervening days of compliance or the intermittent nature of the violation. Assembling such information may be substantially more difficult or impossible at a later date in response to settlement negotiations or at trial.

While the statutory presumption of continuing violation applies in circumstances where the EPA or a state has provided notice, the question of whether a violation is continuing from the time it is deemed to have first occurred is less settled. This issue is most prevalent in NSR enforcement cases, where the EPA alleges a continuing violation for a source's failure to obtain a preconstruction permit. As violations are calculated daily, and the EPA often brings enforcement cases many years after the alleged violation, total penalties can be substantial if failure to obtain a permit is deemed an ongoing violation. Furthermore, whether a violation is considered continuing can be critical in determining whether it is barred by the generally applicable five-year federal statute of limitations.[161] If a violation is more than five years old, the EPA must establish that it continued into the limitations period in order to avoid this bar. The courts that have addressed this issue are unanimous in concluding that the failure to obtain an operating permit constitutes a continuing violation, but are divided on whether failure to obtain a preconstruction permit under the NSR program amounts to such a violation, and thereby bars application of the statute of limitations.[162]

Mobile Source Penalties

Penalty assessment for mobile source violations in administrative and judicial actions, provided for in CAA Section 205(b), are governed by the same penalty assessment factors. With two exceptions, the penalty assessment criteria are virtually identical to the requirements for stationary sources. The following factors must be addressed: the gravity of the violation, the economic benefit or savings (if any) resulting from the violation, the size of the violator's business, the violator's history of compliance with mobile source requirements, the action taken to remedy the violation, the effect of the penalty on the violator's ability to continue in business, and such other matters as justice may require.[163] Unlike the stationary source requirements, however, the mobile source penalty assessment scheme mandates neither considering the violation's duration, including any credible evidence, nor accounting for previous payments by the violator for the same violation.

For mobile source violations, maximum penalties vary depending on the provision violated. Penalties may be assessed up to $27,500 per day for violations of CAA Sections 203(a)(2) (information requests and inspections) and 211(d) (fuels requirements). They may be assessed up to $27,500 per offense for violations of paragraphs (1), (3)(A), (4), and (5) of Section 203(a) (concerning motor vehicles, engines, and emission control components) and for violations of Section 213(d) (nonroad vehicles and engines). Penalties of up to $2,500 per offense are assessable for violations of Section 203(a)(3)(B) (manufacture or sale of emission control defeating devices) and for violations of Section 203(a)(3)(A) (emission control tampering) by any person other than a vehicle manufacturer or dealer.

CAA Section 205 contains no provision comparable to the Section 113(e)(1) clause addressing the duration of the violation based on any credible evidence. However, to the extent the Title II violation at issue is susceptible to continuing violation, the duration of the violation may be addressed under the "gravity of the violation" factor. Similarly, prior payments for the same violation may be addressed under the catchall "as justice may require" provision. Indeed, it would be better practice, and would avoid inconsistency, if the Section 113(e)(1) factors were addressed in all cases, since judges assessing penalties in citizens' suits alleging mobile source violations must apply the stationary source penalty assessment factors in Section 113(e)(1).[164] It would be anomalous to have two separate bodies of penalty assessment case law for mobile source violations based on the gratuitous distinction of whether citizens or the government initiated the action.

Similarly, there is no Title II penalty assessment provision comparable to CAA Section 113(e)(2) concerning the presumption of continuing violation after EPA notice. However, since courts must apply the Section 113(e)(2) presumption in citizens' suit actions, citizens will be able to apply the presumption in their enforcement actions even though the government cannot. Although Section 113(e)(2) does not explicitly allow citizens to issue a notice of violation, the notice requirement may be met by an EPA administrative order or penalty assessment, neither of which precludes a subsequent citizens' suit. Citizens' suits are barred only when the United States or any state has commenced and is diligently prosecuting a *judicial* enforcement action.[165] Under the citizens' suit provisions, once the EPA (or a state) has given the source notice of the violation by administrative action and then failed to diligently prosecute the action judicially, a citizen may maintain an action to invoke the presumption. Whether this situation comes to pass may well depend on the extent to which citizens' suits become a viable force in mobile source enforcement.

The Role of Self-Policing, Self-Disclosure of Violations, and Privileges

Audit Privilege Laws

Businesses that consider conducting environmental compliance audits have traditionally faced the dilemma of what to do if instances of noncompliance were discovered by the audit. On the one hand, voluntary disclosure of the discovered violations might result in an enforcement action and civil penalties. On the other hand, forgoing the audit might allow continued practices of noncompliance indefinitely without detection. Historically, EPA policy guidance sought to encourage sources to conduct audits by promising to treat voluntary disclosures of noncompliance uncovered pursuant to an audit as good faith efforts worthy of penalty mitigation under the EPA's civil penalty settlement policy guidance. As early as 1986, the EPA made a commitment in guidance not to routinely seek audit reports in enforcement investigations.[166] Faced with the unpredictability of the EPA's discretionary enforcement response, however, many businesses considered compliance audits too risky, given the possible costs and liability exposure. Others chose to proceed with the audits but to implement safeguards designed to maximize protection of the audit contents from public disclosure by recognized common-law privileges. In most cases, however, the traditional privileges (i.e., attorney-client, work product, and critical self-evaluation) have proven only partially effective in shielding self-discovered noncompliance information from disclosure to regulatory agencies or the public.[167] As a result of this conundrum, which seemed to discourage self-policing, many state legislatures considered audit privilege laws designed to shield businesses from enforcement where they make, and disclose, voluntary efforts to discover and correct compliance problems.[168]

At least twenty-four states have adopted some form of audit privilege law, and an additional eleven states have adopted self-disclosure policies.[169] Typically, the existing audit privilege laws offer either a qualified evidentiary privilege or immunity from (or the reduction of) penalties for violations discovered during a bona fide compliance audit or pursuant to a comprehensive environmental compliance management system.[170] Most state privilege laws require that corrective action be promptly initiated and place the burden of proving environmental diligence, as well as entitlement to the privilege, on the party claiming it. In some states, the privilege can be defeated based on a showing of fraud, criminal acts, a history of previous environmental violations, waiver, or compelling state need.

Because these laws can provide important benefits, practitioners in states with audit privilege laws should understand the unique procedures and precautions necessary to invoke the shield. Because the EPA has refused to recognize state audit privilege laws, however, compliance with state audit privilege laws will not ensure the vitality of the privilege at the federal level. In 1995, in response to efforts to institute audit privilege laws at the state and federal levels, the EPA underwent a lengthy public reevaluation of its audit policy. The review culminated in an enforcement policy guidance document titled "Incentives for Self-Policing: Discovery, Disclosure, Correction and Prevention of Violations."[171] The policy creates tangible incentives for businesses to self-police and report violations of federal law to the EPA, but the policy also expresses strong opposition to the adoption of state audit privilege laws. As a result, unless federal law is enacted to provide for an audit privilege, the EPA can be expected to take the position in enforcement litigation that state laws are powerless to prevent discovery of such information in a federal enforcement action.[172]

The EPA's Self-Policing Policy

The EPA's self-policing policy is a settlement policy that applies to self-reported violations of federal environmental law. The policy applies to corporate entities that voluntarily discover, disclose, and correct noncompliance. Violations discovered by a compliance audit or an environmental management system (EMS) that comply with the policy will be subject to 100 percent reduction of the gravity-based component of the settlement penalty.[173] Violations that are voluntarily discovered by a means other than an audit or EMS and are otherwise voluntarily reported to the EPA are subject to a 75 percent reduction in the gravity-based penalty. Where the policy applies, the EPA will not recommend criminal prosecution of the corporate entity based on a voluntarily discovered, self-disclosed violation. In addition, the EPA will continue its historical practice of not routinely requesting audit reports when it conducts facility investigations.

The policy establishes nine factors that determine eligibility for penalty mitigation:

1. Systematic discovery
2. Voluntary discovery

3. Prompt disclosure
4. Discovery and disclosure independent of government or third-party suit or action
5. Correction and remediation
6. Recurrence prevented
7. No repeat violations
8. No serious or potential harm
9. Cooperation

An entity requesting relief under the policy bears the burden of demonstrating that each applicable element of the policy has been satisfied.

Systematic discovery requires that the violation be discovered through a qualifying environmental audit or an EMS meeting standards of due diligence.[174] Violations discovered through systematic procedures (i.e., an audit or EMS) are entitled to 100 percent mitigation of the gravity portion of civil penalties provided that the other eight conditions are met. Violations that are discovered in a "nonsystematic" manner are entitled to a 75 percent gravity reduction if the remaining eight factors are met. To qualify as voluntary, a violation must be discovered by means not otherwise mandated by statute, regulation, permit, judicial or administrative order, or consent agreement. For example, violations detected by continuous emissions monitors or other required alternative compliance monitoring in a Title V permit are not eligible, and neither are violations detected by a compliance audit mandated by the terms of a consent order or settlement agreement.

Prompt disclosure means that a violation must be fully reported to the EPA in writing within twenty-one days (or sooner if required by law) after discovery that the violation has occurred or *may* have occurred.[175] In addition, any source must disclose the violation before any regulatory agency begins an inspection or investigation, before notice of a citizens' suit or filing of a third-party complaint, before reporting by a whistle blower, and before imminent discovery of the violation by a regulatory agency.[176] The violation must be corrected and, generally, any harm it caused must be remediated within sixty days. The regulated entity must agree in writing to prevent recurrence of the violation in the future, including, at the EPA's discretion, by agreeing to implement a compliance audit or EMS procedures.

To be eligible, the specific violation, or a closely related one, cannot have occurred within the past three years at the same facility, and the violation cannot be part of a pattern of violations that has occurred at the facility's parent organization within the past five years.[177] The term "violation" is broadly construed to mean any civil or criminal violation of local, state, or federal law or any act or omission for which the regulated entity has received any penalty mitigation. The violation is not required to have been adjudicated or reduced to a settlement agreement. Thus, any violation that has been excused or received penalty mitigation pursuant to a state audit privilege law is subject to the time limits. A field citation issued pursuant to CAA Section 113(d) would also count toward the time bar. In addition, to be eligible to receive penalty mitigation, the regulated entity must fully cooperate with the EPA in investigating and remediating the violation to the EPA's satisfaction and publicly disclosing the relevant facts underlying the violation.

Note that the policy does not apply to actual or potential egregious violations. Thus, violations that result in serious actual harm to human health or the environment are ineligible. Even violations that *may have presented* an imminent and substantial endangerment are excluded. Thus, this provision may allow the EPA to refuse penalty mitigation even when actual harm did not occur, provided the potential for such harm was present. (Under this flexible standard, for example, noncomplying emissions of hazardous air pollutants are highly likely to be viewed as presenting a potential harm.) The policy also precludes violations of judicial or administrative orders, agreements, or decrees from consideration for penalty mitigation.

Although the self-policing policy offers businesses greater incentives to conduct compliance audits or to institute an EMS, the policy contains some important drawbacks worthy of careful consideration before the policy is invoked. For instance, while the EPA will refrain from requesting an "audit report," it has defined the term such that the EPA reserves the prerogative to request the data obtained in the audit and any testimonial evidence concerning the audit. Moreover, the policy against criminal prosecution based on information obtained through an audit or EMS is limited. It does not apply to criminal acts by individual managers, a prevalent corporate management practice or attitude that concealed or condoned violations, or senior corporate managers' conscious involvement in or willful blindness to environmental violations. Accordingly, before deciding to invoke the policy, issues relating to the potential for criminal liability should be carefully considered.

Another factor to consider before invoking the policy is the high degree of discretion and leverage the policy gives to the EPA to insist that an entity improve its existing self-policing system as a condition of penalty mitigation. A source that reports violations discovered pursuant to a compliance audit risks creating the circumstances and building the case for the EPA to mandate the facility's adoption of a complete EMS in return for penalty mitigation. Similarly, an entity with neither an audit nor an EMS program that self-reports a violation may be required to implement self-policing measures as a condition of penalty mitigation. The EPA's definition of the due diligence required of a qualifying EMS appears to be quite exacting, and potentially costly to achieve.

Sources contemplating use of the policy must also consider the implications of the broad public disclosure provisions in the policy. Although the policy may bar subsequent citizens' suits based on the reported information if the violations are embodied in a judicial consent agreement, third-party toxic tort suits cannot be prevented. The enhanced public disclosure of the circumstances underlying the violations may provide unwelcome exposure. In addition, the policy allows mitigation of only the gravity portion of the penalty policy settlement calculation. It does not allow the EPA to waive any significant economic benefit the regulated entity received through noncompliance. Even if the strict terms of the policy cannot be complied with, many of the policy factors will apply to reduce a potential penalty under the EPA's CAA civil penalty settlement policy, using the categories for cooperation and good faith efforts to comply. In addition, the EPA has issued a small business assistance policy that allows the agency to excuse all penalties when a qualifying small business seeks compliance assistance and agrees to remedy violations within a short grace period.[178] The policy applies to businesses that employ fewer than one hundred persons and that have never had a prior violation. Despite its narrow application, qualifying businesses may be able to have the EPA waive the entire penalty, including economic benefit, and keep the fact of the violation confidential from other enforcement entities. Finally, even when the audit policy does not apply, sources can obtain significant benefit by proposing a supplemental environmental project (SEP). Substantial penalties can be offset in return for implementation of a SEP. Acceptable categories of SEPs include certain pollution prevention projects, pollution reduction, environmental restoration, environmental audits, compliance promotion, and efforts to promote emergency preparedness and planning.[179]

The EPA's self-policing policy implies that entities that avail themselves of state audit privilege laws may receive increased EPA enforcement scrutiny under federal law. The policy suggests that the EPA may overfile when the application of a state audit privilege results in an inadequate enforcement response under the EPA's timely and appropriate enforcement guidance.[180] Likely candidates for an EPA overfiling action include violations that cause serious actual harm to the public or the environment and where application of a privilege law allows a violator to retain the economic benefit of noncompliance (e.g., when immunity attaches to a violation disclosed by an audit). Practitioners should anticipate the possibility of subsequent federal enforcement when a state audit privilege law results in serious violations receiving no civil penalties from state authorities. While historically the EPA has rarely exercised its overfiling authority, the issuance of this policy may signal a renewed interest and incentive for the EPA to do so in the future.

The Role of Citizens in CAA Enforcement

Citizens' suit enforcement under the CAA has never been as prevalent as it has historically been under the Clean Water Act. The likely causes of the apparent underuse of the CAA citizens' suit authority can be traced to the lack of authority in the 1977 CAA Amendments to recover civil penalties, a prohibition against suits for wholly past violations, the lack of publicly available source self-monitoring and compliance data, and the absence of a clear compendium of the state and federal CAA requirements applicable to any particular source. The 1990 amendments enhanced the viability of citizens' suits by expanding jurisdiction to wholly past violations in some cases, by the award of civil penalties for CAA violations, and by the creation of operating permits, which catalog the enforceable CAA requirement applicable to sources.[181] In addition, the promulgation of the EPA's credible evidence rule has clarified that a broad scope of evidence is available for proving violations of the CAA, which is critical to citizen suit enforcement.

Pre-Suit Matters: Notice and Jurisdiction

CAA Section 304 authorizes any person to commence a civil action in court against any person alleged to have violated, or to be in present violation of, an emission standard or limitation or an order issued by the EPA or a state requiring compliance with such standards or limitations. The term "emission standard or limitation" is defined to encompass certain mobile source requirements (including fuels, inspection and maintenance programs, and transportation control measures), PSD and nonattainment NSR requirements and permit conditions,[182] stratospheric ozone protection requirements, compliance plans or schedules, any term or condition of a permit issued pursuant to Title V, and any requirement to obtain a permit.[183] Venue is proper in the district court in which the alleged violating source is located.[184] A suit for past violations can be maintained only "if there is evidence that the alleged violation has been repeated."[185] The EPA may intervene as a matter of right in any citizens' suit at any time.[186]

In addition to meeting federal judicial standing requirements,[187] a citizens' suit cannot be maintained unless the plaintiff has given sixty days' prior notice of the suit to the EPA, the state in which the violation occurred, and the alleged violator.[188] Failure to comply with the sixty-day notice provision deprives the court of jurisdiction to entertain the suit.[189] Procedures governing proper timing and content of citizens' suit notices are located at 40 C.F.R. pt. 54.[190] Copies of the complaint must be served on the EPA and DOJ.[191] Although the CAA, like many other environmental statutes, contains no explicit statute of limitations, the general five-year limitation period contained in 28 U.S.C. Section 2462 is presumed to apply to citizens' suits.[192] Citizens that seek to invoke CAA Section 304 must be extremely careful to provide adequate notice as required by the statute and case law since courts will not hesitate to dismiss the case for lack of jurisdiction. In addition, because notice is jurisdictional, a citizen must be equally careful to draft the notice and complaint sufficiently broad so that the notice requirement will be deemed satisfied if the plaintiff's theory of the case changes during the litigation.[193]

In addition, a citizens' suit cannot be maintained if the EPA or the state has "commenced and is diligently prosecuting a civil action in a *court*" of the United States or state before initiation of the citizens' suit (emphasis added).[194] Notably, prior EPA or state *administrative* proceedings do not bar citizens' suits.[195] As administrative penalty procedures become more commonly used by the EPA and states, citizens' suits may cause violators to become subject to multiple prosecutions for the same offense, thus undermining any potential benefit to the regulated community of adjudication or settlement in the administrative forum. However, at least as concerns administrative actions that resulted in a penalty assessment, courts in citizens' suits must take into account any penalties previously paid by the violator for the same violation. This might discourage such suits, especially if courts routinely offset prior assessed penalties.[196]

Proof of Violation

A citizen plaintiff may seek to prove violations of emission limitations by reliance on source self-reported admissions in annual compliance certifications required by CAA Section 114(a)(3) and the operating permit program. The CAA annual compliance certification requirements are modeled on the discharge monitoring reports (DMRs) required under the CWA's National Pollutant Discharge Elimination System program.[197] Numerous courts have found that DMRs qualify as admissions and *prima facie* evidence of liability; compliance certifications should be no different.[198] In addition, as noted above, the EPA has promulgated a rule clarifying that any credible evidence permitted by state or federal rules of evidence may be used to prove a CAA violations.

The definition of emission standards or limitations was changed in the 1990 CAA Amendments to encompass, in addition to numerical emission standards, "any design, equipment, work practice, or operational standard" promulgated under the CAA.[199] Many of these standards will be capable of proof through observation or expert testimony, thus ensuring some potential avenues of citizen enforcement regardless of the implementation of source compliance monitoring and reporting terms in operating permits. In addition, through the Freedom of Information Act citizens will be able to obtain access to any emission data or compliance information in the EPA's possession, including where such information formed the basis for settlement or judgment in the administrative forum. Moreover, state- or EPA-ordered compliance testing will not be necessary to prove violations of monitoring, record-keeping, reporting, and other nonemission limit requirements, provided such requirements are contained in a permit, order, or compliance plan.[200]

Remedies

Proof of violation of the CAA under the citizens' suit provision allows, but does not compel, the court to order injunctive relief. Some courts have limited injunctions to cases where repeated violations are likely.[201] Civil penalties are within the discretion of the judge, though as discussed earlier, the court must address the penalty assessment factors set out in CAA Section 113(e). Citizens are entitled to assert the presumption of continuing violation for penalty assessment purposes, provided they can make the prerequisite prima facie case that the violation was likely to continue and provided that notice of the violation had been given to the alleged violator in accordance with CAA Section 113(e)(2). Instead of requiring civil penalties to be paid into the General Treasury Fund, the 1990 amendments created a special CAA penalty fund into which such citizens' suit penalties would be deposited and made available for use by the EPA to fund air compliance and enforcement activities.[202] In addition, the court in its discretion, and after obtaining the EPA's views, may apply up to $100,000 per suit for use in beneficial mitigation projects that, consistent with the CAA, enhance public health or the environment. In cases in which the EPA is not a party to the action, citizens' suit judgments have no binding effect on the United States. The EPA and the DOJ are entitled to a copy of a proposed consent judgment and are afforded forty-five days from its receipt to submit comments to the court.[203] Appropriate attorneys' fees may be awarded at the court's discretion.[204]

Notes

1. This chapter in the first edition was authored by John S. Rudd.

2. These enforcement actions have been driven by the EPA's interpretation of certain exemptions to NSR requirements, most notably an exception provided for projects that are deemed routine maintenance, repair, and replacement. *See* 40 C.F.R. § 52.21(b)(2)(iii). Defendants in these actions generally contend that the EPA has reinterpreted this exclusion from NSR requirements, and that the EPA's new interpretation of this exception constitutes a "new rule" that could be challenged under federal statutes applicable to agency rule-making activities. *See* United States v. Southern Indiana Gas and Electric Company, No. 99-1692, 2002 U.S. Dist. LEXIS 20936 (S.D. Ind. October 24, 2002) (holding the EPA's interpretation of routine maintenance exception did not constitute a new rule for purposes of a challenge under the Congressional Review Act).

3. EPA, *Annual Report on Enforcement and Compliance Assurance Accomplishments in 1999,* June 2000.

4. EPA, *Protecting the Public and the Environment through Innovative Approaches FY 2001,* Appendix B, Dec. 1, 2002.

5. While many commercial services offer access to some EPA policies and guidance, it may be necessary to contact an EPA regional or headquarters office to obtain access to the most current and comprehensive policy documents. Many of these guidance documents are available through the EPA's Internet Web site or the Technology Transfer Network computer electronic bulletin board maintained by the Office of Air Quality Planning and Standards, both of which are regularly updated. For more information on how to access the OAQPS bulletin board or Web site, see any recent *Federal Register* notice concerning promulgation of a CAA rule.

6. CAA § 114(a)(1). This authority does not apply to new engine and automobile manufacturers as concerns Title II requirements. CAA § 114(a)(1). New automobile and engine testing, monitoring, and inspection are covered by CAA Sections 206 and 208. Otherwise, the language is broad enough to apply to activities related to mobile source requirements for sources other than "manufacturers." The term "manufacturer" is defined in CAA Section 216(1).

7. CAA § 114(b).

8. CAA § 114(c).

9. CAA § 114(a)(1).

10. For example, in the regulatory area, the EPA has relied on Section 114 authority to require a utility in the southwest to permit the EPA to conduct an emissions modeling and transport analysis study, which involved the controlled release of tracer gases into the facility's exhaust gas stack. The tracer gas study, conducted over a ten-month period, was part of a larger effort to track and measure the dispersal of emissions throughout the southwest United States that could lead to visibility impairment at the Grand Canyon and other Class I areas. Implementation of the study required frequent agency access to

the facility, its operating information, records, and emission stacks. *See* Section 114 Letter from David P. Howekamp, Director, Air and Toxics Division, EPA Region 9, to Robert Deitch, Vice President, Southern California Edison Co. (Oct. 31, 1991).

11. The statutory penalty limit of $25,000 per day was adjusted for inflation to $27,500. *See* 40 C.F.R. §§ 19.1 *et. seq.*

12. *See, e.g.,* United States v. Hugo Key & Sons, 731 F. Supp. 1135 (D.R.I. 1989); James T. Price, *Responding to EPA Information Requests,* 5 NAT. RES. & ENV'T 13 (1990) (discussing penalty assessment for failure to comply with information gathering authority under all major environmental statutes).

13. *See* "EPA Requests for Data from Boilermakers Prompt Alarm Among Coal-Fired Utilities," BNA Daily Environment Report, AA-1, July 21, 1998.

14. *Id.*

15. These enforcement actions were part of series of broad-based enforcement initiatives that the EPA undertook to investigate CAA violations on an industrywide scale. In addition to coal-fired utilities, the EPA targeted the pulp and paper industry, the petroleum refining industry, ethanol production plants, and heavy-duty diesel engine manufacturers under such initiatives.

16. CAA § 208(a).

17. *See* 40 C.F.R. § 70.6(c)(2).

18. CAA § 114(d).

19. *See, e.g.,* United States v. Tivian Laboratories, Inc., 589 F.2d 49 (1st Cir. 1978), *cert. denied,* 442 U.S. 942 (1979); Public Service Co. v. EPA, 509 F. Supp. 720 (S.D. Ind. 1981), *aff'd* 682 F.2d 626 (7th Cir. 1982), *cert. denied,* 459 U.S. 1127 (1983); CED's Inc. v. EPA, 745 F.2d 1092 (7th Cir.), *cert. denied,* 471 U.S. 1015 (1984); United States v. Hugo Key and Son, 731 F. Supp. 1135, 1143–44 (D.R.I. 1989); James A. Holtkamp & Linda W. Magleby, *The Scope of EPA's Inspection Authority,* 5 NAT. RES. & ENV'T 16 (1990); Carol S. Holmes and Arnold W. Reitze, Jr., *Inspections under the Clean Air Act,* 1 ENVTL. LAW. 29 (1994).

20. Since mobile source inspection authorities are expressly limited to "officers" or "employees" of the EPA, there is no question that contractors are not authorized by such authority. *See* CAA §§ 206(c), 208(b).

21. Bunker Hill Co. v. EPA, 658 F.2d 1280 (9th Cir. 1981) (upholding use of contractors for inspections); Stauffer Chem. Co. v. EPA, 647 F.2d 1075 (10th Cir. 1981) (denying use of contractors for inspections); United States v. Stauffer Chem. Co., 684 F.2d 1174 (6th Cir. 1982) (same), *aff'd on other grounds,* 464 U.S. 165 (1984). *See also* Aluminum Co. of America v. EPA, 663 F.2d 499 (4th Cir. 1981) (noting that district court allowed use of contract inspector, but not ruling on its legality). Congressional attempts to settle the issue during development of the 1990 CAA were unsuccessful. The Statement of Senate Managers supports the agency's position; the House committee report and explanatory remarks by a House manager of the bill refute the position. *See Chafee-Baucus Statement of Senate Managers,* 136 CONG. REC. S16,933, S16,952–53 (daily ed. Oct. 27, 1990); S. REP. NO. 228, at 369 (1989), *reprinted in* 1990 U.S.C.C.A.N. 3385, 3752; H.R. Rep. No. 490, pt. 1 at 395–96 (1990); 136 CONG. REC. E3714 (daily ed. Nov. 2, 1990), Extension of Remarks by Rep. Dingell.

22. CAA § 206(c).

23. CAA § 208(b).

24. *See* CAA §§ 206(e), 208(c).

25. CAA §§ 203(a)(2), 205(a). *See* S. REP. NO. 228, at 126 (1989) (describing "per day of violation" language in Sections 205(c) and 211(d)(1) to mean for "each day for each violation."). See the proposed Field Citation rule for a related discussion of the CAA Section 113(d)(3) "per day of violation" language. Field Citation Program, 59 Fed. Reg. 22,776, 22,778–80 (1994) (notice of proposed rule making).

26. *Public Service Co. v. EPA*, 509 F. Supp. 720, 722 (S.D. Ind. 1981), *aff'd*, 682 F.2d 626 (7th Cir. 1982), *cert. denied*, 459 U.S. 1127 (1983); *see* Holmes & Reitze, *supra* note 19, at 54.

27. *See* United States v. Tivian Laboratories, Inc., 589 F.2d 49, 53 (1st Cir. 1978), *cert. denied*, 442 U.S. 942 (1979) ("Threats or no, the [EPA's] request for information is not enforceable under the [CAA], nor may fines be imposed, until a court order has been obtained.").

28. Of course, the usual exceptions to warrant requirements apply (e.g., open fields, emergencies, pervasively regulated industry), but are rarely applicable. Holmes & Reitze, *supra* note 19, at 62–68. Title V permits are required to contain terms authorizing entry and inspection. 40 C.F.R. § 70.6(c)(2). Holmes and Reitze characterize the issuance of a permit with entry and inspection authorization terms as tantamount to the facility's blanket grant of consent to inspect without a warrant. Holmes & Reitze, *supra* note 19, at 63.

29. *See* Public Service Co. v. EPA, 509 F. Supp. 720, 725 (S.D. Ind. 1981), *aff'd* 682 F.2d 626 (7th Cir. 1982), *cert. denied*, 459 U.S. 1127 (1983); Marshall v. Barlow's, Inc., 436 U.S. 307 (1978) (OSHA warrantless search unreasonable).

30. *See, e.g.*, EPA v. Alyeska Pipeline Serv. Co., 836 F.2d 443 (9th Cir. 1988) (upholding district court finding that portion of TSCA subpoena request was unreasonable); John A. Hamill, *EPA Administrative Tools: An Inside Perspective*, 4 J. ENVTL. LAW. & LIT. 85, 116–19 (1989); *see, generally,* Holmes & Reitze, *supra* note 19, at 55–71.

31. For a more detailed discussion of how to prepare for and implement an inspection, see Holmes & Reitze, *supra* note 19, at 71–95.

32. CAA § 307(a).

33. The provisions relating to protection of confidential business information and trade secrets are located at 40 C.F.R. pt. 2.

34. *See* 40 C.F.R. §§ 2.301(a)(2) (definition of "emission data"), 2.301(e) (substantive criteria).

35. 40 C.F.R. § 2.301(f).

36. Administrative Procedures Act, 5 U.S.C. § 555(b); *see also* FCC v. Schreiber, 329 F.2d 517, 526 (9th Cir. 1964) (in a fact-finding, nonadjudicative proceeding, counsel may advise client but not make objections on the record), *modified on other grounds*, 381 U.S. 279 (1965); Professional Reactor Operator Society v. NRC, 939 F.2d 1047 (D.C. Cir. 1991) (attorney cannot be excluded from subpoena interview without "concrete evidence" that investigation will be impaired).

37. *See* United States v. Tivian Laboratories, Inc., 589 F.2d 49, 54 (1st Cir. 1978), *cert. denied*, 442 U.S. 942 (1979) (construing pre-1990 CAA § 114 request, and comparing it to subpoena authority).

38. The sufficient cause defense is discussed in a later section. Interestingly, civil penalty actions for failure to comply with subpoenas may be pursued only pursuant to the CAA § 113(d) administrative penalty order authority, and even then only if a subpoena can be construed to be a "requirement or prohibition" of Title III. *Compare* CAA § 113(d)(1)(B), authorizing enforcement of "any requirement or prohibition" of Title III, *with* CAA § 113(a), (b), which authorize enforcement of violations only of Section 303 of Title III. Since Title II contains no provision authorizing civil penalties for subpoena noncompliance, CAA § 113(d) also would have to provide the basis for mobile source subpoena noncompliance penalties.

39. *See* CAA § 113(a)(3), (b)(2). The absence of a judicial forum for the imposition of penalties for failure to comply with an administrative subpoena is difficult to harmonize with the language in the penalty assessment section of the act, which authorizes the "court" to not assess penalties where there is sufficient cause to refuse or fail to comply with a subpoena. See CAA § 113(e)(1).

40. *See* CAA § 113(c)(1).

41. General NSPS notification, record-keeping, monitoring, and reporting requirements are set forth at 40 C.F.R. § 60.7. This provision, for example, requires owners or operators subject to continuous emission monitoring requirements (CEMs) to meet specific quarterly reporting requirements such as reports of excess emissions, start-ups, shutdowns, or malfunctions of any pollution control system. Each of the NSPS standards in 40 C.F.R. pt. 60 specifies additional industry-, source category-, or process-specific requirements.

42. Sources subject to MACT will be subject to general monitoring, record-keeping, and reporting requirements under 40 C.F.R. pt. 63 and specific monitoring and reporting requirements under individual NESHAP. See, for example, the NESHAP for Coke Oven Batteries. 40 C.F.R. § 63.311.

43. CAA § 211(b).

44. *See* 40 C.F.R. pt. 75, which sets out the acid rain control continuous emission monitoring, record-keeping, and reporting requirements.

45. SIP and NSR permitted monitoring and reporting requirements can exceed the minimum reporting requirements that otherwise apply under the CAA. *See* CAA § 116; Union Elec. Co. v. EPA, 427 U.S. 246, 265 (1976); Glazer v. American Ecology Environmental Services, 894 F. Supp. 1029, 1041 (E.D. Tex. 1995).

46. *See* 40 C.F.R. § 60.8(c) (NSPS); 40 C.F.R. § 63.6(e)(3) (HAP); 40 C.F.R. § 70.6(g); *see also* Operating Permits Program and Federal Operating Permits Program; Proposed Rule, 60 Fed. Reg. 45,530, 45,558–61 (1995) (clarifying that states have discretion to not adopt the emergency upset defense and proposing to scale back the scope of the existing Part 70 emergency defense).

47. 58 Fed. Reg. 54,648 (1993), 59 Fed. Reg. 66,844 (1944).

48. 62 Fed. Reg. 54,900.

49. Appalachian Power Co. v. EPA, 208 F.3d 1015 (D.C. Cir. 2000).

50. Clean Air Implementation Project v. EPA, 150 F.3d 1200 (D.C. Cir. 1998).

51. 62 Fed. Reg. 8314.

52. *Clean Air Implementation Project, supra.*

53. *See* CAA Section 504, 42 U.S.C. § 7661c, and 40 C.F.R. §§ 70.6(a)(3) and 70.6(c). Section 70.6(a)(3)(iii)(B) requires the permitting authority to define "prompt" in relation to the degree and type of deviation likely to occur and the applicable requirements. The EPA has interpreted this provision to require reporting generally within two to ten days, but in any event more frequently than semiannually. *See, e.g.,* Clean Air Act Interim Approval of Operating Permit Program; Delegation of Section 112 Standards; Commonwealth of Massachusetts, 61 Fed. Reg. 3827, 3828 (direct final rule).

54. *See* 40 C.F.R. §§ 70.5(d) and 70.6(a)(3)(iii)(A). "Responsible official" is defined for a corporation to mean "a president, secretary, treasurer, or vice-president in charge of a principal business function, or any other person who performs similar policy or decision-making functions for the corporation, or a duly authorized representative of such person" who performs similar managerial functions. 40 C.F.R. § 70.2(1). *See also* Operating Permits Program and Federal Operating Permits Program; Proposed Rule, 60 Fed. Reg. 45,530, 45,561–62 (1995) (clarifying the origin of the existing certification language in F.R.C.P. Rule 11 and proposing to modify the certification language to abolish Rule 11's "reasonableness" standard in favor of the more stringent text of the acid rain compliance certification rule (40 C.F.R. § 72.21(b)(2)), the proposed enhanced monitoring rule, and CWA discharge monitoring reporting requirements).

55. 40 C.F.R. § 70.6(c)(2).

56. *See* 40 C.F.R. § 70.6(c); CAA § 114(a)(3). Criminal sanctions for false statements are proscribed by CAA Section 113(c)(2)(A), 42 U.S.C. § 7413(c)(2)(A). The CAA § 114(a)(3)

compliance assurance monitoring rule-making requirements, discussed earlier, may also specify additional requirements concerning compliance certifications of sources subject to enhanced monitoring.

57. *See* 42 U.S.C. § 7401(a)(3); Train v. NRDC, 421 U.S. 60, 64 (1975) (state and local governments have had "primary responsibility" for "the prevention and control of air pollution at its source").

58. *See* Harmon Industries v. EPA, 191 F.3d 894 (8th Cir. 1999).

59. *See* Alaska v. EPA, 298 F.3d 814, 821 (9th Cir. 2002) (upholding EPA compliance orders issued to source based on state's application of BACT requirements that the EPA deemed insufficient).

60. EPA, *The Timely and Appropriate (T&A) Enforcement Response to High Priority Violation (HPVs)* (December 22, 1998).

61. CAA § 113(a)(3).

62. CAA § 113(a)(3).

63. The one-year duration of the order cannot be renewed to extend the compliance date. CAA § 113(a)(4), 42 U.S.C. § 7413(a)(4).

64. CAA § 113(a)(4), 42 U.S.C. § 7413(a)(4).

65. CAA § 113(a)(4), 42 U.S.C. § 7413(a)(4).

66. CAA § 113(b) and (d).

67. CAA § 113(a)(4).

68. *See* United States v. Hugo Key and Son, 731 F. Supp. 1135, 1144–45 (D.R.I. 1989) (penalty liability assessed for violation of information request and order requiring compliance with information request).

69. For example, where the EPA believes new construction is being undertaken in violation of SIP NSR requirements and it appears the construction might be completed within the thirty-day state SIP notice period, the EPA may issue a stop construction order under CAA § 113(a)(5). *See In re* Chevron USA, Inc., Docket No. 9-94-4 (Sept. 29, 1993) (EPA Region IX CAA Section 113(a)(5) administrative order); *In re* Union Oil Company of California, Docket No. 9-94-8 (Oct. 27, 1993) (same). In these actions, Chevron and Unocal both allegedly commenced construction on reformulated fuels projects without new source permits based on a letter interpretation issued by the South Coast Air Quality Management District (SCAQMD). Both Region IX stop construction orders were immediately stayed by the Ninth Circuit Court of Appeals. Chevron USA, Inc. v. EPA, No. 93-70810 (9th Cir. Oct. 8, 1993); Union Oil Co. of California v. EPA, No. 93-70870 (9th Cir. Nov. 2, 1993) (order granting consolidation of Chevron and Unocal petitions for emergency review and granting emergency stay). However, the appeal was mooted because SCAQMD issued construction permits before the appeal could be heard. *See also* United States v. Allsteel, 25 F.3d 312 (6th Cir. 1994) (staying EPA CAA Section 113(a)(5) stop work order; discussing criminal sanctions).

70. CAA § 113(a)(1), 42 U.S.C. § 7413(a)(1). Courts have clarified that notice is not required when enforcing federal requirements such as HAP emission regulations. *See, e.g.,* United States v. B & W Investment Properties, 38 F.3d 362, 366–67 (7th Cir. 1994) (and cases cited therein).

71. *See* S. Rep. No. 228, 101st Cong., 1st Sess. (1989) at 361–62; H. Rep. No. 490, 101st Cong., 2d Sess. pt. 1 (1990), at 391. Before the 1990 amendments, some federal courts interpreted the notice provision to require that the violation continue beyond the thirty-day notice period before the EPA could proceed under CAA Section 113(a)(1) or (b)(1)(B). *See, e.g.,* United States v. Louisiana-Pacific Corp., 682 F. Supp. 1122, 1127–29 (D. Colo. 1987); United States v. Ford Motor Co., 736 F. Supp. 1539, 1546 (W.D. Mo. 1990).

72. CAA § 113(a)(5).

73. *See* United States v. Solar Turbines, Inc., 732 F. Supp. 535, 538–40 (M.D. Pa. 1989) (dismissed action for civil penalties and injunctive relief under CAA Sections 113(b) and 167 because source properly relied on validly issued state PSD permit to authorize its emissions); *see also* United States v. AM General Corp., 34 F.3d 472 (7th Cir. 1994) (holding that source is not liable for violating preconstruction permit requirements where state issued permit and the EPA failed to make a finding of violation prior to source modification allowed by the permit); *but see* United States v. Campbell Soup Co., Civ-95-1854, 1997 U.S. Dist. LEXIS 3211 (E.D. Cal., Mar. 11, 1997) (state permit decision not bar to federal enforcement). *See also* cases cited in note 69.

74. CAA § 167.

75. *See* CAA § 113(a)(2). Thirty-day public notice is required for federally assumed enforcement of a SIP program and ninety days is required for permit program enforcement. Invoking federal implementation plan (FIP) requirements can take substantially longer. *See* NRDC v. EPA, 57 F.3d 1122, 1123–25 (D.C. Cir. 1995).

76. CAA § 307(b). Lloyd A. Fry Roofing Co. v. EPA, 554 F.2d 885 (8th Cir. 1977) (issuance of § 113(a) administrative compliance order does not constitute "final action"); *accord* Asbestec Constr. Services Inc. v. EPA, 849 F.2d 765 (2d Cir. 1988).

77. The legislative history of the 1990 amendments suggests Congress decided that no new legislative language was necessary and deferred to existing law "which has been interpreted correctly as barring preenforcement review of administrative compliance orders." *Chafee-Baucus Statement of Senate Managers*, 136 Cong. Rec. S16,933, S16,951, S16,953 (Oct. 27, 1990). For detailed discussion of the legislative history of the 1990 amendments on this subject, *see* James Miskiewicz & John S. Rudd, *Civil and Criminal Enforcement of the Clean Air Act After the 1990 Amendments*, 9 Pace Envtl. Law. Rev. 281, 328 (1992).

78. *See* United States v. Allsteel, 25 F.3d 312 (6th Cir. 1994) (finding an EPA stop work order, issued under Sections 113(a)(5) and 167 and issued after the state approved the construction permit, to be "final" action for purposes of pre-enforcement judicial review); *but see* Solar Turbines Inc. v. Seif, 879 F.2d 1073 (3d Cir. 1989) (holding pre-1990 CAA § 167 order not final agency action). Whether a Section 113(a)(5) order is enforceable at all was called into question by the court in United States v. AM General Corp., 34 F.3d 472 (7th Cir. 1994).

79. CAA § 113(d).

80. The EPA has issued waivers of both the dollar limit and the time for filing, though waivers of the time limits are more common.

81. CAA § 113(d)(1)(A) and (C).

82. CAA § 113(d)(2)(A) and Administrative Procedures Act, 5 U.S.C. §§ 554, 556.

83. 40 C.F.R. § 22.19(f). *See* Harwood, *Hearings Before an EPA Administrative Law Judge*, 17 Envtl. L. Rep. (Envtl Law Inst.) 10,441 (1987) for a more comprehensive discussion of Part 22 practice. *See also* http://www.epa.gov/oalj for Rules of Practice and Procedure.

84. *See* EPA, *Guidance on Choosing the Appropriate Forum in Clean Air Act Stationary Source Enforcement Actions* (Oct. 29, 1991). Similar decision criteria have been proposed for the field citation program. *See* Field Citation Program, 59 Fed. Reg. 22,776, 22,781 (1994) (notice of proposed rule making).

85. EPA, *Clean Air Act Stationary Source Civil Penalty Policy* (July 23, 1994, *available at* http://www.epa.gov/compliance/resources/policies/civil/caa/stationary/penpol.pdf).

86. CAA § 205(c)(1). Like the CAA Section 113(d)(1) stationary source penalty order authority, mobile source administrative penalty cap waivers are not subject to judicial review. Contrary to the stationary source penalty order authority, Section 205(b) does not require that the order be issued within one year from the date of the first violation. The EPA has issued a separate penalty policy for mobile source administrative hearings. EPA,

Clean Air Act Mobile Source Policies and Guidance (Section J, Document 16); *Civil Penalty Policy for Administrative Hearings* (Jan. 14, 1993). The EPA enforcement policy compendium includes additional guidance documents concerning mobile source violations (*e.g.*, catalytic converter tampering, engine switching, exhaust systems repairs, diesel and reformulated fuels, etc.).

87. Like stationary source orders, mobile source administrative order hearings are governed by 40 C.F.R. pt. 22. See 40 C.F.R. § 22.01(a)(2).

88. CAA § 205(c)(4).

89. *See* Nancy B. Firestone, *The Environmental Protection Agency's Environmental Appeals Board*, 1 ENVTL. LAW. 1, 17 (1994). The EAB has issued a practice manual that contains important insights concerning the conduct of an appeal before the board. *The Environmental Appeals Board Practice Manual* (Sept. 2002), *available at* http://www.epa.gov/eab/manual.htm.

90. CAA §§ 113(d)(4) and 205(c)(5).

91. CAA §§ 113(d)(5) and 205(c)(6).

92. CAA § 120(a)(2)(A). Note that Section 120 assessments cannot be made for past noncompliance, and that for SIP noncompliance, penalties may assessed only against "major" stationary sources. Noncompliance penalty order actions are governed by regulations codified at 40 C.F.R. pt. 66.

93. 40 C.F.R. § 66.1(a).

94. CAA § 120(d)(3); 40 C.F.R. § 66.11(c).

95. CAA § 120(b)(4)–(5).

96. *See* CAA § 120(a)(2)(B).

97. CAA § 120(a)(1)(B)(i).

98. CAA § 120(f).

99. CAA § 120(e); 40 C.F.R. § 66.81.

100. For example, Section 120 requires that within 180 days from the date a source achieves compliance, the EPA must initiate an additional proceeding to review the noncompliance penalty paid and reimburse, with interest, any overpayment. CAA § 120(d)(4); *see also* 40 C.F.R. pt. 66, subpt. H.

101. However, it is possible to postulate the use of Section 120 in the unusual case where a source obtains economic benefit far in excess of the $25,000 statutory maximum penalty available per day for each violation under CAA Sections 113(b) and (d). In this case, the Section 120 authority would allow the EPA to recoup the full economic advantage. In addition, because Section 120 penalties arguably have no impact on other CAA penalty authorities, the EPA would not be precluded from assessing an additional penalty for deterrence purposes pursuant to Sections 113(b) or (d). *See* CAA § 120(f). *See also* the discussion of penalty assessment criteria.

102. 59 Fed. Reg. 22,776 (May 3, 1994).

103. 67 Fed. Reg. 33,734 (May 13, 2002).

104. CAA § 113(d)(3). Presumably, if the violation does not continue, payment of the citation would operate as a bar to further enforcement for the same violation.

105. For instance, the EPA has issued an administrative emergency order pursuant to Section 7003 of the Resource Conservation and Recovery Act (RCRA), 42 U.S.C. § 6973, to require a municipal waste incinerator to reduce its dioxin emissions. *In re* Solid Waste Authority of Central Ohio, Docket No. V-W-016-94 (Sept. 9, 1994) (Region V Unilateral Administrative Order for Protective Measures). For further discussion of the emergency authorities available to the EPA under various statutes, *see* Clean Air Act; Enforcement Authority Guidance (Guidance on Using the Order Authority under Section 112(r)(9) of

the Clean Air Act, as Amended, and on Coordinated Use with Other Order and Enforcement Authorities), 56 Fed. Reg. 24,393 (1991).

106. See the discussion of judicial review of administrative orders. Courts have upheld this interpretation in reviewing other imminent and substantial endangerment order authorities. *See, e.g.,* United States v. Dale Valentine, 38 ERC 2086 (BNA) (D. Wyo. June 1, 1994) (upholding RCRA § 7003 imminent and substantial endangerment order and holding that defendant was not entitled to pre-enforcement judicial review); *and see* cases cited in note 78.

107. CAA § 303. Consultation in this context is likely to consist of little more than a phone call to state authorities.

108. *See* CAA § 113(b)(2).

109. CAA § 112(r)(9)(A).

110. CAA § 112(r)(2)(A).

111. CAA § 112(r)(2)(A). *See also* 40 C.F.R. pt. 68.

112. Legislative history of the 1990 amendments indicates that Congress may have intended the term "extremely hazardous substances" to include the approximately 360 substances listed under the Emergency Planning and Community Right to Know Act of 1986, 42 U.S.C. § 11001 et. seq. *See* S. REP. NO. 228, 101st Cong., 1st Sess. at 211 (1989).

113. *See* Clean Air Act; Enforcement Authority Guidance (Guidance on Using the Order Authority under Section 112(r)(9) of the Clean Air Act, as Amended, and on Coordinated Use with Other Order and Enforcement Authorities), 56 Fed. Reg. 24,393 (1991).

114. CAA § 306(a).

115. *See* Executive Order No. 11738, 38 Fed. Reg. 25,161 (1973). The Clean Water Act (CWA) also contains a similar federal procurement bar for persons convicted of CWA crimes. CWA § 508(a), 33 U.S.C. § 1368(a).

116. CAA § 306(a). One court has held that the mandatory listing prohibition extends only to the persons convicted, not the facility with whom the government contracts. *See* Southern Dredging Co., Inc. v. United States, 833 F. Supp. 555, 558–59 (D.S.C. 1993) (effect of convictions under the CWA construed). According to this court, a *facility* may be listed only pursuant to the EPA's "discretionary" listing program.

117. *See* Suspension, Debarment and Ineligibility for Contracts, Assistance, Loans and Benefits, 61 Fed. Reg. 28,755 (1996) (final rule making).

118. 40 C.F.R. § 32.321.

119. *See In re* Valmont Indus., Neb. Facility, EPA Contractor Listing Docket No. 07-89-LO68 (Jan. 12, 1990) (CWA removal determination); *In re* Exxon Corp., EPA Contractor Listing Docket No. 02-91-LO34, (Feb. 4, 1992) (construing the condition giving rise to the violation to include Exxon's failure to adequately train and supervise its managers to prevent noncompliance with the CWA); EPA Policy Regarding the Role of Corporate Attitude, Policies, Practices, and Procedures in Determining Whether to Remove a Facility from the EPA List of Violating Facilities Following a Criminal Conviction, 56 Fed. Reg. 64,785 (1991).

120. *See generally,* Jonathan S. Cole, *EPA's Contractor Listing Program: A List You Do Not Want to Make,* 2 FED. FACILITIES ENVTL. J. 129 (1991).

121. 40 C.F.R. § 32.335.

122. CAA § 307(b)(1).

123. CAA § 113(e).

124. 40 C.F.R. pt. 66, subpt. C, provides the procedures for calculating noncompliance penalties.

125. CAA § 205(b) and (c)(2).

126. CAA § 113(b).

127. *See, e.g.,* United States v. B & W Investment Properties, 38 F.3d 362, 367 (7th Cir. 1994); United States v. Hugo Key and Son, 731 F. Supp. 1135, 1140 (D.R.I. 1989); Midwest Suspension and Brake, 824 F. Supp. 713, 725 (E.D. Mich. 1993), *aff'd,* 49 F.3d 1197 (6th Cir. 1995); United States. v. Tzavah Urban Renewal Corp., 696 F. Supp. 1013, 1020–21 (D. N.J. 1988).

128. *See* United States v. SCM Corp., 667 F. Supp. 1110, 1128–30 (D. Md. 1987).

129. CAA § 205(b). Although CAA § 205(b) does not itself specify injunctive relief authority, CAA § 204(a) authorizes injunctive relief for violations of CAA § 203(a) requirements (which incorporates CAA §§ 202 and 213 standards and prohibitions [see CAA § 213(d)]) and Section 211(d)(2) authorizes injunctive relief for violations of Section 211(d)(1) requirements. CAA §§ 204(a), 211(d)(2).

130. Pre-referral negotiations are allowed when the EPA believes the defendant is cooperative and the case amenable to quick settlement. *See* EPA, *Process for Conducting Pre-Referral Settlement Negotiations,* GM-73 (March 9, 1988). The EPA often extends the time frame for filing of the complaint when settlement negotiations appear fruitful.

131. Civil Justice Reform, Exec. Order No. 12,788, ¶ 1.a. (Oct. 23, 1991). 57 Fed. Reg. 2213 (Jan. 21, 1992).

132. Frequently, the agency's applicable civil penalty policy requires economic benefit or BEN, as the EPA refers to it, to be calculated using a computer model developed by the EPA. Because it incorporates conservative assumptions about investment return and interest rates, BEN has been subjected to wide criticism. *See* Robert H. Fuhrman, *A Discussion of Technical Problems with EPA's BEN Model,* 1 ENVTL. LAW. 561 (1995). Private parties can obtain a diskette version of the model and guidance from the National Technological Information Service by calling (703) 487-4650; *see* Calculation of the Economic Benefit of Noncompliance in EPA's Civil Penalty Enforcement Cases, 61 Fed. Reg. 65,391 (1996) (extending request for comment on need to revise BEN program).

133. EPA, *Clean Air Act Stationary Source Civil Penalty Policy* (Oct. 25, 1991). The EPA has also issued numerous enforcement guidances concerning mobile source violations. *See* EPA, *Clean Air Act Mobile Source Policies and Guidance (Section J).* Mobile source violations of the CAA are generally addressed in the administrative forum and often pursuant to an informal NOV settlement policy. *See* S. REP. NO. 228, 101st Cong., 1st Sess. (1989) at 125–26, *reprinted in* 1990 U.S.C.C.A.N. at 3510–11; EPA, *Tampering Settlement Agreement Memorandum* (June 27, 1985). Both the stationary and mobile source civil penalty policies are based on the agencywide *Policy on Civil Penalties* and *A Framework for Statute-Specific Approaches to Penalty Assessments* (EPA General Enforcement Policies GM-21 and GM-22, issued Feb. 16, 1984). In addition, the EPA has also issued numerous more targeted civil penalty policies for specific types of stationary source civil penalty violations (*e.g.,* asbestos NESHAP, vinyl chloride NESHAP, NSR permits, VOCs, CFCs, etc.). In recent years, the EPA's use of penalty policies has been challenged. *See In re* Employers Insurance Co. of Wausau & Group Eight Technology, Inc., Docket No. TSCA-V-C-62-90, 1995 TSCA LEXIS 15, (Sept. 29, 1995) (holding that the EPA must submit proof of the validity of the application of the applicable penalty policy in each enforcement action or conduct notice and comment rule making on each policy), *reversed in part,* EPA EAB, TSCA Appeal No. 95-6 (Feb. 11, 1997). In response to the *Wausau* decision, the EPA issued a policy guidance outlining how penalties should be pleaded and argued in administrative proceedings. EPA, *Guidance on Use of Penalty Policies in Administrative Litigation* (Dec. 15, 1995). The EPA's failure to provide proper notice of its interpretational guidance can create a viable defense to the imposition of penalties. *See* General Electric v. EPA, 53 F.3d 1324 (D.C. Cir. 1995); United States v. Hoechst Celanese Corp., Civ. No. 0:92-1879-17, 27 ELR 20487 (D.S.C., May 10, 1996) (awarding no civil penalty for violations of CAA benzene NESHAP).

134. *See* EPA, *Clean Air Act Stationary Source Civil Penalty Policy* (Oct. 25, 1991).

135. *See* 28 C.F.R. § 50.7.

136. CAA § 113(e)(1).

137. CAA § 113(e)(1).

138. The purpose of this provision, concerning duration of the violation, which is unique to the CAA, was to overturn United States v. Kaiser Steel Corp., No. 82-2623-IH (C.D. Cal. Jan. 17, 1984), which held that the duration of a violation could only be proved by reference test methods, not expert testimony. *See* S. Rep. No. 228, 101st Cong., 1st Sess. (1989) at 366, *reprinted in* 1990 U.S.C.C.A.N. at 3749.

139. This provision clarifies that an absolute defense to liability cannot be presumed simply because of a prior penalty assessment for the same violation. The CWA allows such a defense in certain circumstances. *See* CWA § 1319(g)(6)(A)(iii), 33 U.S.C. § 309(g)(6)(A)(iii).

140. *See Statement of Senate Managers,* 136 Cong. Rec. S16,933, S16,952 (daily ed. Oct. 27, 1990) (penalty assessment criteria intended to be applied "in the same manner under [the CAA] as the similar criteria" in the amended CWA).

141. *See* United States v. B & W Investment Properties, 38 F.3d 362, 368 (7th Cir. 1994); U.S. v. Midwest Suspension and Brake, 824 F. Supp. 713, 735 (E.D. Mich. 1993) (citing U.S. v. A.A. Mactal Constr. Co., 22 Envtl. L. Rep. 21,200 (No. 89-2372) (D. Kan. Mar. 31, 1992)), *aff'd,* 49 F.3d 1197 (6th Cir. 1995); *and see* Atlantic States Legal Foundation v. Tyson Foods, 897 F.2d 1128, 1142 (11th Cir. 1990) (construing CWA penalty assessment factors).

142. *See* Duquesne Light Co. v. EPA, 698 F.2d 456 (D.C. Cir. 1983); American Cyanimid v. EPA, 810 F.2d 493 (5th Cir. 1987).

143. *See* General Motors v. United States, 496 U.S. 530, 541 n.4 (1990); *and see* United States v. Vista Paint Corp., No. 92-55160, 1992 WL 236898, 1992 U.S. App. LEXIS 24747 (9th Cir. Sept. 24, 1992) (unpublished order) (in effect, the court created an additional penalty assessment factor for SIP violations where review of a SIP revision was unreasonably delayed). In addition, courts have held that while good faith efforts to comply and technological infeasibility are not defenses to violation of the CAA, such factors may support penalty reduction. Union Elec. Co. v. EPA, 427 U.S. 246, 256–59 (1976); United States v. Vanguard Corp., 701 F. Supp. 390, 392 (E.D.N.Y. 1988).

144. CAA § 411(a). The statute and regulations mandate that the excess emissions penalty amount be adjusted annually to account for increases in the consumer price index. CAA § 411(c); 40 C.F.R. § 77.6(b). For compliance year 1996, the CPI adjusted cost per ton of excess emissions was $2,454. Acid Rain Notice of Annual Adjustment Factors for Excess Emissions Penalties, 60 Fed. Reg. 52,912 (1995).

145. CAA § 411(e); 40 C.F.R. § 77.1(b). Because the CAA authorizes civil penalties based on the number of days for each violation, violations of acid rain requirements determined by the amount of excess emissions do not readily correspond to a number of *days* of violation. *See* CAA §§ 113(b) and (d). One approach would be to presume each violation to fall on some putative "day" and ascribe a maximum $25,000 penalty to each violation, or excess ton of emissions. Another approach would be to ascribe the violations to each day in the annual averaging period, which would yield a maximum potential penalty of 365 days times $25,000. This multiday averaging period approach finds some support in the legislative history concerning penalty assessment generally although it would allow for a virtually unlimited maximum penalty in the acid rain context. *See* S. Rep. No. 228 at 366, *reprinted in* 1990 U.S.C.A.A.N. at 3749.

146. *See* 40 C.F.R. § 77.6(a).

147. CAA § 113(f).

148. Regulations Governing Awards under Section 113(f) of the Clean Air Act, 59 Fed. Reg. 22,795 (1994) (proposed rule).

149. United States v. Walsh, 8 F.3d 659, 664 (9th Cir. 1993), *cert. denied*, 114 S. Ct. 1830 (1994); Adamo Wrecking Co. v. United States, 434 U.S. 275, 284 (1978); *In re* Norma J. Echevarria, EAB CAA Appeal No. 94-1 (Dec. 21, 1994) at 19–28 (constitutional challenge based on vagueness not reviewable).

150. CAA § 307(b)(1).

151. 40 C.F.R. § 70.4(b)(xii) (state permit program regulations concerning exclusivity of judicial review).

152. CAA § 113(e)(1).

153. 409 U.S. 123 (1908).

154. For a more detailed discussion of the Ex Parte Young line of cases in environmental law, see J. Wylie Donald, *Defending Against Daily Fines and Punitive Damages under CERCLA: The Meaning of "Without Sufficient Cause,"* 19 COL. J. OF ENVTL. LAW 185, 196–206 (1994). *See also* United States v. Tivian Laboratories, Inc., 589 F.2d 49, 53 (1st Cir. 1978), *cert. denied*, 442 U.S. 942 (1979) ("Threats or no, the [EPA's] request for information is not enforceable under the [CAA], nor may fines be imposed, until a court order has been obtained.").

155. *See* Donald, *Defending against Daily Fines and Punitive Damages under CERCLA, supra* note 154. Although the "as justice requires" penalty assessment criteria in CAA § 113(e)(1) would allow judges to avoid an unconstitutional application of the penalty assessment provisions in appropriate cases, the explicit sufficient cause defense assures alleged violators that penalties can be avoided in appropriate challenges.

156. *See, e.g.,* Solid State Circuits Inc. v. United States EPA, 812 F.2d 383, 388–92 (8th Cir. 1987) (and citations therein); United States v. Parsons, 723 F. Supp. 757, 763 (N.D. Ga. 1989), *vacated on other grounds*, 936 F.2d 526 (11th Cir. 1991).

157. As discussed above, while this provision generally does not apply to Title II violations, there appears to be an exception when Title II enforcement proceeds by citizens' suit.

158. CAA § 113(e)(2).

159. *See* United States v. SCM Corp., 667 F. Supp. 1110, 1124–25 (D. Md. 1987); United States v. Kaiser Steel Corp., no. 82-2623-IH (C.D. Cal. Jan. 17, 1984) (court excluded expert testimony bearing on the duration of violation). A similar result was reached in International Paper Co. v. Town of Jay, 41 ERC 1988 (Oct. 6, 1995) (construing local ordinance). *But see* Sierra Club v. Public Service Co. of Colorado, Inc., 894 F. Supp. 1455, 1458–61 (D. Colo. 1995) (upholding citizen enforcement action based on use of non-reference monitoring information).

160. *See* S. REP. NO. 228, 101st Cong., 1st Sess. (1989) at 366, *reprinted in* 1990 U.S.C.C.A.N. at 3749.

161. *See* 28 U.S.C. § 32,321.

162. *See, e.g.,* United States v. Murphy Oil USA, Inc., 143 F. Supp. 2d 1054 (W.D. Wisc. 2001) (holding that failure to obtain a construction permit is a one-time violation that is not continuing, and thus is barred if it falls outside of the limitations period); United States v. Southern Indiana Gas and Electric Co., No. 99-1692, 2002 U.S. Dist. LEXIS 14040 at *14 (S.D. Ind. July 26, 2002) ("[O]perating a facility after it was modified without first obtaining the necessary construction permit may constitute a continuing violation of the relevant operating permit, but it does not constitute a continuing violation of the relevant construction permit."). *But see* United States v. Westvaco Corp., 144 F. Supp. 2d 439 (D.Md. 2001) (holding that failure to obtain a PSD permit constituted a continuing violation and thus the statute of limitations was inapplicable).

163. CAA § 205(b) and (c)(2).

164. *See* CAA § 304(a)(1) (citizen suit authority), CAA § 304(f) (definition of "emission standard or limitation" to include mobile source violations), and CAA § 113(e)(1) (penalty assessment criteria applicable to citizen suits brought pursuant to CAA § 304(a)).

165. CAA § 304(b)(1)(B); and see citizens' suit discussion.

166. EPA, Environmental Auditing Policy Statement, 51 Fed. Reg. 25,004 (1986).

167. *See* David R. Erickson & Sarah D. Mathews, *Environmental Compliance Audits: Analysis of Current Law, Policy, and Practical Considerations to Best Protect Their Confidentiality,* 63 UMKC L. REV. 491 (1995); see also BNA's DUE DILIGENCE GUIDE, Protecting the Confidentiality of Environmental Audits, Commentary and Analysis, § 231:551 (Mar. 1997) (discussing limits of self-critical analysis privilege).

168. For a discussion of the rationale in favor of the legislative adoption of audit privilege protections, see James T. O'Reilly, *Environmental Auditing Privileges: The Need for Legislative Recognition,* 19 SETON HALL L. REV. 119 (1994). Other commentators have argued that audit privilege laws are inappropriate. *See, e.g.,* Craig N. Johnston, *An Essay on Environmental Audit Privileges: The Right Problem, the Wrong Solution,* 25 ENVTL. LAW. 335 (1995); Bennet L. Heart, *The Environmental Audit Privilege: A Step in the Wrong Direction,* TOXICS LAW REP. 305 (BNA) (Aug. 16, 1995).

169. For a list of the states that have adopted audit privilege laws or self-disclosure policies, see the National Conference of State Legislatures Web site at http://www.ncsl.org/programs/esnr/audittub.htm.

170. *See* Erickson & Mathews, *supra* note 167, at 514–20 for a more in-depth discussion of the scope of state audit privilege laws.

171. 60 Fed. Reg. 66,706 (1995) (final policy statement); see also EPA, *Interpretative Guidance for EPA's 1995 Audit Policy* (Jan. 1997) BNA's ENVIRONMENTAL DUE DILIGENCE GUIDE, App. 501.1671.

172. *See* 60 Fed. Reg. at 66,710.

173. 60 Fed. Reg. at 66,711.

174. The EPA defines "due diligence" in great detail in the policy according to the size and nature of the business. *See* 60 Fed. Reg. at 66,710–11.

175. The EPA recently revised its self-disclosure policy to allow twenty-one days for disclosure, as opposed to ten days provided in the initial policy. *See* 65 Fed. Reg. 19,618. In addition, these revisions clarify that the independent discovery condition does not automatically preclude penalty mitigation for multifacility entities, and clarify how prompt disclosure and repeat violation conditions apply to newly acquired companies.

176. 60 Fed. Reg. at 66,711. On this point, the policy is not clear whether the possession of prior knowledge by the regulated entity of the imminence of an inspection, notice or third party report is prohibited.

177. Note, however, that the 2000 revisions to the policy provide that independent discovery conditions do not automatically bar application at multifacility entities. *Id.*

178. EPA, *Enforcement Response Policy for Treatment of Information Obtained through Clean Air Act Section 507 Small Business Assistance Programs* (Aug. 12, 1994); Final Policy on Compliance Incentives for Small Businesses, 61 Fed. Reg. 27,984 (1996) (applicable to all media).

179. See the EPA Interim Revised Supplemental Environmental Projects Policy, 60 Fed. Reg. 24,856 (1995).

180. EPA, *Guidance on the Timely and Appropriate Enforcement Response to Significant Air Pollution Violators* (Feb. 7, 1992).

181. *See* Scott M. DuBoff, *The 1990 Amendments and Section 304: The Specter of Increased Citizen Suit Enforcement,* 7 NAT. RES. & ENV'T. (Fall 1992), at 14.

182. The provision allowing citizen enforcement of permit conditions was added as an amendment during consideration of the bill by the full House. *See* Legislative History of the Clean Air Act Amendments of 1990, at 2570, 2716, comments of Rep. Collins at 2765–67 (describing citizens' suit authority as amended as applying to "Any aspect of a State implementation plan; any aspect of a permit; and the failure to obtain a permit.").

183. CAA § 304(f), 42 U.S.C. § 7604(f). Courts have held that National Ambient Air Quality Standards (NAAQS) are not emission standards or limitations. *See, e.g.,* Coalition Against Columbus Center v. New York, 967 F.2d 764, 769–71 (2d Cir. 1992) (holding SIP standard enforceable and discussing NAAQS case law); Cate v. Transcontinental Gas Pipe Line Corp., 904 F. Supp. 526 (W.D. Va. 1995) (differentiating between emission standards set out in CAA and NAAQS).

184. CAA § 304(c)(1).

185. CAA § 304(a)(1). Courts have not decided exactly what this language means. The legislative history suggests that continuous violations need not be shown; only that two or more past violations occurred. See Statement of Senate Managers, at S16,953. *See also* Adair v. Troy State University of Montgomery, 892 F. Supp. 1401, 1409 (M.D. Ala. 1995) (rejecting the argument that CAA citizen suits cannot be brought for wholly past violations if there is evidence of repeated violations; *but see* Satterfield v. J.M. Huber Corp., 888 F. Supp. 1561, 1564–65 (N.D. Ga. 1994) (finding that jurisdiction depended upon an allegation that the *same* violation had been repeated, and holding that the court lacked jurisdiction because plaintiff did not allege that failure to obtain a permit had been, or could be, repeated); Moran v. Vaccaro, 684 F. Supp. 1201 (S.D.N.Y. 1988) (interpreting 1977 Act).

186. CAA § 304(c)(2).

187. CAA § 304(b)(1)(A). The standing requirement, usually defined to include injury in fact, causation, and redressability, is discussed further in David T. Buente, *Citizen Suits and the Clean Air Act Amendments of 1990: Closing the Enforcement Loop,* 21 ENVTL L. 2233, 2244 (1991); *and see* Lujan v. *Defenders of Wildlife,* 504 U.S. 555, 560–61 (1992); Roy S. Belden, *Preparing for the Onslaught of Clean Air Citizen Suits: A Review of Strategies and Defenses,* 1 ENVTL. LAW. 377, 412–17 (1995).

188. A citizen need not wait sixty days to file suit where the action alleges a violation of CAA § 112(i)(3)(A) or (f)(4) (concerning hazardous air pollutants) or an administrative order issued by the EPA pursuant to CAA § 113(a). CAA § 304(b). *See* Adair v. Troy State University of Montgomery, 892 F. Supp. 1401, 1408–09 (M.D. Ala. 1995) (air toxics).

189. *See* Hallstrom v. Tillamook County, 493 U.S. 20, 31 (1989) (RCRA); Village of Oconomowoc Lake v. Dayton Hudson Corp., 24 F.3d 962, 964–65 (7th Cir. 1994); Glazer v. American Ecology Environmental Services, 894 F. Supp. 1029, 1041–43 (E.D. Tex. 1995).

190. *See* Regulations Governing Prior Notice of Citizen Suits Brought under Section 304 of the Clean Air Act, 56 Fed. Reg. 7870 (1993) (proposed rule); Save Our Health Organization v. Recomp of Minn., 37 F.3d 1334, 1337–38 (8th Cir. 1994) (strictly construing CAA notice content requirements); Glazer v. American Ecology Environmental Services, 894 F. Supp. 1029, 1043 (E.D. Tex. 1995) (notice not sufficiently detailed to support jurisdiction); Fried v. Sungard Recovery Services, Inc., 900 F. Supp. 758, 764–66 (E.D. Pa. 1995) (minimal CAA notice requirements satisfied); Sierra Club v. Tri-State Generation and Transmission Assoc., Inc., Civ. No. 96 N 2368, 1997 U.S. Dist. LEXIS 2464 (D. Colo. Feb. 6, 1997) (upholding sufficiency of CAA notice).

191. CAA § 304(c)(3).

192. United States v. Walsh, 8 F.3d 659, 662 (9th Cir. 1993), cert. denied, 114 S. Ct. 1830 (1994); *see* David T. Buente, *Citizen Suits and the Clean Air Act Amendments of 1990: Closing the Enforcement Loop,* 21 ENVTL. LAW. 2233, 2246 (1991); *see also* 3M Co. v. Browner, 17 F.3d 1453, 1457–59 (general discussion of applicability of 28 U.S.C. § 2462 in TSCA case and holding that five-year statute of limitations runs from date of violation, not date of the EPA discovery); United States v. Campbell Soup Co., Civ-95-1854, 1997 U.S. Dist. LEXIS 3211 (E.D. Cal., Mar. 11, 1997) (failure to obtain a new source review pre-construction permit not a continuing violation that extends the five-year limitations period). United States v. Murphy Oil USA, Inc., 143 F. Supp. 2d 1054 (W.D. Wisc. 2001) (statute of limitations

begin to run at time of construction for CAA preconstruction permit requirements). *But see* United States v. AEP, 136 F. Supp. 2d 808 (S.D. Ohio 2001) (general federal statute of limitations does not apply to claims for equitable or injunctive relief.)

193. *See, e.g.*, Ogden Projects Inc. v. New Morgan Landfill Co., 41 ERC 2064, 2078 (E.D. Pa. Jan. 10, 1996).

194. CAA § 304(b)(1)(B), 42 U.S.C. § 7604(b)(1)(B). *See also* Roy S. Belden, *Preparing for the Onslaught of Clean Air Citizen Suits: A Review of Strategies and Defenses,* 1 ENVTL. LAW. 377, 400–05 (1995).

195. *See* Maryland Waste Coalition v. SCM Corp., 616 1474, 1481 (D. Md. 1985); Baughman v. Bradford Coal Co., 592 F.2d 215, 217 (3d Cir. 1979).

196. CAA § 113(e)(1), 42 U.S.C. § 7413(e)(1).

197. *See* S. REP. NO. 228, 101st Cong., 1st Sess. 368 (1989), *reprinted in* 1990 U.S.C.C.A.N. 3385, 3751.

198. See cases cited in Roy S. Belden, *Preparing for the Onslaught of Clean Air Citizen Suits: A Review of Strategies and Defenses,* 1 ENVTL. LAW. 377, 383 n.28 (1995).

199. CAA § 302(k).

200. *See* CAA § 304(f)(4), which defines emission standard or limitation to include "any permit term or condition," apparently making enforceable any permit "condition."

201. United States v. SCM Corp., 667 F. Supp. 1110, 1128–30 (D. Md. 1987); *Midwest Suspension and Brake,* 824 F. Supp. 713, 738 (E.D. Mich. 1993), *aff'd,* 49 F.3d 1197 (6th Cir. 1995) (refusing to grant injunction merely to enjoin future violations).

202. CAA § 304(g), 42 U.S.C. § 7604(g).

203. CAA § 304(c)(2)–(3), 42 U.S.C. § 7604(c)(2)–(3).

204. CAA § 304(d), 42 U.S.C. § 7604(d). *See* American Petroleum Institute v. EPA, 42 ERC 1008, 1009 (D.C. Cir., Jan. 9, 1996) (attorneys fees are "appropriate" where the party prevailed upon the merits and where the party's litigation furthered the purposes of the statute). For further discussion, see Roger A. Greenbaum and Anne S. Peterson, *The Clean Air Act Amendments of 1990: Citizen Suits and How They Work,* 2 FORDHAM ENVTL. LAW REP. 79, 113–17 (1991).

CHAPTER 18

Criminal Enforcement

JOHN S. RUDD

Introduction

Before the 1990 Clean Air Act (CAA) Amendments, criminal offenses under the CAA were limited to misdemeanors and fines of up to $25,000 per day of violation. In addition, the substantive offenses were restricted primarily to knowing violations of state implementation plans (SIPs), new source performance standards (NSPS), and the National Emissions Standards for Hazardous Air Pollutants (NESHAP).[1] Knowingly making false statements in CAA-required reports, records, and applications and falsifying or tampering with monitoring devices or methods also constituted crimes under the CAA before 1990.[2] In those years CAA criminal prosecutions were relatively rare.[3]

The 1990 amendments greatly expanded the scope of criminal liability for knowing violations to virtually all substantive CAA requirements. The punishment level for existing crimes was raised from misdemeanor to felony, and maximum fines were substantially increased. False-statement crimes were expanded to include knowing omission, concealment, and failure to file required reports. New crimes were also established for knowing and negligent emissions of hazardous air pollutants that pose an endangerment to people. In addition, criminal responsibility was extended to "responsible corporate officers." Restrictions were, however, imposed on finding criminal liability for low-level employees (but not their superiors in management) when exercising ordinary functions or following direct management orders.

Consistent with ongoing trends and policy statements concerning all environmental statutes, criminal investigations and enforcement by the Environmental Protection Agency and the Department of Justice have dramatically risen in recent years. Regarding criminal violations involving corporations, the federal government has also increasingly pursued a policy of targeting criminal prosecutions at senior management officials.[4] Criminal enforcement of the CAA will undoubtedly follow these same trends, especially after the compliance certification requirements, operating permit programs, and hazardous air pollutant standards are fully implemented.[5] Practitioners are reminded that entities convicted of a CAA criminal offense are barred from engaging in government contracts pursuant to CAA Section 306.[6] Counsel familiar with the nuances of CAA criminal enforcement should be consulted as early as possible when circumstances indicate potential criminal liability.[7]

Knowing Violations of CAA Requirements

It is a criminal offense under the CAA to knowingly violate any requirement or prohibition of any rule, order, waiver, or permit, including the following: SIPs, NSPS, requirements regarding hazardous air pollutants under Section 112,[8] inspection and information gathering requests pursuant to Section 114, new source review preconstruction permitting standards, emergency orders, permit conditions, or requirements or prohibitions relating to acid deposition or stratospheric ozone control, or to knowingly violate any requirement for the payment of a fee.[9]

Knowing violation of the enumerated CAA requirements is a felony offense, which for a first violation subjects the convicted person to imprisonment of up to five years, punishment by a fine, or both, in accordance with the general fine provisions of Title 18 of the United States Code.[10] For individuals found guilty of a felony under CAA Section 113(c)(1), such fines can reach a maximum of $250,000 per conviction, or twice the gross pecuniary gain derived from the violation.[11] Organizational defendants convicted of knowing violations of CAA requirements face fines of up to $500,000, or twice the pecuniary gain derived from the violation.[12] For all crimes, except knowing releases of endangering hazardous air pollutants under CAA Section 113(c)(5), "organizational" defendants include corporations, partnerships, associations, states, municipalities and political subdivisions of the state, and any agency, department, or instrumentality of the United States.[13] Under Section 113(c)(5), an organizational defendant does not include the government.[14] A second conviction for the same CAA offense results in the doubling of the maximum fine and period of incarceration.[15]

The criminal provisions of the CAA as amended by the 1990 amendments impose differing standards of criminal liability on employees within an organization based on their position in the hierarchy. Accordingly, the definition of a criminally liable person excludes "an employee who is carrying out his normal activities and who is acting under orders from the employer," unless the employee's violative conduct was "knowing and willful."[16] Like other environmental statutes, the criminal level of scienter required for establishing the *mens rea* element requires only proof beyond a reasonable doubt that a defendant generally intended to commit certain acts, as opposed to a specific intent to violate the regulatory requirements.[17] However, as concerns lower-level employees, the CAA imposes criminal liability only for violations that are "knowing and willful," a standard that would appear to approach a level of scienter warranting proof of specific intent.[18]

Knowingly False Statements and Failure to Pay Fees

Criminal liability may be imposed under the CAA on any person who knowingly makes any false material statement, representation, or certification in a document required to be filed or maintained under the act, including any omission, knowing alteration, or concealment regarding any such application, record, report, plan, or document.[19] In addition, knowingly failing to file, notify, or report as required under the CAA or falsifying, tampering with, failing to install, or rendering inaccurate any monitoring device or method required under the act constitutes a crime under the CAA. Such crimes are defined as felonies subject to imprisonment for up to two years, a fine pursuant to U.S.C. Title 18, or both, as discussed earlier, which maximum punishment is doubled with respect to second convictions.[20] Knowing failure to pay a fee regarding CAA program requirements, except in regards to mobile source requirements under Title II, is subject to misdemeanor penalties (including a doubling of maximum fines and imprisonment for second convictions).[21]

Cognizant of its newly created criminal liability for record keeping, filing, and other crimes of omission, Congress expressed the view that criminal liability ought not to be imposed for "inadvertent errors."[22] In addition, Congress expressed concern that the expanded criminal liability for record-keeping crimes and omissions should not be used in a manner that would deter owners and operators of CAA sources from conducting self-audits. Indeed, Congress specified that criminal penalties under CAA Section 113(c) "should not be applied in a situation where a person, acting in good faith, promptly reports the results of an audit and promptly acts to correct any deviation."[23]

Endangering Releases of Hazardous Air Pollutants

Knowing Releases

Felony criminal liability may be imposed on any person who knowingly releases into the ambient air any hazardous pollutant listed under CAA Section 112 or "any extremely hazardous substance listed pursuant to section 302(a)(2) [of the Emergency Planning and Community Right-to-Know Act (42 U.S.C. § 11002(a)(2))]" if the release negligently places another person in "imminent danger of death or serious bodily injury."[24] Conviction is punishable by a fine pursuant to Title 18, by imprisonment for not more than fifteen years, or both. In addition, upon conviction an organization is subject to a fine of not more than $1 million for each offense.[25] A second conviction results in the doubling of maximum fines and imprisonment.

It is important to note that under this provision criminal liability may be imposed for emissions of air pollutants that are *not* regulated by the CAA. In addition, to obtain a conviction, the government must prove beyond a reasonable doubt that the release was "into the ambient air," which would appear to minimize the potential for criminal liability regarding actions that affect only on-site employees at indoor facilities. Moreover, an affirmative defense is provided when the conduct comprising the violation was consented to by the endangered person, provided that the danger and conduct were "reasonably foreseeable hazards" of an occupation, business, profession, or medical experimentation or treatment.[26] Criminal liability under this paragraph cannot be imposed for emissions of any air pollutant that is in compliance with a CAA emission standard or a Title V operating permit.[27]

The CAA defines the level of knowledge requisite for establishing that an individual knew his or her actions placed another person in imminent danger of death or serious bodily injury.[28] Such liability is limited to "actual awareness or actual belief possessed," and knowledge possessed by someone other than the defendant may not be imputed to the defendant. However, a defendant's possession of actual knowledge may be demonstrated by circumstantial evidence, including that "the defendant took affirmative steps to be shielded from relevant information."[29] The statute also specifically applies all general common-law defenses available under federal criminal law, and it encourages courts to develop "concepts of justification excuse" in light of reason and experience.[30] In addition, government entities are by definition excluded from criminal liability as organizational defendants.[31]

Negligent Releases

In addition to intentional releases of endangering air pollutants, any person who negligently releases into the ambient air a hazardous pollutant listed pursuant to Section 112 of the CAA or Section 302(a)(2) of the Emergency Planning and Community Right-to-Know Act is also subject to criminal liability if the release "negligently places another person in imminent danger of death or serious bodily injury."[32] Conviction of the crime of negligent endangerment under the CAA is a misdemeanor punishable by imprisonment of up to one year and fines imposed pursuant to U.S.C. Title 18. Subsequent convictions result in doubling of both maximum punishments.

Notes

1. CAA § 113(c)(1).

2. CAA § 113(c)(2).

3. Between the fiscal years 1983 and 1992, sixty-eight defendants were charged with crimes under the CAA. By comparison, during the same period 317 defendants faced prosecution under the Resource Conservation and Recovery Act and 205 faced prosecution under the Clean Water Act. See James Miskiewicz & John S. Rudd, *Civil and Criminal Enforcement of the Clean Air Act after the 1990 Amendments,* 9 PACE ENVTL. L. REV. 281, 374 n.370 (1992).

4. *See id.* at 372–73 nn. 364–65.

5. Indeed, recent Environmental Protection Agency statistics indicate that CAA criminal enforcement is already on the rise. During fiscal year 1996, more than 109 files were opened for CAA crimes. Response to Freedom of Information Act Request, National Enforcement Investigations Center (Apr. 14, 1997).

6. See the Chapter 17 discussion under "The Federal Procurement Bar."

7. For a more in-depth treatment of the issues involved in responding to criminal enforcement of environmental laws, see Chapters 6 and 7 in DANIEL RIESEL, ENVIRONMENTAL ENFORCEMENT: CIVIL AND CRIMINAL (Law Journal Seminar-Press, 1997).

8. Before the 1990 amendments, knowing violation of so-called work practice requirements were not subject to criminal liability under the CAA. Adamo Wrecking Co. v. United States, 434 U.S. 275 (1978). The 1990 amendments clarify that work practice standards are

now included within the definition of emissions standards. *See* CAA § 302(k) (defining "emission standard" as "any design, equipment, work practice, or operational standard promulgated" under the CAA); CAA § 112(h) (hazardous air pollutant work practices).

9. *See* CAA § 113(c)(1).

10. *See id.;* 18 U.S.C. § 3571. According to one commentator, the CAA includes criminal liability for failure to pay fees because fee-based economic incentive programs such as the acid rain allowance trading program could not otherwise be enforced. *See* Michael S. Alushin, *Enforcement of the Clean Air Act Amendments of 1990,* 21 ENVTL L. 2217, 2219 (1991).

11. 18 U.S.C. § 3571(b)(3).

12. *Id.* § 3571(c)(3), (d).

13. CAA § 113(c)(6), 302(e).

14. CAA § 113(c)(5)(E).

15. CAA § 113(c)(1).

16. CAA § 113(h).

17. *See* Miskiewicz & Rudd, *supra* note 3, at 381–83 & n.418.

18. CAA § 113(h). There is legislative history, on the other hand, that suggests that Congress may have intended something less than specific intent to convict under the knowing and willful standard. *See* 136 CONG. REC. S16,933, S16,952 (daily ed. Oct. 27, 1990) (statement of Sen. Baucus) ("A person who knows that he is being ordered to commit an act that violates the law cannot avoid criminal liability for such act by hiding behind such internal 'orders.' The 'knowing and willful' standard does not require proof by the government that the defendant knew he was violating the Clean Air Act per se. It is sufficient for the government to prove the defendant's knowledge that he was committing an unlawful act.").

19. CAA § 113(c)(2).

20. *See id.*

21. CAA § 113(c)(3). Note that knowingly failing to pay a fee is also defined as a felony crime under CAA Section 113(c)(1).

22. H.R. CONF. REP. No. 952, at 347–48 (1990) ("The amendments add new criminal sanctions for recordkeeping, filing, and other omissions. These provisions are not meant to penalize inadvertent errors. For criminal sanctions to apply, a source owner or operator must be on notice of the recordkeeping, information, or monitoring requirements in question.").

23. *See id.* at 348 ("Knowledge gained by an individual solely in conducting an audit or while attempting to correct any deficiencies identified in the audit or the audit report itself should not ordinarily form the basis of the intent which results in criminal penalties.").

24. CAA § 113(c)(5)(A).

25. *See id.*

26. CAA § 113(c)(5)(C).

27. CAA § 113(c)(5)(A).

28. Serious bodily injury is defined as "bodily injury which involves a substantial risk of death, unconsciousness, extreme physical pain, protracted and obvious disfigurement or protracted loss or impairment of the function of a bodily member, organ, or mental faculty." CAA § 113(c)(5)(F).

29. CAA § 113(c)(5)(B).

30. CAA § 113(c)(5)(D).

31. CAA § 113(c)(5)(E).

32. CAA § 113(c)(4).

CHAPTER 19

Implementation of Clean Air Act Programs by American Indian Tribes

JILL E. GRANT

The basic framework of the Clean Air Act (CAA) consists of the Environmental Protection Agency (EPA) setting national standards and requirements and the states assuming the primary responsibility for implementing and enforcing those standards and requirements.[1] Before undertaking this responsibility, a state must submit a CAA program to the EPA for approval, showing that the state program satisfies the minimum federal requirements and that the state has adequate legal authority and resources to implement the program. The EPA retains legal authority to bring an enforcement action against a source violating a state-implemented CAA program, and it also retains authority to ensure that the state is implementing the program in question adequately.[2]

This model of cooperative federalism assigns air quality protection responsibilities between the federal government and the states, but it does not provide a role for American Indian tribes. In fact, this gap existed generally in all of the federal environmental statutes; in a few instances, federal regulations already existed that the EPA could apply to tribes,[3] but for the most part sources on tribal lands went unregulated.[4] Congress eventually recognized this omission and amended three of the statutes, including the Clean Air Act, to provide for tribes to assume implementation and enforcement responsibility for federal environmental programs in a manner similar to that assumed by states.[5]

In the 1990 amendments, Congress added Section 301(d) to the CAA.[6] This provision is known as the "treatment as a state" (TAS) provision, and it authorizes the EPA to "treat Indian tribes as states under this Act" so that tribes may develop and implement various CAA programs on their own lands. Section 301(d) fits tribes into the federal-state model of CAA implementation, although a tribe's participation is voluntary. It thus provides for tribes to submit programs under the CAA for the EPA's approval and, if approval is granted, compliance with the tribal programs will satisfy the CAA requirements. This chapter examines the CAA TAS provision, the EPA rule implementing that provision, and other EPA and tribal attempts to provide for implementation of CAA programs in "Indian country."[7]

619

CAA "Treatment as a State"

Requirements for TAS under Section 301(d)

Under Section 301(d)(2), a tribe must meet four criteria to be eligible to be "treated as a state" with respect to any particular CAA program.

1. It must be federally recognized.[8]
2. It must have a "governing body carrying out substantial governmental duties and powers."
3. It must exercise functions that "pertain to the management and protection of air resources within the exterior boundaries of the reservation or other areas within the tribe's jurisdiction."
4. It must be "reasonably expected to be capable, in the judgment of the Administrator, of carrying out" these functions.

A tribe must demonstrate that it meets these TAS eligibility criteria each time it applies for EPA approval for the tribe to implement a CAA program.[9] In addition, the particular CAA program for which the tribe seeks approval must satisfy the various program requirements spelled out in the EPA regulations.

Under Section 301(d), therefore, for a tribe to receive EPA approval to implement a CAA program, a tribe not only must satisfy the specific program requirements, as a state must, but also must meet these four eligibility criteria. The program applied for must be one that the EPA has found is "appropriate" for tribes to implement, as set forth by rule under Section 301(d)(2). If the EPA determines that treatment of tribes as states is inappropriate for particular programs or provisions, the EPA may directly administer CAA provisions in those instances, pursuant to regulations promulgated under Section 301(d)(4). A tribe is not, however, required by the statute to apply for TAS approval for a particular program. If a tribe does not seek TAS approval, it would seem that the EPA must administer the program for the tribe within Indian country, as Section 301(d)(4) appears to acknowledge.[10]

Comparison with TAS Provisions in Other Statutes

Section 301(d) is similar to the TAS provisions in Section 518(e) of the Clean Water Act, 33 U.S.C. Section 1377(e), and Section 1451 of the Safe Drinking Water Act, 42 U.S.C. Section 300j-11. These provisions all require that the four criteria of federal recognition, governmental authority, jurisdiction, and capability be satisfied for a tribe to receive TAS authority. The only significant difference between the three TAS provisions is in the wording of the jurisdiction criterion, and of the three TAS jurisdiction provisions the CAA provision, which was the last to be enacted, provides for approval of tribal programs over the broadest area of land with the most certainty as to the scope of jurisdiction.

The Clean Water Act provides for the narrowest scope of tribal program authority, according to the EPA's interpretation, which construes Section 518(e) of the Clean Water Act to authorize EPA approval of tribal Clean Water Act programs only to the extent that the tribe is implementing the programs within the tribe's reservation.[11] In approving TAS applications under this provision, the EPA has stated that it will interpret the term "reservation" broadly, finding, for example, that it includes tribal trust land outside of formal reservation boundaries.[12] Nevertheless, this is a much narrower definition than the definition of "Indian country" that is usually used to determine tribal jurisdiction for purposes of federal Indian law.[13]

Moreover, under the Clean Water Act a tribe must demonstrate that it has jurisdiction over all land for which it seeks TAS approval, even though the land is within its reservation, since the EPA has declined to find that Congress delegated jurisdiction under the Clean Water Act to tribes within their reservations.[14] This interpretation opens the door to challenges to tribal jurisdiction over nonmembers of the tribe. Under the holding of *Montana v. United States*, such challenges are limited to the assertion of tribal jurisdiction over nonmembers located on nontribal fee lands within reservations.[15] Moreover, the EPA has stated a presumption that water quality affects tribal health and welfare, so that tribal regulation of water quality is likely to meet the *"Montana* exception" providing for tribal jurisdiction over nonmembers with regard to activities that threaten or have some direct effect on the health or welfare of the tribe.[16] These challenges may become broader, however, and extend to tribal regulation of nonmembers regardless of the trust status of the land, if courts extend the reasoning of *Nevada v. Hicks*, discussed further below.

The Safe Drinking Water Act allows a much broader assertion of tribal jurisdiction, requiring simply that the functions to be exercised by the tribe be "within the area of the Tribal Government's jurisdiction."[17] The EPA has interpreted this language to mean "Indian country," as defined in 18 U.S.C. Section 1151, whether or not these lands are within or outside of formal reservation boundaries.[18] The Safe Drinking Water Act still requires the tribe to make a showing of jurisdiction for each area claimed, however, and there is less of a case than under the Clean Water Act that the language of Section 1451 could be interpreted to be a delegation.

The CAA combines the two previous approaches, requiring that the functions to be exercised by the tribe pertain to air resources "within the exterior boundaries of the reservation or other areas within the tribe's jurisdiction."[19] The CAA includes the concept of tribal jurisdiction within the reservation, as in the Clean Water Act, but also recognizes that tribal jurisdiction may extend to the "other areas" of Indian country, as under the Safe Drinking Water Act. Moreover, in part because of the juxtaposition of the two clauses, the EPA found in its rule implementing Section 301(d) that the first clause in Section 301(d)(2)(B) is a legislative grant of authority to tribes over all air resources within the exterior boundaries of their reservations. This finding was upheld in *Arizona Public Service Co. v. EPA*,[20] and leads to the possibility that the similar language in Section 518(e) of the Clean Water Act could also be found to be a delegation.[21]

The CAA TAS section thus is as broad as the Safe Drinking Water Act TAS provision with regard to jurisdiction, but also provides more certainty than the equivalent section under the Safe Drinking Water Act because it constitutes a delegation of authority to tribes over all areas within reservation boundaries, obviating the need for tribes to make any further showing of jurisdiction for such areas.[22]

Grant Provisions

Section 301(d)(1)(B) provides that "subject to the provisions of paragraph 2 [the TAS provisions]," the EPA administrator may provide grant and contract assistance to tribes to carry out programs under the CAA. The EPA has interpreted this provision in its rule implementing Section 301(d) as authorizing the EPA to provide funds to tribes essentially in accordance with existing grant provisions under the CAA, namely, Sections 103 and 105, but with a substantially lower matching requirement under Section 105 for eligible tribes.[23] Section 103 provides for financial assistance with regard to research and development programs, and Section 105 provides for grants to air pollution control agencies. The details regarding the EPA's application of these provisions to tribes are discussed in the next section.

The CAA "Tribal Authority Rule"

Background of the Rule Making

Section 301(d)(2) required the EPA to promulgate a rule by May 15, 1992, "specifying those provisions of [the CAA] for which it is appropriate to treat Indian tribes as States." The agency held a number of meetings with tribal representatives, from spring 1992 to fall 1993, to discuss issues pertaining to the rule. On August 25, 1994, the EPA published a proposed rule in the *Federal Register*.[24] The EPA eventually published the final rule, known as the Tribal Authority Rule (TAR), on February 12, 1998.[25] The TAR was the only one of the TAS rules issued by the EPA to be challenged in court, and the D.C. Circuit upheld the rule in its entirety in *Arizona Public Service*. Nevertheless, the EPA's delay in issuing the final rule has contributed to delays in the development of tribal air programs, which continue to lag behind tribal programs under other environmental statutes.

Main Provisions of the TAR

The TAR creates a new 40 C.F.R. Part 49, entitled Tribal Clean Air Act Authority, and also revises 40 C.F.R. Part 35 to extend the CAA grant provisions to tribes.[26] The rule provides that tribes meeting the four eligibility criteria listed in CAA Section 301(d) and reiterated in Section 49.6 of the rule shall be "treated in the same manner as states" with respect to all provisions of the CAA and implementing regulations except those specifically listed in

Section 49.4. That section excludes tribes only from provisions relating to deadlines and sanctions for failure to meet deadlines, since tribes are not required to obtain treatment as a state under the CAA, and from certain provisions that could require waivers of tribal sovereign immunity. Otherwise, all provisions of the CAA apply to or may be implemented by tribes.

The TAR lays out in Section 49.7 the procedures that tribes must follow to demonstrate eligibility to implement CAA programs. These procedures include submitting a jurisdictional statement that "describes the basis for the tribe's assertion of authority," together with a map of the area over which the tribe asserts authority.[27] In addition, the tribe must submit a statement describing its capability and the capability of its staff to administer the CAA program for which it seeks approval.[28] The TAR also requires the tribe to enter into a memorandum of agreement with the appropriate EPA region to provide for referrals to the EPA for criminal enforcement in circumstances where the tribe lacks criminal jurisdiction.[29] These requirements all are similar to the requirements in the regulations implementing the TAS provisions of the Clean Water Act and the Safe Drinking Water Act. Finally, the TAR requires the EPA regional administrator to notify all "appropriate government entities" of a tribe's application for treatment as a state, and provides for a thirty-day comment period.[30]

The rule also provides for financial assistance to tribes developing or implementing CAA programs, based on existing Sections 103 and 105 of the CAA. In addition, the EPA can provide funding to tribes for environmental program development under the general assistance program (GAP).[31] Under CAA Section 103, states are eligible for federal assistance for the full amount of approved research and development costs, and the TAR does not alter this provision, making it equally applicable to tribes.[32] Moreover, a TAS application is not required to obtain funding under Section 103.[33]

In order to receive funds for air pollution planning and control programs under CAA Section 105, states and tribes without TAS approval must meet a 40 percent matching requirement. Under the TAR, however, if a tribe applies for and receives TAS approval for a Section 105 grant, the tribe is eligible for financial assistance of up to 95 percent of approved program costs for the first two years of a grant award, and up to 90 percent thereafter, as opposed to the 60 percent otherwise awarded under the CAA.[34]

Major Issues Raised by the TAR

The preambles to the proposed and final rules address the following major issues regarding the TAR:

- Tribal jurisdiction under the CAA
- CAA provisions for which it is appropriate to treat tribes as states
- Stringency of tribal requirements
- A "modular" approach to treatment as a state

These issues are discussed in the paragraphs below.

Tribal Jurisdiction under the CAA

In the preamble to the final TAR, the EPA confirmed its position that the language of Section 301(d)(2)(B) is a federal delegation of authority to tribes within their reservations. In the EPA's words, the delegation provides "a federal statutory source of tribal authority over designated areas, whether or not the tribe's inherent authority would extend to all such areas."[35] The EPA explained that its interpretation was based on the plain language of the statute, which differentiates between "the reservation" and "other areas within the tribe's jurisdiction," and also was supported by the legislative history.[36] The EPA also confirmed its interpretation of the term "reservation" as including tribal trust lands located outside of formal reservation boundaries.[37]

The EPA's interpretation was upheld by the D.C. Circuit in *Arizona Public Service Co.* In addition, the court found that, contrary to the arguments of petitioners,[38] tribes are not limited to promulgating tribal implementation plans (TIPs) and issuing redesignations only for reservations, but may do so for all areas of Indian country. Although Sections 110(o) and 164(c),[39] the CAA provisions governing TIPs and redesignations, make reference to "reservation," the court found that these references did not restrict the broader tribal authority recognized in Section 301(d).

The EPA's interpretation of Section 301(d)(2)(B) as a delegation has gained greater significance following the Supreme Court's decision in *Nevada v. Hicks.* The actual holding of *Hicks* is quite narrow: The Court found that a tribal court lacked jurisdiction over a tribal member's claims against state officials executing a search warrant on tribal land on the reservation for crimes allegedly committed off the reservation.[40] The analysis the Court employed to reach this holding is much broader, however. Previously, based on *Montana,* it was assumed that tribes had civil regulatory jurisdiction over anyone within a reservation, except over non-Indians on non-Indian-owned fee land within a reservation. In that situation, unless there was an express Congressional delegation of jurisdiction to the tribe, the tribe had jurisdiction only if it met one of the two exceptions laid out in *Montana,* namely, the tribe must be regulating "the activities of nonmembers who enter consensual relationships with the tribe or its members, through commercial dealing, contracts, leases or other arrangements" or it must be regulating conduct which "threatens or has some direct effect on the political integrity, the economic security, or the health or welfare of the tribe."[41] The Court in *Hicks* applied the *Montana* test to trust land within the reservation, and at least three of the Justices indicated that the *Montana* test should apply in all situations in the future, whenever a tribe asserts civil regulatory or adjudicative authority over non-Indians, regardless of (or with little weight given to) the status of the land at issue.[42] To date, the reasoning of *Hicks* has not been extended, and the one post-*Hicks* environmental case decided at the time of this writing found that *Hicks* did not apply to a challenge to a TAS approval under the Clean Water Act.[43] In any event, since Section 301(d) is a congressional delegation of jurisdiction to tribes, there is no need under the CAA for a tribe to demonstrate its authority over trust lands, regardless of *Hicks.*

CAA Provisions for Which it is Appropriate to Treat Tribes as States

In its proposed rule, the EPA provided that treatment as a state should apply to all provisions of the CAA, with the exception of provisions regarding deadlines for program implementation, sanctions for failure to comply with these deadlines, and certain enforcement provisions. The EPA excepted deadline and sanction provisions because tribes, unlike states, are not required to implement any CAA programs and so cannot logically be penalized for failure to implement programs by a certain date. Similarly, the EPA would not be required to promulgate federal implementation plans (FIPs) by a certain date, although the EPA stated its intention to develop a strategy for achieving federal protection of tribal air resources where necessary, which could include the promulgation of FIPs.[44] Tribes would still, however, be subject to sanctions for failure to implement or enforce an approved EPA program adequately.[45] Criminal enforcement provisions would not apply to tribes because of limits on a tribe's criminal jurisdiction. The EPA proposed instead that a tribe enter into a memorandum of agreement with the EPA for criminal enforcement against non-Indians (and presumably for enforcement of criminal penalties against Indians in amounts above the tribal jurisdictional limit).[46] Otherwise, tribes would be subject to the same requirements as states, modified by the "modular" approach discussed below.

The final TAR confirmed this approach, but added two provisions to the list under 40 C.F.R. Section 49.4, due largely to concerns with tribal sovereign immunity. CAA Section 304[47] authorizes citizens' suits against any person, including any governmental entity, for violations of the CAA. In the proposed TAR, the EPA indicated that the provision should apply to tribes in the same manner as to states.[48] In the final rule, however, the EPA "declin[ed] to announce a position . . . regarding whether tribes are subject to the citizen suit provisions contained in section 304," and instead included Section 304 as one of the provisions listed under 40 C.F.R. Section 49.4 as not being appropriate to apply to tribes.[49] The EPA withdrew from its earlier position because it found it was unclear whether Section 301(d) constitutes a waiver of tribal sovereign immunity, and in particular because tribes, unlike states, are not protected by the Eleventh Amendment, which is specifically referenced in Section 304.

Similarly, the EPA changed its position on the judicial review requirements of CAA Title V. Section 502(b)(6) and (b)(7)[50] provide for judicial review in state court of permit actions or failures to act. Originally, the EPA proposed to extend this requirement to tribes.[51] In the final TAR, the EPA withdrew its proposal, both because of concerns with waivers of tribal sovereign immunity and from a recognition that not all tribes have tribal court systems.[52] Instead, the EPA required tribes to "provide for an avenue for appeal of tribal government action or inaction to an independent review body and for injunctive-type relief to which the Tribe would agree to be bound."[53] This could be accomplished by a voluntary waiver of sovereign immunity in tribal court, or by alternative options which a tribe could develop and propose to the EPA for its approval. The D.C. Circuit upheld the EPA's approach in *Arizona Public Service Co.*[54] The

EPA also stated that it would develop guidance on acceptable alternatives to judicial review,[55] but it has not done so.

Stringency of Tribal Requirements

The EPA proposed that, as in the case of states (and comparable to the Clean Water Act and Safe Drinking Water Act TAS rules), tribal clean air requirements must be as stringent as those in the CAA, and can be more stringent if a tribe so chooses, except where the act expressly preempts or precludes the imposition of stricter standards.[56] The final TAR did not alter this principle. Despite this policy's pervasiveness, however, there have been two suits against the EPA for approving more stringent tribal standards under the Clean Water Act. In both instances, the EPA's approval of the tribal standards was upheld, both at the district court level and on appeal.[57]

Modular Approach to Tribal Implementation of CAA Programs

The EPA recognized in the TAR that tribes may decide to develop only certain CAA programs, and perhaps even only parts of those programs, and not others. First, tribes may have concerns with regard to some types of pollution on their reservations and not others. In addition, tribes may not have the resources to develop more than a few CAA programs, and are not in any event required under the CAA to develop their own programs at all. The EPA therefore proposed that tribes be allowed to engage in a "modular" approach to implementing the CAA: that is, a tribe may request approval of "reasonably severable elements" of programs instead of the entire act or even entire programs.[58] The EPA also suggested that tribes conduct emission inventories and project potential future emissions based on projections of future growth to determine priorities for developing tribal air programs.[59] In addition, the agency indicated that tribes may be permitted to submit partial permit programs for TAS approval, consistent with the EPA's modular approach.[60] The TAR codifies this approach, providing that "a program approval request may be comprised of only partial elements of a Clean Air Act program, provided that any such elements are reasonably severable, that is, not integrally related to program elements that are not included in the plan submittal."[61]

Related TAS Rules

Streamlining Rules

The EPA initially required a tribe to demonstrate compliance with the four TAS criteria listed in CAA Section 301(d) in a separate application from its application for program approval. The same requirement applied to TAS applications under the Clean Water Act and the Safe Drinking Water Act. Moreover, each time that a tribe applied for TAS approval, states were given the opportunity to comment on the application. This process was often duplicative and invited delay. In response to comments on these problems, the EPA articulated a general policy to streamline the TAS application process, in a memorandum dated November 10, 1992.[62] Under this policy, tribes would not need to make a separate, formal TAS application each time they sought approval for a grant or program, as long as they demonstrated that they met the applicable statutory requirements of recognition, governmental authority, jurisdiction, and capability. Moreover, any tribe that met the recognition and governmental authority requirements for TAS under one EPA statute would meet them for all EPA statutes. Tribes still would have to demonstrate jurisdiction and capability on a program-by-program basis, but other governments' comments would not be required for grant applications or in instances when a jurisdictional determination had already been made as part of the EPA approval of tribal standards, and they would be expedited in other instances.

The EPA followed this policy statement in a rule establishing tribal eligibility requirements for receiving financial assistance,[63] and it eventually implemented the policy in a rule establishing eligibility requirements for TAS program authorization for all three environmental statutes with TAS provisions.[64] The latter rule also refined the EPA's position on jurisdictional determinations, finding that although the EPA must make a specific determination of tribal jurisdiction for each program application,

> it will ordinarily make the same determination for other programs unless a subsequent application raises different legal issues. Thus, for example, once the Agency has arrived at a position concerning a boundary dispute, it will not alter that position in the absence of significant new factual or legal information. By contrast, however, a determination that a tribe has inherent jurisdiction to regulate activities in one medium might not conclusively establish its jurisdiction over activities in another medium.[65]

Environmental Program Grants

On January 16, 2001, the EPA published a rule clarifying the procedures applicable to tribal environmental program grants and finalizing a new Performance Partnership Grant (PPG) program for tribes.[66] The rule provides for various environmental program grants to be combined into a single PPG with a single budget and work plan. Although a tribe still needs to apply for the different program grants separately and must meet the individual grant TAS requirements,[67] a PPG allows a tribe to

- Combine different program grants so that it need deal with only one budget (and so account for total expenditures only) and one work plan, which should reduce administrative costs;[68]
- Reduce program match requirements to 5 percent for the first two years and 10 percent thereafter for programs that otherwise would have much higher match requirements (CAA Section 105 grants already meet these criteria);[69]

- Gain more flexibility in the use of the grants, which would no longer need to be tied to individual programs;[70] and
- Negotiate longer funding periods, although the EPA does not recommend periods longer than five years.[71]

The list of eligible programs is in Section 35.501, and includes CAA Section 105 and most other environmental program grants, with the notable exception of Superfund emergency response grants.

The same rule also makes changes to the tribal environmental program grant process in general, with some reduction in administrative burdens. Among the changes made to the general tribal grant requirements are the following:

- Funding periods may be negotiated (although GAP grants not within PPGs may not extend beyond four years);[72]
- EPA approval is no longer required for insignificant changes in work plans;
- Pre-award costs may be reimbursed if identified in the approved grant application;[73] and
- Grants may be awarded to intertribal consortia, as long as all members of the consortium meet the grant requirements and authorize the consortium to apply for the grant. For GAP grants, only a majority of members need meet the eligibility requirements and authorize the consortium to apply for the grant, as long as only those members will "benefit directly" from the grant project and will receive funds.[74]

CAA Program Implementation

As of early 2003, no tribes have received TAS approval for any air programs (other than for Section 105 grants), in contrast to tribal programs under the Clean Water Act and the Safe Drinking Water Act. Many tribes, however, have been undertaking at least preliminary air program activities, such as conducting needs assessments and air emissions inventories. Others have developed or are in the process of developing tribal air quality codes. These codes range from fairly simple documents that set forth basic administrative procedures and adopt air quality standards of particular relevance to the reservation in question to complex codes that incorporate virtually all of the programs under the federal CAA.[75]

Some tribes are most concerned with regulating large sources of air pollution located on their reservations. For example, there are two large coal-fired power plants located within the Navajo Reservation. With the trend toward locating power plants on Indian reservations, moreover, other tribes may find themselves with similar concerns in the near future. Other tribes have smaller but still significant sources of air pollution on their reservations, such as gas compressor stations on the Southern Ute Reservation. Tribes are interested in regulating these sources under a Title V permit program, and several have taken steps toward that goal.

Other tribes, concerned with maintaining the pristine air quality on their reservations, have designated their reservations as Class I areas.[76] Still others, such as the Gila River Indian Community, are concerned with nonattainment problems and are working on tribal implementation plans. Common to all tribes, however, is the practical concern that they cannot address all aspects of the CAA at once, if at all, and the corresponding concern that a strategy be developed to address the gaps in CAA program implementation in Indian country.

Filling the Regulatory Void

EPA Strategy to Address Permitting on Reservations and Fill Gaps in Program Implementation

In the final TAR, the EPA recognized "its general obligation under the CAA to ensure the protection of air quality throughout the nation, including throughout Indian country."[77] The EPA acknowledged that there is currently a gap in regulation of air quality in Indian country, and stated that it had

> undertaken an initiative to develop a comprehensive strategy for implementing the Clean Air Act in Indian country. The strategy will articulate specific steps the Agency will take to ensure that air quality problems in Indian country are addressed, either by EPA or by the tribes themselves.[78]

The EPA has never finalized this strategy, but the preamble to the TAR, the EPA's draft strategy, and its subsequent actions provide a good indication of its plans.

The draft strategy[79] and TAR preamble both endorse a two-step approach, under which the EPA will (1) develop federal rules for CAA programs to enable federal implementation of those programs in Indian country, and at the same time (2) provide support to tribes to enable them to implement their own programs.[80] With respect to the first step, the EPA promulgated federal operating permit rules, to apply to both states and tribes lacking approved Title V permit programs.[81] The EPA also has stated its intent to promulgate rules pertaining to minor source permits; federally enforceable emission limits for both major and minor sources in Indian country; and new source review permits.[82]

The federal operating permit rule in 40 C.F.R. Part 71 in large part mirrors the rule for state and tribal operating permit programs in 40 C.F.R. Part 70. As applied to tribes, the EPA has used Part 71 to issue federal operating permits to Title V sources located within Indian country, since there currently are no approved tribal Part 70 programs. The application of the rule to tribes initially was challenged on a number of grounds, in *Michigan v. EPA*, 963 F.3d 1075 (D.C. Cir. 2001), but in the end the only aspect of the rule that petitioners contested was Section 71.4(b), which provided that the EPA would retain jurisdiction for the purpose of issuing permits over areas for which Indian country status was "in question." This portion of the rule was overturned and remanded to the EPA, because the EPA had not provided any assurances that it would eventually determine the jurisdictional status of these "in question" areas. The EPA subsequently deleted the "in question" language from the rule, thus requiring that it make a determination that an area is Indian country before it may issue a federal operating permit for a source in that area.

The EPA may delegate implementation of Part 71 permits to tribes, just as it may for states, and in at least one instance is considering doing so as a transition to a Part 70 program. In order for a tribe to receive delegation of a Part 71 operating permit program, however, the tribe must demonstrate that its "laws . . . provide adequate authority to carry out all aspects of the delegated program."[83] This requirement is the same as the demonstration tribes must make to receive approval for a Part 70 program; tribes therefore cannot expect to use Part 71 as a means of avoiding jurisdictional issues.

The second step of the EPA's strategy involves building and strengthening tribal capacity to develop tribal CAA programs. The EPA has approached this goal largely through the provision of air program grants and technical training.[84] The EPA's strategy, however, even if it continues to be implemented, still leaves significant gaps in CAA regulation in Indian country, making it imperative that other strategies be considered as well.

FIPs

One solution that has been considered is for the EPA to promulgate FIPs to cover specific sources within reservation boundaries that would otherwise go unregulated until and unless the tribe in question developed and implemented its own standards. The final TAR in fact requires the EPA to promulgate "without unreasonable delay such federal implementation plan provisions as are necessary or appropriate to protect air quality . . . if a tribe does not submit a tribal implementation plan . . . or does not receive EPA approval of a submitted tribal implementation plan."[85] In a few instances, the EPA has attempted to promulgate FIPs for large individual sources, generally incorporating most of the corresponding state requirements into the FIP and thereby federalizing the requirements to make them applicable within Indian country. Recently, however, the EPA proposed several FIPs to cover groups of sources in Indian country in Idaho, Oregon, and Washington (EPA Region 10 excluding Alaska).[86] These proposed rules focus on sources of particulate matter on Indian reservations within the region, and are intended to establish a "base program" to control particulate matter from common types of sources. Nevertheless, in light of the scope of the problem and the time and resources that would be needed to complete the task, it is not realistic to expect the EPA to issue FIPs for virtually all of Indian country.

Additional Strategies

In other instances, tribes have entered into memoranda of understanding (MOUs) with state environment departments in an attempt to coordinate regulation and enforcement of air quality programs pending development of the tribes' capabilities to manage such programs on their own. Such MOUs may also serve as training opportunities for tribal environmental officials, since MOUs often provide for tribal officials to work together with state officials, who have the benefits of more experience and greater resources. Cooperation between states and tribes on enforcement issues, particularly in the case of tribes with heavily checkerboarded reservations, also may lessen the likelihood of jurisdictional disputes.

An alternative is for the EPA to authorize tribes to administer the federal programs that the EPA develops for Indian country (just as the EPA does for states lacking approved CAA programs). The EPA has limited resources to implement federal programs in Indian country, but could both enlist tribal assistance and train tribal environmental staff by delegating the implementation of federal programs to tribes. The federal operating permit regulations already provide for such delegation, to both states and tribes.[87]

Some sources in Indian country are located on land leased from tribes, rather than on private fee land. In another attempt to ensure that such sources comply with environmental requirements, tribes have added or considered adding air quality and other environmental provisions to the leases under which these sources operate. Such provisions, of course, are source-specific and do not address overall issues of air quality. In the case of existing leases, moreover, such provisions may be subject to whatever regulatory restrictions may have been agreed to when the leases were executed.

Finally, it is important for other governmental entities and for facility owners and operators to realize that tribes are already participating in the development of air quality policies and initiatives. The participation of a number of western tribes in the activities of the Grand Canyon Visibility Transport Commission (discussed in Chapter 7) and its successor organization, the Western Regional Air Partnership (discussed in Chapter 5), is one major example. As more tribes develop air quality programs and gain more experience with air quality issues, their participation is likely to grow.

Notes

1. In certain instances, when Congress decided that the need for national uniformity prevailed over other concerns, the EPA is responsible both for setting the federal requirements for a program and for implementing the federal requirements that it establishes. Such is the case for most regulation of mobile sources, regulation of substances that deplete stratospheric ozone, and certain aspects of the acid rain program.

2. There is some question as to whether the EPA may bring an enforcement action once a state (or, presumably, a tribe) implementing an EPA-approved program has already done so, in light of conflicting decisions addressing the issue under the Resource Conservation and Recovery Act (RCRA). *E.g.,* United States v. Elias, 269 F.3d 1003 (9th Cir. 2001), *cert. denied,* 123 S.Ct. 72 (2002), and Harmon Industries, Inc. v. Browner, 191 F.3d 894 (8th Cir. 1999), *reh'g denied* (January 24, 2000). The issue is discussed in Chapter 17.

3. The federal PSD regulations provide an example, 40 C.F.R. pt. 51, subpt. I.

4. Even where applicable federal regulations existed, the EPA often did not have or did not commit the resources to enforce those regulations in Indian country. In some

instances, in particular regarding water-quality standards, states regulated sources in Indian country, despite the states' lack of jurisdiction to do so under basic principles of federal Indian law.

5. The other two statutes are the Clean Water Act, 33 U.S.C. §§ 1251–1387, and the Safe Drinking Water Act, 42 U.S.C. §§ 300f–300j-26. FIFRA, 7 U.S.C. §§ 136–136y, and CERCLA, 42 U.S.C. §§ 9601–9675, contain provisions regarding tribes, but they do not provide for "treatment as a state" to the same degree as the other three statutes. RCRA, 42 U.S.C. §§ 6901–6992k, does not contain any "treatment as a state" provision, and efforts to amend the statute to include such a provision have been unsuccessful.

The EPA also created the American Indian Environmental Office, in 1994, to provide for greater coordination and awareness of tribal issues within the EPA. Organizationally, the AIEO is within the Office of Water, despite efforts to elevate the AIEO to the level of a separate Program Office.

6. 42 U.S.C. § 7601(d).

7. "Indian country" is the area over which there is tribal or federal jurisdiction and is defined in 18 U.S.C. Section 1151 as

(a) all land within the limits of any Indian reservation under the jurisdiction of the United States Government, notwithstanding the issuance of any patent, and, including rights of way running through the reservation, (b) all dependent Indian communities within the boarders [sic] of the United States whether within the original or subsequently acquired territory thereof, and whether within or without the limits of a State, and (c) all Indian allotments, the Indian titles to which have not been extinguished, including rights-of-way running through the same.

Although this definition is codified in the criminal code, it is also used in a civil context. *See, e.g.,* De Coteau v. District County Ct., 420 U.S. 425, 427 n.2 (1975); Oklahoma Tax Commission v. Sac and Fox Nation, 508 U.S. 114 (1993) (holding that whether a tribal member is outside of state's taxing jurisdiction depends on whether member lives in Indian country); Ute Indian Tribe v. Utah, 521 F. Supp. 1072, 1078 n.15 (D. Utah 1981), *aff'd in part, rev'd in part on other grounds,* 716 F.2d 1298 (10th Cir. 1983), *on reh'g* 773 F.2d 1087 (10th Cir. 1985), *cert. denied,* 479 U.S. 994 (1986) (stating that statutory definition of Indian country in the federal criminal code applies to questions of civil jurisdiction as well).

8. *See* CAA § 302(r). The list of federally recognized tribes is printed periodically in the *Federal Register;* the most recent list is at 67 Fed. Reg. 46,328 (July 12, 2002).

9. 40 C.F.R. §§ 49.3, 49.6, 49.7. The tribe may rely on aspects of a previous approval in a subsequent program application, however, 40 C.F.R. § 49.7(a)(8), as discussed further in the text. Also, although a tribe must receive TAS approval to be eligible for the lower match requirements available to tribes under CAA § 105 (*see* 40 C.F.R. § 35.220 and discussion of the TAR in the text), the EPA does not conduct as stringent an examination of a tribe's jurisdiction for grant applications as it does for other program applications, since the EPA's approval of a grant for program development does not constitute approval of tribal regulation of any persons or facilities.

10. Since the states in general do not have jurisdiction in Indian country (although the parameters of state jurisdiction may be changing in light of the Supreme Court's decision in Nevada v. Hicks, 533 U.S. 353 (2001), and other recent cases, discussed later in the text), and since the EPA generally has found that environmental matters satisfy the exceptions in Montana v. United States, 450 U.S. 544 (1981) (regarding tribal jurisdiction over nonmembers of the tribe), and, finally, since the CAA, like the other environmental statutes, applies to the entire nation (*see, e.g.,* CAA § 101(b)(1); Phillips Petroleum Co. v. EPA, 803 F.2d 545,

556 (10th Cir. 1986)), it follows that the EPA has the responsibility to implement CAA programs in Indian country when tribes do not take or are refused delegation.

11. Clean Water Act § 518(e) provides that the EPA may treat a tribe as a state if

(2) the functions to be exercised by the Indian tribe pertain to the management and protection of water resources which are held by an Indian tribe, held by the United States in trust for Indians, held by a member of an Indian tribe if such property interest is subject to a trust restriction on alienation, or otherwise within the borders of an Indian reservation.

12. *See, e.g.,* 58 Fed. Reg. 8172, 8177 (1993); 56 Fed. Reg. 64,876, 64,881 (1991).

13. *See supra* note 8.

14. 56 Fed. Reg. at 64,879–80.

15. 450 U.S. 544 (1981).

16. 56 Fed. Reg. at 64,878–79; *see also* Montana v. EPA, 941 F. Supp. 945 (D. Mont. 1991), *aff'd,* 137 F.3d 1135 (9th Cir.), *cert. denied,* 525 U.S. 921 (1998) (stating that the EPA found that "Montana did not rebut the presumption created by the Tribes' showing that pollution of surface waters traversing or appurtenant to nonmember land would have serious and substantial impact on the Tribes' health and welfare").

17. 42 U.S.C. § 300j-11(b)(1).

18. *See, e.g.,* EPA Determination of the Navajo Nation's Eligibility under Section 1451 of the Safe Drinking Water Act, signed by Felicia Marcus, EPA Regional Administrator, Region IX (October 23, 2000), at 10.

19. CAA § 301(d)(2)(B).

20. 211 F.3d 1280 (D.C. Cir. 2000), *cert. denied sub nom.* Michigan v. EPA, 532 U.S. 970 (2001).

21. *See, e.g.,* Brendale v. Confederated Tribes and Bands of the Yakima Nation, 492 U.S. 408, 428 (1989) (White, J., indicating that Clean Water Act § 518(e) is a delegation); Montana v. EPA, 941 F. Supp. 945, 951, 957 n.10 & n.12 (citing Brendale).

22. The EPA noted in its proposed rule that this interpretation is particularly appropriate since Section 110(o) of the CAA, 42 U.S.C. § 7410(o), already delegates authority to tribes over entire reservations for purposes of tribal implementation plans, the tribal equivalent to a SIP. 59 Fed. Reg. at 43,959 (1994). Section 110(o) provides:

When such [tribal implementation] plan becomes effective in accordance with the regulations promulgated under section 7601(d) of this title, the plan shall become applicable to all areas (except as expressly provided otherwise in the plan) located within the exterior boundaries of the reservation, notwithstanding the issuance of any patent and including rights-of-way running through the reservation.

23. 40 C.F.R. §§ 35.205, 35.220. CAA Sections 103 and 105 are found at 42 U.S.C. §§ 7403 and 7405, respectively.

24. 59 Fed. Reg. 43,956 (1994).

25. 63 Fed. Reg. 7254.

26. The rule also adds a definition of "Indian country" to 40 C.F.R. § 50.1.

27. 40 C.F.R. § 49.7(a)(3). This statement and the map can be quite complex, depending upon the nature of the tribe's jurisdictional claim.

28. 40 C.F.R. § 49.7(a)(4).

29. Tribes generally lack criminal jurisdiction over non-Indians, Oliphant v. Suquamish Indian Tribe, 435 U.S. 191 (1978), and, under the Indian Civil Rights Act, 25 U.S.C. §§ 1301–1341, tribes may impose criminal penalties on Indians only up to one year in jail and $5,000.

30. 40 C.F.R. § 49.9. The EPA issued a subsequent *Federal Register* notice (as a result of the litigation in *Arizona Public Service Co. v. EPA*) clarifying that the EPA would accept comments from the general public as well, and not just from governmental entities. 65 Fed. Reg. 1322 (January 10, 2000).

31. 40 C.F.R. pt. 35, subpt. Q. GAP grants, created under the Indian Environmental General Assistance Program Act of 1992, 42 U.S.C. § 4368b, are not limited to particular programs, such as air programs, but may be used for any tribal environmental programs, and may be used in conjunction with program grants.

32. *See* CAA § 302(b)(5), which provides that a tribal agency meets the definition of "air pollution control agency" required to obtain funding under CAA §§ 103 and 105. At one time, regulations applicable to Section 103 contained a 5 percent match requirement, but this requirement has since been deleted.

33. Thus, without applying for TAS approval under Section 301(d), tribes can obtain funding under Section 103(b)(3) to conduct, for example, an air emissions inventory or other study to assess tribal air quality.

34. 40 C.F.R. §§ 35.205(c), 49.11(b). In interpreting the language of Section 301(d)(5), which on its face provides that tribes may continue to receive funds under Section 105 "until such time as the Administrator promulgates regulations pursuant to this subsection [§ 301(d)]," the EPA proposed that tribes that do not meet the TAS eligibility requirements could be eligible for Section 105 funds subject to the same limitations as states, but that tribes that receive TAS approval could be eligible for funds at a lower matching fund requirement, since the EPA has the authority under Section 301(d)(4) to alter the CAA regulations for tribes when appropriate. 59 Fed. Reg. at 43,973.

35. 63 Fed. Reg. 7254. *See also id.* at 7257: "[B]ecause the Agency is interpreting the CAA as an explicit delegation of federal authority to eligible tribes, it is not necessary for the EPA to determine whether tribes have inherent authority over all sources of air pollution on their reservations."

36. *Id.* at 7254–55.

37. *Id.* at 7258. The EPA also included Pueblos (technically tribal fee lands) as within the meaning of the term "reservation." This interpretation is consistent with the EPA's interpretation of the same term under the Clean Water Act, *see supra* note 13.

38. There was a large group of petitioners in this case, including electric utilities, manufacturing, mining and timber interests, and the state of Michigan.

39. 42 U.S.C. §§ 7410(o), 7474(c).

40. *See* 533 U.S. at 357, n.2 ("Our holding in this case is limited to the question of tribal-court jurisdiction over state officers enforcing state law. We leave open the question of tribal-court jurisdiction over nonmember defendants in general"); *see also id.* at 384 (Ginsburg, J., concurring).

41. 450 U.S. at 565–66. The EPA has consistently interpreted environmental regulation as meeting the second *Montana* exception.

42. Justice Souter's concurring opinion, joined by Justices Kennedy and Thomas, stated that Montana's presumption against tribal jurisdiction should apply to all nonmember conduct, regardless of the status of the land or of the nonmember. Justice O'Connor, joined by Justices Stevens and Breyer, commented that in effect that is what the Court did, although the Court's decision states that it is limited to the question of tribal court jurisdiction over state officers. 533 U.S. at 357, n.2.

43. Wisconsin v. EPA, 266 F.3d 741 (7th Cir. 2001). The court explained that "this case does not involve any question of the tribe's ability to restrict activities of state law enforcement authorities on the reservation, when those officials are investigating off-

reservation crimes, and thus the rule of Hicks, 121 S.Ct. 2304, is not implicated." 266 F.3d at 747.

44. 59 Fed. Reg. at 43,961.

45. *See, e.g.,* CAA §§ 179(a)(4), 502(i)(2).

46. *See supra* note 28.

47. 42 U.S.C. § 7604.

48. 59 Fed. Reg. at 43,978.

49. 63 Fed. Reg. at 7260.

50. 42 U.S.C. § 7661a(b)(6) and (b)(7).

51. 59 Fed. Reg. at 43,972.

52. 63 Fed. Reg. at 7261.

53. *Id.* at 7262.

54. 211 F.3d at 1298–99.

55. 63 Fed. Reg. at 7262.

56. As discussed earlier, the EPA has prescribed uniform national standards for certain air programs, such as the acid rain program, and in such cases tribes and states must implement the federal standards.

57. City of Albuquerque v. Browner, 865 F. Supp. 733 (D.N.M. 1993), *aff'd*, 97 F.3d 415 (10th Cir. 1996); Montana v. EPA, 941 F. Supp. 945 (D. Mont. 1996), *aff'd*, 137 F.3d 1135 (9th Cir.), *cert. denied*, 525 U.S. 921 (1998).

58. 59 Fed. Reg. at 43,968.

59. *Id.*

60. *Id.* at 43,967.

61. 40 C.F.R. § 49.7(c).

62. Memorandum from F. Henry Habicht, Deputy Administrator, to the EPA.

63. 59 Fed. Reg. 13,814 (1994).

64. 59 Fed. Reg. 64,339 (1994).

65. *Id.* at 64,340.

66. 66 Fed. Reg. 3782. The rule was scheduled to become effective on February 15, 2001, but the effective date was delayed until April 17, 2001, 66 Fed. Reg. 9661 (2001), due to a White House memorandum delaying the effective dates of all new and pending regulations from the prior administration, 66 Fed. Reg. 7702 (2001).

67. 40 C.F.R. §§ 35.532(b), 35.535(a).

68. 40 C.F.R. §§ 35.530(b), 35.537.

69. 40 C.F.R. § 35.536.

70. 40 C.F.R. § 35.530(b); 66 Fed. Reg. at 3785.

71. 40 C.F.R. §§ 35.508, 35.532(b).

72. 40 C.F.R. §§ 35.508, 35.548(c).

73. 40 C.F.R. § 35.513.

74. 40 C.F.R. § 35.504.

75. For an example of the latter, see the Navajo Nation Air Pollution Prevention and Control Act, 4 N.N.C. § 1101 *et seq.*

76. For example, the Salish-Kootenai, the Northern Cheyenne, and the Yavapai Apache have made such designations. Tribes were permitted to redesignate their reservations prior to the enactment of CAA Section 301(d), pursuant to the provisions of CAA Section 164 (c), 42 U.S.C. § 7474(c). *See* discussion of *Arizona Public Service, supra*; Arizona Chamber of Commerce v. EPA, 151 F.3d 1206 (1998).

77. 63 Fed. Reg. at 7265.

78. 63 Fed. Reg. at 7263. *See also* 59 Fed. Reg. at 43,961.

79. Strategy for Implementing the Clean Air Act in Indian Country, April 15, 1997.

80. *Id.* at 2; 63 Fed. Reg. at 7263.

81. 40 C.F.R. pt. 71.

82. Strategy at 3–4; 63 Fed. Reg. at 7263–64. The EPA currently is developing a national tribal new source review regulation for minor sources. *See* Tribal Consultation Letter (June 28, 2002), *available at* http://www.epa.gov/air/tribal/announce.html.

83. 40 C.F.R. § 71.10(a).

84. EPA grants support a tribal environmental training program at Northern Arizona University and, more recently, the Tribal Air Monitoring Support Center.

85. 40 C.F.R. § 49.11(a).

86. 67 Fed. Reg. 11,748 (March 15, 2002).

87. 40 C.F.R. § 71.10. This is not a delegation of jurisdiction, however; a tribe still must demonstrate that it has jurisdiction to implement the program, as discussed in the text accompanying note 79.

CHAPTER 20

Rule Making and Judicial Review under the Clean Air Act

WILLIAM F. PEDERSEN[1]

Introduction

This chapter provides an overview of the procedural requirements applicable to Environmental Protection Agency (EPA) rule making under the Clean Air Act (CAA), and of the procedures for judicial review both of promulgated EPA rules and of failure to promulgate rules.

These topics are vital to the practitioner for several reasons. Almost without exception, CAA requirements take effect only through implementing rules that the EPA promulgates. Only by participating in the process for issuing those rules can persons outside the EPA bring their concerns before the agency and seek to shape the result. Should the final rule prove unsatisfactory for any reason, judicial review will generally offer one of the few realistic options for changing it. Similarly, if the EPA has failed to issue some rule of concern, judicial review will often be the most effective way to bring about its issuance.

Moreover, the law applicable to CAA rule making differs in some important respects from the generic law of administrative procedure. In particular, most important CAA rules are issued through specific statutory procedures set out in Section 307(d) that require considerably more of all participants than do the simple notice-and-comment requirements of the Administrative Procedure Act (APA). Similarly, both the CAA—specifically, Sections 307(d) and 304—and the cases under it have established judicial review requirements that differ from those applicable in other contexts.

Since one must deal first with the EPA before turning to the courts, this chapter begins with a description of CAA rule making procedures. It then sets out the rules and standards for judicial review of the EPA's actions, and concludes by discussing how and when the courts can be used to correct EPA inaction by requiring the agency to issue a rule.

EPA Rule-Making Procedures

Section 307(d)

The Scope of 307(d) Coverage

The special statutory features of EPA rule-making procedures are all contained in Section 307(d).[2]

That section contains special rule-making procedures applicable to most—but not all—of the important CAA actions that the EPA takes. They include the promulgation or revision of national ambient air quality standards (NAAQS), of federal implementation plans (FIPs), and of most rules relating to regulation of hazardous air pollutants, as well as all rules concerning fuels, auto emissions standards, ozone-depleting substances, acid rain, protection of visibility, and prevention of significant deterioration (PSD).[3] They are *not* automatically applicable, however, to the EPA rules that establish standards for approving state implementation plans (SIPs), or setting standards for enforcement actions.[4] Moreover, Congress expressly excluded "interpretative rules, general statements of policy, or rules of agency organization, practice, and procedure" from mandatory coverage.[5]

The law allows the EPA to extend Section 307(d) requirements to "such other actions as the Administrator may determine."[6] The EPA does not generally use this authority. However, prudence always requires a check of any individual rule making to see whether Section 307(d) has been invoked.

What Section 307(d) Requires

Section 307(d) builds on the notice-and-comment procedures that the APA prescribes for rule making.[7] When it applies, it requires both the EPA and outside rule-making participants to follow supplementary rules designed to allow these procedures to support a detailed probing of the issues at stake and generate an organized and definable record for judicial review. In particular:

- The EPA must begin the rule-making process by publishing a notice of proposed rule making in the *Federal Register*. Section 307(d) requires the notice to be accompanied by "a statement of its basis and purpose" including a summary of the factual data on which the proposed rule is based, the methodology used in obtaining the data and in analyzing the data, and the major legal interpretations and policy considerations underlying the proposed rule.[8]
- The EPA must establish a rule-making docket, which must include as of the date the proposal is published all documents on which the agency relies to support the proposal.[9] It must also include all drafts of the proposed rule provided to the Office of Management and Budget (OMB).[10]
- Section 307(d)(4) requires the EPA to allow at least thirty days for public comment on the proposed rule.[11] The EPA must also provide an opportunity for a "public hearing."[12] This is an informal "legisla-

tive" type of hearing at which there will be no formal witnesses and no cross-examination.

- The EPA must supplement the docket to include "upon receipt" all comments received on the proposed rule, as well as other documents that "become available after the proposed rule has been published and which the Administrator determines are of central relevance to the rule making"[13] and all drafts submitted to OMB before promulgation.[14]
- The EPA must propose and finally promulgate the rule by publication in the *Federal Register*, as provided under 5 U.S.C. Section 553(b), including a detailed "statement of basis and purpose" (including factual data, analytical methodology, and legal interpretations and policy considerations).[15]
- The EPA, in promulgating the rule, must respond to all significant comments.[16]
- The record for judicial review is limited to the docket items. With limited exceptions as discussed below, "[o]nly an objection to a rule or procedure which was raised with reasonable specificity during the period for public comment (including any public hearing) . . . may be raised during judicial review."[17]

EPA Rule Making beyond 307(d)

Section 307(d) provides only the minimum, legally required procedural framework for CAA rule making. Additional opportunities to take part in and influence regulatory decisions arise from other statutes, EPA custom, and presidential directives. These opportunities arise before a rule is proposed, during the comment period on a proposed rule, and at agencies other than the EPA.

Pre-Proposal Rule-Making Participation

The EPA typically starts work on a rule years before a formal proposal appears in the *Federal Register*. Both statute and executive order require the EPA to publish in the *Federal Register*, twice annually, a list of all "significant" rules under development.[18] This list is commonly called the "regulatory agenda." Moreover, the EPA programs typically place additional information about these rules on their portion of the EPA Web site.

During this pre-proposal phase, the EPA often conducts "outreach" activities to learn the views of its constituencies and to get information from them. The EPA staff are generally very willing (their schedules permitting) to meet with outside groups during this pre-proposal stage.

Accordingly, it should generally be easy to learn about upcoming rules and present any concerns about them to the EPA well before any formal proposal. All experienced administrative practitioners believe that the EPA's views on a rule are easiest to influence during this stage of the rule making, while the agency is still considering the issues and before its views have hardened.

PARTICIPATION AFTER THE RULE HAS BEEN PROPOSED   Many rule makings involve more elaborate formal procedures than a simple sequence of proposal, receipt of comments, and promulgation of a final rule. For particularly complex and controversial actions, the EPA may issue an "Advance Notice of Proposed Rulemaking" in the *Federal Register* well before any formal proposal. If comments on a proposed rule, or other information that the agency obtains after the proposal, raise important new issues, the EPA may reopen the comment period, either generally or on selected topics. Sometimes this reopening takes the form of a "Notice of Availability," which puts selected new information before the public (or, at least, those elements of the public that read the *Federal Register*) and asks for comments on it.

Even the formal comment opportunities on the initial proposal will rarely be limited to the statutory thirty days. Comment periods of sixty or ninety or even 120 days are the norm for significant rules. Moreover, the EPA is generally willing to extend the original comment period upon request if an extension is needed to allow the completion of important comments. Finally, if comments are submitted after the deadline, the EPA states that it may still consider them, although it is no longer legally obliged to do so.[19]

The EPA is often willing to meet with interested groups after the rule has been proposed, and even after the close of the comment period, to discuss their concerns and receive new information and arguments. The EPA staff sometimes try to discourage such meetings by saying they would involve a forbidden "*ex parte* contact," but this claim has no legal standing. The law on this point was settled in the case of *Sierra Club v. Costle*, in which the D.C. Circuit accepted (indeed, endorsed) EPA meetings with outside groups even in the last weeks before a rule was promulgated, as long as the agency made a memorandum of any new factual points of "central relevance" to the rule making and put it in the record.[20]

Another objection to such meetings has more legal substance and requires some precautionary care to avoid legal trouble. The Federal Advisory Committee Act (FACA) forbids agencies to use an outside group as a source of advice unless it has been chartered by the General Services Administration and abides by statutory requirements requiring it to conduct "open" meetings and have a "balanced" membership.[21] Twenty years ago some cases held that a series of agency meetings with a single industry group had created a FACA violation, because the group had been adopted as a preferential source of advice although it was neither chartered, open, nor balanced.[22]

These opinions, if pushed to their limit, would prohibit any outside group of any persuasion from lobbying the executive branch vigorously. Since this would probably violate the constitutional rights of those groups to petition the government,[23] such an extreme interpretation is hard to defend. The EPA practice, which has worked to date, has been to minimize any legal dangers by meeting evenhandedly with groups across the spectrum of opinion and avoid selecting any particular group as a preferred source of advice. Any rule-making meetings in which the EPA participates will probably adhere to that standard. (Since, as discussed earlier, the EPA may write a memorandum summarizing the discussion and put it in the record, it is generally a good idea to write a post-meeting letter to the docket giving your own summary.)

PARTICIPATION IN EPA RULE MAKING BY OTHER PARTS OF THE GOVERNMENT
For about thirty years, a series of executive orders has empowered the OMB to review and comment on proposed and final rules from mission agencies before they are issued.[24] The Office of Information and Regulatory Affairs (OIRA) within OMB exercises this authority. These orders have also required the preparation of detailed "cost-benefit" analyses of the most burdensome rules, and have encouraged agency use of a broad form of cost-benefit analysis in all their regulation.[25] Since President George W. Bush reaffirmed President Clinton's executive order on this subject without changing it, it seems safe to conclude that OMB review in its current form has become a permanent part of the U.S. system of government.

The influence of OMB on particular rules tends to vary with the preferences of the incumbent president. However, in all administrations OIRA has been willing (to a variable extent) to meet with outside groups on particular rules. Generally, a representative from the agency will be invited. Moreover, under the Sierra Club standards, any new factual information of central relevance presented to OMB must be reduced to writing and sent to the EPA for inclusion in the docket. Indeed, OIRA now dockets all outside meetings and comments received on its Web site, http://www.whitehouse.gov/omb/inforeg.

Over the past thirty years Congress has enacted a number of statutes requiring agencies to analyze the impact of their rule makings on particular interests. These requirements were all inspired by the success of the environmental impact statement requirements of the National Environmental Policy Act.[26] However, in 1977 Congress exempted CAA rule makings from the environmental impact statement requirement.[27]

More recent statutes and executive orders have required analysis of the impact of rules on small business and small government entities,[28] on Federalism,[29] on children's health,[30] and on energy supply.[31] Since it appears that none of these requirements is enforceable through judicial review, their utility as advocacy tools is limited.

The most potent of these statutes—the Paperwork Reduction Act—has more teeth.[32] It calls on OMB to devise and enforce a paperwork "budget" for the entire government, and to review all federal agency information collection requests to ten or more persons for their consistency with that budget.[33] If the information collection request is not approved, then no one need comply with it.[34]

Judicial Review

Where to File

Judicial review of all CAA rules is governed by Section 307(b) and Section 307(d)(7). If either (1) the rule falls within a specific list of topics contained in Section 307, or (2) (a) the rule is based on a determination of nationwide scope and effect and (b) the EPA publishes a finding to this effect with the rule, Section 307(b) sets exclusive venue in the U.S. Court of Appeals for the D.C. Circuit.[35] Review of locally or regionally applicable actions takes place in the court of appeals for the "appropriate" circuit.[36]

In most cases the right court will be clear from the facts of the rule making, or the EPA will make the finding of "nationwide scope and effect." Nevertheless, disputes on this point have arisen, and have generated a modest case law.[37]

The courts have held that these choice-of-circuit provisions prescribe venue and not jurisdiction, which means that if a petitioner files in the wrong court the government waives any objection by not raising it.[38] (If the provision were jurisdictional, its application could not be waived.) Upon objection, a court of appeals may transfer a case to a court where venue was proper.[39]

When to File

Section 307 provides for judicial review of any "final action" of the administrator.[40] It also requires any petition for review to be filed within sixty days of publication in the *Federal Register* of the action being challenged.[41] However, if review "is based solely on grounds arising after such sixtieth day, then any petition for review under this subsection shall be filed within sixty days after such grounds arise."[42] Once the sixty days have passed, no regulated entity can raise as a defense to an enforcement action any arguments that it could have raised in a direct challenge to the rule itself.[43] This seemingly straightforward requirement raises legal questions when there is doubt about whether a given action is "final," or "ripe" for judicial review, and when issues that a petitioner wants to litigate arise after the sixty-day deadline has run. Those questions are discussed below.

Finality and Ripeness

Many of the rules that implement the CAA do not *directly* affect regulated entities. Instead, they are "matrix" rules that give instructions to states or permit-issuing agencies on how to exercise their authority in some future regulatory proceeding. The EPA also issues less formal "guidance" to such persons on these same topics. Under the language of Section 307(d), this "guidance," too, may be a reviewable "final" action subject to the sixty-day deadline and bar on the later raising of issues as enforcement defenses.[44]

One might question whether all such matrix rules and guidance meet the traditional "finality" requirements of being definitive and having a direct and immediate effect on day-to-day activities of the petitioners. Even if they are "final," they may not present the issues with enough focus and tangibility to be ripe for judicial review.[45] Yet the statute provides every incentive to seek judicial review early in case of doubt, both to challenge a disputed position as soon as possible, before it can become established in practice, and to avoid any possible cutting off of enforcement defenses.

For many years, this dilemma had little practical importance. Those displeased by rules brought early challenges, which the courts considered without much attention to ripeness or finality issues.

In recent years, however, the D.C. Circuit has begun to find that some CAA matrix rules are not ripe for review.[46] The opinions are not consistent,[47] and may be obsolete since the Supreme Court in the *American Trucking* case summarily rejected ripeness and finality arguments.[48] Given this unsettled legal situation, as a practical matter the need to challenge an unsatisfactory rule early has been diminished little if at all.

Guidance documents raise another "when to file" problem in that they are not typically published in the *Federal Register*. The statute does not prescribe when the time for challenging these actions runs. The only decided case says that it does *not* run till the document is published in the *Federal Register*.[49]

However, it would not be prudent to rely on this single precedent unnecessarily. In those increasingly frequent cases where the document is posted on the EPA's Web site, the safe course would be to file within sixty days of the date of posting.

In a few cases, Congress has expressly provided that EPA actions cannot be challenged in court, on the theory that they can be adequately reviewed at a later stage in the regulatory process.[50]

Late-Arising Issues

In general, the courts have enforced the sixty-day cut-off with respect to issues that litigants could have raised at that time. Some courts have created an exception when complex matrix rules apply to a particular situation in a manner that the litigant could not reasonably have been expected to anticipate at the time the rule was promulgated.[51] In one application of this approach, courts have ruled that when the interpretation of the rules is at issue, the sixty-day period does not begin to run "until a fact-based controversy is ripe for judicial review."[52]

However, Section 307(b) expressly excludes from the sixty-day bar "petitions based solely on grounds arising after such sixtieth day." This language must be read together with a parallel exemption in Section 307(d) (specifically, Section 307(d)(7)(B)) that provides relief from the requirement to raise issues in comments before they can be raised in judicial review. It provides:

> If the person raising an objection [before the reviewing court] can demonstrate to the Administrator that it was impracticable to raise such objection [during the comment period] or if the grounds for such objection arose after the period for public comment (but within the time specified for judicial review), and if such objection is of central relevance to the outcome of the rule, the Administrator shall convene a proceeding

for reconsideration of the rule and provide the same procedural rights as would have been afforded had the information been available at the time the rule was proposed.

Two special features of CAA litigation have arisen from this provision. First, the courts have read it to require a petition for reconsideration before raising *any* issues not mentioned in comments, even if they arose from the agency's own error and raising them in comments would have been absolutely impossible. For example, a preliminary petition may well be required to challenge the EPA's failure to give notice and allow comment when it promulgates a completely unexpected provision in a final rule that had no antecedent in the proposal.[53]

Second, an established procedure for challenging rules that have grown obsolete has been built on this foundation. Under it, the prospective litigant must petition the agency to change the rule. That petition should contain or be accompanied by the new material that the agency is requested to consider. The EPA is legally required to respond to the petition, although the CAA, unlike some other statutes, does not set any deadline for this ruling. When the agency rules on that petition, *that* decision, rather than the rule itself, becomes the potential subject of judicial review.[54]

Stays

Under the general rules of administrative law, both a reviewing court and the agency itself may stay a rule pending judicial review. The CAA, however, provides on its face that no such stay shall exceed three months in length.[55]

The courts have largely drained the force from this provision.[56]

Substantive Judicial Review

The Requirements of Section 307(b)

Section 307(b) expressly sets out the standards for judicial review and reversal of EPA rules. A rule must be overturned if it is

(A) arbitrary, capricious, an abuse of discretion, or otherwise not in accordance with law; (B) contrary to constitutional right, power, privilege, or immunity; (C) in excess of statutory jurisdiction, authority, or limitations, or short of statutory right; or (D) without observance of procedure required by law.[57]

These standards, as the courts have recognized, simply repeat the parallel language of the Administrative Procedure Act and therefore do not change the law.[58]

However, Section 307(d) does contain one apparent change in the applicable legal standards for substantive judicial review. It provides:

In reviewing alleged procedural errors, the court may invalidate the rule only if the errors were so serious and related to matters of such central relevance to the rule that there is a substantial likelihood the rule would have been significantly changed if such errors had not been made.[59]

As we shall see, however, the courts have read this provision so as to largely deprive it of any independent force.

The Case Law on CAA Judicial Review

The outcome of a judicial challenge to a CAA rule will generally be influenced far more by the specific legal and factual merits of that challenge than by any principles drawn from other CAA cases. In addition, the case law is ever changing, so that any detailed survey would become incomplete quickly. For these reasons, this chapter will only briefly survey the case law, using the three categories into which almost all successful challenges to EPA rules fall. These are

- The rule was promulgated without observing proper procedure
- The rule exceeds the agency's legal authority; and
- The rule is arbitrary or capricious.

The Rule Was Promulgated without Observing Proper Procedure

Read literally, the stringent two-part test for reversal prescribed by Section 307(d) requires that the error (1) concern a subject of "central relevance" to the rule and (2) create a "substantial likelihood" that the rule would have been "significantly changed" but for the mistake.

However, the courts by and large have read this provision as simply articulating a rule of "harmless error" aimed at preventing ingenious litigants from using the detailed procedures of Section 307(d) to paralyze the agency.[60] In applying that test, the courts have considered that certain basic or core procedural requirements common to informal rule making under both the APA and the CAA are so fundamental that their violation will result in remand without any case-specific "harmless error" analysis.[61]

Since the "harmless error" rule also applies under the APA,[62] this reading essentially conforms the special procedural review language of Section 307(d) to the existing law, without the "free pass" for agency procedural errors that it might suggest on its face.

The most frequent claims of procedural error arise when a final rule differs in some particular from the proposal, giving rise to arguments that the public was denied its right to comment on the new provision, or when a litigant claims that the agency did not adequately respond to its comments.

In response to the first point, the courts have uniformly held that "[i]ncremental changes are permissible so long as the final rule is a 'logical outgrowth' of the proposals highlighted and discussed during the notice and comment period";[63] or, in an alternative formulation, where "interested persons were sufficiently alerted to likely alternatives to have known what was at stake."[64]

On the other hand, where essential provisions of a rule were provided in a "guidelines" document that was mentioned only in a footnote (that is, the text was not published in the *Federal Register*), that was determined not to constitute sufficient notice.[65]

In response to the second point, the courts, pointing out that a response is required only for "significant" comments, have placed on the litigant the burden of demonstrating that the comments were important enough to require a judicially compelled response.[66] (In any event, a court opinion holding that a rule is flawed solely because the agency failed to adequately explain its position is not likely to have more than tactical significance. Such an opinion does not change the applicable law in any way, or disapprove the agency's policy choices. On remand, often no more will be needed to comply with its requirements than a new piece of paper explaining why the original decision was correct.)

The Rule Exceeds the Agency's Legal Authority

In 1984, in the CAA case *Chevron v. NRDC*, the Supreme Court required reviewing courts to defer to agency interpretations of ambiguous statutory provisions.[67] In now-familiar language, the Court said that, although courts must hold agencies to the "unambiguously expressed intent of Congress" when the legislature has "directly spoken to the precise question at issue."[68]

However, in "step two" cases in which

> the statute is silent or ambiguous with respect to the specific issue, the question for the court is whether the agency's answer is based on a permissible construction of the statute. . . . If Congress has explicitly left a gap for the agency to fill, there is an express delegation of authority to elucidate a specific provision of the statute by regulation."[69]

In such cases the courts must defer to the agency's interpretation.

Over the past twenty years, *Chevron* has set the framework within which litigants challenge agency statutory claims. It applies across the board. Although some have questioned whether *Chevron* deference should apply to an agency's determination that a given disputed question falls within its jurisdiction, it now appears that *Chevron* deference applies here as well.[70]

Chevron has unquestionably strengthened the EPA's ability to prevail on statutory interpretation issues. However, it does *not* mean that the agency now wins every statutory interpretation case. In recent years the EPA has suffered a series of punishing court reversals in which the courts uniformly rejected agency claims that it could issue a given regulation simply because the statute did not forbid it to do so.[71] One court said

> To suggest, as the [agency] effectively does, that *Chevron* step two is implicated any time a statute does not expressly *negate* the existence of a

claimed administrative power . . . is both flatly unfaithful to the principles of administrative law . . . and refuted by precedent.[72]

Chevron deference can vary with the context. For example, a court will "especially defer" to the agency's interpretation when the decision requires "reconciling conflicting policies committed to the Agency's care and expertise under the Act."[73] In addition, courts are "extremely deferential" to the EPA in "cases involving technical rule making" particularly when agency actions involve policy decisions resulting from unclear technical information.[74] When the regulatory scheme is both technical and complex, courts "are especially inclined to uphold an agency's interpretation of its statutory mandate."[75]

As is the case with other executive agencies, the EPA is accorded great deference by the courts when the agency is required to interpret its own regulations.[76] *Chevron* deference also increases to the extent that the agency's position has been consistent over time.[77]

The Rule Is Arbitrary, Capricious, or an Abuse of Discretion

Although it is customary to describe any judicial challenge to a rule as seeking its invalidation for being "arbitrary and capricious," that custom does not accurately reflect the law. Properly speaking, a rule is "arbitrary, capricious, or an abuse of discretion" only when it was promulgated by proper procedures, and falls within the agency's legal authority, and yet is so unreasonable that it still must be invalidated.

This is a hard standard to meet. According to the D.C. Circuit, few rules fail to meet the "arbitrary and capricious" standard of review.[78] Nevertheless, the EPA does lose cases on this ground. For example, the D.C. Circuit struck down an EPA regulation designating methylene diphenyl diisocyanate (MDI) as a high-risk pollutant because the model that the EPA used did not bear a "rational relationship to the known properties of MDI emissions."[79]

Settlement

Many challenges to EPA regulations are brought as much to induce the agency to take another look at the issues considered in the rule making as to invoke the powers of the courts. Filing a court challenge "escalates" the controversy, results in a new set of government employees considering the issue, and provides some incentives to compromise to avoid the risk and cost of litigation.[80] Any agreement between the parties will be embodied in a "settlement agreement." Typically, the government will agree to propose certain regulatory changes, and the private litigants will agree to stay their suit pending final action and dismiss it if the rule is promulgated substantially as proposed.

However, the government has no legal obligation to make these changes—indeed, it would regard such an obligation as improperly allowing the litigants to require decisions that should properly be made through the rule-making process.[81] Moreover, if the government fails to act, or otherwise does not abide by the settlement agreement, restarting the litigation is the only enforcement mechanism. No court order requiring the government to issue a proposed or final rule can be obtained.

Suits to Compel Agency Action

The rule-making procedures and rights and standards for judicial review outlined above apply only once the EPA has begun to consider, or has taken, regulatory action. Nongovernment persons, however, may often be aggrieved by the EPA's *failure* to take action, or long delay in taking it. Such grievances present issues basically different from those posed by affirmative agency action. There will typically be no record and no procedure to organize and analyze the issues for the benefit of the court. At the same time, a decision against the agency has the potential for interfering with its management far more fundamentally than most decisions addressing promulgated rules. When a rule has been promulgated, the agency has already decided to invest the resources necessary to address its subject matter. Judicial review serves only to determine whether the results of that investment conform to applicable legal standards. However, a court that directs an agency to promulgate a rule runs the risk of overriding basic management decisions about where the agency should invest its resources.

Nevertheless, the CAA and the courts have established two methods for compelling agency action. The first and more established approach is a suit to enforce a statutory deadline. The second is a suit to compel agency action unreasonably delayed.

Deadline Suits

Under CAA Section 304(a)(2), citizens may compel the EPA to perform duties that are "not discretionary" by filing an action in an appropriate federal district court. Since there are no jurisdictional or venue restrictions other than those generally applicable to federal litigation, such suits can be filed anywhere in the country. Congress has included scores of mandatory deadlines for hundreds of regulatory actions in the CAA (as it has in most other environmental statutes). Indeed, it is rare in such statutes to find a regulatory power without an initial deadline for exercising it. The courts have found that such statutory deadlines for conducting rule making are classic nondiscretionary duties that may be judicially compelled.[82] As a matter of litigation, deadline suits are extremely simple. One need only file a sixty-day notice of intent to sue,[83] and then file an appropriate complaint when the sixty days have run. Since the existence of a mandatory deadline will generally be indisputably clear, these cases are easy to win. Moreover, the act allows the "prevailing party" to recover its attorneys' fees.[84]

These "deadline" suits are generally brought by environmental groups, and are almost invariably settled. The negotiations often expand to representatives of the interests to be regulated. Negotiations culminate with the filing of a consent decree that the court is asked to enter as a final order. Under long-standing Department of Justice policy, such decrees may only set out a schedule for taking the nondiscretionary actions, and cannot in any way predetermine their content.[85] (Such decisions on content, it is thought, can properly be made only by the competent agency officials acting through the rule-making process.)

Of course, if the EPA is unable to meet what is then a court-ordered deadline, it is forced to seek a modification, which usually spawns a new round of negotiations.

The district court is the forum for deadline suits only where the EPA has not formally deferred a statutory deadline. The 1990 amendments expressly provide that a "final decision of the Administrator [that] defers performance of any nondiscretionary statutory action to a later time" will be reviewed in the U.S. Court of Appeals for the D.C. Circuit.[86]

Unreasonable Delay

Before the 1990 amendments, there was some legal controversy about when or whether courts could require the EPA to issue a rule that had been "unreasonably delayed" but was *not* subject to a statutory deadline. The 1990 amendments resolved that issue by amending Section 304 to expressly allow such suits.[87] They may be brought only in courts within the circuit in which the rule at issue would be reviewed, and advance notice of 180 days is required before filing suit. The legislative history discusses some of the demanding showings that would likely be needed to prevail in such a suit.[88]

Conclusion

In the decade after the EPA's formation in 1970, notice and comment rule making became the dominant form of agency action, and was used to address far more complex and technical subjects than rule making had generally addressed before. Both the standards for judicial review of EPA rules and the specific rule-making procedures of CAA Section 307 were attempts to respond to this new situation.

By now, the very success of these approaches has made them established parts of the legal landscape. Although practitioners must be fully familiar with these procedures so as to exploit their advantages and (even more) avoid their pitfalls, their established nature generally does not leave much room for case-winning arguments in an individual proceeding. Instead, success is likely to come—as it generally does in the law—from attention to the legal and factual details of the particular topic at issue.

Notes

1. This chapter in the first edition was authored by Jeffrey B. Renton and Kathleen M. McFadden.

2. The CAA Amendments of 1977, Pub. L. No. 95-95. enacted § 307, 42 U.S.C. § 7607. *See* H.R. Rep. No. 294, 95th Cong., 1st Sess. III, 27, 318–25 (1977), *reprinted in* 1977 U.S.C.C.A.N. 1077, 1105, 1397–1404. These amendments largely codify the rule-making

procedures suggested by Judge Leventhal in Portland Cement Association v. Ruckelshaus, 486 F.2d 375 (D.C. Cir. 1973), and more fully developed in Pedersen, *Formal Records and Informal Rulemaking*, 85 YALE L.J. 38 (1975)). *See* Union Oil Co. v. EPA, 821 F.2d 678, 681–82 (D.C. Cir. 1987) (the 1977 CAA Amendments "provide new procedural requirements for EPA rulemaking under the Act, requirements more stringent than those previously applicable under the Administrative Procedure Act"). An excellent discussion of the legislative history underlying this provision, including the overall approach of the CAA toward rule making, is provided by Matthew D. McCubbins, *Structure and Process, Politics and Policy: Administrative Arrangements and the Political Control of Agencies*, 75 VA. L. REV. 431 (1989). The author opines that Section 307(d) represents "a new hybrid process (more formal than 'informal rulemaking' but less formal than 'formal rulemaking' [resulting from adjudicatory hearings]) that requires a more elaborate written record and a clearer statement of agency intentions and of the bases for its decisions." *Id.* at 431.

3. *See* CAA §§ 307(d)(1)(A), (B), (C), (E), (G), (I), (K), and (T).

4. Such rules do not directly prescribe SIP or enforcement requirements, but describe how states should use their power to establish SIPs or to enforce specific CAA requirements. Evidently Congress in 1977 did not appreciate the significance that such "matrix rules," one step removed from the actual imposition of regulatory obligations, would eventually assume in the administration of the CAA.

5. Section 307(b) expressly exempts from coverage rules "referred to" in subparagraphs (A) and (B) of 5 U.S.C. § 553(b), which include "interpretative rules, general statements of policy, or rules of agency organization, procedure or practice." *See* General Motors Corp. v. Ruckelshaus, 724 F.2d 979, 983 n.22 (D.C. Cir. 1983) (en banc) (interpretive rules), *cert. denied*, 471 U.S. 1074 (1985); Citizens to Save Spencer County v. EPA, 600 F.2d 844, 875–76 (D.C. Cir. 1979) (same); Automotive Parts Rebuilders Ass'n v. EPA, 720 F.2d 142, 155 (D.C. Cir. 1983) (list of pollution control devices was in the nature of "nonbinding" guidance exempt from the CAA's rule-making procedures).

6. CAA § 307(d)(1)(V).

7. For these procedures, see 5 U.S.C. § 553(b).

8. CAA § 307(d)(3).

9. CAA § 307(d)(2).

10. CAA § 307(d)(4)(B)(ii).

11. CAA § 307(d)(5).

12. *Id.*

13. CAA § 307(d)(4)(B)(i).

14. CAA § 307(d)(4)(B)(ii).

15. CAA § 307(d)(3).

16. CAA § 307(d)(6)(B).

17. CAA § 307(d)(7)(B).

18. 5 U.S.C. § 602(a); Exec. Order No. 12,866, 58 Fed. Reg. 51,735 (Sept. 30, 1993).

19. *See also* Air Pollution Control Dist. v. EPA, 739 F.2d 1071, 1080–81 (6th Cir. 1984) (while the EPA has discretion to consider post-comment-period comments, *ex parte* contacts are inappropriate to the extent that "'documents vital to EPA's support for its rule were submitted so late as to preclude any effective public comment'" (quoting *Sierra Club v. Costle*)).

20. 657 F.2d 298 (D.C. Cir. 1981), *rev'd on other grounds*, 463 U.S. 680 (1983).

21. 5 U.S.C. App. § 1 *et seq.*

22. Public Citizen v. U.S. Dept. of Justice, 491 U.S. 440 (1989); American Petroleum Inst. v. Costle, 665 F.2d 1176, 1189 (D.C. Cir. 1981); National Anti-Hunger Coalition v. Executive Committee of President's Private Sector Survey on Cost Control, 711 F.2d 1071 (D.C. Cir. 1983) (addressing the requirement that advisory committees be "fairly balanced").

23. U.S. Const., Amendment 1, Clause 6.

24. The currently effective Order is Exec. Order 12,866, 3 C.F.R. 638 (1993), 58 Fed. Reg. 51,735 (October 4, 1993).

25. Exec. Order 12,866, § 6(a)(3).

26. 42 U.S.C. § 4332(C).

27. The exemption is not contained in the CAA itself, but in an otherwise long-forgotten statute called the Energy Supply and Environmental Coordination Act, 5 U.S.C. § 793(c).

28. The Regulatory Flexibility Act, 5 U.S.C. § 601–612.

29. Exec. Order 13,132.

30. Exec. Order 13,045.

31. Exec. Order 13,211.

32. 44 U.S.C. §§ 3501–3520.

33. *Id.* at § 3507–3508.

34. *Id.* at § 3512.

35. § 307(b). The list includes the promulgation of NAAQS, emission standards for hazardous air pollutants, emission standards for motor vehicles, and fuels regulations.

36. *Id.* Here, too, Congress inserted a specific list of actions presumed to be "locally or regionally applicable." However, the EPA can override that presumption by finding that a particular action was based on a determination "of nationwide scope and effect."

37. *See, e.g.,* Texas Municipal Power Agency v. EPA, 89 F.3d 858, 866–67 (D.C. Cir. 1996) (articulating the debate between "entirely local" and "local but having national effect"); NRDC v. EPA, 465 F.2d 492, 495 (1st Cir. 1972) (finding that in this case the D.C. Circuit is the appropriate circuit in light of judicial economy, potential inconsistency of interpretation, and convenience to the EPA); Madison Gas & Electric Co. v. EPA, 4 F.3d 529 (7th Cir. 1993) (finding that this case challenges a local element of a national program with only speculative national effect and thus should remain in the 7th Circuit); West Virginia Chamber of Commerce v. Browner, 1998 U.S. App. LEXIS 30621 (4th. Cir. 1998).

38. *See* Texas Municipal Power Agency v. EPA, 89 F.3d 858, 862, 867 (D.C. Cir. 1996) (concluding that Section 7601(b)(1) is a matter of venue, not jurisdiction, and therefore is waivable); State of New York v. EPA, 133 F.3d 987, 990 (7th Cir. 1998) (finding that the question of regional circuit the petition for review should have been filed in a question of venue, and hence waived); National Wildlife Federation v. Browner, 237 F.3d 670, 672–73 (D.C. Cir. 2001).

39. *See* West Virginia Chamber of Commerce, 1998 U.S App. LEXIS at 14–26 (transferring a case from the Fourth Circuit to the D.C. Circuit after finding that the case involved an issue of nationwide scope) (citing Clark & Reid, 804 F.2d 3, 7 (1st Cir. 1986); Dornbusch v. C.I.R., 860 F.2d 611, 614–15 (5th Cir. 1988); Alexander v. C.I.R., 825 F.2d 499, 501–02 (D.C. Cir. 1987); Panhandle Eastern Pipeline Co. v. Federal Power Com., 337 F.2d 249, 252 (10th Cir. 1964); Pearce v. Director, Office Workers' Compensation Programs, 603 F.2d 763, 771 n.3 (9th Cir. 1979) (listing cases in eight circuits holding that courts of appeals have inherent power to transfer cases)).

40. CAA § 307(b).

41. *Id.*

42. *Id.*

43. § 307(b)(2).

44. Harrison v. PPG Indus., Inc., 446 U.S. 578 (1980) (use of "other final action" in Section 307(b)(1) authorizes direct appellate judicial review for a broad range of "final" agency actions); Natural Resources Defense Council v. Thomas, 845 F.2d 1088, 1091 (D.C. Cir. 1988).

45. For a general discussion of these requirements, *see* Whitman v. American Trucking Ass'n, 531 U.S. 457 (2001).

46. *See* Utility Air Regulatory Group v. EPA, 320 F.3d 272 (D.C. Cir. 2002) (manual of instructions not final agency action); Clean Air Implementation Project v. EPA, 150 F.3d 1200 (D.C. Cir. 1998) (matrix rule not ripe for review); Louisiana Action Network v. Browner, 87 F.3d 1379 (D.C. Cir. 1996) (matrix rule not final and challengers do not have standing). *But see* Appalachian Power v. EPA, 208 F.3d 1015 D.C. Cir. 2000) (agency guidance document is ripe and final).

47. Compare Clean Air Implementation Project, *supra*, with Appalachian Power, *supra*.

48. 531 U.S. at 477–481.

49. *See* Missouri v. United States, 109 F.3d 440, 442 (8th Cir. 1997) (finding that the sixty-day limitation cannot begin to run until the EPA actions challenged have been published in the *Federal Register*).

50. *See, e.g.*, § 112(e)(4), which bars judicial review of the listing of a pollutant as a hazardous air pollutant (HAP), or the listing of a source category for regulation. The section expressly provides that these decisions can be reviewed as part of any review of the standard that arose from them.

51. Bethlehem Steel Corp. v. EPA, 723 F.2d 1303, 1306 (7th Cir, 1983) (finding that Bethlehem Steel could still challenge a regulation, even though the sixty-day time limit had expired, because they were "not required to challenge a regulation just because the regulation might some day harm [them]"); Illinois Environmental Protection Agency v. EPA, 947 F.2d 283, 288–89 (7th Cir. 1991) (finding that Illinois EPA was not required to challenge the regulation within the sixty-day time limitation when its impact, if any, was in the future and therefore unknown).

52. General Motors Corp. v. Ruckelshaus, 724 F.2d 979, 985 n.30 (D.C. Cir. 1983), *cert. denied*, 471 U.S. 1074 (1985); *see also* 42 U.S.C. § 7607(b)(1).

53. Natural Resources Defense Council v. Thomas, 805 F.2d 410, 437–38 (D.C. Cir. 1986) (relying on American Petroleum Institute v. Costle, 665 F.2d 1176, 1190–91 (D.C. Cir. 1981), *cert. denied*, 455 U.S. 1034 (1982)).

54. Group against Smog & Pollution, Inc. v. EPA, 665 F.2d 1284, 1289–91 (D.C. Cir. 1981); 42 U.S.C. § 7607(b)(1); *see also* Maine v. Thomas, 874 F.2d 883, 890 (1st Cir. 1989); Oljato Chapter of Navajo Tribe v. Train, 515 F.2d 654, 666 (D.C. Cir. 1975), *rev'd on other grounds*, 870 F.2d 892 (2d Cir. 1989).

55. § 307(d)(7)(B).

56. *See, e.g.*, Natural Resources Defense Council v. EPA, 725 F.2d 761 (D.C. Cir. 1984); *but see* Natural Resources Defense Council v. Reilly, 976 F.2d 36 (D.C. Cir. 1992) (finding that the EPA did not have the authority to extend a stay of a rule).

57. § 307(d)(9).

58. Chemical Mfrs. Ass'n v. EPA, 28 F.3d 1259, 1264–65 (D.C. Cir. 1994). *See also* Motor Vehicle Mfrs. Ass'n v. EPA, 768 F.2d 385, 389 n.6 (D.C. Cir. 1985) ("We find it unnecessary to decide this issue here since the standard we apply (i.e., whether the EPA's actions were in excess of statutory authority or arbitrary and capricious) is the same under either Act [citation deleted]"), *cert. denied*, 474 U.S. 1082 (1986); Small Refiner Lead Phase-Down Task Force v. EPA, 705 F.2d 506, 519 (D.C. Cir. 1983) ("The standard for substantive judicial review of EPA action under the Clean Air Act is taken directly from the APA: The court may reverse only if EPA's action was 'arbitrary, capricious, an abuse of discretion, or otherwise not in accordance with law'") (citing CAA § 307(d)(9)(A) and 5 U.S.C. § 706(2)(A)); *Union Oil Co.*, 821 F.2d at 684 ("Section 307(d)(9)(A) of the Clean Air Act duplicates exactly the APA's prohibition of rulemaking that is 'arbitrary, capricious, an abuse of discretion, or otherwise not in accordance with law'").

59. § 307(d)(8).

60. *See* Union Oil Co. v. EPA, 821 F.2d 678, 684 (D.C. Cir. 1987).

61. Concerned Citizens of Bridesberg v. EPA, Small Refiner Lead Phase-Down Task Force v. EPA, 705 F.2d 506 (D.C. Cir. 1983).

62. Concerned Citizens of Bridesburg v. EPA, 836 F.2d 777, 788–89 (3d Cir. 1987).

63. *Sierra Club,* 657 F.2d at 352–53.

64. Natural Resources Defense Council, Inc. v. EPA, 725 F.2d 761, 773 (D.C. Cir. 1984) (quoting South Terminal Corp. v. EPA, 504 F.2d 646, 659 (1st Cir. 1974).

65. PPG Indus., Inc. v. Costle, 659 F.2d 1239, 1249 (D.C. Cir. 1981); *accord,* MCI Telecommunications Corp. v. FCC, 57 F.3d 1136 (D.C. Cir. 1995).

66. California *ex rel.* Air Resources Board v. EPA, 774 F.2d 1437, 1440, 1441 (9th Cir. 1985). *See also* Lead Indus. Ass'n., Inc. v. EPA, 647 F.2d 1130, 1167 (D.C. Cir.) (finding as not "significant" a comment that failed to oppose the decision being rendered by the EPA), *cert. denied,* 449 U.S. 1042 (1980).

67. Chevron U.S.A. v. Natural Resources Defense Council, 467 U.S. 837, 842–43 (1984).

68. *Id.*

69. *Id.*

70. *See, e.g.,* Mississippi Power & Light Co. v. Mississippi, 487 U.S. 354, 380 (1988) (Scalia, J., concurring) (citing NLRB v. City Disposal Systems, Inc., 465 U.S. 822, 830 n.7 (1984) ("We have never . . . held that such an exception [for issues of statutory jurisdiction] exists to the normal standard of review . . . ; indeed we have not hesitated to defer. . . .")); Commodity Futures Trading Comm'n v. Schor, 478 U.S. 833, 844 (1986) (finding "the CFTC's long-held position that it has the power to take jurisdiction" reasonable and entitled to deference); Singh-Bhathal v. INS, 170 F.3d 943, 945 (9th Cir. 1999) (deferring to an agency's jurisdictional interpretation, because it was "neither clearly erroneous nor inconsistent with the regulations") (citing Thomas Jefferson Univ. v. Shalala, 512 U.S. 504, 512 (1994)).

71. Ethyl Corp. v. EPA, 306 F.3d 1144 (D.C. Cir. 2003); American Petroleum Institute v. EPA, 52 F.3d 1113 (D.C. Cir. 1995); Ethyl Corp. v. EPA, 51 F.3d 1053, 1060 (D.C. Cir. 1995).

72. *Ethyl,* supra, 51 F.3d at 1060.

73. Rybachek v. EPA, 904 F.2d 1276, 1284–85 (9th Cir. 1990) (discussing the Clean Water Act and citing *Chevron,* 467 U.S. at 844).

74. Central Arizona Water Cons. Dist. v. EPA, 990 F.2d 1531, 1540 (9th Cir. 1993) (citing Public Citizen Health Research Group v. Tyson, 796 F.2d 1479, 1505 (D.C. Cir. 1986)), *cert. denied,* 510 U.S. 898, 114 S. Ct. 94 (1993).

75. National Tank Truck Carriers, Inc. v. EPA, 907 F.2d 177, 182–83 (D.C. Cir. 1990) (citing *Chevron,* 467 U.S. at 865).

76. Ohio v. EPA, 784 F.2d 224, 230 (6th Cir. 1986), *aff'd on reh'g,* 798 F.2d 880 (6th Cir. 1986).

77. International Bhd. of Teamsters, Chauffeurs, Warehousemen & Helpers of Am. v. Daniel, 439 U.S. 551, 566 n.20 (1979) (citing U.S. v. National Ass'n of Securities Dealers, 422 U.S. 694, 719 (1975); Saxbe v. Bustos, 419 U.S. 65, 75 (1974)); Skidmore v. Swift & Co., 323 U.S. 134, 139 (1944); American Water Works Ass'n v. EPA, 40 F.3d 1266, 1273 (D.C. Cir. 1994).

78. Chemical Manufacturers Association v. EPA, 28 F.3d 1259, 1264 (D.C. Cir. 1994).

79. *Id.*

80. However, the incentives for the EPA to settle litigation are distinctly less than those that bear on a private person, since government agencies do not bear the costs of their intransigence in litigation to the same extent as private persons.

81. *See* Memorandum from Attorney General Meese to all Assistant Attorneys General and all United States Attorneys, March 13, 1986. This Memorandum is still in effect today.

82. Sierra Club v. Thomas, 828 F.2d 783, 791 (D.C. Cir. 1987) (district courts have jurisdiction under CAA § 304(a)(2) to enforce "date-certain" deadlines.)

83. § 304(b)(2).

84. § 304(d).

85. *See* Meese Memorandum, supra n.80.

86. CAA § 307(b)(2).

87. CAA § 304(a).

88. *See* 1990 Senate Report at 375.

APPENDIX

Air-Related Web Sites

ENVIRONMENTAL PROTECTION AGENCY	http://epa.gov
OFFICE OF AIR AND RADIATION	http://epa.gov/oar
Acronyms used within OAR	http://epa.gov/air/acronyms.html
Air and Radiation Docket and Information Center	http://epa.gov/oar/docket.html
Office of the Assistant Administrator	http://epa.gov/oar/oaraa.html
Office of Policy Analysis and Review	http://epa.gov/oar/opar.html
Office of Program Management Operations	http://epa.gov/oar/opmo.html
Office of Transportation and Air Quality	http://epa.gov/omswww
Office of Air Quality Planning and Standards	http://epa.gov/oar/oaqps
Air Quality Strategies and Standards Division	http://epa.gov/oar/oaqps/cleanair.html
Emissions, Monitoring, and Analysis Division	http://epa.gov/air/oaqps/emad.html
Emissions Standards Division	http://epa.gov/air/oaqps/organization/esd/director.html
Information Transfer and Program Integration Division	http://epa.gov/air/oaqps/organization/itpid/director.html
AIRLinks	http://epa.gov/airlinks
Technology Transfer Network (TTN)	http://epa.gov/ttn
AIRS Executive	http://epa.gov/airs/aexec.html
AirData	http://epa.gov/air/data
Clearinghouse for Inventories & Emission Factors (CHIEF) Software and Tools	http://epa.gov/ttn/chief/software/index.html
Factor Information Retrieval (FIRE) Data System	http://epa.gov/ttn/chief/software/fire/index.html
TANKS Software	http://epa.gov/ttn/chief/software/tanks/index.html
Support Center for Regulatory Air Models	http://epa.gov/scram001
Emission Measurement Center	http://epa.gov/ttn/emc
Small Business Technical Assistance	http://epa.gov/ttn/sbap
The Clean Air Act	http://epa.gov/air/oaq_caa.html
The Plain English Guide to the Clean Air Act	http://epa.gov/oar/oaqps/peg_caa/pegcaain.html
The Green Book	http://epa.gov/oar/oaqps/greenbk
Air Quality Index (AQI)—AIRNow	http://epa.gov/airnow
Air Toxics Information	http://epa.gov/ttn/atw
Health Effects Notebook for Hazardous Air Pollutants	http://epa.gov/ttn/atw/hapindex.html

Air Pollution Monitoring	http://epa.gov/oar/oaqps/ montring.html
National Air Pollutant Emission Trends	http://epa.gov/ttn/chief/trends/ index.html
Office of Atmospheric Programs	http://epa.gov/oar/oap.html
Clean Air Markets Division—Acid Rain Program	http://epa.gov/airmarkets/arp
Ozone Depletion	http://epa.gov/air/ozone/index.html
Climate Protection Partnerships Division	http://epa.gov/cpd
Office of Radiation and Indoor Air	http://epa.gov/oar/oria.html
Radiation Protection Division	http://epa.gov/radiation
Indoor Air Quality Division	http://epa.gov/iaq
Radiation and Indoor Environments National Laboratory	http://epa.gov/radiation/rienl
National Air and Radiation Environmental Laboratory	http://epa.gov/narel

REGIONS

EPA Region 1	http://epa.gov/region1
EPA Region 2	http://epa.gov/region2
EPA Region 3	http://epa.gov/region3
EPA Region 4	http://epa.gov/region4
EPA Region 5	http://epa.gov/region5
EPA Region 6	http://epa.gov/region6
EPA Region 7	http://epa.gov/region7
EPA Region 8	http://epa.gov/region8
EPA Region 9	http://epa.gov/region9
EPA Region 10	http://epa.gov/region10

MISCELLANEOUS

Air Facility System (AFS)	http://epa.gov/compliance/ planning/data/air/afssystem.html
EPA Environmental Appeals Board (EAB)	http://epa.gov/eab
EPA Emergency Prevention, Preparedness and Response Division	http://epa.gov/swercepp
Federal Advisory Committee Act (FACA)	http://epa.gov/ttn/faca
Ozone Transport Assessment Group (OTAG)	http://epa.gov/ttn/naaqs/ozone/rto/ otag/index.html
National Technical Information Service	http://www.ntis.gov/
State and Territorial Air Pollution Program Administrators/Association of Local Air Pollution Control Officials (STAPPA/ALAPCO)	http://www.cleanairworld.org/
Environmental Council of the States (ECOS)	http://www.sso.org/ecos
Air & Waste Management Association	http://www.awma.org
Environmental Law Institute	http://www.eli.org
New Source Review Policy & Guidance Database	http://epa.gov/Region7/programs/ artd/air/nsr/nsrpg.htm
EPA Laws & Legislation	http://epa.gov/epahome/rules.html
EPA—OAR Policy and Guidance Recent Actions	http://epa.gov/ttn/oarpg/ ramain.html
EPA Office of Compliance and Enforcement	http://epa.gov/compliance

GENERAL GLOSSARY
OF ACRONYMS
AND TECHNICAL TERMS

AAU	Assigned Amount Unit
ABT	Averaging, Banking, and Trading
ACO	Administrative Compliance Order
ACT	Alternative Control Technique
AECP	Alternative Emission Control Plan
AEL	Alternative Emission Limitation
ALAPCO	Association of Local Air Pollution Control Officials
ALJ	Administrative Law Judge
APA	Administrative Procedures Act
AQCR	Air Quality Control Region
AQRV	Air Quality–Related Value
ARI	Air Conditioning and Refrigeration Institute
ASE	Automotive Service Excellence
ASTM	American Society of Testing and Materials
BACM	Best Available Control Measure
BACT	Best Available Control Technology
BART	Best Available Retrofit Technology
BDT	Best Demonstrated Technology
CAA	Clean Air Act
CAFE	Corporate Average Fuel Economy
CAM	Compliance Assurance Monitoring
CAP	Compliance Assurance Program
CARB	California Air Resources Board
CASAC	Clean Air Scientific Advisory Committee
CBI	Confidential Business Information
CDM	Clean Development Mechanism
CEMS	Continuous Emissions Monitoring System
CER	Certified Emission Reduction
CERCLA	Comprehensive Environmental Response, Compensation, and Liability Act
CFC	Chlorofluorocarbon
CH_4	Methane

CI	Compression Ignition
CISWI	Commercial and Industrial Solid Waste Incinerator
CMAQ	Congestion Mitigation and Air Quality Improvement Program
CMSA	Consolidated Metropolitan Statistical Area
CNG	Compressed Natural Gas
CO	Carbon Monoxide
CO_2	Carbon Dioxide
COMS	Continuous Opacity Monitoring System
CRARM	Commission on Risk Assessment and Risk Management
CSP	Compliance Supplemental Pool
CTG	Control Technique Guideline
CWA	Clean Water Act
DMR	Discharge Monitoring Report
DOT	Department of Transportation
EAB	Environmental Appeals Board
ECAO	Environmental Criteria and Assessment Office
ECO	Employee Commute Option
EGU	Electric Generating Unit
EMS	Environmental Management System
EPA	Environmental Protection Agency
EPCRA	Emergency Planning and Community Right-to-Know Act
ERC	Early Reduction Credit
ERP	Equipment Replacement Provision
ERU	Emission Reduction Unit
ETBE	Ethel Tertiary-Butyl Ether
ETR	Employer Trip Reduction
EUSGU	Electric Utility Steam Generating Unit
FACA	Federal Advisory Committee Act
FAR	Federal Acquisition Regulation
FCC	Federal Communications Commission
FDA	Food and Drug Administration
FESOP	Federally Enforceable State Operating Permit
FHWA	Federal Highway Administration
FIP	Federal Implementation Plan
FLM	Federal Land Manager
FTA	Federal Transportation Authority
FTP	Federal Test Procedure
GACT	Generally Available Control Technology
GAP	General Assistance Program Act of 1992
GATT	General Agreement on Tariffs and Trade
GHG	Greenhouse Gas

GPA	Geographic Phase-in Area
GPS	Generation Performance Standard
GSA	General Services Administration
GVWR	Gross Vehicle Weight Rating
GWP	Global Warming Potential
H_2S	Hydrogen Sulfide
HAP	Hazardous Air Pollutant
HBFC	Hydrobromofluorocarbon
HC	Hydrocarbon
HCB	Hexachlorobenzene
HCFC	Hydrochlorofluorocarbon
HCHO	Formaldehyde
HEW	Health, Education, and Welfare
HFC	Hydrofluorocarbon
HMIWI	Hospital/Medical/Infectious Waste Incinerator
HNO_3	Gaseous Nitrous Oxide
HON	Hazardous Organics NESHAP

I/M	Inspection and Maintenance
IPP	Independent Power Producer
ISTEA	Intermodal Surface Transportation Efficiency Act
IVD	Intake Valve Deposits

| JI | Joint Implementation |

LAER	Lowest Achievable Emissions Rate
LDT	Light-Duty Truck
LDV	Light-Duty Vehicle
LEV	Low Emission Vehicle
LNBT	Low Nitrogen Oxide Burner Technology
LPG	Liquefied Petroleum Gas
LULUCF	Land Use, Land Use Change, and Forestry
LVW	Loaded Vehicle Weight

MACT	Maximum Achievable Control Technology
MDI	Metered Dose Inhaler or Methylene Diphenyl Diisocyanate
MDPV	Medium-Duty Passenger Vehicles
MEK	Methylethel Ketone
MMT	Methylcyclopentadienyl Manganese Tricarbonyl
MOU	Memorandum of Understanding
MPO	Metropolitan Planning Organization
MSA	Metropolitan Statistical Area
MTBE	Methyl Tertiary-Butyl Ether
MVAC	Motor Vehicle Air Conditioner
MWC	Municipal Waste Combustor

N₂O	Nitrous Oxide
NAA	Nonattainment Area
NAAQS	National Ambient Air Quality Standards
NAICS	North American Industry Classification System
NAPCA	National Air Pollution Control Administration
NAS	National Academy of Sciences
NESCAUM	Northeast States for Coordinated Air Use Management
NESHAP	National Emissions Standards for Hazardous Air Pollutants
NGS	Navajo Generating Station
NHSDA	National Highway System Designation Act
NLEV	National Low Emission Vehicle
NMHC	Nonmethane Hydrocarbons
NMOG	Nonmethane Organic Gas
NO	Nitric Oxide
NO₂	Nitrogen Dioxide
NOₓ	Nitrogen Oxides
NPDES	National Pollutant Discharge Elimination System
NRC	National Research Council
NRDC	Natural Resources Defense Council
NSPS	New Source Performance Standard
NSR	New Source Review
NSRWM	New Source Review Workshop Manual
NTE	Not to Exceed
O₃	Ozone
OAQPS	Office of Air Quality Planning and Standards
OBD	On-Board Diagnostic
OCA	Offsite Consequence Analysis
ODP	Ozone-Depleting Potential
ODS	Ozone-Depleting Substance
OIRA	Office of Information and Regulatory Affairs
OMB	Office of Management and Budget
OPEC	Organization of Petroleum Exporting Countries
OPRG	Oxygenated Fuels Program Reformulated Gasoline
OSHA	Occupational Safety and Health Administration
OSWER	Office of Solid Waste and Emergency Response
OSWI	Other Solid Waste Incinerator
OTAG	Ozone Transport Assessment Group
OTC	Ozone Transport Commission
OTR	Ozone Transport Region
PAL	Plantwide Applicability Limit
Pb	Lead
PCB	Polychlorinated Biphenyl
PCP	Pollution Control Project
PDP	Principal Display Panel

PFC	Perfluorocarbon
PFID	Port Fuel Injector Deposits
PM	Particulate Matter
PM_{10}	Particulate Matter Ten Microns or Less in Diameter
$PM_{2.5}$	Particulate Matter Two and a Half Microns or Less in Diameter
PMN	Premanufacture Notice
POM	Polycyclic Organic Matter
PPG	Performance Partnership Grant
PSD	Prevention of Significant Deterioration
PSM	Process Safety Management
PTE	Potential to Emit
RACM	Reasonably Available Control Measure
RACT	Reasonably Available Control Technology
RBLC	RACT/BACT/LAER Clearinghouse
RBOB	Reformulated Blendstock for Oxygenate Blending
RCRA	Resource Conservation and Recovery Act
RECLAIM	Regional Clean Air Incentives Market
RFP	Reasonable Further Progress
RMP	Risk Management Plan
RMU	Removal Unit
RMRR	Routine Maintenance, Repair, and Replacement
RVP	Reid Vapor Pressure
SAB	Science Advisory Board
SAED	Surfactant Alcohol Ethoxylates and Derivatives
SARA	Superfund Amendments and Reauthorization Act
SCAQMD	South Coast Air Quality Management District
SCRS	Source Category Ranking System
SEA	Selective Enforcement Audit
SEP	Supplemental Environmental Project
SESARM	Southeast States Air Resource Managers
SET	Supplemental Emission Test
SF_6	Sulfur Hexafluoride
SFTP	Supplemental Federal Test Procedure
SI	Spark Ignition
SIC	Standard Industrial Classification
SIP	State Implementation Plan
SNAP	Significant New Alternatives Policy
SO_2	Sulfur Dioxide
SOCMI	Synthetic Organic Chemical Manufacturing Industry
SO_x	Sulfur Oxides
SSS	Supplemental Steady State
STAPPA	State and Territorial Air Pollution Program Administrators
SUV	Sport-Utility Vehicle

TAR	Tribal Authority Rule
TAS	Treatment as a State
TCDD	Tetrachlorodibenzo-P-Dioxin
TCM	Transportation Control Measure
TCSP	Transportation and Community and System Preservation Pilot Program
TEA-21	Transportation Equity Act for the 21st Century
TEAP	Technology and Economic Assessment Panel
TIP	Transportation Improvement Plan or Tribal Implementation Plan
TLEV	Transitional Low Emission Vehicle
TOC	Technical Options Committee
TRI	Toxic Release Inventory
TRS	Total Reduced Sulfur
TSCA	Toxic Substances Control Act
TSP	Total Suspended Particulate
TTN	Technology Transfer Network
TW	Test Weight
ULEV	Ultra Low Emission Vehicle
UNDP	United Nations Development Programme
UNEP	United Nations Environment Programme
UNFCCC	United Nations Framework Convention on Climate Change
USFS	United States Forest Service
VAR	Volume Additive Reconciliation
VMT	Vehicle Miles Traveled
VOC	Volatile Organic Compound
VOL	Volatile Organic Liquid
WEPCO	Wisconsin Electric Power Company
WPC	Wholesale Purchaser-Consumer
WRAP	Western Regional Air Partnership
ZEV	Zero Emission Vehicle

Table of Measurements

g/bhp-hr	Grams per Brake Horsepower Hour
gpm	Grams per Mile
lb/hr	Pounds per Hour
lb/mmBtu	Pounds per Million British Thermal Units
ppm	Parts per Million
psi	Pounds per Square Inch
psig	Pounds per Square Inch Gauge
tpy	Tons per Year
µg Pb/dl	Micrograms Lead per Deciliter
µg/m³	Micrograms per Cubic Meter
µm	Micrometer or Micron

INDEX

NOTE: Boldface numbers indicate illustrations.